REVOLUTIONS IN ROMANTIC LITERATURE:
AN ANTHOLOGY OF PRINT CULTURE,
1780–1832

Revolutions in Romantic Literature: An Anthology of Print Culture, 1780–1832

EDITED BY

Paul Keen

broadview press

NATIONAL LIBRARY OF CANADA CATALOGUING IN PUBLICATION

Revolutions in Romantic Literature: an anthology of print culture, 1780–1832 / edited by Paul Keen.

Includes index.
ISBN 1-55111-352-X

1. English prose literature—18th century. 2. English prose literature—19th century. 3. Great Britain—Intellectual life—18th century—Sources. 4. Great Britain—Intellectual Life—19th century—Sources. 5. Books and reading—Great Britain—History—18th century—Sources. 6. Books and reading—Great Britain—History—19th century—Sources. 7. Social problems—Great Britain—History—18th century—Sources. 8. Social problems—Great Britain—History—19th century—Sources. I. Keen, Paul

PN603.R49 2004   828'.70808   C2003-907047-6

Broadview Press, Ltd. is an independent, international publishing house, incorporated in 1985. Broadview believes in shared ownership, both with its employees and with the general public; since the year 2000 Broadview shares have traded publicly on the Toronto Venture Exchange under the symbol BDP.

We welcome comments and suggestions regarding any aspect of our publications—please feel free to contact us at the addresses below or at broadview@broadviewpress.com.

North America
PO Box 1243,
Peterborough, Ontario
Canada K9J 7H5
3576 California Road,
Orchard Park, NY, USA 14127
Tel: (705) 743-8990;
Fax: (705) 743-8353
email:
customerservice@broadviewpress.com

UK, Ireland, and continental Europe
NBN Plymbridge
Estover Road
Plymouth
UK PL6 7PY
Tel: +44 (0) 1752 202301;
Fax: +44 (0) 1752 202331;
Fax Order Line: +44 (0) 1752 202333;
Cust Ser: cservs@nbnplymbridge.com
Orders: orders@nbnplymbridge.com

Australia and New Zealand
UNIREPS,
University of New South Wales
Sydney, NSW, 2052
Australia
Tel: 61 2 9664 0999;
Fax: 61 2 9664 5420
email: info.press@unsw.edu.au

www. broadviewpress.com

Broadview Press gratefully acknowledges the financial support of the Government of Canada through the Book Publishing Industry Development Program for our publishing activities.

PRINTED IN CANADA

TABLE OF CONTENTS [1]

---

[1] Please note that the texts listed are selections; works are not reproduced in their entirety.

SECTION SEVEN: THE PERIODICAL PRESS

SECTION TEN: A REVOLUTION IN FEMALE MANNERS 233

SECTION ELEVEN: THE SECOND WAVE OF REFORM 271

SECTION TWELVE: BRITISH INDIA

SECTION THIRTEEN: THE SLAVE TRADE   316

INDEX OF AUTHORS AND TITLES   351

PREFACE

Things have changed somewhat since a largely unknown thirty-year-old warned readers of *Lyrical Ballads* that they might "have to struggle with feelings of strangeness and awkwardness" and even "unpleasant feeling(s) of disappointment." Today William Wordsworth enjoys pride of place in many if not most accounts of the poetry of his age. Not only that, but on a more fundamental level, our tendency to identify the literature of what we now call the Romantic period with poetry, or more broadly, with "creative writing," reflects assumptions about the primacy of the imagination that were distinctly at odds with other cultural assumptions and practices in the period. Bearing this in mind helps us to appreciate the polemical stance of Wordsworth's comparison of the immediacy of "the Poet, singing a song in which all human beings join with him," to "The Man of Science, the Chemist and Mathematician" and even "the Historian and Biographer," all of whose efforts were too specialized and too remote from people's everyday experiences to have any comparable importance (383; 395–96). A Romantic anthology that doesn't give a prominent place to Wordsworth's writing in particular, and to poetry in general, risks seeming historically anomalous.

This account of a critical pendulum swing in Wordsworth's favour is not the whole story, though. In recent years, canonical approaches to the period have been challenged by a theoretical shift that has situated literary criticism within a much broader focus that includes an interest in the work of historians, biographers, and even, sometimes, scientists. Much of this has to do with a new approach to the history of writing itself. In 1982, Robert Darnton announced that an intellectual revolution was being launched by scholars who, in pursuing new approaches to the study of literary history, "found themselves crossing paths into a no-man's land located at the intersection of a half-dozen fields of study." Frustrated with the limitations of their individual disciplines, these scholars "decided to constitute a field of their own and to invite in historians, literary scholars, sociologists, librarians, and anyone else who wanted to understand the book as a force in history." Soon "the history of books began to acquire its journals, research centers, conferences, and lecture circuits" (108). This was to be more than a bureaucratic addition that would leave traditional critical practices intact though. Rejecting "the great-man, great-book view of literary history" as a "mystification" of literary production which overlooks the important role of "literary middlemen," Darnton insisted that a non-canonical approach will "open up the possibility of rereading literary history. And if studied in connection with the system for producing and diffusing the printed word, they could force us to rethink our notion of literature itself" (153).

This desire to rethink our most fundamental notions of literature reflects a broader transition that James Clifford describes in *Writing Culture* as a "conceptual shift, 'tectonic' in its implications" in our relation to the disciplinary boundaries that have for a long time helped to define our work in various university departments. Where the division of knowledge established by disciplinary boundaries offered a reassuring sense of the authors who were worth studying and of the sorts of questions that were worth asking, "we ground things, now, on a moving earth" (22). One effect of this has been a self-reflexive interrogation which takes the history of the disciplines, and the question of how this history has helped to define our work, as a focus in itself. When Clifford suggests that we live in a "post-literary" age, he doesn't mean that there is no longer any literature or that books have been rendered obsolete, but that we are no longer quite sure what counts as literature or exactly what its value is (5).

Uprooted from any foundational connection with art or "imaginative expression," the word "literature" is now more commonly approached as a complex historical product formed by and responding to an intricate network of social needs and pressures. All of this has replaced appeals to "higher" aesthetic values with a broader understanding of culture as an ongoing process characterized by the selection and organization of different perspectives. As a result, literature has been transformed from something that made our critical work coherent by providing a framework of shared assumptions, into an area of contestation whose shifting contours form one of the primary elements of our investigations. We are more interested in exploring the different ways that people found of posing and answering questions about the nature of literature than in settling the issue by adjudicating between them.

What does all of this have to do with the Romantic period? There are at least two answers. The first is that the field of Romantic literature was ripe for a reappraisal along these lines because traditional approaches were often notoriously narrow in their focus. Driven in large part by developments in feminist, post colonial, Marxist, New Historicist, and other fields of critical inquiry, this revision has situated itself "beyond Romanticism," as the title of a collection of essays edited by Stephen Copley and John Whale puts it. This change of emphasis has focused our attention on "marginal" writers, many of whom were popular and respected in their own time, but who did not find much of a place within the more restrictive and prescriptive confines of the Great Tradition. More radically, it has also extended into sociological concerns about the publication, dissemination, and consumption of literature, and about literature's relation to other processes of cultural transmission. This revisionary spirit has helped to complicate our understanding of the overlapping and often contradictory pressures and opportunities which these authors were simultaneously being shaped by and responding to.

But the Romantic period is ripe for revision for another reason: not because literature had so narrow a meaning in the period, but because its definition was already subject to all of the uncertainties that James Clifford attributes to our own age. Regardless of our inherited assumptions, the question of the definition of literature was one of the central points of debate in the period, both as an implicit dimension of various other debates and as a topic in its own right. In 1780 the *Monthly Review* claimed that "the term *literary* has yet acquired no appropriate signification in our language" (62:63). This anthology brings together a collection of writings by authors who, in one way or another, responded to the challenge of defining literature with unbounded optimism, melancholic loss, righteous indignation, a wry sense of humour, paranoia, and most of all, an urgent sense of the importance of these exchanges. They displayed a sophisticated self-consciousness about the wider theoretical assumptions that these debates were predicated on, and about the possible consequences of the different positions that were being adopted, that our own historical investigations have not always adequately appreciated.

As many of these writers insisted, these debates were not just *about* literature; they constituted an important part of the literature of the day in their own right. "If former times have enjoyed works of more fancy, and sublimity of imagination, than are given to us," the *Monthly Magazine* observed, just one year before Wordsworth's Preface, "we, in return, possess more useful acquisitions. If they have had their Spencer, Tasso, and Shakespeare, we boast Newton, Locke, and Johnson.—Science, taste, and correction, are indeed the characteristics of the present day" (1799: 7:112). "We complain that this is a Critical age," agreed William Hazlitt in an 1823 article in the *Edinburgh Review*, "and that no great works of Genius appear, because so much is said and written about them; while we ought to reverse the argument, and say, that it is because so many works of genius *have appeared*, that they have left us little or nothing to do, but to think and talk about them" (37:350). Whatever our sense of the period's output of "works of genius," or of Hazlitt's distinction between "works of genius" and critical discussions, the Romantic period was animated by an unprecedented eagerness "to think and talk" about a range of literary issues.

To revise Hazlitt's observation in our own theoretical terms, it was a meta-critical age marked by energetic and seemingly unending discussions about the conditions within which writers were immersed. Literary journals epitomized this worldly sense of literature in the extensive range of subjects they reviewed, from divinity to history to travel writing to scientific treatises to antiquities to geography to poetry and novels to transactions of learned societies, and in the tendency of literary magazines such as the *Gentleman's Magazine* and the *Monthly Magazine* to include their reviews alongside letters to the editor, political information, news of society marriages and deaths, weather reports, and notices of bankruptcies and of patents pending. They provided a vital forum for reflecting on the most fundamental literary dynamics of the age; reviews of individual publications were frequently complemented by astute reflections on many of these more profound and self-reflexive questions about literature itself. It made for popular reading. Authors on the receiving end of negative reviews frequently complained that periodicals reached far more readers on a monthly basis than any single publication could ever hope to. Their dominant cultural presence underlined the fact that, both in terms of the fields of knowledge that were included in it, and the social and economic contexts that it was situated within, literature gained its importance, not through its separation from more secular phenomena into some highly reified mode of "creative" expression, but just the opposite, from its immersion in a busy world where creativity had as much to do with patents pending as lyrical inspiration.

The anthology is organized into thirteen sections, each with its own introduction. This structure is designed to embody many Romantic writers' assumption that literature should be a vehicle for debate, or as William Godwin put it, a means of promoting "the collision of mind with mind," rather than a form of solitary reflection (21). It foregrounds the multiple perspectives that circulated on any topic, and suggests that the literary assumptions which we attribute to the period should be read as uncertainties or particular perspectives rather than inherent truths. The varying length of these excerpts, from a paragraph to several pages, is intended to encourage the reader to pursue these writings in terms of the connections between them rather than approaching each text in isolation. The emphasis is on the conceptual focus of the debates themselves rather than on particular authors or texts. I have preserved stylistic anomalies and grammatical errors in order to reflect both the processes of standardization which characterized the age, and the power of literature as a means of self-legitimation for sometimes minimally educated writers originating outside of the polite classes.

This selection of categories is strategic rather than totalizing. These categories reflect important issues that preoccupied many writers in the period, but they are not the only ones that did so; others could easily have been selected. They suggest how complicated the challenge of conceptualizing the literary field in this period is, and invite questions about alternative possibilities. The contents are equally provisional. Some excerpts would fit well in other categories; every category could easily include other writings than those offered here. These writings have been selected and arranged as one way of illustrating the extent to which Romantic literature was itself marked by an anxious network of tensions and affirmations that reflected a variety of cultural priorities. Rather than evading this sense of contingency, my hope is that this format will affirm the provisional nature of all accounts of literary history. As Section Six, which surveys the historical connections between literature and science suggests, the arrangement of knowledge was one of the most vexing issues in the period.

I don't use the phrase "Print Culture" to suggest an alternative to the literature of the period, but as a means of reflecting as accurately as possible Romantic writers' assumptions about literature as a complex field of writing and reading shaped by a range of commercial, political and social factors—assumptions that were displaced by the emergence of the modern definition of literature which has today become the object of so much critical scrutiny. "Print culture" evokes a society whose self-understanding was fundamentally determined by the prominence of these practices of reading and writing within it. The *Retrospective Review* (1820) situated itself within this widely shared sense that the period offered "a spectacle of what, perhaps, was never before seen in any age, certainly neither Greek nor Roman, that of a whole nation, employing nearly all its leisure hours from the highest to the lowest rank in *reading*—we have been truly called a READING PUBLIC." The *Retrospective* went on to suggest that this seemingly universal commitment to reading compared rather poorly with "the lively Greeks," who "were not a *reading* nation—they were a hearing and a talking people" (iv).

Seven years later, John Stuart Mill voiced a similar ambivalence about the extent to which modern England had become a print culture: "This is a reading age," Mill acknowledged, "and precisely because it is so reading an age, any book which is the result of profound meditation is, perhaps, less likely to be duly and profitably read than at any former period." Whatever the previous century's triumphalist rhetoric about the connections between reading and rational inquiry, the dissemination of printed texts had enervated rather than invigorated the nation's intellectual health: "the public is in the predicament of an indolent man, who cannot bring himself to apply his mind vigorously to his own affairs, and over whom, therefore, not he who speaks wisely, but he who speaks most frequently, obtains the influence" (409–17). Whatever one thought of what the *Retrospective* referred to as "the fertile and luxurious crop of modern literature," the spectacle of so many people reading and (an inevitable corollary) writing, and the sense that, for better or worse, these dynamics had enormous political implications, made the task of understanding more about these developments an undeniable priority (vii).

The political turbulence that spilled over from the French Revolution at the end of the eighteenth century had intensified this awareness of the pressing need to define literature in ways that reinforced particular social perspectives. William Godwin argued in *The Enquirer: Reflections on Education, Manners, and Literature* (1797) that "the cause of political reform, and the cause of intellectual and literary refinement, are inseparably connected" (x). Not everyone agreed, but it was a serious enough claim that it could not be ignored. If, as some critics have argued, the Romantic period marked the last time that Britain had a genuine debate about its fundamental political choices, it was also the last time until our own "post-literary" age that there was any thorough-going debate about the meaning of literature. Nor, as authors in the period were aware, were these two facts unconnected. T.J. Mathias's *The Pursuits of Literature* (1797), published anonymously in four volumes through the mid-1790s, is largely neglected today, but it attracted a storm of attention at the time. And one of Mathias's central points was precisely the degree to which the political debate that exploded in Britain after the beginning of the French Revolution was also a debate about the nature of literature. Mathias's invitation to readers to "consider the nature, variety, and extent of the word, Literature" (238) suggests not only the breadth that was attributed to it, but just as importantly, the urgency and clarity with which writers were trying to decide what this category should include, who ought to be reading and writing it, in what ways the dissemination of written texts ought to be constrained or encouraged, whose intellectual property it was, and what it might be expected to *do*.

This final issue is crucial because it highlights the particularly functional nature of many people's assumptions. It may seem foreign to our own tendency to equate literature with artistic expression, but whether they felt that it was a blessing or a curse, conservative and radical critics agreed that literature had the power to change the world. T.J. Mathias and William Godwin disagreed about whether or not this was a good thing but, as we see in Section One, they coincided (along with many other commentators in the period) in their description of literature as an "engine" of social change—an especially powerful metaphor during the industrial revolution. The relationship between literature and history went in both directions though. As an engine of change, literature had an enormous potential to influence historical events. But these historical developments also had an enormous impact on the claims that different social groups were making about literature. It was not for nothing that the French revolutionaries included a printing press in their parades. Nor were English conservatives and reformers unaware of these implications. Literature had helped to make change possible, but revolutionary changes in France and America fostered a nervous consciousness of the need to address this radical potential.

The best parallel in our own age is not with what we now think of as literature but with our computer-driven information revolution. Literature was embraced in the Romantic period, in strikingly familiar language, as a means of promoting the progress of learning by freeing up information. It was in this spirit that William Godwin spoke of literature in terms of a communicative process rather than a set of discrete texts. In his *Enquiry Concerning Political Justice* (which sold 3,000 copies at the steep price of three guineas a piece), he defined literature as "the diffusion of knowledge through the medium of discussion, whether written or oral" (19). The result, reformers such as Godwin argued, would be the development of a body of rational knowledge that would displace the prejudices and superstitions of a society organized around aristocratic privilege. But this could only happen if literature fulfilled its second function of diffusing these truths throughout an expanding reading public. During an age when democracy remained a limited reality at best, this circulation of fresh ideas was often celebrated as an indomitable moral force. In November 1788, on the eve of the French Revolution, the *Analytical Review* used the occasion of a series of pamphlets between two leading French statesmen to insist that "literature, by enlightening the understanding, and uniting the sentiments and views of men and nations, forms a concert of wills, and a concurrence of action too powerful for armies of tyrants." Literature may not have been the only phenomenon capable of ensuring the success of this process, but for reformist thinkers, at least, it was "the most important by far" (1788: 2: 324).

Like our own information revolution, these aspirations generated a corresponding set of anxieties, even amongst those who were convinced of this general vision. Less sympathetic critics warned that if they were not restricted, these sorts of communicative processes would lead to revolution by encouraging the dissemination of dangerous ideas that were intended to inflame people's understanding rather than appeal to reason. Worse, there would be little way of regulating whose hands these seditious materials could make their way into. Others worried that, quite apart from the dangerous content of these materials, the print revolution was suffering from a staggering crisis of overproduction. So many books and pamphlets were being printed that it was impossible to read them all, and if there were too many being produced to read, how could any individual possibly hope to decide which of them to select? Even more disturbing was the fact that readers often seemed to prefer trivial books to more serious and informative ones. Literature had traditionally been celebrated as a moral antidote to the corrosive effects of fashion and luxury, but by the time of the Romantic period it had itself become a major fashion industry. Its role as a vehicle for the diffusion of knowledge rested on the assumption that the individual only had to recognize the truth in order to regulate his or her behaviour accordingly. But this implied that people wanted to know the truth when it was just as possible to borrow the latest romantic novels from the circulating library.

The educational connotations implicit in many of these debates about literature ensured that these discussions extended to the question of the rights of women. If the diffusion of knowledge was assumed to be empowering, then women authors insisted that women should be allowed to have an enlightenment too. Not only that, but many of them insisted that they ought to be allowed to define the nature of this enlightenment for themselves.

Questions about the role of women in society extended well beyond discussions about literature, but even these broader social debates were often shaped by assumptions about the relationship between power and knowledge that were rooted in literary arguments. Conservative critics insisted that gender differences should manifest themselves in the different genres that women ought to write and read, but for more radical authors such as Mary Wollstonecraft, literature was a force capable of fostering a sense of rational power that would enable women to overcome these culturally-prescribed limitations.

These debates were not fought out in a vacuum but were staged in a range of contexts that reflected a highly fractious network of cultural and political struggles: a succession of legal trials against the authors and publishers of radical books and pamphlets; the efforts of the government to control the circulation of seditious writings through a series of taxes and pieces of legislation; the tendency of literary reviews to proscribe the limits of literary prerogative; and biting satires and polemics, both against the reactionary spirit of the government and against radical working-class and women authors. These debates were also dependent on the technical and economic advances in printing and publishing, and on an increasingly efficient infrastructure that made the dissemination of literature possible.

Ideas about literature were also forged in a global context that ranged from the debate about slavery to explorer narratives in Africa, British North America, and the South Seas, to the political uprisings in Ireland. Connections between literature and empire were particularly rich in the case of British India because the East was so frequently hailed as the birthplace of civilization, and because this narrative of cultural origins provided so convenient a response to nagging moral questions about Britain's conduct in India. Before the exportation of English Studies became a crucial element of imperial policy, the emphasis was on the opposite dynamic: the capacity of foreign literatures to humanize Britain's government of distant lands by instilling a more thorough understanding of the cultural and legal practices of subject peoples. Such a practice would help to contain worries about the linked excesses of imperial conquest and commercial gain by emphasizing an area of untarnished cultural interaction that would be driven by authors' disinterested love of truth. The links between literature and liberty remained alive, but in a strangely transmuted form. Whereas reformers in Britain such as Tom Paine and Mary Wollstonecraft tended to insist on the separation of power and knowledge in order to celebrate the latter as a force capable of resisting the practises of arbitrary government, British writers in the colonies insisted on this separation in order to claim that their philanthropic efforts could coincide with the often notorious activities of the government of British India without being morally compromised by this association. The problem with this ideal was that it continued to be plagued by its own contradictions. Learning might help to soften the excesses of military conquest but, as critics often noted, it relied on those conquests in order to introduce authors to new texts and challenges; it was also associated with a steady transfer of texts and artifacts to Britain that seemed to double rather than displace the tainted promise of easy commercial gain. In any case, by the end of the Romantic period, authors such as Thomas Macaulay were insisting that the real role of literature was not to collect information about degenerate societies but to save those societies from themselves by introducing them to the blessings of English culture.

If the equation of literature with the power of rational debate lay at the bottom of many of these tensions, another group of writers, those we now call the Romantics, insisted on the primacy of the imagination rather than reason, and on the power of inspiration rather than intellectual debate. Knowledge, for the Romantics, was not a set of rational propositions arrived at through research and debate, but a psychologized concept that called the nature of reason into question. Like many of their contemporaries, however, they were preoccupied with the question, "What is it we mean by *literature*?" as Thomas De Quincey put it in his comparison of a literature of power, which stirred the imagination, and a literature of knowledge, which traded in mere "information" (53). The greatest critical achievement of the Romantic poets was not their insistence on the supreme virtues of a certain type of poetry, but of a certain type of literature that reflected this sense of the mercurial nature of human consciousness. Their aesthetic priorities drew on broader cultural trends such as the ballad revival that was associated with figures such as Joseph Ritson and Thomas Percy, and on the popularity of the picturesque and the sublime. None of this should blind us to the differences between these writers, though. As we will see in Section Eight, the power of the imagination may have been a common rallying point, but it could be mobilized towards very different ends.

If the definition of literature that we have inherited today is a more narrow one equated with artistic expression, then this is in many ways a direct result of the tensions of this period. It became all the more attractive to think, with William Wordsworth, of the poet as a man speaking to men if the alternative was either Tom Paine speaking to working-class men or Mary Wollstonecraft speaking to women at a time when revolution was a real possibility. If one of the consequences of these historical processes is that we remain belated Romantics implicitly convinced of the equation between literature and "creative writing," then that predisposition blinds us to the status of this equation as one of the most important developments in the period. Recognizing that this identification of literature with imaginative expression (and especially poetry) was one of many perspectives in the period renews the challenge of exploring the various ways that different writers responded to the question posed by Thomas De Quincey: "What is it we mean by *literature*?"

Works Cited

Analytical Review, or History of Literature, Domestic and Foreign, on an Enlarged Plan. 1788.

British Critic; a New Review. 1793.

Clifford, James. "Introduction." *Writing Culture.* Ed. James Clifford and George E. Marcus. Berkeley: U of California P, 1986.

Copley, Stephen, and John Whale, eds. *Beyond Romanticism: New Approaches to Texts and Contexts, 1780–1832.* London: Routledge, 1992.

Darnton, Robert. *The Kiss of Lamourette: Reflections in Cultural History.* N.Y.: W.W. Norton & Co., 1990.

De Quincey, Thomas. *The Collected Writings of Thomas De Quincey.* Ed. David Masson. Vol. 11. 1897.

Edinburgh Review, or Critical Journal. 1802.

Gentleman's Magazine and Historical Chronicle. 1731.

Godwin, William. *Enquiry Concerning Political Justice.* London, 1793.

____. *The Enquirer: Reflections on Education, Manners, and Literature.* London, 1797.

Mathias, T.J. *The Pursuits of Literature, or What You Will: A Satirical Poem in Dialogue.* 7th edn. 1797.

Mill, John Stuart. *The Collected Works of John Stuart Mill*, ed. J.M. Robson. Vol. 27. U fo Toronto P, 1981–91.

Monthly Review; or Literary Journal, Enlarged. ns. 1790.

Retrospective Review. 1820.

Wordsworth, William. *The Poetical Works of William Wordsworth.* Eds. E. de Selincourt and Helen Darbishire. Vol. 2. Oxford: Clarendon P, 1944.

೧೦೧೦

ACKNOWLEDGEMENTS

It is an axiom of book historians that authors don't write books, they write texts. Books are joint products that involve writing, copy-editing, typesetting, printing, marketing, and a host of other skills. The same is even more true for editors. This anthology is an attempt to collect together a range of critical debates about various aspects of the complex social, political and commercial activity of producing, disseminating and reading books, all of which ran against the grain of an aesthetic ideal of the author—or editor—as autonomous creator. I have benefitted enormously from a long list of assistants and informal advisors. Don LePan reacted with imprudent but welcome enthusiasm when I suggested the idea to him at a conference book exhibit. Julia Gaunce has been unfailingly helpful. Kathryn Brownsey was an enormous help at the copy-editing stage. Broadview's anonymous readers offered important suggestions that have helped to steer this in more interesting and historically representative directions than I had originally envisioned.

This anthology is in many ways an attempt to bridge a gap, one which I suspect many of us feel, between the wealth of primary materials that inform our research and the more limited range of published resources that are at our disposal as teachers. Like many, I wrestled with this problem by producing my own course-books reflecting aspects of the period that I found intriguing and that I wanted to share with students; this is a development of those earlier efforts. To this extent I owe a further debt of gratitude to those students who were subjected to my various course-books, and whose frequently astute responses and unexpected questions helped to sharpen my sense of these materials. Transcribing and proofreading has been a lot of hard work, for which I have to thank a series of research assistants: Janne Cleveland, Jerusha Deweerd, Miranda Foster, Geoff Hajcman, and Andrea Wolsjensky. Footnote materials range from the historically significant to cultural trivia fit for any academic pub quiz. I have relied on and would like to acknowledge my intellectual debt to several reference works including *Oxford Companion to the Romantic Age*, *Oxford Companion to English Literature* (4th and 5th editions), *Blackwell Companion to the Enlightenment*, *Oxford English Dictionary*, and *Funk & Wagnells Standard College Dictionary*, as well as to three on-line resources: Bartleby. com, the Family Education Network, and New Advent. Texts by S.T. Coleridge are reprinted with permission of Princeton University Press. The excerpt from *The Autobiography of Francis Place* is reprinted with permission of Cambridge University Press and Mary Thale, its original editor for Cambridge. More personal thanks are owed to a group of willing footnote collaborators: Jerusha Deweerd, Janne Cleveland, John Barrell, Siobhain Bly, Leanne Groenveld, April London, and Jon Mee. Shane Hawkins was an endlessly helpful source for classical references. Research for the project has been funded by grants from the Social Sciences and Humanities Research Council of Canada and Carleton University. I appreciate their generosity.

SECTION ONE

The Nature of the Word, Literature

Whatever they meant by the word literature, and there was no easy consensus on the subject, most writers in the Romantic period understood something very different than we often do today. Nor did they always agree with each other's definition. But they did share a sense of the broader importance of the issue. The result was a remarkably sophisticated and clear-sighted debate about the definition of literature that highlighted both the multiplicity of contending opinions and the degree to which most (but not all) of those opinions differed from our own tendency to approach literature as a category of aesthetic production that includes primarily poetry, fiction, and drama. It was a debate that moved well beyond formal concerns about the particular qualities of literary texts to social questions about who should be reading what, how the circulation of texts should be facilitated or policed, what sort of effect reading should have on people, and what the consequences of all of this might be for society in general. In his famous radical work, *An Enquiry Concerning Political Justice,* William Godwin defined literature as "the diffusion of knowledge through the medium of discussion, whether written or oral." It is worth insisting on how utterly foreign this perspective is to our own cultural assumptions. Its emphasis on the process of intellectual exchange rather than on particular written works and its disregard for our own dichotomy between "creative" and "critical" expression cannot be insisted on today with any real credibility. When allowed to operate freely, Godwin claimed, "few engines can be more powerful." The radically different tones of the reviews of Godwin's work in the staunchly conservative *British Critic* and the mildly reformist *Monthly Review* suggest the volatile context within which these debates were being conducted. It was, Godwinian reformers might have been tempted to suggest, an example of literature in action.

T.J. Mathias may have been far more concerned about the negative potential of the process of intellectual exchange than Godwin was, but despite their differences, he shared many of Godwin's most important assumptions about literature, and he used the same metaphor (an engine) to describe it: "LITERATURE, *well or ill conducted,* IS THE GREAT ENGINE *by which,* I am fully persuaded, ALL CIVILIZED STATES *must ultimately be supported or overthrown.*" This, like Godwin's comment about "the diffusion of knowledge through the medium of discussion," is an extraordinary claim that cannot possibly be reconciled with our assumptions about literature today, but it was a familiar one to most people in the Romantic period. It is consistent, for instance, with the *Analytical Review*'s comments about the emancipatory power of literature in the context of a pamphlet war between two of France's leading government ministers, M. Necker and

M. de Calonne, over the state of the country's finances. Like Godwin's and Mathias's comments, the fact that this debate was between two political figures suggests the very public role that literature was assumed to play in shaping the social and political life of the nation. Nor, as Hazlitt's discussion of literature in his essay, "The Periodical Press" suggests, should we underestimate the role of the literary reviews in making these exchanges accessible to a broader reading public.

Not everyone in the period shared this tendency to equate literature with critical debate, or to call pamphlets by finance ministers literature. Some people were already beginning to adopt our more modern definition of literature as "creative expression" associated with spiritual insight rather than social issues. Thomas De Quincey's discussion of literature in terms of power was published in 1842, after the period that we normally think of as the Romantic age had ended, but his argument was really a more explicit articulation of a position that was already inherent in William Wordsworth's Preface to the *Lyrical Ballads* and in much of S.T. Coleridge's writings. De Quincey's discussion has strong similarities with Godwin's and Mathias's description of literature as an engine, but for De Quincey the importance of literature lay in its ability to effect a spiritual rather than social transformation. Influenced by his connections with the major Romantic poets, De Quincey's distinction between literatures of knowledge and power offers a particularly clear account of what we now describe as the Romantic emphasis on the value of "creative writing" rather than intellectual exchange. It highlights the tendency, which would persist until fairly recently, to think in terms of the opposition *between* critical and creative expression, rather than in terms of their interfusion. However, as De Quincey himself acknowledged, the division was never clear cut. Leigh Hunt was an advocate of the same aesthetic ideals that De Quincey championed, but what is most striking in Hunt's case is his juxtaposition of poetry with literature as distinct discursive fields. For Hunt, the fates of poetry and literature, by which he meant the more general field of art and science, went hand in hand.

Anna Letitia Barbauld and William Hazlitt envisioned literature more as an imagined community or field of cultural production than as a spiritual or social engine, but they differed slightly in their sense of the health of this community. Barbauld was responding to the government's 1790 decision to uphold the Test Acts which rendered Protestant Dissenters ineligible for political office. For Barbauld, Dissenting authors' high moral standards offered the best proof that the government was mistaken. Her argument prefigures Percy Shelley's characterization of the poet as the unacknowledged legislator of the world, but it did so in terms of a community rather than an individual. Hazlitt was as ambivalent as Barbauld was hopeful in his summation of the dangerous instabilities of modern literature. From his perspective, the greatest enemy of the literary community was not the hostile policies of a repressive government but the permissive character of commercial society in which endless novelty threatened to undermine cultural integrity. But accepting that these changes were inevitable, he declared himself an optimist—a positive stance that was often absent in his other discussions of modern literature. Whatever their different concerns, Barbauld and Hazlitt both recognized that, for better or worse, literature was nothing more than the sum total of the efforts of the people who produced and consumed it—the same thought which attracted Godwin and worried Mathias.

ᘓᘓᘓ

WILLIAM GODWIN
An Enquiry concerning Political Justice, and its Influence on General Virtue and Happiness [1]

THREE PRINCIPAL CAUSES OF MORAL
IMPROVEMENT CONSIDERED

I. *LITERATURE*
Benefits of literature.—Examples.—Essential properties of literature.—Its defects.

II. *EDUCATION*
Benefits of education.—Causes of its imbecility.

III. *POLITICAL JUSTICE*
Benefits of political institution.—Universality of its influence—Proved by the mistakes of society.—Origin of evil.

THERE are three principal causes by which the human mind is advanced towards a state of perfection; literature, or the diffusion of knowledge through the medium of discussion, whether written or oral; education, or a scheme for the early impression of right principles upon the hitherto unprejudiced mind; and political justice, or the adoption of any principle of morality and truth into the practice of a community. Let us take a momentary review of each of these.

I. LITERATURE

FEW engines can be more powerful, and at the same time more salutary in their tendency, than literature. Without enquiring for the present into the cause of this phenomenon, it is sufficiently evident in fact, that the human mind is strongly infected with prejudice and mistake. The various opinions prevailing in different countries and among different classes of men upon the same subject, are almost innumerable; and yet of all these opinions only one can be true. Now the effectual way for extirpating these prejudices and mistakes seems to be literature.

Literature has reconciled the whole thinking world respecting the great principles of the system of the universe, and extirpated upon this subject the dreams of romance and the dogmas of superstition. Literature has unfolded the nature of the human

[1] The most prominent of the middle-class reformers in the 1790s, William Godwin (1756–1836) was famous for his philosophical vision of social change in *An Enquiry concerning Political Justice, and its Influence on General Virtue and Happiness* (1793), for his political thriller novel *Caleb Williams* (1794), and for other more journalistic efforts in the cause of reform. Godwin championed fundamental social and political reforms, and insisted that they could only be achieved through robust intellectual debate, but warned that this required a degree of reflection that was irreconcilable with the mob mentality of a mass movement.

mind, and Locke[1] and others have established certain maxims respecting man, as Newton[2] has done respecting matter, that are generally admitted for unquestionable. Discussion has ascertained with tolerable perspicuity the preference of liberty over slavery; and the Mainwarings, the Sibthorpes, and the Filmers, the race of speculative reasoners in favour of despotism, are almost extinct.[3] Local prejudice had introduced innumerable privileges and prohibitions upon the subject of trade; speculation has nearly ascertained that perfect freedom is most favourable to her prosperity. If in many instances the collation of evidence have failed to produce universal conviction, it must however be considered, that it has not failed to produce irrefragable argument, and that falshood would have been much shorter in duration, if it had not been protected and inforced by the authority of political government.

Indeed, if there be such a thing as truth, it must infallibly be struck out by the collision of mind with mind. The restless activity of intellect will for a time be fertile in paradox and error; but these will be only diurnals, while the truths that occasionally spring up, like sturdy plants, will defy the rigour of season and climate. In proportion as one reasoner compares his deductions with those of another, the weak places of his argument will be detected, the principles he too hastily adopted will be overthrown, and the judgments, in which his mind was

exposed to no sinister influence, will be confirmed. All that is requisite in these discussions is unlimited speculation, and a sufficient variety of systems and opinions. While we only dispute about the best way of doing a thing in itself wrong, we shall indeed make but a trifling progress; but, when we are once persuaded that nothing is too sacred to be brought to the touchstone of examination, science will advance with rapid strides. Men, who turn their attention to the boundless field of enquiry, and still more who recollect the innumerable errors and caprices of mind, are apt to imagine that the labour is without benefit and endless. But this cannot be the case, if truth at last have any real existence. Errors will, during the whole period of their reign, combat each other; prejudices that have passed unsuspected for ages, will have their era of detection; but, if in any science we discover one solitary truth, it cannot be overthrown.

Such are the arguments that may be adduced in favour of literature. But, even should we admit them in their full force, and at the same time suppose that truth is the omnipotent artificer by which mind can infallibly be regulated, it would yet by no means sufficiently follow that literature is alone adequate to all the purposes of human improvement. Literature, and particularly that literature by which prejudice is superseded, and the mind is strung to a firmer tone, exists only as the portion of a few. The multitude, at least in the present state of human society, cannot partake of its illuminations. For that purpose it would be necessary, that the general system of policy should become favourable, that every individual should have leisure for reasoning and reflection, and that there should be no species of public institution, which, having falshood for his basis, should counteract their progress. This state of society, if it did not precede the general dissemination of truth, would at least be the immediate result of it.

---

[1] John Locke (1632–1704), an influential political philosopher whose argument against the divine right of kings in *Two Treatises on Government* (1690) was celebrated by many reformers for its emphasis on the right of individuals to fashion a government that reflects their interests.

[2] Sir Isaac Newton (1642–1727), mathematician and natural philosopher. By the end of the eighteenth century, Newton had become an almost legendary figure amongst advocates of experimental science.

[3] Arthur Mainwaring (1668–1712), Whig polemicist; Sir Christopher Sibthorpe, (*d.* 1632), pamphleteer; Sir Robert Filmer (*c.* 1590–1653), political writer. Godwin is citing them as examples of reactionary thinkers fearful of social and political progress.

But in representing this state of society as the ultimate result, we should incur an obvious fallacy. The discovery of truth is a pursuit of such vast extent, that it is scarcely possible to prescribe bounds to it. Those great lines, which seem at present to mark the limits of human understanding, will, like the mists that rise from a lake, retire farther and farther the more closely we approach them. A certain quantity of truth will be sufficient for the subversion of tyranny and usurpation; and this subversion, by a reflected force, will assist our understandings in the discovery of truth. In the mean time, it is not easy to define the exact portion of discovery that must necessarily precede political melioration. The period of partiality and injustice will be shortened, in proportion as political rectitude occupies a principal share in our disquisition. When the most considerable part of a nation, either for numbers or influence, becomes convinced of the flagrant absurdity of its institutions, the whole will soon be prepared tranquilly and by a sort of common consent to supersede them.

(1793)

MONTHLY REVIEW
Review of *An Enquiry concerning Political Justice, and its Influence on General Virtue and Happiness*. By William Godwin

IT may well be doubted whether, at any period, since the fatal contest between Charles I. and his parliament,[1] the minds of men have been so much awakened to political inquiry, as they are at this moment. If the well-being of society may be said to depend on the progress of political knowledge, it will follow that nothing is so desirable as the earnest pursuit of this inquiry; and what indeed can so effectually promote the peace and welfare of society, as knowledge? Wherefore do men dispute, quarrel, and make war on each other, but in consequence of their mistakes? Who will affirm that devastation and slaughter are good?—and why do these happen, but because of individual and general *ignorance*? Hence, too, arises all the oppression that exists among mankind; from which no system of government, nor of legislation, can free them; though, by unwise legislation and misgovernment, evils may be perpetuated. A general diffusion of knowledge is the only remedy for these evils; and he, who increases its stores, is the most useful of citizens, and the best of benefactors to mankind.

For these reasons, we have no small degree of pleasure in announcing the present work to our readers; as one, which, from the freedom of its inquiry, the grandeur of its views, and the fortitude of its principles, is eminently deserving of attention.—By this eulogium, we would by no means be understood to subscribe to all the principles which these volumes contain. Knowledge is not yet arrived at that degree of certainty, which is requisite for any two men to think alike on all subjects; neither has language attained that consistent accuracy, which can enable them to convey their thoughts, even when they do think alike, in a manner perfectly correct and intelligible to both. These difficulties are only to be overcome by a patient, incessant, and benevolent investigation.

Many of the opinions, which this work contains, are bold; some of them are novel; and some, doubtless, are erroneous:—but that which ought to endear it even to those whose principles it may offend, is the strength of argument adduced in it to prove, that peace and order most effectually promote the happiness after which political reformers are panting;—that, as the progress of knowledge is gradual, political reform ought not to be precipitate;—and that convulsive violence is dangerous,

---

[1] Charles I was executed in 1649 during the English Civil War.

not only to individuals, (for *that* result, comparatively, would be of small account,) but to the general cause of truth. It is the opposite of this principle that inspires the enemies of political inquiry with so much terror; it is the supposition that change must inevitably be attended by the turbulence and injustice of commotion; and that innovation cannot be made, without the intervention of evils more destructive than those which are intended to be reformed. Under the conviction of this philanthropic sentiment, of calm and gradual reform, (which, in its proper place, he has fully illustrated,) Mr. Godwin proceeds, without scruple, first to inquire into present evil, through its essential branches, and next to demonstrate future good.

(1793)

BRITISH CRITIC
Review of *An Enquiry concerning Political Justice, and its Influence on General Virtue and Happiness*. By William Godwin

WHEN we meet a man who frequently and violently extols his own wisdom, knowledge, and sagacity, the obvious, and almost infallible conclusion, is, that he is shallow, ignorant, and foolish. Experience daily shows that this conclusion is not in the least too harsh; and reason fully justifies it, by pronouncing, that no wise man could be so ill-informed, either of his own imperfections, or of the comparative merits of others, as to be guilty of such empty boasting. The reason extends equally to a whole age; and we live in an age which is so perpetually vaunting its own illumination and knowledge, that a consistent reasoner can have little doubt, even from this single symptom, that it must be the most vain, shallow, foolish, and impertinent age, that ever the revolution of time has yet brought into existence. The cause of this absurd vanity is as

ridiculous in this case as in any other. Having been fortunately directed, by a more thinking age, into the right method of investigating facts in natural philosophy, the present generation in Europe, (for of Europe only we speak) has taken some pains in pursuing that method, which is matter of curiosity and entertainment; has collected a great number of facts; and has drawn the natural conclusions from them: and, for this reason, it has very wisely concluded itself to be a most enlightened generation. But setting aside natural and experimental philosophy; which, for the reasons just suggested, has been the hobby-horse of these times, it would have been an odd, and very extraordinary instance of good fortune, if the present race of Europeans had possessed more wisdom than all others, since it most remarkably neglects all methods of acquiring it. Intense study and indefatigable application are almost unheard of; the patience of former students, in searching out whatever could be known on any subject, is held almost incredible; or if not incredible, ridiculous: since it has been found, it seems, that a casual thought upon an abstruse subject decides it better than a profound enquiry; and that wisdom and knowledge come, to *enlightened ages*, like Sir Andrew Aguecheek's reading and writing, *by nature*.[1] All this is so evident, that few pretend to deny the present to be an indolent and superficial age, though at the same time they will extol it as informed and enlightened; putting these detached assertions together, we shall have some thing very like the truth; which is, that it is an indolently informed, and superficially enlightened age: despising all former wisdom, chiefly from not knowing it precisely; and free in assertion rather than enquiry, merely from that impudence which ignorance alone produces, and from a childish love of novelty, unchecked by fear of consequences, or veneration of any principles. Hence is it that a few specious, but

---

[1] William Shakespeare (1564–1616), *Twelfth Night* (1600): I: iii: 28.

not sound, metaphysicians, with not much higher talents, for such purposes, than those of saying bold things in an original or witty manner, and of giving a false colour to paradoxes (which are either new, because they never were before thought worthy to be advanced, or, being old, were given up as too nonsensical to be supported) have been dignified with the title of *philosophers*, conferred, as is usual in such cases, by themselves; but conceded, as is very wonderful, by many others. There is much reason to apprehend that if this *enlightened* age should be succeeded by times of real wisdom and of sound research, the general laugh of posterity will attend those high pretensions which a few have uttered with such courage, and multitudes have admitted with such *levity*.

But, of all the ridiculous circumstances which these propensities have yet produced, there are few more remarkable, than that there should have arisen a person so wildly extravagant as to write and publish, and even one or two to commend, so perfectly chimerical a book as that which is the subject of this article. The author, full of that importance which makes him suppose he shall attract prodigious attention, and excite vast movement, flatters himself he shall become the subject of persecution; and works himself up to a spirit of martyrdom that he may support all the evil this formidable book shall draw upon him. But alas! a much heavier fate than persecution awaits him, and one for which perhaps his mind is not equally prepared; the worst fate that can attend ambitious authorship, and system-making, neglect. Two bulky quartos contain too much reading to be popular; and one pound sixteen is too serious a sum for any man to give, merely to see Mr. Burke's ironical satire upon civil society,[†] and Swift's exaggerated

descriptions of the depravity of man, advanced into a grave system, gravely intended at least, for the conduct of the world.[††] Secure in these great pledges of obscurity, full many a copy have we seen with its title page exposed in a window, with its leaves uncut, till flies and dust had defaced its open front, and many an one, perhaps, shall see descending from the flies above to those of subterraneous London, guiltless of having seduced one wavering mind, or excited even a wish to prosecute, much less to persecute the author.

(1793)

T.J. Mathias
The Pursuits of Literature: A Satirical Poem in Four Dialogues [1]

IN my introduction to the Third Dialogue, feeling the importance of my subject in it's various branches, I asserted that, "LITERATURE, *well or ill conducted*, IS THE GREAT ENGINE *by which*, I am fully persuaded, ALL CIVILIZED STATES *must ultimately be supported or overthrown*." I am now more and more deeply impressed with this truth, if we consider the nature, variety and extent of the word, Literature. We are no longer in an age of ignorance, and information is not partially distributed according to the ranks, and orders, and

the principle which forms the ground-work of Mr. Godwin's book was too absurd to be maintained a moment.

[††] Both these authors are quoted in pp. 9 and 10.

[1] Thomas James Mathias (*c.* 1745–1835) published the first part of his satirical poem, *The Pursuits of Literature*, in 1794. In the mid-to-late 1790s, the ultra-conservative Mathias responded to the revolutionary controversy by publishing three more parts. Its vicious satirical tone coincided with the polarized spirit of the period and earned the poem a great deal of attention amongst like-minded readers. The fact that Mathias continued to publish it anonymously also helped to fuel the public's interest, and led to a lively debate about the identity of the author in conservative literary magazines such as the *Gentleman's*.

[†] Published originally in 1756, and called *A Vindication of Natural Society*; reprinted in a set of *Fugitive Pieces*, published by the Dodsleys in 1761. Written in ridicule of Bolingbroke, on the supposition, that

functions, and dignities of social life. All learning has an index, and every science it's abridgement. I am scarcely able to name any man whom I consider as wholly ignorant. We no longer look exclusively for learned authors in the usual place; in the retreats of academic erudition, and in the seats of religion. Our peasantry now read the *Rights of Man* on mountains, and moors, and by the way side; and shepherds make the analogy between their occupation and that of their governors. Happy indeed, had they been taught to make no other comparison.[1] Our *unsexed* female writers now instruct, or confuse, us and themselves in the labyrinth of politics, or turn us wild with Gallick frenzy.[2]

But there is one publication of the time too peculiar, and too important to be passed over in a general reprehension. There is nothing with which it may be compared. A legislator in our own parliament, a member of the House of Commons of Great Britain, an elected guardian and defender of the laws, the religion, and the good manners of the country, has neither scrupled nor blushed to depict, and to publish to the world, the arts of lewd and systematic seduction, and to thrust upon the nation the most open and unqualified blasphemy against the very code and volume of our religion. And all

this, with his name, style, and title, prefixed to the novel or romance called "The Monk."[3]

(1797)

ANALYTICAL REVIEW

Review of:

1. *Requête au Roi, &c.*—Address to the King, by M. de Calonne. London, 1787.
2. *Réponse de M. de Calonne &c.*—M. Calonne's Reply to M. Necker's Pamphlet published in April 1787, containing the Examination of his Report of the State of the Finances of France in 1774, 1776, 1781, 1783, 1787, &c. London, 1788.
3. *Sur le Compte rendu au Roi, &c.*—Explanations of the Account rendered to the King in 1781. By M. Necker. Paris, 1788.
4. *Motif de M. de Calonne, &c.*—M. de Calonne's Motive for delaying his Refutation of M. Necker's Explanations till the meeting of the States-General. London, 1788.[4]

IF there are circumstances which invariably tend to convert free into absolute governments, there are, fortunately, others which tend, by a process equally certain, to re-establish the dignity and the rights of human nature. Among these last, the most important by far, is the light of literature, widely diffused, and with increasing splendour, by the invention of printing. Literature, by enlightening the understanding, and uniting the sentiments and views of men and nations, forms a concert of wills, and a

---

[1] The "other comparison" that Mathias may have had in mind is to Edmund Burke's notorious but generally misquoted reference to the "swinish multitude" in his *Reflections on the Revolution in France*. Burke was referring to extremist factions but the comment was generally read as a reflection on Burke's condescending attitude to the poor, an insult that quickly became an ironic form of self-identification in the radical movement. Thomas Spence's radical journal, *One Pennyworth of Pig's Meat; or, Lessons for the Swinish Multitude*, is an example.

[2] The reference is to radical women writers such as Helen Maria Williams and Mary Wollstonecraft who published political works on the French Revolution. The word "unsex'd" refers to their insistence that gender difference was culturally produced rather than natural, but more ominously, it also recalls Lady Macbeth's speech before killing Duncan in *Macbeth*. It provided the title for Richard Polwhele's satirical poem, *The Unsex'd Females* (1798), which was dedicated to Mathias.

[3] Matthew Lewis's gothic novel, *The Monk* (1796), was notorious for its risque content.

[4] Jacques Necter (1732–1804), served as director-general of Finances in France from 1776 until he was replaced by Alexandre de Calonne (1734–1802). Necker was reinstated in 1788 in a final attempt to solve France's spiralling fiscal problems. The two men engaged in a very public debate over the true state of France's finances, the various elements of which are reviewed here.

concurrent of action too powerful for the armies of tyrants.

The French nation, better distinguished by the name of Franco-Galli, was the freest in Europe at a period when political liberty, under different forms, was not so rare as it is at present. The gradual encroachments of the executive on the legislative power, mechanical and mercantile employment, riches, luxury, and the very increase in population, at last converted an elective magistrate into an hereditary monarch. But liberty begins to dawn again on France, after a long night of two hundred years. A dispute arises between two ministers of state, concerning the receipt and expenditure of the public revenue. An appeal is made to the nation at large: homage is paid to reason, truth, and justice; and the way is thus prepared for the reign of freedom.

(1788)

Anna Letitia Barbauld[1]
An Address to the Opposers of the Repeal of the Corporation and Test Acts

YOU have set a mark of separation upon us, and it is not in our power to take it off; but it is in our power to determine whether it shall be a disgraceful stigma or an honorable distinction. If, by the continued peaceableness of our demeanour, and the superior sobriety of our conversation,—a sobriety for which we have not yet quite ceased to be distinguished; if, by our attention to literature, and that ardent love of liberty which you are pretty ready to allow us, we deserve esteem, we shall enjoy it. If our rising seminaries should excel in whole-

some discipline and regularity, if they should be schools of morality, and yours, unhappily, should be corrupted into schools of immorality, you will entrust us with the education of your youth, when the parent, trembling at the profligacy of the times, wishes to preserve the blooming and ingenuous child from the degrading taint of early licentiousness. If our writers are solid, elegant, or nervous, you will read our books and imbibe our sentiments, and even your preachers will not disdain, occasionally, to *illustrate* our morality. If we enlighten the world by philosophical discoveries, you will pay the involuntary homage due to genius, and boast of our names when, amongst foreign societies, you are inclined to do credit to your country. If your restraints operate towards keeping us in that middle rank of life where industry and virtue most abound, we shall have the honor to count ourselves among that class of the community which has ever been the source of manners, of population, and of wealth. If we seek for fortune in that track which you have left most open to us, we shall increase your commercial importance. If, in short, we render ourselves worthy of respect, you cannot hinder us from being respected—you cannot help respecting us—and in spite of all names of opprobrious separation, we shall be bound together by mutual esteem and the mutual reciprocation of good offices.

(1790)

Monthly Magazine
Letter

Sir,

LITERATURE is either less cultivated, or less valued in these days than it was in those of our ancestors, for certainly learning does not *now* receive the honours it *then* did. That it is less culti-

---

[1] Anna Letitia Barbauld (1743–1825), a prominent essayist, editor, poet, and author of children's books. This pamphlet reflects her reformist political sympathies. It responds to the defeat of a bill to end the prohibition of Dissenters from political office.

vated, cannot, I think, with any truth be asserted, because the present is denominated a learned age. It must be the universality then, with which it is diffused throughout society; that renders it less valuable: as articles grow cheap, not in proportion to their insignificancy, but their abundance. Great talents, indeed, in any condition of civilized society must inevitably confer a certain degree of power: inasmuch as they render their possessors either useful, or formidable: but scarcely any literary attainments would, I apprehend, raise a writer in these days, to the same degree of eminence and request, as Petrarch, Erasmus, and Politiano[1] enjoyed, in their respective times. We have now amongst us many scholars of great erudition (Parr, Wakefield, Professors Porson and White, &c. &c.):[2] men of distinguished abilities: yet I much question, as haughty as kings were under the feudal system, if any of the princes in being would contend with the same eagerness for their favour, as we learn the various sovereigns of Europe did, for that of Petrarch, or Erasmus.

It has been questioned by some, whether the number of publications, which are annually poured upon the world, have contributed in any proportionable ratio to the encrease of literature? In my opinion, they have *not*. To a liberal and cultivated mind there is certainly no indulgence equal to the luxury of books: but, in works of learning, may not the facilities of information be encreased, until the powers of application and retention be diminished? After admitting that the present is a learned age, it may appear singular to doubt, whether it affords individuals as profoundly learned, (at least, as far as Latin and Greek go,) as some who flourished in the fifteenth and sixteenth centuries.

From these remarks, I would not be understood as wishing to make invidious comparisons between the learning of different ages, or to depreciate that of our own. Upon a fair investigation, there can be no doubt, I think, to which side the scale of general literature would incline. My object simply is, to shew the different direction which letters take, and the different patronage they obtain, in different periods of society. Indeed, learning may more properly be said to *lead* than to *follow* the course of the world: since, though it may, at first, bend to the spirit of the age, it will in the end assuredly direct, and govern it. The general stock of genius is, perhaps, always pretty equal: the opportunities of improving it, and the support it receives, vary with the times. Petrarch and Erasmus were caressed by Popes and princes: Butler, Otway, and Chatterton,[3] not much inferior in merit, were absolutely starved; and Johnson,[4] whose moral works were calculated

---

[1] Francesco Petrarcha (1304–74), an Italian poet and humanist, known for his enthusiasm for Classical culture; Desiderius Erasmus (1466–1536), a Dutch humanist whose often satirical writings are seen as helping to pave the way for the reformation; *Politiano*, Angelo Poliziano (Politiano in English), the name assumed by Agnolo Ambrogini (1454–95), an Italian poet and humanist, Professor of Greek and Latin in the University of Florence, revered for his philological acumen.

[2] Samuel Parr (1747–1825), a Whig controversialist and Latin scholar; Gilbert Wakefield (1756–1801), editor of the *Georgics* (1788), *Horace* (1794), *Lucretius* (1796–99) and some Greek plays, a polemical controversialist who was jailed in 1799 for an anti-war pamphlet. One of his fiercest intellectual antagonists was Richard Porson (1759–1808), Regius professor of Greek at Cambridge; Gilbert White (1720–93), a distinguished natural historian.

[3] Samuel Butler (1612–80), best known for his satirical poetry. His three-part poem *Hudibras* (1663–78), mocked the pretensions of Presbyterians and Independents; Thomas Otway (1652–85), a playwright known for tragedies such as *Don Carlos* (1676), *The Orphan* (1680) and *Venice Preserv'd* (1682) and comedies such as *Friendship in Fashion* (1678), *The Soldier's Fortune* (1678) and *The Atheist* (1684); Thomas Chatterton (1752–70), best known for writing a group of poems which he claimed to have discovered, and which he attributed to a fifteenth-century poet named Thomas Rowley. Chatterton's suicide (though this is uncertain—it may have been an arsenic overdose, taken as a treatment for venereal disease) at a young age made him a favourite with Romantic poets who identified with his brilliance and psychological fragility.

[4] Samuel Johnson (1709–84), a poet, essayist, literary critic, lexicographer, and man of letters, was a dominant literary figure in the eighteenth century.

to delight and improve the age, lived long in distress, and at length received a scanty pension. In some ages, and upon some occasions, it must be admitted, a genius darts upon the world with intellectual powers, that no industry, in the common-course of things, can hope to equal: but this is a *particular* case, and is generally compensated some other way. If former times have enjoyed works of more fancy, and sublimity of imagination, than are given to us, we, in return, possess more useful acquisitions. If they have had their Spencer, Tasso, and Shakespere,[1] we boast Newton, Locke, and Johnson.[2]—Science, taste, and correction, are indeed the characteristics of the present day. Every thing is refined; every thing is grand. We are actually misers in luxury and taste, and have left nothing for posterity. *"Venimus ad summum fortunae"*[3]— We learn our Greek from the Pursuits of Literature, and our morality from Parissot: and I do not see how we are to be outdone either in learning or in dress.

I remain, Sir,&c.&c.

AUSONIUS[4]

Wells, Norfolk, (OCT. 24, 1798)

---

[1] Edmund Spenser (*c.* 1552–99), an English poet best known for *The Faerie Queene* (1590–96); Torquato Tasso (1544–95), an Italian poet remembered for *Jerusalem Delivered* (1580), the epic of a crusade; William Shakespeare (1564–1616), playwright and poet.

[2] John Locke (1632–1704), an influential political philosopher whose argument in *Two Treatises on Government* was celebrated by many reformers for its emphasis on the right of individuals to fashion a government that reflects their interests; Sir Isaac Newton (1642–1727), mathematician and natural philosopher; Samuel Johnson (1709–84), a poet, essayist, literary critic, lexicographer and man of letters, was a dominant literary figure in the eighteenth century.

[3] We have come to the height of fortune.

[4] Dicimus Magmus Ausonius. (*c.* 310–93), the most famous of the learned poets in the second half of the fourteenth century.

EDINBURGH REVIEW
The Periodical Press

A Review of:
The St. James Chronicle—The Morning Chronicle—The Times—The New Times—The Courier, &c.—Cobbett's Weekly Journal—The Examiner—The Observer—The Gentleman's Magazine—The New Monthly Magazine—The London, &c. &c. (1823)[5]

LITERATURE formerly was a sweet Heremitress, who fed on the pure breath of Fame, in silence and in solitude; far from the madding strife, in sylvan shade or cloistered hall, she trimmed her lamp or turned her hourglass, pale with studious care, and aiming only to "make the age to come her own!"[6] She gave her life to the perfecting some darling work, and bequeathed it, dying, to posterity! Vain hope, perhaps; but the hope itself was fruition—calm, serene, blissful, unearthly! Modern literature, on the contrary, is a gay Coquette, fluttering, fickle, vain; followed by a train of flatterers; besieged by a crowd of pretenders; courted, she courts again; receives delicious praise, and dispenses it; is impatient for applause; pants for the breath of popularity; renounces eternal fame for a newspaper puff; trifles with all sorts of arts and sciences; coquettes with fifty accomplishments—*mille ornatus habet, mille decenter,*[7] is the subject of polite conversation; the darling of private parties; the go-between

---

[5] The Edinburgh Review, founded in 1802, was the first of the literary quarterlies, a type of periodical which assumed enormous authority in the early nineteenth century. This article was published anonymously by William Hazlitt (1778–1830), a leading essayist in the period known for his critical work on literature and the fine arts, social and autobiographical reflections, and for his radical political sympathies.

[6] Abraham Cowley (1618–67), "The motto" (1656). A version of the phrase also appears in Thomas Brown (1663–1704), "To the Memory of Mr. John Oldham" (1720).

[7] She has a thousand trifling things, a thousand things which are fitting to her.

in politics; the directress of fashion; the polisher of manners; and, like her winged prototype in Spenser,

"Now this now that, she tasteth tenderly,"[1]

glitters, flutters, buzzes, spawns, dies,—and is forgotten! But the very variety and superficial polish show the extent and height to which knowledge has been accumulated, and the general interest taken in letters.

To dig to the bottom of a subject through so many generations of authors, is now impossible: the concrete mass is too voluminous and vast to be contained in any single head; and therefore, we must have essences and samples as substitutes for it. We have collected a superabundance of raw materials: the grand *desideratum*[2] now is, to fashion and render them portable. Knowledge is no longer confined to the few: the object therefore is, to make it accessible and attractive to the many. The *Monachism* of literature is at an end; the cells of learning are thrown open and let in the light of universal day. We can no longer be churls of knowledge, ascetics in pretension. We must yield to the spirit of change (whether for the better or worse); and "to beguile the time, look like the time."[3] A modern author may (without much imputation of his wisdom) declare for a short life and a merry one. He may be a little gay, thoughtless, and dissipated. Literary immortality is now let on short leases, and he must be contented to succeed by rotation. A scholar of the olden time had resources, had consolations to support him under many privations and disadvantages. A light (that light which penetrates the most clouded skies) cheered him in his lonely cell, in the most obscure retirement: and, with the eye of faith, he could see the meanness of his garb

exchanged for the wings of the Shining Ones, and the wedding-garment of the Spouse. Again, he lived only in the contemplation of old books and old events; and the remote and future became habitually present to his imagination, like the past. He was removed from low, petty vanity, by the nature of his studies, and could wait patiently for his reward till after death. We exist in the bustle of the world, and cannot escape from the notice of our contemporaries. We must please to live, and therefore should live to please. We must look to the public for support. Instead of solemn testimonies from the learned, we require the smiles of the fair and the polite. If princes scowl upon us, the broad shining face of the people may turn to us with a favorable aspect. Is not this life (too) sweet? Would we change it for the former if we could? But the great point is, that *we cannot*! Therefore, let Reviews flourish—let Magazines increase and multiply—let the Daily and Weekly Newspapers live forever! We are optimists in literature, and hold, with certain limitations that in this respect, whatever is, is right!

(1823)

Leigh Hunt
On the Connection and the Mutual Assistance of the Arts and Sciences, and the Relation of Poetry to them All.

from *The Reflector, A Collection of Essays, on Miscellaneous Subjects of Literature and Politics*[4]

THE simple truth seems to be this. The same impulse that carries the mind to poetry, in-

---

[1] Edmund Spenser (c. 1552–99), "Muiopotmos, or The Fate of the Butterflie" (1590).

[2] Desired thing.

[3] William Shakespeare (1564–1616), *Macbeth* (1606): I: v: 62–63.

[4] Leigh Hunt (1784–1859), a prominent editor and journalist, who published several periodicals including, most famously, *The Examiner* (1808–22). *The Reflector* (1810–12), which included Charles Lamb's essays on Shakespeare and Hogarth as well as various accounts of modern poetry alongside vehement political analysis, reflected Hunt's insistence on the importance of fusing cultural and political issues.

clines it to a love of general excellence, and by a most natural sympathy, to connect it with art and science. Pursue the course of poetry in England, and you will find it accompanied with literature. Chaucer,[1] the first of our poets, on reference to the change of our language from the Saxon, of much account, was well acquainted with all literature of his time, and with something better. Cowley[2] was, from his earliest childhood, devoted to study: Milton[3] was unacquainted scarcely with any branch of literature, and would have immortalized his name had he left only his prose works behind him: Dryden[4] possessed a well-furnished mind, and was a prose writer of the most varied excellence: Pope[5] converted all he read and all he saw into harmonious rhyme: Collins,[6] a bard of powerful imagination, had been a deep thinker and a successful student: and Gray,[7] though an enemy to the mathematics, was, in other respects, a most polished, fastidious scholar: poets these of the first eminence among us. They by their literature enriched their poetry; and what they borrowed from the public stock of art and science, they repaid with interest, by the pleasure and instruction which they afford mankind. Similar examples too might be shewn in our own time, to prove that the relation here contended for is real, and that those who have obtained any notice for their poetry, were persons, though in different degrees and, perhaps, different ways, of enlarged and cultivated minds.

"But such writers as Burns"—Such writers as Burns confirm my argument. That story would be poorly, indeed falsely, told, that left Burns gasping for inspiration at the ploughtail. Such a character would not have existed, but for that love of general nature and strength of feeling which in part lead to, and in part constitute, mental improvement. Writers much inferior to Burns prove no less; such as Taylor the Water Poet, and Stephen Duck the Thresher:[8] they considered mental improvement so essential to their pretensions, as to be even ostentatious of the little they knew; and whoever chooses to dip into their poems, will find that the extent of their reading was commensurate, at least, with the reach of their poetry.

(1812)

THOMAS DE QUINCEY
The Poetry of Pope [9]

WHAT is it that we mean by *literature*? Popularly, and amongst the thoughtless, it is held to include everything that is printed in a book. Little logic is required to disturb *that* definition. The most thoughtless person is easily made aware that in the idea of *literature* one essential element is some relation to a general and common interest of man,—so that what applies only to a local, or professional, or merely personal interest, even though presenting itself in the shape of a book, will not belong to Literature. So far the definition is easily narrowed; and it is as easily expanded. For not

---

[1] Geoffrey Chaucer (c. 1343–1400).

[2] Abraham Cowley (1618–67).

[3] John Milton (1608–74).

[4] John Dryden (1631–1700).

[5] Alexander Pope (1688–1744).

[6] William Collins (1721–59).

[7] Thomas Gray (1716–71).

[8] John Taylor (1580–1654), a Thames waterman, became well known for his high-spirited verse and was patronized by Ben Jonson and others; Stephen Duck (1705–56), whose most famous poem was "The Thresher's Labour," began life as a farm labourer but eventually took Holy Orders and became rector of Byfleet in 1752.

[9] Thomas De Quincey (1785–1859), an autobiographer, essayist, editor and novelist in the Romantic and early Victorian periods, was heavily influenced by the aesthetic ideals of S.T. Coleridge and William Wordsworth. De Quincey's essay, "The Poetry of Pope," which appeared in the *North British Review* in 1848, is in many ways a popularization of the arguments in Wordsworth's Preface to the *Lyrical Ballads*.

only is much that takes a station in books not literature; but inversely, much that really *is* literature never reaches a station in books. The weekly sermons of Christendom, that vast pulpit literature which acts so extensively upon the popular mind—to warn, to uphold, to renew, to comfort, to alarm—does not attain the sanctuary of libraries in the ten-thousandth part of its extent. The Drama again,—as, for instance, the finest of Shakspere's plays in England, and all leading Athenian plays in the noontide of the Attic stage,—operated as a literature on the public mind, and were (according to the strictest letter of that term) *published* through the audiences that witnessed[†] their representation some time before they were published as things to be read; and they were published in this scenical mode of publication with much more effect than they could have had as books during ages of costly copying or of costly printing.

Books, therefore, do not suggest an idea coextensive and interchangeable with the idea of Literature; since much literature, scenic, forensic, or didactic (as from lecturers and public orators), may never come into books, and much that *does* come into books may connect itself with no literary interest.[††] But a far more important correction, applicable to the common vague idea of literature, is to be sought not so much in a better definition of literature as in a sharper distinction of the two functions which it fulfils. In that great social organ which, collectively, we call literature, there may be distinguished two separate offices that may blend and often *do* so, but capable, severally, of a severe insulation, and naturally fitted for reciprocal repulsion. There is, first, the literature of *knowledge*; and, secondly, the literature of *power*. The function of the first is—to *teach*; the function of the second is—to *move*: the first is a rudder; the second, an oar or a sail. The first speaks to the *mere* discursive understanding; the second speaks ultimately, it may happen, to the higher understanding or reason, but always *through* affections of pleasure and sympathy. Remotely, it may travel towards an object seated in what Lord Bacon calls *dry* light;[†††] but, proximately, it does and must operate,—else it ceases to be a literature of *power*,—on and through that *humid* light which clothes itself in the mists and glittering *iris* of human passions, desires, and genial emotions. Men have so little reflected on the higher functions of literature as to find it a paradox if one should describe it as a mean or subordinate purpose of books to give information. But this is a paradox only in the sense which makes it honourable to be paradoxical. Whenever we talk in ordinary language of seeking information or gaining knowledge, we understand the words as connected with something of absolute novelty. But it is the grandeur of all truth which *can* occupy a very high place in human interests that it is never absolutely novel to the meanest of minds: it exists eternally by way of germ or latent principle in the lowest as in the highest, needing to be developed, but never to be planted. To be capable of transplantation is the immediate

---

[†] Charles I., for example, when Prince of Wales, and many others in his father's court, gained their known familiarity with Shakspere not through the original quartos, so slenderly diffused, nor through the first folio of 1623, but through the court representations of his chief dramas at Whitehall.

[††] What are called *The Blue Books,*—by which title are understood the folio Reports issued every session of Parliament by committees of the two Houses, and stitched into blue covers,—though often sneered at by the ignorant as so much waste paper, will be acknowledged gratefully by those who have used them diligently as the main wellheads of all accurate information as to the Great Britain of this day. As an immense depository of faithful *(and not superannuated)* statistics, they are indispensable to the honest student. But no man would therefore class the *Blue Books* as literature.

[†††] "Heraclitus saith well in one of his enigmas, *Dry light is ever the best.* And certain it is that the light that a man receiveth by counsel from another is drier and purer than that which cometh from his own understanding and judgment; which is ever infused and drenched in his affections and customs."—*Bacon's Essay on Friendship.*

criterion of a truth that ranges on a lower scale. Besides which, there is a rarer thing than truth,—namely, *power*, or deep sympathy with truth. What is the effect, for instance, upon society, of children? By the pity, by the tenderness, and by the peculiar modes of admiration, which connect themselves with the helplessness, with the innocence, and with the simplicity of children, not only are the primal affections strengthened and continually renewed, but the qualities which are dearest in the sight of heaven,—the frailty, for instance, which appeals to forbearance, the innocence which symbolises the heavenly, and the simplicity which is most alien from the worldly,—are kept up in perpetual remembrance, and their ideals are continually refreshed. A purpose of the same nature is answered by the higher literature, viz. the literature of power. What do you learn from "Paradise Lost"? Nothing at all. What do you learn from a cookery-book? Something new, something that you did not know before, in every paragraph. But would you therefore put the wretched cookery-book on a higher level of estimation than the divine poem? What you owe to Milton is not any knowledge, of which a million separate items are still but a million of advancing steps on the same earthly level; what you owe is *power*,—that is, exercise and expansion to your own latent capacity of sympathy with the infinite, where every pulse and each separate influx is a step upwards, a step ascending as upon a Jacob's ladder from earth to mysterious altitudes above the earth. *All* the steps of knowledge, from first to last, carry you further on the same plane, but could never raise you one foot above your ancient level of earth: whereas the very *first* step in power is a flight—is an ascending movement into another element where earth is forgotten.

Were it not that human sensibilities are ventilated and continually called out into exercise by the great phenomena of infancy, or of real life as it moves through chance and change, or of literature as it recombines these elements in the mimicries of poetry, romance, &c., it is certain that, like any animal power or muscular energy falling into disuse, all such sensibilities would gradually droop and dwindle. It is in relation to these great *moral* capacities of man that the literature of power, as contradistinguished from that of knowledge, lives and has its field of action. The very highest work that has ever existed in the Literature of Knowledge is but a *provisional* work: a book upon trial and sufferance, and *quamdiu bene se gesserit*.[1] Let its teaching be even partially revised, let it be but expanded,— nay, even let its teaching be but placed in a better order,—and instantly it is superseded. Whereas the feeblest works in the Literature of Power, surviving at all, survive as finished and unalterable amongst men. For instance, the *Principia* of Sir Isaac Newton was a book *militant* on earth from the first. In all stages of its progress it would have to fight for its existence: 1st, as regards absolute truth; 2dly, when that combat was over as regards its form or mode of presenting the truth. And as soon as a La Place,[2] or anybody else, builds higher upon the foundations laid by this book, effectually he throws it out of the sunshine into decay and darkness; by weapons won from this book he superannuates and destroys this book, so that soon the name of Newton remains as a mere *nominis umbra*,[3] but his book, as a living power, has transmigrated into other forms. Now, on the contrary, the Iliad, the Prometheus of Æschylus, the Othello or King Lear, the Hamlet or Macbeth, and

---

[1] As long as he will conduct himself well.

[2] Pierre Simon Laplace (1749–1827), French astronomer and mathematician. His most popular work, *Exposition du système du monde* (1796), offered both a summary of the history of astronomy and a hypothesis of the origin of the solar system. His research, published in his famous *Mécanique céleste* (1799–1825, tr. by Nathaniel Bowditch, 1829–39) helped to validate Newton's theory of gravitation.

[3] Shadow of a name.

the Paradise Lost, are not militant but triumphant for ever as long as the languages exist in which they speak or can be taught to speak. They never *can* transmigrate into new incarnations. To reproduce *these* in new forms, or variations, even if in some things they should be improved, would be to plagiarise. A good steam-engine is properly superseded by a better. But one lovely pastoral valley is not superseded by another, nor a statue of Praxiteles by a statue of Michael Angelo.

All the literature of knowledge builds only ground-nests that are swept away by floods, or confounded by the plough; but the literature of power builds nests in aerial altitudes of temples sacred from violation, or of forests inaccessible to fraud. *This* is a great prerogative of the *power* literature; and it is a greater which lies in the mode of its influence. The *knowledge* literature, like the fashion of this world, passeth away. An Encyclopaedia is its abstract; and, in this respect, it may be taken for its speaking symbol—that before one generation has passed an Encyclopaedia is superannuated; for it speaks through the dead memory and unimpassioned understanding, which have not the repose of higher faculties, but are continually enlarging and varying their phylacteries. But all literature properly so called—literature κατ᾽ ἐξοκην,[1]—for the very same reason that it is so

much more durable than the literature of knowledge, is (and by the very same proportion it is) more intense and electrically searching in its impressions. The directions in which the tragedy of this planet has trained our human feelings to play, and the combinations into which the poetry of this planet has thrown our human passions of love and hatred, of admiration and contempt, exercise a power for bad or good over human life that cannot be contemplated, when stretching through many generations, without a sentiment allied to awe.[†] And of this let every one be assured—that he owes to the impassioned books which he has read many a thousand more of emotions than he can consciously trace back to them. Dim by their origination, these emotions yet arise in him, and mould him through life, like forgotten incidents of his childhood.

(1848)

---

[1] Outstanding.

[†] The reason why the broad distinctions between the two literatures of power and knowledge so little fix the attention lies in the fact that a vast proportion of books,—history, biography, travels, miscellaneous essays, &c.,—lying in a middle zone, confound these distinctions by interblending them. All that we call "amusement" or "entertainment" is a diluted form of the power belonging to passion, and also a mixed form; and, where threads of direct *instruction* intermingle in the texture with these threads of *power*, this absorption of the duality into one representative *nuance* neutralises the separate perception of either. Fused into a *tertium quid*, or neutral state, they disappear to the popular eye as the repelling forces which, in fact, they are.

SECTION TWO

The Reading Public

Debates about the reading public were as explicit and as passionately argued as were the debates about the meaning of literature itself. In many ways, the two issues could never be separated. The question of what one thought literature should be necessarily implied a sense of who should be reading it, and what effect it should have on them. For many critics, this generated an even more vivid sense of who should *not* be members of the reading public. This question gained added urgency because of a growing sense that the reading public had expanded in potentially threatening ways. The spectre of the lower orders reading Tom Paine "on mountains, and moors, and by the way side," as T.J. Mathias put it in *The Pursuits of Literature*, threw the broader implications of these debates into stark relief. The importance of these issues was confirmed in a very different context when the Attorney General, trying Paine *in absentia* for seditious libel for *Rights of Man* Part Two, insisted that the greatest proof of Paine's guilt was the ways that it was being disseminated amongst an improper audience. What the prosecutor's more colourful description alluded to was the fact that, unlike Part One, which had cost the same price as Burke's *Reflections on the Revolution in France* (three shillings), Part Two had been released as a cheap sixpenny pamphlet. Paine's defense lawyer, Thomas Erskine, contested this argument that a particular readership ought to imply criminality, but Erskine used the same argument himself five years later as prosecuting attorney when Thomas Williams, Paine's publisher, was tried for seditious libel for releasing a cheap version of the atheistic tract, *Age of Reason*.

The result of all of these politically driven concerns was a very explicit debate about the actual and potential status of the reading public. Conservative critics worried that the spectre of a mass reading public confident of its abilities to participate in the debate about the nature of government threatened to undermine the traditional connections between liberty and print. For the letter writer to the *Gentleman's Magazine* who signed himself Eusebius, educating the lower orders merely made them vulnerable to the stratagems of desperate reformers whose aims ran counter to the best interests of the country. More optimistic authors embraced this expansion of the reading public as a necessary stage in the realization of true liberty. Hazlitt's image of a battering ram offered a vivid depiction of the absolute power of this new reading public once it had developed an accurate sense of its own true interests.

Eusebius's other letter to *Gentleman's*, on novel reading, highlights another source of worry for many commentators. Critics were concerned that an expanded reading public posed a threat, not just to the political stability of the nation, but to its cultural health as well. If, for Eusebius, poorly educated workers were more concerned than they ought to be about the political affairs of their nation, women novel readers (for Eusebius, as for many of his contemporaries, the two were synonymous) were far less serious than they ought to be about the educational potential that reading offered. This fear that people were no longer reading for the right reasons was a common one. Godwin's argument was not with political adversaries so much as with the poetic notion that hard study undermined the supreme power of inspiration. But even Godwin allowed that there was an increasing temptation to read too much rather than to read with any kind of critical rigour. As passionate as Hazlitt's argument for the good judgement of the reading public may have been, he qualified it too, closing with a mock apocalyptic image of the world turned into waste paper as more people turned from readers to authors.

For Coleridge, the term "reading public" was an oxymoron, a prime example of "the misgrowth of our luxuriant activity." Reading, he argued, ought to be what it used to be, an activity reserved for a learned audience that was prepared to give it their serious and passionate attention. But given the fact that this could no longer be the case, Coleridge—unlike Eusebius—insisted that the best solution was not to try to stuff mass literacy back into the historical bottle but to face the problem head-on by developing a national program of education that would teach people to read in suitably controlled ways. Coleridge warned that true education must involve far more than simply teaching the skills of reading and writing, but it was conservatives' emphasis on conditioning the plebeian reading public in order to deprive it of its potential power of self-determination that Willaim Cobbett objected to in his "Letter to Alderman Wood," which appeared in his *Political Register*. Cobbett's career as a veteran political journalist is itself proof of his deep convictions about the power of an expanded reading public, but he recognized the dangers of placing too much faith in reading in situations where it was subject to the overbearing scrutiny and manipulation of political authorities.

On a completely different level, the reading public was being defined through the literary self-representation of various readers. In identifying themselves as cultural consumers, these people implied a corresponding sense of the product they were consuming. Being genteel readers, like the self-image of the *Gentleman's* correspondent, reveling in his latest monthly edition over "a bottle of my oldest port" before a well-made fire after his morning's ride, suggested a correspondingly elevated sense of literature itself. For Leigh Hunt, the world of books was a quasi-aristocratic world that transcended the more sordid issue of property rights. True book-lovers were above worrying about whose books belonged to whom. They existed in a cultural domain that was nearly as autonomous as Hunt's image of his study, walled in with books. Images of readers proliferated throughout this period. We will see more sustained examples in the section on autobiographies. Their ultimate effect was to intensify the emphasis on the prestige that was associated with being the sort of person who was well acquainted with the correct sorts of literature, and who had the correct motives for being so. The challenge, of course, was to establish which types of literature and which motives were the "correct" ones—an exercise that inevitably fueled denunciations of supposedly illegitimate readers and reading habits.

∽∾∽

S.T. Coleridge
The Statesman's Manual: A Lay Sermon[1]

WHEN I named this Essay a Sermon, I sought to prepare the inquirers after it for the absence of all the usual softenings suggested by worldly prudence, of all compromise between truth and courtesy. But not even as a Sermon would I have addressed the present Discourse to a promiscuous audience; and for this reason I likewise announced it in the title-page, as exclusively *ad clerum*; i.e. (in the old and wide sense of the word) to men of *clerkly* acquirements, of whatever profession.[2] I would that the greater part of our publications could be thus *directed*, each to its appropriate class of Readers. But this cannot be! For among other odd burs and kecksies,[3] the misgrowth of our luxuriant activity, we have now a READING PUBLIC [†]—as strange a phrase, methinks, as ever

exclusively for the primitive converts from Judaism, was accommodated to their prejudices, and is of no authority, as a rule of faith, for Christians in general. "The READING PUBLIC in this ENLIGHTENED AGE, and THINKING NATION, by its favorable reception of LIBERAL IDEAS, has long demonstrated the benign influence of that PROFOUND PHILOSOPHY which has already emancipated us from so many absurd prejudices held in superstitious awe by our deluded forefathers. But the *Dark Age* yielded at length to the dawning light of Reason and Common-Sense at the glorious, though imperfect, Revolution. THE PEOPLE can be no longer duped or scared out of their *imprescriptible and inalienable* RIGHT to judge and decide for themselves on all important questions of Government and Religion. The *scholastic jargon* of jarring articles and metaphysical creeds may continue for a time to deform our Church-establishment; and like the grotesque figures in the nitches of our old gothic cathedrals may serve to remind the nation of its former barbarism; but the *universal suffrage* of a FREE AND ENLIGHTENED PUBLIC," &c. &c.!

Among the Revolutions worthy of notice, the change in the nature of the introductory sentences and prefatory matter in serious Books is not the least striking. The same gross flattery which disgusts us in the dedications to individuals in the elder writers, is now transferred to the Nation at large, or the READING PUBLIC: while the Jeremiads of our old Moralists, and their angry denunciations concerning the ignorance, immorality, and irreligion of the *People*, appear (mutatis mutandis, and with an appeal to the worst passions, envy, discontent, scorn, vindictiveness, &c.) in the shape of bitter libels on Ministers, Parliament, the Clergy: in short, on the State and Church, and all persons employed in them. Likewise, I would point out to the Reader's attention the marvellous predominance at present of the *words*, Idea and Demonstration. Every talker now a days has an *Idea*; aye, and he will demonstrate it too! A few days ago, I heard one of the READING PUBLIC, a thinking and independant smuggler, *euphonize* the latter word with much significance, in a tirade against the planners of the late African expedition: *As to Algiers, any man that has half an IDEA in his skull, must know, that it has been long ago dey-monstered, I should say, dey-monstrified*, &c. But, the phrase, which occasioned this note, brings to my mind the mistake of a lethargic Dutch traveller, who returning highly gratified from a showman's caravan, which he had been tempted to enter by the words, THE LEARNED PIG, gilt on the pannels, met another caravan of a similar shape, with THE READING FLY on it, in letters of the same size and splendour. Why, dis is voonders above voonders! exclaims the Dutchman, takes his seat as first comer, and soon fatigued by waiting, and by the very hush and

---

[1] Samuel Taylor Coleridge (1772–1834), a well-known poet, literary critic and social commentator, He was hired in 1816 by the publisher Rest Fenner to write three Lay Sermons addressing the social and political unrest that had begun to grow after the end of the Napoleonic war. These sermons were to be directed to "the higher classes of society" in the first, "the higher and middle classes" in the second, and the labouring classes in the third, which remained unwritten. This extract is from the first Lay Sermon, which was titled *The Statesman's Manual*.

[2] To men of learning.

[3] William Shakespeare (1564–1616), *Henry V* (1599): V: ii: 51–53.

[†] Some participle passive in the diminutive form, ERUDITULORUM NATIO for instance, might seem at first sight a fuller and more exact designation; but the superior force and humor of the former become evident whenever the phrase occurs as a step or stair in a *climax* of irony. By way of example take the following sentences, transcribed from a work *demonstrating* that the New Testament was intended

forced a splenetic smile on the staid countenance of Meditation; and yet no fiction! For our Readers have, in good truth, multiplied exceedingly, and have waxed proud. It would require the intrepid accuracy of a Colquhoun[1] to venture at the precise number of that vast company only, whose heads and hearts are dieted at the two public *ordinaries* of Literature, the circulating libraries and the periodical press. But what is the result? Does the inward man thrive on this regime? Alas! if the average health of the consumers may be judged of by the articles of largest consumption; if the secretions may be conjectured from the ingredients of the dishes that are found best suited to their palates; from all that I have seen, either of the banquet or the guests, I shall utter my *Profaccia*[2] with a desponding sigh. From a popular philosophy and a philosophic populace, Good Sense deliver us!

At present, however, I am to imagine for myself a very different audience. I appeal exclusively to men, from whose station and opportunities I may dare anticipate a respectable portion of that "*sound book learnedness*,"[3] into which our old public schools still continue to initiate their pupils. I appeal to men in whom I may hope to find, if not philosophy, yet occasional impulses at least to philosophic thought. And here, as far as my own experience extends, I can announce one favorable symptom. The notion of our measureless superiority in good sense to our ancestors, so general at the commencement of the French Revolution, and for some years before it, is out of fashion. We hear, at

least, less of the jargon of this *enlightened age*. After fatiguing itself, as performer or spectator in the giddy figure-dance of political changes, Europe has seen the shallow foundations of its self-complacent faith give way; and among men of influence and property, we have now more reason to apprehend the stupor of despondence, than the extravagancies of hope, unsustained by experience, or of self-confidence not bottomed on principle.

In this rank of life the danger lies, not in any tendency to innovation, but in the choice of the means for preventing it. And here my apprehensions point to two opposite errors; each of which deserves a separate notice. The first consists in a disposition to think, that as the Peace of Nations has been disturbed by the diffusion of a false light, it may be re-established by excluding the people from all knowledge and all prospect of amelioration. O! never, never! Reflection and stirrings of mind, with all their restlessness, and all the errors that result from their imperfection, from the *Too much*, because *Too little*, are come into the world. The Powers, that awaken and foster the spirit of curiosity, are to be found in every village: Books are in every hovel. The Infant's cries are hushed with *picture*-books: and the Cottager's child sheds his first bitter tears over pages, which render it impossible for the man to be treated or governed as a child. Here as in so many other cases, the inconveniences that have arisen from a thing's having become too general, are best removed by making it universal.

The other and contrary mistake proceeds from the assumption, that a national education will have been realized whenever the People at large have been taught to read and write. Now among the many means to the desired end, this is doubtless one, and not the least important. But neither is it the most so. Much less can it be held to *constitute* Education, which consists in *educing* the faculties, and forming the habits; the means varying accord-

---

intensity of his expectation, gives way to his constitutional somnulence, from which he is roused by the supposed showman at Hounslow, with a *In what name, Sir! was your place taken? Are you booked all the way for Reading?*—Now a Reading Public is (to my mind) more marvellous still, and in the third tier of 'Voonders above Voonders.'

[1] Patrick Colquhoun (1745–1820). The author of *Treatise on the Police of the Metropolis* (1796).

[2] Good wishes offered before a meal or drink.

[3] William Wordsworth, *The Prelude* III: 398.

ing to the sphere in which the individuals to be educated are likely to act and become useful. I do not hesitate to declare, that whether I consider the nature of the discipline adopted, or the plan of poisoning the children of the poor with a sort of *potential* infidelity under the "*liberal idea*" of teaching those points only of religious faith, in which all denominations agree, I cannot but denounce the so called Lancastrian schools[1] as pernicious beyond all power of compensation by the new acquirement of Reading and Writing.—But take even Dr. Bell's original and unsophisticated plan,[2] which I myself regard as an especial gift of Providence to the *human race*; and suppose this incomparable machine, this vast moral steam-engine to have been adopted and in free motion throughout the Empire; it would yet appear to me a most dangerous delusion to rely on it as if this of itself formed an efficient national education. We cannot, I repeat, honor the scheme too highly as a prominent and necessary part of the great process; but it will neither supersede nor can it be substituted for sundry other measures, that are at least equally important. And these are such measures, too, as unfortunately involve the necessity of sacrifices on the side of the rich and powerful more costly, and far more difficult than the yearly subscription of a few pounds! Such measures as demand more self-denial than the expenditure of time in a committee or of eloquence in a public meeting.

Nay, let Dr. Bell's philanthropic end have been realized, and the proposed modicum of learning universal: yet convinced of its insufficiency to stem up against the strong currents *set in* from an opposite point, I dare not assure myself, that it may not be driven backward by them and become confluent with the evils, it was intended to preclude.

What other measures I had in contemplation, it has been my endeavour to explain elsewhere.[3] But I am greatly deceived, if one preliminary to an efficient education of the laboring classes be not the recurrence to a more manly discipline of the intellect on the part of the learned themselves, in short a thorough re-casting of the moulds, in which the minds of our Gentry, the characters of our future Land-owners, Magistrates and Senators, are to receive their shape and fashion.

(1816)

JOHN STUART MILL
The Present State of Literature[4]

IT is the demand, in literature as in most other things, which calls forth the supply. Among mental as well as among physical endowments, that is most cultivated which is most admired. When the public bestowed so much of its admiration upon skill in cutting throats, that it had very little to spare for any thing else, all the ardent characters betook themselves to the trade of blood, and made it their pride to be distinguished chiefly by the warlike virtues. At other times, when the chief source of reputation was oratorical or poetical merit, every

[1] Joseph Lancaster (1799–1838), author of *Improvements in Education*, worked with the British and Foreign School Society, formed in 1814, to institute a set of schools based on a monitorial system of teaching. Romantic writers such as Coleridge and Southey objected to what they saw as its excessively disciplinarian focus.

[2] Dr. Andrew Bell (1753–1832), was associated with a similar but competing system that emphasized student monitors, creating a kind of pyramid structure in which students taught less advanced students, who in turn taught students who were still less advanced. There was considerable controversy between the proponents of the two approaches. Bell's system was associated with the Church of England; Lancaster's was associated with schools run by Dissenters for the poor.

[3] It is unclear which of his other writings Coleridge is referring to, though he may have had the next Lay Sermon, addressed "To The Higher and Middle Classes," in mind.

[4] John Stuart Mill (1806–73), a political, social and economic philosopher. This passage is from a speech that Mill gave on 16 November, 1827, at a meeting of the London Debating Society.

body who possessed, or thought he possessed genius, was an orator or a poet. There have always been men, who without much aiming at reputation, wrote chiefly to please themselves or to improve their readers. But the grand object of writers in general is success. The qualities most calculated to ensure success, constitute the sole idea they have of merit: they cultivate in their own minds a habit of being pleased with that which they find pleases those to whom they address themselves: their aim is to be read and admired, and the degree in which that aim is successful, is the test by which they try their own merits, and those of others. The weaker minds cannot resist the contagion of the common opinion or the common taste: and such of the stronger as prefer the honour and profit of pleasing others to the satisfaction of pleasing themselves, set the example to their numerous imitators of sailing with the stream.

Assuming therefore as an indisputable truth, that the writers of every age are for the most part what the readers make them, it becomes important to the present question to consider who formed the reading public formerly, and who compose it now. The present age is very remarkably distinguished from all other ages by the number of persons who can read, and what is of more consequence by the number who do. Our working classes have learned to read, and our idle classes have learned to find pleasure in reading, and to devote a part of that time to it, which they formerly spent in amusements of a grosser kind. That human nature will be a gainer, and that in a high degree by this change, no one can be more firmly convinced than I am: but it will perhaps be found, that the benefit lies rather in the ultimate, than in the immediate effects. Reading is necessary; but no wise or even sensible man was ever made by reading alone. The proper use of reading is to be subservient to thinking. It is by those who read to think, that knowl-

edge is advanced, prejudices dispelled, and the physical and moral condition of mankind is improved. I cannot however perceive that the general diffusion (so remarkable in our own day) of the taste for reading, has yet been accompanied by any marked increase in taste for the severer exercises of the intellect; that such will one day be its effect, may fairly be presumed; but it has not yet declared itself: and it is to the immense multiplication in the present day of those who read but do not think, that I should be disposed to ascribe what I view as the degeneracy of our literature.

In former days the literati and the learned formed a class apart: and few concerned themselves with literature and philosophy except those who had leisure and inclination to form their philosophical opinions by study and meditation, and to cultivate their literary taste by the assiduous perusal of the most approved models. Those whose sole occupation was pleasure, did not seek it in books, but in the gaieties of a court, or in field sports and debauchery. The public for which authors wrote was a small but, to a very considerable degree, an instructed public; and their suffrages were only to be gained by thinking to a certain extent profoundly and by writing well. The authors who were then in highest reputation are chiefly those to whom we now look back as the ablest thinkers and best writers of their time. No doubt there were many blockheads among the reading public in those days, as well as in our own, and the blockheads often egregiously misplaced their admiration, as blockheads are wont: but the applause of the blockheads was not then the object aimed at even by those who obtained it, and they did not constitute so large and so influential a class of readers, as to tempt any writer of talent to lay himself out for their admiration. If an author failed of obtaining the suffrages of men of knowledge and taste, it was for want of powers, not from the misapplication of them. The case is now altered. We live in a refined age, and there is a corresponding refinement in our amusements. It is now the height of *mauvais ton*[1] to be drunk, neither is it any longer considered decorous among gentlemen, that the staple of their conversation should consist of bawdy. Reading has become one of the most approved and fashionable methods of killing time, and the number of persons who have skimmed the surface of literature is far greater than at any previous period of our history. Our writers therefore find that the greatest success is now to be obtained by writing for the many; and endeavouring all they can to bring themselves down to the level of the many, both in their matter and in the manner of expressing it.

(1827)

NEW MONTHLY MAGAZINE
The Influence of Books[2]

PUBLIC opinion, then, is the atmosphere of liberal sentiment and equitable conclusions; books are the scale in which right and wrong are fairly tried; and all false weights or sinister motives being excluded, and the balance placed in the hands of a sufficient number of competent judges, and adjusted by the abstract merits of the case alone, speculative truth necessarily becomes practical justice, the moment it is referred to and enforced by a tribunal which is as powerful as it is impartial and disinterested. Set ten persons to read a book, and nine out of the ten will agree in their opinion of the characters and sentiments; at least so far as to

admire any striking traits of generosity, and to condemn any flagrant abuse of power, because neither they, nor anyone immediately belonging to them, is concerned. Remove the veil of self-love, and the sense of right and wrong is neither slow nor dull. But in books, and in a more refined and civilized state of society, everything is subjected to this severe and at the same time imposing ordeal. The mind is habituated to form its taste, and to indulge its likings or antipathies, according to this comprehensive view, and the more humane and enlightened impulse it receives from it; our preposterous pretensions are brought froward, and their grossness and deformity seen through, so that we are ashamed to own them or to act upon them: we learn in the same manner to sympathize in the interest of others, which to the eye of reason prefer just claims, to that of the imagination delightful ones; the private will (warped before by headstrong indulgence and by narrow views) is conformed to the standard of public good, almost without our knowing it; and man becomes by means of his studies, his amusements, and his intellectual attachments, an *ideal* and abstracted, and therefore a disinterested and *reclaimed* character. The reading public—laugh at it as we will, abuse it as we will—is, after all (depend upon it), a very rational animal, compared with a feudal lord and his horde of vassals. In a rude and barbarous age or clime, a man never sees beyond himself or his immediate circle; all beyond that circle is hid, all within it is exaggerated and distorted: his own passions, grounded on selfish and sensual objects, take the lead; he forms his enmities or his friendships by accident or interest: if rich and powerful, he holds the neighborhood in awe, can bribe by promises, or terrify by threats; if poor, he is the slave of the nearest tyrant, is too ignorant to exert his understanding, too dependant to think that his soul is his own; there is no measure of right and wrong but the strong arm, the bloody

---

[1] Bad form.

[2] The *New Monthly Magazine*, edited by Thomas Campbell, was a literary miscellany. This essay, which appeared anonymously, was by William Hazlitt (1778–1830), a leading essayist in the period known for his critical work on literature and the fine arts, social and autobiographical reflections, and for his radical political sympathies. This article appeared anonymously.

hand; will and passion are the only law, truth is as little known as justice; the ability to make an injury or an insult good is held a sufficient warrant to commit it, and cruelty and fraud are only counteracted by their own excess, and one scene of profligacy and blood shed avenged and succeed by another. I deny that this state of things can continue long after the invention of printing, of the diffusion of letters, or that it must not find its corrective and a more legitimate standard of thinking and acting in science, history and romance. The owner of a baronial castle could do as he pleased, as long as he had only to account to his tenants, or the inhabitants of the adjacent hamlet, for his unjustifiable proceedings, to crush their feeble opposition, or silence their peevish discontent; but when public opinion was brought to bear upon his conduct, he could no more stand against it than against a train of artillery placed on the opposite heights to batter down his stronghold, and let daylight into its dark and noisome dungeons. Just so the Modern Philosophy "bores through his castle-walls, and farewell Lord!"[1] Formerly, neither the vassal nor his lord could read or write, and knew nothing but what they suffered or inflicted: now the meanest mechanic can both read and write, and the only danger seems to be that every one, high and low, rich and poor, should turn author, and the whole world be converted into waste paper.

(1828)

POLITICAL REGISTER
Letter to Alderman Wood, on the Subject of Teaching the Children of the Poor to Read[2]

SIR,

I SEE, from accounts published in the newspapers, that you are taking great pains to establish a school upon the Lancasterian plan, the main object of which appears to be to teach poor children to *read*, and particularly to *read the Bible*. I have, for some months, had an intention to address you upon this subject, and to state to you my reasons for believing, that an act, arising solely from your benevolent disposition, is not, with sufficient clearness, founded in reason, and that it is not likely to produce the good which you certainly have in view.

The subject naturally divides itself into two parts: or, rather, presents two questions for discussion: 1st. Whether, under the present circumstances, in this country, the teaching of poor children *to read generally* be likely to do good; and, 2nd, Whether it be likely to do good to teach them *to read the Bible*.

Whatever men may think about reading the Bible; however their opinions may differ as to the utility of reading this particular Book, the number is very small, indeed, who think that the teaching of poor children to *read generally* is not a good past all dispute. To that very small number, however, I belong; and my opinion decidedly is, that, under the present circumstances of this country, the teaching of poor children to read generally is calcu-

---

[1] William Shakespeare (1564–1616), *Richard II* (1595): III: ii: 169.

[2] The *Political Register*, founded in 1802, was written and published by William Cobbett (1763–1835), the best known of the radical journalists in this period. Sir Matthew Wood (1768–1843), first baronet, Alderman of Cripplegate Without, 1807, Lord Mayor 1815–16 and 1816–17, and MP for the city, 1817–43, was a popular figure amongst reformers. This article appeared in the December 11, 1813 edition.

lated to produce *evil* rather than *good*; for which opinion I will now proceed to offer you my reasons, and not without some hope of being able to convince you, that your money, laid out in pots of beer to the parents, would be full as likely to benefit the community.

The *utility* of reading consists in the imparting knowledge to those who read; knowledge dispels ignorance. Reading, therefore, naturally tends to enlighten mankind. As mankind becomes enlightened, they become less exposed to the arts of those who would enslave them. Whence reading naturally tends to promote and ensure the liberties of mankind. "How, then," you will ask, "can you object to the teaching of the children of the ignorant to read?" But, Sir, when we thus describe the effects of reading, we must always be understood as meaning, the reading works which convey *truth* to the mind; for, I am sure, that you will not deny, that it is possible for a person to become by reading more ignorant than he was before. For instance, a child has *no knowledge* of the source whence coals are drawn; but, if, in consequence of what he read, he believes coals to be made out of clay, he is more ignorant than he was before he read; because falsehood is farther from truth than is the absence of knowledge. A child, in the neighbourhood of Loretto, who had been happy enough to escape the lies of the priests, would know nothing at all of the origin of the Virgin Mary's House at that famous resort of pilgrims;[1] but, if he had read the history of the Bees' House, he would believe that it came thither, flying across the sea from Palestine; and he would, of course, be a great deal *more ignorant* than if he had never read the said history.[2]

Thus, then, reading does not tend to enlighten men, unless what they read convey *truth* to their minds. The next question is, therefore, whether, under the present circumstances of this country, the children of the poor are likely to come at truth by reading; which question, I think, we must decide in the negative.

You will please to observe, that I am not now speaking of the Bible, or of works upon religion. Those I shall notice by-and-by. I am now speaking of *reading in general*. To those who object to the teaching of children to read the Bible, as being above their capacity to comprehend, it is usually answered, that if children learn to read the Bible, they will inevitably read *other things*; and that out of *reading* will proceed *light*, and the means of giving the people true notions of their *rights* in society. But, here again it is taken for granted, that what they will read, after they have been taught to read the Bible, will be calculated to give them *true notions*, and will inculcate the principles upon which men ought to be governed.

Now, Sir, is this the fact? Does the press in this country send forth works calculated to produce such an effect? That is to say, are its productions *generally* of this description? Or, to put the question more closely, is the *major part* of its productions of this description? Because, if it send forth more productions which are calculated to give *false* notions, than of productions which are calculated to give *true* notions, it follows, of course, that reading, generally, must tend to the increase of a belief in falsehood, which no one will deny to be the worst species of ignorance.

Let us see, then, what is the real state of this *press*; this vaunted press, which, in ninety-nine

---

[1] Loretto is a pilgrimage site in Italy, known as "The Shrine of our Lady," marking the legendary place where the house of Mary and Joseph of Nazareth was said to have been transported by angels in the thirteenth century.

[2] In the next edition of the *Register* (December 18, 1813), Cobbett announced that "In the *printing* of my last letter a gross error, or, rather, interpolation, was made, where 'the history of the *Bees'* House' is spoken of. I never heard of such a history, and am utterly at a loss to conceive how the blunder could have been committed."

hundredths of the publications which issue from it, is represented as being FREE. Let us see what is the real state of this press.

In the first place, a man is liable, if he write, or print, or publish any thing, which the Attorney-General (an officer *appointed by the Crown* and *removable at pleasure*) chooses to prosecute him for; any man who does this is liable to be prosecuted, and to be punished in a manner much more severe than a great part of the persons convicted of felony. You yourself remember (and I shall always retain a grateful recollection of your goodness upon the occasion), that I, for writing an article, respecting the treatment of the Local Militia at the town of Ely, was sent to pass two years of my life in a place where there were felons, and men actually found guilty of unnatural crimes. Many of the felons, at that time in Newgate, were punished with a shorter term of imprisonment than I was; to say nothing of the *fine*, a sum equal to what may be fairly deemed a fourth part of the average earnings of any literary man's whole life.

And, who will say, that, if he venture to utter what is calculated to displease men in power, he will escape such punishment? There are no laws, which set bounds to his pen; there is no settled rule of law which enables him to know what is criminal and what is not criminal. He is prosecuted if the King's officer chooses to prosecute him; and the jury, by whom he is tried, is specially nominated by another officer of the Crown, the accused party having the privilege of objecting to twelve out of forty-eight of the persons so nominated. The Attorney-General may, if he please, commence a prosecution and *not proceed in it*. He may keep a criminal charge hanging over the head of any writer as long as he chooses; and, with the consent of a Judge, he may hold the party to bail for his appearance for as long a time as he chooses to keep the charge suspended over his head. So that such writer, during his whole

life-time, may have a criminal charge kept suspended over his head, and, without forfeiting his recognizances and those of his sureties, he cannot, during his whole life-time, quit the country, or be absent at any one term; for, at any term, whenever his accuser pleases, though, perhaps, after his witnesses are dead, he may be commanded to come and take his trial.

On the *other hand*, the Attorney-General may, if he chooses, drop the prosecution, and that, too, at whatever time he may please to drop it. After having charged a writer with a crime, he may keep the charge suspended over his head for months or years; and then, without even leave of the Court, and *without assigning any reason at all*, he may *wholly withdraw the charge*, and relieve the poor creature and his family from their fears.

This is the state of our press as it is affected by the *law*. And, under such circumstances, is it to be expected, that the press will convey, freely convey, *truths* to the people? For, you will be particular in bearing in mind, that the *truth* of any writing, so far from being a *justification* of the author, is not permitted to be *pleaded* in his defence. To utter *truth*, therefore, respecting the measures of the government, the administration of the laws, the weight or the mode of collecting the taxes, the treatment of the army or the navy, the conduct of the clergy, the creeds of the Church; to utter *truth* respecting any of these may, in the eye of the law, be a greatly criminal act, and may subject the utterer to a punishment more severe than that inflicted on a great part of the felons.

We are not inquiring here, whether this law of the press be good or bad. There are those who assert it to be full of justice and wisdom. We will not, therefore, raise a dispute upon the point. We will content ourselves with observing that such *is* the law; and, then, we have only to determine, whether, under such a law, the press is likely to be the vehicle of *truth*. There are those, who say, that it ought not to be permitted to convey, in an undisguised manner, truths, upon all public matters and concerning all public men, to the people. Very well; but, if this to be the case, can the reading of the productions of this press tend to dispel ignorance; can it tend to *enlighten* the people? Can it be any public benefit, can it further the cause of public liberty, to teach the children of the poor to *read*?

Let us, if you please, trace one of these poor boys in his progress of reading, after he has been taught, at your Lancaster school, to read in the Bible. He is, you will please to observe, not going to live in the house of a father or a master, who has the means or the capacity to direct his studies in any particular channel. He has no one to tell him what publications he ought to look upon as good and what as bad. He has no one to point out to him what is the production of venality and what is not. He must take things promiscuously as they come before him. He has no guide; no criterion of truth; nothing to excite his doubts of the veracity of his author; but must swallow every thing which chance sends into his hands. What, then, will be the probable course of his reading? "*Children's Books*," as they are called, he will naturally begin with. As far as these consist of *sheer nonsense*, they may do his mind little harm; but, past all dispute, it is impossible for them to have the smallest tendency towards *enlightening* that mind. If they rise only a little above the nonsensical, look at them, and you will find, that from one end to the other, their tendency is to inculcate *abject submission*. His next series are ballads and songs, which, if they step out of nonsense, go at once into the national braggings, which, while they are applauded as the means of keeping up the spirit of people, have been one cause of plunging us into, and of prolonging, those wars, which have occasioned our enormous debts and taxes, and have led to the filling of the country with all those military

establishments, heretofore regarded as so dangerous to the liberties of England. Addison, who was a very vile politician, approved of these means of keeping alive what is called "the *honest prejudices* of Englishmen."[1] What a base idea! To inculcate undisguisedly the praiseworthiness of *keeping the people in ignorance*; and that, too, for the *good of the country*, and by the means *of the press*! Honest prejudices! That is to say, an honest *belief in falsehoods*; an *honest belief that falsehood is truth*! One cannot help hating the man, who could avow such an idea.

If your pupil live in the country, his standard book will, in all likelihood, be MOORE'S ALMANACK,[2] that universal companion of the farmers and labourers of England. Here he will find a perpetual spring of knowledge; a *daily* supply, besides an extra portion monthly. Here are *signs* and *wonders* and *prophecies*, in all which he will believe as implicitly as he does in the first chapter of Genesis. Nor will he want a due portion of politics. To keep a people in a state of profound ignorance; to make them superstitious and slavish, there needs little more than the general reading of this single book. The poor creature, who reads this book, and who believes that the compiler of it is able to foretel when it will rain and when it will snow, is very little more enlightened that those men who believe most firmly that St. Dunstan took the Devil by the nose;[3] and, there is no doubt in my mind, that, if that legend were now published, they would believe it. You will

---

[1] Joseph Addison (1672–1719), best known for his contributions to Sir Richard Steele's *Tatler* in 1709–11 and collaboration with Steele on the *Spectator* in 1711–12. Addison was closely associated with the Whig party.

[2] Francis Moore (1657–1714), a physician, began an almanac in 1700 called *Vox Stellarum, an Almanac for 1701 with Astrological Observations*. Popular with the common people but despised by the well educated, it combined herbal remedies with astrology. It continued to be published throughout the next two centuries.

[3] An eleventh-century legend tells that the devil tempted St. Dunstan (*c.* 910–88) while he was a Benedictine monk. A skilled metal worker, he seized the devil's nose with tongs.

say, perhaps, that it is only the very lowest of the people who believe in the prophecies of Moore's Almanack; but, is it not the very lowest description of people whom you are attempting to teach? And, when they get out of your hands, must they not be left to themselves? You certainly do not mean to follow them to their hovels to superintend their reading.

But, the greatest source of your pupil's knowledge, the great source of that *light*, which he is to acquire, will be the NEWSPAPERS. Here he will find a constant and copious supply. And of *what*? Of *truth*? Will he here find bold and impartial statements of facts? Will he here find plain and fearless censure of public wrong-doers? Will he here see the cause of the oppressed manfully espoused, and the oppressor painted in colours calculated to rouse against him the hatred of mankind? You know, Sir, that he will not. You know, that he will find the reverse of all this. You know, that he will find falsehoods, upon every subject of nature; praises of all those who have power to hurt or to reward, and base calumnies on all those, who, in any degree, make themselves obnoxious to power. "Yes," say you, in the ardour of your zeal, "but, there are *exceptions*, my friend; there are *some* of the public papers of a different description." *Some*? How many, Sir? How many out of the 300 or 400 which are published in the kingdom? Are there *ten*? Suppose there are *twenty*. Then there are twenty chances to one against your pupil's imbibing the *truth*; there are twenty chances to one that his reading will produce in him an increase of ignorance, instead of pouring light into his mind. Besides, what is he to find in the very best of these public prints? Will he find anything like *free discussion*? Suppose a venal wretch to fill his columns with praises of a wicked man in power. Will any one of your twenty newspapers dare freely to investigate those columns, and by bringing proof of the

wickedness of the men in power, show their falsehood? You know well, Sir, that no one would dare to do this; you know that no writer, in his sober senses, would think of doing it. What, then, is the undeniable conclusion? Why, this: that the praise, reaching the mind of your *reader*, and remaining uncontradicted, his reading must deceive him; must give him false notions; must, as to a matter of great public importance, make him *more ignorant* than he would have been if he had never been able to read; must make him the partisan of a man, to whom he ought, in duty to his country, to be opposed. We often hear it said, "Let us have *discussion*, discussion will *do good*." But, Sir, what does *discussion* mean? It means, the arraying, by one person, of all *the* facts, and *all* the arguments that he can muster up, against the facts and arguments of another. It does not mean open-mouthed statement and argument on one side, while, on the other, the combatant is muzzled, is compelled, for his safety, to suppress his facts, and is only permitted tremblingly to state in parables, and argue by hypothesis. In short, *discussion* demands a perfectly unshackled use of all that the mind suggests; and, if this be denied, there is *no discussion*. The Bishop of Llandaff *answered* Mr. Paine;[1] his Lordship *discussed* the matter with Thomas. But, Thomas's publishers were prosecuted by the Attorney-General, and his book was suppressed; while that of the Bishop not only had leave to circulate freely, but was forced into circulation by all the aid that zealous churchmen and other Christians could give it. I am not here speaking of the propriety or impropriety of this; but, it must be confessed, I think, that it was a singular sort of *discussion*. Yet, of very nearly the same stamp are all the discussion that your pupils will find in our public prints. If, for instance, a report be published of a trial in a court of justice, accompanied with

---

[1] Richard Watson, Bishop of Llandaff wrote an *Apology for the Bible* (1796) in response to Thomas Paine's *Age of Reason*.

astonishing praises of the wisdom and integrity of "the Learned Judge;" and, if some one were to think that the decision evinced no such qualities in the learned personage, but, rather, the contrary; would he be much inclined to impart his thoughts to the public? If, in a moment of ungovernable zeal, he were freely to discuss such praises, and draw from his facts and arguments an opposite conclusion, would he not, when he came to see his writing in print, set himself down as ruined? Why, then, talk of *discussion*? Discuss, indeed, we may, and freely, too, all question relating to the qualities of trees and herbs. There is no danger in writing about dung or potatoes or cabbages. Here your pupils will have a large field; but, as to politics, law, and religion, the army or the navy, peace or war; as to all those subjects interesting to man as a member of society, they will assuredly meet with nothing, issuing from the press of this country, worthy of the name of *discussion*.

Why, then, teach the children of the poor to read? Why waste, in this pursuit, either money or time; seeing that, if you succeed, your success must necessarily tend to the increase of error and to the debasement of the people? It is not the *mere capability of reading* that can raise man in the scale of nature. It is the *enlightening* of his mind; and, if the capability of distinguishing words upon paper does not tend to enlighten him, that acquirement is to be considered as nothing of any value.

The great length of this letter makes me fear to proceed further at present; and, therefore, I conclude with an expression of my sincere respect for your character and your motives.

WM. COBBETT.

Botley, 8th *Dec.* 1813.

(1813)

WILLIAM GODWIN
Of Learning [1]
from *The Enquirer: Reflections on Education, Manners and Literature*

HOW much eloquent invective has been spent in holding up to ridicule the generation of book-worms! We have been told, that a persevering habit of reading, kills the imagination, and narrows the understanding; that it overloads the intellect with the notions of others and prevents its digesting them, and, by a still stronger reason, prevents it from unfolding its native powers; that the man who would be original and impressive, must meditate rather than hear, and walk rather than read. He that devotes himself to a methodical prosecution of his studies, is perhaps allowed some praise for his industry and good intention; but it is at the same time insinuated, that the only result to be expected from such ill-placed industry, is a plentiful harvest of laborious dulness.

It is no wonder that this sort of declamation has been generally popular. It favours one of the most fundamental passions of the human mind, our indolence. To acquaint ourselves profoundly with what other men have thought in different ages of the world, is an arduous task; the ascent of the hill of knowledge is steep, and it demands the most unalterable resolution to be able to conquer it. But this declamation presents to us every discourage-ment, and severs all the nerves of the soul. He that is infected by it, no longer "girds up the loins of his mind;"[†] but surrenders his days to unenterprising indulgence. Its effect is like that of a certain religious creed,[3] which, disclaiming the connection between motives and action, and between one

---

[1] William Godwin (1756–1836), a prominent middle-class reformer.

[†] Peter 1:13.

[3] This reflects some interpretations of Calvinism's principle of predestination.

action and another, instructs its votaries to wait, with pious resignation, for the influx of a supernatural strength which is to supersede the benefit of our vigilance and exertions.

Nothing however can be more ill founded than this imputed hostility between learning and genius. If it were true, it is among savages only that we ought to seek for the genuine expansion of the human mind. They are, of all their kind, the most undebauched by learning, and the least broken in upon by any regular habits of attention. In civilised society, and especially among that class in civilised society who pay any attention to intellectual pursuits, those who have the greatest antipathy to books, are yet modified in a thousand ways by the actual state of literature. They converse with men who read, though they disdain to read themselves. A sagacious observer might infer beforehand, in its principal outlines, what a self-educated man could do, from a previous knowledge of the degree of improvement existing in the country he inhabited. Man in society is variously influenced by the characters of his fellow men; he is an imitative animal, and, like the camelion, owes the colour he assumes, to the colour of the surrounding objects. But, if men the most austerely and cynically independent in this respect, must be so deeply affected by literature and books at second hand, it were surely better to go at once to the fountainhead, and drink of the spring in all its purity.

The opinion here combated, seems to have originated in the most profound ignorance of the intellectual nature of man. Man taken by himself is nothing. In the first portion of his life, he is more ignorant and worthless that the beasts. For all that he has, he is indebted to collision. His mother and his nurse awaken his mind from its primeval sleep. They imbue it in various respects with subtlety and discrimination. They unfold the understanding, and rouse in turn the whole catalogue of the passions.

The remaining sections of the history of man, are like the first. He proceeds forward, as he commenced. All his improvements have communication for their source.

Why are men not always savages? Because they build upon one another's structures. Because "one man labours, and other men enter into the fruits of his labour."[1] It is thus that the species collectively seems formed to advance, and one generation, casualties and extraordinary revolutions being excepted, to improve upon the attainments of another. The self-educated man seems to propose, as far as possible, to divest himself of this fundamental advantage.

If I would do well in any art or science, I should think nothing could be more necessary for me, than carefully to enquire in the first instance what had been done already. I should otherwise most likely only write over again in a worse manner, what had been repeatedly written before I was born. It would be the most atrocious absurdity to affirm, that books may be of use to other men, but not to an author. He of all men wants them most. If on the other hand they be without utility, for what reason is he an author?

When we compare the knowledge of any subject to be acquired from books, with that to be acquired from conversation, it is astonishing how unequal they will ordinarily be found. Books undertake to treat of a subject regularly; to unfold it part by part till the whole is surveyed; they are entirely at our devotion, and may be turned backward and forward as we please; it is their express purpose to omit nothing that is essential to a complete delineation. They are written in tranquillity, and in the bosom of meditation: they are revised again and again; their obscurities removed, and their defects supplied. Conversation on the other hand is fortuitous and runs wild; the life's blood of truth is filtrated and diluted, till much of its essence is gone. The

---

[1] John 4:38.

intellect that depends upon conversation for nutriment, may be compared to the man who should prefer the precarious existence of a beggar, to the possession of a regular and substantial income.

One of the most prevailing objections to a systematical pursuit of knowledge, is that it imposes upon us a methodical industry, and by consequence counteracts the more unlicensed and dignified sallies of the mind. But the industry which books demand, is of the same species as the industry requisite for the development of our own reflections; the study of other men's writings, is strikingly analogous to the invention and arrangement of our own. A better school cannot be devised for the improvement of individual mind, than for it thus to collate itself with other minds in a state of the highest and most persevering exertion. It is to be feared that, if industry be not early formed, and if that indolence, which in one form or other is always our motive for neglecting books and learning, be uniformly indulged, the mind will never rouse itself to an undaunted subtlety of thought, or acquire the constancy requisite for the invention and execution of any great undertaking.

The reason why reading has fallen into a partial disrepute is, that few men have sufficiently reflected on the true mode of reading. It has been affirmed by astronomers, that the spots discoverable in the disk of the sun, are a species of fuel calculated to supply its continual waste, and that, in due time, they become changed into the substance of the sun itself. Thus in reading: if the systems we read, were always to remain in masses upon the mind, unconcocted and unaltered, undoubtedly in that case they would only deform it. But, if we read in a just spirit, perhaps we cannot read too much: in other words, if we mix our own reflections with what we read; if we dissect the ideas and arguments of our author; if, by having recourse to all subsidiary means, we endeavour to clear the recollection of

him in our minds; if we compare part with part, detect his errors, new model his systems, adopt so much of him as is excellent, and explain within ourselves the reason of our disapprobation as to what is otherwise. A judicious reader will have a greater number of ideas that are his own passing through his mind, than of ideas presented to him by his author. He sifts his merits, and bolts his arguments. What he adopts from him, he renders his own, by repassing in his thoughts the notions of which it consists, and the foundation upon which it rests, correcting its mistakes, and supplying its defects. Even the most dogmatical branches of study, grammar and mathematics, supply him with hints, and give a turn to his meditations. Reading and learning, when thus pursued, not only furnish the most valuable knowledge; but afford incitements to the mind of a thousand denominations, and add a miraculous sort of finishing to its workmanship which could have been bestowed by no other means. It furnishes, what is of all things most important, occasions for approbation and disapprobation. It creates a certain manliness of judgement, not indebted for its decisive character to partiality and arrogance, but truth by its own light, even while it never divests itself of the sobriety of scepticism, and accommodated to the office of producing conviction in its intimates and hearers.

(1797)

SIR ARCHIBALD MACDONALD
Speech as Prosecution in the
Seditious-Libel Trial of Thomas Paine for
Rights of Man *Part Two* [1]

GENTLEMAN, the publication in question was not the first of its kind which this Defendant

---

[1] Sir Archibald Macdonald (1747–1826), Attorney-General and therefore head of the prosecution in Paine's 1792 seditious-libel trial.

sent forth into the world. This particular publication was preceded by one upon the same subjects, and handling, in some measure, the same topics. That publication, although extremely reprehensible, and such as, perhaps, I was not entirely warranted in overlooking, I did overlook, upon this principle, that it may not be fitting and prudent at all times, for a public prosecutor to be sharp in his prosecutions, or to have it said that he is instrumental in preventing any manner of discussion coming under the public eye, although, in his own estimation, it may be very far indeed from that which is legitimate and proper discussion. Reprehensible as that book was, extremely so, in my opinion, yet it was ushered into the world under circumstances that led me to conceive that it should be confined to the judicious reader, and when confined to the judicious reader, it appeared to me that such a man would refute as he went along.

But, gentlemen, when I found that another publication was ushered into the world still more reprehensible than the former; that in all shapes, in all sizes, with an industry incredible, it was either totally or partially thrust into the hands of all persons in this country, of subjects of every description; when I found that even children's sweetmeats were wrapped up with parts of this, and delivered into their hands, in the hope that they would read it; when all industry was used, such as I describe to you, in order to obtrude and force this upon that part of the public whose minds cannot be supposed to be conversant with subjects of this sort, and who cannot therefore correct as they go along, I thought it behoved me upon the earliest occasion, which was the first day of the term succeeding this publication, to put a charge upon record against its author.

Gentlemen, to whom are the positions that are contained in this book addressed? They are addressed, Gentlemen, to the ignorant, to the credulous, to the desperate: to the desperate all government is irksome; nothing can be so palatable to their ears as the comfortable doctrine that there is neither law nor government amongst us.

The ignorant and the credulous, we all know to exist in all countries; and perhaps exactly in proportion as their hearts are good and simple, are they an easy prey to the crafty who have the cruelty to deceive them.

(1792)

Thomas Erskine
Speech as Prosecution in the Seditious-Libel Trial of Thomas Williams for Publishing Age of Reason, by Thomas Paine [1]

A FREE and unlicensed press, *in the just and legal sense of the expression*, has led to all the blessings both of religion and government, which Great Britain or any part of the world at this moment enjoys, and it is calculated to advance mankind to still higher degrees of civilization and happiness.—But this freedom, like every other, must be limited to be enjoyed, and like every human advantage, may be defeated by its abuse. An intellectual book, however erroneous, addressed to the intellectual world upon so profound and complicated a subject, can never work the mischief which this Indictment is calculated to repress.—Such works will only incite the minds of men enlightened by study, to a closer investigation of a subject well worthy of their deepest and continued contemplation.—The powers of the mind are given for human improvement in the progress of human existence.—The changes produced by such reciprocations of lights and intelligences are certain in their progressions, and make their way imperceptibly, by

---

[1] Thomas Erskine (1750–1823), the leading defendant of political prisoners in the 1790s, including those charged with treason in 1794.

the final and irresistible power of truth. But this book has no such object, and no such capacity:—it presents no arguments to the wise and enlightened. On the contrary, it treats the faith and opinions of the wisest with the most shocking contempt, and stirs up men, without the advantages of learning, or sober thinking, to a total disbelief of every thing hitherto held sacred; and consequently to a rejection of all the laws and ordinances of the state, which stand only upon the assumption of their truth.

(1797)

GENTLEMAN'S MAGAZINE
Letter: On Reading Novels

MR. URBAN,[1]

THE generality of young people are fond of this amusement; and some parents indulge them in it, under an idea that it is innocent, and gives them a knowledge of the world; but, let them beware of encouraging the perusal of such books without a proper discrimination. Of all reading, that of novels is the most frivolous, and frequently the most pernicious. Many of them suggest false notions of life, inflame the imagination, deprave the judgement, and vitiate the heart. A lady, whose mind is not engaged in more useful, or capable of more rational, employment, sends her servant to the Circulating Library;[2] and he returns loaded with volumes, containing pathetic tales of love and madness; tales, which fill her head with the most

ridiculous chimeras; with romantic schemes of gallantry; with an admiration of young rakes of spirit; with dreams of conquests, amorous interviews, and matrimonial excursions; with a detestation of all prudential advice, impatience of controul, love of imaginary liberty, and an abjuration of all parental authority. In most of our novels, such infatuating and inflammatory notions are excited, such scenes of villainy and vice are laid open, as should never be communicated to the female mind. The criminal projects of a romantic hero are usually placed in the most agreeable light; his arts of seduction; his flattery, his insinuating address, his personal accomplishments, his gallantry and gaiety, his enterprising spirit, are set off to the highest advantage. By these means, vice generally becomes familiar, and no longer excites that horror and detestation which it ought to create.

A young woman, who employs her time in reading novels, will never find amusement in any other sort of books. Her mind will be soon debauched by licentious description, and lascivious images; and she will, consequently, remain the same frivolous and insignificant creature through life; her mind will become a magazine of trifles and follies, or rather impure and wanton ideas. Her favourite novels will never teach her the social virtues, the qualifications of domestic life, the principles of her native language, history, geography, morality, the precepts of Christianity, or any other useful science. For the generality of those compositions, which are thrown out upon the world by idle scribblers, silly women, or impertinent coxcombs in literature, are crude and hasty effusions, written in mean and vulgar language, or with an affected pomp of expression, and abound with characters, images, and sentiments, of levity and licentiousness.

I do not, however, pretend to assert, that all novels are equally despicable. The severest critic must allow, that there are several productions of this

---

[1] Sylvanus Urban was the fictional name of the Editor of *Gentleman's Magazine.* The letter-to-the-editor section was a prominent element of each issue.

[2] Circulating libraries were notorious symbols of the frivolous nature of modern literature. They were associated by critics such as Eusebius with carrying the worst modern novels to a predominantly female readership. These descriptions frequently referred to them in language that suggested a virus traveling through the nation.

kind not unworthy of his attention. I should think a person destitute of taste who should dislike the works of some ingenious writers in this department of literature. But, it is necessary to make a proper distinction between the works of real genius, and the trifling contents of a Circulating Library; between Gil Blas[1] and an insipid tale of love and gallantry; between the memoirs of an illustrious patriot, or an eminent writer, and those of a fortune-hunter, or a lady of pleasure. I have received, I confess, much real pleasure and information, from the writings of Fielding,[2] and even from the perusal of Pompey the Little;[3] but, I should think myself excessively idle were I to devote a considerable part of my time to an amusement of this kind. I would seldom take up a novel but at a time when I had either no opportunity to pursue more instructive and useful studies, or after I had fatigued myself with business of importance. At such intervals a great man may be allowed to trifle; and even this engagement is infinitely better than idleness, and a total vacuity of thought. "I pity," says the celebrated lord Falkland,[4] "an unlearned gentleman in a rainy day." Nothing certainly can be more despicable than the sight of an empty head gazing out at a window for amusement in the street! To such a genius I would recommend some innocent novel, rather that the sacrifice of several hours to the mere gratification of the eye, or a contemptible *lounge*.

(1797)

---

[1] A picaresque romance by the French novelist and dramatist, Alain René Le Sage, published 1715–35. It was translated into English by Tobias Smollett in 1749.

[2] Henry Fielding (1707–54), English novelist and dramatist best known for the novels and *Joseph Andrews* (1742) and *Tom Jones* (1746).

[3] A satire in the form of the narrative of the life of a lap-dog, by Francis Coventry (1725–54). Published in 1751.

[4] Lucius Cary Falkland (*c.* 1610–43), an articulate statesmen known for his sympathy for the most liberal thinkers of his day.

GENTLEMAN'S MAGAZINE
Letter: Eusebius's Final Reply on the Subject of Sunday Schools [5]

MR. URBAN,

IT has been observed by some persons of prudence, and knowledge of mankind, that the scheme of which I am speaking, detached from a constant attention to the habit of industry, has been artfully encouraged by our Reforming Societies,[6] for the purpose of *illuminating* the common people of England, for rendering them capable of reading their *edifying* publications, and openings their eyes to the *glorious* advantages of liberty and equality.

It is a well attested fact, that no less than 400 copies of Paine's Age of Reason[7] were, on one market-day, distributed, *gratis*, among the ordinary farmers, servants, and laborers, at York, in a cheap and commodious edition, in order to disseminate its principles, and extend its *illuminating* influence among the vulgar. Those who have received a tincture of scholarship at a Sunday school, without any regular discipline for the rest of the week, will be proper subjects for their purpose, and no doubt, will be the first to derive instruction from the luminous pages of this precious reformer. It would have been useless, it would have been throwing their

---

[5] A previous letter by the correspondent who signed himself Eusebius declaiming against the idea of Sunday schools had sparked a lively controversy in the Letters section of ensuing editions. *Gentleman's* was known as a relatively conservative literary magazine and its readership would have reflected this, but even for most conservatives, the idea of Sunday schools, and by implication, of teaching the lower orders to read, had become politically acceptable. This excerpt is from Eusebius's final response to the debate that his letter had prompted.

[6] Societies whose mandate was to seek political reform. The most famous of these was the London Corresponding Society, some of whose leaders were tried for treason in 1794.

[7] Thomas Paine's *Age of Reason* (1793) was widely denounced as being an atheistic critique of Christianity that was consistent with his desire for radical political reform.

pearls before swine to have *stuffed* these edifying publication into the pockets of illiterate rustics.

Whenever industry is made a leading principle in our establishments for the benefit of the poor, the effect will be proportionately advantageous to the community. This, this is the parent of all domestic comfort, the great preservative of peace, order, regularity, and subordination, in society; the foundation of arts, manufacturers, and commerce; in short, it is the only basis of our national prosperity. This, and this only, is the great principle in which the nation is interested, and which ought to be the primary object of every public charity for "meliorating" the condition of the poor.

When this is in any degree neglected, or made a subordinate consideration, all theoretical introduction will be proportionately insignificant. It will be like the good seed falling by the wayside. The young disciple will bear his instructor; but, when he escapes from his task master, and finds that idleness, liberty, and equality, are more agreeable than "drudgery," "the devil cometh, and taketh away the word out of his heart,"[1] and he falls a sacrifice to his own passions, or the artifices of some factious declaimer.

To the neglect of industry in the lowest classes of mankind may be ascribed all the licentiousness, all the riots, all the beggary, which we meet with in every part of the three kingdoms. And how are these abominations to be prevented? Not by alienating the minds of the poor from labor; not by teaching them Dyche and Dilworth;[2] not by raising their ideas above their station; not by giving them a small portion of scholastic learning and mental improvement on Sundays, and then leave them to idleness, fighting, strolling, and thievery, all the rest of the week; but by obliging them to *work*, and earn their livelihood by some useful occupation. This is the highest and most substantial charity, and is calculated to render the lowest ranks of mankind useful and *happy* in their respective stations.

The piety of our ancestors has amply provided for the instruction of the poor, by erecting in almost every village a place for public instruction, and the adoration of the Supreme Being; where the most ignorant creature may learn his duty to his creator and his fellow creatures, and become habituated to seriousness, regularity, and devotion. Let young people be obliged to attend their respective churches, and be inured to some honest and laborious occupation for six days in the week; and, with few exceptions, they will become quiet and useful members of society.

Eusebius is no enemy to instruction; but he still insists that industry in the lowest classes of society is better than scholarship; and that to give them the latter without the former, is to put swords into their hands, which may be instrumental to their own destruction.

(1798)

GENTLEMAN'S MAGAZINE
Letter: Some former Articles Reviewed by an old Correspondent

MR. URBAN *Cornwall, Nov. 20*

THERE is scarcely a greater entertainment that I receive, than from the expectation and enjoyment of your valuable Monthly Repository. It reaches me, in this distant quarter, about the tenth or twelfth day after its publication; and I am free to say, that I return with keenness from my morning's ride, in expectation that Peter has brought the Gentleman's Magazine from the neighbouring

---

[1] Luke 8:12.

[2] Thomas Dyche (*d.* 1733), author of *A Guide to the English Tongue* (1707) and *The Spelling Dictionary* (1725); Thomas Dilworth (*d.* 1780), author of *A New Guide to the English Tongue* (1740).

market-town. He knows my trim, and prepares for me accordingly; and I generally find the fire fresh poked up, the hearth swept clean, and my cushion plumped-up in the easy chair. The rogue too brings up a bottle of my oldest port, sets it before the fire, and then quits the room, to prepare for the approaching dinner.

Left thus alone with my favourite Intelligencer, my entertainment commences. I con over the pages which contain the opinions of your various correspondents: I mark the modest essays of the Tyro, the bolder genius of the more approved Scholar, and the clearness and comprehension of the Veteran in learning. Hence I feel myself amused and instructed; and what is of no small moment, a happier man.

(1789)

LEIGH HUNT
My Books[1]

SITTING, last winter, among my books, and walled round with all the comfort and protection which they and my fireside could afford me; to wit, a table of high-piled books at my back, my writing-desk on one side of me, some shelves on the other, and the feeling of the warm fire at my feet; I began to consider how I loved the authors of those books,—how I loved them, too, not only for the imaginative pleasures they afforded me, but for their making me love the very books themselves, and delight to be in contact with them. I looked sideways at my *Spenser*, my *Theocritus*, and my *Arabian Nights*; then above them at my Italian poets; then behind me at my *Dryden* and *Pope*, my romances, and my *Boccaccio*; then on my left side at my *Chaucer*, who lay on a writing desk; and

thought how natural it was in C. L.[2] to give a kiss to an old folio, as I once saw him do to *Chapman's Homer*.[3] At the same time I wondered how he could sit in that front room of his with nothing but a few unfeeling tables and chairs, or at best a few engravings in trim frames, instead of putting a couple of arm-chairs into the back-room with the books in it, where there is but one window. Would I were there, with both the chairs properly filled, and one or two more besides! "We had talk, sir,"—the only talk capable of making one forget the books.

I entrench myself in my books equally against sorrow and the weather. If the wind comes through a passage, I look about to see how I can fence it off by a better disposition of my movables; if a melancholy thought is importunate, I give another glance at my *Spenser*. When I speak of being in contact with my books, I mean it literally. I like to lean my head against them. Living in a southern climate, though in a part sufficiently northern to feel the winter, I was obliged, during that season, to take some of the books out of the study, and hang them up near the fireplace in the sitting-room, which is the only room that has such a convenience.[4] I therefore walled myself in, as well as I could, in the manner above mentioned. I took a walk every day, to the astonishment of the Genoese, who used to huddle against a piece of sunny wall, like flies on a chimney-piece; but I did this only that I might so much the more enjoy my *English* evening. The fire

[2] Charles Lamb (1775–1834), a prominent poet and essayist.

[3] Edmund Spenser (*c.* 1552–99), best known for *The Faerie Queene* (1590–96); Theocritus, a Greek pastoral poet from the third century B.C.; *Arabian Nights*, a collection of stories in Arabic known in Europe through Antoine Galland's early eighteenth-century translation into French; John Dryden (1631–1700), poet, dramatist and essayist; Alexander Pope (1688–1744), poet and essayist; Giovanni Boccaccio (1313–75), Italian writer and humanist; Geoffrey Chaucer (*c.* 1345–1400), English poet best known for *Canterbury Tales* (*c.* 1387); George Chapman (1559–1634), English dramatist best known for his translation of Homer.

[1] Leigh Hunt (1786–1859), a well-known editor and journalist.

[4] Hunt lived in Italy from 1822–23.

was a wood fire instead of a coal; but I imagined myself in the country. I remember at the very worst that one end of my native land was not nearer the other than England is to Italy.

While writing this article I am in my study again. Like the rooms in all houses in this country which are not hovels, it is handsome and ornamented. On one side it looks towards a garden and the mountains; on another to the mountains and the sea. What signifies all this? I turn my back upon the sea; I shut up even one of the side windows looking upon the mountains, and retain no prospect but that of the trees. On the right and left of me are book-shelves; a bookcase is affectionately open in front of me; and thus kindly enclosed with my books and the green leaves, I write. If all this is too luxurious and effeminate, of all luxuries it is the one that leaves you the most strength. And this is to be said for scholarship in general. It unfits a man for activity, for his bodily part in the world; but it often doubles both the power and the sense of his mental duties; and with much indignation against his body, and more against those who tyrannise over the intellectual claims of mankind, the man of letters, like the magician of old, is prepared "to play the devil" with the great men of this world, in a style that astonishes both the sword and the toga.

I do not like this fine large study. I like elegance. I like room to breathe in, and even walk about, when I want to breathe and walk about. I like a great library next my study; but for the study itself, give me a small snug place, almost entirely walled with books. There should be only one window in it, looking upon trees. Some prefer a place with few or no books at all—nothing but a chair or a table, like Epictetus;[1] but I should say that these were philosophers, not lovers of books, if I did not recollect that

Montaigne was both.[2] He had a study in a round tower, walled as aforesaid. It is true, one forgets one's books while writing—at least they say so. For my part, I think I have them in a sort of sidelong mind's-eye; like a second thought, which is none—like a waterfall or a whispering wind.

I dislike a grand library to study in. I mean an immense apartment, with books all in Museum order, especially wire-safed. I say nothing against the Museum itself, or public libraries. They are capital places to go to, but not to sit in; and talking of this, I hate to read in public, and in strange company. The jealous silence; the dissatisfied looks of the messengers; the inability to help yourself; the not knowing whether you really ought to trouble the messengers, much less the gentleman in black, or brown, who is, perhaps, half a trustee; with a variety of other jarrings between privacy and publicity, prevent one's settling heartily to work. They say "they manage these things better in France;" and I dare say they do; but I think I should feel still more *distrait* in France, in spite of the benevolence of the servitors, and the generous profusion of pen, ink, and paper. I should feel as if I were doing nothing but interchanging amenities with polite writers.

A grand private library, which the master of the house also makes his study, never looks to me like a real place of books, much less of authorship. I cannot take kindly to it. It is certainly not out of envy; for three parts of the books are generally trash, and I can seldom think of the rest and the proprietor together. It reminds me of a fine gentleman, of a collector, of a patron, of Gil Blas and the Marquis of Marialva; of anything but genius and comfort. I have a particular hatred of a round table (not *the* Round Table, for that was a dining one) covered and irradiated with books, and never met with one

[1] A Phrygian philosopher in the middle of the first century, A.D.

[2] Michel Eyquem de Montaigne (1533–92), celebrated in the period as an early and influential essayist. His *Essais* appeared originally in 1580, and then in an enlarged edition in 1588.

in the house of a clever man but once. It is the reverse of Montaigne's Round Tower. Instead of bringing the books around you, they all seem turning another way, and eluding your hands.

Conscious of my propriety and comfort in these matters, I take an interest in the bookcases as well as the books of my friends. I long to meddle and dispose them after my own notions. When they see this confession, they will acknowledge the virtue I have practiced. I believe I did mention his book-room to C. L., and I think he told me that he often sat there when alone. It would be hard not to believe him. His library, though not abounding in Greek or Latin (which are the only things to help some persons to an idea of literature), is anything but superficial. The depth of philosophy and poetry are there, the innermost passages of the human heart. It has some Latin too. It has also a handsome contempt for appearance. It looks like what it is, a selection made at precious intervals from the book-stalls;—now a Chaucer at nine and twopence; now a Montaigne or a Sir Thomas Browne at two shillings; now a Jeremy Taylor; a Spinoza; an old English Dramatist, Prior, and Sir Philip Sidney; and the books are "neat as imported." The very perusal of the backs is a "discipline of humanity." There Mr. Southey takes his place again with an old Radical friend: there Jeremy Collier is at peace with Dryden: there the lion, Martin Luther, lies down with the Quaker lamb, Sewell: there Guzman d'Alfarache thinks himself fit company for Sir Charles Grandison, and has his claims admitted. Even the "high fantastical" Duchess of Newcastle, with her laurel on her head, is received with grave honours, and not the less for declining to trouble herself with the constitutions of her maids.[1] There

is an approach to this in the library of W. C., who also includes Italian among his humanities. W. H.,[2] I believe, has no books, except mine; but he has Shakespeare and Rousseau by heart. N.,[3] who, though not a book-man by profession, is fond of those who are, and who loves his volume enough to read it across the fields, has his library in the common sitting-room, which is hospitable. H. R.'s[4] books are all too modern and finely bound, which however, is not his fault, for they were left him by will,—not the most kindly act of the testator. Suppose a man were to bequeath us a great japan chest three feet by four, with an injunction that it was always to stand on the tea-table. I remember borrowing a book of H. R., which, having lost, I replaced with a copy equally well bound. I am not sure I should have been in such haste, even to return the book, had it been a common-looking volume; but the splendour of the loss dazzled me into this

---

[1] Sir Thomas Browne (1605–82), his *Christian Morals* was edited by Samuel Johnson in 1756; Jeremy Taylor (1613–67), a religious writer best known for *A Discourse of the Liberty of Prophesying* (1646), which espoused the principle of religious toleration; Benedict de Spinoza (1632–77), a philosopher whose ideas were aligned with the pantheis-tic principles of Romantic poets such as S. T. Coleridge; Matthew Prior (1664–1721), a poet, dramatist and essayist. Robert Southey (1774–1843) had by this time distanced himself from his earlier radical politics. He was no longer on cordial terms with his former ally, Coleridge; Jeremy Collier (1650–1726), best known for his *Short View of the Immorality and Profaneness of the English Stage* (1698); Martin Luther (1483–1546), the leader of the Reformation in Germany; William Sewell (1653–1720), author of *History of the Rise, Increase and Progress of the Christian People called Quakers* (1717); Guzman d'Alfa-rache, the protagonist of a Spanish picaresque romance of the same name by Mateo Aleman (translated into English in 1622). He is at times a scullion, thief, gentleman, beggar, soldier and page to a cardinal and a French ambassador; Sir Charles Grandison, the genteel hero of Samuel Richardson's novel *The History of Sir Charles Grandison* (1754); Margaret Cavendish, Duchess of Newcastle (1623–73), best known for her first work, *Poems and Fancies* (1653). Her work was both praised and dismissed. Although she appeared deliberately to have espoused singularity in dress and manners, much of her prose has an engaging and honest directness, notably in her apologies for her own audacity in writing at all, being a woman.

[2] William Hazlitt (1778–1830).

[3] Vincent Novello.

[4] Henry Crabb Robinson (1775–1867), a barrister by profession, but best known for his reflections on many of the leading literary figures of his age.

ostentatious piece of propriety. I set about restoring it as if I had diminished his fortunes, and waived the privilege a friend has to use a man's things as his own. I may venture upon this ultra-liberal theory, not only because candour compels me to say that I hold it to a greater extent, with Montaigne, but because I have been a meek son in the family of book-losers. I may affirm, upon a moderate calculation, that I have lent and lost in my time (and I am eight-and-thirty), half-a-dozen decent-sized libraries,—I mean books enough to fill so many ordinary bookcases. I have never complained; and self-love, as well as gratitude, makes me love those who do not complain of me.

I own I borrow books with as much facility as I lend. I cannot see a work that interests me on another person's shelf, without a wish to carry it off; but, I repeat, that I have been much more sinned against than sinning in the article of non-return; and am scrupulous in the article of intention.

I yield to none in my love of bookstall urbanity. I have spent as happy moments over the stalls as any literary apprentice boy who ought to be moving onwards. But I confess my weakness in liking to see some of my favourite purchases neatly bound. The books I like to have about me most are—Spenser, Chaucer, the minor poems of Milton, the *Arabian Nights*, Theocritus, Ariosto, and such old good-natured speculations as Plutarch's *Morals*.[1] For most of these I like a plain, good, old binding, never

mind how old, provided it wears well; but my *Arabian Nights* may be bound in as fine and flowery a style as possible, and I should love an engraving to every dozen pages. Book-prints of all sorts, bad and good, take with me as much as when I was a child: and I think some books, such as Prior's Poems, ought always to have portraits of the authors. Prior's airy face with his cap on is like having his company. From early association, no edition of Milton pleases me so much as that in which there are pictures of the devil with brute ears, dressed like a Roman General.

I take our four great English poets to have all been fond of reading. Milton and Chaucer proclaim themselves for hard sitters at books. Spenser's reading is evident by his learning; and if there were nothing else to show for it in Shakespeare, his retiring to his native town, long before old age, would be a proof of it. It is impossible for a man to live in solitude without such assistance, unless he is a metaphysician or mathematician, or the dullest of mankind; and any country town would be solitude to Shakespeare, after the bustle of a metropolis and a theatre. Doubtless he divided his time between his books, and his bowling-green, and his daughter Susanne. It is pretty certain, also, that he planted, and rode on horseback; and there is evidence of all sorts to make it clear, that he must have occasionally joked with the blacksmith, and stood godfather for his neighbours' children.

(1823)

---

[1] Theocritus (*c.* 300–260 B.C.), a poet active in the golden age of Alexandrian poetry; Ariosto Ludovico (1474–1533), an Italian poet.

SECTION THREE

Literary Autobiographies

Ironically and perhaps appropriately, the most famous reader in the Romantic period may well have been a character in a novel. The monster in Mary Shelley's *Frankenstein*, who is himself the product of an Enlightenment thirst for knowledge taken to extremes, describes "the science of words or letters" as "a godlike science" with which he, like his creator, "ardently desired to become acquainted." Victor Frankenstein's creature may been forced to go to greater lengths than most to satisfy this desire, but it was a common one in the period. Nor were references to it limited to seemingly endless depictions of reading in novels, poems, plays and critical writings. Numerous individuals recorded their own encounters with the printed word in an assortment of autobiographical contexts ranging from private diaries to published autobiographies. In doing so they laid claim to a complex and sometimes contradictory network of privileges that were associated with literacy.

The transformative potential implicit in the sorts of descriptions of print culture that we have encountered in previous sections—a powerful engine capable of ridding the world of error and superstition, and reforming or even overturning governments—added an overtly political dimension to more individualist notions of improvement that were traditionally associated with reading as education. But an acquaintance with literature was celebrated for conferring benefits that were in many ways the opposite of these reformist suggestions. Where one view of the importance of literacy implied a democratic faith in the ability of a proper education to enfranchise individuals of all ranks by transforming them into thoughtful citizens, an alternative perspective reinforced hierarchical difference by enshrining literacy (in the sense of being well read) as a defining feature of the difference between the polite and the vulgar. In Thomas Henry's essay, *On the Advantages of Literature and Philosophy in general, and especially on the consistency of Literary and Philosophical with Commercial Pursuits*, which he presented to the Literary and Philosophical Society of Manchester in 1781, Henry argued that "a taste for polite literature, and the works of nature and art, is essentially necessary to form the Gentleman, and will always distinguish him more completely from the vulgar, than any advantage he can derive from wealth, dress, or titles." In case his audience missed the civic implications of this distinction, Henry made the point in more explicitly political terms: "How great is the contrast between the characters of the elegant scholar, and the man whose uncultivated mind feels no restraint, but those which the laws of his country impose!"

Depending on the ways that one portrayed one's self, it was possible to suggest that one's encounter with literature reflected either, or in varying degrees, both of these emphases. The selections from the four autobiographies included here use a variety of strategies to make these points. All four emphasize the author's lowly beginnings; the grammatical irregularities that characterize these works—especially the memoirs of the three men—highlight the extent to which their education was achieved despite their lowly social position. There are, however, as many differences as there are similarities. The shoemaker-turned-bookseller, James Lackington, situated his book within the class dynamics highlighted by Thomas Henry by carrying on a spirited debate with his well-bred detractors in the book's dedication and then again in the preface to the second edition. For Lackington, a love of reading (the result of his youthful conversion to Methodism) was inseparable from his commitment to selling books. Lackington's entrepreneurial savvy made him a wealthy man, but he also delighted in the idea that by selling books cheaply, he had helped to enrich the lives of ordinary people.

Like Lackington, Mary Robinson's autobiography is a tale of unwavering determination to overcome life's obstacles, but the challenges Robinson faced were sexual as well as financial. Her father's infidelities and financial recklessness were repeated in the vices of her husband. Given her own frequently demonized personal life after splitting with her husband, Robinson's emphasis on these struggles helps to present her as a morally proper and victimized woman in a world of "duplicity and sorrow." The book's gothic tone emphasized the gendered nature of her struggle to contend with "the perseverance of sorrow" that characterized her life. Robinson turned to literature as a cathartic outlet for her own sufferings, and, with the family in jail as a result of her husband's debts, as a source of income. In doing so she very quickly attracted the attention of one of the most prestigious and, in her own way, controversial names of her age, the Duchess of Devonshire, who took a strong personal interest in Robinson's plight. Robinson became an extremely successful author in the 1790s, but in some ways her career reinforced rather than released her from her problems. Authorship may have helped to alleviate the emotional burden of her sufferings, but as a profession it was, she insisted, "a *destroying labour*" that only exacerbated her afflictions.

William Gifford's autobiography appeared as the Preface to his translation of the satires of Juvenal, the completion of which forms one of the threads in his account of triumphing over his "humble and obscure state, poor beyond the common lot." Like Lackington and Place, Gifford's is an extraordinary tale of self-education and determination in which his literary inclinations were frequently at odds with more practical concerns. Because of Gifford's political conservatism[1] (in 1809 he became the editor of the staunchly Tory *Quarterly Review*), his tale is less a celebration of working class improvement than a record of his individual merits, aided by a succession of increasingly prestigious patrons. Francis Place's life story is filled with the same spirit daunting adversity and unwavering determination. But where Gifford's narrative is tempered by a polite tone of due humility in the face of his more illustrious patrons, Place's tale of his rise from childhood poverty to affluence is laced with a suggestion of the egotism of the self-made man. It is, however,

---

[1] See William Hazlitt's characterization of Gifford in Section 11.

also one of working-class pride in "the improvement which has since taken place among the *People*." Written decades after his immersion in the volatile world of radical politics in the 1790s (he was a leading member of London's dominant reformist group, the London Corresponding Society), Place's life story is an implicit legitimation, not only of his desire for personal improvement, but of the enlightened character of the radical movement itself. His ultimate prosperity is offered as a vindication of his own ambitions, but it is a vindication that he is careful to extend to his former peers in the radical movement. Place's memoirs offer one of the most vivid existing accounts of London Corresponding Society meetings. Like the other autobiographies in this section, it is also a compelling depiction of the centrality of literature in these personal and political struggles.

ຕະຕະ

JAMES LACKINGTON
Memoirs of the Forty-Five First Years of the Life of James Lackington, Bookseller

PREFACE
TO THE
SECOND AND SUBSEQUENT EDITIONS.

"'Tis nothing new, I'm sure you know,
For those who write, their works to show;
And if they're prais'd, and render'd vain,
'Tis ten to one they write again:
And then they read it o'er with care,
Correcting here, and adding there." MRS SAVAGE.[1]

THE first edition of my Memoirs was no sooner published, than my old envious friends, mentioned in the third class of my dedication,[2] found out that it was "d—d stuff! d—d low!" the production of a *cobler*, and only fit to amuse that honourable fraternity, or to line their garrets and stalls; and many gentlemen, who are my customers, have informed me that, when they ask for them at several shops, they received for an answer, that they had already too much waste paper, and would not increase it by keeping Lackington's Memoirs: and some kindly added, "You need not be in haste to purchase, as in the course of the Christmas holidays, Mr Birch in Cornhill will wrap up all his mince-pies with them, and distribute them through the town for the public good. Thus

"With all the eunuch's melancholy spite,
They growl at you, because they cannot write;
A gloomy silence, envy's pang imparts,
Or some cold hint betrays their canker'd hearts."[3]

---

[1] Source unidentified.

[2] James Lackington (1746–1815), a self-educated bookseller famous for his innovative commercial practices, including his commitment to selling at the cheapest possible prices. The first edition of Lackington's *Memoirs* had begun with a triple dedication: to "THE PUBLIC," whose attentions Lackington held in high regard; to "RESPECTABLE...BOOKSELLERS," who had responded to his efforts with "candour and liberality;" and to "those sordid and malevolent BOOKSELLERS," to "whose assiduous and unwearied labours to injure his reputation" Lackington responded, "I'll give every one a smart lash in my way." It is to this final group, which dismissed him as an unqualified upstart, that Lackington is responding in the Preface to the second edition. The second edition and all subsequent editions included both his initial dedication and his later response to his "old envious friends."

[3] Source unidentified.

But the rapid sale of this Life soon caused them to alter their stories; and I was very much surprised to hear that several of those gentlemen, who had scarce done exclaiming, "Vile trash! beneath all criticism!" &c. began to praise the composition; and on looking into the English Review, I found that the editors had filled seven pages in reviewing these Memoirs, and had bestowed much praise on the author. I was then ready to conclude, that their generous and manly impartiality had, in a miraculous manner, effected the conversion of others. But I was soon convinced, that meanness can never be exchanged for generosity; and that those who had been "unclean were unclean still;" or, as Churchill says,

"That envy, which was woven in the frame
At first, will to the last remain the same.
Reason may drown, may die, but envy's rage,
Improves with time, and gathers strength from age." [1]

It seems that several of those liberal-minded men, being prodigiously mortified at the increasing sale of my Life, applied to different authors in order to get one of them to father my book: but those authors, either from principle, or from knowing that my manuscript was kept in my shop for the inspection of the public, or from some other motive, refused to adopt the poor bantling: and not only so, but laughed at, and exposed the mean contrivance, to the very great disappointment of those *kind and honest-hearted friends of mine.*

"'Tis hard to say, what mysteries of fate,
What turns of fortune, on poor writers wait;
The party slave will wound him as he can,
And damn the merit, if he hates the man."
                                        W. HARTE. [2]

That I might not be justly charged with ingratitude, I take this opportunity of thanking my friends, customers, and the public, for their candid reception of my volume; the sale of which, and the encomiums I have received on the subject, both by letter and otherwise, have far exceeded my most sanguine and self-flattering expectations; I very sensibly feel the obligation! Their generosity has overwhelmed me! I am overpaid, and remain their debtor!

[In the opening pages, Lackington described his early childhood and adolescence. Due to his family's poverty, Lackington was not able to attend school, but at the age of ten, a local baker hired him to sell pies. It was during this period that Lackington acquired some knowledge of trade. He lived with the baker until he was fourteen, at which point he was hired by George Bowden as an apprentice.]

At the time that I was bound apprentice, my master had two sons, the eldest about seventeen years old, the youngest fourteen. The eldest had just been baptized, and introduced as a member of the Arianistical dipping community where my master and his family attended. [3] The boy was a very sober industrious youth, and gave his father and mother much pleasure. The youngest was also a good lad. Thus everything continued well for some time after I had been added to the family. Both of the boys had very good natural parts, and had learned to read, write, keep accounts, &c. But they had been at schools where no variety of books had been introduced, so that all they had read was the bible. My master's whole library consisted of a school-size

---

[1] Charles Churchill (1731–64), *An Epistle to William Hogarth* (1763): 441–44.

[2] Walter Harte (1709–74), "To A Young Lady, with Mr. Fenton's Miscellany" (1727).

[3] An evangelical Christian community, probably related to the Baptists. Arianism, a religious sect founded on the teachings of the fourth-century priest, Arius, was viewed with suspicion by the Church of England for its improper sense of Christ's divinity. Arius believed that Christ was a supernatural creature not quite human and not quite divine, created by rather than coeval with God.

bible, Watts's Psalms and Hymns, Foot's Tract on Baptism, Culpepper's Herbal, the History of the Gentle Craft, an old imperfect volume of Receipts in Physic, Surgery, &c., and the Ready Reckoner.[1] The ideas of the family were as circumscribed as their library. My master called attention to business and working hard, "minding the main chance." On Sundays all went to meeting; my master on that day said a short grace before dinner, and the boys read a few chapters in the bible, took a walk for an hour or two, then read a chapter or two more.

Thus was the good man's family jogging easily and quietly on, no one doubting but he should go to heaven when he died, and every one hoping it would be a good while first.

"A man should be religious, not superstitious." [2]

But, alas! the dreadful crisis was at hand that put an end to the happiness and peace of this little family. I had been an apprentice about twelve or fifteen months, when my master's eldest son George happened to go and hear a sermon by one of Mr Wesley's preachers, and who had left the plough-tail to preach the *pure* and *unadulterated* Gospel of Christ.[3] By this sermon the fallow ground of poor George's heart was ploughed up, he was now persuaded that the innocent and good life he had led would only sink him deeper into hell; in short, he found out that he had never been converted, and of course was in a state of damnation without benefit of clergy. But he did not long continue in this damnable state, but soon became one of

"———— The sanctified band,
Who all holy mysteries well understand."

SIMKIN.[4]

He persuaded himself that he had passed through the *new birth*, and was quite sure that his name was registered in the Book of Life, and (to the great grief of his parents) he was in reality become a *new creature*.

"'Twas methodistic grace that made him toss and tumble,
Which in his entrails did like a jalap rumble."

OVID's *Epist. Burlesqued*.[5]

George had no sooner made things sure for himself, than he began to extend his concern to his father, mother, brother, and me; and very kindly gave us to understand that he was sure we were in a very deplorable state, "without hope, and without God in the world," being under the curse of the Law.

This created in me a desire for knowledge, that I might know who was right and who was wrong. But to my great mortification, I could not read. I

[1] Isaac Watts (1674–1748), a Dissenting minister, wrote verse and prose for children. He published *Songs Attempted in Easy Language for the Use of Children* in 1715; William Foot (1707–82), author of *a Plain Account of the Ordinance of Baptism; The English Physician: or an Astrologo-Physical Discourse of the Vulgar Herbs of this Nation* (1653), by Nicholas Culpepper (1616–54), an English physician committed to treating the poor, often for free, and translating medical texts from Latin in order to make them more accessible to the disenfranchised; *The Gentle Craft* (*c.* 1599), by Thomas Deloney (1543–1600), a silk weaver and ballad writer, fiction writer, and pamphleteer, offered a vivid and humorous account of contemporary London, as well as "shewing what famous men have been shoe-makers in time past in this land with their worthy deeds and great hospitality"; *The Book of Knowledge: Treating of the Wisdom of the Ancients*, by Erra Pater, a pseudonym for William Lilly (1602–81), included "several choice receipts in physic and surgery"; *The Ready Reckoner, or Trader's Most Useful Assistant, in Buying and Selling All Sorts of Commodities Either Wholesale or Retail*, by Daniel Fenning, promised to show "at one view the amount or value of any number or quantity of goods or merchandise from one farthing to twenty shillings, either by the long or short hundred, half hundred or quarter, pound or ounce, ell or yard, &c. &c. In so plain and easy a manner, that persons quite unacquainted with arithmetic may hereby ascertain the value of any number of hundreds, pounds, ounces, ells or yards, &c."

[2] Aulus Gellius (*c.* A.D. 117–80), *Noctes Atticae* 4: 9: 1.

[3] A sarcastic reference to Methodists' reputation for assuming a highly exclusive sense of Christian righteousness.

[4] Source unidentified.

[5] Source unidentified.

knew most of the letters, and a few easy words, and I set about learning with all my might. My mistress would sometimes instruct me, and having three-halfpence per week allowed me by my mother, this money I gave to John (my master's youngest son) and for every three-halfpence he taught me to spell one hour. This was done in the dark, as we were not allowed a candle after we were sent up stairs to bed.

I soon made a little progress in reading; in the mean time I also went to the Methodist meeting. There, as "enthusiasm is the child of melancholy," I caught the infection.[1] The first that I heard was one Thomas Bryant, known in Taunton by the name of the Damnation Preacher (he had just left off cobbling soles of another kind.) His sermon frightened me most terribly. I soon after went to hear an old Scotchman, and he assured his congregation that they would be damned, and double damned, and treble damned, and damned for ever, if they died without what he called *faith*.

"Conj'rers like, on fire and brimstone dwell,
And draw each moving argument from hell."
SOAME JENYNS.[2]

This marvellous doctrine and noisy rant and enthusiasm soon worked on my passions, and made me believe myself to be really in the damnable condition that they represented; and in this miserable state I continued for about a month, being all that time unable to work myself up to the proper key.

The enthusiastic notions[3] which I had imbibed, and the desire I had to be talking about religious mysteries, &c. answered one valuable purpose; as it caused me to embrace every opportunity to learn to read, so that I could soon read the easy parts of the

bible, Mr Wesley's hymns, &c. and every leisure minute was so employed.

In the winter I was obliged to attend my work from six in the morning until ten at night. In the summer half year I only worked as long as we could see without candle; but notwithstanding the close attention I was obliged to pay to my trade, yet for a long time I read ten chapters in the bible every day: I also read and learned many hymns, and as soon as I could procure some of Mr Wesley's tracts, sermons, &c. I read them also; many of them I perused in Cloacina's temple,[4] (the place where my lord Chesterfield advised his son to read the classics; but I did not apply them, after reading, to the farther use that his lordship hints at).

I had such good eyes, that I often read by the light of the moon, as my master would never permit me to take a candle into my room, and that prohibition I looked upon as a kind of persecution, but I always comforted myself with the thoughts of my being a dear child of God; and as such, that it was impossible for me to escape persecution from the children of the devil, which epithets I very *piously* applied to my good master and mistress. And so ignorantly and imprudently zealous (being a real Methodist) was I for the good of their precious souls, as sometimes to give them broad hints of it, and of the dangerous state they were in.

[*Lackington eventually moved to Bristol, where he met John Jones, a shoemaker, with whom he immersed himself in reading.*]

My friend Mr Jones was my secretary, who before I came to live with him had not the least relish for books, and I had only read a few enthusiastic authors, together with Pomfret's poems;[5] this

[1] Source unidentified.

[2] Soame Jenyns (1704–87), *An Essay on Virtue* (1770).

[3] Enthusiasm was a term for a visionary intensity that many people felt bordered on delusion or even madness.

[4] The bathroom. "Cloaca" is a sewage drain.

[5] John Pomfret (1667–1702), best remembered for his poem *The Choice* (1700), which extolled the virtues of a quiet country estate.

last I could almost repeat by memory; however, I made the most of my little stock of literature, and strongly recommended the purchasing of books to Mr Jones. But so ignorant were we on the subject, that neither of us knew what books were fit for our perusal, nor what to enquire for, as we had scarce ever heard or seen even any title pages, except a few of the religious sort, which at that time we had no relish for. So that we were at a loss how to encrease our small stock of science. And here I cannot help thinking that had Fortune thrown proper books in our way, we should have imbibed a just taste for literature, and soon made some tolerable progress; but such was our obscurity, that it was next to impossible for us ever to emerge from it.

> "The mind untaught, in vain,
> Her powers, tho' blooming vigour nourish,
> Hopes in perfect pride to flourish;
> Culture must her might maintain."
>
> MR. PICKERTON[1]

As we could not tell what to enquire for, we were ashamed to go into the booksellers' shops; and I assure you that there are thousands now in England in the very same situation; many, very many have come to my shop, who have discovered[2] an enquiring mind, but were totally at a loss what to ask for, and who had no friend to direct them.

> "——————— Reason grows apace, and calls
> For the kind hand of an assiduous care.
> Delightful task! To rear the tender thought,
> To teach the young idea how to shoot,
> To pour the fresh instruction o'er the mind,
> To breathe th' enlivening spirit, and to fix
> The gen'rous purpose in the glowing breast."
>
> THOMSON.[3]

---

[1] Source unidentified.

[2] Revealed.

[3] James Thomson (1700–48), *The Seasons* (1726–30): "Spring" (1728): 1150–56.

One day, as my friend Jones and I were strolling about the fair that is annually held in and near St. James's church-yard, we saw a stall of books, and in looking over the title-pages, I met with Hobbes's Translation of Homer's Iliad and Odyssey. I had somehow or other heard that Homer was a great poet, but unfortunately I had never heard of Pope's translation of him, so we very eagerly purchased that by Hobbes. At this stall I also purchased Walker's Poetical Paraphrase of Epictetus's Morals: and home we went, perfectly well pleased with our bargains.[4]

We that evening began with Hobbes's Homer, but found it very difficult for us to read, owing to the obscurity of the translation, which together with the indifferent language, and want of poetical merit in the translator, somewhat disappointed us; however, we had from time to time, many a hard puzzling hour with him.

But as to Walker's Epictetus, although that had not much poetical merit, yet it was very easy to be read, and as easily understood. The principles of the *stoics* charmed me so much, that I made the book my companion wherever I went and read it over and over in raptures, thinking that my mind was secured against all the smiles and frowns of fortune.

[*In 1770, Lackington married his childhood sweetheart, Nancy Smith, who subsequently became seriously ill and was confined to bed for six months. Lackington blamed her illness on his wife's move from the countryside to "the sedentary life and very bad air" in Bristol. When she recovered, they left Bristol and*

---

[4] Thomas Hobbes (1588–1679), is best known for the pessimistic view of human nature which informed his philosophical work, *Leviathan*. In 1674–75 he published a translation of Homer in quatrains. Alexander Pope (1688–1744) published translations of Homer's *Iliad* in 1715–20 and *Odyssey* in 1725–26 with the assistance of William Broome and Elijah Fenton. Ellis Walker (?) wrote *The Morals of Epictetus: A Poetical Paraphrase of Epictetus' Encheiridion* (1690).

relocated to Taunton, seven miles from her previous home. They eventually moved to London, where wages were better.]

At this time I was as visionary and superstitious as ever I had been at any preceeding period, for although I had read some sensible books, and had thereby acquired a few rational ideas, yet, having had a methodistical wife for near three years, and my keeping methodistical company, together with the gloomy notions which in spite of reason and philosophy I had imbibed during the frequent, long, and indeed almost constant illness of my wife, the consequence was, that those few rational or liberal ideas which I had before treasured up, were at my coming to London in a dormant state, or borne down by the torrent of enthusiastic whims, and fanatical chimeras.

———— "Oh! what a reasonless machine
Can superstition make the reas'ner man!"
MALLET's *Mahomet*.[1]

So that as soon as I procured a lodging and work, my next enquiry was for Mr Wesley's gospel-shops: and on producing my class and band tickets from Taunton I was put into a class, and a week or two after admitted into a band.

But it was several weeks before I could firmly resolve to continue in London; as I really was struck with horror for the fate of it, more particularly on Sundays, as I found so few went to church, and so many were walking and riding about for pleasure, and the lower class getting drunk, quarrelling, fighting, working, buying, selling, &c. I had seen so much of the same kind in Bristol, that I often wondered how God permitted it to stand; but

London I found infinitely worse, and seriously trembled for fear the measure of iniquity was quite full, and that every hour would be its last. However, I at length concluded, that if London was a second Sodom, I was a second Lot; and these comfortable ideas reconciled me to the thoughts of living in it.[2]

After our room was furnished, as we still enjoyed a better state of health than we did at Bristol and Taunton, and had also more work and higher wages, we often added something or other to our stock of wearing apparel.

"Industrious habits in each bosom reign,
And industry begets a love of gain,
Hence all the good from opulence that springs."
GOLDSMITH.[3]

Nor did I forget the old book-shops: but frequently added an old book to my small collection; and I really have often purchased books with the money that should have been expended in purchasing something to eat; a striking instance of which follows:

At the time we were purchasing household goods we kept ourselves very short of money, and on Christmas eve we had but half-a-crown left to buy a Christmas dinner. My wife desired that I would go to market and purchase this festival dinner, and off I set for that purpose; but in the way I saw an old book-shop, and I could not resist the temptation of going in; intending only to expend sixpence or nine-pence out of my half-a-crown. But I stumbled upon Young's Night Thoughts—forgot my dinner—down went my half-crown—and I hastened home, vastly delighted with the acquisition.[4] When my wife asked me where was our

---

[1] James Miller (1706–44) and John Hoadly (1711–76), *Mahomet the Imposter: A Tragedy* (1744): v: i: 4–5. A translation of Voltaire's play, *Le Fanatisme, ou Mahomet le prophète* (1741).

[2] Genesis 18:1–23.

[3] Oliver Goldsmith (c. 1730–74), *The Traveller, or a Prospect of Society* (1764): 299–301.

[4] *The Complaint, or Night Thoughts on Life, Death, and Immortality* (1742–44), the best known poem of Edward Young (1683–1765).

Christmas dinner, I told her it was in my pocket.—
"In your pocket (said she); that is a strange place!
How could you think of stuffing a joint of meat
into your pocket?" I assured her that it would take
no harm. But as I was in no haste to take it out, she
began to be more particular, and enquired what I
had got, &c. On which I began to harangue on the
superiority of intellectual pleasures over sensual
gratifications, and observed that the brute creation
enjoyed the latter in a much higher degree than
man. And that a man, that was not possessed of
intellectual enjoyments, was but a two-legged brute.

I was proceeding in this strain; "And so, (said
she,) instead of buying a dinner, I suppose you
have, as you have done before, being buying books
with the money?"

"Pray what is the value of Newton or Locke?
 Do they lessen the price of potatoes or corn?
When poverty comes, can they soften the shock,
 Or teach us how hunger is patiently borne?
You spend half your life-time in poring on books;
 What a mountain of wit must be cramm'd in that skull!
And yet, if a man were to judge by your looks,
 Perhaps he would think you confoundedly dull."[1]

I confessed I had bought Young's Night
Thoughts "And I think (said I) that I have acted
wisely; for had I bought a dinner we should have
eaten it tomorrow, and the pleasure would have
been soon over, but should we live fifty years
longer, we shall have the Night Thoughts to feast
upon." This was too powerful an argument to
admit of any farther debate; in short, my wife was
convinced. Down I sat, and began to read with as
much enthusiasm as the good doctor possessed
when he wrote it; and so much did it excite my
attention as well as approbation, that I retained the
greatest part in my memory. A couplet of Persius, as
Englished, might have been applied to me:

"For this you gain your meagre looks,
 And sacrifice your dinner to your books."[2]

Sometime in June 1774, as we sat at work in our
room, Mr Boyd, one of Mr Wesley's people, called
and informed me that a little shop and parlour were
to be let in Featherstone street, adding, that if I was
to take it, I might there get some work as a master.
I without hesitation told him that I liked the idea,
and hinted that I would sell books also. Mr Boyd
then asked me how I came to think of selling books?
I informed him that until that moment it had never
once entered into my thoughts; but that when he
proposed my taking the shop it instantaneously
occurred to my mind, that for several months past
I had observed a great increase in a certain old book
shop; and that I was persuaded I knew as much of
old books as the person who kept it. I farther
observed, that I loved books, and that if I could but
be a bookseller I should then have plenty of books
to read, which was the greatest motive I could
conceive to induce me to make the attempt. My
friend on this assured me, that he would get the
shop for me, and with a loud laugh added, "When
you are lord mayor, you shall use all your interest to
get me made an alderman." Which I engaged not to
forget to perform.

"In all my wanderings round the world of care,
 In all my grief—and God has giv'n my share—
I still had hopes to see some better days."[3]

My private library at this time consisted of
Fletcher's Checks to Antinomianism, &c. 5 vol-
umes; Watts's Improvement of the Mind; Young's
Night Thoughts; Wake's Translation of the
Apostolical Epistles; Fleetwood's Life of Christ; the

---

[1] Source unidentified.

[2] Persius, or Aulus Persius Flaccus (34–62), a Roman satirical poet. *Satires* III: 85–86.

[3] Oliver Goldsmith (1728–74), *The Deserted Village* (1770): 85–87.

first twenty numbers of Hinton's Dictionary of the Arts and Sciences; some of Wesley's journals, and some of the pious lives published by him; and about a dozen other volumes of the latter sort, besides odd magazines, &c.[1] And to set me up in style, Mr Boyd recommended me to the friends of a holy brother lately gone to heaven, and of whom I purchased a bagful of old books, chiefly divinity, for a guinea.

Soon after I commenced bookseller I became acquainted with what Pope calls "the noblest work of God," an honest man.[2] This was Mr John Dennis, an oilman in Cannon street (father of the present John Dennis, bookseller.) This gentleman had often visited me during my long illness,[3] and having seen me tranquil and serene when on the very point of death, he formed a favourable conclusion that I too must be an honest man, as I had so quiet a conscience at such an awful period. Having retained these ideas of me after my recovery, and being perfectly well acquainted with my circumstances, he one day offered to become a partner in my business, and to advance money in proportion to my stock. This confidential offer I soon accepted:

early in 1778 he became partner; and we very soon laid out his money in second-hand books, which increased the stock at once to double.

I soon after this proposed printing a sale catalogue, to which, after making a few objections, Mr Dennis consented. This catalogue of twelve thousand volumes (such as they were) was published in 1779. My partner's name was not in the title-page, the address was only "J. Lackington and Co., No. 46, Chiswell street." This our first publication produced very opposite effects on those who perused it; in some it excited much mirth, in others an equal proportion of anger. The major part of it was written by me, but Mr Dennis wrote many pages of it, and as his own private library consisted of scarce, old, mystical and alchymical books, printed above a century ago, many of them in bad condition, this led him to insert *neat* in the catalogue to many articles, which were only neat when compared with such as were in very bad condition; so that when we produced such books as were called neat in our catalogue, we often got ourselves laughed at, and sometimes our neat articles were heartily damned. We had also a deal of trouble on another score: Mr Dennis inserted a number of articles without the authors' names, and assured me that the books were well known, and to mention the authors was often useless. The fact was, Mr Dennis knew who wrote those articles; but was soon convinced that many others did not, as we were often obliged to produce them merely to let our customers see who were the authors. We however took twenty pounds the first week the books were on sale, which we thought a large sum. The increase of our stock augmented our customers in proportion, so that Mr Dennis, finding that his money turned to a better account in book-selling than in the funds, very soon lent the stock near two hundred pounds, which I still turned to a good account. We went on very friendly and prosperously for little more than two years; when

---

[1] Reverend John William Fletcher (1729–85), wrote *Checks to Antinomianism*, in response to the disputes between the Arminians and Calvinists (1771); Isaac Watts (1674–1748), *The Improvement of the Mind: Or, a Supplement to the Art of Logick: Containing a Variety of Remarks and Rules for the Attainment and Communication of Useful Knowledge, in Religion, in the Sciences, and in Common Life* (1741); William Wake (1657–1737), author of *Translation of the Apostolical Epistles* (1693); Reverend John Fleetwood (?), *The Life of Our Lord and Saviour Jesus Christ: From His Incarnation to His Ascension into Heaven* (?); Reverend J. H. Hinton (?), co-author of *Supplement to the Oxford Encyclopædia: or, Dictionary of Arts, Sciences, and General Literature* (?); John Wesley (1703–91) published twenty-three collections of hymns and a collected prose works. His journal blended an account of his religious activism with social observations.

[2] Alexander Pope (1688–1744), *An Essay on Man*, Epistle IV (1734): 244.

[3] Lackington fell ill in September 1775. His wife, who fell ill less than two weeks later, died on 9 November of that year. Having only recently recovered from his own illness, Lackington remarried 30 January 1776.

one night Mr Dennis hinted that he thought I was making purchases too fast, on which I grew warm, and reminded him of an article in our partnership agreement, by which I was to be sole purchaser, and was at liberty to make what purchases I should judge proper. I also reminded him of the profits which my purchases produced, and he reminded me of his having more money in the trade than I had. We were indeed both very warm; and on my saying, that if he was displeased with any part of my conduct, he was at liberty to quit the partnership, he in great warmth replied that he would. The above passed at Mr Dennis's house in Hoxton square; I then bade him good night. When Mr Dennis called at the shop the next day, he asked me if I continued in the same mind I was in the preceding night? I assured him that I did. He then demanded of me whether I insisted on his keeping his word to quit the partnership? I replied, I did not insist on it, as I had taken him a partner for three years, nearly one third part of which time was unexpired; but I added, that as I had always found him strictly a man of his word, I supposed he would prove himself so in the present instance, and not assert one thing at night and another in the morning. On which he observed, that as he was not provided with a shop, he must take some time to look for one. I told him that he might take as long a time as he thought necessary. This was in March 1780. He appointed the twentieth of May following. On that day we accordingly dissolved the partnership; and, as he had more money in the trade than myself, he took my notes for what I was deficient, which was a great favour done to me. We parted in great friendship, which continued to the day of his death; he generally called every morning to see us, and learn our concerns, and we constantly informed him of all that had passed the preceding day; as how much cash we had taken, what were the profits, what purchases we had made, what bills we had to pay,

&c., and he sometimes lent me money to help to pay them.

At his death he left behind him in his private library the best collection of scarce valuable mystical and alchymical books that ever was collected by one person. In his lifetime he prized these kind of books above everything; in collecting them he never cared what price he paid for them. This led him to think, after he became a bookseller, that other book-collectors should pay their money as freely as he had done his, which was often a subject of debate between him and me, as I was for selling everything cheap, in order to secure those customers already obtained, as well as increase their numbers.

For several years together I thought I should be obliged to desist from purchasing a large number of any one article; for although by not giving any credit I was enabled to sell very cheap, yet the heavy stock of books in sheets often disheartened me, so that I more than once resolved to leave off our chasing all such articles where the number was very large. But, somehow or other, a torrent of business suddenly poured in upon me on all sides, so that I very soon forgot my resolution of not making large purchases, and now find my account in firmly adhering to that method; and being universally known for making large purchases, most of the trade in town and country, and also authors of every description, are continually furnishing me with opportunities. In this branch of trade it is next to impossible for me ever to have any formidable rivals, as it requires an uncommon exertion, as well as very uncommon success, and that for many years together, to rise to any great degree of eminence in that particular line. This success must be attained too without the aid of *novelty*, which I found to be of very great service to me: and should any person begin on my plan, and succeed extremely well, he could never supercede me, as I am still enlarging my business every year, and the more it is extended the cheaper I can afford to sell; so that though I may be pursued, I cannot be overtaken, except I should (as some others have done) be so infatuated and blinded by prosperity, as to think that the public would continue their favours, even though the plan of business were reversed. But as the first king of Bohemia kept his country shoes by him, to remind him from whence he was taken, I have put a motto on the doors of my carriage, constantly to remind me to what I am indebted for my prosperity, viz.

"SMALL PROFITS DO GREAT THINGS"

And I assure you that reflecting on the means by which I have been enabled to support a carriage adds not a little to the pleasure of riding in it. I believe I may, without being deemed censorious, assert, that there are some who ride in their carriages, who cannot reflect on the means by which they were acquired with an equal degree of satisfaction.

(1791; 1792)

MARY ROBINSON
Memoirs of Mary Robinson. Written by Herself. [1]

A T the period when the antient city of Bristol was besieged by Fairfax's army, the troops being stationed on a rising ground in the vicinity of the suburbs, a great part of the venerable MIN-STER was destroyed by the cannonading before Prince Rupert surrendered to the enemy;[2] and the beautiful Gothic structure, which at this moment fills the contemplative mind with melancholy awe, was reduced to but little more than one half of the original fabric. Adjoining to the consecrated hill, whose antique tower resists the ravages of time, once stood a monastery of monks of the order of St Augustine. This building formed a part of the spacious boundaries which fell before the attacks of the enemy, and became a part of the ruin, which never was repaired, or re-raised to its former Gothic splendours.

On this spot was built a private house, partly of simple and partly of modern architecture. The front faced a small garden, the gates of which opened to the Minister-Green (now called the College-Green): the west side was bounded by the Cathedral, and the back was supported by the antient cloisters of St Augustine's monastery. A spot more calculated to inspire the soul with mournful meditation can scarcely be found amidst the monuments of antiquity.

In this venerable mansion there was one chamber whose dismal and singular constructure left no doubt of its having been a part of the original monastery. It was supported by the mouldering arches of the cloisters; dark, Gothic, and opening on the minster sanctuary, not only by casement windows that shed a dim mid-day gloom, but by a narrow winding staircase, at the foot of which an iron-spiked door led to the long gloomy path of cloistered solitude. This place remained in the situation in which I describe it in the year 1776, and probably may, in a more ruined state, continue so to this hour.

In this awe-inspiring habitation, which I shall henceforth denominate the Minster-house, during a tempestuous night, on the twenty-seventh of

---

[1] Mary "Perdita" Robinson (1758–1800), a well-known actress, poet, novelist, and polemical writer. At the height of her popularity as an actress in the late 1770s and early 1780s, she was closely linked with fashionable London, and became the subject of gossip for her notorious liaison with the eighteen year old Prince of Wales. In the 1790s she aligned herself with reformist politics. In 1798 she published (under the pseudonym Anne Frances Randall) *A Letter to the Women of England, on the Injustice of Mental Insubordination.* Her daughter Elizabeth completed and in 1801, a year after her mother's death, published Robinson's *Memoirs.*

[2] During the English civil war in the seventeenth century.

November 1758, I first opened my eyes to this world of duplicity and sorrow. I have often heard my mother say that a more stormy hour she never remembered. The wind whistled round the dark pinnacles of the minster tower, and the rain beat in torrents against the casements of her chamber. Through life the tempest has followed my footsteps; and I have in vain looked for a short interval of repose from the perseverance of sorrow.

In my early days my father was prosperous, and my mother was the happiest of wives. She adored her children; she devoted her thoughts and divided her affections between them and the tenderest of husbands. Their spirits now, I trust, are in happier regions, blest, and re-united for ever.

If there could be found a fault in the conduct of my mother towards her children, it was that of a too unlimited indulgence, a too tender care, which but little served to arm their breast against the perpetual arrows of moral vicissitude. My father's commercial concerns were crowned with prosperity. His house was opened by hospitality, and his generosity was only equalled by the liberality of fortune: every day augmented his successes: every hour seemed to increase his domestic felicity, till I attained my ninth year, when a change took place as sudden as it was unfortunate, at a moment when every luxury, every happiness, not only brightened the present, but gave promise of future felicity: a scheme was suggested to my father, as wild and romantic as it was perilous to hazard, which was no less than that of establishing a whale fishery on the coast of Labrador; and of civilizing the Esquimaux Indians, in order to employ them in the extensive undertaking. During two years this eccentric plan occupied his thoughts by day, his dreams at night: all the smiles of prosperity could not tranquilize the restless spirit: and, while he anticipated an acquirement of fame, he little considered the perils that would attend his fortune.

In order to facilitate this plan, my father deemed it absolutely necessary to reside at least two years in America. My mother, who felt an invincible antipathy to the sea, heard his determination with grief and horror. All the persuasive powers of affection failed to detain him; all the pleadings of reason, prudence, a fond wife, and an infant family, proved ineffectual. My father was determined on departing, and my mother's unconquerable timidity prevented her being the companion of his voyage. From this epocha I date the sorrows of my family.

Many months elapsed, and my mother continued to receive the kindest letters from that husband, whose rash scheme filled her bosom with more regret and apprehension. At length the intervals became more frequent and protracted. The professions of regard, no longer flowing from the heart, assumed a laboured style, and seemed rather the efforts of honourable feeling than the involuntary language of confidential affection. My mother felt the change, and her affliction was infinite.

At length a total silence of several months awoke her mind to the sorrows of neglect, the torture of compunction: she now lamented the timidity which had divided her from a husband's bosom, the natural fondness which had bound her to her children;—for, while her heart bled with sorrow and palpitated with apprehension, the dreadful secret was unfolded,—and the cause of my father's silence was discovered to be a new attachment;—a mistress, whose resisting nerves could brave the stormy ocean, and who had consented to remain two years with him in the frozen wilds of America.

This intelligence nearly annihilated my mother, whose mind, though not strongly organized, was tenderly susceptible. She resigned herself to grief. I was then at an age to feel and to participate in her sorrows. I often wept to see her weep: I tried all my little skill to soothe her, but in vain: the first shock was followed by calamities of a different nature.

The scheme in which my father had embarked his fortune failed, the Indians rose in a body, burst his settlement, murdered many of his people, and turned the produce of their toil adrift on the wide and merciless ocean. The *noble* patrons of his plan deceived him in their assurances of marine protection, and the island of promise presented a scene of barbarous desolation. This misfortune was rapidly followed by other commercial losses: and to complete the vexations which pressed heavily on my mother, her rash husband gave a bill of sale of his whole property, by the authority of which we were obliged to quit our home, and to endure those accumulated vicissitudes for which there appeared no remedy.

Within a few days of our arrival in London we were placed for education in a school at Chelsea. The mistress of this seminary was perhaps one of the most extraordinary women that ever graced, or disgraced, society: her name was Meribah Lorrington. She was the most extensively accomplished female that I ever remember to have met with: her mental powers were no less capable of cultivation than superiorly cultivated. Her father, whose name was Hull, had from her infancy been the master of an academy at Earl's Court, near Fulham; and early after his marriage losing his wife, he resolved on giving his daughter a masculine education. Meribah was early instructed in all the modern accomplishments, as well as in classical knowledge. She was mistress of the Latin, French, and Italian languages; she was said to be a perfect arithmetician and astronomer, and possessed the art of painting on silk to a degree of exquisite perfection. But, alas! with all these advantages she was addicted to one vice, which at times so completely absorbed her faculties, as to deprive her of every power, either mental or corporeal. Thus, daily and hourly, her superior acquirements, her enlightened understanding, yielded to the intemperance of her ruling infatuation, and every power of reflection seemed lost in the unfeminine propensity.

All that I ever learned I acquired from this extraordinary woman. In those hours when her senses were not intoxicated, she would delight in the task of instructing me. She had only five or six pupils, and it was my lot to be her particular favourite. She always, out of school, called me her little friend, and made no scruple of conversing with me (sometimes half the night, for I slept in her chamber) on domestic and confidential affairs. I felt for her a very sincere affection, and I listened with peculiar attention to all the lessons she inculcated. Once I recollect her mentioning the particular failing which disgraced so intelligent a being: she pleaded, in excuse of it, the immitigable regret of a widowed heart, and with compunction declared that she flew to intoxication as the only refuge from the pang of prevailing sorrow. I continued more than twelve months under the care of Mrs Lorrington, during which period my mother boarded in a clergyman's family at Chelsea. I applied rigidly to study, and acquired a taste for books, which has never, from that time, deserted me. Mrs Lorrington frequently read to me after school hours, and I to her: I sometimes indulged my fancy in writing verses, or composing rebuses;[1] and my governess never failed to applaud the juvenile compositions I presented to her. Some of them, which I preserved and printed in a small volume shortly after my marriage, were written when I was between twelve and thirteen years of age; but as love was the theme of my poetical phantasies, I never showed them to my mother, till I was about to publish them.

I was now near fourteen years old, and my mother began to foresee the vicissitudes to which my youth might be exposed, unprotected, tenderly

---

[1] Puzzles representing words, phrases, or sentences using letters, numerals, pictures, etc., whose names have the same sounds as the words represented.

educated, and without the advantages of fortune. My father's impracticable scheme had impoverished his fortune, and deprived his children of that affluence which, in their infancy, they had been taught to hope for. I cannot speak of my own person, but my partial friends were too apt to flatter me. I was naturally of a pensive and melancholy character; my reflections on the changes of fortune frequently gave me an air of dejection which perhaps excited an interest beyond what might have been awakened by the vivacity or bloom of juvenility.

Shortly after my mother had established herself at Chelsea, on a summer's evening, as I was sitting at the window, I heard a deep sigh or rather a groan of anguish, which suddenly attracted my attention. The night was approaching rapidly, and I looked towards the gate before the house, where I observed a woman evidently labouring under excessive affliction; I instantly descended and approached her. She, bursting into tears, asked whether I did not know her. Her dress was torn and filthy;—she was almost naked;—and an old bonnet, which nearly hid her face, so completely disfigured her features that I had not the smallest idea of the person who was then almost sinking before me. I gave her a small sum of money, and inquired the cause of her apparent agony: she took my hand and pressed it to her lips.—"Sweet girl," said she, "you are still the angel I ever knew you!"—I was astonished; she raised her bonnet—her fine dark eyes met mine. It was Mrs Lorrington—I led her to my chamber, and, with the assistance of a lady who was our French teacher, I clothed and comforted her. She refused to say how she came to be in so deplorable a situation; and took her leave. It was in vain that I entreated, that I conjured her to let me know where I might send to her. She refused to give me her address, but promised that in a few days she would call upon me again. It is impossible to

describe the wretched appearance of this accomplished woman! The failing to which she had now yielded, as to a monster that would destroy her, was evident even at the moment when she was speaking to me. I saw no more of her: but to my infinite regret I was informed some years after, that she had died, the martyr of premature decay, brought on by the indulgence of her propensity to intoxication, in the workhouse—of Chelsea!

The finishing points of my education I received at Oxford house, Marylebone: I was at this period within a few months of fifteen years of age, tall, and nearly such as my partial friends, the few whose affections have followed me from childhood, remember me. My early love for lyric harmony had led me to a fondness for the more sublime scenes of dramatic poetry. I embraced every leisure moment to write verses; I even fancied that I could compose a tragedy, and more than once unsuccessfully attempted the arduous undertaking.

The dancing master at Oxford-house, Mr Hussey, was then ballet master of Covent-garden theatre.[1] Mrs Hervey, the governess, mentioned me to him as possessing an extraordinary genius for dramatic exhibitions. My figure was commanding for my age and (my father's pecuniary embarrassments augmenting by the failure of another American project) my mother was consulted as to the propriety of my making the stage my profession. Many cited examples of females who, even in that perilous and arduous situation, preserved an unspotted fame, inclined her to listen to the suggestion, and to allow of my consulting some master of the art, as to my capability of becoming an ornament to the theatre.

Previous to this idea my father had again quitted England: he left his wife with assurances of goodwill—his children with all the agonies of parental

---

[1] Covent-Garden and Drury Lane were the two principal theatres in London.

regret. When he took leave of my mother, his emphatic words were these—I shall never forget them—"Take care that no dishonour falls upon my daughter. If she is not safe at my return I will annihilate you." My mother heard the stern injunction, and trembled while he repeated it.

I was, in consequence of my wish to appear on the stage, introduced to Mr Hull of Covent-garden theatre; he then resided in King-street, Soho. He heard me recite some passages of the character of Jane Shore, and seemed delighted with my attempt. I was shortly after presented, by a friend of my mother's, to Mr Garrick: Mr Murphy, the celebrated dramatic poet, was one of the party; and we passed the evening at the house of the British Roscius in the Adelphi.[1] This was during the last year that he dignified the profession by his public appearance. Mr Garrick's encomiums were of the most gratifying kind. He determined that he would appear in the same play with me on the first night's trial; but what part to choose for my *début* was a difficult question. I was too young for any thing beyond the girlish character; and the dignity of tragedy afforded but few opportunities for the display of such juvenile talents. After some hesitation, my tutor fixed on the part of Cordelia. His own Lear can never be forgotten.

I now found myself an object of attention whenever I appeared at the theatre. I had been too often in public not to be observed; and it was buzzed about that I was the juvenile pupil of Garrick,—the promised Cordelia. My person improved daily; yet a sort of dignified air, which from a child I had acquired, effectually shielded me

from the attacks of impertinence or curiousity. Garrick was delighted with every thing I did. He would sometimes dance a minuet with me, sometimes request me to sing the favourite ballads of the day; but the circumstance which most pleased him, was my tone of voice, which he frequently told me closely resembled that of his favourite Cibber.[2]

Every attention which was now paid to me augmented my dear mother's apprehensions. She fancied every man a seducer, and every hour an hour of accumulating peril! I know what she was doomed to feel, for that Being who formed my sensitive and perpetually aching heart knows that *I have since felt it.*

Among other friends who were in the habit of visiting my mother, there was one, a Mr Wayman, an attorney of whom she entertained the highest opinion. He was distinguished by the patronage of Mr Cox, and his reputation required no other voucher. One evening a party of six was proposed for the following Sunday; with much persuasion my mother consented to go, and to allow that I should also attend her. Greenwich was the place fixed on for the dinner; and we prepared for the day of recreation. It was then the fashion to wear silks. I remember that I wore a nightgown of pale blue lustring, with a chip hat, trimmed with ribbands of the same colour. Never was I dressed so perfectly to my own satisfaction; I anticipated a day of admiration;—Heaven can bear witness that, to me, it was a day of fatal victory!

On our stopping at the Star and Garter, at Greenwich, the person who came to hand me from the carriage was our opposite neighbour in Southampton-buildings. I was confused; but my mother was indignant! Mr Wayman presented his

---

[1] David Garrick (1717–79), famous as both an actor for his Shakespearean roles and for his part in managing Drury Lane, was highly praised in Charles Churchill's play, *The Rosciad* (1761), which offered satirical sketches of prominent actors of the day; Arthur Murphy (1727–1805) wrote comedies, tragedies, and farces; the Adelphi, built after Robert and James Adams leased the site of Durham House in 1768, was London's finest riverside building.

[2] Colley Cibber (1671–1757), an actor and playwright. He became Poet Laureate in 1730, and was attacked by poets such as Alexander Pope.

young friend—that friend who was ordained to be MY HUSBAND.

Our party dined; and early in the evening we returned to London. Mr Robinson remained at Greenwich for the benefit of the air, being recently recovered from a fit of sickness. During the remainder of the evening, Mr Wayman expatiated on the many good qualities of his friend Mr Robinson: spoke of his future expectations from a rich old uncle; of his probable advancement in his profession; and, more than all, of his enthusiastic admiration of me.

A few days after, Mr Robinson paid my mother a visit. We had now removed to Villars-street, York-buildings; my mother's fondness for books of a moral and religious character was not lost upon my new lover; and elegantly bound editions of Hervey's *Meditations*,[1] with some others of a similar description, were presented, as small tokens of admiration and respect. My mother was beguiled by these little interesting attentions, and soon began to feel a strong predilection in favour of Mr Robinson.

Every day some new mark of respect augmented my mother's favourable opinion; till Mr Robinson became so great a favourite, that he seemed to her the most perfect of existing beings. Just at the period my brother George sickened for the small-pox: my mother idolized him; he was dangerously ill:—Mr Robinson was indefatigable in his attentions, and my appearance on the stage was postponed till the period of his perfect recovery. Day and night Mr Robinson devoted himself to the task of consoling my mother, and of attending to her darling boy; hourly, and indeed momentarily, Mr Robinson's praises were reiterated with enthusiasm by my mother. He was "the kindest, the best of mortals!", the least addicted to worldly follies—and

the man, of all others, who she should adore as a *son-in-law*.

My brother recovered, at the period when I sickened from the infection of his disease. I felt little terror at the approaches of a dangerous and deforming malady; for, I know not why, but personal beauty has never been to me an object of material solicitude. It was now that Mr. Robinson exerted all his assiduity to win my affections; it was when a destructive disorder menaced my features, and the few graces that nature had lent them,[2] that he professed a disinterested fondness: every day he attended with the zeal of a brother; and that zeal made an impression of gratitude upon my heart, which was the source of all my succeeding sorrows.

During my illness Mr Robinson so powerfully wrought upon the feelings of my mother that she prevailed on me to promise, in case I should recover, to give him my hand in marriage. The words of my father were frequently repeated, not without some innuendos that I refused my ready consent to an union with Mr Robinson, from a blind partiality to the libertine Captain ******.[3] Repeatedly urged and hourly reminded of my father's vow, I at last consented; and the bans were published while I was yet lying on a bed of sickness;—I was then only a few months advanced in my sixteenth year.

As soon as the day of my wedding was fixed, it was deemed necessary that a total revolution should take place in my external appearance. I had till that period worn the habit of a child; and the dress of a woman so suddenly assumed sat rather awkwardly upon me. Still so juvenile was my appearance, that even two years after my union with Mr Robinson I was always accosted with the appellation of *Miss*, whenever I entered a shop, or was in company with strangers. My manners were no less childish than

---

[1] James Hervey (1714–58), *Meditations Among the Tombs, Reflections in a Flower Garden, and Contemplations on the Night* (1746–47).

[2] Small pox.

[3] This unnamed man had already expressed a romantic interest in Robinson but was discovered to already be married.

my appearance; only three months before I became a wife, I had dressed a doll.

Of those who frequented our house Lord Lyttelton was most decidedly my abhorrence; I knew that he frequently led my husband from the paths of domestic confidence to the haunts of profligate debasement. Towards me his Lordship affected great indifference; he has even in my presence declared, that no woman under thirty years of age was worth admiring; that even the antiquity of forty was far preferable to the insipidity of sixteen; and he generally concluded his observations by hoping he had not made "the *pretty child* angry".

I soon discovered that his intercourse with Lord Lyttelton produced a very considerable change in Mr Robinson's domestic deportment. They were constantly together, and the neglect which I experienced began to alarm me. I dedicated all my leisure hours to poetry: I wrote verses of all sorts; and Mr Robinson having mentioned that I had purposed appearing on the stage previous to my marriage, in the character of Cordelia, Lord Lyttelton facetiously christened me the Poetess Corry.

One forenoon Lord Lyttelton called in Hatton-garden, as was almost his daily custom, and, on finding that Mr Robinson was not at home, requested to speak to me on business of importance. I found him seemingly much distressed. He informed me that he had a secret to communicate of considerable moment both to my interest and happiness. I started. "Nothing, I trust in heaven, has befallen my husband!" said I with a voice scarcely articulate. Lord Lyttelton hesitated. "How little does that husband deserve the solicitude of such a wife!" said he; "but", continued his Lordship, "I fear that I have in some degree aided in alienating his conjugal affections. I could not bear to see such youth, such merit, so sacrificed"—"Speak briefly, my Lord," said I.—"Then", replied Lord Lyttelton, "I must inform you, that your husband is the most

false and undeserving of that name! He has formed a connection with a woman of abandoned character; he lavishes on her those means of subsistence which you will shortly stand in need of."

"I do not believe it," said I, indignantly.— "Then you shall be convinced," answered his Lordship—"but remember, if you betray me, your true and zealous friend, I must fight your husband; for he will never forgive my having discovered his infidelity."

"It cannot be true," said I. "You have been misinformed."

"Then it has been by the woman who usurps your place in the affections of your husband," replied Lord Lyttelton: "from her I received the information: her name is Harriet Wilmot: she resides in Soho: your husband daily visits her."—I thought I should have fainted: but a torrent of tears recalled the ebbing current of my heart, and I grew proud in fortitude, though humbled in self-love.

"Now," said Lord Lyttelton, "if you are a woman of spirit, you will be *revenged*!" I shrunk with horror, and would have quitted the room. "Hear me," said he. "You cannot be a stranger to my motives for thus cultivating the friendship of your husband; my fortune is at your disposal. Robinson is a ruined man; his debts are considerable, and nothing but destruction can await you. Leave him! Command my powers to serve you."

I would hear no more— broke from him, and rushed out of the apartments. My sensations, my sufferings were undescribable.

I immediately took an hackney coach, and proceeded to Prince's-street, Soho;—Lord Lyttelton having given me the address of my rival. Language cannot begin to describe what I suffered till I arrived at the lodgings of Miss Wilmot. The coachman knocked, a dirty servant girl opened the door. Her mistress was not at home, I quitted the coach and ascended to the drawing-room; where the servant left me, after informing me that Miss W. would return in a very short time. I was now left alone.

I opened the chamber-door which led from the drawing-room: a new white lustring sacque and petticoat lay on the bed. While I was examining the room, a loud knocking at the street door alarmed me. I re-entered the front apartment, and waited with a palpitating bosom till the being whose triumph had awakened both my pride and resentment, appeared before me.

She was a handsome woman, though evidently some years older than myself. She wore a dress of printed Irish muslin, with a black gauze cloak and a chip hat, trimmed with pale lilac ribbons; she was tall, and had a very pleasing countenance: her manner was timid and confused; her lips as pale as ashes. I commiserated her distress, desired her not to be alarmed, and we took our seats, with increased composure.

"I came to inquire whether or not you are acquainted with a Mr Robinson," said I.

"I am," replied Miss Wilmot. "He visits me frequently." She drew off her glove as she spoke, and passing her hand over her eyes, I observed on her finger a ring, which I knew to have been my husband's.

"I have nothing more to say," added I, "but to request that you will favour me with Mr Robinson's address, I have something which I wish to convey to him." She smiled, and cast her eyes over my figure: my dress was a morning *dishabille*[1] of India muslin: with a bonnet of straw: and a white lawn cloak bordered with lace.

"You are Mr Robinson's wife," said she with a trembling voice: "I am sure that you are; and probably this ring was yours; pray receive it—"

I declined taking the ring. She continued: "Had I known that Mr Robinson was the husband of such a woman—"

---

[1] A state of being partly or negligently dressed.

I rose to leave her.— She added: "I never will see him more—unworthy man—I never will again receive him." I could make no reply; but rose and departed.

On my return to Hatton-garden I found my husband waiting dinner. I concealed my chagrin; we had made a party that evening to Drury-lane theatre, and from thence to a select concert at the Count de Belgeioso's in Portman square. Lord Lyttelton was to join us at both places. We went to the play; but my agitation had produced such a violent headache that I was obliged to send an apology for not keeping our engagement at the Imperial Ambassador's.

On the following morning I spoke to Mr Robinson respecting Miss Wilmot. He did not deny that he knew such a person; that he had visited her; but he threw all the blame of his indiscretion on Lord Lyttelton. He requested to know who had informed me of his conduct. I refused to tell; and he had too high an opinion of his false associate to suspect him of such treachery.

[*The Robinsons' problems were reaching a crisis point. The problem of Mr. Robinson's infidelity was compounded by his lavish habits and by the failure of Robinson's father to relieve their subsequent debts. Robinson was not, as he had intimated prior to the marriage, the nephew and heir of a Mr. Harris, from whom he expected to inherit a fortune, but Harris's illegitimate son.*]

From Hatton-garden we removed to a house, which was lent to us by a friend at Finchley. Mr Robinson had much business to transact in London, and I was almost perpetually alone at Finchley. Of our domestic establishment there was only one who did not desert us, and he was—a Negro!—one of that despised degraded race, who wear the colour on their features which too often characterizes the hearts of their fair and unfeeling oppressors. I have found, during my journey through life, that the two male domestics who were most attached to my interest, and most faithful to my fortunes, were both *Negros*!

At length the expected, though, to me, most perilous moment arrived, which awoke a new and tender interest in my bosom, which presented to my fondly beating heart my child,—my Maria. I cannot describe the sensations of my soul at the moment when I pressed the little darling to my bosom, my maternal bosom; when I kissed its hands, its cheeks, its forehead, as it nestled closely to my heart, and seemed to claim that affection which has never failed to warm it. She was the most beautiful of infants! I thought myself the happiest of mothers: her first smile appeared like something celestial,—something ordained to irradiate my dark and dreary prospect of existence.

My little collection of Poems, which I had arranged for publication, and which had been ready ever since my marriage, I now determined to print immediately.[1] They were indeed trifles, very trifles—I have since perused them with a blush of self-reproof, and wondered how I could venture on presenting them to the public. I trust that there is not a copy remaining, excepting that which my dear *partial* mother fondly preserved, and which is now in my possession.

A short time after Mr Robinson was arrested. Now came my hour of trial. He was conveyed to the house of a sheriff's officer, and in a few days, detainers were lodged against him to the amount of twelve hundred pounds, chiefly the arrears of annuities, and other demands from Jew creditors; for I can proudly and with truth declare, that he did not at that time, *or at any period since*, owe fifty pounds for *me*, or to any tradesman on *my* account whatever. He was, therefore, after waiting three weeks in the custody of the sheriff's officer (during which time I never left him for a single hour, day or night) obliged to submit to the necessity of becoming a captive.

What I suffered during this tedious captivity!—My little volume of Poems sold but indifferently: my health was considerably impaired; and the trifling income which Mr Robinson received from his father was scarcely sufficient to support him. I will not enter into a tedious detail of vulgar sorrow, of vulgar scenes; I seldom quitted my apartment,[2] and never till the evening, when for air and exercise I walked on the racquet-ground with my husband.

Having much leisure and many melancholy hours, I again turned my thoughts towards the Muses. I chose *Captivity* for the subject of my pen, and soon composed a quarto poem of some length; it was superior to my former productions; but it was full of defects, replete with weak or laboured lines. I never now read my early compositions without a suffusion on my cheek, which marks my humble opinion of them.

At this period I was informed that the Duchess of Devonshire[3] was the admirer and patroness of literature; with a mixture of timidity and hope I sent Her Grace a neatly bound volume of my Poems, accompanied by a short letter apologizing for their defects, and pleading my age as the only excuse for their inaccuracy. My brother, who was a charming youth, was the bearer of my first literary offering at the shrine of nobility. The Duchess admitted him; and with the most generous and amiable sensibility inquired some particulars respecting my situation, with a request that on the following day I would make her a visit.—

---

[1] *Poems by Mrs. Robinson* (1775).

[2] Jail cell.

[3] Georgiana Cavendish (1757–1806), an aristocrat who achieved a celebrity status as a woman of fashion, society hostess, writer and patron. She was known for her active Whig political sympathies, which led to her very controversial public role in the 1784 election campaign, and for her passion for gambling.

I knew not what to do. Her liberality claimed my compliance; yet, as I had never, during my husband's long captivity, quitted him for half an hour, I felt a sort of reluctance that pained the romantic firmness of my mind, while I meditated what I considered a breach of my domestic attachment. However, at the particular and earnest request of Mr Robinson, I consented; and accordingly accepted the Duchess's invitation.

To describe the Duchess's look and manner when she entered the back of the drawing-room of Devonshire-house,[1] would be impracticable; mildness and sensibility beamed in her eyes, and irradiated her countenance. She expressed her surprise at seeing so young a person, who had already experienced such vicissitude of fortune; she lamented that my destiny was so little proportioned to what she was pleased to term my desert, and with a tear of gentle sympathy requested that I would accept a proof of her good wishes. I had not words to express my feelings, and was departing, when the Duchess requested me to call on her very often, and to bring my little daughter with me.

Were I to describe one half of what I suffered, during fifteen months captivity, the world would consider it as the invention of a novel. But Mr Robinson knows what I endured, and how patiently, how correctly I suited my mind to the strict propriety of wedded life: he knows that my duty as a wife was exemplary, my chastity inviolate; he knows that neither poverty nor obscurity, neither the tauntings of the world nor his neglect, could tempt me even to the smallest error: he knows that I bore my afflicting humiliations with a cheerful, uncomplaining spirit; that I toiled honourably for his comfort; and that my attentions were exclusively dedicated to him and my infant.

The period now arrived when Mr Robinson, by setting aside some debts, and by giving fresh bonds and fresh securities for others, once more obtained his liberty. I immediately conveyed the intelligence to my lovely patroness the Duchess of Devonshire, and she wrote me a letter of kind congratulation: she was then at Chatsworth.[2]

Mr Robinson having once more obtained his liberty, how were we to subsist honourably and above reproach? He applied to his father, but every aid was refused; he could not follow his profession, because he had not completed his articles of clerkship.[3] I resolved on turning my thoughts towards literary labour, and projected a variety of works, by which I hoped to obtain at least a decent independence. Alas! how little did I then know either the fatigue or the hazard of mental occupations! How little did I foresee that the day would come, when my health would be impaired, my thoughts perpetually employed, in so destructive a pursuit! At the moment that I write this page I feel in every fibre of my brain the fatal conviction that it is a *destroying labour.*

It was at this moment of anxiety, of hope, of fear, that my thoughts once more were turned to a dramatic life;[4] and, walking with my husband in St James's Park, late in the autumn, we were accosted by Mr Brereton of Drury-lane theatre. I had not seen him during the last two years, and he seemed rejoiced in having met us. At that period we lodged at Lyne's the confectioner in Old Bond-street. Mr Brereton went home and dined with us; and after dinner the conversation turned on my partiality to the stage, which he earnestly recommended as a scene of great promise to what he termed my

1 The Duke and Duchess of Devonshire's winter residence. It was one of the great aristocratic mansions built in the fashionable west end of London during the eighteenth century.

2 Their summer residence, located in Derbyshire.

3 He had not yet finished his training to be a lawyer.

4 Mary Robinson's dramatic career had ended when she was married. Her new husband regarded it as an undignified and scandalous occupation.

promising talents. The idea rushed like electricity through my brain: I asked Mr Robinson's opinion, and he now readily consented to my making the trial. He had repeatedly written to his father, requesting even the smallest aid towards our support until he could embark in his profession; but every letter remained unanswered, and we had no hope but in our own mental exertions.

An appointment was made in the Green-room of Drury-lane theatre. Mr Garrick, Mr Sheridan, Mr Brereton, and my husband, were present; I there recited the principal scenes of Juliet (Mr Brereton repeating those of Romeo), and Mr Garrick, without hesitation, fixed on that character as the trial of my *début*.

[*Robinson's autobiography goes on to narrate her illustrious career on stage and, as a result of her celebrity, her infamous relationship with the Prince of Wales, who in 1779 promised to settle £20,000 on her as a basis for their liaison, a pledge he would renege on when he broke off the relationship the next year. Her death on 26 December 1800 prevented Robinson from going on to describe her rise to literary fame as a poet, novelist, and political writer in the 1790s. The* Memoirs *were completed and published by her daughter Maria in 1801.*]

(1801)

WILLIAM GIFFORD, ESQ.
The Satires of Decimus Junius Juvenalis and of Aulus Persius Flaccus, Translated Into English Verse. Prefaced by a Life of Gifford.[1]

---

[1] William Gifford (1756–1827), a leading conservative satirist. His enthusiastic support of Tory causes was rewarded in 1797 when he was appointed editor of the *Anti-Jacobin* newspaper, and even more profoundly, in 1809, when he became the editor of the *Quarterly Review*, Britain's leading conservative quarterly.

I AM about to enter on a very uninteresting subject: but all my friends tell me that it is necessary to account for the long delay of the following Work; and I can only do it by adverting to the circumstances of my life. Will this be accepted as an apology?

I know but little of my family, and that little is not very precise: My great-grandfather (the most remote of it, that I ever recollect to have heard mentioned) possessed considerable property at Halsbury, a parish in the neighbourhood of Ashburton; but whether acquired or inherited, I never thought of asking, and do not know.

He was probably a native of Devonshire, for there he spent the last years of his life; spent them too, in some sort of consideration, for Mr. T. (a very respectable surgeon of Ashburton) loved to repeat to me, when I first grew into notice, that he had frequently hunted with his hounds.[†]

My father was a good seaman, and was soon made second in command in the Lyon, a large armed transport in the service of government: while my mother (then with child of me) returned to her native place, Ashburton, where I was born, in April, 1756.

The resources of my mother were very scanty. They arose from the rent of three or four small fields, which yet remained unsold. With these, however, she did what she could for me; and as soon as I was old enough to be trusted out of her sight, sent me to a schoolmistress of the name of Parret, from whom I learned in due time to read. I cannot boast much of my acquisitions at this school; they consisted merely of the contents of the

---

[†] The matter is of no consequence—no, not even to thyself. From my family I derived nothing but a name, which is more perhaps, than I shall leave: but (to check the sneer of rude vulgarity,) that family was among the most ancient and respectable of this part of the country, and, not more than three generations from the present, was counted among the wealthiest.—Σχιας οναρ! ["Dream of a shadow," from Pindar Pythian Ode 8.95. The full phrase is "man is but a dream of a shadow."]

"Child's Spelling Book" but from my mother, who had stored up the literature of a country town, which, about half a century ago, amounted to little more than what was disseminated by itinerant ballad-singers, or rather, readers, I had acquired much curious knowledge of Catskin, and the Golden Bull, and the Bloody Gardener,[1] and many other histories equally instructive and amusing.

My father returned from sea in 1764. He had been at the siege of the Havannha;[2] and though he received more than a hundred pounds for prize money, and his wages were considerable; yet, as he had not acquired any strict habits of economy, he brought home but a trifling sum. The little property yet left was therefore turned into money; a trifle more was got by agreeing to renounce all future pretensions to an estate at Totness;[†] and with this my father set up a second time as a glazier[3] and house painter. I was now about eight years old, and was put to the freeschool,[4] (kept by Hugh Smerdon,) to learn to read, and write and cipher. Here I continued about three years, making a most wretched progress, when my father fell sick and died. He had not acquired wisdom from his misfortunes, but continued wasting his time in unprofitable pursuits, to the great detriment of his business. He loved drink for the sake of society, and to this he fell a martyr; dying of a decayed and ruined constitution before he was forty. The town's-people thought him a shrewd and sensible man, and regretted his death. As for me, I never greatly loved him; I had not grown up with him; and he was too prone to repulse my little advances to familiarity, with coldness, or anger. He had certainly some reason to be displeased with me, for I learned little at school; and nothing at home, though he would now and then attempt to give me some insight into his business. As impressions of any kind are not very strong at the age of eleven or twelve, I did not long feel his loss; nor was it a subject of much sorrow to me, that my mother was doubtful of her ability to continue me at school, though I had by this time acquired a love for reading.

I never knew in what circumstances my mother was left: most probably they were inadequate to her support, without some kind of exertion, especially as she was now burthened with a second child about six or eight months old. Unfortunately she determined to prosecute my father's business; for which purpose she engaged a couple of journeymen,[5] who, finding her ignorant of every part of it, wasted her property, and embezzled her money. What the consequence of this double fraud would have been, there was no opportunity of knowing, as, in somewhat less than a twelvemonth, my poor mother followed my father to the grave. She was an excellent woman, bore my father's infirmities with patience and good humour, loved her children dearly, and died at last, exhausted with anxiety and grief more on their account than her own.

I was not quite thirteen when this happened; my little brother was hardly two; and we had not a relation nor a friend in the world. Every thing that was left, was seized by a person of the name of Carlile, for money advanced to my mother. It may be supposed that I could not dispute the justice of his claims; and as no one else interfered, he was suffered to do as he liked. My little brother was sent to the alms-house, whither his nurse followed him

---

[1] Typical subjects of popular chapbooks.

[2] England, at war with Spain during the Seven years War (1756–63) captured Havana on 13 August 1762 after a two month siege.

[†] This consisted of several houses, which had been thoughtlessly suffered to fall into decay, and of which the rents had been so long unclaimed, that they could not now be recovered, unless by an expensive litigation.

[3] One who fits windows, doors, etc., with panes of glass.

[4] These schools, which provided a free education, were privately endowed, often by local tradesmen who had become wealthy.

[5] Workers who have completed their apprenticeship in skilled trades or crafts.

out of pure affection; and I was taken to the house of the person I have just mentioned, who was also my godfather. Respect for the opinion of the town (which, whether correct or not, was, that he had amply repaid himself by the sale of my mother's effects) induced him to send me again to school, where I was more diligent than before, and more successful. I grew fond of arithmetick, and my master began to distinguish me: but these golden days were over in less than three months. Carlile sickened at the expense; and, as the people were now indifferent to my fate, he looked round for an opportunity of ridding himself of a useless charge. He had previously attempted to engage me in the drudgery of husbandry.[1] I drove the plough for one day to gratify him; but I left it with a firm resolution to do so no more; and in despite of his threats and promises, adhered to my determination.

He proposed to send me on board one of the Torbay fishing boats; I ventured, however, to remonstrate against this, and the matter was compromised by my consenting to go on board a coaster.[2] A coaster was speedily found for me at Brixham, and thither I went when little more than thirteen.

My master, whose name was Full, though a gross and ignorant, was not an ill-natured, man; at least, not to me: and my mistress used me with unvarying kindness; moved perhaps by my weakness and tender years. In return, I did what I could to requite her, and my good will was not overlooked.

It will be easily conceived that my life was a life of hardship. I was not only a "shipboy on the high and giddy mast,"[3] but also in the cabin, where every menial office fell to my lot: yet if I was restless and discontented, I can safely say, it was not so much on

account of this, as of my being precluded from all possibility of reading; as my master did not possess, nor do I recollect seeing during the whole time of my abode with him, a single book of any description, except the Coasting Pilot.

On Christmas day (1770) I was surprised by a message from my godfather, saying that he had sent a man and horse to bring me to Ashburton and desiring me to set out without delay. My master, as well as myself, supposed it was to spend the holidays there; and he therefore made no objection to my going. We were, however, both mistaken.

Since I had lived at Brixham, I had broken of all connexion with Ashburton. I had no relation there but my poor brother, who was yet too young for any kind of correspondence; and the conduct of my godfather towards me, did not intitle him to any portion of my gratitude, or kind remembrance. I lived therefore in a sort of sullen independence on all I had formerly known, and thought without regret of being abandoned by every one to my fate. But I had not been overlooked. The women of Brixham, who traveled to Ashburton twice a week with fish, and who had known my parents, did not see me without kind concern, running about the beach in a ragged jacket and trousers. They mentioned this to the people of Ashburton, and never without commiserating my change of condition. This tale often repeated, awakened at length the pity of their auditors, and, as the next step, their resentment against the man who had reduced me to such a state of wretchedness. In a large town, this would have had little effect; but in a place like Ashburton, where every report speedily becomes the common property of all the inhabitants, it raised a murmur which my godfather found himself either unable or unwilling to encounter: he therefore determined to recall me; which he could easily do, as I wanted some months of fourteen, and was not yet bound.

---

[1] Farming.

[2] A vessel employed in sailing along the coast.

[3] William Shakespeare (1564–1616), *2 Henry 4* III: i: 18–20.

All this, I learned on my arrival; and my heart, which had been cruelly shut up, now opened to kinder sentiments, and fairer views.

After the holidays I returned to my darling pursuit, arithmetick: my progress was now so rapid, that in a few months I was at the head of the school, and qualified to assist my master (Mr. E. Furlong) on any extraordinary emergency. As he usually gave me a trifle on those occasions, it raised a thought in me, that by engaging with him as a regular assistant, and undertaking the instruction of a few evening scholars, I might, with a little additional aid, be enabled to support myself. God knows, my ideas of support at this time were of no very extravagant nature. I had, besides, another object in view. Mr. Hugh Smerdon (my first master) was now grown old and infirm; it seemed unlikely that he should hold out above three or four years; and I fondly flattered myself that, notwithstanding my youth, I might possibly be appointed to succeed him. I was in my fifteenth year, when I built these castles: a storm, however, was collecting, which unexpectedly burst upon me, and swept them all away.

On mentioning my little plan to Carlile, he treated it with the utmost contempt; and told me, in his turn, that as I had learned enough, and more than enough, at school, he must be considered as having fairly discharged his duty; (so, indeed, he had;) he added, that he had been negotiating with his cousin, a shoemaker of some respectability, who had liberally agreed to take me without a fee, as an apprentice. I was so shocked at this intelligence, that I did not remonstrate; but went in sullenness and silence to my new master, to whom I was soon after bound,[†] till I should attain the age of twenty-one.

The family consisted of four journeymen, two sons about my own age, and an apprentice some-

what older. In these there was nothing remarkable; but my master himself was the strangest creature!—He was a Presbyterian, whose reading was entirely confined to the small tracts published on the Exeter Controversy.[1] As these (at least, his portion of them) were all on one side, he entertained no doubt of their infallibility, and being noisy and disputacious, was sure to silence his opponents; and became, in consequence of it, intolerably arrogant and conceited. He was not, however, indebted solely to his knowledge of the subject for his triumph: he was possessed of Fenning's Dictionary,[2] and he made a most singular use of it. His custom was to fix on any word in common use, and then to get by heart the synonym, or periphrasis by which it was explained in the book; this he constantly substituted for the simple term, and as his opponents were commonly ignorant of his meaning, his victory was complete.

With such a man I was not likely to add much to my stock of knowledge, small as it was; and, indeed, nothing could well be smaller. At this period, I had read nothing but a black letter romance[3] called Parismus and Parismenus, and a few loose magazines which my mother had brought

---

[†] My indenture, which now lies before me, is dated the 1st of January, 1772.

[1] Sometimes known as the Prayer Book Rebellion, it was fought between old and new Protestants. Tensions that had been reinforced by the introduction of the new Prayer Book in 1549 were ignited when Sir Walter Ralegh's father, riding out of Exeter in July of that year, upbraided a women for saying her rosary. The woman interrupted the service which was then underway at her local church, and enthused the congregation with a spirit of revolt which was fortified by suspicions that Ralegh's reformed Protestant zeal reflected gentry plans to steal their property. The conflict escalated into a military battle in which Ralegh was taken prisoner, and which only ended when Lord Grey arrived with a troop of Italian mercenaries. The conflict remained an important historical event; there were special sermons in Exeter every year to commemorate the "delivery" of the city.

[2] Daniel Fenning (1751–67), author of *The Royal English Dictionary or Treasury of the English Language* (1761), as well as the *Universal Spelling Book* (1756) and several other textbooks.

[3] "Black letter" was a form of type, associated in the period with popular texts of dubious literary quality.

from South Molton. With the Bible, indeed, I was well acquainted; it was the favourite study of my grandmother, and reading it frequently with her, had impressed it strongly on my mind; these then, with the Imitation of Thomas à Kempis, which I used to read to my mother on her deathbed, constituted the whole of my literary acquisitions.

As I hated my new profession with a perfect hatred, I made no progress in it; and was consequently little regarded in the family, of which I sunk by degrees into the common drudge: this did not much disquiet me, for my spirits were now humbled. I did not however quite resign the hope of one day succeeding to Mr. Hugh Smerdon, and therefore secretly prosecuted my favourite study, at every interval of leisure.

These intervals were not very frequent; and when the use I made of them was found out, they were rendered still less so. I could not guess the motives for this at first; but at length I discovered that my master destined his youngest son for the situation to which I aspired.

I possessed at this time but one book in the world: it was a treatise on Algebra, given to me by a young woman, who had found it in a lodging-house. I considered it as a treasure; but it was a treasure locked up; for it supposed the reader to be well acquainted with simple equation, and I knew nothing of the matter. My master's son had purchased Fenning's Introduction: this was precisely what I wanted; but he carefully concealed it from me, and I was indebted to chance alone for stumbling upon his hiding-place. I sat up for the greatest part of several nights successively, and, before he suspected that his treatise was discovered, had completely mastered it. I could now enter upon my own; and that carried me pretty far into the science.

This was not done without difficulty. I had not a farthing on earth, nor a friend to give me one: pen, ink, and paper, therefore, (in despite of the

flippant remark of Lord Orford,[1]) were, for the most part, as completely out of my reach, as a crown and sceptre. There was indeed a resource; but the utmost caution and secrecy were necessary in applying to it. I beat out pieces of leather as smooth as possible, and wrought my problems on them with a blunted awl: for the rest, my memory was tenacious, and I could multiply and divide by it, to a great extent.

Hitherto I had not so much as dreamed of poetry: indeed I scarcely knew it by name; and, whatever may be said of the force of nature, I certainly never "lisp'd in numbers."[2] I recollect the occasion of my first attempt: it is; like all the rest of my non-adventures, of so unimportant a nature, that I should blush to call the attention of the idlest reader to it, but for the reason alleged in the introductory paragraph. A person, whose name escapes me, had undertaken to paint a sign for an ale-house: it was to have been a lion, but the unfortunate artist produced a dog. On this awkward affair, one of my acquaintance wrote a copy of what we called verse: I liked it; but fancied that I could compose something more to the purpose: I made the experiment, and by the unanimous suffrage of my shopmates was allowed to have succeeded. Notwithstanding this encouragement, I thought no more of verse, till another occurrence, as trifling as the former, furnished me with a fresh subject: and thus I went on, till I had got together about a dozen of them. Certainly, nothing on earth was ever so deplorable: such as they were, however, they were talked of in my little circle, and I was sometimes invited to repeat them, even out of it. I never committed a line to paper for two reasons; first, because I had no paper; and secondly—perhaps I might be excused

---

[1]   Horace Walpole, 4th Earl of Orford (1717–97), in a letter to George Montagu, July 30, 1752.

[2]   Alexander Pope (1688–1744), "Epistle to Dr. Arbuthnot" (1731–34): 128.

from going further; but in truth I was afraid, as my master had already threatened me, for inadvertently hitching the name of one of his customers into a rhyme.

The repetitions of which I speak were always attended with applause, and sometimes with favours more substantial: little collections were now and then made, and I have received sixpence in an evening. To one who had long lived in the absolute want of money, such a resource seemed a Peruvian mine: I furnished myself by degrees with paper, &c. and what was of more importance, with books of geometry, and of the higher branches of algebra, which I cautiously concealed. Poetry, even at this time, was no amusement of mine: it was subservient to other purposes; and I only had recourse to it, when I wanted money for my mathematical pursuits.

But the clouds were gathering fast. My master's anger was raised to a terrible pitch by my indifference to his concerns, and still more by the reports which were daily brought to him of my presumptuous attempts at versification. I was required to give up my papers, and when I refused, my garret was searched, my little board of books discovered and removed, and all future repetitions prohibited in the strictest manner.

This was a very severe stroke, and I felt it most sensibly; it was followed by another severer still; a stroke which crushed the hopes I had so long and so fondly cherished, and resigned me at once to despair. Mr. Hugh Smerdon, on whose succession I had calculated, died, and was succeeded by a person not much older than myself, and certainly not so well qualified for the situation.

In this humble and obscure state, poor beyond the common lot, yet flattering my ambition with day-dreams which, perhaps, would never have been realized, I was found in the twentieth year of my age by Mr. William Cookesley, a name never to be pronounced by me without veneration. The lamen-table doggerel which I have already mentioned, and which had passed from mouth to mouth among people of my own degree, had by some accident or other reached his ear, and given him a curiosity to inquire after the author.

It was my good fortune to interest his benevolence. My little history was not untinctured with melancholy, and I laid it fairly before him: his first care was to console; his second, which he cherished to the last moment of his existence, was to relieve and support me.

Mr. Cookesley was not rich: his eminence in his profession, which was that of a surgeon, procured him, indeed, much employment; but in a country town, men of science are not the most liberally rewarded: he had besides, a very numerous family, which left him little for the purposes of general benevolence: that little, however, was cheerfully bestowed, and his activity and zeal were always at hand to supply the deficiencies of his fortune.

On examining into the nature of my literary attainments, he found them absolutely nothing: he heard, however, with equal surprise and pleasure, that amidst the grossest ignorance of books, I had made a very considerable progress in the mathematicks. He engaged me to enter into the details of this affair; and when he learned that I had made it in circumstances of peculiar discouragement, he became more warmly interested in my favour, as he now saw a possibility of serving me.

The plan that occurred to him was naturally that which had so often suggested itself to me. There were indeed several obstacles to be overcome; I had eighteen months yet to serve; my handwriting was bad, and my language very incorrect; but nothing could slacken the zeal of this excellent man; he procured a few of my poor attempts at rhyme, dispersed them amongst his friends and acquaintance, and when my name was become somewhat familiar to them, set on foot a subscription for my relief. I still preserve the original paper; its title was not very magnificent, though it exceeded the most sanguine wishes of my heart: it ran thus, "A Subscription for purchasing the remainder of the time of William Gifford, and for enabling him to improve himself in Writing and English Grammar." Few contributed more than five shillings, and none went beyond ten-and-sixpence: enough, however, was collected to free me from my apprenticeship[†] and to maintain me for a few months, during which I assiduously attended the Rev. Thomas Smerdon.

In two years and two months from the day of my emancipation, I was pronounced by Mr. Smerdon, fit for the University. The plan of opening a writing school had been abandoned almost from the first; and Mr. Cookesley looked round for some one who had interest enough to procure me some little office at Oxford. This person, who was soon found, was Thomas Taylor, Esq. of Denbury, a gentleman to whom I had already been indebted for much liberal and friendly support. He procured me the place of Bib. Lect. at Exeter College; and this, with such occasional assistance from the country as Mr. Cookesley undertook to provide, was thought sufficient to enable me to live, at least, till I had taken a degree.

During my attendance on Mr. Smerdon I had written, as I observed before, several tuneful trifles, some as exercises, others voluntarily, (for poetry was now become my delight,) and not a few at the desire of my friends.[††] When I became capable,

however, of reading Latin and Greek with some degree of facility, that gentleman employed all my leisure hours in translations from the classicks; and indeed I scarcely know a single school-book, of which I did not render some portion into English verse. Among others, JUVENAL engaged my attention, or rather my master's, and I translated the tenth Satire for a holiday task. Mr. Smerdon was much pleased with this, (I was not un-delighted with it myself,) and as I was now become fond of the author, he easily persuaded me to proceed with him; and I translated in succession, the third, the fourth, the twelfth, and, I think, the eighth Satires. As I had no end in view but that of giving a temporary satisfaction to my benefactors, I thought little more of these, than of many other things of the same nature, which I wrote from time to time, and of which I never copied a single line.

On my removing to Exeter College, however, my friend, ever attentive to my concerns, advised me to copy my translation of the tenth Satire, and present it, on my arrival, to the Rev. Dr. Stinton, (afterwards Rector,) to whom Mr. Taylor had given me an introductory letter: I did so, and it was kindly received. Thus encouraged, I took up the first and second Satires, (I mention them in the order they were translated,) when my friend, who had sedulously watched my progress, first started the idea of going through the whole, and publishing it by subscription,[1] as a scheme for increasing my means of subsistence. To this I readily acceded, and

---

[†] The sum my master received was six pounds.

[††] As I have republished one of our old poets, it may be allowable to mention that my predilection for the drama began at an early period. Before I left school, I had written two tragedies, the Oracle and the Italian.

My qualifications for this branch of the art may be easily appreciated; and, indeed, I cannot think of them without a smile.—These rhapsodies were placed by my indulgent friend, who thought well of them, in the hands of two respectable gentlemen who undertook to convey them to the manager of——: I am ignorant of their fate. The death of Mr. Cookesley broke every link of my connexion with the

majority of my subscribers, and when subsequent events enabled me to renew them, I was ashamed to inquire after what was most probably unworthy of concern.

[1] A method of publishing based on a list of committed purchasers or subscribers. This was often viewed as a compromise between conventional patronage relations and the more unstable realities of the modern book trade. This arrangement provided a degree of security for authors, but eminent names on the subscription list also conveyed a prestige on the author and the book which could help to promote it with a wider audience.

finished the thirteenth, eleventh, and fifteenth Satires: the remainder were the work of a much later period.

When I had got thus far, we thought it a fit time to mention our design; it was very generally approved of by my friends; and on the first of January, 1781, the subscription was opened by Mr. Cookesley at Ashburton, and by myself at Exeter College.

So bold an undertaking so precipitately announced, will give the reader, I fear, a higher opinion of my conceit than of my talents; neither the one nor the other, however, had the smallest concern with the business, which originated solely in ignorance: I wrote verses with great facility, and I was simple enough to imagine that little more was necessary for a translator of Juvenal! I was not, indeed, unconscious of my inaccuracies: I knew that they were numerous, and that I had need of some friendly eye to point them out, and some judicious hand to rectify or remove them: but for these, as well as for every thing else, I looked to Mr. Cookesley, and that worthy man, with his usual alacrity of kindness, undertook the laborious task of revising the whole translation. My friend was no great Latinist, perhaps I was the better of the two; but he had taste and judgment, which I wanted. What advantages might have been ultimately derived from them, there was unhappily no opportunity of ascertaining, as it pleased the Almighty to call him to himself by a sudden death, before we had quite finished the first Satire. He died with a letter of mine, unopened, in his hands.

This event, which took place on the 15th of January, 1781, afflicted me beyond measure.[†] I was not only deprived of a most faithful and affectionate friend, but of a zealous and ever active protector, on whom I confidently relied for support: the sums that were still necessary for me, he always collected; and it was to be feared that the assistance which was not solicited with warmth, would insensibly cease to be afforded.

In many instances this was actually the case: the desertion, however, was not general; and I was encouraged to hope, by the unexpected friendship of Servington Savery, a gentleman who voluntarily stood forth as my patron, and watched over my interests with kindness and attention.

Some time before Mr. Cookesley's death, we had agreed that it would be proper to deliver out, with the terms of subscription, a specimen of the manner in which the translation was executed.[††] To obviate any idea of selection, a sheet was accordingly taken from the beginning of the first Satire. My friend died while it was in the press.

After a few melancholy weeks, I resumed the translation; but found myself utterly incapable of proceeding. I had been so accustomed to connect the name of Mr. Cookesley with every part of it, and I laboured with such delight in the hope of giving him pleasure, that now, when he appeared to have left me in the midst of my enterprize, and I was abandoned to my own efforts, I seemed to be engaged in a hopeless struggle, without motive or end: and his idea, which was perpetually recurring to me, brought such bitter anguish with it, that I shut up the work with feelings bordering on distraction.

The lapse of many months had now soothed, and tranquillized my mind, and I once more returned to the translation, to which a wish to serve a young man surrounded with difficulties, had in-

---

[†] I began this unadorned narrative on the 15th of January, 1801: twenty years have therefore elapsed since I lost my benefactor and my friend. In the interval I have wept a thousand times at the recollection of his goodness: I yet cherish his memory with filial respect; and at this period, my heart sinks within me at every repetition of his name.

[††] Many of these papers were distributed; the terms, which I extract from one of them, were these: "The work shall be printed in quarto, (without notes,) and be delivered to the Subscribers in the month of December next.

"The price will be sixteen shillings in boards, half to be paid at the time of subscribing, the remainder on delivery of the book."

duced a number of respectable characters to set their names; but alas, what a mortification! I now discovered, for the first time, that my own inexperience, and the advice of my too, too partial friend, had engaged me in a work, for the due execution of which, my literary attainments were by no means sufficient. Errors and misconceptions appeared in every page. I had, perhaps, caught something of the spirit of Juvenal, but his meaning had frequently escaped me, and I saw the necessity of a long and painful revision, which would carry me far beyond the period fixed for the appearance of the volume. Alarmed at the prospect, I instantly resolved (if not wisely, yet I trust honestly) to renounce the publication for the present.

In pursuance of this resolution, I wrote to my friend in the country, (the Rev. Servington Savery,) requesting him to return the subscription money in his hands, to the subscribers. He did not approve of my plan; nevertheless he promised, in a letter, which now lies before me, to comply with it; and, in a subsequent one, added that he had already begun to do so.

For myself, I also made several repayments; and trusted a sum of money to make others, with a fellow collegian, who, not long after, fell by his own hands in the presence of his father. But there were still some whose abode could not be discovered, and others, on whom to press the taking back of eight shillings would neither be decent nor respectful: even from these I ventured to flatter myself that I should find pardon, when on some future day I should present them with the Work, (which I was still secretly determined to complete,) rendered more worthy of their patronage, and increased by notes, which I now perceived to be absolutely necessary, to more than double its proposed size.

In the leisure of a country residence, I imagined that this might be done in two years: perhaps I was not too sanguine: the experiment, however, was not made, for about this time a circumstance happened, which changed my views, and indeed my whole system of life.

I had contracted an acquaintance with a person of the name of ———, recommended to my particular notice by a gentleman of Devonshire, whom I was proud of an opportunity to oblige. This person's residence at Oxford was not long, and when he returned to town, I maintained a correspondence with him by letters. At his particular request, these were enclosed in covers, and sent to Lord GROS-VENOR: one day I inadvertently omitted the direction, and his Lordship, necessarily supposing the letter to be meant for himself, opened and read it. There was something in it which attracted his notice; and when he gave it to my friend, he had the curiosity to inquire about his correspondent at Oxford; and, upon the answer he received, the kindness to desire that he might be brought to see him upon his coming to town: to this circumstance, purely accidental on all sides, and to this alone, I owe my introduction to that nobleman.

On my first visit, he asked me what friends I had, and what were my prospects in life; and I told him that I had no friends, and no prospects of any kind. He said no more; but when I called to take leave, previous to returning to college, I found that this simple exposure of my circumstances had sunk deep into his mind. At parting, he informed me that he charged himself with my present support, and future establishment; and that till this last could be effected to my wish, I should come and reside with him. These were not words, of course: they were more than fulfilled in every point. I did go, and reside with him; and I experienced a warm and cordial reception, a kind and affectionate esteem, that has known neither diminution nor interruption, from that hour to this, a period of twenty years![†]

In his Lordship's house I proceeded with Juvenal, till I was called upon to accompany his son (one of the most amiable and accomplished young noblemen that this country, fertile in such characters, could ever boast) to the continent. With him, in two successive tours, I spent many years; years of which the remembrance will always be dear to me, from the recollection that a friendship was then contracted, which time and a more intimate knowledge of each other, have mellowed into a regard that forms once the pride and happiness of my life.

It is long since I have been returned and settled in the bosom of competence and peace: my translation frequently engaged my thoughts, but I had lost the ardour and the confidence of youth, and was seriously doubtful of my abilities to do it justice. I have wished a thousand times that I could decline it altogether; but the ever-recurring idea that there were people of the description already mentioned, who had just and forcible claims on me for the due performance of my engagement, forbad the thought; and I slowly proceeded towards the completion of a work in which I should never have engaged, had my friend's inexperience, or my own, suffered us to suspect for a moment the labour, and the talents of more than one kind, absolutely necessary to its success in any tolerable degree. Such as I could make it, it is now before the Publick.

—— majora canamus.[1]

(1802)

[†] I have a melancholy satisfaction in recording that this revered friend and patron lived to witness my grateful acknowledgment of his kindness. He survived the appearance of the translation but a very few days, and I paid the last sad duty to his memory, by attending his remains to the grave. To me—this laborious work has not been happy: the same disastrous event that marked its commencement, has embittered its conclusion; and frequently forced upon my recollection the calamity of the rebuilder of Jericho, "He laid the foundation thereof in Abiram, his first born, and set up the gates thereof in his youngest son, Segub." 1806.

[1] Let us sing greater things.

FRANCIS PLACE
The Autobiography of Francis Place [2]

MY father at the time of his marriage was I conclude a Journeyman Baker. The earliest account I can remember to have heard of him, was, that he was a Journeyman Baker and worked at Clapham, whence he came home to my mother every saturday night, at her lodgings in the Borough of Southwark, bringing with him a loaf and a parish pudding.[††] After this he became a master Baker, I believe in the Borough, and had a flourishing business, but his propensity for drinking and gaming ruined him. At one sitting he lost every thing he had in the world, even the furniture of his house and the good will of his business, having done this and executed the requisite assignments of his property, he took himself off without the knowledge of my mother and she was turned into the Street; she took a lodging and maintained herself by needlework, to which she had applied herself during the time my father worked as journeyman. For several months my mother heard nothing of my father but was at length informed by letter that he had resided for some time at Plymouth, was ill of a fever and not expected to recover. She raised all the money she could and set out for Plymouth. Travelling at that time was a slow process if compared with its present rate by means of Stage Coaches, and before she could reach Plymouth he was convalescent, they staid there some time and then set out for London, and travelled on foot a considerable part of the way. I have heard my mother give an account of their crossing Salisbury Plain a distance of 21 miles

---

[2] Francis Place (1771–1854) was a leading member of the radical London Corresponding Society in the 1790s, and in the radical movement in the early decades of the next century. He was the author of numerous pamphlets on social and political issues.

[††] A parish pudding is a compound of materials taken from every body's dish and baked in the oven.

on a day in which it rained from morning till night. There was at that time no house on the plain nor any sort of shelter.

On their arrival in London they took lodgings in the Borough again, probably as being better known there than any where else and more likely to procure employment and credit than in a strange place. At the age of four years I was sent to school to an old woman in Bell Yard Temple Bar and with her I remained until I was sent to another school in Wine Office Court Fleet Street when I was about seven years of age. At this old womans school it can scarcely be said that I learned any thing, all I knew, when I left it, was how to read in Dilworth's Spelling Book[1] and that too badly.

In another court called Kings head Court at the top of Wine Office Court was a sort of finishing day school, where latin was pretended to be taught, as well as bookkeeping and Navigation The boys in this school were stout lads, and matches used to be made for two of the small boys in our school to fight one of the large boys in the other school. In these battles I was generally one of the combatants and was almost always victorious.

At a short distance was another large school exactly such an one as ours kept by a Mr Bird, and between the two war was almost constantly waged, sometimes school fought school sometimes half a dozen or more from each side had regular sets to in the presence of both schools. The whole affair was systematically conducted—a large place called Gough Square was the arena and each school took its station across the space leaving an open area in the middle between them, victory was sometimes in favour of one side sometimes on the other side. Neither school ever obtained preeminence for more than a week or two.

There is nothing like these schools now, they abounded at the time I am speaking of and the conduct of all was alike. From this school I and my brother were removed to another school of a similar sort; a small school in Windsor court near the New Church in the Strand. It never contained more than forty boys seldom so many. The school room was on the third floor and at one corner of it was a smaller room for girls. The master, a Mr Bowis was a good man, greatly beloved by his pupils.

As the time approached when I was to be put out in the world, Mr Bowis was directed to have me taught Ingrossing and German Text, both of which I learned in a very short time, as any boy may easily do. I was to be pushed on in arithmetic that I might get through the Rule of three,[2] I had however without my father knowing any thing of the matter gone through all the rules in common arithmetic and vulgar fractions, had he known it, it would not have made any difference, he would have supposed that they proceeded the rule of three. Yet ignorant as he was of arithmetic; he had a method of his own by which he could calculate values by his head more rapidly and quite as correctly as I could do by my arithmetical process.

Mr Bowis must have been an ordinary man in respect to learning—he was not learned in any thing, but at the time I was under his care he seemed to me, to be a prodigiously learned man and a very wise one. He took pains with his scholars and taught them as well as he was able. He gave them good advice, pointed out to them the probable situations they would fill when men and did all he could by advice and by quoting examples to induce them to be industrious, humane careful and respectable. To the advice he gave me, and the care in

---

[1] Thomas Dilworth (*d.* 1780), wrote *A New Guide to the English Tongue* (1740).

[2] The rule of three is the method whereby a fourth number can be determined from a sequence of three proportionally related numbers; engrossing was a style of handwriting suitable to legal documents; German Text was a style used in wills and in the opening of legal documents.

other respects which he took of me I can trace the germs of many right notions, and much of the faculty which served me well when I became a man, namely, the talent of distinguishing, of separating matters and drawing conclusions. This dexterity and power of reasoning kept me from more extensive evils in my youth, than those I fell into, and prevented many evil consequences which others who were not so well taught in these particulars could not avoid.

The progress made in refinement of manners and morals seems to have gone on simultaneously with the improvements in Arts Manufactures and Commerce. The impulse was given about sixty years ago, it moved slowly at first but has been constantly increasing its velocity. Some say we have refined away all our simplicity and have become artificial, hypocritical, and upon the whole worse than we were half a century ago. This is a common belief, but it is a false one, we are a much better people now than we were then, better instructed, more sincere and kind hearted, less gross and brutal, and have fewer of the concomitant vices of a less civilized state.

[*Place found settled employment with a breeches maker, Mr. Pike, and then met the woman who would become his wife, who was working as a serving girl at the pastry-cook's shop next door. Together they decided that Place, having been discharged by Pike, would find work where he could while building towards his ultimate goal of running his own business.*]

It may be supposed that I led a miserable life but I did not I was very far indeed from being miserable at this time when my wife came home at night, we had always something to talk about, we were pleased to see each other, our reliance on each other was great indeed, we were poor, but we were young, active cheerful, and although my wife at times

doubted that we should get on in the world, I had no such misgivings.

My landlady's husband was at home only about two hours in the evening and when the weather was wet, and cold I used to sit in her room and thus saved the expense of firing.[†]

My landlady furnished me with occupation, she brought home books from the chambers she had care of, and exchanged them for others as often as I wished. My good schoolmaster had implanted in me a love for reading, and a desire for information which was by no means wholly neglected even while I was an apprentice, I always found some time for reading, and I almost always found the means to procure books, useful books, not Novels. My reading was of course devoid of method, and very desultory. I had read in English the only language in which I could read, the histories of Greece and Rome, and some translated works of Greek and Roman writers. Hume Smollett, Fieldings novels and Robertsons works, some Hume Essays, some Translations from french writers, and much on geography—some books on Anatomy and Surgery, some relating to Science and the Arts, and many Magazines. I had worked all the Problems in the Introduction to Guthries Geography, and had made some small progress in Geometry. I now read Blackstone, Hale's Common Law, several other Law

---

[†] A curious dissertation might be written on the way in which poor honest respectable persons spend the small sums which come into their hands. On many occasions I have had my attention drawn to the notions entertained by gentlemen and Ladies with whom I have become acquainted respecting the value and the expenditure of small sums by poor people, and have had great difficulty to make them obtain even a glimpse of a poor persons notions on the same subject. Few indeed among the rich can comprehend why a poor person should "look at both sides of a penny before he or she spends it" or the calculations that are made respecting how many things must not be had, how many had, for the sixpence, before it is parted with.

Books, and much Biography.[1] This course of reading was continued for several years until the death of my landlady, she was a very good sort of woman and was a friend of ours as long as she lived, her husband was a plodding stupid sort of a fellow whom we seldom saw and with whom there was no particular intimacy.

Some time before I was married I became a member of the Breeches Makers Benefit Society, for the support of the members when sick, and to bury them when dead. I paid my subscription regularly, but I never attended at the public house at which the club was held excepting on the evenings when the Stewards were chosen. The club though actually a benefit club, was intended for the purpose of supporting the members in a strike for wages. It had now in the Spring of 1793 about £250 in its chest which was deemed sufficient a strike was agreed upon and the men left their work.

As I had not been at the club house for more than three months, and had now no acquaintance with any one in the trade, I was neither aware of the intention to strike, nor of the strike when it took place. The first I heard of it was from Mr Bristow.[2] On taking some work home one evening; he instead of giving me more as I expected gave me my discharge. I asked the reason, he would assign none, and I reproached him with acting unjustly, and in a way, I should not have done towards him, he then alluded to the strike to which he supposed I was a party. I assured him that I had never heard of any intention amongst the men to strike, and had no

knowledge whatever on the subject, but that which he had imparted. He was a kind and reasonable man. He told me he was satisfied, I had not and would not deceive him, he was he said sorry to discharge me, but that at a meeting of the masters it had been agreed that every leather breeches maker who was employed to make stuff breeches[3] should be at once discharged to prevent them assisting those who had struck. Allison[4] discharged me next day. Thus at once were our hopes destroyed and our views obscured.

The whole, or nearly the whole, of the eight months when I was not employed was not lost. I read many volumes in history, voyages, and travels, politics, law and Philosophy. Adam Smith and Locke and especially Humes Essays and Treatises, these latter I read two or three times over, this reading was of great service to me, it caused me to turn in upon myself and examine myself in a way which I should not otherwise have done. It was this which laid the solid foundation of my future prosperity, and completed the desire I had always had to acquire knowledge. Reading of Hume put me on improving myself in other ways. I taught myself decimals, equations, the square cube and biquadrate roots. I got some knowledge of Logarithmes, and some of Algebra. I readily got through a small school book of Geometry and having an odd volume the 1st of Williamsons Euclid[5] I attacked it vigorously and perseveringly. Williamsons is by no means the best book on the subject, yet I am still of opinion that it is the best book I could have had, for the purpose of teaching myself. My progress was for some time very slow, I was perplexed between

---

[1] David Hume (1711–76), Scottish philosopher and historian; Tobias Smollett (1721–71), novelist, editor of the *Critical Review*, historian, and travel writer; Henry Fielding (1707–54), best known for the novels *The History of Tom Jones* (1749) and *Joseph Andrews* (1742); William Robertson (1721–93), a popular historian; Sir William Blackstone (1723–80), the principal legal commentator of the age; Sir Matthew Hale (1609–76), author of *History of the Common Law of England* (1713).

[2] Mr. Bristow was one of Place's occasional employers.

[3] Trousers made out of woven material, usually wool.

[4] Mr. Allison had become Place's most regular employer.

[5] James Williamson (1735–1810), *the Elements of Euclid: with Dissertations Intended to Assist and Encourage a Critical Examination of These Elements as the Most Effectual Means of Establishing a Juster Taste upon Mathematical Subjects than That Which at Present Prevails* (1781).

quantity and number and could not readily abstract myself from the consideration of numbers. I suspect that this has its baleful influence on all who learn arithmetic before they acquire any knowledge of Geometrical figures and definitions of them, which by experience I now know may be taught to children without much difficulty, and which being taught, assist the learner to a great extent when he comes to be taught Mathematics, as a science. Often and often did I find my self at fault and was as often obliged to turn back again, I was sometimes brought to a standstill, and at times almost despaired of making further progress. Williamsons Euclid is preceded by five dissertations, these I read carefully working the problems as I went on. I have no doubt that I should have had less difficulty had I not been impressed with a persuasion of the great difficulty of acquiring the information I sought. The volume contained the first six books of Euclid. With labour such as few would take and difficulties such as few would encounter I got through the six books, but not at all to my satisfaction. I knew no one of whom I could ask a question or receive any kind of instruction, and the subject was therefore at times very painful. I had acquired a good deal of information and was upon the whole well pleased with my progress. I was beginning the book again when Mr Allison sent for me and this for a time put an end to my studies.

On the 28 of April 1794 My wife had her second child a girl whom we named after her Elizabeth, we had been hard at work all day and I had been out at business in the evening, my wife had been putting the room in order when she was taken in labour, and when I came home I found her in that state. At her first lying in she was attended by a woman, but as we were not quite satisfied with her treatment, we resolved to have a man of some reputation, and one had been engaged, two guineas were laid by for him, and as good clothes had been

provided for the child as any working man could reasonably desire. She was delivered at two o clock in the morning. Our room was on the second floor, the landlady of the house was with my wife, and I was invited to sit in the room on the first floor.[1] In this room was a number of books, and among them every thing which had been published by Thomas Paine, all these I had read and cheap editions were in my possession; but here was one which I had not seen, namely "the Age of Reason" Part 1.[2] I read it with delight. It was the first deeistical[3] book I ever saw, excepting the writings of David Hume. I had lived in the house about two months, but there had been no other communication between me and my landlord than a friendly salutation, but the quantity and kind of books I found in his room made me desirous of his acquaintance.

My Landlord made me a chest of drawers of solid mahogany, so contrived that they might be taken in halves, and yet without the appearance in front of being two chests. He also made me a mahogany dining table. He was paid for these articles partly in money, partly in cloaths. We had now quite enough furniture for one room all good and nearly all new. We really wanted nothing now for personal comfort, and could this state of things have been continued we should have saved money and I should have become a master tradesman. But the hopes of a man who has no other means than those of his own hands to help himself are but too often illusory, and in a vast number of cases, the disappointments are more than can be steadily met, and men give up in despair; become reckless, and after a life of poverty end their days prematurely in

[1]   Place and his wife had moved since living in the house where they shared the fireplace with their landlady.

[2]   Thomas Paine's *Age of Reason* (1793) was widely denounced as being an atheistic critique of Christianity that was consistent with his own desire for radical political reform.

[3]   A disposition to freethinking that became associated in the Romantic period with popular radical politics.

misery. The misfortune is the greater too as it is only the better sort of persons to whom this happens. To the careful saving moral men and women who have set their hearts on bettering their condition and have toiled day and night in the hope of accomplishing their purpose. None but such as they can tell how disappointment preys on them, how as the number of their children increases, hope leaves them, how their hearts sink as toil becomes useless, how adverse circumstances force on them those indescribable feelings of their own degradation which sinks them gradually to the extreme of wretchedness. Others there are in much larger numbers whose views are narrower, they who hoped and expected to keep on in a decent way who never expected to rise in the world and never calculated on extreme poverty. I have seen a vast many such, who when the evil day has come upon them, have kept on working steadily but hopelessly more like horses in a mill, or mere machines than human beings, their feelings blunted, poor stultified moving animals, working on yet unable to support their families in any thing like comfort, frequently wanting the common necessaries of life, yet never giving up until "misery has eaten them to the bone," none knowing none caring for them, no one to administer a word of comfort, or if an occasion occured which might be of service to them, none to rouse them to take advantage of it. All above them in circumstances, calumniating them, classing them with the dissolute, the profligate and the dishonest, from whom the character of the whole of the working people is taken. Yet I have witnessed in this class of persons, so despised so unjustly judged of by their betters, virtues which I have not seen, to the same extent as to means, among any other description of the people. Justice will never perhaps be done to them because they may never be understood, because it is not the habit for men to care for others beneath them in rank, and because they who

employ them will probably never fail to look grudgingly on the pay they are compelled to give them for their services, the very notion of which produces an inward hatred of them, a feeling so common that it is visible in the countenance and manners in nearly every one who has to pay either journeymen, labourers, or servants.

My Landlord, the Cabinet Maker was a member of the London Corresponding Society,[1] and at his request I also became a member. This was in the month of June 1794. On the 12 of May Thomas Hardy the Secretary[2] was seized by order of the Government on a pretended charge of High Treason, and about the same time ten others on the same charge, Thomas Holcroft[3] whom it was also intended should be seized avoided them and was at large till the time of trial approached when he surrendered himself. The London Corresponding Society was like the Society of the Friends of the people[4] and the Society for Constitutional Information[5] established to provide a reform in the Representation of the people in the House of Commons.

The violent proceedings of the Government frightened away many of the members of the society

---

[1] The most formidable popular organization for political reform in the 1790s. Founded in 1792, by 1795 it had as many as 5,000 members. The LCS drew on a primarily artisan base

[2] Thomas Hardy (1752–1832), founder of the London Corresponding Society.

[3] Thomas Holcroft (1745–1809), a playwright, novelist, and journalist known for his radical political sympathies.

[4] Society of the Friends of the People was founded in April 1792 to promote parliamentary reform according to the strictly English (rather than revolutionary French) principles that had been suggested in 1780. It included many prominent Whigs such as Charles James Fox and Richard Brinsley Sheridan, but also more radical elements, particularly amongst its members in Scotland. James Mackintosh, author of *Vindiciae Gallicae*, was also a leading member.

[5] A leading reform association during the campaign for political reform in the 1780s. The SCI had a more "respectable" or middle- and upper-class base than the LCS, but the principles that it advocated were embraced by the popular reform movement of the nineteenth century.

and its number was very considerably diminished. Many persons however, of whom I was one, considered it meritorious, and the performance of a duty to become members, now that it was threatened with violence, and its founder and secretary was persecuted. This improved the character of the society as most of those who joined it were men of decided character, sober, thinking men, not likely to be easily put from their purpose.

In this society I met with many inquisitive clever upright men and among them I greatly enlarged my acquaintance. They were in most if not in all respects superior to any with whom I had hitherto been acquainted. We had book subscriptions, similar to the breeches clubs, before mentioned,[1] only the books for which any one subscribed were read by all the members in rotation who chose to read them before they were finally consigned to the subscriber. We had Sunday evening parties at the residences of those who could accommodate a number of persons. At these meetings we had readings, conversations and discussions. There was at this time a great many such parties, they were highly useful and agreeable.

The usual mode of proceeding at these weekly meetings was this. The chairman, (each man was chairman in rotation,) read from some book a chapter or part of a chapter, which as many as could read the chapter at their homes the book passing from one to the other had done and at the next meeting a portion of the chapter was again read and the persons present were invited to make remarks thereon, as many as chose did so, but without rising. Then another portion was read and a second invitation was given—then the remainder was read and a third invitation was given when they who had

not before spoken were expected to say something. Then there was a general discussion. No one was permitted to speak more than once during the reading The same rule was observed in the general discussion, no one could speak a second time until every one who chose had spoken once, then any one might speak again, and so on till the subject was exhausted—these were very important meetings, and the best results to the parties followed.

As I could not doubt of success whenever I should get into business, so I was resolved to give my children the best possible education which my circumstances would afford, I also resolved as much as possible to put my self in a condition to assist them while they were young, and to judge of their progress as they grew up. I therefore determined to obtain some knowledge of the French Language, but how to accomplish this was a great difficulty on account of the expense. It was however overcome. There was in the London Corresponding Society a man named Hitchins, a strange creature in his appearance and odd in his manners, very profound and pompous, which so ill suited his short squat figure as to make him appear ridiculous, he used to talk with great self complacency of his skill in teaching and he was well qualified to teach as far as the acquisition of such learning as he was acquainted with went, he followed the old method of giving a task but no explanation, if it was learned by rote all was well if not he became angry. To explain and remove difficulties was beneath his dignity. He had never once reflected on the truth that it is of little importance by what means the learner acquires the information he stands in need of, and that it is in the power of the teacher frequently to convey as much information in a few minutes as an ignorant scholar might be a week in acquiring without assistance. His notion was the old one, that unless the learner did every thing for himself, he did nothing, and he was therefore a bad teacher. This I

---

[1] A group that Place had belonged to, where members pooled dues which they paid on a regular basis. The money would pay for a new pair of breeches for a series of winners, whose names were drawn in a lottery style at regular intervals.

did not previously know and he was the only person I could find who was willing to teach for so small a sum as I could afford to pay. With this Mr Hitchins I made an agreement to receive an hours instruction twice a week in the french language, provided I could procure four others to join me so that he should receive half a crown a week for his services. I found four. They were all members of the London Corresponding Society and all of them confidential friends of mine and mostly so of one another. I used to plod at the French Grammar as I sat at my work, the book being fixed before me I was diligent also in learning all I could after I left off working at night. My progress was rapid and I soon discovered that our teacher was not well qualified to teach us in some particulars. We therefore resolved to procure a Frenchman if possible. After some seeking we found an Emigrant Priest a kind considerate attentive man, a scholar, who was well calculated to teach; we all of us progressed rapidly under his guidance. I usually when I had done with my french, read some book every night and having left the Corresponding Society I never went from home in the evening I always learned and read for three hours and sometimes longer, the books I now read were french; Helvetius Rousseau and Voltaire.[1] I never wanted books and could generally borrow those I most desired to peruse. I borrowed french books from two members of the Society a Mr. Webbe, was one, his father and I believe he himself—was a musician, a musical composer as I heard, he was a very precise careful young man who occasionally employed me. The other was a Mr Williams a Law Student, he lent me books but never employed me.

---

[1] Claude Arien Helvetius (1715–71); Jean-Jacques Rousseau (1712–78); Voltaire, the name assumed by François Marie Arouet (1694–1778). Despite their philosophical differences, these three writers were seen as important forerunners of the French Revolution.

The moral effects of the Society were considerable. It induced men to read books, instead of wasting their time in public houses, it taught them to respect themselves, and to desire to educate their children. It elevated them in their own opinions, It taught them the great moral lesson "to bear and forbear." The discussions in the divisions, in the sunday evenings readings, and in the small debating meetings, opened to them views which they had never before taken. They were compelled by these discussions to find reasons for their opinions, and to tolerate others. It gave a new stimulus to an immense number of men who had been but in too many instances incapable of any but the grossest pursuits, and seeking nothing beyond mere sensual enjoyments. It elevated them in society. Of all this among multitudes of other proofs a very striking one occurred on the anniversary of the acquittal of Thomas Hardy on the 5th November 1822 at the Crown and Anchor Tavern in the Strand, at this dinner about two hundred persons were present. I attended the first anniversary in 1795 but had never been at any other between 1795 and this in 1822. In 1795, I was a journey man breeches maker. In 1822 I had retired from business. At this meeting I was recognized by no less than twenty four persons who had been delegates from divisions and members of the General Committee of the Society when I was chairman. I had not seen more than one or two of them for upwards of twenty years several I had never seen since 1797–or 1798 all of them recognized me, but I could not recognize many of them until names and circumstances were mentioned. The greetings were mutually agreeable, of these twenty four men, twenty at the least of them were Journey men or shopmen at the time when they were delegates to the General Committee of the Society, they were now all in business all flourishing men. Some of them were rich most of them had families of children to whom they had given or were then giving good educations. The society had been to a very considerable extent the means, and in some of the cases the whole means of inducing them to desire to acquire knowledge the consequence of which was their bringing up a race of men and women as superior in all respects to what they would otherwise have been as can well be conceived. It is more than probable that a circumstance like this never before occurred. That so many persons from among the delegates alone should still be alive, in good health and in good circumstances and should from sympathy assemble in one room is a very extraordinary circumstance, a plain and positive proof of high moral conduct and right feeling which never was surpassed, if indeed it ever was equaled. But if twenty four such men were found in one room at one time, how many such men must there be in the whole country. It must be concluded that compared with the whole number of delegates and even with the whole number of members the number of persons of the same sort must be very large. I know many well doing men who were members but not delegates, and yet my acquaintance with the members out of the committee was not large. Every such person with whom I ever conversed has acknowledged the benefit he derived, and the knowledge he obtained from having been a member of the society, whilst I never heard of any one man who was made worse in consequence of his having been a member of the society.

Vague declamation against the society should then go for nothing, nor should any attention be paid to the accusation of any one be his rank or condition whatever it may, unless he can shew that as much evil was done to individuals and to the public as I have shewn good was done. This is however impossible and I may I am sure safely affirm that the London Corresponding Society was a great moral cause of the improvement which has since taken place among the *People*.

(1824)

Section Four

The Book Trade

Many of the literary debates that we are exploring in this anthology were bound up with broader political issues such as the campaign for government reform, questions about the social role of women, or the connections between literature and empire. But there was also much discussion about print culture as an exciting but potentially monstrous phenomenon in itself. And in one way or another, this discussion had to do with the fact that authors, publishers and readers existed within a thriving but turbulent literary marketplace. Earlier authors had maintained a genteel distance from the idea of writing for profit, preferring to secure patronage from aristocrats who were capable of bestowing both money and prestige on them. Some authors still maintained this pose in the Romantic period, but although most condemned mercenary writers who were motivated solely or primarily by a thirst for profit, they generally acknowledged that, for better or worse, market realities were a central part of any writer's life. Good writers might well be motivated by loftier goals than a love of money, they agreed, but this did not eliminate the need to earn a living. Nor did it shelter them from the various afflictions that were frequently associated with the literary marketplace, such as judicial decisions about copyright, or the ever-popular target of booksellers, whose exploitative instincts were a favourite topic with the writers from whom they derived their wealth.

The question of copyright, or of literary property, had been a prominent one throughout the eighteenth century. In 1710, the world's first copyright statute, known as the Act of the 8th of Anne, established an author's ownership of his or her work for a fourteen-year period, to be renewed for another fourteen years if the author was still alive. It was a significant step, not least because it established the author as an important element of these debates. Before the introduction of this Act, literary property was regulated by a guild known as the Stationer's Company. Books registered with the Stationer's Company could not be republished by other booksellers. This arrangement established a perpetual "copy," but significantly, the opportunity was only available to members of the Stationer's Company, which included booksellers and printers, but not authors. The statute of the 8th of Anne introduced authors into the equation by "Vesting the Copies of Books in the Authors," but it also muddied the legal and literary waters.

The central issue was the question of whether the 1710 Act reinforced the perpetual copyright established by common law within the time frame defined by the Act, or destroyed it altogether in favour of the Act's more limited arrangements. This ambiguity resulted in a string of trials throughout the eighteenth century that provided a public forum for debates about literary property. These were complemented by a lively pamphlet war waged on both sides of what was essentially a commercial struggle between a monopoly of establishment London booksellers, whose dominance could be preserved if the copyrights they already possessed were perpetual, and their Scottish rivals, who were intent on breaking this monopoly by exploiting the fourteen-year limit. The result was a complicated blend of legal and literary discourses that raised pressing questions about the unruly connections between culture and commerce: What did the phrase "literary property" actually mean? Did it refer to intangible ideas or material products? To put it another way, what did the purchaser actually buy—the printed pages or the ideas they conveyed—and what did it entitle him or her to do with them? What notions of authorship were these debates predicated on? How, since they were ultimately concerned with the ability to make writing profitable, were ideas about authorial distinction to be integrated with the effects of commerce?

The statute of the 8th of Anne was formally titled "A Bill for the Encouragement of Learning by Vesting the Copies of Printed Books in the Authors, or Purchasers, of Such Copies, during the Times therein Mentioned," and critics on both sides of the copyright debate based their case on this emphasis on literature as a means of developing and diffusing knowledge. Proponents of perpetual copyright insisted that literary production would decline if authors could not be sure of extending the fruits of their labour to their descendants; opponents of perpetual copyright argued that the very ideal of the diffusion of knowledge was at odds with the restrictive effects of perpetual copyright. These sentiments repeated themselves in various forms. The *Gentleman's Magazine*'s obituary for the well-known publisher Joseph Johnson lauded Johnson's resistance to restrictive forms of "typographical luxury" that made literature visually appealing but more expensive.

These legal battles culminated in the landmark case of *Donaldson v. Becket,* tried before the House of Lords in 1774. The case was in many ways a replay of a similar trial five years earlier. In 1769, Andrew Millar, who owned the copyright to James Thomson's poem, *The Seasons,* sued a Scottish publisher, Robert Taylor, who had reprinted an edition of the work in 1769. The case was tried in the King's Bench, where Taylor argued that under the terms of the 1710 Act, the copyright had expired, but the judges upheld Millar's claim to a perpetual copyright. In 1774, a London bookseller named Thomas Becket, having purchased the copyright to *The Seasons* from Millar's executors, filed a claim against the Edinburgh bookseller Alexander Donaldson, who had reprinted an edition of it. This time, the House of Lords reversed the 1769 decision, effectively destroying perpetual copyright.

The result was an explosion of new editions of older texts by a variety of less established booksellers, a development that intensified the volatility of the literary marketplace. But this did not end legal debates over these issues. In part this was because of a changing interpretation of one aspect of the Act, which required that all authors registering their books for copyright submit one of them to each of a list of designated libraries. As the Act was amended over the years, new libraries were added to the list until, by the early nineteenth century, the number had grown to eleven. The real change, though, was a new ruling which stipulated that authors were required to donate these eleven copies whether they opted to secure their copy or not. Some authors had formerly calculated that their book was expensive enough to produce, and aimed at a select enough audience, that it was not worth sacrificing free copies to insure themselves from pirate editions. But a case fought by the University of Cambridge (one of the eleven copyright libraries) in 1810 resulted in a ruling which stipulated that the trade-off was no longer optional. The author of a letter to the *Gentleman's Magazine* explaining why a promised book had failed to appear, protested that this ruling, which required him to donate eleven copies even though he would simply have foregone the protection that was made available through the Act, had made it financially impossible to publish the book. He denounced this legal shift for its "prejudicial consequences to Literature and Science," but perhaps predictably, the copyright libraries made their case in similar terms: literature was best served, they suggested, by having copies of every publication available at the nation's most important lending institutions.

The shoemaker-turned-bookseller James Lackington discovered that questions about accessibility were not wholly bound up with copyright issues. Early in his career as a bookseller, Lackington learned that the book trade was a tightly controlled monopoly of established booksellers who conspired to maintain an artificially high price for books by destroying remaindered copies. Such a practice, he argued, ran counter to the liberating ethos of literature generally, which implied that the book trade should be governed by the laws of supply and demand in order to guarantee maximum accessibility. Instead of this, he discovered that the publishing industry, far from seeking to extend itself to new readerships, was explicitly designed to limit the number of people who could buy books. Lackington built up a successful business selling cheap copies of remaindered texts, and championed himself as someone who was helping to encourage a revolution in the reading habits of the general public.

Both Isaac D'Israeli and the anonymous author of *An Address to the Parliament of Great Britain, on the Claims of Authors to Their Own Copy Right* argued that particular legal issues were ultimately an expression of this more profound shift—the arrival of what D'Israeli called "*a new state of society.*... We became a reading people; and then the demand for books naturally produced a new order of authors, who traded in literature." The *Address* agreed that it was useless to search for relevant legal precedents because earlier societies lacked contemporary Britain's cultural and commercial realities: "Literature was not then a trade. Genius was but of little value as a saleable commodity, and the whole of this kind of property was in the hands of the Booksellers.... From this time the names of Milton, Dryden, and Newton, produced a new era in literature and science, and literary property became more and more an object of consideration." Legal decisions had an enormous impact on the rights and the related cultural status of various sorts of booksellers and authors, but in this larger perspective, they were themselves merely symptoms of far broader and more fundamental social changes.

The statute of the 8th of Anne vested the ownership of copy in the author, but the fact that eighteenth-century legal battles over copyright were almost always waged by booksellers highlighted a central tension in the literary world. Authors may have owned their copyright, but they generally sold this to whichever bookseller agreed to publish their work, a situation that led to frequent charges of callous exploitation. As D'Israeli put it, "authors continue poor, and booksellers become opulent; an extraordinary result!" The *Gentleman's Magazine*'s obituary for Johnson celebrated "his true regard for the interests of Literature," but many writers were skeptical that booksellers had a "true regard" for anything but their own interests. D'Israeli dismissed the possibility that booksellers might behave more selflessly as a romantic delusion: booksellers were "but commercial men. A trader can never be deemed a patron, for it would be romantic to purchase what is not saleable; and where no favour is conferred, there is no patronage."

Like them or not, however, booksellers were an undeniable and often useful element of modern literature. Nor were authors wholly negative about their commercial counterparts. Whether he always approved of booksellers' ways or not, Coleridge warned all aspiring authors to forego the temptation "to deviate from the ordinary mode of publishing a work by *the trade*." Even D'Israeli allowed that an earlier mercenary spirit which reduced the bookseller to "a mere trader in literature has disappeared." Authors, booksellers, and readers were bound together in a dense and frequently vexing network of social, economic, and legal relations that was effectively redefining literature and reimagining the social distinction of authors. In doing so they inevitably raised new questions about the role of all of the different elements of the infrastructure that made the circulation of texts possible.

❧❧❧

JAMES LACKINGTON
Memoirs of the Forty-Five First Years of the Life of James Lackington, Bookseller [1]

WHEN I was first initiated into the various manœuvers practised by booksellers, I found it customary among them, (which practice still continues,) that when any books had not gone off so rapidly as expected, or so fast as to pay for keeping them in store, they would put what remained of such articles into private sales, where only booksellers are admitted, and of them only such as were invited by having a catalogue sent them. At one of these sales, I have frequently seen seventy or eighty thousand volumes sold after dinner, including books of every description, good, bad, and indifferent; by this means they were distributed through the trade.

When first invited to these trade sales, I was very much surprised to learn that it was common for such as purchased remainders to destroy one half or three fourths of such books, and to charge the full

---

[1] James Lackington (1746–1815), a self-educated bookseller famous for his innovative commercial practices, including his commitment to selling at the cheapest possible prices.

publication price, or nearly that, for such as they kept on hand; and there was a kind of standing order amongst the trade, that, in case any one was known to sell articles under the publication price, such a person was to be excluded from trade sales; so blind were copy-rightholders to their own interest.

For a short time I cautiously complied with this custom; but I soon began to reflect that many of these books so destroyed possessed much merit, and only wanted to be better known; and that if others were not worth six shillings they were worth three, or two, and so in proportion, for higher or lower-priced books.

From that time I resolved not to destroy any books that were worth saving, but to sell them off at half, or a quarter, of the publication prices. By selling them in this cheap manner I have disposed of many hundred thousand volumes, many thousands of which have been intrinsically worth their original prices. This part of my conduct, however, though evidently highly beneficial to the community, and even to booksellers, created me many enemies among the trade; some of the meaner part of whom, instead of employing their time and abilities in attending to the increase of their own business aimed at reducing mine; and by a variety of pitiful insinuations and dark inuendoes, strained every nerve to injure the reputation I had already acquired with the public, determined (as they wisely concluded) thus to effect my ruin; which indeed they daily prognosticated, with a demon-like spirit, must inevitably very speedily follow. This conduct however was far from intimidating me, as the effect proved directly opposite to what they wished for and expected, and I found the respect and confidence of the public continually increasing, which added very considerably to the number of my customers: it being an unquestionable fact that, before I adopted this plan, great numbers of persons were very desirous of possessing some particular

books, for which however (from various motives) they were not inclined to pay the original price; as some availed themselves of the opportunity of borrowing from a friend, or from a circulating library, or having once read them, though they held the works in esteem, might deem them too dear to purchase; or they might have a copy by them, which from their own and family's frequent use (or lending to friends) might not be in so good a condition as they could wish, though rather than purchase them again at the full price they would keep those they had; or again, they might be desirous to purchase them to make presents of, or they might have a commission from a correspondent in the country, or abroad, and wish to gain a small profit on the articles for their trouble, not to mention the great numbers that would have been given to the poor.

Thousands of others have been effectually prevented from purchasing, (though anxious so to do) whose circumstances in life would not permit them to pay the full price, and thus were totally excluded from the advantage of improving their understandings, and enjoying a rational entertainment. And you may be assured that it affords me the most pleasing satisfaction, independent of the emoluments which have accrued to me from this plan, when I reflect what prodigious numbers in inferior or reduced situations of life have been essentially benefitted in consequence of being thus enabled to indulge their natural propensity for the acquisition of knowledge on easy terms: nay, I could almost be vain enough to assert, that I have thereby been highly instrumental in diffusing that general desire for reading now so prevalent among the inferior orders of society, which most certainly, though it may not prove equally instructive to all, keeps them from employing their time and money, if not to bad, at least to less rational purposes.

How happy should I have deemed myself in the earlier stage of my life, if I could have met with the opportunity which every one capable of reading may now enjoy, of obtaining books at so easy a rate: had that been the case, the catalogue of my juvenile library would have made a more respectable appearance, and I might possibly have been enabled when I purchased Young's "Night Thoughts"[1] for a Christmas dinner, to have at the same time bought a joint of meat, and thus enjoyed both a mental and corporeal feast, as well as pleased my wife, (which I need not inform you the ladies say every good husband ought to do.)

I cannot help observing that the sale of books in general has increased prodigiously within the last twenty years. According to the best estimation I have been able to make, I suppose that more than four times the number of books are sold now than were sold twenty years since. The poorer sort of farmers, and even the poor country people in general, who before that period spent their winter evenings in relating stories of witches, ghosts, hobgoblins, &c., now shorten the winter nights by hearing their sons and daughters read tales, romances, &c.; and on entering their houses, you may see Tom Jones, Roderick Random,[2] and other entertaining books, stuck up on their bacon racks, &c. If John goes to town with a load of hay, he is charged to be sure not to forget to bring home "Peregrine Pickle's Adventures;"[3] and when Dolly is sent to market to sell her eggs, she is commissioned to purchase, "The History of Pamela Andrews."[4] In short, all ranks and degrees now read.

But the most rapid increase of the sale of books has been since the termination of the late war.[5]

A number of book-clubs are also formed in every part of England, where each member subscribes a certain sum quarterly to purchase books; in some of these clubs the books, after they have been read by all the subscribers, are sold among them to the highest bidders, and the money produced by such sale, is expended in fresh purchases, by which prudent and judicious mode each member has it in his power to become possessed of the work of any particular author he may judge deserving a superior degree of attention; and the members at large enjoy the advantage of a continual succession of different publications, instead of being restricted to a repeated perusal of the same authors; which must have been the case with many, if so rational a plan had not been adopted.

I have been informed, that when circulating libraries were first opened, the booksellers were much alarmed, and their rapid increase added to their fears, and led them to think that the sale of books would be much diminished by such libraries. But experience has proved that the sale of books, so far from being diminished by them, has been greatly promoted, as from those repositories many thousand families have been cheaply supplied with books, by which the taste for reading has become much more general, and thousands of books are purchased every year by such as have first borrowed them at those libraries, and after reading, approving of them, become purchasers.

Circulating libraries have also greatly contributed towards the amusement and cultivation of the other sex; by far the greatest part of ladies have now a taste for books.

---

[1] "The Complaint, or Night Thoughts on Life, Death, and Immortality" (1742–45), the best-known poem of Edward Young (1683–1765).

[2] *The History of Tom Jones* (1749) by Henry Fielding (1707–54); *The Adventures of Roderick Random* (1748) by Tobias Smollet (1721–71).

[3] *The Adventures of Peregrine Pickle* (1751) by Tobias Smollet (1721–71).

[4] *Pamela, or Virtue Rewarded* (1740) by Samuel Richardson (1689–1761).

[5] The American Revolution.

" ——Learning, once the man's exclusive pride,
Seems verging fast towards the female side." [1]

It is true that I do not, with Miss Mary Wolstonecraft, "earnestly wish to see the distinction of sex confounded in society," not even with her exception, "unless where love animates the behaviour." [2] And yet I differ widely from those gentlemen who would prevent the ladies from acquiring a taste for books; and as yet I have never seen any solid reason advanced why ladies should not polish their understandings, and render themselves fit companions for men of sense. And I have often thought that one great reason why some gentlemen spend all their leisure hours abroad, is, for want of rational companions at home; for, if a gentleman happens to marry a fine lady, as justly painted by Miss Wolstonecraft, or the square elbow family drudge, as drawn to the life by the same hand, I must confess that I see no great inducement that he has to desire the company of his wife, as she scarce can be called a rational companion, or one fit to be entrusted with the education of her children; and even Rousseau is obliged to acknowledge, that it "is a melancholy thing for a father of a family, who is fond of home, to be obliged to be always wrapped up in himself, and to have nobody about him to whom he can impart his sentiments." [3] Lord Lyttle

ton advises well in the two following lines:

"Do you, my fair, endeavour to possess
An elegance of mind, as well as dress." [4]

I cannot help thinking that the reason why some of the eastern nations treat the ladies with such contempt, and look upon them in such a degrading point of view, is owing to their marrying them when mere children, both as to age and understanding, which last being entirely neglected, they seldom are capable of rational conversation, and of course are neglected and despised. [5] But this is not the case with English ladies; they now in general read, not only novels, although many of that class are excellent productions, and tend to polish both the heart and head; but they also read the best books in the English language, and many read the best works in various languages; and there are some thousands of ladies who come to my shop, that know as well what books to chuse, and are as well acquainted with works of taste and genius as any gentlemen in the kingdom, notwithstanding the sneer against novel-readers, &c.

The Sunday-schools are spreading very fast in most parts of England, which will accelerate the diffusion of knowledge among the lower classes of the community and in a very few years exceedingly increase the sale of books. Here permit me earnestly to call on every honest bookseller (I trust my call

---

[1] William Cowper (1731–1800), *The Progress of Error* (1782): 429–30.

[2] "An earnest wish has just flown from my hearty to my head, and I will not stifle it though it may excite a horse-laugh.—I do earnestly wish to see the distinction of sex confounded in society, unless where love animates the behaviour." *Vindication of the Rights of Woman*, Chapter 4.

[3] Jean Jacques Rousseau (1711–78), *Émile* (1762). The passage also appears within a much longer passage cited in Wollstonecraft's *Rights of Woman* (Chapter 5:1), from which Lackington had just quoted. Wollstonecraft cites it in the context of her condemnation of Rousseau's more usual insistence on the importance of maintaining womens' innocence by depriving them of an education. Wollstonecraft's point, which Lackington shares, is that enlightened men would

be happier sharing their lives with a compatible (and thus an educated) partner. The first edition appeared in 1791, the year before the publication of Wollstonecraft's *Rights of Woman*. Lackington's references to it were incorporated in subsequent editions.

[4] First Baron George Lord Lyttleton (1709–73), *Advice to a Lady* (1733): 27–28. Also the author of *Commonsense, or, The Englishman's Journal* (1737–43), Lyttleton was a friend of Pope, Shenstone, and Fielding, and a liberal patron of literature. It is he whom Thomson addresses in *The Seasons*.

[5] Islamic cultures were frequently cited by British writers as examples of societies which systematically mistreated women.

will not be in vain) as well as on every friend to the extension of knowledge, to unite (as *you* I am confident will) in a hearty Amen.

(1791; 1792)

GENTLEMAN'S MAGAZINE
Bibliographic Account of the late Mr. Joseph Johnson[1]

DIED, on *December* 20, greatly regretted by his numerous friends, Mr. JOSEPH JOHNSON, of St. Paul's Church-yard, a most respectable member of the Society of Booksellers in London, and for some years past considered as the Father of the Trade.

The character Mr. Johnson established by his integrity, good sense, and honourable principles of dealing, soon raised him to eminence as a publisher; and many of the most distinguished names in science and literature during the last half century appear in works which he ushered to the world. Of a temper the reverse of sanguine, with a manner somewhat cold and indifferent, and with a decided aversion to all arts of puffing and parade, the confidence and attachment he inspired were entirely the result of his solid judgement, his unaffected sincerity, and the friendly benevolence with which he entered into the interests of all who were connected with him. Although he was not remarkable for the encouragement he held out to Authors—the consequence of his being neither sanguine nor pushing; yet it was his invariable rule, when the success of a work surpassed his expectations, to

make the Writer a partaker in the emolument, though he lay under no other obligation to do so than his own notions of justice and generosity. The kindness of his heart was equally conspicuous in all the relations of life. His house and purse were always open to the calls of friendship, kindred, or misfortune; and perhaps few men of his means and condition have done more substantial services to persons whose merits and necessities recommended them to his notice.

It is well known that Mr. Johnson's literary connexions have lain in great part among the free Enquirers both on religious and political topicks. He was himself, on conviction, a friend to such large and liberal discussion as is not inconsistent with the peace and welfare of Society, and the preservation of due decorum towards things really respectable. But these were limits within which both by temper and principle, he wished to see such discussion confined; for turbulence and sedition were utterly abhorrent from his nature. When, therefore, for the unconscious offence of selling a few copies of a pamphlet of which he was not the publisher, and which was a reply to one of which he has sold a much larger number, the opportunity was taken of involving him in a prosecution that brought upon him the infliction of fine and imprisonment, it was by many considered as the ungenerous indulgence of a long-hoarded spleen against him on account of publications not liable to legal censure, though displeasing to Authority.[2] It is gratifying, however, to relate, that during the height of party animosity, so little was he regarded personally as a party-man, that he continued to number among his intimate friends, several worthy persons of opposite sentiments and connexions, who, with himself, were capable of considering a man's perfor-

---

[1] Joseph Johnson (1738–1809), a widely respected publisher and bookseller with close ties to London's Unitarian populace. As a publisher he promoted a range of reform-oriented political, religious, and scientific texts which reflected the rationalist and Dissenting intellectual commitments of Unitarianism. In 1788 Johnson and Thomas Christie founded the *Analytical Review*, which was also known for its reformist allegiances.

[2] In 1798 Johnson was arrested for selling Gilbert Wakefield's anti-war pamphlet, *Address to the People of Great Britain*, in his bookshop in St. Paul's Churchyard.

mance of the duties of life apart from his speculative opinions.

Although the majority of his publications were of the theological and political class, yet the number of those in science and elegant literature was by no means inconsiderable. Besides all the scientific writings of Dr. Priestley,[1] he published many important works in Medicine and Anatomy; and others in different branches of knowledge. Two Poets of great modern celebrity were by him first introduced to the Publick—Cowper and Darwin.[2] The former of these, with the diffidence, and perhaps the despondency, of his character, had actually, by means of a friend, made over to him his two volumes of Poems on no other condition than that of securing him from expence; but when the Publick, which neglected the first volume, had discovered the rich mine opened in "The Task," and assigned the Author his merited place among the first-rate English Poets, Mr. Johnson would not avail himself of his advantage, but displayed a liberality which has been warmly acknowledged by that admirable though unfortunate person.

It is proper to mention that his true regard for the interests of Literature rendered him an enemy to that typographical luxury which, joined to the necessary increase of expence in printing, has so much enhanced the price of new books as to be a material obstacle to the indulgence of a laudable and reasonable curiosity by the reading Publick. On this principle he usually consulted cheapness rather than appearance in his own publications; and if Authors were sometimes mortified by this preference, the purpose of extensive circulation was better served.

Stoke Newington, Dec. 31st, 1809.

ISAAC D'ISRAELI
The Case of Authors Stated,
Including the History of Literary Property[3]

JOHNSON has dignified the booksellers as "the patrons of literature,"[4] which was generous in that great author, who had written well and lived but ill all his life on that patronage. Eminent booksellers, in their constant intercourse with the most enlightened class of the community, that is, with the best authors and the best readers, partake of the intelligence around them; their great capitals, too, are productive of good and evil in literature; useful when they carry on great works, and pernicious when they sanction indifferent ones. Yet are they but commercial men. A trader can never be deemed a patron, for it would be romantic to purchase what

---

[1] Joseph Priestley (1733–1804), a leading theologian, political theorist, chemist, and educational pioneer. In 1791 the *Monthly Review* called him "the literary wonder of the present times" (5:303), but Priestley's outspoken and often radical positions made him a controversial figure in the era of the French Revolution. On July 14, 1791, Priestley's house and library were destroyed by a Church-and-King mob in Birmingham. In 1794 he emigrated to the United States to escape the ongoing threat of violent attack.

[2] William Cowper (1731–1800). His autobiographical poem, *The Task* (1785) had an important influence on later poets such as William Wordsworth and S. T. Coleridge; like them, Cowper celebrated the rural world as a healing antithesis to the jarring realities of the modern urban world; Erasmus Darwin (1731–1802), a physician, poet, inventor, and theorist in medicine, agriculture, and female education. His *Zoonomia; or, The Laws of Organic Life* (1794–96) offered an early version of the theory of evolution that would be more famously propounded by his grandson, Charles.

[3] Isaac D'Israeli (1766–1848) failed to achieve his early dream of poetic success but established himself as a well-known and generally respected literary critic. D'Israeli published several collections of essays on contemporary literary issues.

[4] In his *Life of Johnson*, James Boswell notes that in a letter to Bennet Langton in January 1759, Johnson referred to his publisher Dodsley as his "patron." Johnson's letter to the Earl of Chesterfield in February 1755, mocking the Earl's belated offer of support for Johnson's Dictionary, was widely seen as a manifesto of authorial revolt against aristocratic patronage in favour of a more professionalized orientation towards booksellers and the reading public.

is not saleable; and where no favour is conferred, there is no patronage.

Authors continue poor, and booksellers become opulent; an extraordinary result! Booksellers are not agents for authors, but proprietors of their works; so that the perpetual revenues of literature are solely in the possession of the trade.

Is it then wonderful that even successful authors are indigent? They are heirs to fortunes, but by a strange singularity they are disinherited at their birth; for, on the publication of their works, these cease to be their own property. Let that natural property be secured, and a good book would be an inheritance, a leasehold or a freehold, as you choose it; it might at least last out a generation, and descend to the author's blood, were they permitted to live on their father's glory, as in all other property they do on his industry.[†] Something of this nature has been instituted in France, where the descendants of Corneille and Moliere[1] retain a claim on the theatres whenever the dramas of their great ancestors are performed. In that country, literature has ever received peculiar honours—it was there decreed, in the affair of Crebillon,[2] that literary productions are not seizable by creditors.[††]

The history of literary property in this country might form as ludicrous a narrative as Lucian's "true history."[3] It was a long while doubtful whether any such thing existed, at the very time when booksellers were assigning over the perpetual copyrights of books, and making them the subject of family settlements for the provision of their wives and children! When Tonson, in 1739, obtained an injunction to restrain another bookseller from printing Milton's "Paradise Lost," he brought into court as a proof of his title an assignment of the original copyright, made over by the sublime poet in 1667, which was read. Milton received for this assignment the sum which we all know—Tonson and all his family and assignees rode in their carriages with the profits of the five-pound epic.[†††]

[†] The following facts will show the value of *literary property*; immense profits and cheap purchases! The manuscript of "Robinson Crusoe" ran through the whole trade, and no one would print it; the bookseller who did purchase it, who, it is said, was not remarkable for his discernment, but for a speculative turn, got a thousand guineas by it. How many have the booksellers since accumulated? Burn's "Justice" was disposed of by its author for a trifle, as well as Buchan's "Domestic Medicine;" these works yield annual incomes. Goldsmith's "Vicar of Wakefield" was sold in the hour of distress, with little distinction from any other work in that class of composition; and "Evelina" produced five guineas from the niggardly trader. Dr. Johnson fixed the price of his "Biography of the Poets" at two hundred guineas; and Mr. Malone observes, the booksellers in the course of twenty-five years have probably got five thousand. I could add a great number of facts of this nature which relate to living writers; the profits of their own works for two or three years would rescue them from the horrors and humiliation of pauperism. It is, perhaps, useful to record, that, while the compositions of genius are but slightly remunerated, though sometimes as productive as " the household stuff" of literature, the latter is rewarded with princely magnificence. At the sale of the Robinsons, the copyright of "Vyse's Spelling-book" was sold at the enormous price of 2200*l.*, with an *annuity* of fifty guineas to the author!

[1] Pierre Corneille (1606–84), the pseudonym of Jean Baptiste Poquelin (1622–73), who also used the more famous pseudonym of and Molière.

[2] Prosper Jolyot de Crébillon (1674–1762), French dramatist, was presented with a pension and a post in the Royal Library in 1745.

[††] The circumstance, with the poet's dignified petition, and the King's honourable decree, are preserved in "Curiosities of Literature," vol.i. p. 406.

[3] Lucian (*c.* 115–200), a Greek writer, author of *True History*, a fantastic tale parodying incredible adventure stories.

[†††] The elder Tonson's portrait represents him in his gown and cap, holding in his right hand a volume lettered "Paradise Lost"—such a favourite object was Milton and copyright! Jacob Tonson was the founder of a race who long honoured literature. His rise in life is curious. He was at first unable to pay twenty pounds for a play by Dryden, and joined with another bookseller to advance that sum; the play sold, and Tonson was afterwards enabled to purchase the succeeding ones. He and his nephew died worth two hundred thousand pounds.—Much old Tonson owed to his own industry; but he was a mere trader. He and Dryden had frequent bickerings; he insisted on receiving 10 000 verses for two hundred and sixty-eight pounds, and poor Dryden threw in the finest Ode in the language towards the number. He would pay in the base coin which was then current; which was a loss to the poet. Tonson once complained to Dryden, that he had only received 1446 lines of his translation of Ovid for his Miscellany for fifty guineas, which he had calculated at the rate

The verbal and tasteless lawyers, not many years past, with legal metaphysics, wrangled like the schoolmen, inquiring of each other, "whether the *style* and *ideas* of an author were tangible things; or if these were a *property*, how is *possession* to be taken, or any act of *occupancy* made on mere intellectual *ideas*." Nothing, said they, can be an object of property but which has a corporeal substance; the air and the light, to which they compared an author's ideas, are common to all; ideas in the MS. state were compared to birds in a cage; while the author confines them in his own dominion, none but he has a right to let them fly; but the moment he allows the bird to escape from his hand, it is no violation of property in any one to make it his own. And to prove that there existed no property after publication, they found an analogy in the gathering of acorns, or in seizing on a vacant piece of ground; and thus degrading that most refined piece of art formed in the highest state of society, a literary production, they brought us back to a state of nature; and seem to have concluded that literary property was purely ideal; a phantom which, as its author could neither grasp nor confine to himself, he must entirely depend on the public benevolence for his reward.[†]

The Ideas, that is, the work of an author, are "tangible things." "There are works," to quote the words of a near and dear relative, "which require great learning, great industry, great labour, and great capital, in their preparation. They assume a palpable form. You may fill warehouses with them, and freight ships; and the tenure by which they are held is superior to that of all other property, for it is original. It is tenure which does not exist in a doubtful title; which does not spring from any adventitious circumstances; it is not found—it is not purchased—it is not prescriptive—it is original; so it is the most natural of all titles, because it is the most simple and least artificial. It is paramount and sovereign, because it is a tenure by creation."[††]

There were indeed some more generous spirits and better philosophers fortunately found on the same bench; and the identity of a literary composition was resolved into its sentiments and language, besides what was more obviously valuable to some persons, the print and paper. On this slight principle was issued the profound award which accorded a certain term of years to any work, however immortal. They could not diminish the immortality of a book, but only its reward. In all the litigations respecting literary property, authors were little considered—except some honourable testimonies due to genius, from the sense of WILLES,[1] and the eloquence of MANSFIELD.[2] Literary property was still disputed, like the rights of a parish common. An honest printer, who could not always write grammar, had the shrewdness to make a bold effort in this scramble, and perceiving that even by this last favourable award all literary property would necessarily centre with the booksellers, now stood forward for his own body—the printers. This rough advocate observed that "a few persons who call themselves *booksellers*, about the number of *twenty-five*, have kept the *monopoly of books and copies* in their hands, to the entire exclusion of all others, but more especially to the *printers*, whom they have always held it a rule never to let become purchasers

---

of 1518 lines for forty guineas; he gives the poet a piece of critical reasoning, that he considered he had a better bargain with "Juvenal," which is reckoned "not so easy to translate as Ovid." In these times such a mere trader in literature has disappeared.

[†] Sir James Burrows' Reports on the question concerning Literary Property. 4 to. London 1773.

[††] Mirror of Parliament, 3529.

[1] Sir John Willes (1685–1761), presided as judge in several copyright cases, in which he was known for his allegiance to the principle that authors had a legal right to their writings as personal property derived from their labour.

[2] The first Earl of Mansfield (William Murray) (1705–93), a preeminent and often controversial judicial authority, defended the rights of authors in various copyright trials throughout the eighteenth century.

in *copy.*" Not a word for the *authors*! As for them, they were doomed by both parties as the fat oblation: they indeed sent forth some meek bleatings; but what were AUTHORS, between judges, booksellers, and printers? the sacrificed among the sacrificers!

All this was reasoning in a circle. LITERARY PROPERTY in our nation arose from *a new state of society.* These lawyers could never develope its nature by wild analogies, nor discover it in any common-law right; for our common law, composed of immemorial customs, could never have had in its contemplation an object which could not have existed in barbarous periods. Literature, in its enlarged spirit, certainly never entered into the thoughts or attention of our rude ancestors. All their views were bounded by the necessaries of life; and as yet they had no conception of the impalpable, invisible, yet sovereign dominion of the human mind—enough for our rough heroes was that of the seas! Before the reign of Henry VIII. great authors composed occasionally a book in Latin, which none but other great authors cared for, and which the people could not read. In the reign of Elizabeth, ROGER ASCHAM[1] appeared—one of those men of genius born to create a new era in the history of their nation. The first English author who may be regarded as the founder of our *prose style* was Roger Ascham, the venerable parent of our *native literature.* At a time when our scholars affected to contemn the vernacular idiom, and in their Latin works were losing their better fame, that of being understood by all their countrymen, Ascham boldly avowed the design of setting an example, in his own words, TO SPEAK AS THE COMMON PEOPLE, TO THINK AS WISE MEN. His pristine English is still forcible without pedantry, and still beautiful

without ornament.[†] The illustrious BACON[2] condescended to follow this new example in the most popular of his works. This change in our literature was like a revelation; these men taught us our language in books. We became a reading people; and then the demand for books naturally produced a new order of authors, who traded in literature. It was then, so early as in the Elizabethan age, that *literary property* may be said to derive its obscure origin in this nation. It was protected in an indirect manner by the *licensers* of the press; for although that was a mere political institution, only designed to prevent seditious and irreligious publications, yet, as no book could be printed without a licence, there was honour enough in the licensers not to allow other publishers to infringe on the priviledge granted to the first claimant. In Queen Anne's time, when the office of licensers was extinguished, a more liberal genius was rising in the nation, and *literary property* received a more definite and a more powerful protection. A limited term was granted to every author to reap the fruits of his labours; and Lord Hardwicke pronounced this statute "a universal patent for authors."[3] Yet, subsequently, the subject of *literary property* involved discussion; even at so late a period as in 1769 it was still to be litigated. It was then granted that originally an author had at common law a property in his work, but that the act of Anne took away all copy-

---

[†] See "Amenities of Literature" for an account of this author.

[2] Francis Bacon (1561–1626), renowned for his philosophical and literary achievements. The former included *The Advancement of Learning* (1605) which divided knowledge into three fields: history, poetry and philosophy. Bacon's *Essays*, published in three editions of increasing size in 1597, 1612, and 1625, were his chief literary contribution. Like Ascham, Bacon was known for his commitment to an accessible prose style.

[3] Philip Yorke, second Earl of Hardwicke (1720–90), presided as judge in many of the most important copyright trials of the eighteenth century. This quote is probably from the *Millar v. Taylor* case (1769) in which Hardwicke declared that "The Statute of Queen Ann might be considered as a standing patent to authors."

---

[1] Roger Ascham (1515–68), author of the posthumously published *Schoolmaster*, was revered for his commitment to a simple English prose style.

right after the expiration of the terms it permitted.[1]

As the matter now stands, let us address an arithmetical age—but my pen hesitates to bring down my subject to an argument fitted to "these coster-monger times."[†] On the present principle of literary property, it results that an author disposes of a leasehold property of twenty-eight years, often for less than the price of one year's purchase! How many living authors are the sad witnesses of this fact, who, like so many Esaus, have sold their inheritance for a meal![2] I leave the whole school of Adam Smith to calm their calculating emotions concerning "that unprosperous race of men" (sometimes this master-seer calls them "unproductive") "commonly called *men of letters*," who are pretty much in the situation which lawyers and physicians would be in, were these, as he tells us, in that state when "*a scholar* and *a beggar* seem to have been very nearly *synonymous terms*"—and this melancholy fact that man of genius discovered, without the feather of his pen brushing away a tear from his lid—without one spontaneous and indignant groan![3]

Authors may exclaim, "we ask for justice, not charity." They would not need to require any favour, nor claim any other than that protection which an enlightened government, in its wisdom

and its justice, must bestow. They would leave to the public disposition the sole appreciation of their works; their book must make its own fortune; a bad work may be cried up, and a good work may be cried down; but Faction will soon lose its voice, and Truth acquire one. The cause we are pleading is not the calamities of indifferent writers, but of those whose utility or whose genius long survives that limited term which has been so hardly wrenched from the penurious hand of verbal lawyers. Every lover of literature, and every votary of humanity has long felt indignant at that sordid state and all those secret sorrows to which men of the finest genius, or of sublime industry, are reduced and degraded in society. Johnson himself, who rejected that perpetuity of literary property which some enthusiasts seemed to claim at the time the subject was undergoing the discussion of the judges, is, however, for extending the copyright to a *century*. Could authors secure this, their natural right, literature would acquire a permanent and a nobler reward; for great authors would then be distinguished by the very profits they would receive from that obscure multitude whose common disgraces they frequently participate, notwithstanding the superiority of their own genius. Johnson himself will serve as a proof of the incompetent remuneration of literary property. He undertook and he performed an Herculean labour, which employed him so many years that the price he obtained was exhausted before the work was concluded—the wages did not even last as long as the labour! Where, then, is the author to look forward, when such works are undertaken, for a provision for his family, or for his future existence? It would naturally arise from the work itself, were authors not the most ill-treated and oppressed class of the community. The daughter of MILTON need not have craved the alms of the admirers of her father, if the right of authors had been better protected; his own "Paradise Lost" had then been her

---

[1] The 1769 ruling in the case of *Millar v. Taylor* actually upheld the notion of perpetual copyright. It was the 1774 case of *Donaldson* v. *Becket* which ruled that the Act erased common law claims.

[†] A coster-monger, or Costard-monger is "A dealer in apples, which are so called because they are shaped like a *costard,* i.e. a man's head." *Steevens.*—Johnson explains the phrase eloquently: "In these times when the prevalence of trade has produced that meanness, that rates the merit of everything by money."

[2] Hebrews 12:15–16.

[3] *Wealth of Nations* (Book 1 Ch.10). In his discussion of "That unprosperous race of men commonly called men of letters," Smith suggested that "the greater part of them have been educated for the church, but have been hindered by different reasons from entering into holy orders. They have generally, therefore, been educated at the public expence, and their numbers are everywhere so great as commonly to reduce the price of their labour to a very paultry recompence."

better portion and her most honourable inheritance. The children of BURNS would have required no subscriptions; that annual tribute which the public pay to the genius of their parent was their due, and would have been their fortune.

Authors now submit to have a shorter life than their own celebrity. While the book markets of Europe are supplied with the writings of English authors, and they have a wider diffusion in America than at home, it seems a national ingratitude to limit the existence of works for their authors to a short number of years, and then to seize on their possession for ever.

(1812)

ANONYMOUS
An Address to the Parliament of Great Britain, on the Claims of Authors to Their Own Copy Right.
By a Member of the University of Cambridge

THE right of Authors to their own Copy has been often brought under consideration: the opinions of the ablest Lawyers and the most enlightened men were divided on the subject. The House of Lords, however, at last, decided for the public, and it is no longer a legal question; but as there is now a bill pending in Parliament to amend the Statute of the 8th of Anne, respecting literary property, the present Address is offered, to show how the question stands at this time among the parties concerned.

Authors are deprived of the *common law-right* to their own labors, because it was feared that, by permitting them to have an exclusive property in their literary works, the public would he injured. This is the substance of every argument, however ingeniously diversified, that has been used, to show the necessity of limiting the duration of literary property to the author; and, the general principle of expediency, the only plausible argument to wrest it from him.

When the great question of *copy-right* first underwent a full discussion, the only Judge in the King's Bench who opposed it as the author's property, was Mr. Justice Yates; with him it was considered as of a nature too incorporeal and evanescent to have a specific value, yet he allowed it to be sufficiently substantial to exist for a term of years, to be circumscribed by the law, and to be protected by it.

A speech made to a public assembly, a public lecture for which the author is paid by his audience, a sermon preached by a Bishop from his manuscript, or a charge delivered by an Archdeacon to the diocesan clergy; are not too evanescent to be protected; not by Statute, but by *common law*; and no man is permitted to derive any profit from either, *except the author,* even though the sale should be confined to the very persons to whom the instruction, advice, or information, were given. This is the law as it now stands, and is founded upon the principles of the common law of England.[†] It is therefore clear that it is not the *incorporeal nature of ideas* which has created the real difficulty of securing them to the author, and of acknowledging him to be true owner; but he is deprived of his ownership as a measure of policy. At this time, I trust, it

---

[†] Upon this point, my Lord Mansfield has thus expressed himself:—No *disposition*, no *transfer* of *paper* upon which the composition is written, marked, or impressed, (though it gives the power to print and publish) can be construed a *conveyance of copy*, without the author's express *consent to print and publish*; much less against his will.

"The property of the copy, *thus narrowed*, may equally go down from generation to generation, and possibly continue for ever; though neither the author nor his representatives should have any manuscript whatsoever of the work, original, duplicate, or transcript."

With respect to copy-right *after* publication, he adopts this opinion: "He who pays for a literary composition buys the *improvement, knowledge, or amusement*, he can derive from it: but the *right* to the work itself, the copy-right, remains in *him* whose industry composed it. The buyer might *as truly* claim the *merit of the composition* by his purchase, as the right of *multiplying copies* and *reaping the benefits*."

will not be difficult to show, that the guardians of the public entertained groundless apprehensions on this point.

That the question of *copy-right* may be clearly and distinctly before the reader, I will first recite the Acts of the Legislature, which have been made at different times in aid of literature.

The Licensing Act of the 13th and 14th of Charles II compelled all Printers and Booksellers to enter whatever they printed in the Register of the Stationers' Company,[1] and enacted that all Printers should reserve three copies of every newly-printed book; one for his Majesty's library, and one for each of the Universities of Oxford and Cambridge. This Act expired on the 9th of May, 1679. It was afterwards revived, but finally expired in 1694.

In the 8th year of Anne, an Act was made for the *encouragement of learning*, by which the author, or his assignee, possesses an exclusive copy-right for fourteen years, and is enabled to recover penalties for the invasion of his property; and if the author should survive that term, the same privileges extend to fourteen years more: and of all newly-printed books, by this statute, nine copies of each are given to the six Universities of England and Scotland, and the Libraries of his Majesty, Sion College, and the Advocates' Library in Edinburgh; and lest books should be sold at too high a price, the Act contains a provisionary clause, vesting a power in certain persons therein named, to regulate the same according to their judgment.[†]

By an Act for the suppression of Seditious Societies, made in the 31st of George III. c. 79. §.

29., one copy of every book printed is to be deposited with the printer.

By an Act of the 41st of George III. c. 107., the author is compelled to give two additional copies to Trinity College, and the King's Inns in Dublin.

By these several Acts, the author is now deprived of twelve copies of every book he prints.

After various Star-chamber[2] regulations for printing, and charters granted to a body of Booksellers, to guard against the disseminating *heretical, schismatical, blasphemous, seditious, and treasonable books*, an Act was passed in the 13th and 14th years of the reign of Charles the Second, to continue in force for two years only, to compel all Printers to enter the works they printed in the Register of the Stationers' Company.[††] This Licensing Act invested the Stationers' Company with great power, and gave them a complete monopoly of the whole trade, with all its ramifications, of printing and bookselling, and the importation of foreign literature, and for which, in return, they were to act as watchful agents for the Crown, to protect it from slander and detraction, and to give three copies of every book they published, as specified in the Act. The author here is entirely left out of the question; nor, indeed, can it be said that his interest was much involved in it. The Act itself was only to last two years. Literature was not then a trade. Genius was but of little value as a saleable commodity, and the

---

[1] A guild of printers, bookbinders, and booksellers, incorporated in 1577. The Stationer's Company was initially created by Queen Mary as a way of controlling the dissemination of seditious literature, but the fact that booksellers entered their "copy" in its register gave the Company power to control the security of copyright.

[†] This last clause, thirty years afterwards, being found to be wholly useless, was repealed in the 12 of George II. c. 36.

[2] A secret court, abolished in 1641. Originally named after the stars on the ceiling of the Westminster Palace apartment where it met, the Star-Chamber was frequently used as a synonym for arbitrary judicial authority.

[††] The first charter of the Stationers' Company originally comprehended 97 persons, who were Booksellers, Stationers, Printers, or persons connected with these occupations. It was granted in the year 1556, and it recited that the grant was made *to prevent the renewal of great and detestable heresies*. It authorised the members of the Company to search for books, &c. and though the Crown had no right over the trade of printing, it was ordered, "that no man should exercise the mystery of printing unless he was of the Stationers' Company, or had a license."

whole of this kind of property was in the hands of the Book sellers; the small donation, therefore, of three copies of every work they printed, was a very inconsiderable equivalent for the great advantages which were given to them by the Act.

From this time the names of Milton, Dryden, and Newton, produced a new era in literature and science, and literary property became more and more an object of consideration to the trader, though it remained of little importance to the author.

By this Act it is evident that, if books were not entered in the register-book of the Stationers' Company, no claim by the English universities was supposed to exist, which was clearly founded upon this plain reason, that if a book was not entered, it could claim no benefit under the statute, and with this impression of its interest and meaning, it was always an affair of calculation by the author or bookseller, whether nine copies were more, or less, than equivalent to the risk of the work's being pirated; and if the risk was thought to be less, it was not entered: this was the case with respect to two of the most expensive works ever published in this country,—Boydell's Shakespeare, and Macklin's Bible:[†] it was thought by the proprietors of these works, that the protection offered to them by the Act of Anne, was not equivalent to the nine copies, and therefore these works were not entered at the Stationers' Hall; neither did the universities take any exception to this discretionary power, in these, or in any other similar instances, from the passing the Act of Anne, 1709, till the year 1810, when the University of Cambridge tried their claim against Walker, for a copy of Fox's History of James II. and obtained a verdict on the *letter of the statute*.

This is a brief statement of what the Stationers'

---

† John Boydell (1719–1804), the engraver and publisher who, with his nephew Josiah Boydell, opened the Shakespeare Gallery, containing thirty-four paintings of subjects from Shakespeare by leading artists in London in 1789; Thomas Macklin (1760–1800), editor/publisher of a popular version of the bible.

Company supposed they had obtained by the Act of Anne, and the extent of what they believed the Parliament intended to grant, so far as concerned the protection of their property, and their remedy by law; nor was it till the year 1774, in the case of Donaldsons and Becket, sixty-six years afterwards, that the booksellers discovered that this Act, which was meant to protect their property, in reality took it away.

From the decision in the House of Lords, which took place upon this occasion, nine judges out of twelve decided that the author's property in his own productions was more valuable before the statute of the 8th of Anne than since: in other words, the statute of the 8th of Anne abridged his right, so that from the misconception of the nature of this Act, as by subsequent interpretation it has been understood, the author had his right *taken* away, and his property *given* away at the same time, and without receiving any compensation. And it ought to be remembered, that the property thus given away, is not *imaginary* and *evanescent*.

As early as the establishment of the Stationers' Company, there are records entered upon their books, which show their belief of the existence of a common-law principle which gave to the owners of intellectual property as entire and exclusive a right as could be possessed by manual labor or by purchase.

In the year 1559, persons were fined for *printing other men's* COPIES, and in 1573, there are entries which take notice of the *sale of the* COPY, and the *price*.

In 1582, there are entries of an express proviso, "that if it be found *any other has right to any of the copies*, then the *licence*, touching such of the copies *so belonging to another*, shall be *void*."

Such cases, and many more might be cited, show that, down to the Act of Anne, there could have been no doubt entertained, by the body of booksellers, of the permanency and perpetuity of their literary property: and how far, in their opinion, this statute affected their common-law right, may be clearly seen in the progress of an action brought by seventeen booksellers of London against twenty-four booksellers of Edinburgh, in the year 1746, to recover damages under the statute for an invasion of their property, in which they insist that the statute of the 8th of Anne gave an additional security by penalties during a limited time, to property which existed *before*: and that it was a declaratory Act and a penal statute, and that the Court of Chancery had always understood it in this sense, and given relief accordingly.

Sir Joseph Jekyll, in 1735, granted an injunction to restrain one Walker from printing the *Whole Duty of Man*, because it was considered to belong to the plaintiff *Eyre*, though the book had been originally published in 1657.

Lord Talbot, in 1736, granted an injunction against one Falkner, an Irish bookseller, for printing Pope's and Swift's *Miscellamies*, the property of the plaintiff, Motte.

Lord Hardwicke, in 1739, in the case of *Tonson and others*, against *Walker*, granted an injunction to prevent the defendant from printing Paradise Lost. The original assignment was made in 1667. These were severally acquiesced under. And in the case of *Millar* against *Taylor*, for printing Thomson's Seasons, in 1768, in the Court of King's Bench, before Lord Mansfield, Mr. Justice Yates, Aston, and Willes, it was decided by the Court, that the COPY of a book, or literary composition, belonged to the author by the COMMON-LAW, and that the COMMON-LAW RIGHT of authors, to the copy-right of their *own* works, was not taken away by the statute of Anne. This decision of the Judges of the Court of King's Bench was only a confirmation of what had been uniformly understood to be the law of the land, as well before as after the passing the Act of the 8th of Anne. But in the case of Donaldsons and Becket, in 1774, the House of Lords made a new decree, and voted the common-law right to be merged in the statute of Anne.

Previously to this time, the universities of England and Scotland, and the three public schools of Eton, Westminster, and Winchester, had entertained the same opinion as the Company of Stationers with respect to the perpetuity of literary property; but on this decision of the Lords, they petitioned Parliament to bring in a Bill for the *advancement of learning*, to secure to themselves a perpetual copy-right in all books which had heretofore been deemed their property, or which might at any future time become so; and to this effect an Act was passed in the 15th year of his present Majesty.[1]

Thus the universities preserved their perpetual copy-right; the King also retains his copy-right for ever by common law; but the authors lost theirs by an Act which was meant to strengthen the power of the Stationers' Company, and to give an additional protection and security to their property.

Before the case of Millar and Taylor was argued in the Court of King's Bench, in 1768, no legal investigation had ever been made of the nature and extent of the right of COPY; and here it was decided, in favor of the authors, as a common-law right, notwithstanding the statute of Anne. When the opinions of the Judges were taken in the House of Lords, in the case of Donaldsons and Becket, respecting the common-law right of authors to their *own copy*, before the statute, nine Judges of the twelve decided, that the literary productions of an author were as much his own property as that which belongs to any other man, produced by his manual labor; and that an exclusive and perpetual copy-right belonged to him, or his assignee, at *common-law,* upon the same principles of natural justice. And, as to literary works *before* publication,

[1] 1775.

however they may be circulated orally, or given away by transcript, the Judges have been always *unanimous*, that the sole and exclusive right of such works belongs to the author, and so it is now received, as the common law of England.

If the same statements and reasoning which led to these conclusions in the minds of such men as Lord Hardwicke and Lord Mansfield, in 1768, had been fully brought before the legislature in the reign of Anne, it is difficult to conceive that any act could have passed for the *encouragement and benefit of learned men*, which, to use Lord Mansfield's words, should be in direct opposition to natural principles, moral justice, and the fitness of things.

At common law, every one enjoys the reward of his labor, and he enjoys it for ever; and, as Mr. Christian[1] has well expressed it, if any private right ought to be preserved more sacred and inviolable than another, it is that where the most extensive benefit flows to mankind from the labor by which it is acquired; and intellectual property, though differing from the substantial form of tangible things; yet, under whatever denomination of right it may be classed, it is founded upon the same principles of general utility to society, which is the basis of all other moral rights and obligations.

Thus considered, an author's copy-right ought to be esteemed an inviolable right, established in sound reason and abstract morality.

(1813)

SIR EGERTON BRYDGES, BART. M.P.
Reasons for a Further Amendment of the Act 54 Geo. III. C. 156: Being an Act to Amend the Copyright Act of Queen Anne.[2]

ADVERTISEMENT.

IN consequence of the Motion which the Author is about to bring forward in the House of Commons for Leave to bring in a Bill to amend the late Copyright Act, which was passed on the 29th of July, 1814, he has been induced to put into print the following *Reasons*, though very hastily drawn; conceiving that a due and leisurely consideration of them will prove their force and justice.

London, June 17, 1817.

IN the following pages I propose, briefly to enquire into the history and provisions of the Act 54 Geo. III. C. 156, entitled, "*An Act to amend the several Acts for the Encouragement of Learning, by securing the Copies and Copyrights of Printed Books, to the Authors of such Books or their Assigns*:" for the purpose of ascertaining,

1. Whether the said Act has answered the purposes, and produced the remedies, for which it was passed?
2. Whether it has not created, either intentionally, or from some incorrectness in the wording of it, new grievances, so considerable as to call loudly for another interference of Parliament?

It would now be wasting time to establish by authority or argument the property which an Author has in the issue of his own brain. The principle of Copyright is no longer disputed, either

---

[1] Edward Christian (d. 1823), professor of common law at Downing College, Cambridge, was the author of *A Vindication of the Right of the Universities of Great Britain to a Copy of Every New Publication* (1807).
  Christian was the instigator of Cambridge's decision to enforce its right to every text published.

[2] Sir Egerton Brydges (1762–1836), a writer, editor, and genealogist. He was the author of *Four Tracts on Copyright 1817–18*. He sat as an M.P. from 1812–18 and rarely spoke though he took an active part in debates about copyright.

as a matter of justice or law. The difficulty has arisen in devising means to enforce and protect that right.

The best and clearest account of this may be given in a passage extracted from some lately recovered Letters of Thomas Carte, the Historian,[1] on this subject, published in 1735, when a Bill was brought in, to render the Act of Queen Anne more effectual.

"To call the securing of this property an unjust design, and an invasion of the natural rights of mankind, will scarce appear a true suggestion to any one that considers the natural right which Authors have in their Works, and the legal right which both they and their assigns have in their Copies. 'Tis certain that no printer since the invention of the art of printing, ever had, in England, a right to print the Works of another man, without his consent. There ever was a property in all Books here printed; and for the making of it known, the better to prevent all invasion thereof, when the Stationers were incorporated,[2] all Authors, and the proprietors to whom they sold their Copies, constantly entered them in the Register of that Company, as their property."

It becomes, however, a matter, not of mere curiosity, but of great use to the purposes of the present discussion, to trace the progress of the steps in Parliament for the protection of Copyright. It will a little surprise those who have been misled, by the advocates for the Universities, to believe that the claims of those Universities have been an inseparable condition coetaneous[3] with the interference of Parliament in the protection of Copyright, to learn that nearly seventy years before the act of Q. Anne, Parliament unequivocally declared the property of Copyright, and denounced penalties for the in-

fringement of it. And this, without requiring the tax of a single copy.

"If ever," (continues the Letter-writer in 1735,) "there was a danger of the invasion of Copyright, it was in 1641, when the licentiousness of the press was carried to the greatest height; and there wanted not persons to insinuate to the Members of the then House of Commons, that it would be convenient to lay all Copies open for every printer that pleased to publish them. On this occasion, Featley, Burgers, Gouge, Byfield, Calamy, Seaman, and several other divines, favourites of the prevailing party in that House, thought it proper to sign a paper, declaring, 'that, to their knowledge, very considerable sums of money had been paid by Stationers and Printers to many Authors, for the Copies of such useful Books as had been imprinted; in regard whereof (they say) we conceive it to be both just and necessary that they should enjoy a property for the sole imprinting of their Copies; and we further declare, that, unless they do so enjoy a property, all Scholars will be utterly deprived of any recompense from the Stationers or Printers, for their studies or labour in writing or preparing Books for the press.'"

In 1813 and 1814, the owners of Copyright sought an amendment of the act of Q. Anne, according to the construction given to it by the Court of King's Bench in 1812, in the case of the University of Cambridge and Bryer, by which it was decided that the Universities were entitled to eleven copies of every work printed and published, or re-published with additions, whether entered at Stationers' Hall or not.[4]

This was a claim which had never been in the contemplation of either party, from the passing the

---

[1] Thomas Carte (1686–1754), author of *General History of England* (1747).

[2] 1577.

[3] Of the same historical period.

[4] Authors had the option of not availing themselves of the copyright privileges endowed by the Stationer's Company if they did not register their book with them. Authors could decide, in other words, that the book was so expensive to produce, and was aimed at so elect an audience, that the cost of securing copyright (in terms of the number of copies that would have to be donated) outweighed the risk of piracy.

act in the reign of Queen Anne till 1805, when such a construction of the act was first put forth by Mr. Montagu, or Professor Christian. The owners of Copyright felt that if such was the correct construction of the act, as it stood, they were entitled to petition Parliament to amend what was so obviously contrary to the intention of all parties; and at the same time so grievous a burden on them, and such a discouragement to literature.

The claimants, however, of the eleven copies felt resolved to surrender nothing of the advantages thus gained; and being powerful bodies, widely connected with every part of the Empire, they carried on their opposition with too much success.

The petitioners urged the justice of their title to relief by various statements and proofs in print as well as otherwise, to which no answer was made which has ever appeared to my mind to carry even plausibility. They prayed, that, if the tax was to be levied where no protection was even asked, the wantonness of demand might at least be checked by the claimants being ordered to pay some small proportion (say a third or a fourth) of the price. The claimants would yield nothing. They said "We will have everything; whether you ask protection or not: and we will pay, nothing!"

(1817)

GENTLEMAN'S MAGAZINE
Letter: Mr. Fisher's Publication on Stratford-upon-Avon[1]

MR. URBAN,   *May* 20

OBSERVING myself publicly called upon by one of your Correspondents[2] to explain why a publication which was commenced in the year 1803 upon Paintings discovered at Stratford-upon-Avon in Warwickshire, has not yet been completed in the manner then proposed, I feel it to be a duty which I owe to the publick, to afford the required explanation.

The work in question, Mr. Urban, was undertaken at a period when the practical interpretation of the Copy-right Act, of the 8th year of Queen Anne, had, *for exactly a century preceding*, left authors and publishers at liberty to judge for themselves, how far the protection held out in that Act was desirable to them at the price they were called on to pay for it, *viz. eleven copies*;[†] and according to the decision of their own judgements, it was optional with them either to register their works under the provisions of this and a subsequent Act, and thus to sacrifice 11 copies; or to omit such registration, and leave their works open to piracy.

Estimating, from the character of my work, its probable circulation at a very small number, and considering the laborious manner in which every copy was to be finished in colours; convinced also of the impossibility of any profitable piracy under these circumstances (and I conceive nothing but the hope of profit will induce piracy), I resolved on executing an impression of only 120 copies of the Paintings at a *polyautographic* press; by the eventual sale of which impression, chiefly amongst students in Antiquity, I expected to obtain a very small remuneration for my labour.

For the accomplishment of my design, I had obtained access to Materials original and interesting, beyond the general run of topographical publications; and, in the confidence of success, I certainly did intimate a purpose of completing the work by the addition of copper-plates and *copious letter-press*, thereby intending a memoir of the ancient Fraternity or Guild of Holy Cross at Stratford-upon-Avon, at whose cost these Paintings were executed,

---

[1] Thomas Fisher (1781?–1836), an antiquarian and contributor to several leading periodicals.

[2] See *Gentleman's Magazine* 87 (1817):328.

[†] Only Nine editions previous to the Act of 54 Geo. III. EDIT.

to be compiled from the authentic records of the Corporation.

But, unfortunately, while the materials for the Fourth Part were in a state of considerable progress a question was brought under legal discussion, arising out of an *unconditional* claim made by one of the eleven privileged Bodies, to receive from the proprietors of all works, without *purchase*, and without *exception*, one copy of every literary performance; even although it might not be deemed expedient by the Author to claim the protection of the Act of Queen Anne for the Copyright.

Mr. Brougham's arguments against this claim in the court of King's Bench appeared to me at the time, and have ever since appeared to me, just and convincing; those of the opposite party had this obvious defect, that they led to a result prejudicial to that Literature which the Act of Queen Anne, in its preamble, expressly professed to befriend. A decision, however, was obtained, favourable to the claim; on the legal validity of which there could be no question, whatever doubts might exist as to its accuracy.

When in consequence of this decision, it was deemed necessary by the Booksellers and Publishers to apply to Parliament for an alteration of the Law (then recently after 100 years of uniform operation, explained to their prejudice, and to the prejudice of all possessors of literary property), I was one of, I believe, only two private persons, who, perceiving literary property to be very materially affected by the change, petitioned the Legislature against the Act. A copy of my Petition to Parliament I inclose, should you deem it worth preserving in your Magazine; from which it will appear that I only solicited the Legislature by adopting a certain Clause, to leave me at liberty to publish my works without being subject to the heavy tax, and to take upon myself the risk of having my copyright invaded.[1]

That this apparently reasonable request was not granted, is to me indeed a matter of regret as it respects my own property, greatly depreciated by the change; but much more do I conceive it to be a matter of complaint to the British publick, as it respects the superior labours of other persons; for unquestionably England will suffer the loss of many valuable original scientific works, which might have been published in small impressions, had it not been for the operation of this Act of Queen Anne, under the decision of the Court of King's Bench; and of the further Act of the Session before the last, by which the obnoxious claims have been established. The Act of Anne, thus explained and applied, is oddly enough described *to be an Act to encourage learned men to write useful books.*

Under these altered circumstances, I conceive myself justified in declining either to involve myself in the predicament of attempting to evade the Law, which is repugnant to my feelings—or of submitting to an unreasonable loss of property, which I have a right to avoid,—or, as a remaining alternative, to involve myself in legal disputes with powerful and wealthy Bodies, who, with ample funds, and a host of legal retainers, have, by an extraordinary plea of poverty, obtained the sanction of the Legislature to their claim.

To the yet unpublished Plates of my Stratford-upon-Avon the Subscribers[2] will be welcome, as soon as I can put them together; and I am not yet so far advanced in life but that I entertain a hope of being enabled to complete my original design, when the Legislature shall have perceived, as it unquestionably must in a very few years perceive, the

---

[1] The petition was included in the *Gentleman's Magazine* after Mr. Fisher's letter.

[2] A method of publishing based on a list of committed purchasers or subscribers. This was often viewed as a medium between conventional patronage relations and the more unstable realities of the modern book trade. This arrangement provided a degree of security for authors, but eminent names on the subscription list also conveyed a prestige on the author and the book that could help to promote it with a wider audience.

prejudicial consequences to Literature and Science, of the Law as it now stands.

Yours, &c. T. FISHER.

(1817)

S.T. Coleridge
Advice to Young Authors

from *Biographia Literaria.*[1]

An imprudent man of common goodness of heart, cannot but wish to turn even his imprudences to the benefit of others, as far as this is possible. If therefore any one of the readers of this semi-narrative should be preparing or intending a periodical work, I warn him, in the first place, against trusting in the number of names on his subscription list. For he cannot be certain that the names were put down by sufficient authority; or (should that be ascertained) it still remains to be known, whether they were not extorted by some over zealous friend's importunity; whether the subscriber had not yielded his name, merely from want of courage to answer, no! and with the intention of dropping the work as soon as possible. One gentleman procured me nearly a hundred names for THE FRIEND,[2] and not only took frequent opportunity to remind me of his success in his canvas, but laboured to impress my mind with the sense of the obligation, I was under to the subscribers; for (as he very pertinently admonished me) "*fifty-two shillings* a year was a large sum to be bestowed on one individual, where there were so many objects of charity with strong claims to the assistance of the benevolent." Of these hundred patrons ninety threw up the publication before the fourth number,

without any notice; though it was well known to them, that in consequence of the distance, and the slowness and irregularity of the conveyance, I was compelled to lay in a stock of *stamped* paper[3] for at least eight weeks beforehand; each sheet of which stood me in five pence previous to its arrival at my printer's; though the subscription money was not to be received till the twenty-first week after the commencement of the work; and lastly, though it was in nine cases out of ten impracticable for me to receive the money for two or three numbers without paying an equal sum for the postage.

In confirmation of my first caveat, I will select one fact among *many*. On my list of subscribers, among a considerable number of names equally flattering, was that of an Earl of Cork, with his address. He might as well have been an Earl of Bottle, for aught *I* knew of him, who had been content to reverence the peerage in abstracto, rather than in concretis. Of course THE FRIEND was regularly sent as far, if I remember right, as the eighteenth number: i.e. till a fortnight before the subscription was to be paid. And lo! just at this time I received a letter from his Lordship, reproving me in language far more lordly than courteous for my impudence in directing my pamphlets to him, who knew nothing of me or my work! Seventeen or eighteen numbers of which, however, his Lordship was pleased to retain, probably for the culinary or post-culinary conveniences of his servants.

Secondly, I warn all others from the attempt to deviate from the ordinary mode of publishing a work by *the trade*. I thought indeed, that to the purchaser it was indifferent, whether thirty per cent. of the purchase-money went to the booksellers or to the government; and that the convenience of receiving the work by the post at his own door would give

---

[1] Samuel Taylor Coleridge (1772–1834), a well-known poet, literary critic, and social commentator. The *Biographia Literaria* was an ambitious blend of literary criticism, philosophy, and autobiography.

[2] Thomas Clarkson (1760–1846).

[3] The Stamp Act of 1712 imposed a tax on periodicals depending on the number of pages used. The tax was increased in the Romantic period as an attempt to curb the circulation of the radical press.

the preference to the latter. It is hard, I own, to have been labouring for years, in collecting and arranging the materials; to have spent every shilling that could be spared after the necessaries of life had been furnished, in buying books, or in journies for the purpose of consulting them or of acquiring facts at the fountain head; then to buy the paper, pay for the printing, &c. all at least fifteen per cent. beyond what *the trade* would have paid; and then after all to give thirty per cent. not of the net profits, but of the gross results of the sale, to a man who has merely to give the books shelf or warehouse room, and permit his apprentice to hand them over the counter to those who may ask for them; and this too copy by copy, although if the work be on any philosophical or scientific subject, it may be years before the edition is sold off. All this, I confess, must seem an hardship, and one, to which the products of industry in no other mode of exertion are subject. Yet even this is better, far better, than to attempt in any way to unite the functions of author and publisher. But the most prudent mode is to sell the copy-right, at least of one or more editions, for the most that *the trade* will offer. By few only can a large remuneration be expected; but fifty pounds and ease of mind are of more real advantage to a literary man, than the *chance* of five hundred with the *certainty* of insult and degrading anxieties. I shall have been grievously misunderstood, if this statement should be interpreted as written with the desire of detracting from the character of booksellers or publishers. The individuals did not make the laws and customs of their trade, but as in every other trade take them as they find them. Till the evil can be proved to be removable and without the substitution of an equal or greater inconvenience, it were neither wise or manly even to complain of it. But to use it as a pretext for speaking, or even for thinking, or feeling, unkindly or opprobriously of the tradesmen, as *individuals*, would be something worse than unwise

or even than unmanly; it would be immoral and calumnious! My motives point in a far different direction and to far other objects, as will be seen in the conclusion of the chapter.

A learned and exemplary old clergyman, who many years ago went to his reward followed by the regrets and blessings of his flock, published at his own expense two volumes octavo,[1] entitled, a new Theory of Redemption. The work was most severely handled in the Monthly or Critical Review, I forget which, and this unprovoked hostility became the good old man's favorite topic of conversation among his friends. Well! (he used to exclaim) in the SECOND edition, I shall have an opportunity of exposing both the ignorance and the malignity of the anonymous critic. Two or three years however passed by without any tidings from the bookseller, who had undertaken the printing and publication of the work, and who was perfectly at his ease, as the author was known to be a man of large property. At length the *accounts* were written for; and in the course of a few weeks they were presented by the *rider* for the house, in person. My old friend put on his spectacles, and holding the scroll with no very firm hand, began—*Paper, so much*: O moderate enough—not at all beyond my expectation! *Printing, so much*: well! moderate enough! *Stitching, covers, advertisements, carriage, &c. so much.*—Still nothing amiss. *Selleridge* (for orthography is no necessary part of a bookseller's literary acquirements) £3. 3s. Bless me! only three guineas for the what d'ye call it? the selleridge? No more, Sir! replied the rider. Nay, but that is *too* moderate! rejoined my old friend. Only three guineas for *selling* a thousand copies of a work in two volumes? O Sir! (cries the young traveller) you have mistaken the word. There have been none of them *sold*; they have been sent back from London long ago; and

---

[1] A page size (6" by 9½") obtained by folding a printer's sheet into eight leaves.

this £3. 3s. is for the *cellaridge*, or warehouse-room in our book *cellar*. The work was in consequence preferred from the ominous cellar of the publisher's, to the author's garret; and on presenting a copy to an acquaintance the old gentleman used to tell the anecdote with great humor and still greater good nature.

With equal lack of worldly knowledge, I was a far more than equal sufferer for it, at the very outset of my authorship. Toward the close of the first year from the time, that in an inauspicious hour I left the friendly cloysters, and the happy grove of quiet, ever honored Jesus College, Cambridge,[1] I was persuaded by sundry Philanthropists and Anti-polemists[2] to set on foot a periodical work, entitled THE WATCHMAN, that (according to the general motto of the work) *all might know the truth, and that the truth might make us free!*[3] In order to ex-empt it from the stamp-tax, and likewise to contrib-ute as little as possible to the supposed guilt of a war against freedom, it was to be published on every eighth day, thirty-two pages, large octavo, closely printed, and price only FOUR-PENCE. Accord-ingly with a flaming prospectus, *"Knowledge is Power,"* &c. *to cry the state of the political atmosphere*, and so forth, I set off on a tour to the North, from Bristol to Sheffield, for the purpose of procuring customers, preaching by the way in most of the great towns, as an hireless volunteer, in a blue coat and white waistcoat, that not a rag of the woman of Babylon might be seen on me.[4]

My campaign commenced at Birmingham; and my first attack was on a rigid Calvinist, a tallow chandler by trade. He was a tall dingy man, in whom length was so predominant over breadth, that he might almost have been borrowed for a foundery[5] poker. O that face! a face κατ' ἔμφασιν![6] I have it before me at this moment. The lank, black, twine-like hair, *pingui-nitescent*,[7] cut in a strait line along the black stubble of his thin gunpowder eye brows, that looked like a scorched *after-math* from a last week's shaving. His coat collar behind in perfect unison, both of colour and lustre with the coarse yet glib cordage, that I suppose he called his hair, and which with a *bend* inward at the nape of the neck (the only approach to flexure in his whole figure) slunk in behind his waistcoat; while the countenance lank, dark, very *hard*, and with strong perpendicular furrows, gave me a dim notion of some one looking at me through a *used* gridiron,[8] all soot, grease, and iron! But he was one of the *thor-ough-bred*, a true lover of liberty, and (I was in-formed) had proved to the satisfaction of many, that Mr. Pitt was one of the horns of the second beast in the Revelations, *that spoke like a dragon.*[9] A person, to whom one of my letters of recommenda-tion had been addressed, was my introducer. It was a new event in my life, my first *stroke* in the new business I had undertaken of an author, yea, and of an author trading on his own account. My compan-ion after some imperfect sentences and a multitude of hums and haws abandoned the cause to his client; and I commenced an harangue of half an hour to Phileleutheros,[10] the tallow-chandler, varying my notes through the whole gamut of eloquence from the ratiocinative to the declamatory, and in the latter from the pathetic to the indignant. I argued, I described, I promised, I prophecied; and beginning with the captivity of nations I ended with

---

[1] Coleridge left Cambridge in 1794.

[2] Opponents of war.

[3] Coleridge's journal, *The Watchman*, ran from 1 March to 13 May .

[4] Revelation 17:6.

[5] A workplace where metal is cast into moulds.

[6] Par excellence.

[7] Shining with fat.

[8] A framed set of metal bars used for broiling.

[9] Revelation 13:11.

[10] One who loves freedom.

the near approach of the millenium, finishing the whole with some of my own verses describing that glorious state out of *the Religious Musings*:

> ——————— Such delights,
> As float to earth, permitted visitants!
> When in some hour of solemn jubilee
> The massive gates of Paradise are thrown
> Wide open: and forth come in fragments wild
> Sweet echoes of unearthly melodies,
> And odors snatch'd from beds of Amaranth,
> And they that from the chrystal river of life
> Spring up on freshen'd wings, ambrosial gales!
>
> *Religious Musings*, 1.356.[1]

My taper man of lights listened with perseverant and praiseworthy patience, though (as I was afterwards told on complaining of certain gales that were not altogether ambrosial) it was a *melting* day with him. And what, Sir! (he said after a short pause) might the cost be? *Only* FOUR-PENCE (O! how I felt the anti-climax, the abysmal bathos of that *four-pence!*) *only four-pence, Sir, each number, to be published on every eighth day.* That comes to a deal of money at the end of a year. And how much did you say there was to be for the money? *Thirty-two pages, Sir! large octavo, closely printed.* Thirty and two pages? Bless me, why except what I does in a family way on the Sabbath, that's more than I ever reads, Sir! all the year round. I am as great a one, as any man in Brummagem, Sir! for liberty and truth and all them sort of things, but as to this (no offence, I hope, Sir!) I must beg to be excused.

Conscientiously an opponent of the first revolutionary war, yet with my eyes thoroughly opened to the true character and impotence of the favorers of revolutionary principles in England, principles which I held in abhorrence (for it was part of my political creed, that whoever ceased to act as an *individual* by making himself a member of any *society* not sanctioned by his Government, forfeited the rights of a citizen)—a vehement anti-ministerialist, but after the invasion of Switzerland a more vehement anti-gallican, and still more intensely an anti-Jacobin, I retired to a cottage at Stowey, and provided for my scanty maintenance by writing verses for a London Morning Paper.[2] I saw plainly, that literature was not a profession, by which I could expect to live; for I could not disguise from myself, that whatever my talents might or might not be in other respects, yet they were not of the sort that could enable me to become a popular writer; and that whatever my opinions might be in themselves, they were almost equi-distant from all the three prominent parties, the Pittites, the Foxites, and the Democrats. Of the unsaleable nature of my writings I had an amusing memento one morning from our own servant girl. For happening to rise at an earlier hour than usual, I observed her putting an extravagant quantity of paper into the grate in order to light the fire, and mildly checked her for her wastefulness; la, Sir! (replied poor Nanny) why, it is only "WATCHMEN."

(1817)

---

[1] S.T. Coleridge, *Religious Musings: A Desultory Poem, Written on Christmas' Eve, in the Year of our Lord, 1794.* ll. 364–72. (The line number Coleridge gives in the text is erroneous.)

[2] The *Morning Post.* Coleridge contributed poetry and prose pieces to the newspaper, which was reformist in its sympathies.

SECTION FIVE

The Vanity Fair of Knowledge: Literary Fashions

Concerns about the book trade were compounded by the ironic fact that, for many writers, literature had become *too* popular. Coleridge may have affected surprise at the size and enthusiasm of the reading public, which he dismissed as a "misgrowth of our luxuriant activity," but as almost everyone admitted, literature was one of the most fashionable trends of a fashion-crazed era. Hannah More warned that the prevailing superficiality of literary taste both reflected and reinforced "the general habits of fashionable life." She insisted that "real knowledge and real piety, though they have gained in many instances, have suffered in others from that profusion of little, amusing, sentimental books with which the youthful library overflows." Part of the problem, she explained, was that minds were weakened far more quickly by "frivolous reading" than they could ever be enlightened by "books of solid instruction." To go to a dinner-party without having read the latest novel, or at least without knowing enough about it to be able to pretend to have read it, William Hazlitt cautioned, was to seem dangerously out of touch. This fashionable status exacerbated concerns that instead of serving as a corrective, literature had become part of the moral rot in a society that was addicted to conspicuous consumption.

Vicesimus Knox's gloomy diagnosis that "idle curiosity" had triumphed over "all desire of increasing the store of knowledge," was amplified by critics' frequent lament that novelty was many readers' highest priority. Amongst fashionable readers, he added, the first question put to librarians was "have you any thing new?" Hazlitt professed to be mystified by "the rage manifested by the greater part of the world for reading New Books" given the endless numbers of old books that went unread. But, he accepted, "there is a fashion in reading as well as in dress, which lasts only for the season." Hazlitt put the modern rage of novelty—what he called "this idle, dissipated turn"—down to a reaction against an earlier insistence on the exclusive merit of classical authors. It was only natural that the pendulum had shifted, Hazlitt acknowledged, but he nonetheless wondered what good "the diffusion of knowledge" was "if we do not gain an enlargement and elevation of views" that would transcend "this exclusive, upstart spirit." For Hazlitt and Knox, as for so many of their peers, the popularity of the reading habit with fashionable society constituted a serious threat to, rather than the culmination of, the progress of learning.

The great scapegoat for critics of modern reading habits was romantic novels, or what a letter to the *Gentleman's Magazine* promoting the formation of subscription libraries as a means of combating these problems called "the corruptive trash of our common circulating libraries." The negative effects of this sort of reading were closely connected in many critics' minds with the promiscuous availability of circulating libraries, which were frequently portrayed as traveling the country like viruses, making the latest "corruptive trash" all too easily available to the sorts of readers who were most vulnerable to their negative influence. Hannah More's vivid description of the "hot-bed of a circulating library" conveys critics' sense of how unnatural the situation was. They warned that these sorts of books tended to inculcate an overwrought sensibility and give young ladies false expectations. In her review of *Edward and Harriet, or the Happy Recovery*, for the *Analytical Review,* Mary Wollstonecraft argued that "ridicule should direct its shafts against this fair game, and, if possible, deter the thoughtless from imbibing the wildest notions, the most pernicious prejudices; prejudices which influence the conduct, and spread insipidity over social converse." Ridicule did not prove to be much of a deterrent though. As Anna Barbauld noted, romantic novels may have been "condemned by the grave, and despised by the fastidious; but their leaves are seldom found unopened, and they occupy the parlour and the dressing-room while productions of higher name are often gathering dust upon the shelf."

Nor was the problem simply that books offering only idle distraction had crowded out those more serious works preferred by grave and fastidious scholars. Learning itself had become a fashion craze, but with predictably mixed results. The *Monthly Review* acknowledged that "perhaps there never was a period in which abridgments of books on comprehensive subjects so much abounded as at the present. Abridgments of divinity, philosophy, history, and the *belles lettres*, are published almost every month." This was not, the *Monthly* concluded, wholly a bad thing, in that "it peculiarly contributes to the diffusion of knowledge," but it questioned "whether a superficial knowledge thus acquired has not a tendency rather to inspire vanity and self-conceit, than to enlighten the understanding or to rectify the heart." More was predictably skeptical about these "swarms of *Abridgments, Beauties,* and *Compendiums,* which form too considerable a part of a young lady's library," and which "may be considered in many instances as an infallible receipt for making a superficial mind." Problems with literary quality generally were exacerbated by the way books circulated, in the "hot-beds" of circulating libraries or excerpted in anthologies that appealed to readers' indolence.

All of this was reinforced by the book-trade's tendency to resort to marketing strategies that confirmed critics' fears that, in literary matters as elsewhere, appearances counted more than substance. The letter to the *Gentleman's* recommending the formation of subscription libraries warned that "among the many luxuries of the present day," none was "more hostile to the general welfare of society" than the book-trade's growing dependence on "the mechanical embellishments of literature." Striking an equally melodramatic pose, T.J. Mathias insisted that if this "needlessly expensive manner of publishing" was not stopped, "Literature will destroy itself." The superficiality of a frivolous age where appearances counted more than substance was replicated in readers' preference for elegant appearances over the knowledge contained in books. Hazlitt warned that this was an inevitable consequence of the spread of literacy. "The taste for literature becomes superficial, as it becomes universal." Rather than merely keeping pace with these problems though, literature had become one of the worst examples of "the scramble and lottery for fame in the present day."

The real problem with all of this, Isaac D'Israeli suggested, was that as books became more popular, literary figures became more commonplace. Earlier times paid "the highest honours…to the Literary Character," but the modern obsession with reading was making it difficult to command the same kind of respect. "What Alexander feared, when he reproached Aristotle for rendering learning popular, has happened to modern literature; learning and talents have ceased to be learning and talents, by an universal diffusion of books, and a continued exercise of the mind." Authors' status declined as their profession expanded, until the only popularity they commanded was as a kind of spectacle on par with circus exhibits. "Men of the world are curious to have a glance at a celebrated Author, as they would be at some uncommon animal," or as children would "the reflections of a magic lanthorn." It was "the age of Authors," but only in the most demeaning sense: "writing is an interminable pursuit, and the raptures of publication have a great chance of becoming a permanent fashion."

It was not merely that there were more authors, but that, as with reading, authors' motivation had been corrupted by the prevailing culture of fashionable display. A letter to the *Gentleman's Magazine* observed that whereas in feudal times, "it was deemed essential to the character of a *gentleman*, either to fight a duel, or to rescue a princess:—*now*, if he would appear with credit to the world, it is equally essential 'to write a book.'" Amongst fashionable circles, it was not enough merely to know of the most recent literary novelties; authorship itself had become a prerequisite. Not only that, but quantity counted more than quality. Better to write several novels than spend too long working on one serious project. "Who are those ever multiplying authors, that with unparalleled fecundity are overstocking the world with their quick succeeding progeny?" asked Hannah More: "They are novel writers; the easiness of whose productions is at once the cause of their own fruitfulness, and of the almost infinitely numerous race of imitators to whom they give birth."

The Enlightenment ideal of literature as a basis for extended discussion presupposed a community of rational individuals who were both readers and authors, absorbing each others' ideas and responding in ways that fostered important debates. But this vision found its parodic double in what More described as the tendency of "a thorough paced novel reading Miss, at the close of every tissue of a hackney'd adventures," to exclaim "And I too am an author!" As the letter to the *Gentleman's* about the character of the modern gentleman pointed out, these problems corrupted what ought to be a "cordial friendship" between readers and authors based on a shared respect for genuine literary merit into "a constant state of warfare" in which both groups worked to promote their interests to the detriment of the other. Clearly this wasn't always the case. As both Hannah More and the *Gentleman's* correspondent suggested, bad novelists enjoyed a sense of perfect unity with their readers, whose degraded tastes they shared. But more serious authors were unsettled by an acrimonious sense that their intellectual commitments were out of step with the spirit of their age. Tensions between authors and booksellers, which were inflamed by debates about copyright, were reinforced by these struggles between authors and readers to determine the importance of particular types of literature, and of the social distinction of the people who produced and consumed them.

හවෙ

VICESIMUS KNOX
*Of Reading Novels and Trifling Books
Without Discrimination.*[1]

from *Winter Evenings: or, Lucubrations of
Life and Letteres*

Belli libelli, lepidi, novi libelli.[2]   IGNORAMUS.

SIR,   *Bath, July* 20, 1786.

As I came hither to relax myself from the fatigues of a profession which requires great application and confinement, I am resolved to make use of all the methods which this ingenious and polite place has invented for the valuable purpose of killing time. Accustomed to reading as I have always been, I cannot omit books while I seek the means of amusement; but I am forbidden by my physician to read any thing but what is called summer reading, and therefore I am a frequent lounger at the circulating library.[3] By the way, I beg leave to give you a hint, that if you do not contrive to make your Winter Evenings summer reading, they will not be much noticed in the repository of knowledge, where I am now writing you this letter.

As I often sit and read in the library, I have an opportunity of hearing what books are in the most request; and I am frequently not a little diverted with observing the great eagerness with which tomes, totally unknown to me, who have made books the study of my life, are demanded of the librarian. The first question on entering the shop I found to be universally—Have you any thing new? I should have supposed that the publications of the last year would have deserved this epithet; but I found by observation that scarcely any thing is esteemed new but what is just advertised, and almost wet from the press. Curiosity seems to be the great stimulus of the subscribers; idle curiosity, as I may call, it, since it seems to seek its own gratification independently of all desire of increasing the store of knowledge, improving the taste, or confirming the principles.

I have smiled at hearing a lady admire the delicacy of sentiment which the author of some novel, which she had just been reading, must possess, though I knew it to be the production of some poor hireling; destitute of learning and taste, knowledge of life and manners, and furnished with the few ideas he had by reading the novels of a few preceding years. He had inserted in the title-page,

---

[1] Vicesimus Knox (1752–1821), a periodical essayist. Knox published three volumes of essays on contemporary social and literary issues entitled *Winter Evenings: or, Lucubrations on Life and Letters*, the idea being that each essay constituted entertainment for a winter evening's reading. This "letter" was one of many brief essays by Knox which adopted the epistolary form—a frequent practice by periodical writers in the period.

[2] Pretty little books, witty new little books.

[3] Circulating libraries were synonymous in the period with the problems of modern literature. They were virtually always depicted as disseminating the latest and worst romantic novels to an eager female audience.

By a Lady, and various conjectures were often hazarded in my hearing concerning the authoress. Some hinted that they were acquainted with her, and that it was a lady of quality. Others knew it to be written by acquaintance of their own; while all agreed in asserting, it must be by a lady, the sentiments were so characteristically delicate and refined. You may conjecture how much I was disposed to laugh when I knew it to be the production of a comb-maker in Black Boy Alley.

I confess I had been much more conversant in a college library than in a circulating one, and could not therefore but be astonished at the number of volumes which the students would devour. The *Helluo Librorum*, or Glutton of Books, was a character well known at the university, and mentioned by the ancients; but I believe their idea of him is far exceeded by many a fair subscriber at the circulating library. I have known a lady read twenty volumes in a week during two or three months successively. To be sure they were not bulky tomes, such as those of which it was predicated that a great book was a great evil. The print in the pages of most of them, to speak in the mechanical style of mensuration, were three inches by one and a half, and the blank paper exceeded the printed in quantity by at least half on a moderate computation.

Now, Sir, I am not one of those who mean austerely to censure this mode of reading; for I am of opinion that it is often very innocent, and sometimes not without considerable advantage. There are certainly many novels which, though little known in the literary world, are not without merit, and of a very virtuous tendency. Most of them tend to recommend benevolence and liberality; for it is the fashion of the age to affect those qualities; and I really think, as conversation is usually conducted, scarcely so many opportunities occur of imbibing benevolent and virtuous sentiments from it as from the decent books of a circulating library: I say

decent, for I am sorry to observe, that in the multitude of new books which the librarians are obliged to purchase, some have a tendency to diffuse every kind of evil which can mislead the understanding and corrupt the heart.

The danger of indiscriminately reading whatever has the recommendation of novelty induced me to take up my pen and write to you, hoping that I might suggest a caution on the subject to some of your fair readers, who, I am sure, have recourse to a circulating library solely to improve and amuse themselves while under the hair-dresser's operation.

They would, I think, do right to enquire the character of every book they read before they take it into their dressing room, and shew the same caution in the choice of their circulating library books as they would of their company.

Your's, &c. SENEX.[1]

(1788)

Gentleman's Magazine
Letter:
Libraries recommended in Market Towns

Mr Urban, *Jan. 3.*

AMONG the many luxuries of the present day, none appears to me more hostile to the general welfare of society than that which begins so extensively to prevail in the useful art of printing, and the other branches of the bookselling business. Science now seldom makes her appearance without the expensive foppery of gilding, lettering, and unnecessary engravings, hot-pressing, and an extent of margin as extravagant as a court-lady's train. The inferior orders of society can scarce get a sight of her; and, to make matters worse, cheapness in editing is almost exclusively attended to in novels,

---

[1] Old man.

which, with a few exceptions, are no better than manuals of lust, quixotism, and dissipation.

I am aware that no remonstrance to the worshipful company of Stationers[1] on this head will be of any avail, while the public taste gives such encouragement to their splendid labours. But if those of the middling classes, who are not solely taken with the mechanical embellishments of literature, will exert themselves in establishing private subscription-libraries, each within his own neighbourhood, the evil here alluded to may, in a great degree, be remedied. To perceive the advantages and feasibility of such a plan, requires but little consideration. Let us suppose such a library begun by a few reading, public-spirited men, in a market town, in any part of England. Any person above a state of penury, residing within five miles of that town, may, without inconvenience, become a member, inasmuch as he will always have, once or twice a week at the least, an opportunity of sending, or receiving, books; and the monthly subscription need not be more than one shilling. Within this circle we may reasonably expect to find fifty subscribers, whose yearly contribution for the purchase of books would amount to thirty pounds, without being felt by any member. Now, on this moderate scale, the society would, in twenty years, have insensibly laid out in the purchase of moral and instructive books, of its own choice, no less than 600£.

A valuable collection like this, would, in the family of every subscriber, prove a general luminary to the human mind, and effectually exclude all the corruptive trash of our common circulating libraries. Of the happy and progressive influence of such

an institution on the public taste and sentiments, I have for some years been a witness in the town of Lewes, Sussex. The subscription library there began in January 1786, with about ten members, and as many volumes; but, in the course of eight years only, it has already to boast of sixty members, and about a thousand well-selected volumes; and as the rules adopted by this society may be of some use to similar institutions in their infancy, I request you will be so kind, Mr. Urban, as to give them a place in your Miscellany. Yours, &c. Z.

(1794)

T.J. MATHIAS
The Pursuits of Literature: [2]
A Satirical Poem in Four Dialogues

I CONDEMN the general and needlessly expensive manner of publishing most pamphlets and books at this time. If the present rage of printing on fine, *creamy* wire-woven, *vellum*, hot-pressed paper is not stopped, the injury done to the eye from reading, and the shameful expence of the books, will in no very long time annihilate the desire of reading, and the possibility of purchasing. *No new work whatsoever* should be published in *this* manner, or Literature will destroy itself.

(1797)

---

[1] A guild of printers, bookbinders, and booksellers, incorporated in 1577. The Stationer's Company was initially created by Queen Mary as a way of controlling the dissemination of seditious literature, but the fact that booksellers entered their "copy" in its register gave the Company power to control the security of copyright.

[2] Thomas James Mathias (*c.* 1745–1835) published the first part of his satirical poem, *The Pursuits of Literature*, in 1794. In the mid-to-late 1790s, the ultra-conservative Mathias responded to the revolutionary controversy by publishing three more parts. Its vicious satirical tone coincided with the polarized spirit of the period and earned the poem a great deal of attention amongst like-minded readers. The fact that Mathias continued to publish it anonymously also helped to fuel the public's interest, and led to a lively debate about the identity of the author in conservative literary magazines such as the *Gentleman's*.

ISAAC D'ISRAELI
Preface to *An Essay on the Manners and Genius of the Literary Character*[1]

THE LITERARY CHARACTER has, in the present day, singularly degenerated in the public mind. The finest compositions appear without exciting any alarm of admiration, they are read, approved, and succeeded by others; nor is the presence of the Author considered, as formerly, as conferring honour on his companions; we pass our evenings sometimes with poets and historians, whom it is probable will be admired by posterity, with hardly any other sensation than we feel from inferior associates.

The youth who has more reading than experience, and a finer imagination than a sound logic, will often be surprised when he compares the splendid facts stored in his memory, with the ordinary circumstances that pass under his eye. In the history of all ages, and of all nations, he observes the highest honours paid to the Literary Character. Statues, tombs, festivals, and coronations, croud in glittering confusion, while when he condescends to look around him, he perceives the brilliant enchantment dissolved, and not a vestige remains of the festivals and the coronations.

Before I attempt to alledge a reason for a singular revolution in the human mind, I shall arrange a few striking facts of the numerous honours which have been paid to the Literary Character.

I must not dwell on the distinctions bestowed on the learned by the Greeks and the Romans; their temples, their statues, their games, and fleets dis-patched to invite the Student; these honours were more numerous and splendid than those of modern ages. I must not detail the magnificent rewards and the high veneration paid by the Persians, the Turks, the Arabians, the Chinese, &c. The Persian Ferdosi[2] received sacks of gold for his verses; the Arabs have sent ambassadors to congratulate poets on the success of their works; Mahomet took off his mantle to present to an Author; and literature in China confers nobility. But I pass this romantic celebrity, to throw a rapid glance on our own Europe.

Not to commence more remotely than at the thirteenth century, when Nobles, and even Kings, aspired to literature. Authors, of course, were held in the highest estimation. Fauchet[3] and Pasquier[4] inform us, that the learned received magnificent dresses, steeds richly caparisoned, and arms resplendent with diamonds and gold. The Floral games at Toulouse were established; and three prizes of golden flowers were reserved for the happy poets. It was in the fourteenth century that the Italians raised triumphal arches, tombs, and coronations, for distinguished Authors. Ravenna[5] erected a marble tomb to the memory of Dante;[6] Certaldo[7] a statue to Boccaccio,[8] and Petrarch[9] was at once invited by the city of Rome and the court of France, to receive the crown of laurel. Rome was preferred, and there he was publickly crowned with such magnificence of pomp, and ceremonies so splendid and numerous, that his own imagination could not have

---

[1] Isaac D'Israeli (1766–1848) failed to achieve his early dream of poetic success but established himself as a well-known and generally respected literary critic. D'Israeli published several collections of essays on contemporary literary issues. D'Israeli's son, Benjamin, the future novelist and Prime Minister of England, described *An Essay on the Manners and Genius of the Literary Character* as "the most delightful of his [father's] works."

[2] A medieval Persian poet (born *c.* 950). The great epic poet of Iran.

[3] Claude Fauchet (1530–1601), French historian and antiquary.

[4] Étienne Pasquier (1529–1615), French jurist and man of letters.

[5] A city in northern Italy. The site of Dante's tomb.

[6] Dante Alighieri (1265–1321), author of the *Divine Comedy*.

[7] An Italian city. Born in Paris, Boccaccio was educated in Certaldo and Naples.

[8] Giovanni Boccaccio (1313–75), Italian poet and storyteller, author of the *Decameron*.

[9] Francesco Petrarca (1304–74), poet.

surpassed the realities of this triumph.[†] Tasso[1] died the evening of his coronation. In the fifteenth century, Sannazarius[2] received from the Venetians for six verses, six hundred pistoles, and poets were kissed by princesses. Later times saw the phlegmatic Hollander raise a statue to the excellent Erasmus.[3] Let us not omit that Charles IX. of France reserved apartments in his palace, and even wrote a poetical epistle to Ronsard;[4] and Bais[5] received a silver image of Minerva[6] from his native city. Charles V. and Francis I. in the sixteenth century, poured honours, preferments, and gifts, on the learned of their age.

[†] I lament much that Dr. Burney, whose learning excels my praise, and whose elegance is not inferior to his learning, has treated this subject with great levity. He says, in his valuable History of Music, vol.2. p.332, that this was a censureable vanity—and that "the blame can only be laid on his youth, or rather on *the practice of the times.*" And he continues in a strain of ridicule to censure these testimonies of national sensibility. But I observe, that the learned Doctor, while he smiles at this popular display and vanity, has prefixed to his performance *his own portrait* in (what some may consider) *the affected posture of beating time,* painted by Reynolds, and engraved by Bartolozzi. The Doctor makes an animated appearance; but this *public exhibition* of Burney, has not less vanity than that of Petrarch; must not we apply to the Doctor his own words, and "lay the blame on his youth, or rather *on the practice of the times?*"

The error of Dr. Burney, in this instance, proceeds from his not confessing that there was *no vanity* in the coronation of Petrarch; for the love of glory is something very superior to vanity.

[1] Torquato Tasso (1544–95), an Italian poet remembered for *Jerusalem Delivered* (1580).

[2] Jacopo Sannazaro (1458–1530), an Italian and Latin poet. In his youth Sannazaro wrote a work in mingled verse and prose entitled "Arcadia," in which he described the pastoral life according to the traditions of the ancients. This work had great success; it was translated and imitated, and in the sixteenth century had about sixty editions.

[3] Desiderius Erasmus (1466–1536), a Dutch humanist whose often satirical writings are seen as helping to pave the way for the reformation.

[4] Pierre de Ronsard (1524–85), French poet. Named poet royal, he was the author of the love poems *Sonnets pour Hélène* (1578).

[5] Possibly a reference to the Belgian theologian, Michael Baius (1513–89), who studied philosophy and theology at Louvain and held various chairs there. Charles V made him professor of scriptural interpretation.

[6] The Roman goddess of wisdom and of arts and trades.

Literary merit was the road to promotion, and seignories and abbeys, seats in the state council, and ambassadorships were bestowed upon the Literary Character.

Since all this is truth, yet at present appears much like fiction, it may be enquired if our ancestors were wiser than we, or we more wise than our ancestors.

It is to be recollected, that before the art of printing existed, great Authors were like their works, very rare; learning was then only obtained by the devotion of a life. It was long after the art of multiplying works at pleasure was discovered, that the people were capable of participating in the novel benefit; what Alexander feared, when he reproached Aristotle for rendering learning popular, has happened to modern literature; learning and talents have ceased to be learning and talents, by an universal diffusion of books, and a continued exercise of the mind. Authors became numerous, but as the body of the people, till within the present century, was sufficiently unenlightened, their numbers were not yet found inconvenient; and as dictionaries were not yet formed, every man was happy to seise on whatever particles of knowledge accident offered; so late as the middle of this century, Translators were yet esteemed, and Compilers were yet respected.

But since, with incessant industry, volumes have been multiplied, and their prices rendered them accessible to the lowest artisans, the Literary Character has gradually fallen into disrepute. It may be urged that a superior mind, long cultivated, and long exercised, adorned with polite, and enriched with solid letters, must still retain it's pre-eminence among the inferior ranks of men; and therefore may still exact the same respect from his fellow-citizens, and still continue the dignity of an Author with the same just claims as in preceding ages.

I believe, however, that he who would be reverenced as an Author has only one resource; and that is, by paying to himself that reverence, which will be refused by the multitude. The respect which the higher classes shew to the Literary Character, proceeds from habitual politeness, and not from any sensibility of admiration; and that this is true, appears from this circumstance, that, should the Literary Character, in return, refuse to accommodate himself to their regulations, and have not the art of discovering what quality they expect to be remarked in themselves, he will be soon forsaken; and he may say what Socrates did at the court of Cyprus, "what I know is not proper for this place, and what is proper for this place, I know not." Men of the world are curious to have a glance at a celebrated Author, as they would be at some uncommon animal; he is therefore sometimes exhibited, and spectators are invited. A croud of frivolists gaze at a Man of Letters, and catch the sounds of his ideas, as children regard the reflections of a magic lanthorn.[†]

Nor will the Literary Character find a happier reception among others if he exacts an observance of his dignity. Authors are a multitude; and it requires no inconsiderable leisure and intelligence to adjust the claims of such numerous candidates.

De Foe called the last age, the age of Projectors,[1] and Johnson has called the present, the age of Authors. But there is this difference between them; the epidemical folly of projecting in time cures itself, for men become weary with ruination; but writing is an interminable pursuit, and the raptures of publication have a great chance of becoming a permanent fashion. When I reflect that every literary journal consists of 50 or 60 publications, and that of these, 5 or 6 at least are capital performances, and the greater part not contemptible, when

I take the pen and attempt to calculate, by these given sums, the number of volumes which the next century must infallibly produce, my feeble faculties wander in a perplexed series, and as I lose myself among billions, trillions, and quartillions, I am obliged to lay down my pen, and stop at infinity.

"Where all this will end, God only knows,"[2] is the reflection of a grave historian, in concluding the Memoirs of his Age. Nature has, no doubt, provided some concealed remedy for this future universal deluge. Perhaps in the progress of science, some new senses may be discovered in the human character, and this superfluity of knowledge may be essential to the understanding. We are considerably indebted, doubtless, to the patriotic endeavours of our grocers and trunkmakers, whom I respect as the alchemists of literature; they annihilate the gross bodies, without injuring the finer spirits.

We are, however, sincerely to lament that the dignity of great Authors is at all impaired. Every kind of writers find a correspondent kind of readers, and the illiterate have their admirers, and are of some use. But it is time that we should distinguish between Authors, and submit ourselves to respect those, from whom we acquire instruction, and to cherish those, from whom we derive the most elegant of our amusements.

(1795)

Monthly Review
Review of *A View of Universal History, from Creation to the Present Time.* By the Rev. J. Adams.[3]

PERHAPS there never was a period in which abridgments of books on comprehensive sub-

---

[†] The observation of the great Erasmus on Men of Letters, is not less just than admirable. He said, that they were like the great figures in the tapestries of Flanders, which lose their effect, when not seen at a distance.

[1] Opportunists or schemers.

[2] Source unidentified.

[3] John Adams (1750?–1814), a volunteer compiler of books for young readers.

jects so much abounded as at the present. Abridgments of divinity, philosophy, history, and the *belles lettres*, are published almost every month; and the writings of some of the most approved authors of the last and present age have been garbled and retailed under the appellation of BEAUTIES, &c:—the beauties of Johnson, Sterne, Goldsmith, &c. This practice is justified by some plausible arguments; the strongest of which seems to be that it peculiarly contributes to the diffusion of knowledge; but whether a superficial knowledge thus acquired has not a tendency rather to inspire vanity and self-conceit, than to enlighten the understanding or to rectify the heart, may be questioned; and it must be allowed, even by those who are most partial to such compendiums, that they may tend to draw off the attention of young students from those original writers, whose reputation has been consecrated by the approbation of successive ages, and who have ever been considered as our best guides in the pursuit of wisdom, and her constant associate, virtue. It has likewise been alleged that they may prove unfavourable to those habits of application and attention, without which it is impossible to make a real progress in any branch of learning: but, whatever may be the force of such objections, abridgments are too flattering to the indolence of mankind not to meet with readers and advocates: and after all, they may really be of much use, by smoothing the way to knowledge, and making it pleasant to those who might be discouraged from pursuing it by more rugged and tedious paths.

(1796)

HANNAH MORE
Strictures on the Modern System of Female Education[1]

[1] Hannah More (1745–1833) was often celebrated, and had frequently been remembered, as Mary Wollstonecraft's conservative antagonist, but this appraisal has been complicated by a recognition of

CHAP. VII.

On female study, and initiation into knowledge.—Error of cultivating the imagination to the neglect of judgement.—Books of reasoning recommended.

As this little work by no means assumes the character of a general scheme of education, the author has purposely avoided expatiating largely on any kind of instruction; but so far as it is connected, either immediately or remotely, with objects of a moral or religious nature. Of course she has been so far from thinking it necessary to enter into the enumeration of those books which are useful in general instruction, that she has forborne to mention any. With such books the rising generation is far more copiously and ably furnished than any preceding period had been; and out of an excellent variety the judicious instructor can hardly fail to make such a selection as shall be beneficial to the pupil.

But while due praise ought not to be withheld from the improved methods of communicating the elements of general knowledge; yet is there not some danger that our very advantages may lead us into error, by causing us to repose so confidently on the multiplied helps which facilitate the entrance into learning, as to render our pupils superficial through the very facility of acquirement? Where so much is done for them, may they not be led to do too little for themselves? May there not be a moral disadvantage in possessing them with the notions

the reformist vision implicit in her critique of fashionable society, a stance which had a surprising amount in common with Wollstonecraft's own middle-class antagonism to contemporary excesses. A growing estimation of More's importance also reflects an awareness of her central literary status in the period as a dramatist, poet, educational pioneer, and political writer in the Rights of Man and Rights of Woman controversies, but also in the struggle to abolish the slave trade. She was an eminent member of the Blue Stocking Circle, a group of learned women committed to the eighteenth-century ideal of polite conversation.

that learning may be acquired without diligence and labour? Sound education never *can* made a "primrose path of dalliance."[1] Do what we will we cannot *cheat* children into learning or *play* them into knowledge, according to the smoothness of the modern creed.

Will it not be ascribed to a captious singularity if I venture to remark that real knowledge and real piety, though they have gained in many instances, have suffered in others from that profusion of little, amusing, sentimental books with which the youthful library overflows? Abundance has its dangers as well as scarcity. In the first place may not the multiplicity of these alluring little works increase the natural reluctance to those more dry and uninteresting studies, of which after all, the rudiments of every part of learning *must* consist? And, secondly, is there not some danger (though there are many honourable exceptions) that some of those engaging narratives may serve to infuse into the youthful heart a sort of spurious goodness, a confidence of virtue? And that the benevolent actions with the recital of which they abound, when they are not made to flow from any source but feeling, may tend to inspire a self-complacency, a self-gratulation, a "stand by, for I am holier than thou?" May they not help to infuse a love of popularity and an anxiety for praise, in the place of that simple and unostentatious rule of doing whatever good we do, *because it is the will of God?* The universal substitution of this would tend to purify the worldly morality of many a popular little story. And there are few dangers which good parents will more carefully guard against than that of giving their children a mere political piety; that sort of religion which just goes to make people more respectable, and stand well with the world.[†]

There is a certain precocity of mind which is much helped on by these superficial modes of instruction; for frivolous reading will produce its correspondent effect, in much less time than books of solid instruction; the imagination being liable to be worked upon, and the feeling to be set a going, much faster than the understanding can be opened and the judgement enlightened. A talent for conversation should be the result of education, not its precursor; it is a golden fruit when suffered to ripen gradually on the tree of knowledge; but if forced in the hot-bed of a circulating library, it will turn out worthless and vapid in proportion as it was artificial and premature. Girls who have been accustomed to devour frivolous books, will converse and write with far greater appearance of skill as to style and sentiment at twelve or fourteen years old, than those of a more advanced age who are under the discipline of severer studies; but the former having early attained to that low standard which had been held out to them, became stationary; while the latter, quietly progressive, are passing through just gradations to a higher strain of mind; and those who early begin with talking and writing like women, commonly end with thinking and acting like children.

The swarms of *Abridgments*, *Beauties*, and *Compendiums*, which form too considerable a part of a young lady's library, may be considered in many instances as an infallible receipt for making a superficial mind. The *names* of the renowned characters in history thus became familiar in the mouths of those who can neither attach to the idea of the person, the series of his actions, nor the peculiarities of his character. A few fine passages from the poets (passages perhaps which derived their chief beauty from their position and connec-

---

[1] William Shakespeare (1564–1616), *Hamlet* (1601): I: iii: 55.

[†] An ingenious (and in many respects useful) French Treatise on Education, has too much encouraged this political piety; by sometimes considering religion as a thing of human convention; as a thing

creditable rather than commanded: by erecting the doctrine of expediency in the place of Christian simplicity; and wearing away the spirit of truth, by the substitution of occasional deceit, equivocation, subterfuge, and mental reservation.

tion) are huddled together by some extract-maker, whose brief and disconnected patches of broken and discordant materials, while they inflame young readers with the vanity of reciting, neither fill the mind nor form the taste: and it is not difficult to trace back to their shallow sources the hackney'd quotations of certain *accomplished* young ladies, who will be frequently found not to have come legitimately by any thing they know: I mean, not to have drawn it from its true spring, the original works of the author from which some *beauty-monger* has severed it. Human inconsistency in this, as in other cases, wants to combine two irreconcileable things; it strives to unite the reputation of knowledge with the pleasures of idleness, forgetting that nothing that is valuable can be obtained without sacrifices, and that if we would purchase knowledge we must pay for it the fair and lawful price of time and industry.

This remark is by no means of general application; there are many valuable works which from their bulk would be almost inaccessible to a great number of readers, and a considerable part of which may not be generally useful. Even in the best written books there is often superfluous matter; authors are apt to get enamoured of their subject, and to dwell too long on it: every person cannot find time to read a longer work on any subject, and yet it may be well for them to know something on almost every subject; those therefore, who abridge voluminous works judiciously, render service to the community. But there seems, if I may venture the remark, to be a mistake in the *use* of abridgments. They are put systematically into the hands of youth, who have, or ought to have leisure for the works at large; while abridgements seem more immediately calculated for persons in more advanced life, who wish to recal something they had forgotten; who want to restore old ideas rather than acquire new ones; or they are useful for persons immersed in the

business of the world who have little leisure for voluminous reading. They are excellent to refresh the mind, but not competent to form it.

Perhaps there is some analogy between the mental and bodily conformation of women. The instructor therefore should imitate the physician. If the latter prescribe bracing medicines for a body of which delicacy is the disease, the former would do well to prohibit relaxing reading for a mind which is already of too soft a texture, and should strengthen its feeble tone by invigorating reading.

By softness, I cannot be supposed to mean imbecility of understanding, but natural softness of heart, with that indolence of spirit which is fostered by indulging in seducing books and in the general habits of fashionable life.

I mean not here to recommend books which are immediately religious, but such as exercise the reasoning faculties, teach the mind to get acquainted with its own nature, and to stir up its own powers. Let not a timid young lady start if I should venture to recommend to her, after a proper course of preparation, to swallow and digest such strong meat, as Watt's or Duncan's little book of Logic, some parts of Mr. Locke's Essay on the Human Understanding, and Bishop Butler's Analogy.[1] Where there is leisure, and capacity, and an able counsellor, works of this nature might be profitably substituted in the place of so much English Sentiment, French Philosophy, Italian Poetry, and fantastic German imagery and magic wonders. While such enervating or absurd books sadly disqualify the reader for solid pursuit or vigorous thinking, the studies here recommended would act upon the constitution of the mind as a kind of

---

[1] Isaac Watt (1674–1748), author of *Logick; or the Right Use of Reason in the Enquiry after Truth* (1726); William Duncan (1717–60), author of *Cicero's Select Orations, The Elements of Logick* (1748); John Locke (1632–1704), author of *Essay Concerning Human Understanding* (1690); Bishop Joseph Butler (1692–1752), author of *The Analogy of Religion, Natural and Revealed* (1736).

alterative, and, if I may be allowed the expression, would help to brace the intellectual stamina.

This is however by no means intended to exclude works of taste and imagination, which must always make the ornamental part, and of course a very considerable part of female studies. It is only suggested that they should not form them entirely. For what is called dry tough reading, independent of the knowledge it conveys, is useful as an habit and wholesome as an exercise. Serious study serves to harden the mind for more trying conflicts; it lifts the reader from sensation to intellect; it abstracts her from the world and its vanities; it fixes a wandering spirit, and fortifies a weak one; it divorces her from matter; it corrects that spirit of trifling which she naturally contracts from the frivolous turn of female conversation, and the petty nature of female employment; it concentrates her attention, assists her in a habit of excluding trivial thoughts, and thus even helps to qualify her for religious pursuits. Yes; I repeat it, there is to woman a Christian use to be made of sober studies; while books of an opposite cast, however unexceptionable they may be sometimes found in point of expression; however free from evil in its more gross and palpable shapes, yet by their very nature and constitution they excite a spirit of relaxation, by exhibiting scenes and ideas which soften the mind; they impair its general powers of resistance, and at best feed habits of improper indulgence, and nourish a vain and visionary indolence, which lays the mind open to error and the heart to seduction.

Far be it from me to desire to make scholastic ladies or female dialecticians;[1] but there is little fear that the kind of books here recommended, if thoroughly studied, and not superficially skimmed, will make them pedants or induce conceit; for by shewing them the possible powers of the human mind, you will bring them to see the littleness of their own, and to get acquainted with the mind and to regulate it, does not seem the way to puff it up. But let her who is disposed to be elated with her literary acquisitions, check her vanity by calling to mind the just remark of Swift, "that after all her boasted acquirements, a woman will generally speaking, be found to possess less of what is called learning than a common school-boy."[2]

Neither is there any fear that this sort of reading will convert ladies into authors. The direct contrary effect will likely to be produced by the perusal of writers who throw the generality of readers at such an unapproachable distance. Who are those ever multiplying authors, that with unparalleled fecundity are overstocking the world with their quick succeeding progeny? They are novel writers; the easiness of whose productions is at once the cause of their own fruitfulness, and of the almost infinitely numerous race of imitators to whom they give birth. Such is the frightful facility of this species of composition, that every raw girl while she reads, is tempted to fancy that she can also write. And as Alexander,[3] on perusing the Iliad,[4] found by congenial sympathy the image of Achilles in his own ardent soul, and felt himself the hero he was studying; and as Corregio,[5] on first beholding a picture which exhibited the perfection of the Graphic art, prophetically felt all his own future greatness, and cried out in rapture, "And I too am a painter!" so a thorough paced novel reading Miss, at the close of every tissue of a hackney'd adventures, feels within herself the stirring impulse of corresponding genius, and triumphantly exclaims, "And I too am an author!" The glutted imagination soon overflows with the redundance of cheap sentiment and plenti-

---

[1] Masters of argument or disputation.

[2] "A Letter to a Very Young Lady on her Marriage," in Swift and Pope's *Miscellanies in Prose and Verse* (1735; 5 volumes, 1727–36).

[3] Alexander the Great (345–322 B.C.), king of Macedon.

[4] Greek epic poem attributed to Homer (c. 9th–8th century B.C.).

[5] Antonio Allegri da Correggio (1494–1534), an Italian painter.

ful incident, and by a sort of arithmetical proportion, is enabled by the perusal of any three novels to produce a fourth; till every fresh production, like the progeny of Banquo, is followed by

> Another, and another, and another! [†]

Is a lady, however destitute of talents, education, or knowledge of the world, whose studies have been completed by a circulating library, in any distress of mind? the writing a novel suggests itself as the best soother of her sorrows! Does she labour under any depression of circumstances? writing a novel occurs as the readiest receipt for mending them! And she solaces herself with the conviction that the subscription which has been given to her importunity or her necessities, has been given to her genius. And this confidence instantly levies a fresh contribution for a succeeding work. Capacity and cultivation are so little taken into the account, that writing a book seems to be now considered as the only sure resource which the idle and the illiterate have always in their power.

May I be indulged in a short digression to remark, though rather out of its place, that the corruption occasioned by these books has spread so wide, and descended so low, that not only among milleners,[1] mantua-makers,[2] and other trades where numbers work together, the labour of one girl is frequently sacrificed that she may be spared to read those mischievous books to the others; but the Author has been assured by clergymen, who have witnessed the fact, that they are procured and greedily read in the

wards of our Hospitals! an awful hint, that those who teach the poor to read, should not only take care to furnish them with principles which will lead them to abhor corrupt books, but should also furnish them with such books as shall strengthen and confirm their principles.[††]

(1799)

GENTLEMAN'S MAGAZINE
Letter: A Modern Requisite towards the Character of a Gentleman

MR. URBAN,   *Wells, Norfolk, Aug. 22.*

"Tu ne cede malis, sed contra audentior ito." [3] Æneid vi.

THE pursuits of men are constantly varying with the varying fashions of the times in which they live. In the days when the feudal spirit had possession of the public mind, it was deemed essential to the character of a *gentleman*, either to fight a duel, or to rescue a princess:—*now*, if he would appear with credit to the world, it is equally essential "to write a book."

This rule is so absolute as to admit few exceptions.—And this circumstance accounts, better than any apologies of the authors, for the many confused, incompetent, and ignorant works which we every day meet with.

When the French affairs were in a state of extreme

[†] It is surely not necessary to state, that no disrespect can be here intended to those females of real genius and correct character, some of whose justly admired writings in this kind, are accurate histories of life and manners, and striking delineations of character. It is not *their* fault if their works have been attended with the consequences which usually attend good originals, that of giving birth to a multitude of miserable imitations.

[1] One who makes or sells women's hats.

[2] One who makes women's cloaks.

[††] The above facts furnish no argument on the side of those who would keep the poor in ignorance. Those who cannot *read* can *hear*, and are likely to hear to worse purpose than those who have been better taught. And that ignorance furnishes no security for integrity either in morals or politics, the late revolts in more than one country, remarkable for the ignorance of the poor, fully illustrates. It is earnestly hoped that the above facts may tend to impress ladies with the importance of superintending the instruction of the poor, and of making it an indispensable part of their charity to give them moral and religious books.

[3] Though you do not wish to, proceed and go forth boldly. *Æneid* VI: 96.

depression, in consequence of an outrageous circulation of assignats; we are told, that the cry in the committees of finance was,—"issue more paper." —This issuing of more paper, to cure a redundancy of that article; without any *substratum* of public credit, was the warm water and bleeding, of the renowned Dr. Sangrado,[1] to an eptosciated patient.—The practice appears ridiculous to us I own: yet it is in strict conformity with an axiom of the healing art, which says,—"vomitus vomitu curatur."[2]

At present, if a man of fashion wish to distinguish himself,—*he writes a book.*—Should this fail, as it is odds but it do, he writes another; and then a third: still bearing in mind the maxim of the committee,—"issue more paper."

In a celebrated hunt in the interior of the kingdom it was customary with the members to suspend their determination about the merits of a newcomer, until they had put the preliminary question,—"how many horses does he keep?"—The same rule prevails, and with equal justice, in judging of an author,—How many books has he written? But though every man is, by the courtesy of the land, at liberty to write, provided he write nothing inconsistent with the safety of the Constitution; yet it has justly been observed, that there has never been discovered any secret to compel[†] men to *read.* This surely, Sir, is a great *desideratum* in literature.— Since, so far from any cordial friendship, such as might naturally be expected, between parties so correlative as writers, and readers, being observable; it is evident, that there has always been a constant warfare,—attended with no small degree of stratagem on each side.

The principals in this contest have, like the principals in most contests, taken certain coadjutors; who, though they at first appeared to act a secondary part in the affair, have ultimately had a very leading hand in determining the result.—The *authors* in alliance with the booksellers, avail themselves of the exterior recommendations of advertisements,— puffs,—vignettes,—title-pages,—superfine royal,— superb engravings, &c. &c.—while the *readers,* no less dexterous,—call in the assistance of indices,— extracts,—heads of chapters,—*converzationis*; and thus get the character of a book, and are enabled to quote from it, without the drudgery of perusal.

This superficial way of reading produces an equally superficial way of thinking. And thus men, becoming learned without labour, impose upon the multitude, and not unfrequently upon themselves. Confidence, where it is connected with splendid talents, is but the necessary consequence of comparison; and will often meet with indulgence from the world.—But the garb of wisdom, without the substance, cannot reasonably expect the same treatment.—It were, indeed, devoutly to be wished, that men of great talents,—would learn from the Apostle, "not to think of themselves more highly than they ought to think, but to think soberly."[3]—Yet a competent opinion of their own merits, or, as the Irishman calls it, a modest assurance, is a virtue in which the wits of each hemisphere of time have never been deficient.

Yours, &c.   AUSONIUS[4]

(1799)

---

[1] In the French picaresque novel *Gil Blas* (1715) by Alain-Rene Le Sage (1668–1747), Dr. Sangrado insists that blood is not necessary for life, and that hot water can not be administered too plentifully into the system.

[2] Vomit attends to vomit.

[†] If any person has discovered this secret, it must be our friend, Mr. Urban; who gives monthly to the publick,—a journal, at once literary, moral, and entertaining.

[3] Paul in Romans 12:3.

[4] Dicimus Magmus Ausonius. (*c.* 310–93). The most famous of the learned poets in the second half of the fourth century.

ANNA LETITIA BARBAULD[1]
*On the Origin and Progress of
Novel-Writing*

A COLLECTION of Novels has a better chance of giving pleasure than of commanding respect. Books of this description are condemned by the grave, and despised by the fastidious; but their leaves are seldom found unopened, and they occupy the parlour and the dressing-room while productions of higher name are often gathering dust upon the shelf. It might not perhaps be difficult to show that this species of composition is entitled to a higher rank than has been generally assigned it. Fictitious adventures, in one form or other, have made a part of the polite literature of every age and nation. These have been grafted upon the actions of their heroes; they have been interwoven with their mythology; they have been moulded upon the manners of the age,—and, in return, have influenced the manners of the succeeding generation by the sentiments they have infused and the sensibilities they have excited.

If the end and object of this species of writing be asked, many no doubt will be ready to tell us that its object is,—to call in fancy to the aid of reason, to deceive the mind into embracing truth under the guise of fiction:

> *Cosi a l'egro fanciul porgiamo aspersi*
> *Di soave licor gli orli del vaso,*
> *Succhi amari, ingannato in tanto ei beve,*
> *E da l' inganno suo vita riceve.* [2]

---

[1] Anna Letitia Barbauld (1743–1825), a prominent essayist, editor, poet, and author of children's books. In 1810 she edited a 50 volume edition of *The British Novelists*. This passage is from the edition's introduction.

[2] Torquato Tasso, (1544–96), poet and dramatist. *Gerusalemme Liberata* (Jerusalem Delivered) (1575): "So when the draught we give to the sick child,/ The vessel's edge we touch with syrup sweet;/ Cheated, he swift drinks down the bitter brew,/ And from the cheat receives his life anew."

with such-like reasons equally grave and dignified. For my own part, I scruple not to confess that, when I take up a novel, my end and object is entertainment; and as I suspect that to be the case with most readers, I hesitate not to say that entertainment is their legitimate end and object. To read the productions of wit and genius is a very high pleasure to all persons of taste, and the avidity with which they are read by all such shows sufficiently that they are calculated to answer this end. Reading is the cheapest of pleasures: it is a domestic pleasure. Dramatic exhibitions give a more poignant delight, but they are seldom enjoyed in perfection, and never without expense and trouble. Poetry requires in the reader a certain elevation of mind and a practiced ear. It is seldom relished unless a taste be formed for it pretty early. But the humble novel is always ready to enliven the gloom of solitude, to soothe the languor of debility and disease, to win the attention from pain or vexatious occurrences, to take man from himself, (at many seasons the worst company he can be in,) and, while the moving picture of life passes before him, to make him forget the subject of his own complaints. It is pleasant to the mind to sport in the boundless regions of possibility; to find relief from the sameness of every-day occurrences by expatiating amidst brighter skies and fairer fields; to exhibit love that is always happy, valour that is always successful; to feed the appetite for wonder by a quick succession of marvelous events; and to distribute, like a ruling providence, rewards and punishments which fall just where they ought to fall.

It is sufficient therefore, as an end, that these writings add to the innocent pleasures of life; and if they do no harm, the entertainment they give is a sufficient good. We cut down the tree that bears no fruit, but we ask nothing of a flower beyond its scent and its colour. The unpardonable sin in a novel is dullness: however grave or wise it may be, if its author possesses no powers of amusing, he has no business to write novels; he should employ his pen in some more serious part of literature.

(1810)

MONTHLY MAGAZINE
On Reading New Books [1]

"And what of this new book, that the whole world make such a rout about?"—STERNE.

I CANNOT understand the rage manifested by the greater part of the world for reading New Books. If the public had read all those that have gone before, I can conceive how they should not wish to read the same work twice over; but when I consider the countless volumes that lie unopened, unregarded, unread, and unthought-of, I cannot enter into the pathetic complaints that I hear made, that Sir Walter writes no more—that the press is idle—that Lord Byron is dead. If I have not read a book before, it is, to all intents and purposes, new to me, whether it was printed yesterday or three hundred years ago. If it be urged that it has no modern, passing incidents, and is out of date and old-fashioned, then it is so much the newer; it is farther removed from other works that I have lately read, from the familiar routine of ordinary life, and makes so much more addition to my knowledge. But many people would as soon think of putting on old armour, as of taking up a book not published within the last month, or year at the utmost. There is a fashion in reading as well as in dress, which lasts only for the season. One would imagine that books were, like women, the worse for being old;[†] that they have a pleasure in being read for the first time; that they open their leaves more cordially; that the spirit of enjoyment wears out with the spirit of novelty; and that, after a certain age, it is high time to put them on the shelf. This conceit seems to be followed up in practice. What is it to me that another—that hundreds or thousands have in all ages read a work? Is it on this account the less likely to give me pleasure, because it has delighted so many others? Or can I taste this pleasure by proxy? Or am I in any degree the wiser for their knowledge? Yet this might appear to be the inference. *Their* having read the work may be said to act upon us by sympathy, and the knowledge which so many other persons have of its contents deadens our curiosity and interest altogether. We set aside the subject as one on which others have made up their minds for us (as if we really could have ideas in their heads), and are quite on the alert for the next new work, teeming hot from the press, which we shall be the first to read, criticise, and pass an opinion on. Oh, delightful! To cut open the leaves, to inhale the fragrance of the scarcely dry paper, to examine the type, to see who is the printer (which is some clue to the value that is set upon the work), to launch out into regions of thought and invention never trod till now, and to explore characters that never met a human eye before—this is a luxury worth sacrificing a dinner-party, or a few hours of a spare morning to. Who, indeed, when the work is critical and full of expectation, would venture to dine out, or to face a coterie of blue-stockings[2] in the evening, without having gone through this ordeal, or at least without hastily turning over a few of the first pages, while dressing, to be able to say that the beginning does not promise much, or to tell the name of the heroine?

---

[1] This article appeared in the *Monthly Magazine* signed with William Hazlitt's initials. William Hazlitt (1778–1830) was a leading essayist in the period known for his critical work on literature and the fine arts, social and autobiographical reflections, and for his radical political sympathies.

[†] "Laws are not like women, the worse for being old."—*The Duke of Buckingham's Speech in the House of Lords, in Charles the Second's Time.*

---

[2] An informal group of women intellectuals committed to the eighteenth-century ideal of polite conversation. It was frequently the target of misogynist critiques of ambitious literary women.

Books have been so multiplied in our days (like the Vanity Fair of knowledge[1]), and we have made such progress beyond ourselves in some points, that it seems at first glance as if we had monopolised every possible advantage, and the rest of the world must be left destitute and in darkness. This is the *cockneyism* (with leave be it spoken) of the nineteenth century. We must always make some allowance for a change of style, which those who are accustomed to read none but works written within the last twenty years neither can nor will make. When a whole generation read, they will read none but contemporary productions. The taste for literature becomes superficial, as it becomes universal and is spread over a larger space. When ten thousand boarding-school girls, who have learnt to play on the harpsichord, are brought out in the same season, Rossini[2] will be preferred to Mozart,[3] as the last new composer. Is it not provoking with us to see the *Beggar's Opera*[5] cut down to two acts, because some of the allusions are too broad, and others not understood? And in America—that Van Diemen's Land of letters[5]—this sterling satire is hooted off the stage, because fortunately they have no such state of manners as it describes before their eyes; and because, unfortunately, they have no conception of any thing but what they see. America is singularly and awkwardly situated in this respect. It is a new country with an old language; and while every thing about them is of a day's growth, they are constantly applying to us to know what to think of it, and taking their opinions from our books and newspapers with a strange mixture of servility and of the spirit of contradiction. They are an independent state in politics: in literature they are still a colony from us—not out of their leading strings, and strangely puzzled how to determine between the Edinburgh and Quarterly Reviews. We have naturalised some of their writers, who had formed themselves upon us. This is at once a compliment to them and to ourselves. Amidst the scramble and lottery for fame in the present day, besides puffing,[6] which may be regarded as the hot-bed of reputation, another mode has been attempted by *transplanting* it; and writers who are set down as drivellers at home, shoot up great authors on the other side of the water; pack up their all—a title-page and sufficient impudence; and a work, of which *the flocci-nauci-nihili-pili-fication*, in Shenstone's phrase,[7] is well known to every competent judge, is *placarded* into eminence, and "flames in the forehead of the morning sky"[8] on the walls of Paris or St. Petersburgh. Some reputations last only while the possessors live, from which one might suppose that they gave themselves a character for genius: others are cried up by their gossiping acquaintances, as long as they give dinners, and make their houses

---

[1] In Paul Bunyan's *Pilgrim's Progress* (1678), a fair that goes on perpetually in the town of Vanity and symbolizes worldly ostentation and frivolity. Hazlitt's reference reflects the opinion, common in the period, that too great a stress on the importance of learning had reduced it to an empty pose that was made still worse by the endless numbers of new books being published.

[2] Gioacchino Antonio Rossini (1792–1868), Italian operatic composer best known for *The Barber of Seville* (1816).

[3] Wolfgang Amadeus Mozart (1756–91), Austrian composer and pianist. Despite some critics' appreciation of Mozart's artistic genius, his work attracted limited interest in English theatres during the period.

[4] A musical play by John Gay, first produced in 1728, written partly in response to Jonathon Swift's suggestion that a Newgate pastoral "might make an odd pretty sort of thing."

[5] Now called Tasmania, Van Diemen's Land was synonymous for many British with primitive or uncivilized wilderness.

[6] Strategically arranged positive reviews.

[7] The trivialization. From the correspondence of the poet William Shenstone (1714–63). The phrase, which Shenstone used again in a subsequent publication, was popular with romantic writers such as William Hazlitt, Charles Lamb, and Walter Scott, all of whom used it. The phrase is based on the words, "Flocci, nauci, nihili, pili," which formed the beginning of a rule in old Latin grammar textbooks which brings together a number of words meaning "of no account."

[8] John Milton (1608–1674), *Lycidas* (1637): 171.

places of polite resort; and, in general, in our time, a book may be considered to have passed the ordeal that is mentioned at all three months after it is printed. Immortality is not even a dream a boy's conceit; and posthumous fame is no more regarded by the author than by his bookseller.[†]

This idle, dissipated turn seems to be a set-off to, or the obvious reaction of, the exclusive admiration of the ancients, which was formerly the fashion; as if the sum of human intellect rose and set at Rome and Athens, and the mind of man had never exerted itself to any purpose since. The ignorant, as well as the adept, were charmed only with what was obsolete and far-fetched, wrapped up in technical terms and in a learned tongue. Those who spoke and wrote a language which hardly any one at present even understood, must of course be wiser than we. Time, that brings so many reputations to decay, had embalmed others and rendered them sacred. From an implicit faith and overstrained homage paid to antiquity, we of the modern school have taken too strong a bias to what is new; and divide all wisdom and worth between ourselves and posterity,—not a very formidable rival to our self-love, as we attribute all its advantages to ourselves, though we pretend to owe little or nothing to our predecessors. About the time of the French Revolution, it was agreed that the world had hitherto been in its dotage or its infancy; and that Mr. Godwin, Condorcet, and others were to begin a new race of men—a new epoch in society.[1] Every thing up to

that period was to be set aside as puerile or barbarous; or, if there were any traces of thought and manliness now and then discoverable, they were to be regarded with wonder as prodigies—as irregular and fitful starts in that long sleep of reason and night of philosophy. In this liberal spirit Mr. Godwin composed an Essay, to prove that, till the publication of *The Enquiry concerning Political Justice*, no one knew how to write a word of common grammar, or a style that was not utterly uncouth, incongruous, and feeble.[2] Addison, Swift, and Junius[3] were included in this censure. The English language itself might be supposed to owe its stability and consistency, its roundness and polish, to the whirling motion of the French Revolution. Those who had gone before us were, like our grandfathers and grandmothers, decrepit, superannuated people, blind and dull; poor creatures, like flies in winter, without pith or marrow in them. The past was barren of interest—had neither thought nor object worthy to arrest our attention; and the future would be equally a senseless void, except as we projected ourselves and our theories

---

[†] When a certain poet was asked if he thought Lord Byron's name would live three years after he was dead, he answered, "Not three days, Sir!" This was premature: it has lasted above a year. His works have been translated into French, and there is a *Caffé Byron* on the Boulevards. Think of a *Caffé Wordsworth* on the Boulevards!

[1] William Godwin (1756–1836), was the most prominent of middle-class reformers, famous for his philosophical vision of social change in *An Enquiry concerning Political Justice, and its Influence on General Virtue and Happiness* (1793), for his political thriller novel *Caleb Williams* (1794) and for other more journalistic efforts in the cause of reform; Jean Antoine Nicolas Caritat Condorcet (1743–94), a leading

member of a group known as the philosophes in France. Many linked their religious scepticism and commitment to rational enquiry to the late-eighteenth-century crisis of cultural fragmentation that helped to precipitate the French Revolution.

[2] In a seven-part essay at the end of *The Enquirer* (1797), Godwin attempted to demonstrate that "the English language was never in so high a state of purity and perfection, as in the present reign of king George the third," in part by demonstrating "the bad taste which displays itself in the phrases of the old writers."

[3] Joseph Addison (1672–1719), best known for his contributions to Sir Richard Steele's *Tatler* in 1709–11 and collaboration with Steele on the *Spectator* in 1711–12. Addison was closely associated with the Whig party; Jonathan Swift (1667–1745), a leading member of what by the Romantic period had already become known as the Augustan writers in the early eighteenth century. Author of *Gulliver's Travels* (1726) and various satirical pieces such as *The Battle of the Books* (written in 1697 and published in 1704) and *A Modest Proposal for Preventing the Children of Poor People from being a Burden to their Parents or the Country* (1729); Junius, the pseudonym of the author of a series of radical pamphlets that appeared in the *Public Advertiser* from 1769–1771.

into it. There is nothing I hate more than I do this exclusive, upstart spirit.

If, with the diffusion of knowledge, we do not gain an enlargement and elevation of views, where is the benefit? If, by tearing asunder names from things, we do not leave even the name or shadow of excellence, it is better to let them remain as they were; for it is better to have something to admire than nothing—names, if not things—the shadow, if not the substance—the tinsel, if not the gold. All can now read and write equally; and, it is therefore presumed, equally well. Any thing short of this sweeping conclusion is an invidious distinction; and those who claim it for themselves or others are *exclusionists* in letters. Every one at least can call names—can invent a falsehood, or repeat a story against those who have galled their pragmatical pretensions by really adding to the stock of general amusement or instruction. Every one in a crowd has the power to throw dirt: nine out of ten have the inclination. It is curious that, in an age when the most universally-admitted claim to public distinction is literary merit, the attaining this distinction is almost a sure title to public contempt and obloquy.[†] They cry you up, because you are unknown, and do not excite their jealousy; and run you down, when they have thus distinguished you, out of envy and spleen at the very idol they have set up. A public favourite is "kept like an apple in the jaw of an ape—first mouthed, to be afterwards swallowed. When they need what you have gleaned, it is but squeezing you, and spunge, you shall be dry again."[1] At first they think only of the pleasure or advantage they receive: but, on reflection, they are mortified at

the superiority implied in this involuntary concession, and are determined to be even with you the very first opportunity. What is the prevailing spirit of modern literature? To defame men of letters. What are the publications that succeed? Those that pretend to teach the public that the persons they have been accustomed unwittingly to look up to as the lights of the earth are no better than themselves, or a set of vagabonds or miscreants that should be hunted out of society.[††] Hence men of letters, losing their self-respect, become government-tools, and prostitute their talents to the most infamous purposes, or turn *dandy*[2] *scribblers*, and set up for gentlemen authors in their own defence.

(1827)

[†] Is not this partly owing to the disappointment of the public at finding any defect in their idol?

[1] William Shakespeare (1566–1616), *Hamlet* (1600): IV: ii: 16–19.

[††] An old friend of mine, when he read the abuse and billingsgate poured out in certain Tory publications, used to congratulate himself upon it as a favourable sign of the times, and of the progressive improvement of our manners. Where we now called names, we formerly burnt each other at the stake; and all the malice of the heart flew to the tongue and vented itself in scolding, instead of crusades and *auto-da-fés*—the nobler revenge of our ancestors for a difference of opinion. An author now libels a prince; and, if he takes the law of him or throws him into gaol, it is looked upon as a harsh and ungentlemanly proceeding. He, therefore, gets a dirty Secretary to employ a dirty bookseller, to hire a set of dirty scribblers, to pelt him with dirt and cover him with blackguard epithets—till he is hardly in a condition to walk the streets. This is a hard measure, no doubt, and base ingratitude on the part of the public, according to the imaginary dignity and natural precedence which authors take of kings; but the latter are men, and will have their revenge where they can get it. They have no longer their old summary appeal—their will may still be good—to the dungeon and the dagger. Those who "speak even of dignities" may, therefore, think themselves well off in being merely *sent to Coventry*; and, besides, if they have *pluck*, they can make a Parthian retreat, and shoot poisoned arrows behind them. The good people of Florence lift up their hands when they are shewn the caricatures in the Queen's Matrimonial Ladder and ask if they are really a likeness of the king?

[2] A man who is excessively interested in cultivating a fashionable appearance.

SECTION SIX

The Arts and Sciences

Like the word "literature," the word "science" was used in the Romantic period in a range of ways that are sometimes at odds with our current sense of it. Recognizing these confusions between inherited and emergent assumptions about science, especially as it related to literature or more broadly, "the arts," is crucial to any understanding of these historically-defined fields. This section opens with nine brief extracts that illustrate some of these various nuances. In many ways, the issue was the extent of common ground or difference between the various intellectual fields, or the division of knowledge between what we refer to today as the disciplines. Sometimes, as with the *Monthly Review*'s account of John Pinkerton's *An Inquiry into the History of Scotland* or James Lackington's description of his self-education, "science" and "literature" were used interchangeably to refer to the pursuit of knowledge. The *Gentleman's Magazine* blurred the categories in a different way in their review of Sheridan and Henderson's *Practical Method of Reading and Reciting* English *Poetry*, by combining process and content in their reference to "that most important science, the art of reading." The *Monthly Magazine*'s obituary for Samuel Paterson fused the two in yet another way, lauding Paterson's groundbreaking efforts in "the science of literary history, and the art of bibliography," or the arrangement of the different fields of knowledge within some larger domain known as literature. At other times, as in the *Gentleman Magazine*'s 1795 Preface or the Preface to the *Encyclopedia Britannica*, "Science" and "the Arts" were referred to in ways that reflect our modern sense of the divide between these domains. The choice was not always clearly one or the other. The *British Critic*'s reference to "almost every branch of science and literature," in their review of James Pettit Andrews's *History of Great Britain,* suggested no stable sense of either the distance or proximity between the two words (though, the review implies, they were both connected to the field of history writing). In part, these categorical confusions reflected the social conditions of scientific enquiry in the period. The more illustrious works associated with the Royal Society were complemented by the industrious effort of endless other formal and informal societies, such as the Society for the Encouragement of Arts, Commerce, and Manufactures in Great Britain, and the Birmingham Lunar Society, in which intellectuals such as Joseph Priestley, Thomas Beddoes, and Erasmus Darwin mixed with pioneer industrialists such as Josiah Wedgwood, Matthew Boulton, and James Watt, the inventor of the modern steam engine. These contexts encouraged a range of connected enquiries rather than emphasizing their distinction, and grounded them in a confident sense of the commercial context within which they would become valuable.

Elsewhere, the question had less to do with disciplinary divisions, or the relation between science and literature as categories, than with the particular qualities that were attributed to science. Because of the reformist overtones of the eighteenth-century celebration of knowledge as power, discussions of science were inevitably bound up with the political debates that intensified after the outbreak of the French Revolution. Whereas the 1795 Preface in the *Gentleman's Magazine* characterized the intellectual world as a redemptive community of kindred souls engaged in a shared pursuit of knowledge that transcended factional divides, Joseph Priestley, in *Experiments and Observations on Air*, equated science with the progress of knowledge in an overtly politicized way. Like William Godwin's description of literature, Priestley offered a dynamic vision of an ever-expanding and necessarily incomplete body of knowledge fueled by intellectual exchange that would not be limited to discreet disciplinary categories. Priestley insisted that this inexorable and increasingly rapid progress of knowledge would inevitably extend to political debates as well—a thinly veiled radical democratic manifesto. These overt political suggestions were characteristic of the often avowedly political and egalitarian sympathies which character-ized Britain's complex provincial scientific world.

Often, the pursuit of new forms of knowledge went hand in hand with the exploration of previously unexamined regions. Captain James Cook's journeys, particularly in the South Seas, were a widely noted example. As the Preface to *Dissertations and Miscellaneous Pieces relating to the History and Antiquities, the Arts, Sciences, and Literature, of Asia* suggests, this pursuit of knowledge beyond Britain's borders was celebrated in overtly political ways as an endeavour that would simultaneously dignify Britain's imperial activities and "spread the advantages of knowledge through a region" that had previously been deprived of these advantages. This celebration of the prepolitical world of learning as a domain that transcended national borders provided an especially appealing counterbalance to the age's intense ethical debates about Britain's growing presence in India.

The spectres of imperial aggression abroad and Jacobin revolution at home were not the only controversies haunting science. Discussions of the social nature of the pursuit and dissemination of knowledge inevitably fueled tensions between an Enlightenment desire to promote the circulation of new ideas, and fears that unprincipled researchers and undereducated audiences would combine to subdue genuine intellectual pursuits. Two reviews in the *Monthly Review* reflect this tension. In its discussion of "the delicate art of Dyeing," the *Monthly* rejected the isolationist tendencies of "antient" scientists who "shrunk from the contamination of plebeian approach" in favour of modern science's immersion in "the active scenes of life." But in its discussion of animal magnetism, the *Monthly* was equally wary of the possibility that the rigorous work of respectable scientists was being drowned out by the carnivalesque excesses of a culture besotted with the "*ignus fatuus*" of intellectual charlatans.

Erasmus Darwin's poem, *The Loves of the Plants*, was viewed with political suspicion, not because of any particular political views that it espoused, but because the sexually liberated and polygamous world it presented in its description of various plants seemed to promote a community freed from the traditional restraints of social decorum. It was a threatening gesture that drew predictably hostile responses. *The Anti Jacobin, or Weekly Examiner*, parodied Darwin's poem with its *Love of Triangles*. In his conservative polemic, *The Unsex'd Females*, Richard Polwhele defended the literary excellence of Darwin's "admirable poem," but he nonetheless warned that "Botany has lately become a fashionable amusement with the ladies. But how the study of the sexual system of plants can accord with female modesty, I am not able to comprehend." Nor was it just the ladies. Polwhele expressed disgust with the fact that "I have, several times, seen boys and girls botanizing together."

Humphry Davy's message was as politically conservative as Priestley's was radical, but his arguments here are even more revealing in their dialogue with Wordsworth's comments in his Preface to the *Lyrical Ballads*. Davy and Wordsworth were both engaged in establishing the cultural authority of their particular discipline. Ironically, and perhaps because of this, the two men ended up making almost identical claims about the universality and the particular relevance of their chosen field. In his *A Discourse Introductory to a Course of Lectures on Chemistry*, Davy insisted that chemistry was important because of both its range and immediacy: it "has for its objects all the substances found upon our globe," but it was also connected to "the processes and operations of common life." For Wordsworth, it was the other way around: "the man of science seeks truth as a remote and unknown benefactor," whereas the poet "rejoices in the presence of truth as our visible friend and hourly companion." What they all agreed upon was, in Davy's words, the central role "of the invention of printing" in promoting "the diffusion of knowledge."

ↄ҉ↄↄ

MONTHLY REVIEW
Review of *An Inquiry into the History of Scotland Preceding the Reign of Malcolm III or the Year 1056*. By John Pinkerton.[1]

IN the acquisition of knowledge, the human mind generally takes great delight, as men of letters, from their own experience, will readily admit: but, as it is not in the power of any individual to investigate, deeply, every branch of literature, it is natural for a lover of knowledge, gladly to avail himself of the labours of others who have cultivated those branches of science which he has not, perhaps, had leisure to study.

On these principles, we rejoiced to see the present work announced to the public; as it professed to investigate an important subject, which has long been involved in great obscurity; and we took

---

[1] John Pickerton (1758–1826), Scottish antiquary and historian.

the earliest opportunity of perusing it with attention:—nor were we so far disgusted at the rude and inelegant manner of this author, as to throw aside the book: we were willing to overlook these imperfections, from the expectation of benefitting by the useful information which we hoped to obtain. Though we have not been *entirely* disappointed in this respect, yet, on finishing the perusal of this Inquiry, we are forced to say, that the labour of wading through such a chaos has not been fully compensated by the portion of real and useful knowledge which we have been able to collect.

"It is much to be lamented, that accuracy and penetration are so rare in works written upon antiquarian subjects. In every country, if the most foolish books were to be named, it is believed that the antiquarian class would be immediately condescended on. One would imagine that, in such subjects, quite a different mode of reasoning is allowed, than is employed in treating any other branch of science. Instead of facts, we find mere imagination; instead of argument, only groundless conjecture, supported by such incoherent and inconclusive sophistry, as must argue a deranged understanding, if exerted on any other literary department."

These are the words of Mr. Pinkerton; and we are sorry to admit that there is some truth in the observation; and are still more concerned to be obliged, as we are, for the sake of truth, to allow, that the present work can scarcely be admitted as an exception to it.

(1790)

JAMES LACKINGTON
Memoirs of the First Forty-Five Years of the Life of James Lackington [1]

MY friend Mr. Jones was my secretary, who before I came to live with him had not the least relish for books, and I had only read a few enthusiastic authors, together with Pomfret's poems;[2] these last I could almost repeat by memory; however, I made the most of my little stock of literature, and strongly recommended the purchasing of Books to Mr. Jones. But so ignorant were we on the subject, that neither of us knew what books were fit for our perusal, nor what to enquire for, as we had scarce ever heard or seen even any *title pages*, except a few of the religious sort, which at that time we had no relish for. So that we were at a loss how to encrease our small stock of science.

(1791; 1792)

BRITISH CRITIC
Review of *The History of Great Britain, Connected with the Chronology of Europe: With Notes,&c. containing Anecdotes of the Times, Lives of the Learned, and Specimens of their Works. Vol. I. From Caesar's Invasion to the Deposition and Death of Richard II.*
By James Pettit Andrews, F.A.S.[3]

IT is not necessary at this time of day to assert, that, in almost every branch of science and literature, the industry and abilities of our countrymen have rendered themselves conspicuous. The fact is

---

[1] James Lackington (1746–1815), a self-educated bookseller famous for his innovative commercial practices, including his commitment to selling at the cheapest possible price.

[2] John Pomfret (1667–1702), best remembered for his poem *The Choice* (1700), which extolled the virtues of a quiet country estate.

[3] James Petit Andrews (1737?–97), an antiquary and historian.

allowed, even by those not generally disposed to praise us. In the branch of national history, activity has been so far from deficient, that a laborious enquirer, whom we are happy to call our friend, has been able to enumerate near three thousand volumes, which relate, directly or indirectly, to that subject. That in this number there is no one general history of the country which in all respects deserves approbation, may seem extraordinary, yet it is true. The faults of Rapin[1] and his continuator are well known. Hume,[2] in the early periods, is remarkably deficient; in the latter, not impartial; and the spirit of irreligion, which even here appears occasionally, is such that they who feel the importance of sacred truths, can neither peruse his work with pleasure, nor unequivocally commend it with honesty. Mr. Andrews has written annals of England, accompanied by chronological notices of other countries, in a form entirely new. Most convenient for reference, and well calculated to aid and impress the memory of the young student. He has supplied the lecturer with a most valuable text-book, the historian with an excellent book of reference, the man of literary leisure with a rational and instructive amusement, and even the indolent with a copious store of lively and uncommon anecdote, and matters of various curiosity, diligently collected, and pleasingly delivered.

(1794)

---

[1] Paul de Rapin (1661–1725), whose *History of England* was translated into English by Ralph Tindal, who published a two volume "Continuation after Rapin's death.

[2] David Hume (1711–76), philosopher, essayist, and author of *History of Great Britain* (1754–62).

Gentleman's Magazine
Review of Sheridan and Henderson's
Practical Method of Reading and Reciting English *Poetry; designed as an Introduction to Dr.* Enfield's *"Speaker."*

IT is much to be lamented that greater pains are not bestowed, in our public schools and seminaries, with respect to that most important science the art of reading. To those young gentlemen destined for the pulpit or the bar it is of infinite importance. It is especially required in a *clergyman* that he should read well; and not a little injury has been done to the cause of Religion by the drawling, miserable, school-boy manner in which the lessons are read, the prayers recited, and the sermons delivered, by too many of the Clergy. We heartily wish (though utter enemies to what some call reformation) for a reformation on *this point*. A minister who reads with perspicuity, elegance, and grace, will ever be popular, and, consequently, will have his sphere of usefulness widely extended.

(1798)

Monthly Magazine
A Tribute to the Memory of the Late Excellent and Celebrated Bibliographer, Mr. Samuel Paterson[3]

IN order to give a satisfactory account of Mr. Paterson's merit as a bibliographer, a short digression on the progress and state of the theoretical and practical part of such learned avocations, during the two preceding generations appears necessary. Our readers may thereby form an opinion of the several

---

[3] Samuel Paterson (1725–1802). Initially unsuccessful as a bookseller and then auctioneer, Paterson gained more renown as a bibliographer or theorist of the arrangement of books and, by extension, the organization of knowledge itself.

gradations in which he found, he established, and he left the science of literary history, and the art of bibliography.

The knowledge of bibliography and literary history bears, perhaps, the most recent date, in the annals of the human mind: it is the happy result of those persevering inquiries into the intellectual and active powers of man, through which we have been able to refer to their common stock, and to trace back to their root the manifold, diverging, and apparently unconnected branches of the tree of knowledge; and it is also the immediate consequence of that overgrowing and amazing scientific wealth, from which we have endeavoured to take the most valuable materials, and the most conducive method, for our exertions and improvement. It must, however, be acknowledged that no regular work, nor any detailed precept was ever given, to forward these pursuits, by the eminent metaphysicians of the last century, notwithstanding the early advice of Sir Francis Bacon;[1] that the bibliographical science, like most others, has an accidental and rather obscure origin; that neither England nor France, nor any other country, justly considered as the native seat of genius, had issued a publication of the kind; and that the ultimate fame for the introduction of this new branch of studies must be ascribed to a nation rather noted for want of brilliant talents. In fact, the first man who attempted to give a sketch of universal bibliography was the learned and laborious Christopher Augustus Hermann, Professor in the University of Gottingen, in 1718. He then published his known work— "Conspectus Republicae Literariae, sive Via ad Historiam Literariam,"[2] which gradually went through seven editions, the last of which was published in Han-

over, in 1763. Numberless other works, analogous to this, were published in the same interval, in Germany, which it is unnecessary to mention in this article.

No sooner had this swarm of laborious *eruditi* paved the way to the knowledge of authors and books, and opened this new field of scientific pursuits, than it became an additional acquisition to the philosophy of the age. It was duly experienced that the detailed notice of the gradual steps of our predecessors, in the several departments of knowledge, was necessary to carry into execution the precept of Lord Verulam, to teach sciences historically; how this preliminary knowledge might enable the inquirers, to ascertain the precise point from which they should begin their course; how an exact partition of labour, and a convenient method of classification, could assist the powers of judgement and of memory; and how this very method of classification might be subservient to the arrangement of a library, or, in other words, to the regular and local disposition of objects that are the occasion of our ideas, and give a fuller scope to our faculties.

This was the progress and the state of bibliographical knowledge, when Mr. Paterson entered upon the profession of it. His superior talents, already assisted by a proportionate practice, soon enabled him to judge of what had hitherto been done in the historical and systematical part of these pursuits, to imagine what still remained to be done in either way, and to adopt the best practical principles for the conduct of his avocations. He regretted that no system of universal bibliography and literary history had ever been exhibited since the attempt of Professor Hermann, except perhaps the Sketch late given by Dr. Meusel, in Germany.[3] He was aware that a work of this kind, capable of representing in one point of view the intellectual pursuits of several

---

[1] Francis Bacon (1561–1626), author of *The Advancement of Learning* (1605) which divided knowledge into three fields: history, poetry and philosophy. In 1618 he became Lord Veralum.

[2] *Survey of the Republic of Letters, Or the Way to a History of Literature.*

[3] Dr. Meusel (1749–1807), *Philosophische and Kritische Untersuchungen über das Alte testament und dessen Göttlichkeit, besonders über die Mosaiche Religion* (1785).

nations, and of an infinite number of individuals in every age to connect the scientific annals of each generation with their proper links; to notice in their due times, place and gradation, all the names who have gradually contributed to the improvement of the human mind, and to describe every publication, with the circumstances by which it was attended, would be utterly impossible for any one man to execute—impossible, even if the writer should possess all the mental powers in the highest degree of perfection. The learning of Selden,[1] and the genius of Bacon, combined together, would prove unequal to the task. And he was wont to repeat on the subject the proverbial expression of Struvius, that "it would be easier to remove the mountain Atlas than to compose an universal literary history."[2] The impossibility however of performing a complete work of this kind was not with him a reason why nothing should be undertaken towards effecting the purpose, if not by one man, at least by a society of men. Any partial and inadequate performance was, in his opinion, better than an utter destitution!

(1803)

Encyclopaedia Britannica
Or, a Dictionary of Arts, Sciences, and Miscellaneous Literature; Enlarged and Improved. The Fourth Edition.[3]

Preface

IN the present improved state of science, of literature, and of all those arts which are connected with the progress and improvement of society, it is surely unnecessary to dwell on the importance of a work, the chief object of which is to exhibit a view of those great and interesting subjects. If science, while its beneficial influence is felt in all the common pursuits of life, affords scope at the same time to the greatest exertions of human genius; if literature is both the delight and ornament of those by whom it is cultivated; and if history, by bringing under our review the great course of human affairs, enables us to draw lessons for our future conduct from the unerring experience of the past, there can be no question as to the importance of a work comprising so many objects of deep and general interest to mankind. It deserves also to be remarked, that many of those great discoveries which have effected a revolution in science, and which have gradually introduced the most striking changes into the affairs of the world, have been the fruit not of accident, but of the most painful and abstruse inquiries; and that the great powers of invention and genius necessary to explore those intricate paths, do not by any means imply the same capacity of plain and familiar illustration;—those who possess those rare endowments being, on the contrary, rather averse to waste their precious talents on what appears to them to be the natural employment of more ordinary minds. It is hardly necessary, however, to point out to the reader how greatly the cause of philosophy must be promoted, when its important truths, in place of being confined to the speculative few, are expounded in popular works, and in this manner diffused among all classes of the community, so as to be the common topics of men's discourse,—thus adding to their innocent and laudable recreations, and setting to work at the same time, in the cause of literature and science, an additional stock of talent and exertion. Such being the obvious advantages arising from a well-digested account of Science, of Literature, and of General History, we shall not enlarge farther on the utility of the present work. As in such an undertaking,

[1] John Seldon (1584–1654), an eminent lawyer and man of letters.
[2] Burcardos Gottholdus Struvius (1671–1738), historian of philosophy and jurisprudence.
[3] The *Encyclopaedia Brittanica* began publication in sixpenny parts in 1760 and was released as a three volume edition in 1771.

however, the execution is of as much importance as the plan, we shall endeavour, as shortly as possible, to satisfy the reader that, in that particular, no pains nor expence have been spared to render the present edition as perfect as possible, and to give it a fair claim to that share of popularity and reputation, so amply enjoyed by the ENCYCLOPÆDIA BRITAN-NICA from the first moment of its publication.

In so complicated a work, it is obviously of infinite importance to preserve a clear and accurate arrangement, so as to give unity and consistency to its various parts; for it is evident that, without constant attention to method and order, such a work may be rendered in a great measure useless: and though it may still be an immense and valuable register of knowledge, the reader may search through its pages without any clue to guide him to the object of his inquiries. It is in this particular that the first rude essays[1] towards a compilation of this kind are so extremely defective. The alphabet, in place of being employed in the humble function of an index to the matter contained in the work, was made supreme arbiter of the whole arrangement; and the different sciences, instead of following their natural order, were cut down into detached parts, out of which no great whole could possibly be formed. In this view the alphabet, far from conducing to clearness, became an instrument of disorder; and its only use appeared to be, to save the writers to whom we allude from the trouble of a more accurate or philosophical arrangement. Those obvious defects in all the most popular dictionaries of arts and sciences were observed by Mr Chambers,[2] the compiler of a very valuable work of this kind himself; and, in speaking of the labours of his predecessors, he particularly censures

the inattention to method, so visible in every part of their performances.

But although the arrangement of the Cyclopædia of Mr Chambers is much preferable to that of any former work of this kind, it is still liable to many of those objections for which he censures his predecessors. Even if his original plan had been carried into effect with complete success, and all the articles in different parts of his work had been so managed, as, when reunited, to have made so many complete systems, the number of references was still so great that no reader could possibly have submitted to the trouble of combining them.

Of this inconveniency, inseparable from a mere *dictionary* of arts and sciences, the original compilers of the Encyclopædia Britannica were fully aware; and they resolved, in the conduct of their work, to adopt such a plan as should completely free it from this objection. They were as fully convinced as their predecessors of the utility of a separate explanation of every technical term, and of the necessity also of noticing, in detail, many topics which it would be proper more fully to illustrate in the general account of the respective sciences to which they belonged. They were sensible, however, at the same time, how greatly the progress of useful knowledge is facilitated by systematical arrangement, and how necessary it is for those to think methodically who expect to benefit mankind by their labours. They have accordingly endeavoured, in place of the awkward expedient of a prefatory analysis, adopted by Mr Chambers, to exhibit a clear and satisfactory account of the several arts and sciences under their proper denominations, and to explain at the same time the subordinate articles under their technical terms.

(1810)

---

[1] Attempts.

[2] Ephraim Chambers (*c.* 1680–1740), author of *Cyclopaedia*, the first English Encyclopaedia, published in 1728.

MONTHLY REVIEW
Review of *Experimental Researches Concerning the Philosophy of Permanent Colours*. By Edward Bancroft.[1]

THE science of nature cultivated in antient times, unsupported by observation, was dissipated in idle abstractions and airy subtleties, which might fascinate the minds of its chosen votaries, but shrunk from the contamination of plebeian approach. A line of perpetual separation was drawn between the philosopher and the artist, attended with all the mischievous consequences generally annexed to established orders in society. The former, secluded from the great school of the world, abused his talent in decking out the phantoms of a prolific imagination; while the latter, directed by no general views, but urged by the incessant calls of interest, was imperceptibly led, as accident suggested, to the discovery of many valuable facts; obscured, however, and incumbered by a copious mixture of error and absurdity. It is the peculiar boast of the present age, that philosophy has emerged from the shades of retirement, to mingle in the active scenes of life. Those mysteries, which craft or ignorance employed to veil their operations, have gradually vanished, or have sunken into contempt; and a liberal curiosity, awakened and inflamed, advances its inquiries in all directions. The mass of knowledge accumulated among artists during the lapse of ages, and the new facts which are continually developed by varying their procedures, afford abundant materials with which we may build and improve rational theories. Nor are there wanting signal instances of discoveries, the most important in their application to practice, which have originated in the minds of speculative men. This alliance, so happily formed between speculation and action, between the sciences and the arts, has therefore proved reciprocally beneficial. Its influence has already, in a very perceptible degree, sweetened the various conditions of life; and perhaps it is finally destined to change the fortunes of the human race.

Chemistry is a science the most intimately connected with the arts, and which, within these few years, has been cultivated with uncommon ardour and with the happiest success. The system lately promulgated by the philosophical chemists in France,—the most perfect, certainly, which the present state of our knowledge will admit,—seems calculated, by its resistless beauty and simplicity, to gain a general reception and an extensive spread. It was in that country, likewise, that the most unwearied pains were taken to assist and direct the operations of the artist by the lights of science; and these noble efforts in some measure counteracted the blighting influence of despotic sway, and contributed to maintain its distinguished rank among nations. In the delicate art of Dyeing, the French have been unrivaled.

Owing to delay in the composition of this work, Dr. Bancroft has been anticipated in several points by other writers, particularly by M. Berthollet: but, notwithstanding this, he has produced much new and valuable matter; and his general concurrence, with some exceptions, in the system of that respectable chemist is a farther testimony of the solidity of the principles on which it is founded. The Doctor appears to possess no common portion of ingenuity, and he everywhere discovers accuracy, sagacity, and judgement. Not dazzled by the glitter of false theory, he stops to ponder and discuss; and his work is replete with extensive information and curious historical learning. Its composition is easy and perspicuous; the descriptions of the processes are full, without being tedious; and the perusal of

---

[1] Edward Bancroft (1744–1821), politician, naturalist, and chemist.

the whole is fitted to instruct and entertain the artist and the man of science.

(1795)

MONTHLY REVIEW
Review of FLORENTII JACOBI VOLTELEN [1]
Oratio, &c. i. e. An Oration delivered in the University of Leydon.
By F. J. Voltelen, on his retiring from the Office of Rector Magnificus.

IT is somewhat mortifying to the cautious experimental philosopher, who examines his ground and measures every step in his pursuit of science, to observe that the men, who boldly soar in the regions of enthusiasm,[2] should attract the attention and admiration of the multitude, while he is left almost solitary with his facts and inductions! It is humiliating that, after such incessant pains have been taken, to free the mind from superstition, with all its horrors, to dispel charms, annihilate evil dæmons, exorcise *exorcists,* and break the conjuror's wand, that the warm imagination of a few adventurers, should be able so speedily to recall them; and thus expose the present age, that boasts of its superior light and knowledge, to be again overrun with legions of fancied beings and fancied payers! Shall the *ignus fatuus* of a swampy ground, be always preferred to the riches of assiduous cultivation?

These reflections naturally present themselves, when the duties of our office oblige us to advert to the subject of *animal magnetism*:[3] which has, of late,

engaged so much of the attention of learned and unlearned, gentle and simple, in different parts of Europe; and which, we learn, is making considerable progress among our neighbours, the *Dutch.*

However we may oppose every explanation given by the advocates for animal magnetism, as being highly unphilosophical and absurd; yet it is universally acknowledged that, in the midst of much empyricism, collusion, credulity, and exaggeration, effects of a very extraordinary nature are occasionally produced by some of their manœuvres. The regular practitioner has more than once felt his obligations to bold and sanguine *irregulars*, for the discovery of very active medicaments. By yielding, though with reluctance, to the facts, and by investigating the nature of the medicine, and the cases in which it was salutary or pernicious, the former has frequently rescued a dangerous weapon from the hands of the unskilful, and has given it a very important place in the *Materia Medica*.[4] We are convinced that the obstinate denial of every effect from animal magnetism, has afforded an occasion of triumph to the abettors of magnetism, and has increased the number of their proselytes; as the admission of facts of which they had ocular demonstration naturally prepares the multitude, who are not able to discriminate, for a firm belief of the *principles* on which it is pretended that these facts are founded; and those principles being *visionary*, they are farther prepared to credit every extravagant assertion that is made of their influence.

(1791)

---

[1] Floris Jacobus Voltelen (1754–1795).

[2] A deluded state of fervour.

[3] Also known as mesmerism after the teachings of Franz Anton Mesmer, animal magnetism postulated a mysterious power that enabled one to induce hypnosis. It was a highly popular but much derided topic which had largely gone out of vogue by the end of the eighteenth century before gaining the attention of Romantic poets such as S.T. Coleridge and Percy Shelley.

[4] Medical literature.

Gentleman's Magazine

PREFACE

In time of peril and alarm, when, for wise and salutary reasons, providence permits the sagacity of the wise to be frustrated by the artifices of wicked men, and the triumphs of moral virtue to be for a while suspended, the mind can rest upon no base so strong, or feelings so consolatory, as the consciousness of having done its duty.

With such emotions Mr. Urban enters upon a new year; and, although somewhat depressed, in common with all those who are not proselytes to a new philosophy, he looks upon his labours of the year that is past, with a manly confidence. He boldly avows that no principles can be imputed to him but such as necessarily proceed from loyalty as a subject, benevolence as a man, impartiality as a critick, and a general love of genius and talents wherever they appear. He has acted, and will act, upon a system of conduct, which, equally defying the institutions of prejudice, malignity, and disappointment, at once elevates and secures the mind, from the reach of mean and contemptible passions. At the same time, therefore, that he repeats his acknowledgements to the publick, for the undiminished success which still continues to accompany his exertions, he again holds forth his accustomed invitation, without distinction of sect or party, to all who may think proper to exercise their talents, in whatever pursuit, for the elucidation of what is obscure, or the promotion of what is useful, in any branch of Science or the Arts. Neither will he take his leave of the numerous circle whose friendship is his pride, and whose assistance he may boast, or of that publick whose approbation stamps its valued sanction on his labours, without offering his serious prayer to the Father of Good, that all sorrow for past, or terror of future calamity, may be speedily obliterated by the return of peace, the extinction of animosities, the oblivion of injuries, and the circulation of benevolence to an extent, which may embrace every quarter of the globe.

(1795)

Dissertations and Miscellaneous Pieces Relating to the History and Antiquities, the Arts, Sciences, and Literature, of Asia[1]

PREFACE

It is a consideration which cannot but afford the utmost pleasure to a reflecting mind, that the Arts and Sciences, which are rapidly advancing towards a state of perfection in EUROPE, are not confined to that quarter of the globe. In the East, where Learning seems to be extinguished, and Civilization nearly lost, amidst the contention of avarice and despotism, a spirit of enquiry hath gone forth, which, aided by the ardour of Philosophy, promises to dissipate the gloom of ignorance, and to spread the advantages of knowledge through a region where its effects may be expected to be most favourable to the general interests of society.

To the exertions of one Gentleman,[2] whose various excellencies panegyric might display in the warmest terms, without being charged with extravagance, the ENGLISH settlements in the EAST INDIES are indebted for an institution which has already exhibited specimens of profound research, of bold investigation, and of happy illustration, in various subjects of literature;—subjects which, until the present times, had not exercised the faculties of EUROPEANS; but which, being produced to publick notice, will enlarge the bounds of knowledge,

---

[1] A compilation of works by members of the Asiatic Society formed by Sir William Jones.

[2] Sir William Jones (1726–95), the preeminent Orientalist of the late eighteenth century.

increase the stock of information, and furnish materials for future Philosophers, Biographers, and Historians.

That so much has already been achieved by an infant Society, will be a subject of surprize to those who have not considered the powers of genius and industry to overcome obstacles. From what has already appeared at CALCUTTA, a judgement may be formed of what may hereafter be expected. The stores of Oriental Literature being now accessible to those who have ability to make a proper use of them, intelligence hitherto locked up, it may be hoped, will delight and inform the enquirers after the History, Antiquities, Arts, Sciences, and Literature of ASIA.

Two Volumes of the Society's Transactions have been already published; but these have been so sparingly distributed in GREAT BRITAIN that few have had the opportunity of being informed of their contents, or of judging of their value. This circumstance has induced the Editor to select the contents of the present volumes from them and the Asiatic Miscellany, for the amusement and instruction of the publick. They are such as will confer honour on their authors, and afford entertainment to their readers. They contain a noble specimen of the talents of our countrymen inhabiting a distant quarter of the globe, employing themselves sedulously and honourably in extending the credit and establishing the reputation of BRITONS in new and unexplored regions of Science and Literature.

(1793)

JOSEPH PRIESTLEY
Experiments and Observations on Different Kinds of Air and Other Branches of Natural Philosophy [1]

Dedication:
To HIS ROYAL HIGHNESS
GEORGE PRINCE OF WALES,

SIR,

IN dedicating this work to your ROYAL HIGH-NESS, I express my own earnest wish and that of many others, that to your other excellent qualities your ROYAL HIGHNESS may add a disposition to patronize a branch of science, in the extension of which the natives of Great Britain have ever borne a distinguished part, and which has for its object the benefit of all mankind.

It is by increasing our knowledge of *nature*, and by this alone, that we acquire the great art of commanding it, of availing ourselves of its *power*, and applying them to our own purposes; true *science* being the only foundation of all those *arts* of life, whether, relating to peace or war, which distinguish *civilized* nations from those which we term *barbarous*; a distinction not less conspicuous than that between some nations of *men* and some species of *brutes*. And that branch of this great science to which the subject of this work relates, viz. *chemistry* is perhaps of more various and extensive use than any other part of natural knowledge; and by the application that is now given to it, it is continually growing in relative magnitude and importance.

It is true that we are indebted to the poverty of many persons for some of the most simple and effectual modes of operating in chemistry; *necessity* having in this, as well as in many other cases, been the happy *mother of invention*. But in some cases it is well known that the most promising projects have

---

[1] Joseph Priestley (1733–1804) was a leading theologian, political theorist, chemist, and educational pioneer. Amongst his scientific interests, Priestley was known for his experiments on the nature of air. Like many Dissenters, Priestley was committed to the pursuit of knowledge through critical debate in scientific contexts and as the basis

of political reform. In 1791 the *Monthly Review* called him "the literary wonder of the present times" (5: 303), but Priestley's outspoken and often radical positions made him a controversial figure in the era of the French Revolution. On July 14, 1791, Priestley's house and library were destroyed by a Church-and-King mob in Birmingham. In 1794 he emigrated to the United States to escape the ongoing threat of violent attack.

become abortive for want of the means that were necessary to carry them into execution. For in this science mere *observation* and *reflection* will not carry a man far. He will frequently have occasion to put the substances which he examines into various new situations, and observe the result of circumstances, which, without *expence*, as well as *labour*, he can have no opportunity of knowing.

Hence it is that the greatest and happiest effects may be expected from the patronage of science by persons of your ROYAL HIGHNESS'S rank and expectations, whose wishes and inclinations are often alone sufficient to give a turn to the taste and pursuits of the rich and great. And hitherto almost every country in Europe can boast of more persons among their nobility, and men of fortune, who are devoted to scientifical pursuits, than Great Britain.

In some countries the sciences seem to require the support of princes, or of the community, by pensions and establishments. In ours these aids are unnecessary. Our *Royal Society*, which gives none but honorary rewards, is all that is wanted in the way of *establishment*; and it has been, and is, eminently useful. In this country patronage is not wanted for those who cultivate the sciences, but rather for the sciences themselves; to give them their due value and consideration, to apply the influence which the great possess over the minds and opinions of men, in directing their tastes to useful pursuits, and thus to incite a sufficient number of able inquirers to explore the hidden powers which the Deity has impressed on matter.

Considering your ROYAL HIGHNESS as destined to be the future sovereign of this country, I cannot wish you greater glory or happiness, than that you should consider it as consisting, not in the *extent*, but in the *flourishing state*, of your dominions, to which *science*, *manufactures*, and *commerce* (each the true source of the other) will most eminently contribute; and that you should not be dazzled by the flattering, but often fatal, idea of extending what is called the *royal prerogative*; but rather study to give your subjects every power which they can exercise for their own advantage. And whatever flatterers may suggest, the people (each of them giving his whole attention to those things in which he is most interested) will always be able to do more for themselves than the most enlightened and best disposed princes can do for them.

As a person whose deliberate judgment has led him to dissent from the mode of religion by law established in this country, permit me, Sir, to express something more than a wish, that, as the future sovereign of Great Britain you will be the equal father of all your subjects; and that in your reign every man will meet with encouragement and favour in proportion to the services he renders his country, and the credit he is to it.[1]

There has of late years been a wonderful concurrence of circumstances tending to expand the human mind, to shew the inconvenience attending all *establishments*, civil or religious, formed in times of ignorance, and to urge the reformation of them. Let these be suffered to operate without obstruction; and have the true magnanimity to let no impediment be thrown in the way of the efforts of the more enlightened part of the community to improve the state of it in any respect.

A sovereign conducting himself by these liberal maxims will rank among the few truly *great and good princes*, whose object has not been themselves, and their personal glory and power, but the real good of their country; and not *that* only, or exclusively, but the benefit of all the human race. A character thus supported will be admired, and beloved, when that of other princes, generally, but falsely, called *great*, will be consigned to what is worse than oblivion, the detestation of all good men.

---

[1] As a religious Dissenter or non-Anglican, Priestley was barred from civic office and from attending Oxford or Cambridge.

That your ROYAL HIGHNESS may prove a truly patriot king, an ornament to human nature, and a blessing to your country, and to mankind, is the sincere wish, and prayer, of

YOUR ROYAL HIGHNESS'S,

    Most obedient

        And most humble servant,

                J. PRIESTLEY.

BIRMINGHAM,
March 24, 1790.

THE PREFACE

WHEN, for the sake of a little more reputation, men can keep brooding over a new fact, in the discovery of which they might, possibly, have very little real merit, till they think they can astonish the world with a system as *complete* as it is *new*, and give mankind a high idea of their judgment and penetration; they are justly punished for their ingratitude to the fountain of all knowledge, and for their want of a genuine love of science and of mankind, in finding their boasted discoveries anticipated, and the field of honest fame pre-occupied, by men, who, from a natural ardour of mind engage in philosophical pursuits, and with an ingenuous simplicity immediately communicate to others whatever occurs to them in their inquiries.

As to myself, I find it absolutely impossible to produce a work on this subject that shall be any thing like *complete*. Every publication I have frankly acknowledged to be very imperfect, and the present, I am as ready to acknowledge, is so. But, paradoxical as it may seem, this will ever be the case in the progress of natural science, so long as the works of God are, like himself, infinite and inexhaustible. In completing one discovery, we never fail to get an imperfect knowledge of others, of which we could have had no idea before; so that we cannot solve one doubt without creating several new ones.

No philosophical investigation can be said to be completed, which leaves any thing unknown that we are prompted by it to wish we could know relating to it. But such is the necessary connection of all things in the system of nature, that every discovery bring to our view many things of which we had no intimation before, the complete discovery of which we cannot help wishing for; and whenever these discoveries are completed, we may assure ourselves they will farther increase this kind of dissatisfaction.

The greater is the circle of light, the greater is the boundary of the darkness by which it is confined. But, notwithstanding this, the more light we get, the more thankful we ought to be. For by this means we have the greater range for satisfactory contemplation. In time the bounds of light will be still farther extended; and from the infinity of the divine nature, and the divine works, we may promise ourselves an endless progress in our investigation of them: a prospect truly sublime and glorious. The works of the greatest and most successful philosophers are, on this account, open to our complaints of their being imperfect.

This rapid process of knowledge, which, like the progress of a wave of the sea, of sound, or of light from the sun, extends itself not this way or that way only, but *in all directions*, will, I doubt not, be the means, under God, of extirpating *all* error and prejudice, and of putting an end to all undue and usurped authority in the business of *religion*, as well as of *science*; and all the efforts of the interested friends of corrupt establishments of all kinds, will be ineffectual for their support in this enlightened age; though, by retarding their downfall, they may make the final ruin of them more complete and glorious. It was ill policy in Leo X. to patronize polite literature. He was cherishing an enemy in disguise. And the English hierarchy (if there be any thing unsound in its constitution) has equal reason to tremble even at an air pump, or an electrical machine.

But, though I have little doubt, from the train that things are visibly in, that philosophical discoveries in general will go on with an accelerated progress (as indeed they have done ever since the revival of letters in Europe) it would be too rash to infer, from the present flattering appearances, that any particular expedition into the undiscovered regions of science will be crowned with more distinguished success than another. Nothing is more common, in the history of all the branches of experimental philosophy, than the most unexpected revolutions of good or bad success. In general, indeed, when numbers of ingenious men apply themselves to one subject, that has been *well opened*, the investigation proceeds happily and equably. But, as in the history of *electricity*, and now in the discoveries relating to *air*, light has burst out from the most unexpected quarters, in consequence of which the greatest matters of science have been obliged to recommence their studies, from new and simpler elements; so it is also not uncommon for a branch of science to receive a check, even in the most rapid and promising state of its growth.

It is true that the rich and the great in this country give less attention to these subjects than, I believe, they were ever known to do, since the time of Lord Bacon, and much less than men of rank and fortune in other countries give to them. But with us this loss is made up by men of leisure, spirit, and ingenuity, in the middle ranks of life, which is a circumstance that promises better for the continuance of this progress in useful knowledge than any noble or royal patronage. With us, also, politics chiefly engage the attention of those who stand foremost in the community, which, indeed, arises from the *freedom* and peculiar *excellence* of our constitution, without which even the spirit of men of letters in general, and of philosophers in particu-

lar, who never directly interfere in matters of government, would languish.

It is rather to be regretted, however, that, in such a number of nobility and gentry, so very few should have any taste for scientifical pursuits, because, for many valuable purposes of science, *wealth* gives a decisive advantage. If extensive and lasting *fame* be at all an object, literary, and especially scientifical pursuits, are preferable to political ones in a variety of respects. The former are as much more favourable to the display of the human faculties than the latter, as the *system of nature* is superior to any *political system* upon earth.

I also cannot help expressing a wish that during the establishment of peace in Europe (and happily it is not in the power of any state to be always at war) we may see every obstruction to the progress of knowledge, which is equally friendly to all states, removed. Taxes on the importation of books, and other articles of literature, are so impolitic, as well as illiberal, that it is earnestly wished that something may be stipulated by contending powers for abolishing them. There are statesmen whose minds are sufficiently enlarged to see that philosophy gives an ample equivalent for the exemption.

I might enlarge much more than I have done in this preface on the *dignity*, and *utility*, of experimental philosophy; but shall only observe farther, that it is nothing but a superior knowledge of the laws of nature, that gives Europeans the advantage they have over the Hottentots,[1] or the lowest of our species. Had these people never known Europeans, they could not have formed an idea of any mode of life superior to their own, though it differs but little from that of the brutes. In like manner, science advancing, as it does, with an accelerated progress, it may be taken for granted, that mankind some centuries hence will be as much superior to us in

---

[1] South African aboriginals, though the term was used more generally as a negative reference to uncivilized and culturally inferior individuals.

knowledge, and improvements in the arts of life, as we now are to the Hottentots, though we cannot have any conception what that knowledge, or what those improvements, will be. It is enough for us to see that nature is inexhaustible, that it is a rich mine, in which we shall never dig in vain, and that it is open to infinitely more labourers than are now employed in exploring its contents, or in digging for them.

(1790)

ERASMUS DARWIN
The Loves of the Plants [1]

CANTO I.

DESCEND, ye hovering Sylphs! aerial Quires,
And sweep with little hands your silver lyres;
With fairy foot-steps print your grassy rings,
Ye Gnomes! Accordant to the tinkling strings;
5 While in soft notes I tune to oaten reed
Gay hopes, and amorous sorrows of the mead.—
From giant Oaks, that wave their branches dark,
To the dwarf Moss, that clings upon their bark,
What Beaux and Beauties croud the gaudy groves,

10 And woo and win their vegetable Loves. [†]
How Snow-drops cold, and blue-eyed Harebels blend
Their tender tears, as o'er the stream they bend;
The love-sick Violet, and the Primrose pale
Bow their sweet heads, and whisper to the gale;
15 With secret sighs the Virgin Lily droops,
And jealous Cowslips hang their tawny cups.
How the young Rose in beauty's damask pride
Drinks the warm blushes of his bashful bride;
With honey'd lips enamour'd Woodbines meet,
20 Clasp with fond arms, and mix their kisses sweet .—

Stay thy soft-murmuring waters, gentle Rill;
Hush, whispering Winds, ye rustling Leaves, be still;
Rest, silver Butterflies, your quivering wings;
Alight, ye Beetles, from your airy rings;
25 Ye painted Moths, your gold-eyed plumage furl,
Bow your wide horns, your spiral trunks uncurl;
Glitter, ye Glow-worms, on your mossy beds;
Descend, ye Spiders, on your lengthen'd threads;
Slide here, ye horned Snails, with varnish'd shells;
30 Ye Bee-nymphs, listen in your waxen cells!—

BOTANIC MUSE! who in this latter age
Led by your airy hand the Swedish sage, [2]
Bad his keen eye your secret haunts explore
On dewy dell, high wood, and winding shore;
35 Say on each leaf how tiny Graces dwell;
How laugh the Pleasures in a blossom's bell;
How insect-Loves arise on cob-web wings,
Aim their light shafts, and point their little stings

---

[1] Erasmus Darwin (1731–1802), a physician, poet, inventor, and theorist in medicine, agriculture, and female education. His *Zoonomia; or, The Laws of Organic Life* (1794–96) offered an early version of the theory of evolution that would be more famously propounded by his grandson, Charles Darwin's *The Loves of the Plants* (1789) represented an attempt to make science interesting to a wider audience through an appeal to the imagination. The poem adopted the classificatory system established by the Swedish botanist Carolus Linnaeus in order to depict the sex life of plants. The poem's celebration of a polygamous world was linked by conservative critics to the political excesses of the age. The poem was parodied by George Canning's *Love of Triangles* in the *Anti-Jacobin Review*. In his ultra-conservative attack on proto-feminist radicals in the poem *The Unsex'd Females* (1798), Richard Polwhele reported with disgust that "I have, several times, seen boys and girls botanizing together." Despite conservatives' hostility, however, the poem met with great success. In 1791 Darwin published *Loves of the Plants* and *The Economy of Vegetation* together as *The Botanic Garden*.

[†] *Vegetable Loves.* Linneus the celebrated Swedish naturalist, has demonstrated, that all flowers contain families of male or females, or both; and on their marriages has constructed his invaluable system of Botany.

[2] Carolus Linnaeus (1707–78), Swedish naturalist and founder of modern botany.

"First the tall CANNA[†] lifts his curled brow
40 Erect to heaven, and plights his nuptial vow;
The virtuous pair, in milder regions born,
Dread the rude blast of Autumn's icy morn;
Round the chill fair he folds his crimson vest,
And clasps the timorous beauty to his breast.

45 Thy love, CALLITRICHE,[††] *two* Virgins share,
Smit with thy starry eye and radiant hair;—
On the green margin sits the youth, and laves
His floating train of tresses in the waves;
Sees his fair features paint the streams that pass,
50 And bends for ever o'er the watery glass.

Two brother swains of COLLIN'S[†††] gentle name,
The same their features, and their forms the same,
With rival love for fair COLLINIA sigh,
Knit the dark brow, and roll the unsteady eye.
55 With sweet concern the pitying beauty mourns,
And sooths with smiles the jealous pair by turns.

When the young Hours amid her tangled hair
Wove the fresh rose-bud, and the lily fair,

Proud GLORIOSA[††††] led *three* chosen swains,
60 The blushing captives of her virgin chains.—
—When Time's rude hand a bark of wrinkles spread
Round her weak limbs, and silver'd o'er her head,
Three other youths her riper years engage,
The flatter'd victims of her wily age.
65 So NINON pruned her wither'd charms, and won
With harlot-smiles her gay unconscious son;—
Clasp'd in his arms she own'd a mother's name,
Shook her grey locks, and tittering mock'd his flame;
With mad despair he plunged the guilty dart,
70 And life and love gush'd mingled from his heart!

Sopha'd on silk, amid her charm-built towers,
Her meads of asphodel, and amaranth bowers,
Where Sleep and Silence guard the soft abodes,
In sullen apathy PAPAVER[†††††] nods.
75 Faint o'er her couch in scintillating streams

[†] *Canna.* Cane, or Indian Reed. One male and one female inhabit each flower. It is brought from between the tropics to our hot-houses, and bears a beautiful crimson flower; the seeds are used as shot by the Indians, and are strung for prayer-beads in some catholic countries.

[††] *Callitriche.* Fine-Hair, Stargrass. One male and two females inhabit each flower. The upper leaves grow in the form of a star, whence it is called Stellaria Aquatica by Ray and others; its stems and leaves float far on the water, and are often so matted together, as to bear a person walking on them. The male sometimes lives in a separate flower.

[†††] *Collinsonia.* Two males one female. I have lately observed a very singular circumstance in this flower; the two males stand widely diverging from each other, and the female bends herself into contact first with one of them, and after some time leaves this, and applies herself to the other. It is probable one of the anthers may be mature before the other? See note on Gloriosa, and Genista. The females in Nigella, devil in the bush, are very tall compared to the males; and bending over in a circle to them, give the flower some resemblance to a regal crown. The female of the epilobium angustifolium, role bay willow herb, bends down amongst the males for several days, and becomes upright again, when impregnated.

[††††] *Gloriosa.* Superba. Six males one female. The petals of this beautiful flower with three of the stamens, which are first mature, hang down in apparent disorder; and the pistil bends at nearly a right angle to insert its stigma amongst them. In a few days, as these decline, the other three stamens bend over, and approach the pistil. In the Fritillaria Persica, the six stamens are of equal lengths, and the anthers lie at a distance from the pistil, and three alternate ones approach first; and, when these decline, the other three approach: in the Lithrum Salicaria, (which has twelve males and one female) a beautiful red flower, which grows on the banks of rivers, six of the males arrive at maturity, and surround the female sometime before the other six; when these decline, the other six rise up, and supply their places. Several other flowers have in similar manner two sets of stamina of different ages, as Adoxa, Lychnis, Saxifraga. See Genista. Perhaps a difference in the time of their maturity obtains in all those flowers, which have numerous stamens.

[†††††] *Papaver.* Poppy. Many males, many females. The plants of this class are almost all of them poisonous; the finest opium is procured by wounding the heads of large poppies with a three-edged knife, and tying muscle shells to them to catch the drops. In small quantities it exhilarates the mind, raises the passions, and invigorates the body; in large ones it is succeeded by intoxication, languor, stupor and death. It is customary in India for a messenger to travel above a hundred miles without rest or food, except an appropriated bit of opium for himself, and a larger one for his horse at certain stages. The emaciated and decrepit appearance with the ridiculous and idiotic gestures of the opium-eaters in Constantinople is well described in the memoirs of Baron de Tott.

Pass the thin forms of Fancy and of Dreams;
Froze by enchantment on the velvet ground
Fair youths and beauteous ladies glitter round;
On crystal pedestals they seem to sigh,
Bend the stiff knee, and lift the unmoving eye.

(1789)

HUMPHRY DAVY
A Discourse, Introductory to a Course of Lectures on Chemistry [1]

CHEMISTRY is that part of natural philosophy which relates to those intimate actions of bodies upon each other, by which their appearances are altered, and their individuality destroyed.

This science has for its objects all the substances found upon our globe. It relates not only to the minute alterations in the external world, which are daily coming under the cognizance of our senses, and which in consequence, are incapable of affecting the imagination, but likewise to the great changes, and convulsions in nature, which, occurring but seldom, excite our curiosity, or awaken our astonishment.

Chemistry, considered as a systematic arrangement of facts, is of later origin than most of the other sciences; yet certain of its processes and operations have been always more or less connected with them; and, lately, by furnishing new instruments and powers of investigation, it has greatly

contributed to increase their perfection, and to extend their applications.

Fortunately for man, all the different parts of the human mind are possessed of certain harmonious relations; and it is even difficult to draw the line of distinction between the sciences; for as they have for their objects only dead and living nature, and as they consist of expressions of facts more or less analogous, they must all be possessed of certain ties of connection, and of certain dependencies on each other. The man of true genius who studies science in consequence of its application,—pointing out to himself a definite end, will make use of all the instruments of investigation which are necessary for his purposes; and in the search of discovery, he will rather pursue the plans of his own mind than be limited by the artificial divisions of language. Following extensive views, he will combine together mechanical, chemical, and physiological knowledge, whenever this combination may be essential; in consequence his facts will be connected together by simple and obvious analogies, and in studying one class of phenomena more particularly, he will not neglect its relations to other classes.

But chemistry is not valuable simply in its connections with the sciences, some of which are speculative and remote from our habitual passions and desires; it applies to most of the processes and operations of common life; to those processes on which we depend for the gratification of our wants, and which in consequence of their perfection and extension by means of scientific principles, have become the sources of the most refined enjoyments and delicate pleasures of civilized society.

It is difficult to examine any of our common operations or labours without finding them more or less connected with chemistry. By means of this science man has employed almost all the substances in nature either for the satisfaction of his wants or the gratification of his luxuries. Not contented with

---

[1] Humphry Davy (1778–1829), chemist and scientific lecturer, and after 1802, professor of chemistry at the Royal Institution. Davy was an intimate of William Wordsworth and S. T. Coleridge, and helped Wordsworth edit the second edition of *Lyrical Ballads* in 1800. In his lectures and essays, Davy attempted to synthesize the worlds of science and the arts. Davy's public lectures became a fashionable attraction, in part because support from aristocratic patrons enabled Davy to offer his audiences visually spectacular demonstrations. Despite his early associations with radicals such as Joseph Priestley, Erasmus Darwin, and William Godwin, Davy insistently connected the ideal of scientific inquiry to a belief in the importance of a conservative social order.

what is found upon the surface of the earth, he has penetrated into her bosom, and has even searched the bottom of the ocean for the purpose of allaying the restlessness of his desires, or of extending and increasing his power. He is to a certain extent ruler of all the elements that surround him ; and he is capable of using not only common matter according to his will and inclinations, but likewise of subjecting to his purposes the ethereal principles of heat and light. By his inventions they are elicited from the atmosphere; and under his control they become, according to circumstances, instruments of comfort and enjoyment, or of terror and destruction.

To be able indeed to form an accurate estimate of the effects of chemical philosophy, and the arts and sciences connected with it, upon the human mind, we ought to examine the history of society, to trace the progress of improvement, or more immediately to compare the uncultivated savage with the being of science and civilization.

But, though improved and instructed by the sciences, we must not rest contented with what has been done; it is necessary that we should likewise do. Our enjoyment of the fruits of the labours of former times should be rather an enjoyment of activity than of indolence; and, instead of passively admiring, we ought to admire with that feeling which leads to emulation.

Science has done much for man, but it is capable of doing still more; its sources of improvement are not yet exhausted; the benefits that it has conferred ought to excite our hopes of its capability of conferring new benefits; and in considering the progressiveness of our nature, we may reasonably look forward to a state of greater cultivation and happiness than that we at present enjoy.

As a branch of sublime philosophy, chemistry is far from being perfect. It consists of a number of collections of facts connected together by different relations but as yet it is not furnished with a precise and beautiful theory. Though we can perceive, develope, and even produce, by means of our instruments of experiment, an almost infinite variety of minute phænomena, yet we are incapable of determining the general laws by which they are governed; and in attempting to define them, we are lost in obscure, though sublime imaginations concerning unknown agencies. That they may be discovered, however, there is every reason to believe. And who would not be ambitious of becoming acquainted with the most profound secrets of nature, of ascertaining her hidden operations, and of exhibiting to men that system of knowledge which relates so intimately to their own physical and moral constitution?

At the beginning of the seventeenth century very little was known concerning the philosophy of the intimate actions of bodies on each other; and before this time, vague ideas, superstitious notions, and inaccurate practices, were the only effects of the first efforts of the mind to establish the foundations of chemistry. Men either were astonished and deluded by their first inventions so as to become visionaries, and to institute researches after imaginary things, or they employed them as instruments for astonishing and deluding others, influenced by their dearest passions and interests, by ambition, or the love of money. Hence arose the dreams of alchemy concerning the philosopher's stone, and the elixir of life. Hence, for a long while the other metals were destroyed or rendered useless by experiments designed to transmute them into gold; and for a long while the means of obtaining earthly immortality were sought for amidst the unhealthy vapours of the laboratory. These views of things have passed away, and a new science has gradually arisen. The dim and uncertain twilight of discovery, which gave to objects false or indefinite appearances, has been succeeded by the steady light of truth, which has shown the external world in its distinct forms, and in its true relations to human powers. The composition of the atmosphere, and the properties of the gases, have been ascertained; the phænomena of electricity have been developed; the lightnings have been taken from the clouds; and lastly, a new influence has been discovered, which has enabled man to produce from combinations of dead matter effects which were formerly occasioned only by animal organs.

The human mind has been lately active and powerful; but there is very little reason for believing that the period of its greatest strength is passed; or even that it has attained its adult state. We find in all its exertions not only the health and vigour, but likewise the awkwardness of youth. It has gained new powers and faculties; but it is as yet incapable of using them with readiness and efficacy. Its desires are beyond its abilities; its different parts and organs are not firmly knit together, and they seldom act in perfect unity.

Unless any great physical changes should take place upon the globe, the permanency of the arts and sciences is rendered certain, in consequence of the diffusion of knowledge by means of the invention of printing; and those words which are the immutable instruments of thought, are become the constant and widely-diffused nourishment of the mind, the preservers of its health and energy. Individuals, in consequence of interested motives or false views, may check for a time the progress of knowledge; moral causes may produce a momentary slumber of the public spirit; the adoption of wild and dangerous theories, by ambitious or deluded men, may throw a temporary opprobrium on literature; but the influence of true philosophy will never be despised; the germs of improvement are sown in minds even where they are not perceived, and sooner or later the spring-time of their growth must arrive.

In reasoning concerning the future hopes of the human species, we may look forward with confidence to a state of society in which the different orders and classes of men will contribute more effectually to the support of each other than they have hitherto done. This state indeed seems to be approaching fast; for in consequence of the multiplication of the means of instruction, the man of science and the manufacturer are daily becoming more nearly assimilated to each other. The artist who formerly affected to despise scientific principles, because he was incapable of perceiving the advantages of them, is now so far enlightened, as to favour the adoption of new processes in his art, whenever they are evidently connected with a diminution of labour. And the increase of projectors,[1] even to too great an extent, demonstrates the enthusiasm of the public mind in its search after improvement. The arts and sciences also are in a high degree cultivated, and patronized by the rich and privileged orders. The guardians of civilization and of refinement, the most powerful and respected part of society, are daily growing more attentive to the realities of life; and, giving up many of their unnecessary enjoyments in consequence of the desire to be useful, are becoming the friends and protectors of the labouring part of the community. The unequal division of property and of labour, the difference of rank and condition amongst mankind, are the sources of power in civilized life, its moving causes, and even its very soul; and in considering and hoping that the human species is capable of becoming more enlightened and more happy, we can only expect that the great whole of society should be ultimately connected together by means of knowledge and the useful arts; that they should act as the children of one great parent, with one determinate end, so that no power may be rendered useless, no exertions thrown away. In this view we

---

[1] People who form projects, with the negative connotation of schemers.

do not look to distant ages, or amuse ourselves with brilliant, though delusive dreams concerning the infinite improveability of man, the annihilation of labour, disease, and even death. But we reason by analogy from simple facts. We consider only a state of human progression arising out of its present condition. We look for a time that we may reasonably expect, for a bright day of which we already behold the dawn.

In common society, to men collected in great cities, who are wearied by the constant recurrence of similar artificial pursuits and objects, and who are in need of sources of permanent attachment, the cultivation of chemistry and the physical sciences may be eminently beneficial. For in all their applications they exhibit an almost infinite variety of effects connected with a simplicity of design. They demonstrate that every being is intended for some definite end or purpose. They attach feelings of importance even to inanimate objects; and they furnish to the mind means of obtaining enjoyment unconnected with the labour or misery of others.

To the man of business, or of mechanical employment, the pursuit of experimental research may afford a simple pleasure, unconnected with the gratification of unnecessary wants, and leading to such an expansion of the faculties of the mind as must give to it dignity and power. To the refined and fashionable classes of society it may become a source of consolation and of happiness, in those moments of solitude, when the common habits and passions of the world are considered with indifference. It may destroy diseases of the imagination, owing to too deep a sensibility; and it may attach the affections to objects, permanent, important, and intimately related to the interests of the human species. Even to persons of powerful minds, who are connected with society by literary, political, or moral relations, an acquaintance with the science that represents the operations of nature cannot be

wholly useless. It must strengthen their habits of minute discrimination; and by obliging them to use a language representing simple facts, may tend to destroy the influence of terms connected only with feeling. The man who has been accustomed to study natural objects philosophically, to be perpetually guarding against the delusions of the fancy, will not readily be induced to multiply words so as to forget things. From observing in the relations of inanimate things fitness and utility, he will reason with deeper reverence concerning beings possessing life; and perceiving in all the phenomena of the universe the designs of a perfect intelligence, he will be averse to the turbulence and passion of hasty innovations, and will uniformly appear as the friend of tranquillity and order.

(1802)

WILLIAM WORDSWORTH
Preface to *Lyrical Ballads* [1]

ARISTOTLE, I have been told, hath said, that poetry is the most philosophic of all writing: it is so: its object is truth, not individual and local, but general, and operative; not standing upon external testimony, but carried alive into the heart by passion; truth which is its own testimony, which gives strength and divinity to the tribunal to which it appeals, and receives them from the same tribu-

---

[1] William Wordsworth (1770–1850) had been an early enthusiast of the French Revolution, but after becoming disenchanted with the cause of radical reform, turned to the imagination as an alternative revolutionary force capable of fostering spiritual renewal. Part of this involved Wordsworth's exaltation of poetry above other forms of writing. Humphry Davy had actually helped to edit the initial version of the Preface, published in 1800, but when Wordsworth revised in two years later for a new edition, Wordsworth countered Davy's own remarks about the cultural importance of science by emphasizing the scientist's subordinate position in relation to the poet. Their writings form an intriguing dialogue in an important moment in the evolution of the intellectual disciplines.

nal. We have no knowledge, that is, no general principles drawn from the contemplation of particular facts, but what has been built up by pleasure, and exists in us by pleasure alone. The man of science, the chemist and mathematician, whatever difficulties and disgusts they may have had to struggle with, know and feel this. However painful may be the objects with which the anatomist's knowledge is connected, he feels that his knowledge is pleasure; and where he has no pleasure he has no knowledge. What then does the poet? He considers man and the objects that surround him as acting and reacting upon each other, so as to produce an infinite complexity of pain and pleasure; he considers man in his own nature and in his ordinary life as contemplating this with a certain quantity of immediate knowledge, with certain convictions, intuitions, and deductions which by habit become of the nature of intuitions; he considers him as looking upon this complex scene of ideas and sensations, and finding every where objects that immediately excite in him sympathies which, from the necessities of his nature, are accompanied by an overbalance of enjoyment.

To this knowledge which all men carry about with them, and to these sympathies in which without any other discipline than that of our daily life we are fitted to take delight, the poet principally directs his attention. He considers man and nature as essentially adapted to each other; and the mind of man as naturally the mirror of the fairest and most interesting qualities of nature. And thus the poet, prompted by this feeling of pleasure which accompanies him through the whole course of his studies, converses with general nature with affections akin to those, which, through labour and length of time, the man of science has raised up in himself, by conversing with those particular parts of nature which are the objects of his studies. The knowledge both of the poet and the man of science is pleasure;

but the knowledge of the one cleaves to us as a necessary part of our existence, our natural and unalienable inheritance; the other is a personal and individual acquisition, slow to come to us, and by no habitual and direct sympathy connecting us with our fellow-beings. The man of science seeks truth as a remote and unknown benefactor; he cherishes and loves it in his solitude: the poet, singing a song in which all human beings join with him, rejoices in the presence of truth as our visible friend and hourly companion. Poetry is the breath and finer spirit of all knowledge; it is the impassioned expression which is in the countenance of all science. Emphatically may it be said of the poet, as Shakespeare hath said of man, "that he looks before and after."[1] He is the rock of defence of human nature; an upholder and preserver, carrying every where with him relationship and love. In spite of difference of soil and climate, of language and manners, of laws and customs, in spite of things silently gone out of mind and things violently destroyed, the poet binds together by passion and knowledge the vast empire of human society, as it is spread over the whole earth, and over all time. The objects of the poet's thoughts are every where; though the eyes and senses of man are, it is true, his favourite guides, yet he will follow wheresoever he can find an atmosphere of sensation in which to move his wings. Poetry is the first and last of all knowledge—it is as immortal as the heart of man. If the labours of men of science should ever create any material revolution, direct or indirect, in our condition, and in the impressions which we habitually receive, the poet will sleep then no more than at present, but he will be ready to follow the steps of the man of science, not only in those general indirect effects, but he will be at his side, carrying sensation into the midst of the objects of the science itself. The remotest discoveries of the chemist, the

---

[1] *Hamlet* IV: iv: 37.

botanist, or mineralogist, will be as proper objects of the poet's art as any upon which it can be employed, if the time should ever come when these things shall be familiar to us, and the relations under which they are contemplated by the followers of these respective sciences shall be manifestly and palpably material to us as enjoying and suffering beings. If the time should ever come when what is now called science, thus familiarized to men, shall be ready to put on, as it were, a form of flesh and blood, the poet will lend his divine spirit to aid the transfiguration, and will welcome the being thus produced, as a clear and genuine inmate of the household of man.—It is not, then, to be supposed that any one, who holds that sublime notion of poetry which I have attempted to convey, will break in upon the sanctity and truth of his pictures by transitory and accidental ornaments, and endeavour to excite admiration of himself by arts, the necessity of which must manifestly depend upon the assumed meanness of his subject.

(1802)

HUMPHRY DAVY
Address of the President on Taking the Chair of the Royal Society, for the First Time; December 7th, 1820.—on the Present State of That Body, and on the Progress and Prospects of Science.[1]

---

[1] Humphry Davy (1778–1829), chemist and scientific lecturer, and after 1802, professor of chemistry at the Royal Institution, Davy was an intimate of Wordsworth and S. T. Coleridge, and helped Wordsworth edit the second edition of *Lyrical Ballads* in 1800. In his lectures and essays, Davy attempted to synthesize the worlds of science and poetry. Davy's public lectures became a fashionable attraction with a broad populace, in part because support from aristocratic patrons enabled Davy to offer his audiences visually spectacular demonstrations. Despite his early associations with radicals such as Joseph Priestley, Erasmus Darwin, and William Godwin, Davy insistently connected the ideal of scientific inquiry to a belief in the importance of a conservative social order.

GENTLEMEN,

I HAVE, on a former occasion,[†] returned you my thanks for the distinguished honour you have done me in electing me your President. I have stated to you my entire devotion to your interests, and to the cause of science. I do not mean to indulge in any further expression of my feelings on this occasion, except to say that they are deep, and will be permanent.

But I think it my duty, before I enter upon the details of common business, to devote a few words to the present state of the Royal Society,[2] its relations to other scientific bodies, and the prospects and hopes of science.

When the Royal Society was instituted, it stood alone in Britain; and the associations of learned men that were formed soon after, in different parts of the empire, for pursuing natural science, were either dependent or affiliated societies. But, in these latter times, the field of knowledge has become so extensive, and its objects so various, that separate and independent bodies have arisen for registering observations and collecting facts, each in a different department. It would be impossible that our records, as they are now published at our own expense, should contain histories of the multifarious phenomena of all the kingdoms of nature, of all the observations made in zoology, botany, mineralogy, geology, and practical astronomy. It is satisfactory, therefore, to know that institutions exist for preserving and publishing such histories in detail.

I trust that, with these new societies, we shall always preserve the most amicable relations, and that we shall mutually assist each other; and that they, recollecting our grand object, which is to establish principles on inductive reasoning and

---

[†] At the anniversary dinner, November 30.

[2] Founded in 1660, the Royal Society was the oldest and most prestigious scientific society in Britain.

experiments, and to make useful applications in science, will, should any discoveries be made by their members respecting general laws, or important facts observed, which seem to lead to purposes of direct utility, do us the honour to communicate them to us. They will have no dishonourable place in being published in those records, which remain monuments of all the country has possessed of profound in experimental research, or ingenious in discovery, or sublime in speculative science, from the time of Hooke and Newton, to that of Maskelyne and Cavendish.[1]

I am sure there is no desire in this body to exert anything like patriarchal authority, in relation to these institutions; or, indeed, if there were such a desire, it could not be gratified. But I trust there may exist in the new societies, that feeling of respect and affection for the Royal Society, which is due to the eldest brother, to the first-born of the same family; and that we shall co-operate, in perfect harmony, for one great object, which, from its nature, ought to be a bond of union and of peace, not merely amongst the philosophers of the same country, but even amongst those of different nations.

When, by the unrivaled power of one great genius,[2] and the industry and talent of his illustrious disciples, the laws of the motions of the great masses of matter composing the universe were discovered, and most of the physical phenomena connected with them solved, it appeared as if the field of scientific research were exhausted, as if the rich crops taken from the soil had rendered it sterile, and

that little was left for the ingenuity and labour of future inquirers; time, however, has proved how unfounded was this opinion, and how nearly approaching to infinite, are the objects of natural philosophy. Scarcely has any period of thirty years passed without offering a train of important discoveries, and every new truth or new fact has led to new researches; becoming, as it were, a centre of light, from which rays have proceeded in different directions, showing to us unexpected objects; so that this kind of knowledge is as inexhaustible, as the resources of the human mind; and philosophers, like the early cultivators in a great new continent, by every acquisition they make, discover new and extensive uncultivated spots beyond.

Gentlemen, to conclude, I trust in all our researches we shall be guided by that spirit of philosophy, awakened by our great masters, Bacon and Newton; that sober and cautious method of inductive reasoning which is the germ of truth and of permanency in all the sciences. I trust that those amongst us who are so fortunate as to kindle the light of new discoveries, will use them, not for the purpose of dazzling the organs of our intellectual vision, but rather to enlighten us, by showing objects in their true forms and colours; that our philosophers will attach no importance to hypotheses, except as leading to the research after facts so as to be able to discard or adopt them at pleasure, treating them rather as parts of the scaffolding of the building of science, than as belonging either to its foundations, materials, or ornaments; that they will look, where it be possible, to practical applications in science, not, however, forgetting the dignity of their pursuit, the noblest end of which is, to exalt the powers of the human mind, and to increase the sphere of intellectual enjoyment, by enlarging our views of nature, and of the power, wisdom, and goodness of the Author of nature.

---

[1] Robert Hooke (1635–1703), physicist and mathematician, and inventor; Sir Isaac Newton (1642–1727), mathematician and natural philosopher; Nevil Maskelyne (1732–1811), astronomer; Henry Cavendish (1731–1810), known for his experiments on air and electricity.

[2] Sir Isaac Newton (1642–1727), mathematician and natural philosopher. By the end of the eighteenth century, Newton had become an almost legendary figure amongst advocates of experimental science.

Gentlemen, the Society has a right to expect from those amongst its Fellows, gifted with adequate talents, who have not yet laboured for science, some proofs of their zeal in promoting its progress; and it will always consider the success of those who have already been contributors to our volumes, as a pledge of future labours.

Let us then labour together, and steadily endeavour to gain what are perhaps the noblest objects of ambition—acquisitions which may be useful to our fellow-creatures. Let it not be said, that, at a period when our empire was at its highest pitch of greatness, the sciences began to decline; let us rather hope that posterity will find, in the Philosophical Transactions of our days, proofs that we were not unworthy of the times in which we lived.

(1827)

SECTION SEVEN

The Periodical Press

William Hazlitt's observation that "We often hear it asked, *Whether Periodical Criticism is, upon the whole, beneficial to the cause of literature?*" was not simply a rhetorical one. The importance or, alternatively, the abuse of the periodical press was a ubiquitous topic in literary debates in this age. The one thing that virtually all of the participants in these debates could agree on, was the overwhelming presence of the periodicals in Romantic print culture. Their sheer popularity, combined with an authority that was frequently attributed to their critical judgements, gave them a degree of sovereignty within the republic of letters that, for many commentators, was at odds with the interests of authors and readers. Almost everyone accepted the potential value of the periodicals; criticism of them tended to be focussed on abuses that marred their otherwise important role. As a letter to the editor of the *Monthly Magazine* put it, "the Establishment of literary journals has certainly been an event of the greatest consequence in the republic of letters. It has been the means of diffusing knowledge far and wide, and of kindling a love of learning, where the seeds of genius would otherwise, in all likelihood, have perished in wretched torpidity. It has also been of infinite service to the interests of science, and to the useful arts of life, by examining into, and making generally known, the discoveries and improvements of ingenious men. The art of literary composition has, moreover, been vastly improved; the principles of language have been better ascertained; and the qualities of a just and elegant style have been exactly determined hereby." The *Monthly Review* made the same point more succinctly: "Among all the modes which have been devised for the purpose of diffusing knowledge among mankind, none is so effectual as that of periodical publications." The *Analytical* agreed that the role of "a respectable Journal" was "to diffuse knowledge, and to advance the interests of science, of virtue and morality." The emphasis in all of these comments is on the periodicals' crucial role in "diffusing knowledge," or, in other words, of promoting the exchange of ideas and the enlightenment and extension of the reading public—a function that many of the writers that we have seen in earlier sections equated with literature itself.

Periodicals took several forms. Literary reviews such as the *Monthly Review* and the *Critical Review* were wholly composed of reviews of published works; literary magazines such as the *Gentleman's Magazine*, the *Monthly Magazine*, and the *European Magazine* combined a shorter section of reviews with a range of offerings that included letters to the editor, original poetry, domestic and international political news, births and deaths notices, business information, and weather and agricultural reports. The variety reflected the age's predisciplinary character; literature (even in the broader sense of all printed texts) was not to be isolated from these more worldly concerns. On the contrary, reviews of new books took their place alongside accounts of new patents and recent bankruptcies. Any one issue of the literary reviews introduced readers to political pamphlets, historiographies, travelogues, sermons, medical treatises, poetry collections, novels, plays, and various types of scientific studies, all arranged less in terms of genre than by the individual publication's importance. The periodicals' heterogeneity embodied the eighteenth-century ideal of a public sphere of enlightened individuals engaged in a progressive communicative process, but this heterogeneity was balanced by a reassuring sense of structural regularity. Periodicals were not designed to be read and discarded; they were intended to be bound in semi-annual or tri-annual volumes that included prefaces, tables of contents, and indices. In this way they offered permanence and encyclopaedic breadth as serialized but highly standardized accounts of the history of literature. Literary reviews and magazines generally appeared in monthly editions until 1802 when the *Edinburgh Review*—the first of the great quarterlies—broke with convention by offering less frequent editions containing longer articles on a select number of topics.

As the *Retrospective Review* pointed out, periodicals had actually played two very different but equally important historical roles. With the invention of printing in the fifteenth century, periodicals had played a crucial function in spreading a familiarity with literature in societies where print was not yet widely disseminated. They helped to create a reading public, and in doing so they encouraged more people to participate in debates on a range of topics by publishing their own ideas. By the Romantic period, however, many critics argued that periodicals also had a different job to do. They had been so successful in encouraging people to participate in this exchange of published ideas that they were now called upon to protect readers from an excess of publications. Because "the inundation of paper and print" threatened to overwhelm people's ability to assimilate new ideas in a responsible way, periodicals had taken on the job of acting as filters, offering readers a brief introduction to new publications along with some indication of their worth. As the *Retrospective* put it, they served as "dykes or mud-banks…for the purpose of being interposed between the public and the threatened danger." This latter role did not wholly eclipse the former. Instead, periodicals were expected to fulfill both functions simulta- neously, exercising a corrective presence by protecting readers from shoddy publications and encouraging their interest in more worthwhile ones.

There was, however, an inevitable tension between these descriptive and prescriptive functions. According to many commentators, this inherent contradiction was inflamed by modern literary critics' tendency to be gratuitously insulting in order to attract attention. "Having cleared a ring for themselves under the false pretext of a public cause," the *Retrospective* warned, modern journals "have ceased to exhibit themselves in any other character than that of intellectual gladiators; with literature for an arena—the public for spectators—and weapons poisoned with party malice and personal slander." There are few more graphic denunciations of the erosion of an enlightened public sphere mediated by print, but it was a common accusation. Reviewers were accused of holding an unfair advantage over authors because they published their reviews anonymously and because they could rely on a far greater readership than most individual publications could ever hope to attain. These problems were exacerbated by persistent rumours of covert deals between publishers and reviewers to "puff" particular publications by giving them unduly positive reviews. This problem seemed especially troubling because many periodicals were owned by publishers who had a vested interest in generating good publicity for their own books. A still more severe charge that was frequently directed at the periodicals was that they had been infected with the malice of party spirit. In the volatile atmosphere of a revolutionary age, the periodicals were celebrated for nurturing literature's role as a pre-political intellectual community guided by a love of truth that precluded the prejudices of factional argument. But as political debates intensified and views became polarized, the reviews were forced to take sides. Whatever their professions to intellectual objectivity, it became virtually impossible to avoid the problem of seeming to base their opinions about the quality of a publication on the author's explicit or supposed ideological leanings. These problems meant that authors had little chance of getting a fair hearing in a uniquely important venue, but as critics emphasized, it also deprived readers of their important right of thinking for themselves. What almost everyone did agree on was the fact that, for better or worse, periodicals were reaching a wider audience every month than most individual publications could ever hope to attract. Partly because of this, they were frequently hailed as an important form of literature in themselves, rather than merely as a body of critical commentary on literature. Periodicals have been the subject of an increasing body of important research in recent years, but their serial nature has helped to ensure their relative scarcity in courses on eighteenth-century and Romantic literature. Whatever these pedagogical obstacles, few forms of literary production offer a more compelling glimpse of the age's preoccupations and anxieties.

⁊⊃⊱⊃

THE ANALYTICAL REVIEW, OR, HISTORY OF LITERATURE, DOMESTIC AND FOREIGN, ON AN ENLARGED PLAN

TO THE PUBLIC

AT a time when Literary Journals are more numerous than useful, it seems necessary to state to the public, the reasons that have induced us to undertake the publication of a new one.

The true design of a Literary Journal is, in our opinion, to give such an account of new publications, as may enable the reader to judge of them for himself. Whether the Writers ought to add to this their own judgement, is with us a doubtful point. If their account be sufficiently accurate and full, it seems to supersede the necessity of any addition of their own.

The want of time to draw up faithful accounts and abstracts of books, or the want of room to insert them when executed, introduced the practice, of the *Journalists* themselves giving final judgement on the works that came before them. And while this was done with candour and with impartiality, by persons competent to the task, it could not be condemned.

The most respectable of the earlier *Critics*, M. Le Clerc, M. de la Roche, &c.[1] while they gave their own opinion of books, did not lose sight of the necessity of enabling their readers to judge for themselves, by such accounts and extracts, as were sufficient for that purpose. But in later times, the writers of literary journals, flattered by the attention paid to their decisions, and gratified by the influence they have obtained over authors, have filled their publications with little else than their own opinions and judgements. The old Journalists appear, only to introduce their *Principals,* while the modern ones seem to mention these, only to bring forward *themselves.* To tell what is contained in a book, which ought to be their *great object,* is become with them a *secondary matter:* amidst the splendour of their remarks the original author is often eclipsed; and amidst the multitude of their criticisms, he is overwhelmed and lost.

We would not be understood to condemn all critical remarks—When *well-founded* and *candid,* they are undoubtably useful. But certainly the public take up a Work of this kind, not so much to learn the opinion of the critic, as with a view to be enabled to judge of a book for themselves. And wherever this GRAND ORIGINAL END is neglected; wherever a superficial or no analysis[2] is given of a book, and no specimen from which the

reader can form any accurate judgement of it; then we conceive the true design of such a work is not accomplished.

But this is not all. Reviewers have engaged in *wars* with authors; and men without a name, from the shade of obscurity in which they were concealed, have ventured to abuse at random the first literary characters. In many cases they have entirely lost sight of that modesty, which ought always to accompany him, who being a private individual, presumes to speak to the public at large, and have set themselves up as a kind of oracles, and distributed from their dark thrones, decisions to regulate the ideas and sentiments of the literary world.

When Literary Journalists make themselves parties in great controverted questions, they take an unfair advantage of an Author, because the circulation of their publication is much greater than that of his. They may mistake his meaning, or shamefully pervert it, and though he may make a complete defence against their attacks, yet his labour is in vain: the whole world reads the objections, while his answer scarcely extends beyond the narrow circle of his own friends. Thus the sale of his work, as far as their credit extends, is impeded. The consequence has been, that they have gradually lost that *impartiality* which we hold to be essential to their character, and have in many cases become mere party men, who wrote apparently for no other purpose, but to pull down or build up particular systems. Mysterious transactions have taken place between Authors or Booksellers and Reviewers, and the respectable part of the public, suspecting that there was more of this dishonourable business done than really was the case, have lost their confidence in such Critics; and thus the character and reputation of the journals have been injured and degraded.

Beside these reasons, which have induced us to meditate, for some time past, the publication of a New work of this kind, we might mention others.

---

[1] Jean Le Clerc (1657–1736) editor of the literary journal *Bibliothèque choisie* (1703–18). Michel de la Roche (?), editor of the literary journals *Bibliothèque angloise* (1717–27), designed to convey literary news from England to the continent, and *Memoirs of Literature* (1710–14), which published reviews and news in English of scholarly works on the Continent.

[2] A descriptive account.

The plan of the earlier Journalists who took in fewer books and gave a fuller account of them, appears to us preferable to that of the moderns, who, by taking in many, give an imperfect account of all. The press groans with trifling and temporary publications, while the number of truly STANDARD works, which add to the stock of human knowledge, and will live beyond a day, is very small indeed. Of these only, a large account ought to be given, and such a one as Le Clerc used to give; an account that in some degree conveyed to the reader the knowledge of the book—of the rest it is sufficient to put down the titles, or to give a very brief character.

Could we pursue our own plan it would be to have one purely analytical. The true idea of a Literary Journal is to give the history of the republic of letters. Yet so far as their own opinion of books might be deemed important, the public would not be entirely deprived of it in such a Work. A full analysis would always shew, that they deemed a book of importance, a slight account, or total silence, would convey a tacit censure, without the indelicacy of personal abuse toward an author. While they paid a more particular attention to, and gave a larger account than any other Journalists do, of the few truly great works which occasionally appear from the press, they ought to be equally full and accurate in giving a list of the titles of the rest, and should endeavour in some brief expression to covey a true and candid idea of their value.

Anecdotes which may in any shape illustrate the history or Fate of a work, would be in no wise inconsistent with the plan of such a Journal. Facts, which admit of no doubt, can raise no controversy. In relating them, the Writers give no opinion of their own; they appear only as they ought to appear, the HISTORIANS of the Republic of Letters.

It may be thought a very easy matter to write such a journal as is now described, but those who have made the experiment have found it by no means so simple. To do it in some way is indeed easy; but to do it in the best way, to tell all that ought to be told, and nothing more, and that in the fewest words possible, is very difficult.

Such was the plan we had formed to ourselves of a Literary Journal, which we are sure would have been truly useful, and of which every year would have rendered the preceding volumes more valuable. But on weighing the matter fully, a very material objection occurred to us, viz. that the work, though esteemed by the learned and thinking few, would not be sufficiently adapted to the taste of the public at large, and hence fail to meet with encouragement equal to the extraordinary labour that would be required in executing it. On this account we have resolved not to attempt it on the *pure* analytical plan, but to take it up on another, which shall partly coincide with our own ideas, and partly with that pursued by the rest of our brethren. We adopt this, not as the best plan, but as the best that can be put in practice. This New Journal will appear monthly. It will have more of an analytical cast in it than any other, and on that account we shall call it, The ANALYTICAL REVIEW.[†]

In the judgements given on books, the writers will endeavour to conduct themselves with the degree of modesty which is most suitable to their character. Where absurdity and immorality are attempted to be imposed on the public, they will certainly think themselves authorized to raise the rod of criticism, but will not deem themselves entitled to interfere in a dictatorial manner, when authors of approved learning and genius have produced a work containing an elaborate chain of

---

[†] From this title, however, the public is not to expect that we are to give an analysis of *every* publication. A quarto volume monthly would not be sufficient to comprise this, nor would it be of real value to the public: for it is well known that by far the greatest number are unimportant or deserve censure: these will be mentioned with a short character.

facts and arguments, nor pretend by the hasty reading of an hour to confute the labour of years.

It has been proposed to us to receive from authors an analysis of their own works, and in some cases this may be desirable. Certainly no one is so well qualified to tell what is contained in a book as he who wrote it. But at the same time we must add, that all such analyses must be subject to revisal, and to such alterations as we judge necessary; because some authors, from the influence of particular motives, may be led to give too superficial an account of their works, while others, and these the far greater number, over-rating the importance of their own publications, may furnish more extended accounts than we could, in justice to our readers, insert.

A full list of the titles of all new publications will be given. The literary news will be revived, and as early information as can be procured, will be given of foreign literature.

Communications of literary intelligence, are earnestly solicited, and will be properly attended to: letters from foreign corespondents may be written either in Latin, French, Italian, Spanish, or German.

In this work, which we hope to render deserving of the countenance of the Public, we are promised the support of some of the most respectable and learned characters. We shall only add, that it will be our highest ambition to give to the world a respectable Journal, one that shall tend to diffuse knowledge, and to advance the interests of science, of virtue and morality. We shall therefore hope for the encouragement of every friend to the best interests of mankind.

(1788)

Gentleman's Magazine and Historical Chronicle

PREFACE

ON the Completion of a SIXTIETH VOLUME we may again be allowed to make the most grateful Acknowledgments for the Succession of Favour, which has so long enabled us to stand conspicuous in the foremost Rank of Monthly Journalists.

We assume no Merit beyond that of being the brief, but faithful, Reporters of the Chronicle of the Times; and of selecting from the Variety of excellent Contributions which we receive what, in our best Judgement, we think most conducive to the general Fund of public Entertainment and Instruction. It is to our Correspondents that the Reader is principally indebted for the valuable Materials with which our Pages are constantly filled, by Writers of the first Eminence.

Useful Inventions and Improvements in all Branches of Science, and even the Record of unsuccessful Projects, have regularly been registered in our Miscellany. The Admirers of Biography, which has become a favourite Amusement of the present Age, will find here the most copious Stores of Information; and that frequently in the truest Picture that can be given, by the genuine Letters of such eminent Characters as best deserve to be perpetuated. The Natural Historian, the Antiquary, the Philosopher, and the Studious in Polite Literature of every Description, may also meet with their favourite Object of Research, and mutually give and receive that Instruction which we are proud of being the Instruments of conveying to public Notice.

In Politicks, the present Year has been pregnant with Events of the highest Importance both to Church and State; and those it has been our Study to detail with the strictest Impartiality. And in this Volume, we may confidently assert, will be found a satisfactory Narrative of the Proceedings of the National Assembly in France, and of that ever-memorable Federation, which an elegant Female Writer[†], who went to Paris on purpose to be a Spectator of it, calls "the most sublime Spectacle that ever was represented on the "Theatre of the Earth.""[1]

We shall only add, that the very great and flattering Encouragement our Labours continue to receive is an additional Incentive to a steady Pursuit of the Path we have already trod, and to a chearful Continuance of future Exertions.

Dec. 31, 1790.

MONTHLY REVIEW
Review of *The Patriot: or, Political, Moral, and Philosophical Repository, consisting of Original Pieces, and Selections from Writers of Merit, a Work calculated to disseminate those Branches of Knowledge among all Ranks of People, at a small Expence.*
By a Society of Gentlemen.

AMONG all the modes which have been devised for the purpose of diffusing knowledge among mankind, none is so effectual as that of periodical publications; and certainly no subject is more proper for such publication, than the general science of politics, so interesting, and, we will add, so intelligible to the community at large. It is with pleasure that we announce to the public a work of this kind, undertaken, as far as we are able to judge from the contents of the numbers before us, by persons sufficiently qualified to assist in enlightening the public mind.

The declared purpose of *The Patriot* is to open a channel of universal communication on the important subjects expressed in the title of the work, at a price which shall be within the reach of almost every individual. The editors avow themselves the friends of liberty in general, and of the British constitution in particular; and they invite every friend to truth, liberty, and mankind, to assist them in disseminating sound principles of policy, and in promoting public spirit, and public virtue. They declare it to be one of their first objects, to diffuse a general conviction of the importance of an equal representation of the people. Their professed intention is, to pursue the middle path between the well-intended, but perhaps too great, ardour of some of the friends to reformation, on the one part, and the abject timidity of those, who cherish prejudices, however contemptible, because they are prejudices, on the other. They solicit the correspondence of all, who shall think proper to communicate their sentiments and opinions in the dispassionate and sober garb, which such a publication requires.

(1792)

MONTHLY MAGAZINE

MR. EDITOR,
THE Establishment of literary journals has certainly been an event of the greatest consequence in the republic of letters. It has been the means of diffusing knowledge far and wide, and of kindling a love of learning, where the seeds of genius would otherwise, in all likelihood, have perished in wretched torpidity. It has also been of infinite service to the interests of science, and to the useful arts of life, by examining into, and making generally known, the discoveries and improvements of ingenious men. The art of literary composition

---

[†] Miss WILLIAMS, whose Letters from France, lately published, do her much credit.

[1] Helen Maria Williams (c. 1761–1827), *Letters Written in France in the Summer of 1790, to a Friend in England* (1790).

has, moreover, been vastly improved; the principles of language have been better ascertained; and the qualities of a just and elegant style have been exactly determined hereby.

These, together with numerous other advantages, might be enumerated, and dilated upon, in reviewing the pretensions of periodical criticism.

Yet, not withstanding all these important benefits accruing from literary journals, justice compels the examiner to notice some flagrant abuses which have disgraced the monthly reports of literature.

The grand charge which may be brought against all our literary journals, without a single exception, is their being tinctured with a party spirit. The religious or political opinions of a literary reviewer ought not, by any means, to have an influence upon his mind while he is engaged in examining the merits of a book which comes under his critical eye. If they should, the man is the most unfit person in the world to bear the office which he has assumed, because he wants that coolness and indifference of mind which seems to be a grand requisite in the judicial or censorial character. Some reviewers, instead of being impartial reporters, and contenting themselves with summing up the merits of a work, become controversialists, and enter the lists against the author with all the ardour and petulance of professed disputants. This is undoubtably acting very unjustly, both towards the writer and the public. The one has the misfortune of having his arguments misrepresented, and his whole treatise condemned in an extensive publication, the decrees of which are received almost as infallible by thousands of readers. Another disadvantage under which he labours in this instance is the being opposed by a combatant who is sheltered under an impervious veil, while he is held up to ridicule. If he replies in a separate tract to the decisions of the reviewer, his vindication will probably have but a very confined sale, at least compared with that of the work with which he has to contend.

The public also are very unfairly dealt with by this mode of conduct; for the right of judgement is hereby taken out of their hands. I regard the court of criticism in a similar light to a court of judicature, where the bench has no authority whatever to dictate a verdict, but only to sum up the evidence with clearness, and to lay down the law with impartiality and precision, leaving the judgement with the reader.

I am sorry to observe, that there are too many readers who feel the greatest pleasure in this kind of reviewing; and the critics, sensible of this, endeavour to accommodate their criticisms to this vitiated taste, by throwing into their remarks as much of the *sal atticus*[1] as possible. Some indeed, are more profuse in sprinkling the critical brine than others; but this generally happens to be the case with those who have hardened themselves in the profession, and whose feelings are grown callous to the sensibility of an author suffering under their operations. There are, it must be confessed, a few critics who have not quite lost sight of what may properly be called the *morality of criticism*; but even they find that their critiques are not so favourably received by the public as they deserve to be, from the want of that which they cannot bring themselves to make use of with the freedom of their less tender-hearted brethren.

The great source of all this evil appears to be in the secrecy which covers the critical tribunals. Were these literary censors to affix their names to their respective articles, or at least in the title pages of their publications, they would be more cautious how they give loose to intemperate wit, and would be under the necessity of taking more pains with, and manifesting more candour to, an author's productions, than they now feel themselves disposed to do.

I am, Sir, your's   W
(1799)

---

[1] Athenian satire.

SAMUEL PRATT
Gleanings in England:
Descriptive of the Countenance,
Mind, and Character of the Country.[1]

KNOW then, my friend[2] that amongst our inno-vations, we have literary statutes at large, and codes of criticism in abstract, with which the noble art, just mentioned,[3] has no more to do, than with Breslaw's art of Trickery.[4] Those codes and statutes, indeed, much more resemble the mighty magic of the miracle-worker last named, than any of the regular bred practitioners of old, or of modern times. Circumscribed mortals! *they* could only work by rule and measure, the rule of reason, and the measure of right: but the critical Breslaws of Great Britain, might make Longinus,[5] and all other book legislators blush, to think they had exhausted so many years in studying a *science* which their succes-sors have proved, requires no study, nor any science at all. Why, Sir, we have biographers, who know only, that the subjects of their memoirs, were born within the century, and if not still alive, must certainly be dead; but who, with these slight materi-als, can story us from the swathing cloaths to the shroud; can catalogue the minutiæ of soul and body, vices and virtues, weigh to the fraction of a scruple, even to the weight of a split hair, or thistle-down thrice divided, the natural stock of sense and nonsense, ascertaining each man's share—in short,

chartists, who draw maps of our morality, with our black sea, and our red sea, our depths and our shal-lows, our Scylla and our Charybdis,[6] and all coloured and discoloured, and lined and interlined, curved and straightened, even like the map of the world itself.

Yea, and we have critics, who on the like princi-ples, and the like stock of ingenuity and informa-tion, deal wholesale and retail in the trade of lampoonery, or panegyric; but, by a singular inver-sion of common rules, it is a species of fame for an author, or for his book to become the subject of the former, and a kind of disgrace to find himself, or his composition, the *burden* of the latter.

—Peaceful plunder to all such.—You know the remark of Pope.[†] A poetical axiom that has ex-panded itself through every country, and has a place in every memory. Its truth, indeed, will travel down to all ages, and continue unimpaired till the earth shall be freed of noxious reptiles. But as the animal-cula of the mind, like those of the air and earth, are, doubtless, among the evils entailed upon us by the Fall, and will probably, more or less, annoy us till our eternal Rise, they have, I perceive, derived a consequence to which they are not entitled, even while I have been describing their filthy nature.

I have to discourse with your enlightened mind, my friend, on a matter of more weight, as to the office of literary criticism.

There cannot be a doubt but that while the liberty of the press, as to the freedom of publica-tion, shall be sacred—and on this side of licentious-ness, it ought to be uncontrolled—it is equally just that the sense and nonsense which indiscriminately issue from the immense vehicle of communication, should be subject to vigilant examination; otherwise

---

[1] Samuel Pratt (1749–1814), author of poetry, essays, travelogues, letters, plays, and anthologies. *Gleanings of England* was a series of miscellaneous reflections in the form of a travelogue.

[2] *Gleanings* was structured as a series of letters to a friend.

[3] Literary criticism.

[4] Philip Breslaw (1726–1800), who, in his act at the Haymarket in 1781, was the first magician to employ mind reading.

[5] Longinus (c. 213–273), Greek rhetorician and philosopher. Acknowledged author of *On the Sublime*, though this attribution is now disputed.

[6] In Greek mythology, two monsters dwelling on the Sicilian coast, between which one had to navigate. A metaphor for the need to steer between two dangerous extremes.

[†] "Destroy his web, and sophistry? In vain
The creature's at his dirty work again."

the whole world would be over-run with abortions of the mind. We want the assistance of some guides, who will take upon themselves the trouble of separating the good from the bad, and wade through the troubled deep of literature, in order, if we may be permitted a continuation of the figure, to collect the pearls and gems, and to describe the useless weeds, whether swimming on the surface, or lying at the muddy bottom. A stupendous labour if we consider the great disproportion betwixt the former and the latter. Applying this to the case in point, and it is by no means inapposite, a reader unused to such arduous undertakings, can image to himself no task so overwhelming as that of being left unaided to search for instruction in the mass of productions which are every year piled, mountain high, before him. We will even suppose whatever is most beautiful in fancy, captivating to the heart, and informing to the intellect, under his eye; but he startles at the view of the enormous *quantity*, nor can any degree of excellence in the *quality* reconcile, or, indeed, justify him,—in a life so brief, and so connected with other duties as the present,—to the immeasurable fatigue of such a task. Even if there should be found a few persevering spirits, endowed with a fortitude to peruse all that comes to hand, the profit would be no ways answerable to the pain by which it must be procured. For this reason, it would be proper that there should be some professional inspectors to direct our choice, even were literary excellence and defect nearly equal. But when the average is on a ratio of at least ninety in the hundred in the scale of compositions *dead weight*, there is not, perhaps, any office so necessary as his, who, with patient circumspection, will examine the great account betwixt wisdom and folly, and settle the balance.

It is not, therefore, possible to conceive a more useful institution than that of a Literary Journal, when conducted with various ability and inflexible justice; nor can it be denied that a great variety of articles, in every branch of literature, have been analysed on these principles; and a due proportion of good has thence resulted to the community.

We have to boast even at this day, of great and noble critics; and from most, indeed, in all of our Literary Journals, we find substantial evidence of unimpeachable judgement and unwarped integrity. It is not, however, to be expected, that any human association composed of many members, should be conducted on principles uniformly sagacious and correct. Were they to write apart, and consult together ultimately, there must even then often be a clash of sentiment, a dissonance of opinion.

Yet, I am persuaded, the critics above-described, are the very persons who must reprobate the virulences, and regret the errors for which they are made responsible. The literary body cannot be supposed to separate, or seem to move a limb independently;—much less to commit themselves, and confederate against each other, by deploring the want of candour in some of their colleagues, and of capacity in others. Thus from their not being associated by congeniality, or chosen by consent—and yet under a kind of compact to hold together, and by the good faith that should be preserved in all treaties, bound to support one another in the way of a common cause—the errors, incongruities, adulations and virulences, which are observed occasionally to disfigure their journals, attach indiscriminately to all.

A man must write from the spirit of envy, or from pique, or ignorance, if he assents not to these arguments because there is monthly confirmation of them. And of the authors who have, individually, to complain of uncandid treatment, or partial representation, there cannot be one who has genius and candour, in his own mind and heart, but must see and feel there is often just criticism, in the very publication where his *own* performance may be slighted or aspersed.

If, therefore, like every other valuable institution, abuse has crept into this; if prejudice and prepossession too often vault into the chair, and instead of its becoming a *Judgement-seat*, where the labours of the human mind are to have a fair trial, it is frequently a *secret Tribunal*, where the judges are wholly unknown, and the facts judged, so unfairly selected and argued, although formed into the most serious charges, that the work which ought to be condemned is acquitted, and the production that deserves to receive distinguished honours,—is, by this ungenerous artifice, supposed to be guilty of all the imperfections imputed to it.—

If, what by a misnomer is called criticism, the mutilated parts of a book are sometimes given as specimens of its general character—If, in offering an author's argument without reference to the context—by which alone its force or feebleness is to be determined—the most important and admirable reasoning is torn from its antecedent and consequent, like a limb hacked from the body, and presented in a mangled state, to serve as a measure for the harmony and beauty of the whole; or if, which is not more generous, or reasonable, a frequently licentious, sometimes malignant display is made of ill-grounded *ridicule*—a power, by which all things, the most grave and sacred, however happy they may be, in their conception and delivery—are discoloured, distorted, tending to excite the very reverse impression of that they probably *would* have made, on a mind unseduced by the intemperate sally of misapplied or ill-tempered wit—and all this to indulge the miserable propensity of raising a laugh against what, even at worst, is, perhaps, the best effort of its author to please the public; and who, possibly, in the bitterness of his disappointment, weeps not only over the loss of that daily bread which the scorner earns by his taunts, but which the industrious author has often earned more honestly than his critic—if,

while it must be owned there are numberless objects, which deserve to be assailed by all the powers of wit, this dangerous talent snatches the honest morsel from the lip of Genius, for the paltry triumph of saying "a good thing;"—if those compositions which deserve our reverence, and which, perhaps, have delighted even the defamer himself privately, have, nevertheless, been publicly sacrificed—If the attempt to turn performances of indubitable merit and labour into ridicule, by shewing them under absurd circumstances, is but too successfully practised. If, "the sovereigns of Reason, and the artificers and purveyors of our most exquisite pleasures,"—those of the intellect are unquestionably of that order—if the rightful Critic upon the human understanding, is, by the common and inevitable lot of all corporate bodies, thus unfortunately mixt with those critical usurpers, who with pontifical pride, fulminate their defamatory bulls against Genius and Learning, in ignorant pomposity or in rude impertinence—If such accusations are well founded, depend upon it, those who are the true protectors, advocates, and guardians of Literature—the TRUE critics—even while by a sacred duty they are constrained to reprehend, punish, or wholly condemn some of the votaries of Science and the Muses, *they* are the persons most touched and aggrieved whenever the numerous pettifoggers of Literature, any of those unprincipled usurpers with whom, by imperious circumstances, they may be blended, have perplexed or lost the cause of real Genius or Learning. The verdict, it is true, is always given by the PUBLIC—our Literary Grand Jury—but, if by false reasoning, or false impression, by partial evidence, or by corrupt influence, it is practised upon and misguided, the sentence would of course be unjust, though it might have the sanction of a majority of the council and of the judges.

(1799)

The Reflector, A Collection of Essays, on Miscellaneous Subjects of Literature and Politics [1]

PROSPECTUS

THE REFLECTOR will be an attempt to improve upon the general character of Magazines, and all the town knows, that much improvement of this kind may be effected without any great talent. Reform of periodical writing is as much wanted in Magazines, as it formerly was in Reviews, and still is in Newspapers. It is true, there are still to be found some agreeable and instructive articles in the Magazines— a few guineas thrown by richer hands into the poor's box:—indolent genius will now and then contribute a lucky paragraph. But the field is either given up to the cultivation of sorry plants, or it is cut up into a petty variety of produce to which every thing important is sacrificed. It is needless to descant on the common lumber that occupies the greater portion of these publications—on the want of original discussion; or the recipes for and against cooking and coughing; or the stale jests; or the plagiarisms; or the blinking pettiness of antiquarianism, which goes toiling like a mole through every species of rubbish, and sees no object so stupendous as an old house or a belfry. These flimsy publications, though unworthy of notice in themselves, are injurious to the taste of the town in more than one respect, inasmuch as they *make a shew of employing the Arts,* while they are only degrading and wasting them.

(1812)

---

[1] *The Reflector* (1810–12), was published by Leigh Hunt (1784–1859), who did most of the writing for it, though it also included work by various friends including Charles Lamb, who contributed important essays on Shakespeare and Hogarth. Its inclusion of various accounts of modern poetry alongside vehement political analysis reflected Hunt's insistence on the importance of fusing cultural and political issues.

S.T. Coleridge
The Author's Obligations to Critics, and the Probable Occasion

from *Biographia Literaria* [2]

TO anonymous critics in reviews, magazines, and news-journals of various name and rank, and to satirists with or without a name, in verse or prose, or in verse-text aided by prose-comment, I do seriously believe and profess, that I owe full two thirds of whatever reputation and publicity I happen to possess. For when the name of an individual has occurred so frequently, in so many works, for so great a length of time, the readers of these works (which with a shelf or two of BEAUTIES, ELEGANT EXTRACTS and ANAs,[3] form nine-tenths of the reading of the reading public[†]) cannot but be

---

[2] Samuel Taylor Coleridge (1772–1834), a well-known poet, literary critic, and social commentator. The *Biographia Literaria* was an ambitious blend of literary criticism, philosophy, and autobiography.

[3] Various titles for miscellaneous collections of extracts. ANAS referred to the suffix which was added to a proper name to form a title. For example, Johnsoniana.

[†] For as to the devotees of the circulating libraries, I dare not compliment their *pass-time*, or rather *kill-time*, with the name of *reading*. Call it rather a sort of beggarly daydreaming, during which the mind of the reader furnishes for itself nothing but laziness and a little mawkish sensibility; while the whole *materiel* and imagery of the doze is supplied *ad extra* by a sort of mental *camera obscura* manufactured at the printing office, which *pro tempore* fixes, reflects and transmits the moving phantasms of one man's delirium, so as to people the barrenness of an hundred other brains afflicted with the same trance or suspension of all common sense and all definite purpose. We should therefore transfer this species of *amusement*, (if indeed those can be said to retire *a musis*, who were never in their company, or relaxation be attributable to those, whose bows are never bent) from the genus, *reading*, to that comprehensive class characterized by the power of reconciling the two contrary yet co-existing propensities of human nature, namely; indulgence of sloth, and hatred of vacancy. In addition to novels and tales of chivalry in prose and rhyme, (by which last I mean neither rhythm nor metre) this genus comprizes as its species, gaming, swinging, or swaying on a chair or gate; spitting over a bridge; smoking; snuff-taking; *tete a tete* quarrels after dinner between husband and wife; conning word by word all the advertisements of the daily

familiar with the name, without distinctly remembering whether it was introduced for an eulogy or for censure. And this becomes the more likely, if (as I believe) the habit of perusing periodical works may be properly added to Averrhoe's catalogue of ANTI-MNEMONICS, or weakeners of the memory.[1] But where this has not been the case, yet the reader will be apt to suspect, that there must be something more than usually strong and extensive in a reputation, that could either require or stand so merciless and long-continued a cannonading. Without any feeling of *anger* therefore (for which indeed, on my own account, I have no pretext) I may yet be allowed to express some degree of *surprize*, that after having run the critical gauntlet for a certain class of faults which I *had*, nothing having come before the judgement-seat in the interim, I should, year after year, quarter after quarter, month after month (not to mention sundry petty periodicals of still quicker revolution, "or weekly or diurnal"[2]) have been for at least 17 years consecutively dragged forth by them into the foremost ranks of the *proscribed*, and forced to abide the brunt of abuse, for faults directly opposite, and which I certainly had not.[3] How shall I explain this?

As long as there are readers to be delighted with calumny, there will be found reviewers to calumni-

ate. And such readers will become in all probability more numerous, in proportion as a still greater diffusion of literature shall produce an increase of sciolists; and sciolism[4] bring with it petulance and presumption. In times of old, books were as religious oracles; as literature advanced, they next became venerable preceptors; they then descended to the rank of instructive friends; and as their numbers increased, they sunk still lower to that of entertaining companions; and at present they seem degraded into culprits to hold up their hands at the bar of every self-elected, yet not the less peremptory, judge, who chuses to write from humour or interest, from enmity or arrogance, and to abide the decision (in the words of Jeremy Taylor) "of him that reads in malice, or him that reads after dinner."[5]

The same gradual retrograde movement may be traced, in the relation which the authors themselves have assumed towards their readers. From the lofty address of Bacon: "these are the meditations of Francis of Verulam, which that posterity should be possessed of, he deemed *their* interest:"[6] or from dedication to Monarch or Pontiff, in which the honor given was asserted in equipoise to the patronage acknowleged from P I N D A R'S

— ἐπ᾽ἄλλοι-
σι δ᾽ἄλλοι μεγάλοι. τὸ δ᾽ἔσχατου-
φοῦται βασιλεῦσι. μηκέτι
Πάπταινε πόρσιον.
Ε ἴη σέ τε τούτου
Ὑψοῦ κρόυου πατεῖυ, ἐμέ
Τε τοσσάδε υικαφόροις
Ὁμιλεῖυ, πρόφαυτου σοφίανν καθ᾽ Ἑλ-

---

advertizer in a public house on a rainy day, &c. &c. &c.

[1] A misattribution. Not Averroes, but an Arabic writer, Burhān al-Dīn. Coleridge knew of him by way of a footnote in Jean Baptiste de Boyer, Marquis d'Argens's *Kabbalistische Briefe* (1773–77), which refers to *Semita sapientiae* (Paris 1646), a Latin translation of an anonymous Arabic manuscript, later known to be by Burhān al-Dīn, which discusses "some causes for loss of memory." This information is from James Engell and W. Jackson Bate's edition of *Biographia Literaria* (Princeton UP, 1983): 49–50, note 3.

[2] John Gay, "In the Present State of Wit" (1711).

[3] Of the almost one hundred references to Coleridge in articles and reviews from 1798–1814, the majority were positive. The editors of Coleridge's *Collected Works* note the irony of the fact that one of the most negative discussions of Coleridge was written by Robert Southey, who Coleridge was preparing to defend against negative reviews.

---

[4] Pretentious and superficial knowledge.

[5] Jeremy Taylor (1613–67), a religious writer best known for *A Discourse of the Liberty of Prophesying* (1646), which espoused the principle of religious toleration. The quote is from the Epistle Dedicatory of Taylor's *Collection of Polemical Discourses* (1674).

[6] Coleridge's translation of Francis Bacon's *Procemium to the Great Instruction* (1620).

λαυας ὲόυτα παντᾶ.
OLYMP. OD. I.[1]

Poets and Philosophers, rendered diffident by their very number, addressed themselves to "*learned* readers;" then, aimed to conciliate the graces of "the *candid* reader;" till, the critic still rising as the author sunk, the amateurs of literature collectively were erected into a municipality of judges, and addressed as THE TOWN! And now finally, all men being supposed able to read, and all readers able to judge, the multitudinous PUBLIC, shaped into personal unity by the magic of abstraction, sits nominal despot on the throne of criticism. But, alas! as in other despotisms, it but echoes the decisions of its invisible ministers, whose intellectual claims to the guardianship of the muses seem, for the greater part, analogous to the physical qualifications which adapt their oriental brethren for the superintendence of the Harem.[2]

In the present age "perituræ parcere chartæ"[3] is emphatically an unreasonable demand. The merest trifle, he[4] ever sent abroad, had tenfold better claims to its ink and paper, than all the silly criticisms, which prove no more, than that the critic was not one of those, for whom the trifle was written; and than all the grave exhortations to a greater reverence for the public. As if the passive page of a book, by having an epigram or doggrel tale impressed on it, instantly assumed at once loco-motive power and a sort of ubiquity, so as to flutter and buz in the ear of the public to the sore annoyance of the said mysterious personage. But what gives an additional and more ludicrous absurdity to these lamentations is the curious fact, that if in a volume of poetry the critic should find poem or passage which he deems more especially worthless, he is sure to select and reprint it in the review; by which, on his own grounds, he wastes as much more paper than the author, as the copies of a fashionable review are more numerous than those of the original book; in some, and those the most prominent instances, as ten thousand to five hundred.

(1817)

RETROSPECTIVE REVIEW

INTRODUCTION

THE accumulation of books has ever been regarded with some degree of jealousy—an inundation of paper and print seems to have been thought as formidable to the ideas of men, as an inundation of water to their houses and cattle. In these latter times, the danger to be apprehended has been deemed so imminent, that various dykes or mud-banks have been established and supported, for the purpose of being interposed between the public and the threatened danger. Reviews have sprung up as rapidly, and as well armed, as the fabled warriors from the teeth sown by Cadmus,[5] to stand in the gap in the hour of need; but it has been "whispered in the state,"[6] that, like the same sons of the earth, these self-elected champions, neglecting the public weal, have turned their arms against each

---

[1] "Some men are great in one thing; others in another: but the crowning summit is for kings. Refrain from peering too far. Heaven grant that thou mayest plant thy feet on high, so long as thou livest, and that I may consort with victors for all my days, and be foremost in the lore of song among Greeks in every land." *Olympian Odes* 1:113–16. The author, Peter Pindar (c. 522–443 B.C.), was a Greek lyric poet, the majority of whose poems were odes celebrating victories in the games at Olympia and elsewhere.

[2] Castration.

[3] "To spare paper that would be wasted anyway." Juvenal, *Satires* 1:18.

[4] Robert Southey, whose mistreatment by critics Coleridge is denouncing.

[5] Mythological figure reputed to have sown the seeds of a dead serpent, from which sprang the descendants of the noble family of Thebes.

[6] Source unidentified.

other—that having cleared a ring for themselves under the false pretext of a public cause, they have ceased to exhibit themselves in any other character than that of intellectual gladiators; with literature for an arena—the public for spectators—and weapons poisoned with party malice and personal slander.

That the number of books has been increasing—is increasing—and ought to be diminished—is the deliberate resolution even of those who esteem themselves friendly to literature. That a great book is a great evil, is stamped with the sanction of ages—it has passed into a proverb. If, however, the evil of a book is to be measured by its bulk, the mischief *we* shall do is small; while at the same time, the good we propose to effect, if estimated on a scale of this kind, is such as must call down upon us the approbation of all favourers of the proverb—since it is one of our objects, and indeed no small part of the design of this work, to reduce books to their *natural* size; a process which we apprehend will compress many a distended publication into a very insignificant tenement. Let no man weep, as the Thracians did, over the birth of a child, and cry, "another book is born unto the world!"[1] For the space we shall empty is greater than that which we hope to fill, should even our future labours ever rival the "piled heaps" of the most favoured periodical that exists.

The only real evil to be apprehended from the enormous increase in the number of books is, that it is likely to distract the attention, and dissipate the mind, by inducing the student to read many, rather than much. The alluring catalogue of attractive title-pages unfixes the attention, and causes the eye to wander over a large surface, when it ought to be intently turned upon a small though fertile spot. It induces a passion for reading as an end, and not as a means—merely to satisfy an appetite, and not to

strengthen the system, and enrich the powers of original thinking. It makes learned men, and not wise men. Hobbes, on being asked why he did not read more? answered, if I read as much as other men, I should know as little. True it is, that for the purpose of supplying the place of constant companions, of suggesting never failing subjects of reflection, and of exercising and gratifying the imagination, a few choice and venerable authors are amply sufficient. "Make," says Bishop Watson, "Bacon then, and Locke, and why should I not add, that sweet child of nature Shakespeare, your chief companions through life, let them be ever upon your table, and when you have an hour to spare, spend it upon them; and I will answer for their giving you entertainment and instruction as long as you live." [2]

The practice of these times, it is needless to say, is as unlike that here recommended, as it can well be; the British public are almost solely occupied by the productions which daily issue from the press; newspapers, reviews, pamphlets, magazines, the popular poetry, the fashionable romances, together with new voyages and travels, occupy the reading time, and fix the attention of the people—The old and venerable literature of the country, which has, as much as any thing, tended to make us what we are, is treated with distant reverence—its noble works, which every one is ashamed not to know—which every one pretends to know, and which far too few are acquainted with, are much oftener talked of than read. Their authors are apotheosized, but seldom worshipped,—their brilliant but temperate lustre neglected for the glaring meteors, which are hanging their short-lived blaze every where in the heavens—It is time to look back—the enervating effects of a literature of this kind are too obvious—the uncompromising vigor of intellect, and the sturdy and unshrinking adherence to principle, which have been distinguishing character-

[1] Source unidentified.

[2] Source unidentified.

istics of Englishmen, cannot for any length of time resist the relaxing power of so diluted a diet. Never was education so common as at present—never were books so commonly dispersed, so multifariously read. We present a spectacle of what, perhaps, was never before seen in any age, certainly neither Greek nor Roman, that of a whole nation, employing nearly all its leisure hours from the highest to the lowest rank in *reading*—we have been truly called a READING PUBLIC. The lively Greeks were not a *reading* nation—they were a hearing and a talking people—they fed the mind through the ear, and not through the eye; historians and poets were not so much read as heard—Thus they became a thinking, talking, enlightened nation—free of speech, brilliant in wit, restless, active, boasting, audacious, and arrogant—but they were not a *reading* nation. For one library, the Greeks had a hundred theatres for plays, music, spectacles—, groves and academies for disputation—forums for orators—and gymnasia and palæstræ,[1] for exercise and conversation. The invention of paper in the eleventh, and of printing in the fifteenth century, are as cheering to the lovers of humanity, as the sea-birds and sea-weeds, signs of approaching land, are to the wearied and despairing navigator, who is darkly tracking an unknown and pathless ocean. The fertile and luxurious crop of modern literature then appeared above the earth—the richness of the soil, which had lain fallow for so long a time, during which it had only borne the rank weeds of scholastic subtlety, mingled indeed with the wild but romantic flowers of chivalrous feudality, as well as the greenness and freshness of the productions themselves, all encouraging animating hopes of an abundant harvest. Since that time, books have become a common and current coin; every city and every town has its mint—they are almost numberless. A catalogue of all the books that have been

printed, would of itself fill a little library. The knowledge of their external qualities, and the adventitious circumstances attending their formation or history, has become a science—professors devote their lives to it, with an enthusiasm not unworthy of a higher calling—they have earned the name of *bibliomaniacs*. Vast collections of books are esteemed the pride and glory of the countries or cities fortunate enough to possess them. The Vatican boasts its millions—the Laurentian, Ambrosian, and other libraries of Italy, the Bibliotheque du Roi at Paris, the enormous collection at the British Museum, our university and college libraries, particularly the Bodleian, while they are proud monuments of the ingenuity and all-reaching, all-fathoming mind of man; yet must strike the heart of the student that enters them with despair, should he aim at attaining universal knowledge through the medium of books.

No study is more interesting, and few more useful, than the history of literature,—which is in fact, the history of the mind of man. This observation leads us to the chief object of this introduction, namely, a more particular statement of our views in sending forth the "Retrospective Review," one of whose most valuable and important departments, it is the intention of the editors, to assign to the history of literature.

The design of this Review of past literature, had its origin in the decisively modern direction of the reading of the present day—it is an attempt to recal the public from an exclusive attention to new books, by making the merit of old ones the subject of critical discussion. The interesting form and manner of the present Reviews it is intended to preserve; though from the nature of the work, and from our unfeigned horror of either political or personal invective, we shall neither pamper the depraved appetites of listless readers, by piquant abuse—nor amuse one part of the public, by hold-

---

[1] Wrestling schools.

ing up another to scorn and mockery,—at any rate, we shall not be driven to a resource of this description through a paucity of interesting matter which we may legitimately present to our readers. While the present Reviews are confined to the books of the day, *we* have the liberty of ranging over the whole extent of modern literature. Criticism, which when able and just, is always pleasing, we shall combine with copious and characteristic extracts, analyses, and biographical accounts, so as in some measure to supply the dearth of works on the history of literature in our own language.

We shall not pay exclusive homage to the mighty in intellect—to those of heavenly mould, who, like the giants of old, are the offspring of the gods and the daughters of men—far from it—many others less imposing, whether in philosophy, poetry, or general literature, from which any thing original in design, profound in thought, beautiful in imagination, or delicate in expression, can be extracted, will be considered worthy of a place in this work.

We shall also, by a careful selection of particular extracts, not only endeavour to give an idea of the mode and style of individual authors, but to furnish a collection of specimens of the greatest part of our writers, so as to exhibit a bird's-eye view of the rise and progress of our literature. The utility of such a work to the student, in abridging his labour, and thereby increasing his gratification, is obvious —whilst to him, who reads only for his own amusement, it will have the attraction of a various literary miscellany, without extracting from him a too rigid attention; and as it is our design to mingle the useful with the agreeable in due proportions, it may not be to him even without its value and instruction.

(1820)

EDINBURGH REVIEW
The Periodical Press

A Review of:
The St. James Chronicle—The Morning Chronicle—The Times—The New Times— The Courier, &c.—Cobbett's Weekly Journal—The Examiner—The Observer—The Gentleman's Magazine—The New Monthly Magazine—The London, &c. &c.[1]

WE often hear it asked, *Whether Periodical Criticism is, upon the whole, beneficial to the cause of literature?* And this question is usually followed up by another, which is thought to settle the first, *Whether Shakespeare could have written as he did, had he lived in the present day?* We shall not attempt to answer either of these questions: But we will be bold to say, that we have at least one author at present, whose productions spring up free and numberless, in the very hotbed of criticism—a large and living refutation of the chilling and blighting effects of such a neighbourhood. "But would not the author of Waverley himself," resumes our tritical querist, "have written better, if he had not had the fear of the periodical press before his eyes?" We answer, that he has no fear of the periodical press; and that we do not see how, in any circumstances, he could have written better than he does. "But a single exception does not disprove the rule." But he is not a single exception. Is there not Lord Byron? Are there not many more?—only that we are too near them to scan the loftiness of their pretensions, or to guess at their unknown duration. Genius carries on an unequal strife with Fame; nor

---

[1] The *Edinburgh Review*, founded in 1802, was the first of the literary quarterlies, a type of periodical which assumed enormous authority in the early nineteenth century. This article was published by William Hazlitt (1778–1830), a leading essayist known for his critical work on literature and the fine arts, social and autobiographical reflections, and for his radical political sympathies.

will our bare word (if we durst presume to give it) make the balance even. Time alone can show who are the authors of mortal or immortal mould; and it is the height of wilful impertinence to anticipate its award, and assume, because certain living authors are new, that they never can become old.

Waving, however, any answer to these ingenious questions, we will content ourselves with announcing a truism on the subject, which, like many other truisms, is pregnant with deep thought,—*viz. That periodical criticism is favourable—to periodical criticism.* It contributes to its own improvement—and its cultivation proves not only that it suits the spirit of the times, but advances it. It certainly never flourished more than at present. It never struck its roots so deep, nor spread its branches so widely and luxuriantly. Is not the proposal of this very question a proof of its progressive refinement? And what, it may be asked, can be desired more than to have the perfection of one thing at any one time? If literature in our day has taken this decided turn into a critical channel, is it not a presumptive proof that it ought to do so? Most things find their own level; and so does the mind of man. If there is a preponderance of criticism at any one period, this can only be because there are subjects, and because it is the time for it. We complain that this is a Critical age; and that no great works of Genius appear, because so much is said and written about them; while we ought to reverse the argument, and say, that it is because so many works of genius *have appeared*, that they have left us little or nothing to do, but to think and talk about them—that if we did not do that, we should do nothing so good—and if we do this well, we cannot be said to do amiss!

It has been urged as one fatal objection against periodical criticism, that it is too often made the engine of party-spirit and personal invective. This is an abuse of it greatly to be lamented; but in fact, it only shows the extent and importance of this branch of literature, so that it has become the organ of every thing else, however alien to it. The current of political and individual obloquy has run into this channel, because it has absorbed every topic. The bias to miscellaneous discussion and criticism is so great, that it is necessary to insert politics in a sort of sandwich of literature, in order to make them at all palatable to the ordinary taste. The war of political pamphlets, of virulent pasquinades, has ceased, and the ghosts of Junius and Cato, of Gracchus and Cincinnatus,[1] no longer "squeak and gibber"[2] in our modern streets, or torment the air with a hubbub of hoarse noises. A Whig or Tory *tirade* on a political question, the abuse of a public character, now stands side by side in a fashionable Review, with a disquisition on ancient coins, or is introduced right in the middle of an analysis of the principles of taste. This is a violation, no doubt, of the rules of decorum and order, and might well be dispensed with: but the stock of malice and prejudice in the world is much the same, though it has found a more classical and agreeable vehicle to vent itself. Mere politics, mere personal altercation, will not go down without an infusion of the Belles-Lettres and the Fine Arts. This makes decidedly either for the refinement or the frivolity of our taste. It is found necessary to poison or to sour the public mind, by going to the well-head of polite literature and periodical criticism,—which shows plainly how many drink at that fountain, and will drink at no other.

Over-refinement, however, cannot be charged as the failing of most of our periodical publications. Some are full of polemical orthodoxy—some of methodistical deliration—some inculcate servility, and others preach up sedition—some creep along in a series of dull truisms and stale moralities—while others, more "lively, audible, and full of vent,"[3]

---

[1] These classical names were favourite pseudonyms of radical writers.

[2] William Shakespeare (1564–1616), *Hamlet* (1600): I: i: 126.

[3] Shakespeare, *Coriolanus* (1607–08): IV: 5: 238.

subsist on the great staple of falsehood and person-ality, and enjoy all the advantages that result from an entire contempt for the restraints of decency, consistency, or candour. There is no pretence, indeed, or concealment of the principles on which such works are conducted: and the reader feels almost as if he were admitted to look in on a club of thorough-going hack authors, in their moments of freedom and exaltation. There is plenty of *slang-wit* going, and some shrew remark. The pipes and tobacco are laid on the table, with a set-out of oysters and whisky, and bludgeons and sword-sticks in the corner! A profane parody is recited, or a libel on an absent member—and songs are sung in mockery of their former friends and employers. From foul words they get to blows and broken heads; till drunk with ribaldry, and stunned with noise, they proceed to throw open the windows and abuse the passengers in the street, for their want of religion, morals, and decorum! This is a modern and an enormous abuse, and requires to be cor-rected.

The illiberality of the Periodical Press is "the sin that most easily besets it."[1] We have already ac-counted for this from the rank and importance it has assumed, which have made it a necessary engine in the hands of party. The abuse, however, has grown to a height that renders it desirable that it should be crushed, if it cannot be corrected; for it threatens to overlay, not only criticism and letters, but to root out all common honesty and common sense from works of the greatest excellence, upon large classes of society. All character, all decency, the plainest matter of fact, or deductions of reason, are made the sport of a nickname, an innuendo, or a bold and direct falsehood. The continuance of this nuisance rests not with the writers, but with the public; it is they that pamper it into the monster it is; and, in order to put an end to the traffic, the best

way is to let them see a little what sort of thing it is which they encourage. Both of the extreme parties in the State, the Ultra-Whigs as well as the Ul-tra-Royalists, have occasionally trespassed on the borders of this enormity: but it is only the worst part of the Ministerial Press that has had the temp-tation, the hardihood, or the cowardice to make literature the mere tool and creature of party-spirit; and, in the sacredness of the cause in which it was embarked, to disregard entirely the profligacy of the means. It was pious and loyal to substitute abuse for argument, and private scandal for general argument. Knowledge, writing, the press was found to be the great engine that governed public opinion; and the scheme therefore was, to make it recoil upon itself, and act in a retrograde direction to its natural one. Prejudice and power had a provocation to this extreme and desperate mode of defense, in their instinctive jealousy of any opposition to their sentiments or will. They felt that reason was against them—and therefore it was necessary that they should be against reason,—they felt, too, that they could extend impunity to their agents and accom-plices, whom they could easily screen from reprisals. Conscious that they were no match for modern philosophers and reformers in abstract reasoning, they paid off their dread of their talents and princi-ples by a proportionable contempt for their persons, for which no epithets could be too mean or hateful. These were therefore poured out in profusion by their satellites. The nicknames, the cant phrases, too, were all in favour of existing institutions and opinions, and were easily devised in a contest where victory, not truth, was the object. The warfare was therefore turned into this channel from the first; and what passion dictated, a cunning and merce-nary policy has continued.

The beauty of it is, that there is generally no reparation or means of redress. From the nature of the imputations, it is frequently impossible distinctly to refute them, or to gain a hearing to the refutation. A young poet comes forward: an early and favourable notice appears of some boyish verses of his in the Examiner,[1] independently of all political opinion. That alone decides his fate; and from that moment he is set upon, pulled in pieces, and hunted into his grave by the whole venal crew in full cry after him. It was crime enough that he dared to accept praise from so disreputable a quarter. He should have thrown back his bounty in the face of the donor, and come with his manuscript in his hand, to have poetical justice dealt out to him by the unbiassed author of the Baviad and Mæviad![2] His tenderness and beauties would then have been exalted with *faint* praise, instead of being mangled and torn to pieces with ruthless, unfeeling rage; his faults would have been gently hinted at, and attributed to youth and inexperience; and his profession, instead of being made the subject of loud ribald jests by vile buffoons, would have been introduced to enhance the merit of his poetry. But a different fate awaited poor Keats! His fine fancy and powerful invention were too obvious to be treated with mere neglect; and as he had not been ushered into the world with the court-stamp upon him, he was to be crushed as a warning to genius how it keeps company with honesty, and as a sure means of inoculating the ingenuous spirit and talent of the country with timely and systematic servility! We sometimes think that writers are alarmed at the praises that even *we* bestow upon them, lest it

should preclude them from the approbation of the authorized sources of fame!

This system thus pursued is intended to amount, and in fact does amount, to a prohibition to authors to write, and to the public to read any works that have not the Government mark upon them. The professed object is to gag the one, and hoodwink the others, and to persuade the world that all talent, taste, elegance, science, liberality and virtue, are confined to a few hack-writers and their employers. One would think the public would resent this gross attempt to impose on their understandings, and encroach on their liberty of private judgment. When a gentleman is reading a new work, of which he is beginning to form a favourable opinion, is it to be borne that he should have it snatched out of his hands, and tossed into the dirt by a retainer of the *literary police*? Can he be supposed to pick it up afterwards, either to read himself, or to lend it to a friend, sullied and disfigured as it is? But the truth we fear is, that the public, besides their participation in the same prejudices, are timid, indolent, and easily influenced by a little swaggering and an air of authority. They like to amuse their leisure with reading a new work; and if they have more leisure, have no objection to fill it up with listening to an abuse of the writer. If they approve of candour and equity in the abstract, they do not disapprove of a little scandal and tittle-tattle by the by. They take in a disgusting publication, because it is "amusing and clever"—that is, full of incredible assertions which make them stare, and of opprobrious epithets applied to high characters, which, by their smartness and incongruity, operate as a lively stimulus to their ordinary state of ennui.

It used to be the boast of English gentlemen, that their political contentions were conducted in a spirit, not merely of perfect fairness, but of mutual courtesy and urbanity; and that, even among the lower orders, quarrels were governed by a law of

---

[1] The June 1, and July 6, 1817 editions of Leigh Hunt's *Examiner* carried a positive review of Keats's *Poems* (1817), which it hailed as "one of the greatest evidences" of a rebirth of British poetry. Keats's association with the reformist *Examiner* made him the target of hostile reviews in *Blackwood's Edinburgh Magazine* and *Quarterly Magazine*. Keats's supporters frequently blamed the vehemence of these critical attacks for Keats's early death.

[2] William Gifford, editor of the royalist *Quarterly Review*. See Hazlitt's description of Gifford in Section 12: The Second Wave of Revolution, and Gifford's account of his life in Section Three: Literary Autobiographies.

honour and chivalry, which proscribed all base advantages, and united all the spectators against him by whom *a foul blow* was given or attempted. We trust that this spirit is not yet extinguished among us; and that it will speedily assert itself, by trampling under foot that base system of mean and malignant defamation, by which our Periodical Press has recently been polluted and disgraced. We would avoid naming works that desire nothing so much as notoriety; but it is but too well known, that the work of intimidation and deceit, of cruel personality and audacious fabrication, has been carried on, for several years, in various periodical publications, daily, weekly, monthly, and quarterly,—that it has been urged with unrelenting eagerness in the metropolis, in spite of the public discountenance of the leaders of the party which it disgraces by its pretended support; and then propagated into various parts of the country, for purposes of local annoyance. It is equally well known and understood too, that this savage system of bullying and assassination is no longer pursued from the impulse of angry passions or furious prejudices, but on a cold-blooded mercenary calculation of the profits which idle curiosity, and the vulgar appetite for slander, may enable its authors to derive from it. Where this is to stop, we do not presume to conjecture,—unless the excess leads to the remedy, and the distempered appetite of the public be surfeited, and so die. This is by no means an unlikely, and, we hope, may be a speedy consummation. In the mean time, the extent and extravagance of the abuse has already had the effect, not only of making individual attacks less painful or alarming, but even, in many cases, of pointing out to the judicious the proper objects of their gratitude and respect. For ourselves, at least, we do not hesitate to acknowledge, that, when we find an author savagely and perseveringly attacked by this gang of literary retainers, we immediately feel assured, not only that he is a good writer, but an honest man; and if a statesman is once selected as the butt of outrageous abuse in the same quarter, we consider it as a satisfactory proof that he has lately rendered some signal service to his country, or aimed a deadly blow at corruption.   (1823)

Section Eight

Romantic Literature

Many of the comments that we have seen about literature so far describe it as a communicative vehicle promoting the exchange of ideas, and diffusing the knowledge that would result from these exchanges throughout an expanding and increasingly educated reading public. This vision was largely an urban one. Whether in London or in the provincial centres, the virtual reality of intellectual communities mediated by print was rooted in a network of social spaces that included coffee houses, taverns, libraries, bookstores, debating clubs, and literary and philosophical societies. Literature promised a way to extend the discussions that occurred in these places to all motivated participants. William Godwin's description of literature, which we saw in Section One, is a particularly clear example of this perspective. But many writers favoured another perspective grounded in a strikingly different definition of "knowledge" and "truth," and in an equally contrary understanding of human nature. Because of these different assumptions, these writers tended to espouse "creative" rather than "critical" writing. We have seen a discussion of this aesthetic vision in Thomas De Quincey's comparison of a literature of power and a literature of knowledge, also in Section One. For those who favoured De Quincey's perspective, truth was fragmentary rather than totalizing, discontinuous rather than progressive, and spiritual as much as social; it was a mode of apprehension, a tribute to the power of the imagination, more than a set of authenticated facts. For these Romantics, as we now refer to them (they would have been surprised and more than a little horrified to hear the word applied to them), ideas about literature were rooted in a psychologised sense of human complexity rather than an enlightenment ideal of rational individuals guided by a desire to know the facts and an innate willingness to be swayed by the stronger argument. Underlying these characteristics was an implied sense of the benefits of the reading experience that aligned it with our modern inclination to think of literature in terms of imaginative expression rather than the earlier ideal of the republic of letters.

This approach had its roots in the age's broader fascination with bardic poets and ancient ballads, a trend that is reflected in the work of literary historians such as Thomas Percy (*Reliques of Ancient English Poetry* [1765]), Thomas Warton (*History of English Literature, 1100–1603* [1774–81]), and Joseph Ritson (*Select Collection of English Songs* [1783]). Their celebration of the prophetic figure of the bard and of the communal aspects of ballads marked a dramatic turn away from an earlier preoccupation with classical influences in favour of an antiquarian enthusiasm for local histories and folkloric traditions—a field of interest that included both eminent researchers and seemingly endless amateurs such as many of the contributors to the *Gentleman's Magazine*, whose Correspondence section offered a rich supply of antiquarian material. This trend informed the ideas of Romantic writers in three important ways: it focussed on the provinces rather than on London; it implied a preference for primitive energy over refined elegance; and it suggested a concern with a popular rather than an elite cultural history.

This fascination with local histories throughout Britain blended with Romantic writers' insistence that the profound mysteries of the human psyche could not simply be ignored in the quest for rational progress, an emphasis which translated into a preference for intimate social networks cultivated in rural contexts where the inner resources of the individual could be nurtured, rather than the alienating urban bustle of endless debate. They favoured a turn to the educational and restorative power of nature rather than the intellectual world of urban society, and to the tropes of the picturesque and the sublime, aesthetic modes that were antithetical to an Enlightenment confidence in scientific experiment and abstract certainties. Enlightenment contentions that the light of truth, developed through rational debate, would banish the darkness of superstition and prejudice, was at odds with the picturesque's celebration of irregularity, rusticity, and the beauty of ruins, and with descriptions of the sublime as an experience of being temporarily overwhelmed and intellectually disabled by an irresistible force that defied comprehension.

Ironically, although these writers championed the spontaneous power of inspired intuition over critical enquiry, and of poetry over rational explication, many of them responded with remarkable sophistication to the theoretical question of their aesthetic priorities. In doing so they highlighted both the complexities implicit in their celebration of the protean power of the imagination, and the variety of different political perspectives that this faith could be used to support. William Wordsworth's description of "the great national events which are daily taking place, and the increasing accumulation of men in cities, where the uniformity of their occupations produces a craving for extraordinary incident, which the rapid communication of intelligence hourly gratifies," gathered together in a single vision the converging forces of the French Revolution, industrial revolution, and information revolution in print. Haunted by his experience of Parisian violence, Wordsworth argued that poetry was crucial because it served as a humanizing force in an age where everything seemed to be conspiring to dehumanize. In doing so, it salvaged the possibility of a healthy individualism which, in turn, minimized the possibility of mass violence. This essential role, he insisted, made poetry the most influential form of literature and the poet the most elevated social figure.

For Shelley, poetry had a much more radical and activist role. Confronted by the widening gap between the rich and the poor, Shelley dismissed the Enlightenment emphasis on reason as a tool of the very social hierarchy which rational debate was supposed to undermine. As he rather unpoetically put it in the *Defence*, the "rich have become richer, and the poor have become poorer." In place of reason, which had not lived up to reformers' expectations, Shelley embraced the imagination's potential to offer a genuine critical perspective on the endless sorts of information that people were being swamped with. Even more importantly, he suggested, the imagination was a force capable of inspiring people to act in radically subversive ways on the basis of these insights.

In an age of controversy, it probably wasn't surprising that these literary interventions did not go unnoticed. Critics such as Francis Jeffrey (writing for the *Edinburgh Review*) and Leigh Hunt complained about what they saw as the Lake Poets' celebration of eccentricity. In a review of Robert Southey's poem, *Thalaba*, Jeffrey denounced the "*sect of poets*, that has established itself in this country within these ten or twelve years" as the "most formidable conspiracy that has lately been formed against sound judgement in matters poetical." As a noted political activist who was also closely associated with poets such as Percy Shelley and John Keats, Hunt offered a more complex and ambivalent response. He recognized the importance of Wordsworth's efforts, but he also charged Wordsworth with failing to live up to his own potential by cultivating a love of solitude that negated any real capacity to engage with the real complexities of modern life.

Many writers shared Hunt's ambivalence. In "On Artificial Taste," published anonymously as a letter to the editor in the April 1797 *Monthly Magazine*, Mary Wollstonecraft questioned the popular distinction between nature and the artificialities of the social world by arguing that "a taste for rural scenes, in the present state of society, appears to be very often an artificial sentiment, rather inspired by poetry and romances, than a real perception of the beauties of nature." The Romantics may be remembered today as nature poets but for Wollstonecraft, ironically, the celebration of nature was itself part of the artificialities of the age, a fashionable urban pose rather than a genuine rural phenomenon. Even so, Wollstonecraft went on to celebrate a primitivist vision of poetry as an unmediated expression of powerful but often fleeting impressions nurtured by "local manners" and "popular prejudices." For Humphry Davy, a noted scientist who had helped Wordsworth to revise the Preface, rational enquiry and imaginative expression did not need to be thought of as mutually exclusive predispositions. However obscure the workings of mechanical sciences may have been, the "natural sciences" were closely aligned with the arts in their capacity to evoke powerful imaginative responses. The tensions between all of these positions represent one of the most energetic and compelling areas of critical debate in the period. Nor should this be surprising. These writers lived in a time when literature was charged with instigating major cultural and political crises. It was hardly likely that the leading poets of the day could have escaped this spirit of dissension. In many ways, their poetry is all the more interesting because they didn't.

⁊∾⊱

WILLIAM GILPIN
*Three Essays: On Picturesque Beauty;
On Picturesque Travel; and On Sketching
Landscape: to which is added a poem,
on Landscape Painting* [1]

ESSAY I. ON PICTURESQUE BEAUTY

DISPUTES about beauty might perhaps be involved in less confusion, if a distinction were established, which certainly exists, between such objects as are *beautiful,* and such as are *picturesque*—between those, which please the eye in their *natural state*; and those, which please from some quality, capable of being *illustrated by painting*.

Ideas of beauty vary with the objects, and with the eye of the spectator. The stone-mason sees beauties in a well-jointed wall, which escape the architect, who surveys the building under a different idea. And thus the painter, who compares his object with the rules of his art, sees it in a different light from the man of general taste, who surveys it only as simply beautiful.

As this difference therefore between the *beautiful,* and the *picturesque* appears really to exist, and must depend on some peculiar construction of the object; it may be worth while to examine, what that peculiar construction is. We inquire not into the *general sources of beauty,* either in nature, or in representation. This would lead into a nice, and scientific discussion, in which it is not our purpose to engage. The question simply is, *What is that quality in objects, which particularly marks them as picturesque?*

In examining the *real object*, we shall find, one source of beauty arises from that species of elegance, which we call *smoothness*, or *neatness*; for the terms are nearly synonymous. The higher the marble is polished, the brighter the silver is rubbed, and the more the mahogany shines, the more each is considered as an object of beauty: as if the eye delighted in gliding smoothly over a surface.

In the class of larger objects the same idea prevails. In a pile of building we wish to see neatness in every part added to the elegance of the architecture. And if we examine a piece of improved pleasure-ground, every thing rough, and slovenly offends.

Thus then, we suppose, the matter stands with regard to *beautiful objects in general*. But in *picturesque representation* it seems somewhat odd, yet perhaps we shall find it equally true, that the reverse of this is the case; and that the ideas of *neat* and *smooth,* instead of being picturesque, in reality strip the object, in which they reside, of all pretensions to *picturesque beauty*.—Nay, farther, we do not scruple to assert, that *roughness* forms the most essential point of difference between the *beautiful,* and the *picturesque*; as it seems to be that particular quality, which makes objects chiefly pleasing in painting.—I use the general term *roughness*; but properly speaking roughness relates only to the surfaces of bodies: when we speak of their delineation, we use the word *ruggedness*. Both ideas however equally enter into the picturesque; and both are observable in the smaller, as well as in the larger parts of nature—in the outline, and bark of a tree, as in the rude summit, and craggy sides of a mountain.

ESSAY II. ON PICTURESQUE TRAVEL

IN treating of picturesque travel, we may consider first it's object; and secondly it's sources of amusement.

---

[1] William Gilpin (1724–1800), a clergyman and travel writer within Britain, was an authority in debates about the picturesque, as well as in various related debates in the fields of literature, art, and landscape gardening. *Three Essays* is Gilpin's theoretical discussion of the aesthetic principals underlying his accounts of picturesque beauty in popular locales such as the River Wye and the Isle of Wight.

It's object is beauty of every kind, which either art, or nature can produce: but it is chiefly that species of *beauty*, which we have endeavoured to characterize in the preceding essay under the name of *picturesque*. This great object we pursue through the scenery of nature. We seek it among all the ingredients of landscape—trees—rocks—broken-grounds—woods—rivers—lakes—plains—valleys—mountains—and distances. These objects *in themselves* produce infinite variety. No two rocks, or trees are exactly the same. They are varied, a second time, by *combination*; and almost as much, a third time, by different *lights, and shades*, and other aerial effects. Sometimes we find among them the exhibition of a *whole*; but oftener we find only beautiful *parts*.

That we may examine picturesque objects with more ease, it may be useful to class them into the *sublime*, and the *beautiful*; tho, in fact, this distinction is rather inaccurate. *Sublimity alone* cannot make an object *picturesque*. However grand the mountain, or the rock may be, it has no claim to this epithet, unless it's form, it's colour, or it's accompaniments have *some degree of beauty*. Nothing can be more sublime, than the ocean: but wholly unaccompanied, it has little of the picturesque. When we talk therefore of a sublime object, we always understand, that it is also beautiful: and we call it sublime, or beautiful, only as the idea of sublimity, or of simple beauty prevail.

But it is not only the *form*, and the *composition* of the objects of landscape, which the picturesque eye examines; it connects them with the atmosphere, and seeks for all those various effects, which are produced from that vast, and wonderful storehouse of nature. Nor is there in traveling a greater pleasure, than when a scene of grandeur bursts unexpectedly upon the eye, accompanied with some accidental circumstance of the atmosphere, which harmonizes with it, and gives it double value.

Besides the *inanimate* face of nature, it's *living forms* fall under the picturesque eye, in the course of travel; and are often objects of great attention. The anatomical study of figures is not attended to: we regard them merely as the ornament of scenes. In the human figure we contemplate neither *exactness of form*; nor *expression*, any farther than it is shewn in *action*: we merely consider general shapes, dresses, groups, and occupations; which we often find *casually* in greater variety, and beauty, than any selection can procure.

In the same manner animals are the objects of our attention, whether we find them in the park, the forest, or the field. Here too we consider little more, than their general forms, actions, and combinations. Nor is the picturesque eye so fastidious as to despise even less considerable objects. A flight of birds has often a pleasing effect. In short, every form of life, and being may have it's use as a picturesque object, till it become too small for attention.

But among all the objects of art, the picturesque eye is perhaps most inquisitive after the elegant relics of ancient architecture; the ruined tower, the Gothic arch, the remains of castles, and abbeys. These are the richest legacies of art. They are consecrated by time; and almost deserve the veneration we pay to the works of nature itself.

Thus universal are the objects of picturesque travel. We pursue *beauty* in every shape; through nature, through art; and all it's various arrangements in form, and colour; admiring it in the grandest objects, and not rejecting it in the humblest.

After the *objects* of picturesque travel, we consider it's *sources of amusement*—or in what way the mind is gratified by these objects.

We might begin in moral stile; and consider the objects of nature in a higher light, than merely as amusement. We might observe, that a search after beauty should naturally lead the mind to the great origin of all beauty; to the

————first good, first perfect, and first fair.[1]

But tho in theory this seems a natural climax; we insist the less upon it, as in fact we have scarce ground to hope, that every admirer of *picturesque beauty*, is an admirer also of the *beauty of virtue*; and that every lover of nature reflects, that

> Nature is but a name for an *effect*,
> Whose cause is God.————[2]

If however the admirer of nature can turn his amusements to a higher purpose; if it's great scenes can inspire him with religious awe; or it's tranquil scenes with that complacency of mind, which is so nearly allied to benevolence, it is certainly the better. *Apponat lucro.*[3] It is so much into the bargain; for we dare not *promise* him more from picturesque travel, than a rational, and agreeable amusement. Yet even this may be of some use in an age teeming with licentious pleasure; and may in this light at least be considered as having a moral tendency.

We are most delighted, when some grand scene, tho perhaps of incorrect composition, rising before the eye, strikes us beyond the power of thought— when the *vox faucibus hæret*,[4] and every mental operation is suspended. In this pause of intellect; this *deliquium*[5] of the soul, an enthusiastic sensation of pleasure overspreads it, previous to any

examination by the rules of art. The general idea of the scene makes an impression, before any appeal is made to the judgment. We rather *feel*, than *survey* it.

From this correct knowledge of objects arises another amusement; that of representing, by a few strokes in a sketch, those ideas, which have made the most impression upon us. There may be more pleasure in recollecting, and recording, from a few transient lines, the scenes we have admired, than in the present enjoyment of them. If the scenes indeed have *peculiar greatness*, this secondary pleasure cannot be attended with those enthusiastic feelings, which accompanied the real exhibition. But, in general, tho it may be a calmer species of pleasure, it is more uniform, and uninterrupted. It flatters us too with the idea of a sort of creation of our own; and it is unallayed with that fatigue, which is often a considerable abatement to the pleasures of traversing the wild, and savage parts of nature.—After we have amused *ourselves* with our sketches, if we can, in any degree, contribute to the amusement of others also, the pleasure is surely so much enhanced.

But altho the picturesque traveler is seldom disappointed with *pure nature*, however rude, yet we cannot deny, but he is often offended with the productions of art. He is disgusted with the formal separations of property—with houses, and towns, the haunts of men, which have much oftener a bad effect in landscape, than a good one. He is frequently disgusted also, when art aims more at beauty, than she ought. How flat, and insipid is often the garden-scene! how puerile, and absurd! the banks of the river how smooth, and parallel! the lawn, and it's boundaries, how unlike nature! Even in the capital collection of pictures, how seldom does he find *design, composition, expression, character*, or *harmony* either in *light*, or *colouring*! and how often does he drag through saloons, and rooms of state, only to hear a catalogue of the names of masters!

---

[1] Alexander Pope (1688–1744), *An Essay on Man* (1733–34), Epistle II, l 24.

[2] William Cowper (1731–1800), *The Task* (1785), VI, "The Winter Walk at Noon," 223–24.

[3] Reckon it as profit.

[4] Voice sticks in the throat.

[5] Eclipse or failure.

The more refined our taste grows from the *study of nature*, the more insipid are the *works of art*. Few of it's efforts please. The idea of the great original is so strong, that the copy must be pure, if it do not disgust. But the varieties of nature's charts are such, that, study them as we can, new varieties will always arise: and let our taste be ever so refined, her works, on which it is formed (at least when we consider them as *objects*,) must always go beyond it; and furnish fresh sources both of pleasure and amusement.

(1792)

MONTHLY MAGAZINE
On Artificial Taste [1]

To the Editor of the Monthly Magazine.

SIR,

A TASTE for rural scenes, in the present state of society, appears to me to be very often an artificial sentiment, rather inspired by poetry and romances, than a real perception of the beauties of nature; but, as it is reckoned a proof of refined taste to praise the calm pleasure which the country affords, the theme is exhausted; yet, it may be made a question, whether this romantic kind of declamation has much effect on the conduct of those who leave, for a season, the crowded cities in which they were bred.

I have been led into these reflections by observing, when I have resided for any length of time in the country, how few people seem to contemplate nature with their own eyes. I have "brushed the dew away" [2] in the morning; but, pacing over the print-less grass, I have wondered that, in such delightful situations, the sun was allowed to rise in solitary majesty, whilst my eyes alone hailed its beautifying beams. The webs of the evening have still been spread across the hedged path, unless some labouring man, trudging to work, disturbed the fairy structure; yet, in spite of this supineness, on joining the social circle, every tongue rang changes on the pleasures of the country.

Having frequently had occasion to make the same observation, in one of my solitary rambles, I was led to endeavour to trace the cause, and likewise to enquire why the poetry, written in the infancy of society, is most natural: which, strictly speaking (for natural is a very indefinite expression) is merely to say, that it is the transcript of immediate emotions, when fancy, awakened by the view of interesting objects, in all their native wildness and simplicity, was most actively at work. At such moments, sensibility quickly furnishes similes, and the sublimated spirits combine with happy facility—images, which spontaneously bursting on him, it is not necessary coldly to ransack the understanding or memory, till the laborious efforts of judgment exclude present sensations, and damp the fire of enthusiasm.

The effusions of a vigorous mind will, nevertheless, ever inform us how far the faculties have been enlarged by thought, and stored with knowledge. The richness of the soil even appears on the surface; and the result of profound thinking often mixing with playful grace in the reveries of the poet, smoothly incorporates with the ebullitions of animal spirits, when the finely-fashioned nerve vibrates acutely with rapture, or when relaxed by soft melancholy, a pleasing languor prompts the long-drawn sigh, and feeds the slowly falling tear.

---

[1] This article, by Mary Wollstonecraft, appeared anonymously in the *Monthly Magazine* in April 1797 (3: 279–82). Mary Wollstonecraft's husband, William Godwin, reprinted it with the title "On Poetry and Our Relish for the Beauties of Nature" in *Posthumous Works of the Author of a Vindication of the Rights of Woman* in1798.

[2] Source unidentified.

The poet, the man of strong feelings, only gives us a picture of his mind when he was actually alone, conversing with himself, and marking the impression which nature made on his own heart. If, during these sacred moments, the idea of some departed friend—some tender recollection, when the soul was most alive to tenderness, intruded unawares into his mind, the sorrow which it produced is artlessly, but poetically, expressed; and who can avoid sympathizing?

Love of man leads to devotion. Grand and sublime images strike the imagination. God is seen in every floating cloud, and comes from the misty mountain to receive the noblest homage of an intelligent creature—praise. How solemn is the moment, when all affections and remembrances fade before the sublime admiration which the wisdom and goodness of God inspires, when he is worshiped in a temple not made with hands,[1] and the world seems to contain only the mind that formed and contemplates it! These are not the weak responses of ceremonial devotion; nor to express them would the poet need another poet's aid. No: his heart burns within him, and he speaks the language of truth and nature, with resistless energy.

Inequalities, of course, are observable in his effusions; and a less vigorous imagination, with more taste, would have produced more elegance and uniformity. But as passages are softened or expunged, during the cooler moments of reflection, the understanding is gratified at the expence of those involuntary sensations which like the beauteous tints of an evening sky, are so evanescent, that they melt into new forms before they can be analyzed. For, however eloquently we may boast of our reason, man must often be delighted he cannot tell why, or his blunt feelings are not made to relish the beauties which nature, poetry, or any of the imitative arts afford.

It would be a philosophical enquiry, and throw some light on the history of the human mind, to trace, as far as our information will allow us, the spontaneous feelings and ideas which have produced the images that now frequently appear unnatural, because they are remote, and disgusting, because they have been servilely copied by poets, whose habits of thinking, and views of nature must have been different; for the understanding seldom disturbs the current of our present feelings without dissipating the gay clouds which fancy has been embracing; yet, it silently gives the colour to the whole tenor of them, and the reverie is over when truth is grossly violated, or imagery introduced, selected from books, and not from local manners, or popular prejudices.

In a more advanced state of civilization, a poet is rather a creature of art, than of nature; the books that he peruses in his youth, become a hot-bed, in which artificial fruits are produced, beautiful to the common eye, though they want the true hue and flavour. His images do flow from his imagination, but are servile copies; and, like the works of the painters who copy ancient statues when they draw men and women of their own times, we acknowledge that the features are fine, and the proportions just, but still they are men of stone: insipid figures, that never convey to the mind the idea of a portrait taken from the life, where the soul gives spirit and homogeneity to the whole form. The silken wings of fancy are shrivelled by rules, and a desire of attaining elegance of diction occasions an attention to words, incompatible with sublime impassioned thoughts.

A boy of abilities, who has been taught the structure of verse at school, and been roused by emulation to compose rhymes whilst he was reading works of genius, may, by practice, produce pretty verses, and even become what is often termed an elegant poet. But though it should be allowed that

---

[1] Revelation 21:22.

books conned at school may lead some youths to write poetry, I fear they will never be the poets who charm our cares to sleep, or extort admiration. They may diffuse taste, and polish the language, but I am apt to conclude that they will seldom have the energy to rouse the passions which amend the heart.

And, to return to the first object of discussion, the reason why most people are more interested by a scene described by a poet, than by a view of nature, probably arises from the want of a lively imagination. The poet contrasts the prospect, and, selecting the most picturesque part in his camera,[1] the judgment is directed, and the whole attention of the languid faculty turned towards the objects which excited the most forcible emotions in the poet's heart, firing his imagination; the reader consequently feels the enlivened description, though he was not able to receive a first impression from the operations of his own mind.

Besides, it may be further observed, that uncultivated minds are only to be moved by forcible representations. To rouse the thoughtless, objects must be contrasted, calculated to excite tumultuous emotions. The unsubstantial picturesque forms which a contemplative man gazes on, and often follows with ardour till mocked by a glimpse of unattainable excellence, appear to them the light vapours of a dreaming enthusiast, who gives up the substance for the shadow. It is not within that they seek amusement—their eyes are rarely turned on themselves; of course, their emotions, though sometimes fervid, are always transient, and the nicer perceptions which distinguish the man of taste are not felt, or make such a slight impression as scarcely to excite any pleasurable sensations. Is it surprising, then, that fine scenery often overlooked by those who yet may be delighted by the same imagery concentrated and contrasted by the poet? But even this numerous class is exceeded by witlings, who, anxious to appear to have wit and taste, do not allow their understandings or feelings any liberty: for instead of cultivating their faculties, and reflecting on their operations, they are busy collecting prejudices, and are pre-determined to admire what the suffrage of time announces excellent; not to store up a fund of amusement for themselves, but to enable them to talk.

These hints will assist the reader to trace some of the causes why the beauties of nature are not forcibly felt, when civilization and its canker-worm, luxury, have made considerable advances. Those calm emotions are not sufficiently lively to serve as a relaxation to the voluptuary, or even for the moderate pursuers of artificial pleasures. In the present state of society, the understanding must bring back the feelings to nature, or the sensibility must have attained such native strength, as rather to be sharpened than destroyed by the strong exercise of passions.

That the most valuable things are liable to the greatest perversion, is, however, as trite as true. For the same sensibility, or quickness of senses, which makes a man relish the charms of nature, when sensation, rather than reason, imparts delight, frequently makes a libertine of him, by leading him to prefer the tumult of love, a little refined by sentiment, to the calm pleasure of affectionate friendship, in whose sober satisfactions reason, mixing her tranquillizing convictions, whispers that content, not happiness, is the reward, or consequence, of virtue in this world.

W.Q.
(1797)

---

[1] Camera obscura, a darkened chamber or box used to form an image of external images on paper placed at the focus of a double convex lens.

MONTHLY MAGAZINE
On the Characteristics of Poetry

To the Editor of the Monthly Magazine

SIR,

The following Essays were read some time in the year 1794, to a Literary Society in Liverpool. If you think them worthy of a place in your Miscellany, they are much at your service, together with the best wishes of your's,

P.F.

MANKIND may be divided into two classes, consisting of those that are conversant with the productions of literature, and those that entirely disregard them. The former class may be subdivided into those that are "pleased they know not why, and care not wherefore"—and those that enquire into the principles of their pleasures, and bring them to be measured by the standard of reason. It is one thing to be moved—another to enquire by what instruments our emotions are occasioned. The former predicament allies us to the literary vulgar, the latter associates us with philosophers.

Notwithstanding the contempt that has been showered in such abundance upon critical enquiries into the principles of works of taste and genius, to these enquiries the human mind is irresistibly impelled. In this respect the creation of the mind stands upon the same footing as the works of God. The delight and astonishment which men experienced at the sight of the wonders of nature, led to an investigations of their causes; and became the germ of what is termed natural philosophy. And the appearance of exquisite literary productions led men to investigate the principles whence flowed the pleasure with which they refreshed the soul: and this gave rise to philosophical criticism.

But it is a fact well known to those who have formed the slightest habit of reflection, that many subjects which appear most familiar and comprehensible, are in reality most difficult of investigation. The mental faculties are, perhaps, never put more intensely on the stretch than in endeavouring to explain an axiom: and when we set about analyzing and reducing to system, ideas that are daily and hourly floating on the surface of our minds, we meet with more perplexity than we were at first aware of. These observations are surely not irrelevant when they are prefixed to an attempt at an enquiry into the nature and characteristics of poetry.

Whose breast has not been warmed by the muses? Where is the man whose feelings are so firmly bound by the frost of reason as to be impenetrable to the influence of "Sacred Song?" I would not dishonour the present assembly so much as to suppose that we had a brother of this description. But if anyone be inclined to doubt the difficulty of the enquiry into which it is our business to enter, I shall defend my assertions by the high authority of the investigator of the life and writings of Homer. Having looked into his book for assistance in the task which I unwarily undertook, I found the following passage, that strongly reminded me of the friends of Job, who are so generally known under the character of "miserable comforters."[1]

The subject is of a nature so delicate as not to admit of a direct definition; for if ever the *je ne sçais quoi*[2] was rightly applied, it is to the powers of poetry and the faculty that produces it. To go about to describe it, would be like attempting to define inspiration, or that glow of fancy, or effusion of

---

[1] Job 2:11–13. When God allows Satan to tempt Job to curse God for allowing him numerous traumas and misfortunes, Job's friends come to offer support, but instead question what he may have done to deserve God's wrath. Their "comfort" is therefore anything but a comfort to Job.

[2] I do not know what.

soul, which a poet feels while in his fit; a sensation so strong, that they express it only exclamations, adjurings, and rapture.

The word *Poet*, in its original import, signifies Creator. As names are not always arbitrarily applied, but are frequently significant of the nature of the ideas which they represent, perhaps the name itself of Poetry may serve as a clue to direct us in our present enquiry. And it is one of the noblest qualities of Poetry that it opens to the mind a new creation. The poet enjoys the invaluable privilege of ranging through the boundless field of possibilities, and selecting his objects according to the impulse of his fancy and discretion of his judgment. Like our first father "the world is all before him where to choose."[1] What is striking and interesting, he makes prominent in his picture; what is offensive, deformed, or gross in species, he conceals and softens. In what have been termed the dull realities of life, a thousand nameless circumstances intervene, to check the enthusiastic interest which our hearts are disposed to take in any specific occurrence. These circumstances the poet has a prescriptive right to exclude from his representations. His heroes are freed from a connection with the grosser incidents that occur in life—his heroines are purified from the imperfections of the female nature. Though he cannot go beyond the materials which the station and powers of man supply, yet he can, by a combination of these, produce beings and situations that interest us the most; the better powers of fiction, to which they owe their birth, are concealed from us. Like the favoured statuary of Greece, he is surrounded by naked beauties, from each of which he selects its peculiar excellency, and produces a whole, which, though strictly natural, surpasses the realities of nature.

The mathematician, in his investigation of truth, is strictly confined to the narrow path of reason.

The same may be said of the philosopher. The slightest deviation into the fields of imagination frustrates their pursuit, and blasts their laurels. The historian must found his reputation upon a patient investigation of facts, and beware of giving the loosened reins to his inventive talents. The orator, indeed, calls fancy to the aid of reason; but she ought to be strictly an auxiliary. If his edifice be not founded on the basis of reason it will fall, together with its embellishments, to the ground. In oratory, fancy embellishes the operations of judgment; but as poetry is a creative art, imagination is its primary cause, and judgment a secondary agent, pruning the luxuriant shoots of fancy.

No. II

In the course of our last discussion, we seemed to be unanimously of opinion, that the grand characteristic, the *sine quâ non*[2] of poetry, consists in its capacity of pressing the mind with the most vivid pictures. Indeed, the maxim *ut pictura poesis*,[3] is amply illustrated whenever poetry is in any shape the subject of investigation. The terms of the painter's art then insensibly creep into the discourse, and model our phraseology.

Pursuing, then, this idea, we may perhaps lay it down as the grand and leading end of poetry, to make a strong and lively impression on the feelings. In her operations she hurries us far beyond the reach of the voice of sober judgment, and captivates by exciting the aid of the passions. Here, then, we see the cause of the mighty energy of verse, nor wonder at the efficaciousness that has been ascribed to the muses. For how easily are mankind guided by those that possess the happy art of awakening or allaying their feelings. Though all unconscious of

---

[1] John Milton (1608–1674), *Paradise Lost* (1667): XII: 646.

[2] Greatest attribute.

[3] "As is painting, so is poetry," from Horace (65–8 B.C.), *Ars Poetica* (*c.* 13 B.C.): 361.

being under the guidance of another, they turn obedient to the rein. They are roused to insurrection, or moderated to peace, by him who can touch with a skilful hand, the master springs that regulate the motions of their minds. When Brutus ascends the rostrum, the words of truth and soberness are heard, and plain integrity convinces the judgment. But, when Anthony displays the bloody robe, and points to the wounds of Cæsar, reminding the people that this was once their darling benefactor—the multitude are melted to sorrow, and at last roused from pity to fury and revenge.

Here, then, this Essay might, perhaps, with propriety, have been closed. But I must rely upon your candour, for the admission of a few more observations, which may, perhaps, tend to illustrate the point to which this enquiry has led us:

The end of poetry, it is said, is an impression upon the feelings.—But as there is an intimate connection between feeling and action, so that where the one appears, the other 'follows hard upon,'[1] if the foregoing observations be true, we may expect to find that the actions of mankind are, in some measure, influenced by the Muses.

And if we look to the simpler ages of society, when we can best distinguish the grand outlines of the human character, where the springs that actuate the conduct of man are, in a manner, bared for inspection, we shall find this to have been the case. In the infancy of states, poetry is a method equally captivating and efficacious of forming the dispositions of the people, and kindling in their hearts that love of glory which is their country's safeguard and defence. Whether we look to the cold regions of Scandinavia, or the delicious clime of Greece, we find, that when society has made a certain progress, mankind are strongly influenced by a love of song, and listen, with raptured attention, to the strains that record the tale of other times, and the deeds of heroes of old. They listen till they imbibe the enthusiasm of warfare, and in the day of battle, the hero's arm has not unfrequently been nerved by the rough energy of the early bard.—Whether Ossian strike the chords in the Hall of Shells, or Phemius attune his voice at the banquet of Ulysses,[2] the principle by which they operate on the soul of the hearers is the same, and they accord in urging them by great examples, to deeds of high renown.

But, indeed, what occasion have we to search into the dust of antiquity for examples of the influence of verse upon human conduct? The transactions of our own times may teach us, that as strong feelings generate poetic language, so poetic language inspires the mind with, at least, a temporary enthusiasm, and thus impels to action. In this country, the fervour or loyalty has of late been blown into a blaze, and for this event the parties interested are not a little indebted to the assistance of the muses. And when the Marseillois Hymn echoed through the ranks of the French army, at the field of Jemappe,[3] we need not wonder that "the spear of Liberty was weilded with classic grace,"[4] and that the energy of heroism was communicated with the sound.

(1797)

---

[1] Source unidentified.

[2] Ossian, a legendary Gaelic poet, was remembered by most people in the Romantic period in connection with James Macpherson, who published translations of two poems that he claimed had been written by Ossian, but which turned out to be his own creation; The heroic figure Phemius was a singer in the court of Ulysses on Ithaca.

[3] A military victory by the Revolutionary army in 1792.

[4] Source unidentified.

CHARLES LLOYD
Edmund Oliver[1]

YOU will hear Edmund, in the circles of London, that the society and frequent intercourse of fellow beings which towns only admit of, are necessary to the growth of mind; to calling forth the activities of the intellect: that men of genius are found in clusters, and that frequent collision is the only mean of eliciting truth. So far am I from admitting this as a fact, that I would exactly reverse the proposition: and insist that no greatness of character, no vastness of conception were ever nursed except in solitude, and seclusion.

Conversation, when indulged in with simplicity of intention is well as a relief from the more irksome duties of life: much may be done too, where a strict intimacy exists between two persons, by the unlimited communication of ideas. But I firmly believe that nothing more tends to fritter away genius, and level down the sublimity of original thought than the constant habit of attack and defence, of intellectual gladiatorship, adopted in literary and argumentative circles. Truth is seldom or never discovered where a third person is present to witness the triumph of one party, and the defeat of the other. Our passions are enlisted, in these situations, indiscriminately on the side of virtue or vice; and we usually revolt from, rather than yield to, an opinion announced by a successful attack on our conversational powers: we associate with the principle of shame our defeat, and frequently afterwards, be it ever so true, think of it with disgust.

This crusading spirit, which modem philosophy encourages, that disposition of giving "an identity to imaginary aggregates," seems to me by no means favourable to social usefulness. By attempting a great deal we often do nothing: it is not loose declamations, or an harangue of general and popular application, that will eradicate habits, disentangle the foldings of prejudice, and regenerate the mind. No! we must have gained the confidence of the person we wish to reform; cultivated sympathies with him; and twined ourselves round his heart. We must be sentient before we can be rational beings: he therefore, who would tell me, that I must love a whole without attaching myself to parts of that whole, requires that I should attain an end without using the means, possess the principles without sentiments or impressions to support them, and find an interest in what is to me objectless and undefined!

(1798)

WILLIAM WORDSWORTH
Preface to *Lyrical Ballads*[3]

IT is supposed, that by the act of writing in verse an Author makes a formal engagement that he will gratify certain known habits of association; that he not only thus apprizes the Reader that certain classes of ideas and expressions will be found in his book, but that others will be carefully excluded. This exponent or symbol held forth by metrical

---

[1] Charles Lloyd (1775–1839), a poet and novelist who lived with S.T. Coleridge, who was to act as his tutor, in late 1796 and early 1797. *Edmund Oliver* is an epistolary novel that addresses many of the broader Romantic concerns and priorities in an overtly revolutionary context. Coleridge objected to what he saw as an unflattering portrait of himself in its protagonist. This passage combines two letters on the same subject from Charles Maurice, the moral centre of the novel and a firm advocate of an introspective rural lifestyle, to Edmund, the novel's protagonist, who has been lured to London by radical politics and an unwise romantic attachment, both of which appeal to his unstable personality.

[2] William Wordsworth (1770–1850), now widely regarded as the pre-eminent poet of his day, had been an early enthusiast of the French Revolution, but after becoming disenchanted with the cause of radical reform, turned to the imagination as an alternative revolutionary force capable of fostering spiritual renewal. His Preface to the *Lyrical Ballads* was widely viewed as a manifesto announcing the coming of age of a new era in English poetry.

language must in different æras of literature have excited very different expectations: for example, in the age of Catullus, Terence, and Lucretius and that of Statius or Claudian;[1] and in our own country, in the age of Shakespeare and Beaumont and Fletcher, and that of Donne and Cowley, or Dryden, or Pope.[2] I will not take upon me to determine the exact import of the promise which by the act of writing in verse an Author, in the present day, makes to his Reader; but I am certain, it will appear to many persons that I have not fulfilled the terms of an engagement thus voluntarily contracted. They who have been accustomed to the gaudiness and inane phraseology of many modern writers, if they persist in reading this book to its conclusion, will, no doubt, frequently have to struggle with feelings of strangeness and awkwardness: they will look round for poetry, and will be induced to inquire by what species of courtesy these attempts can be permitted to assume that title. I hope therefore the Reader will not censure me, if I attempt to state what I have proposed to myself to perform; and also (as far as the limits of a preface will permit), to explain some of the chief reasons which have determined me in the choice of my purpose: that at least he may be spared any unpleasant feeling of disappointment, and that I myself may be protected from the most dishonourable accusation which can be brought against an Author, namely, that of an indolence which prevents him from endeavouring to ascertain what is his duty, or, when his duty is ascertained, prevents him from performing it.

The principal object, then, which I proposed to myself in these Poems was to choose incidents and situations from common life and to relate or describe them, throughout, as far as was possible, in a selection of language really used by men; and, at the same time, to throw over them a certain colouring of imagination, whereby ordinary things should be presented to the mind in an unusual way; and, further, and above all, to make these incidents and situations interesting by tracing in them, truly though not ostentatiously, the primary laws of our nature: chiefly, as far as regards the manner in which we associate ideas in a state of excitement. Low and rustic life was generally chosen, because in that condition, the essential passions of the heart find a better soil in which they can attain their maturity, are less under restraint, and speak a plainer and more emphatic language; because in that condition of life our elementary feelings co-exist in a state of greater simplicity, and, consequently, may be more accurately contemplated, and more forcibly communicated; because the manners of rural life germinate from those elementary feelings; and, from the necessary character of rural occupations, are more easily comprehended; and are more durable; and lastly, because in that condition the passions of men are incorporated with the beautiful and permanent forms of nature. The language, too, of these men is adopted (purified indeed from what appear to be its real defects, from all lasting and rational causes of dislike or disgust) because such men hourly communicate with the best objects from which the best part of language is originally derived; and because, from their rank in society and the sameness and narrow circle of their intercourse, being less under the influence of social vanity they convey their feelings and notions in simple and unelaborated expressions. Accordingly, such a language, arising out of repeated experience and regular feelings, is a more permanent, and a far

---

[1] Gaius Valerius Catullus (c. 84–c. 54 B.C.), Publius Terentius Afer (?190–159 B.C.), Tiber Lucretius Carus (?99–55 B.C.), Publius Papinius Statius (c. 45–96), and Claudius Claudianus (c. 395–404), were Roman poets.

[2] William Shakespeare (1564–1616), Francis Beaumont (1584–1616), John Fletcher (1579–1625), John Donne (1572–1631), Abraham Cowley (1618–67), John Dryden (1631–1700), and Alexander Pope (1688–1744) were English poets and dramatists.

more philosophical language, than that which is frequently substituted for it by Poets, who think that they are conferring honour upon themselves and their art, in proportion as they separate themselves from the sympathies of men, and indulge in arbitrary and capricious habits of expression, in order to furnish food for fickle tastes, and fickle appetites, of their own creation.[†]

I cannot be insensible of the present outcry against the triviality and meanness both of thought and language, which some of my contemporaries have occasionally introduced into their metrical compositions; and I acknowledge that this defect where it exists, is more dishonorable to the Writer's own character than false refinement or arbitrary innovation, though I should contend at the same time that it is far less pernicious in the sum of its consequences. From such verses the Poems in these volumes will be found distinguished at least by one mark of difference, that each of them has a worthy *purpose*. Not that I mean to say, that I always began to write with a distinct purpose formally conceived; but I believe that my habits of meditation have so formed my feelings, as that my descriptions of such objects as strongly excite those feelings, will be found to carry along with them a *purpose*. If in this opinion I am mistaken I can have little right to the name of a Poet. For all good poetry is the spontaneous overflow of powerful feelings; but though this be true, Poems to which any value can be attached, were never produced on any variety of subjects but by a man who being possessed of more than usual organic sensibility had also thought long and deeply. For our continued influxes of feeling are modified and directed by our thoughts, which are indeed the representatives of all our past feelings; and as by contemplating the relation of these

general representatives to each other, we discover what is really important to men, so by the repetition and continuance of this act feelings connected with important subjects will be nourished, till at length, if we be originally possessed of much organic sensibility, such habits of mind will be produced that by obeying blindly and mechanically the impulses of those habits we shall describe objects and utter sentiments of such a nature and in such connection with each other, that the understanding of the being to whom we address ourselves, if he be in a healthful state of association, must necessarily be in some degree enlightened, his taste exalted, and his affections ameliorated.

I will not suffer a sense of false modesty to prevent me from asserting, that I point my Reader's attention to this mark of distinction, far less for the sake of these particular Poems than from the general importance of the subject. The subject is indeed important! For the human mind is capable of being excited without the application of gross and violent stimulants; and he must have a very faint perception of its beauty and dignity who does not know this, and who does not further know, that one being is elevated above another, in proportion as he possesses this capability. It has therefore appeared to me, that to endeavour to produce or enlarge this capability is one of the best services in which, at any period, a Writer can be engaged; but this service, excellent at all times, is especially so at the present day. For a multitude of causes, unknown to former times, are now acting with a combined force to blunt the discriminating powers of the mind, and unfitting it for all voluntary exertion to reduce it to a state of almost savage torpor. The most effective of these causes are the great national events which are daily taking place, and the increasing accumulation of men in cities, where the uniformity of their occupations produces a craving for extraordinary incident, which the rapid communication of intelli-

---

[†] It is worth while here to observe that the affecting parts of Chaucer are almost always expressed in language pure and universally intelligible even to this day.

gence hourly gratifies. To this tendency of life and manners the literature and theatrical exhibitions of the country have conformed themselves. The invaluable works of our elder writers, I had almost said the works of Shakespeare and Milton, are driven into neglect by frantic novels, sickly and stupid German tragedies, and deluges of idle and extravagant stories in verse.—When I think upon this degrading thirst after outrageous stimulation, I am almost ashamed to have spoken of the feeble effort with which I have endeavoured to counteract it; and, reflecting upon the magnitude of the general evil, I should be oppressed with no dishonorable melancholy, had I not a deep impression of certain inherent and indestructible qualities of the human mind, and likewise of certain powers in the great and permanent objects that act upon it which are equally inherent and indestructible; and did I not further add to this impression a belief, that the time is approaching when the evil will be systematically opposed, by men of greater powers, and with far more distinguished success.

Taking up the subject, then, upon general grounds, I ask what is meant by the word Poet? What is a Poet? To whom does he address himself? And what language is to be expected from him? He is a man speaking to men: a man, it is true, endued with more lively sensibility, more enthusiasm and tenderness, who has a greater knowledge of human nature, and a more comprehensive soul, than are supposed to be common among mankind; a man pleased with his own passions and volitions, and who rejoices more than other men in the spirit of life that is in him; delighting to contemplate similar volitions and passions as manifested in the goings-on of the Universe, and habitually impelled to create them where he does not find them. To these qualities he has added a disposition to be affected more than other men by absent things as if they were present; an ability of conjuring up in himself

passions, which are indeed far from being the same as those produced by real events, yet (especially in those parts of the general sympathy which are pleasing and delightful) do more nearly resemble the passions produced by real events, than any thing which, from the motions of their own minds merely, other men are accustomed to feel in themselves; whence, and from practice, he has acquired a greater readiness and power in expressing what he thinks and feels, and especially those thoughts and feelings which, by his own choice, or from the structure of his own mind, arise in him without immediate external excitement.

(1802)

EDINBURGH REVIEW
Review of *Thalaba, the Destroyer: A Metrical Romance.* By Robert Southey.[1]

POETRY has this much, at least, in common with religion, that its standards were fixed long ago, by certain inspired writers, whose authority it is no longer lawful to call in question; and that many profess to be entirely devoted to it, who have no *good works* to produce in support of their pretensions. The catholic poetical church, too, has worked but few miracles since the first ages of its establishment; and has been more prolific, for a long time, of doctors than of saints: it has had its corruptions, and reformation also, and has given birth to an infinite variety of heresies and errors, the followers of which have hated and persecuted each other as

---

[1] This review by Francis Jeffrey (1773–1850), the editor of the influential *Edinburgh Review,* marked the first entry in Jeffrey's ongoing campaign against the poetic innovations of William Wordsworth and the "Lake School" of poets. This review is actually of a poem by Robert Southey (1774–1843), a friend and literary ally of Wordsworth, but Jeffrey uses the occasion to question the literary and moral efficacy of writing poetry in the language of rural peasants, and addressing their daily concerns.

cordially as other bigots.

The author who is now before us, belongs to a *sect* of poets, that has established itself in this country within these ten or twelve years, and is looked upon, we believe, as one of its chief champions and apostles. The peculiar doctrines of this sect, it would not, perhaps, be very easy to explain; but, that they are *dissenters* from the established systems in poetry and criticism, is admitted, and proved indeed, by the whole tenor of their compositions. Though they lay claim, we believe, to a creed and a revelation of their own, there can be little doubt, that their doctrines are of *German* origin, and have been derived from some of the great modern reformers in that country. Some of their leading principles, indeed, are probably of an earlier date, and seem to have been borrowed from the great apostle of Geneva.[1]

The disciples of this school boast much of its originality, and seem to value themselves very highly, for having broken loose from the bondage of ancient authority, and re-asserted the independence of genius. Originality, however, we are persuaded, is rarer than mere alteration; and a man may change a good master for a bad one, without finding himself at all nearer to independence. That our new poets have abandoned the old models, may certainly be admitted; but we have not been able to discover that they have yet created any models of their own; and are very much inclined to call in question the worthiness of those to which they have transferred their admiration.

The authors of whom we are now speaking, have, among them, unquestionably, a very considerable portion of poetical talent, and have, consequently, been enabled to seduce many into an admiration of the false taste (as it appears to us) in which most of these productions are composed. They constitute, at present, the most formidable conspiracy that has lately been formed against sound judgement in matters poetical; and are entitled to a larger share of our censorial notice, than could be spared for an individual delinquent. We shall hope for the indulgence of our readers, therefore, in taking this opportunity to inquire a little more particularly into their merits, and to make a few remarks upon those peculiarities which seem to be regarded by their admirers as the surest proofs of their excellence.

Their most distinguishing symbol, is undoubtedly an affectation of great simplicity and familiarity of language. They disdain to make use of the common poetical phraseology, or to ennoble their diction by a selection of fine or dignified expressions. There would be too much *art* in this, for that great love of nature with which they are all of them inspired; and their sentiments, they are determined shall be indebted, for their effect, to nothing but their intrinsic tenderness or elevation. There is something very noble and conscientious, we will confess, in this plan of composition; but the misfortune is, that there are passages in all poems that can neither be pathetic nor sublime; and that, on these occasions, a neglect of the establishments of language is very apt to produce absolute meanness and insipidity.

The followers of simplicity are, therefore, at all times in danger of occasional degradation; but the simplicity of this new school seems intended to ensure it. *Their* simplicity does not consist, by any means, in the rejection of glaring or superfluous ornament,—in the substitution of elegance to splendour,—or in that refinement of art which seeks concealment in its own perfection. It consists, on the contrary, in a very great degree, in the positive and *bona fide* rejection of art altogether, and in the bold use of those rude and negligent

---

[1] Jean-Jacques Rousseau (1712–78), originally from Geneva. Rousseau's celebration of natural man over the vices of modern society and his introspective focus made Rousseau a favourite of Romantic writers.

expressions, which would be banished by a little discrimination. One of their own authors, indeed, has very ingenuously set forth, (in a kind of manifesto, that preceded one of their most flagrant acts of hostility[1]), that it was their capital object to adapt to the uses of poetry, the ordinary language of conversation among the middling and lower orders of the people.

What advantages are to be gained by the success of this project, we confess ourselves unable to conjecture. The language of the higher and more cultivated orders may fairly be presumed to be better than that of their inferiors: at any rate, it has all those associations in its favour, by means of which a style can ever appear beautiful or exalted, and is adapted to the purposes of poetry, by having been long consecrated to its use. The language of the vulgar, on the other hand, has all the opposite associations to contend with; and must seem unfit for poetry, (if there were no other reason), merely because it has scarcely ever been employed in it. A great genius may indeed overcome these disadvantages; but we scarcely conceive that he should court them. We may excuse a certain homeliness of language in the productions of a ploughman or a milkwoman; but we cannot bring ourselves to admire it in an author, who has had occasion to indite odes to his college-bell, and inscribe hymns to the Penates.[2]

The low-bred heroes, and interesting rustics of poetry, have no sort of affinity to the real vulgar of this world; they are imaginary beings, whose characters and language are in contrast with their situation; and please those who can be pleased with them, by the marvellous, and not by the nature of such a combination. In serious poetry, a man of the middling or lower order *must necessarily* lay aside a great deal of his ordinary language; he must avoid

errors in grammar and orthography; and steer clear of the cant of particular professions, and of every impropriety that is ludicrous or disgusting: nay, he must speak in good verse, and observe all the graces in prosody and collocation.[3] After all this, it may not be very easy to say how we are to find him out to be a low man, or what marks can remain of the ordinary language of conversation in the inferior orders of society. If there be any phrases that are not used in good society, they will appear as blemishes in the composition, no less palpably than errors in syntax or quantity; and if there be no such phrases, the style cannot be characteristic of that condition of life, the language of which it professes to have adopted. All approximation to that language, in the same manner, implies a deviation from that purity and precision, which no one, we believe, ever violated spontaneously.

It has been argued, indeed, (for men will argue in support of what they do not venture to practise), that as the middling and lower orders of society constitute by far the greater part of mankind, so, their feelings and expressions should interest more extensively, and may be taken, more fairly than any other, for the standards of what is natural and true. To this, it seems obvious to answer, that the arts that aim at exciting admiration and delight, do not take their models from what is ordinary, but from what is excellent; and that our interest in the representation of any event, does not depend upon our familiarity with the original, but on its intrinsic importance, and the celebrity of the parties it concerns. The sculptor employs his art in delineating the graces of Antinous or Apollo, and not in the representation of those ordinary forms that belong to the crowd of his admirers. When a chieftain perishes in battle, his followers mourn more for him, than for thousands of their equals that may have fallen around him.

---

[1] Wordsworth's Preface to the *Lyrical Ballads*.

[2] The Roman household Gods.

[3] Arrangement in proper order.

After all, it must be admitted, that there is a class of persons (we are afraid they cannot be called *readers),* to whom the representation of vulgar manners, in vulgar language, will afford much entertainment. We are afraid, however, that the ingenious writers who supply the hawkers and ballad-singers, have very nearly monopolized that department, and are probably better qualified to hit the taste of their customers, than Mr Southey, or any of his brethren, can yet pretend to be. To fit them for the higher task of original composition, it would not be amiss if they were to undertake a translation of Pope or Milton into the vulgar tongue, for the benefit of those children of nature.

A splenetic and idle discontent with the existing institutions of society, seems to be at the bottom of all their serious and peculiar sentiments. Instead of contemplating the wonders and the pleasures which civilization has created for mankind, they are perpetually brooding over the disorders by which its progress has been attended. They are filled with horror and compassion at the sight of poor men spending their blood in the quarrels of princes, and brutifying their sublime capabilities in the drudgery of unremitting labour. For all sorts of vice and profligacy in the lower orders of society, they have the same virtuous horror, and the same tender compassion. While the existence of these offences overpowers them with grief and confusion, they never permit themselves to feel the smallest indignation or dislike towards the offenders. The present vicious constitution of society alone is responsible for all these enormities: the poor sinners are but the helpless victims or instruments of its disorders, and could not possibly have avoided the errors into which they have been betrayed. Though they can bear with crimes, therefore, they cannot reconcile themselves to punishments; and have an unconquerable antipathy to prisons, gibbets, and houses of correction, as engines of oppression, and instru-

ments of atrocious injustice. While the plea of moral necessity is thus artfully brought forward to convert all the excesses of the poor into innocent misfortunes, no sort of indulgence is shewn to the offences of the powerful and rich. Their oppressions, and seductions, and debaucheries, are the theme of many an angry verse; and the indignation and abhorrence of the reader is relentlessly conjured up against those perturbators of society, and scourges of mankind.

(1802)

Leigh Hunt
The Feast of the Poets [1]

IF Mr. Wordsworth is at present under a cloud,[2] it is one, we see, of a divinity's wearing; and he may emerge from it, whenever he pleases, with a proportionate lustre. May he speedily do so! There is nobody who would be prouder to hail that new morning than myself. Apollo should have another Feast on purpose to welcome it. It certainly appears to me, that we have had no poet since the days of Spenser and Milton,—so allied in the better part of his genius to those favoured men, not excepting

---

[1] Leigh Hunt (1784–1859), a well-known editor and journalist. In 1814, Hunt published a longer version of *The Feast of the Poets*, a poem which had first appeared in Hunt's journal, *The Reflector* (1811). Using the literary conceit of Apollo holding sessions to judge the worth of contemporary poetry, Hunt offered a wide-ranging summation of the strengths and weaknesses of the poets of his day.

[2] These views on William Wordsworth were part of an extended set of footnotes to the poem. By 1814 the notes were considerably longer than the poem itself. The lines about Wordsworth that are referred to here are:

When Apollo, in pity, to screen him from sight,
Threw round him a cloud that was purple and white,
The same that of old us'd to wrap his own shoulders,
When coming from heaven, he'd spare the beholders.
The bard, like a second Æneas, went home in't,
And lives underneath it, it seems, at this moment.

even Collins,[1] who saw farther into the sacred places of poetry than any man of the last age. Mr. Wordsworth speaks less of the vulgar tongue of the profession than any writer since that period; he always thinks when he speaks, has always words at command, feels deeply, fancies richly, and never descends from that pure and elevated morality, which is the native region of the first order of poetical spirits.

It may be asked me then, why with such opinions as I entertain of the greatness of Mr. Wordsworth's genius, he is treated as he is in the verses before us. I answer, because he abuses that genius so as Milton or Spenser never abused it, and so as to destroy those great ends of poetry, by which it should assist the uses and refresh the spirits of life. From him, to whom much is given, much shall be required. Mr. Wordsworth is capable of being at the head of a new and great age of poetry; and in point of fact, I do not deny that he is so already, as the greatest poet of the present;—but in point of effect, in point of delight and utility, he appears to me to have made a mistake unworthy of him, and to have sought by eccentricity and by a turning away from society, what he might have obtained by keeping to his proper and more neighbourly sphere.

The theory of Mr. Wordsworth,—if I may venture to give in a few words my construction of the curious and, in many respects, very masterly preface to the Lyrical Ballads, is this;—that owing to a variety of existing causes, among which are the accumulation of men in cities and the necessary uniformity of their occupations,—and the consequent craving for extraordinary incident, which the present state of the world is quick to gratify, the taste of society has become so vitiated and so accustomed to gross stimulants, such as "frantic novels, sickly and stupid German tragedies, and deluges of *idle* and *extravagant* stories in verse," as to require

the counteraction of some simpler and more primitive food, which should restore to readers their true tone of enjoyment, and enable them to relish once more the beauties of simplicity and nature;—that, to this purpose, a poet in the present age, who looked upon men with his proper eye, as an entertainer and instructor, should chuse subjects as far removed as possible from artificial excitements, and appealing to the great and primary affections of our nature;—thirdly and lastly, that these subjects, to be worthily and effectively treated, should be clothed in language equally artless.

Now the object of the theory here mentioned has clearly nothing in the abstract, that can offend the soundest good sense or the best poetical ambition. In fact, it is only saying, in other words, that it is high time for poetry in general to return to nature and to a natural style, and that he will perform a great and useful work to society, who shall assist it to do so.

But how is our passion for stimulants to be allayed by the substitution of stories like Mr. Wordsworth's? He wishes to turn aside our thirst for extraordinary intelligence to more genial sources of interest, and he gives us accounts of mothers who have gone mad at the loss of their children, of others who have killed their's in the most horrible manner, and of hard-hearted masters whose imaginations have revenged upon them the curses of the poor. In like manner, he would clear up and simplicize our thoughts; and he tells us tales of children that have no notion of death, of boys who would halloo to a landscape nobody knew why, and of an hundred inexpressible sensations, intended by nature no doubt to affect us, and even pleasurably so in the general feeling, but only calculated to perplex or sadden us in our attempts at analysis. Now it appears to me, that all the craving after intelligence, which Mr. Wordsworth imagines to be the bane of the present state of society, is a healthy

---

[1] William Collins (1721–59), a poet celebrated in the Romantic period for his lyrical intensity.

appetite in comparison to these morbid abstractions: the former tends, at any rate, to fix the eyes of mankind in a lively manner upon the persons that preside over their interests and to keep up a certain demand for knowledge and public improvement;—the latter, under the guise of interesting us in the individuals of our species, turns our thoughts away from society and men altogether, and nourishes that eremitical[1] vagueness of sensation,—that making a business of reverie,—that despair of getting to any conclusion to any purpose, which is the next step to melancholy or indifference.

To conclude this inordinate note: Mr. Wordsworth, in objecting to one extreme, has gone to another,—the natural commencement perhaps of all revolutions. He thinks us over-active, and would make us over-contemplative,—a fault not likely to extend very widely, but which ought still to be deprecated for the sake of those to whom it would. We are, he thinks, too much crowded together, and too subject, in consequence, to high-fevered tastes and worldly infections. Granted:—he, on the other hand, lives too much apart, and is subject, we think, to low-fevered tastes and solitary morbidities;—but as there is health in both of us, suppose both parties strike a bargain,—he to come among us a little more and get a true sense of our action,—we to go out of ourselves a little oftener and acquire a taste for his contemplation. We will make more holidays into nature with him; but he, in fairness, must earn them, as well as ourselves, by sharing our working-days:—we will emerge oftener into his fields, sit dangling our legs over his styles, and cultivate a due respect for his daffodils; but he, on the other hand, must grow a little better acquainted with our streets, must put up with our lawyers, and even find out a heart or so among our politicians:—in short, we will recollect that we have hearts and brains, and will feel and ponder a little more to purify us as

spirits; but he will be good enough, in return, to cast an eye on his hands and muscles, and consider that the putting these to their purposes is necessary to complete our part on this world as organized bodies.

Here is the good to be done on both sides; and as society, I believe, would be much bettered in consequence, so there is no man, I am persuaded, more capable that Mr. Wordsworth, upon a better acquaintance with society, to do it the service. Without that acquaintance, his reputation in poetry may be little more salutary than that of an Empedocles in philosophy [2] or a Saint Francis in religion:—with it, he might revive the spirit, the glory, and the utility of a Shakespeare.

(1814)

HUMPHRY DAVY
Parallels Between Art and Science [3]

THE characters of the poet and painter have been often compared: and the analogy between their objects and their methods is so striking, as to have been generally felt and acknowledged. Visible images constitute the great charm of poetry, and they are the elements of painting: and the end of both arts is to represent the admirable in nature, and to awaken pleasurable, useful, or noble feelings. Painting, however, appeals to the eye by immediate characters; it possesses a stronger chain of associa-

---

[1] Characteristic of one leading a hermit-like existence.

[2] Empedocles: Greek philosopher *c.* 495–435 B.C.

[3] Humphry Davy (1778–1829), chemist and scientific lecturer, and after 1802, professor of chemistry at the Royal Institution, Davy was an intimate of Wordsworth and S. T. Coleridge, and helped Wordsworth edit the second edition of *Lyrical Ballads* in 1800. In his lectures and essays, Davy attempted to synthesize the worlds of science and poetry. Davy's public lectures became a fashionable attraction with a broad populace, in part because support from aristocratic patrons enabled Davy to offer his audiences visually spectacular demonstrations. Despite his early associations with radicals such as Joseph Priestley, Erasmus Darwin, and William Godwin, Davy insistently connected the ideal of scientific inquiry to a belief in the importance of a conservative social order.

tion with passion; it is a more distinct and energetic language, and acts first by awakening sensation and then ideas. Poetry is less forcible; for it operates only by imagination and memory, and not by immediate impression; unless indeed in the performances of the drama, or in impassioned recitation. A representation by words is inferior in strength to representation by images; but it has the advantage in being more varied, and capable of a more extensive application. It speaks of sentiments and thoughts and affections, which can never be delineated by the pencil; and it has within its power, not only the world of sensation, but likewise the world of intellect.

The mechanical arts and the fine arts can hardly be compared; the objects of the first being utility, of the last, pleasure. The mechanical arts delight us only indirectly, and by indistinct associations; the fine arts either directly, or by immediate associations. The steam-engine may be an object of wonder, as connected with the power by which it was produced, and the power which it exerts; but to understand its beneficial effects requires extensive knowledge, or a long detail of facts. Mechanism in general is too complicated to produce any general effect of pleasure. Inventions are admired by the multitude, more on account of their novelty or strangeness, than on account of their use or ingenuity. The watch which is the guide of our time, is employed and considered with indifference: but we pay half-a-crown to see a self-moving spider of steel.

In the truths of the natural sciences there is, perhaps, a nearer analogy to the productions of the refined arts. The contemplation of the laws of the universe is connected with an immediate tranquil exaltation of mind, and pure mental enjoyment. The perception of truth is almost as simple a feeling as the perception of beauty; and the genius of Newton, of Shakespeare, of Michael Angelo, and of Handel,[1] are not very remote in character from each other. Imagination, as well as reason, is necessary to perfection in the philosophical mind. A rapidity of combination, a power of perceiving analogies, and of comparing them by facts, is the creative source of discovery. Discrimination and delicacy of sensation, so important in physical research, are other words for taste; and the love of nature is the same passion, as the love of the magnificent, the sublime, and the beautiful.

The pleasure derived from great philosophical discoveries is less popular and more limited in its immediate effect, than that derived from the refined arts; but it is more durable and less connected with fashion or caprice. Canvas and wood, and even stone, will decay. The work of a great artist loses all its spirit in the copy. Words are mutable and fleeting; and the genius of poetry is often dissipated in translation. The compositions of music may remain, but the hand of execution may be wanting. Nature cannot decay: the language of her interpreters will be the same in all times. It will be an universal tongue, speaking to all countries, and all ages, the excellence of the work, and the wisdom of the Creator.

(1807)

PERCY SHELLEY
A Defence of Poetry[2]

POETRY is ever accompanied with pleasure: all spirits on which it falls open themselves to

---

[1] Sir Isaac Newton (1642–1727), renowned scientist; William Shakespeare (1564–1616), dramatist and poet; Buonarroti Michelangelo (1475–1564), Florentine painter, sculptor, architect, and poet; George Frederic Handel (1685–1759), German composer who lived in England after the age of 27.

[2] Percy Shelley (1792–1822), was one of the most notorious of the second-generation Romantic poets. After being expelled from Oxford University for publishing *The Necessity of Atheism* (1811), which he co-

receive the wisdom which is mingled with its delight. In the infancy of the world, neither poets themselves nor their auditors are fully aware of the excellence of poetry: for it acts in a divine and unapprehended manner beyond and above consciousness; and it is reserved for future generations to contemplate and measure the mighty cause and effect in all the strength and splendour of their union. Even in modern times no living poet ever arrived at the fullness of his fame; the jury which sits in judgment upon a poet, belonging as he does to all time, must be composed of his peers: it must be empanelled by Time from the selectest of the wise of many generations. A Poet is a nightingale, who sits in darkness and sings to cheer its own solitude with sweet sounds; his auditors are as men entranced by the melody of an unseen musician, who feel that they are moved and softened yet know not whence or why.

But poets have been challenged to resign the civic crown to reasoners and mechanists on another plea.[1] It is admitted that the exercise of the imagination is most delightful, but it is alleged that that of reason is more useful. Let us examine as the grounds of this distinction, what is here meant by utility. Pleasure or good, in a general sense, is that which the consciousness of a sensitive and intelligent being seeks, and in which, when found, it acquiesces.

There are two modes or degrees of pleasure, one durable, universal and permanent; the other transitory and particular. Utility may either express the means of producing the former or the latter. In the former sense, whatever strengthens and purifies the affections, enlarges the imagination, and adds spirit to sense, is useful. But the meaning in which the author of *The Four Ages of Poetry* seems to have employed the word utility is the narrower one of banishing the importunity of the wants of our animal nature, the surrounding men with security of life, the dispersing the grosser delusions of superstition, and the conciliating such a degree of mutual forbearance among men as may consist with the motives of personal advantage.

Undoubtedly the promoters of utility, in this limited sense, have their appointed office in society. They follow the footsteps of poets, and copy the sketches of their creations into the book of common life. They make space, and give time. Their exertions are of the highest value, so long as they confine their administration of the concerns of the inferior powers of our nature within the limits due to the superior ones. But whilst the sceptic destroys gross superstitions, let him spare to deface, as some of the French writers have defaced, the eternal truths charactered upon the imaginations of men. Whilst the mechanist abridges, and the political economist combines, labour, let them beware that their speculations, for want of correspondence with those first principles which belong to the imagination, do not tend, as they have in modern England, to exasperate at once the extremes of luxury and want. They have exemplified the saying, "To him that hath, more shall be given; and from him that hath not, the little that he hath shall be taken away."[2] The rich have become richer, and the poor have become poorer; and the vessel of the state is

---

wrote with T.J. Hogg, Shelley gravitated to William Godwin's circle of rationalist reformers in London. Shelley's thought integrated the intellectual legacy of the radical Enlightenment with Romantic poets' love of the sublime and deification of the imagination as a revolutionary power. *A Defence of Poetry* responds to two arguments made in Thomas Love Peacock's essay *The Four Ages of Poetry* (1820). The first is that the quality of poetry diminishes as society becomes progressively more civilized; the second, which Shelley is responding to in this section, is that poets are less valuable to society than more pragmatic or utilitarian social reformers. The *Defence* was published posthumously in 1840.

[1] This section picks up where Shelley shifts from the first part of his argument, about the historical nature of poetry, to the second, which contrasts poets' important social role with the more pragmatic but ultimately less important role of utilitarian social reformers.

[2] Matthew 25:49.

driven between the Scylla and Charybdis[1] of anarchy and despotism. Such are the effects which must ever flow from an unmitigated exercise of the calculating faculty.

It is difficult to define pleasure in its highest sense; the definition involving a number of apparent paradoxes. For, from an inexplicable defect of harmony in the constitution of human nature, the pain of the inferior is frequently connected with the pleasures of the superior portions of our being. Sorrow, terror, anguish, despair itself, are often the chosen expressions of an approximation to the highest good. Our sympathy in tragic fiction depends on this principle; tragedy delights by affording a shadow of the pleasure which exists in pain. This is the source also of the melancholy which is inseparable from the sweetest melody. The pleasure that is in sorrow is sweeter than the pleasure of pleasure itself. And hence the saying, "It is better to go to the house of mourning, than to the house of mirth."[2] Not that this highest species of pleasure is necessarily linked with pain. The delight of love and friendship, the ecstasy of the admiration of nature, the joy of the perception and still more of the creation of poetry is often wholly unalloyed.

The production and assurance of pleasure in this highest sense is true utility. Those who produce and preserve this pleasure are poets or poetical philosophers.

The exertions of Locke, Hume, Gibbon, Voltaire, Rousseau,[†3] and their disciples, in favour of oppressed and deluded humanity, are entitled to the gratitude of mankind. Yet it is easy to calculate the degree of moral and intellectual improvement which the world would have exhibited, had they never lived. A little more nonsense would have been talked for a century or two; and perhaps a few more men, women, and children, burnt as heretics. We might not at this moment have been congratulating each other on the abolition of the Inquisition in Spain.[4] But it exceeds all imagination to conceive what would have been the moral condition of the world if neither Dante, Petrarch, Boccaccio, Chaucer, Shakespeare, Calderon, Lord Bacon, nor Milton,[5] had ever existed; if Raphael and Michael Angelo had never been born; if the Hebrew poetry had never been translated; if a revival of the study of Greek literature had never taken place; if no monuments of ancient sculpture had been handed down to us; and if the poetry of the religion of the ancient world had been extinguished together with its belief. The human mind could never, except by the intervention of these excitements, have been awakened to the invention of the grosser sciences, and that application of analytical reasoning to the aberrations of society, which it is now attempted to exalt over the direct expression of the inventive and creative faculty itself.

We have more moral, political and historical wisdom, than we know how to reduce into practice; we have more scientific and economical knowledge than can be accommodated to the just distribution

---

[1] Two monsters positioned, in Greek myths, on either side of the strait between Italy and Sicily. Commonly used as a metaphor for the dangers inherent in verging towards alternative extremes: here, too little or too much government control.

[2] Ecclesiastes 7:2.

[†] I follow the classification by the author of *The Four Ages of Poetry;* but he was essentially a poet. The others, even Voltaire, were mere reasoners.

[3] John Locke (1632–1704), David Hume (1711–76), Edward Gibbon (1737–94), Voltaire (the pseudonym of François-Marie Arouet, 1694–1778), and Jean-Jacques Rousseau (1742–78), were prominent eighteenth-century thinkers frequently associated in different ways with the Enlightenment.

[4] The Inquisition had been temporarily suspended in 1820.

[5] Dante Aligheri (1265–1321), Florentine poet; Francesco Petrarca (1304–74), Italian poet and humanist; Giovanni Boccaccio (1313–75), Italian writer and humanist; Geoffrey Chaucer (c. 1343–1400), English poet; William Shakespeare (1564–1616), English dramatist and poet; Pedro Calderon de la Barca (1600–81), Spanish dramatist; Francis Bacon (1561–1626), English philosopher, essayist, and historian; John Milton (1608–74), English poet.

of the produce which it multiplies. The poetry in these systems of thought, is concealed by the accumulation of facts and calculating processes. There is no want of knowledge respecting what is wisest and best in morals, government, and political economy, or at least, what is wiser and better than what men now practise and endure. But we let "*I dare not* wait upon *I would,* like the poor cat in the adage."[1] We want the creative faculty to imagine that which we know; we want the generous impulse to act that which we imagine; we want the poetry of life: our calculations have outrun conception; we have eaten more than we can digest. The cultivation of those sciences which have enlarged the limits of the empire of man over the external world, has, for want of the poetical faculty, proportionally circumscribed those of the internal world; and man, having enslaved the elements, remains himself a slave. To what but a cultivation of the mechanical arts in a degree disproportioned to the presence of the creative faculty, which is the basis of all knowledge, is to be attributed the abuse of all invention for abridging and combining labour, to the exasperation of the inequality of mankind? From what other cause has it arisen that these inventions which should have lightened, have added a weight to the curse imposed on Adam? Thus poetry and the principle of self, of which money is the visible incarnation, are the God and Mammon[2] of the world.

The first part of these remarks[3] has related to poetry in its elements and principles; and it has been shown, as well as the narrow limits assigned them would permit, that what is called poetry, in a restricted sense, has a common source with all other forms of order and of beauty, according to which the materials of human life are susceptible of being arranged, and which is poetry in an universal sense.

The second part will have for its object an application of these principles to the present state of the cultivation of poetry, and a defence of the attempt to idealize the modern forms of manners and opinions, and compel them into a subordination to the imaginative and creative faculty. For the literature of England, an energetic development of which has ever preceded or accompanied a great and free development of the national will, has arisen as it were from a new birth. In spite of the low-thoughted envy which would undervalue contemporary merit, our own will be a memorable age in intellectual achievements, and we live among such philosophers and poets as surpass beyond comparison any who have appeared since the last national struggle for civil and religious liberty. The most unfailing herald, companion, and follower of the awakening of a great people to work a beneficial change in opinion or institution, is poetry. At such periods there is an accumulation of the power of communicating and receiving intense and impassioned conceptions respecting man and nature. The persons in whom this power resides, may often as far as regards many portions of their nature, have little apparent correspondence with that spirit of good of which they are the ministers. But even whilst they deny and abjure, they are yet compelled to serve, the power which is seated upon the throne of their own soul. It is impossible to read the compositions of the most celebrated writers of the present day without being startled with the electric life which burns within their words. They measure the circumference and sound the depths of human nature with a comprehensive and all-penetrating spirit, and they are themselves perhaps the most sincerely astonished at its manifestations; for it is less their spirit than the spirit of the age. Poets are

---

[1] William Shakespeare (1564–1616), *Macbeth* (1606): I: vii: 43–44.

[2] The opposed forces of moral purity and individual selfishness.

[3] Shelley intended the existing *Defence* to be the first part of a larger essay that was never completed.

the hierophants[1] of an unapprehended inspiration; the mirrors of the gigantic shadows which futurity casts upon the present; the words which express what they understand not; the trumpets which sing to battle, and feel not what they inspire; the influence which is moved not, but moves. Poets are the unacknowledged legislators of the world.

(1821)

---

[1] Priests.

SECTION NINE

Reflections on the Revolution in France

These readings are organized into three clusters of texts that reflect different aspects of the complex intersections between the French Revolution and debates in Britain about print culture. The fact that the Revolution was widely seen, by both its supporters and its critics, as the culmination of an Enlightenment emphasis on critical enquiry as an engine of reform meant that it inevitably raised questions about the proper limits and role of a reading public. Not for nothing did the French revolutionaries carry printing presses in their civic processions and set aside a day in the revolutionary calendar for the celebration of public opinion. Across the Channel, British printing presses were busier than ever before with a frenzied book and pamphlet war about the virtues of radical reform and literature's role in promoting it. It was in this context that T. J. Mathias issued his warning, which we saw in Section One, that "LITERATURE, *well or ill conducted*, IS THE GREAT ENGINE *by which*, I am fully persuaded, ALL CIVILIZED STATES *must ultimately be supported or overthrown.*"

Mathias's invitation to "consider the nature, variety and extent of the word, Literature" was taken up by authors from a wide range of political persuasions and personal backgrounds. In a pamphlet entitled *Slight Observations Upon Paine's Pamphlet* (1791), Thomas Green expressed his "disgust," having changed "the air and comfort of the country, for the business of London," only to discover that, as a result of the debate initiated by Edmund Burke and inflamed by Thomas Paine, "the people here are actually mad, and I am apprehensive, almost literally speaking, of being bitten." No sooner had he settled in at his preferred coffee house than he was bombarded by "a multitude of questions" about Burke's and Paine's literary efforts "with an eagerness which astonished me." Green may have been exaggerating for rhetorical effect, but there is no doubt that Burke's and Paine's tracts were the most important examples of a political debate that flourished throughout Britain in the early stages of the French Revolution as thinkers from all political positions were forced to engage with questions about the social character of literature.

Edmund Burke had been a prominent member of the Whig movement in Britain for decades, but in *Reflections on the Revolution in France* (1790) he offered a scathing critique of the Revolution that was reinforced by a broader rejection of the underlying principles of the reform movement generally, including the Enlightenment claim that literature could help to transform society by encouraging debate. Instead, he insisted that personal intuition, or as he memorably put it, inherited prejudices, were a better basis for social order than intellectual exchange. Burke's opponents gleefully noted the irony that his denunciation of the authority of the public sphere only invigorated debate on the relations between power, knowledge, and print culture. It was in many ways a very literary debate. One of the first responses, Mary Wollstonecraft's *Vindication of the Rights of Men*, focused on "the latent spirit of tyranny" inherent in a literary style that indulged in "slavish paradoxes" at the expense of rational debate. Paine's *Rights of Man* made the same point in an accessible style that was reinforced by the efforts of political societies to distribute cheap or free versions of it in formats such as question-and-answer dialogues, ballads set to familiar tunes, and posters.

These debates were complemented by a series of legislative interventions designed to curb the circulation of cheap political texts by imposing new taxes, and to strengthen criminal prosecutions by passing initiatives such as the Royal Proclamation Against Seditious Writings and Publications, ratified on 21 May 1792, which urged magistrates to pursue the authors, printers and disseminators of seditious writings. One of the most infamous victims of this newly intensified criminal surveillance was Paine himself, who was arrested and tried *in absentia* (he had already fled to France to participate in the Revolution) for seditious-libel for *Rights of Man* Part Two. As we saw in the Attorney General's Speech in Section Two, Paine's popularizing efforts were as much an issue as were the ideas he was communicating. The trial drew attention to important questions about the legal status of a text's price and audience, and the means by which it was being circulated. In his *Letter Addressed to the Addressers of the Late Proclamation*, written in the summer after he had fled to France, Paine ironically praised the role of both the trial and the Royal Proclamation for making these issues explicit.

The extreme popularity of Paine's *Rights of Man* sparked a multitude of conservative replies. They responded to the dangers of the growing republican sentiment in Britain, but they focused even more on the dangers of political pamphlets written by opportunists whose intention was not to promote the diffusion of knowledge but to encourage unrest, in order, as Frederick Hervey put it, "that they may live on the wrecks of ruined states." Conservatives were quick to emphasize their appreciation of the importance of the freedom of the press but, they argued, this freedom only applied to those authors who understood the importance of restricting these exchanges to readers who shared their respect for the difference between ideas and actions. Among this group, the most radical ideas could be suggested because they could be confident that these ideas would be considered without necessarily being acted upon. But the security of this arrangement was being undermined by authors who deliberately courted the attention of readers who did not possess the education necessary to read these tracts in a suitably critical spirit.

Because these debates were strategic as much as intellectual, authors on both sides worked hard to appeal to as broad a readership as possible. The two texts which comprise the second part of this section offer compelling examples of conservative and radical satirical responses to the question of the political force of books. Hannah More's pamphlets, known as the *Cheap Repository Tracts*, were written in the style of popular broadsheets in order to dissuade plebeian readers from joining the reform movement, and were backed by a powerful campaign determined to ensure that they arrived into the hands of a maximum number of readers. In *Village Politics*, the well-intentioned but gullible Tom has been upset by his encounter with a book named *Rights of Man*. Luckily for Tom, the local blacksmith, Jack, is on hand to set him straight by helping Tom to see that his lot is not so bad, and that radical reform was no kind of solution for right-thinking British people. More's pamphlet may have implied that ordinary villagers like Tom were not up to reading tracts on weighty political issues, but her own pamphlet was an adroit attempt to influence a popular reading audience. Daniel Isaac Eaton was a prominent reformist publisher and author who was frequently arrested during the 1790s, each time publishing a copy of the trial proceedings in order to reinforce his point about the double standards of British justice. In *The Pernicious Effects of the Art of Printing upon Society, Exposed*, Eaton mocked both the defensiveness of conservatives and their irrational fears of the supposedly disastrous effects of the printed word. The intensity of the reaction that he depicts may seem like little more than shrewd comic effect today, but he was presenting a careful study of the apocalyptic demise predicted by many of those who were fearful of the effects of a mass readership in Britain.

The three texts which comprise the final part of this section offer an outstanding example of the complexities of the debate over the spectre of a mass reading public, which intensified as the revolutionary crisis reached its peak after the Treason trials of late 1794, when the government failed in its attempt to convict the leading members of the radical reform movement, and lasted until two bills designed to further suppress seditious writings and political organization were passed into law a year later. John Bowles' argument pushed the conservative position to new extremes by rejecting the possibility of a distinction between responsible and destructive forms of an extended public debate. For Bowles, the reformers' emphasis on enlightened discussion rather than violence was merely a sign of their ingenious duplicity. Alluding to John Thelwall, whom he referred to as "The Lecturer, who makes a livelihood by the sale of his Seditious Poison," Bowles insisted that reformers only indulged in rhetoric about the importance of peaceful deliberation because they knew that this was the best way of generating the greatest violence in the long run.

Bowles was certainly correct in emphasizing reformers' commitment to rational debate as an engine of change. Speaking at one of two mass outdoor meetings in late 1795, just weeks before the government passed its infamous "gagging acts" aimed at curbing seditious writings and political organization, John Thelwall offered a perfect vision of this nonviolent pursuit of reform through mass critical debate. Straddling the boundaries between oral and print cultures, Thelwall announced that he was accompanied by a short-hand writer in order that he might be safe from misrepresentations, and that his speech might find a still wider audience in pamphlet form. He offered the example of the violent excesses of the French Revolution as a lesson in the importance of enlightening the general populace through debate before any meaningful political change could be realized. Not everyone was convinced by Thelwall's confidence in a mass reform movement though. As a middle-class reformer, William Godwin's *Considerations* objected to the efforts of working-class political groups such as the London Corresponding Society. Reform was too precious a goal to be entrusted to the wrong hands, he argued. Mass public meetings were the opposite of critical reflection, which needed to be pursued in less intemperate circumstances. Far from learning from the negative example of the French Revolution, Godwin suggested, radical groups such as the London Corresponding Society had patterned themselves after its most extreme elements. But, he also insisted, this did not warrant the British government's assault on literature's important role as means of exchanging ideas. Tellingly, for Godwin, Lord Grenville's bill, which set new limits on the freedom of the press, cited a precedent from 1571, an era when modern literature had not yet achieved its function as a means of sustaining an extended reading public. All of these political tensions brought new clarity and urgency to questions about the nature of literature—a subject which, in turn, rested on the related question of the social demographics of the reading community.

∽∾∾

EDMUND BURKE
Reflections on the Revolution in France and on the Proceedings in Certain Societies in London Relative to that Event. [1]

INFLUENCED by the inborn feelings of my nature, and not being illuminated by a single ray of this new-sprung modern light, I confess to you, Sir,[2] that the exalted rank of the persons suffering, and particularly the sex, the beauty, and the amiable qualities of the descendant of so many kings and emperors, with the tender age of royal infants, insensible only through infancy and innocence of the cruel outrages to which their parents were exposed, instead of being a subject of exultation, adds not a little to my sensibility on that most melancholy occasion.

It is now sixteen or seventeen years since I saw the queen of France, then the dauphiness, at Versailles; and surely never lighted on this orb, which she hardly seemed to touch, a more delightful vision. I saw her just above the horizon, decorating and cheering the elevated sphere she just began to move in,—glittering like the morning-star, full of life, and splendor, and joy. Oh! what a revolution! and what an heart must I have, to contemplate without emotion that elevation and that fall! Little did I dream that when she added titles of veneration to those of enthusiastic, distant, respectful love, that she should ever be obliged to carry the sharp antidote against disgrace concealed in that bosom; little

[1] Edmund Burke (1729–97), a significant eighteenth-century literary figure known for his *A Philosophical Enquiry into the Origin of our Ideas of the Sublime and the Beautiful* (1757) and, after his entry into politics in 1765, a leading member of the Whig party, but then in the 1790s for his outspoken denunciation of the French Revolution. Burke championed a range of reformist causes and led an unsuccessful attempt to impeach Warren Hastings, the Governor General of Bengal for the conduct of the East India Company. His *Reflections* was seen by many of his Whig colleagues as an act of political apostasy, a critique of both the Revolution and the central Enlightenment principles of rational debate as a motor of reform.

[2] The *Reflections* was written as a letter to a correspondent in France.

did I dream that I should have lived to see such disasters fallen upon her in a nation of gallant men, in a nation of men of honour and of cavaliers. I thought ten thousand swords must have leaped from their scabbards to avenge even a look that threatened her with insult.—But the age of chivalry is gone.—That of sophisters, œconomists, and calculators, has succeeded; and the glory of Europe is extinguished for ever. Never, never more, shall we behold that generous loyalty to rank and sex, that proud submission, that dignified obedience, that subordination of the heart, which kept alive, even in servitude itself, the spirit of an exalted freedom. The unbought grace of life, the cheap defence of nations, the nurse of manly sentiment and heroic enterprize is gone! It is gone, that sensibility of principle, that chastity of honour, which felt a stain like a wound, which inspired courage whilst it mitigated ferocity, which ennobled whatever it touched, and under which vice itself lost half its evil, by losing all its grossness.

This mixed system of opinion and sentiment had its origin in the antient chivalry; and the principle, though varied in its appearance by the varying state of human affairs, subsisted and influenced through a long succession of generations, even to the time we live in. If it should ever be totally extinguished, the loss I fear will be great. It is this which has given its character to modern Europe. It is this which has distinguished it under all its forms of government, and distinguished it to its advantage, from the states of Asia, and possibly from those states which flourished in the most brilliant periods of the antique world. It was this, which, without confounding ranks, had produced a noble equality, and handed it down through all the gradations of social life. It was this opinion which mitigated kings into companions, and raised private men to be fellows with kings. Without force, or opposition, it subdued the fierceness of pride and power; it obliged sovereigns to submit to the soft collar of social esteem, compelled stern authority to submit to elegance, and gave a domination vanquisher of laws, to be subdued by manners.

But now all is to be changed. All the pleasing illusions, which made power gentle, and obedience liberal, which harmonized the different shades of life, and which, by a bland assimilation, incorporated into politics the sentiments which beautify and soften private society, are to be dissolved by this new conquering empire of light and reason. All the decent drapery of life is to be rudely torn off. All the superadded ideas, furnished from the wardrobe of a moral imagination, which the heart owns, and the understanding ratifies, as necessary to cover the defects of our naked shivering nature, and to raise it to dignity in our own estimation, are to be exploded as a ridiculous, absurd, and antiquated fashion.

The vanity, restlessness, petulance, and spirit of intrigue of several petty cabals, who attempt to hide their total want of consequence in bustle and noise, and puffing, and mutual quotation of each other, makes you imagine that our contemptuous neglect of their abilities is a mark of general acquiescence in their opinions. No such thing, I assure you. Because a half a dozen grasshoppers under a fern make the field ring with their importunate chink, whilst thousands of great cattle, reposed under the shadow of the British oak, chew the cud and are silent, pray do not imagine, that those who make the noise are the only inhabitants of the field; that of course, they are many in number; or that, after all, they are other than the little shrivelled, meagre, hopping, though loud and troublesome insects of the hour.

You see, Sir, that in this enlightened age I am bold enough to confess, that we are generally men of untaught feelings; that instead of casting away all our old prejudices, we cherish them to a very considerable degree, and, to take more shame to

ourselves, we cherish them because they are prejudices; and the longer they have lasted, and the more
generally they have prevailed, the more we cherish
them. We are afraid to put men to live and trade
each on his own private stock of reason; because we
suspect that this stock in each man is small, and
that the individuals would do better to avail themselves of the general bank and capital of nations,
and of ages. Many of our men of speculation,
instead of exploding general prejudices, employ
their sagacity to discover the latent wisdom which
prevails in them. If they find what they seek, and
they seldom fail, they think it more wise to continue the prejudice, with the reason involved, than
to cast away the coat of prejudice, and to leave
nothing but the naked reason; because prejudice,
with its reason, has a motive to give action to that
reason, and an affection which will give it permanence. Prejudice is of ready application in the
emergency; it previously engages the mind in a
steady course of wisdom and virtue, and does not
leave the man hesitating in the moment of decision,
sceptical, puzzled, and unresolved. Prejudice renders a man's virtue his habit; and not a series of
unconnected acts. Through just prejudice, his duty
becomes a part of his nature.

Your literary men, and your politicians, and so
do the whole clan of the enlightened among us,
essentially differ in these points. They have no
respect for the wisdom of others; but they pay it off
by a very full measure of confidence in their own.
With them it is a sufficient motive to destroy an old
scheme of things, because it is an old one. As to the
new, they are in no sort of fear with regard to the
duration of a building run up in haste; because
duration is no object to those who think little or
nothing has been done before their time, and who
place all their hopes in discovery. They conceive,
very systematically, that all things which give
perpetuity are mischievous, and therefore they are

at inexpiable war with all establishments. They
think that government may vary like modes of
dress, and with as little ill effect. That there needs
no principle of attachment, except a sense of present
conveniency, to any constitution of the state. They
always speak as if they were of opinion that there is
a singular species of compact between them and
their magistrates, which binds the magistrate, but
which has nothing reciprocal in it, but that the
majesty of the people has a right to dissolve it
without any reason, but its will. Their attachment
to their country itself, is only so far as it agrees with
some of their fleeting projects; it begins and ends
with that scheme of polity which falls in with their
momentary opinion.

By the vast debt of France a great monied
interest had insensibly grown up, and with it a great
power. By the ancient usages which prevailed in
that kingdom, the general circulation of property,
and in particular the mutual convertibility of land
into money, and of money into land, had always
been a matter of difficulty. Family settlements,
rather more general and more strict than they are in
England, the *jus retractus*,[1] the great mass of landed
property held by the crown, and by a maxim of
French law held unalienably, the vast estates of the
ecclesiastic corporations,—all these had kept the
landed and monied interests more separated in
France, less miscible,[2] and the owners of the two
distinct species of property not so well disposed to
each other as they are in this country.

In this state of real, though not always perceived
warfare between the noble ancient landed interest,
and the new monied interest, the greatest because
the most applicable strength was in the hands of the
latter. The monied interest is in its nature more
ready for any adventure; and its possessors more

---

[1] The *jus retractus* was an ancient law enabling the heirs to repurchase
any parts of their ancestors' estate that had been previously sold.

[2] Mixable.

disposed to new enterprizes of any kind. Being of a recent acquisition, it falls in more naturally with any novelties. It is therefore the kind of wealth which will be resorted to by all who wish for change.

Along with the monied interest, a new description of men had grown up, with whom that interest soon formed a close and marked union; I mean the political Men of Letters. Men of Letters, fond of distinguishing themselves, are rarely averse to innovation. Since the decline of the life and greatness of Lewis the XIVth, they were not so much cultivated either by him, or by the regent, or the successors to the crown; nor were they engaged to the court by favours and emoluments so systematically as during the splendid period of that ostentatious and not impolitic reign. What they lost in the old court protection, they endeavoured to make up by joining in a sort of incorporation of their own; to which the two academies of France,[1] and afterwards the vast undertaking of the Encyclopædia,[2] carried on by a society of these gentlemen, did not a little contribute.

The literary cabal had some years ago formed something like a regular plan for the destruction of the Christian religion. This object they pursued with a degree of zeal which hitherto had been discovered only in the propagators of some system of piety. They were possessed with a spirit of proselytism in the most fanatical degree; and from thence, by an easy progress, with the spirit of persecution according to their means.[†] What was not to be done towards their great end by any direct or immediate act, might be wrought by a longer process through the medium of opinion. To command that opinion, the first step is to establish a dominion over those who direct it. They contrived to possess themselves, with great method and perseverance, of all the avenues of literary fame. Many of them indeed stood high in the ranks of literature and science. The world had done them justice; and in favour of general talents forgave the evil of their peculiar principles. This was true liberality; which they returned by endeavouring to confine the reputation of sense, learning, and taste to themselves or their followers. I will venture to say that this narrow, exclusive spirit has not been less prejudicial to literature and to taste, than to morals and true philosophy. These Atheistical fathers have a bigotry of their own; and they have learnt to talk against monks with the spirit of a monk. But in some things they are men of the world. The resources of intrigue are called in to supply the defects of argument and wit. To this system of literary monopoly was joined an unremitting industry to blacken and discredit in every way, and by every means, all those who did not hold to their faction. To those who have observed the spirit of their conduct, it has long been clear that nothing was wanted but the power of carrying the intolerance of the tongue and of the pen into a persecution which would strike at property, liberty, and life.

Writers, especially when they act in a body, and with one direction, have great influence on the public mind; the alliance therefore of these writers with the monied interest had no small effect in removing the popular odium and envy which attended that species of wealth. These writers, like

---

[1] There were actually several Academies or learned societies which this reference might have applied to. The Académie Français was often described by conservatives as a breeding ground of sedition and atheism.

[2] The *Encyclopédie*, an enormous project associated with the French Enlightenment, was linked to *philosophes* such as Diderot, d'Alembert, and Condillac.

[†] This (down to the next paragraph) and some other parts, here and there, were inserted, on his reading the manuscript, by my lost son. [inserted 1803]

the propagators of all novelties, pretended to a great zeal for the poor, and the lower orders, whilst in their satires they rendered hateful, by every exaggeration, the faults of courts, of nobility, and of priesthood. They became a sort of demagogues. They served as a link to unite, in favour of one object, obnoxious wealth to restless and desperate poverty.

(1790)

MARY WOLLSTONECRAFT
Vindication of the Rights of Men, in a Letter to the Right Honourable Edmund Burke; occasioned by his Reflections on the Revolution in France [1]

SIR,

IT is not necessary, with courtly insincerity, to apologize to you for thus intruding on your precious time, not to profess that I think it an honour to discuss an important subject with a man whose literary abilities have raised him to notice in the state. I have not yet learned to twist my periods, nor, in the equivocal idiom of politeness, to disguise my sentiments, and imply what I should be afraid to utter: if, therefore, in the course of this epistle, I chance to express contempt, and even indignation, with some emphasis, I beseech you to believe that it is not a flight of fancy; for truth, in morals, has ever

[1] Mary Wollstonecraft (1759–97), best known for her radical political tracts on the Rights of Man and Rights of Woman controversies, was also a novelist, educational theorist (and teacher—before becoming an author she had opened a school with her two sisters and a friend, Fanny Blood), travel writer, and literary critic for Joseph Johnson's *Analytical Review*. Wollstonecraft's *Vindication of the Rights of Men*, which appeared in the same year as Burke's *Reflections*, was one of the first published responses. In it, Wollstonecraft attacked Burke's emotional response to what should be a rational issue, and his sentimental attention to the sufferings of the wealthy at the expense of any consideration of the less glamourous problems of the rank and file—points that would quickly become central radical responses in the pamphlet war that followed.

appeared to me the essence of the sublime; and in taste, simplicity the only criterion of the beautiful. But I war not with an individual when I contend for the *rights of men* and the liberty of reason.

You see I do not condescend to cull my words to avoid the invidious phrase, nor shall I be prevented from giving a manly definition of it, by the flimsy ridicule which a lively fancy has interwoven with the present acceptation of the term. Reverencing the rights of humanity, I shall dare to assert them, not intimidated by the laugh that you have raised, or waiting till time has wiped away the compassionate tears which you have elaborately laboured to excite.

From the many just sentiments interspersed through the letter before me, and from the whole tendency of it, I should believe you to be, though a vain, yet a good man, and for this weakness a knowledge of human nature enables me to discover such extenuating circumstances, in the very texture of your mind, that I am ready to call it amiable, and separate the public from the private character.

I know that a lively imagination renders a man particularly calculated to shine in conversation and in these desultory productions; and the instantaneous applause which his eloquence extorts is at once a reward and a spur. Once a wit and always a wit, is an aphorism that has received the sanction of experience; but the man who with scrupulous anxiety endeavors to support that character, can never nourish by reflection any profound, or, if you please, metaphysical passion. Ambition becomes only the tool of vanity, and Reason, the weathercock of unrestrained feelings, is employed to varnish over the faults which she ought to have corrected.

Sacred, however, would the infirmities and errors of a good man be, in my eyes, if they were only displayed in a private circle; if the venial fault only rendered the wit anxious, like a celebrated beauty, to raise admiration on every occasion, and excite emotion, instead of the calm reciprocation of mutual esteem and unimpassioned respect. Such vanity enlivens social intercourse, and forces the little great man to be always on his guard to secure his throne; and an ingenious man, who is ever on the watch for conquest, will, in his eagerness to exhibit his whole store of knowledge, furnish an attentive observer with some useful information, calcined[1] by fancy and formed by taste.

And though some dry reasoner might whisper that the arguments were superficial, and should even add, that the feelings which are thus ostentatiously displayed are often the cold declamation of the head, and not the effusions of the heart—what will these shrewd remarks avail, when the witty arguments and ornamental feelings are on a level with the comprehension of the fashionable world, and a book is found very amusing? Even the Ladies, Sir, may repeat your sprightly sallies, and retail in theatrical attitudes many of your pathetic exclamations. Sensibility is the *manie* of the day, and compassion the virtue which is to cover a multitude of vices, whilst justice is left to mourn in sullen silence, and balance truth in vain.

In life, an honest man with a confined understanding, is frequently the slave of his habits and the dupe of his feelings, whilst the man with a clearer head and colder heart makes the passion of others bend to his interest; but truly sublime is the character that acts from principle, and governs the inferior springs of activity without slackening their vigour, whose feelings give vital heat to his resolves, but never hurry him into the feverish eccentricities.

However, as you have informed us that respect chills love, it is natural to conclude, that all your pretty flights arise from your pampered sensibility; and that, vain of this fancied pre-eminence of organs, you foster every emotion till the fumes,

mounting to your brain, dispel the sober suggestions of reason. It is not in this view surprising, that when you should argue you become impassioned, and that reflection inflames your imagination, instead of enlightening your understanding.

Quitting now the flowers of rhetoric, let us, Sir, reason together; and, believe me, I should not have meddled with these troubled waters, in order to point out your inconsistencies, if your wit had not burnished up some rusty, baneful opinions, and swelled the shallow current of ridicule till it resembled the flow of reason, and presumed to be the test of truth.

I shall not attempt to follow you through "horse-way and foot-path;"[2] but, attacking the foundation of your opinions, I shall leave the superstructure to find a center of gravity on which it may lean till some strong blast puffs it into the air; or your teeming fancy, which the ripening judgement of sixty years has not tamed, produces another Chinese erection, to stare, at every turn, the plain country people in the face, who bluntly call such an airy edifice—a folly.[3]

I glow with indignation when I attempt, methodically, to unravel your slavish paradoxes, in which I can find no fixed first principle to refute; I shall not, therefore, condescend to shew where you affirm in one page what you deny in another; and how frequently you draw conclusions without any previous premises:—it would be something like cowardice to fight with a man who had never exercised the weapons which his opponent chose to combat with.

I know that you have a mortal antipathy to reason; but, if there is any thing like argument, or first principles, in your wild declamation, behold the result:—that we are to reverence the rust of

---

[1] To treat a substance by heating it to a high temperature. Wollstonecraft is referring to what many reformers denounced as Burke's overly emotional (rather than rational) response.

[2] William Shakespeare (1564–1616), *King Lear* (1605): IV: i: 55.

[3] The vogue for Chinese architecture was frequently cited by critics as evidence of the depravity of popular tastes.

antiquity, and term the unnatural customs, which ignorance and mistaken self-interest have consolidated, the sage fruit of experience: nay, that, if we do discover some errors, our *feelings* should lead us to excuse, with blind love, or unprincipled filial affection, the venerable vestiges of ancient days. These are gothic notions of beauty—the ivy is beautiful, though it insidiously destroys the trunk from which it receives support.

There appears to be such a mixture of real sensibility and fondly cherished romance in your composition, that the present crisis carries you out of yourself; and since you could not be one of the grand movers, the next *best* thing that dazzled your imagination was to be a conspicuous opposer. Full of yourself, you make as much noise to convince the world that you despise the revolution, as Rousseau[1] did to persuade his contemporaries to let him live in obscurity.

Reading your Reflections warily over, it has continually and forcibly struck me, that had you been a Frenchman, you would have been, in spite of your respect for rank and antiquity, a violent revolutionist; and deceived, as you now probably are, by the passions that cloud your reason, have termed your romantic enthusiasm an enlightened love of your country, a respect for the rights of men. Your imagination would have taken fire, and have found arguments, full as ingenious as those you now offer, to prove that the constitution, of which so few pillars remained, that constitution which time had almost obliterated, was not a model sufficiently noble to deserve close adherence. And, for the English constitution, you might not have had such a profound veneration as you have lately acquired; nay, it is not impossible that you might have entertained the same opinion of the English

Parliament, that you professed to have during the American war.[2]

(1790)

THOMAS PAINE
Rights of Man:
Being an Answer to Mr. Burke's Attack
on the French Revolution[3]

PART ONE

AMONG the incivilities by which nations or individuals provoke and irritate each other, Mr. Burke's pamphlet on the French Revolution is an extraordinary instance. Neither the People of France, nor the National Assembly, were troubling themselves about the affairs of England, or the English Parliament; and that Mr. Burke should commence an unprovoked attack upon them, both in parliament and in public, is a conduct that cannot be pardoned on the score of manners, nor justified on that of policy.

Every thing which rancour, prejudice, ignorance, or knowledge could suggest, are poured forth in the copious fury of near four hundred pages. In the strain and on the plan Mr. Burke was writing, he might have written on to as many thousands. When the tongue or the pen is let loose in a frenzy of passion, it is the man, and not the subject, that becomes exhausted.

---

[1]   Jean-Jacques Rousseau (1712–78) disavowed Parisian life in favour of a more modest existence consistent with his critique of the corruption of modern civilization.

[2]   Reformers made much of the fact that Burke, who until 1790, had been a prominent member of the more liberal Whig party, had supported the American side in the recent war with Britain.

[3]   Thomas Paine (1737–1809), radical author and activist. Paine played important roles in the American and French Revolutions (though he barely escaped execution in the latter) and in the reform movement in 1790s Britain. *Rights of Man*, which appeared in two parts in 1791 and 1792, was neither the first nor the most intellectually ambitious response to Burke's *Reflections*, but its ability to address complex issues in a straightforward and accessible language made it enormously popular with the artisan and shop-keeper classes that formed the heart of the radical reform movement in the period.

I know a place in America called Point-no-Point; because as you proceed along the shore, gay and flowery as Mr. Burke's language, it continually recedes and presents itself at a distance before you; but when you have got as far as you can go, there is no point at all. Just thus it is with Mr. Burke's three hundred and fifty-six pages. It is therefore difficult to reply to him. But as the points he wishes to establish, may be inferred from what he abuses, it is in his paradoxes that we must look for his arguments.

As the tragic paintings by which Mr. Burke has outraged his own imagination, and seeks to work upon that of his readers, they are very well calculated for theatrical representation, where facts are manufactured for the sake of show, and accommodated to produce, through the weakness of sympathy, a weeping effect. But Mr. Burke should recollect that he is writing History, and not *Plays*; and that his readers will expect truth, and not the spouting rant of high-toned exclamation.

When we see a man dramatically lamenting in a publication intended to be believed, that, "*The age of chivalry is gone!*" that "*The glory of Europe is extinguished for ever!*" that "*The unbought grace of life*" (if any one knows what it is), "*the cheap defence of nations, the nurse of manly sentiment and heroic enterprize, is gone!*" and all this because the Quixot age of chivalry nonsense is gone, what opinion can we form of his judgment, or what regard can we pay to his facts? In the rhapsody of his imagination, he has discovered a world of wind-mills, and his sorrows are, that there are no Quixots to attack them.[1]

Not one glance of compassion, not one commiserating reflection, that I can find throughout his book, has he bestowed on those who lingered out the most wretched of lives, a life without hope, in the most miserable of prisons.[2] It is painful to behold a man employing his talents to corrupt himself. Nature has been kinder to Mr. Burke than he is to her. He is not affected by the reality of distress touching his heart, but by the showy resemblance of it striking his imagination. He pities the plumage, but forgets the dying bird. Accustomed to kiss the aristocratical hand that hath purloined him from himself, he degenerates into a composition of art, and the genuine soul of nature forsakes him. His hero or his heroine must be a tragedy-victim expiring in show, and not the real prisoner of misery, sliding into death in the silence of a dungeon.

Lay then the axe to the root, and teach governments humanity. It is their sanguinary punishments which corrupt mankind.

As it is not difficult to perceive, from the enlightened state of mankind, that hereditary Governments are verging to their decline, and that Revolutions on the broad basis of national sovereignty, and Government by representation, are making their way in Europe, it would be an act of wisdom to anticipate their approach, and produce Revolutions by reason and accommodation, rather than commit them to the issue of convulsions.

From what we now see, nothing of reform in the political world ought to be held improbable. It is an age of Revolutions, in which every thing may be looked for. The intrigue of Courts, by which the system of war is kept up, may provoke a confedera-

---

[1] In *Don Quixote de la Mancha* (1605), a satirical romance by Cervantes, the protagonist thinks that he is on a chivalric mission against what he assumes to be enemies, including a group of windmills, which he thinks are giants. In the opening pages of the *Reflections*, Burke had implicitly applied the ironic epithet to the French Revolutionaries, aligning them with "the metaphysic Knight of the Sorrowful Countenance." Equating revolutionaries with the idealistic but misguided Quixote was a common practice amongst conservatives in

the period. In his attack on women reformers, *The Unsex'd Females* (1798), Richard Polwhele denounced Mary Wollstonecraft and those women that he saw as being in sympathy with her as "the female Quixotes of the new philosophy."

[2] The Bastille was hated by reformers as a symbol of the tyranny of the *ancien regime*.

tion of Nations to abolish it: and an European Congress, to patronize the progress of free Government, and promote the civilization of Nations with each other, is an event nearer in probability, than once were the revolutions and alliance of France and America.

FINIS

PART TWO [1]

INTRODUCTION

WHAT Archimedes said of the mechanical powers, may be applied to Reason and Liberty: "*Had we,*" said he, "*a place to stand upon, we might raise the world.*"

The revolution of America presented in politics what was only theory in mechanics. So deeply rooted were all the governments of the old world, and so effectually had the tyranny and the antiquity of habit established itself over the mind, that no beginning could be made in Asia, Africa, or Europe, to reform the political condition of man. Freedom had been hunted round the globe; reason was considered as rebellion; and the slavery of fear had made men afraid to think.

But such is the irresistible nature of truth, that all it asks, and all it wants, is the liberty of appearing. The sun needs no inscription to distinguish him from darkness; and no sooner did the American governments display themselves to the world, than despotism felt a shock, and man began to contemplate redress.

All hereditary government is in its nature tyranny. An heritable crown, or an heritable throne, or by what other fanciful name such things may be called, have no other significant explanation than that mankind are heritable property. To inherit a government, is to inherit the people, as if they were flocks and herds.

We have heard the *Rights of Man* called a *levelling* system; but the only system to which the word *levelling* is truly applicable, is the hereditary monarchical system. It is a system of *mental levelling*. It indiscriminately admits every species of character to the same authority. Vice and virtue, ignorance and wisdom, in short, every quality, good or bad, is put on the same level. Kings succeed each other, not as rationals, but as animals. It signifies not what their mental or moral characters are. Can we then be surprised at the abject state of the human mind in monarchical countries, when the government itself is formed on such an abject levelling system?—It has no fixed character. To day it is one thing; to-morrow it is something else. It changes with the temper of every succeeding individual, and is subject to all the varieties of each. It is government through the medium of passions and accidents. It appears under all the various characters of childhood, decrepitude, dotage, a thing at nurse, in leading-strings, or in crutches. It reverses the wholesome order of nature. It occasionally puts children over men, and the conceits of non-age[2] over wisdom and experience. In short, we cannot conceive a more ridiculous figure of government, than hereditary succession, in all its cases, presents.

Whether I have too little sense to see, or too much to be imposed upon; whether I have too much or too little pride, or of anything else, I leave out of the question; but certain it is, that what is called monarchy, always appears to me a silly, contemptible thing. I compare it to something kept behind a curtain, about which there is a great deal of bustle and fuss, and a wonderful air of seeming solemnity; but when, by any accident, the curtain

[1] Part Two of *Rights of Man* appeared in 1792, and offered a radical model of government based on Paine's experience in America, where he had been an active member of the Revolution. Unlike Part One, which had been sold for three shillings, the same price as Burke's *Reflections*, Part Two was also released as a six-penny pamphlet, a strategy that saw him charged with seditious-libel.

[2] Nonage: the period of legal infancy.

happens to be open, and the company see what it is, they burst into laughter.

(1791–92)

ANONYMOUS
Remarks on Mr. Paine's Pamphlet, Called the Rights of Man[1]

MEN of sanguine temper often form violent opinions on the most speculative points, and enter with warmth into the agitation of questions, in the matter of which they are very little concerned; but when men embrace, defend and disseminate the principles of a book, in the subject of which they are not interested, with a zeal, which, supposing them to be so, would be extraordinary, it is natural to look for some other motives for their conduct:—whether the late proceedings in France are justifiable or not—whether Mr. Burke's or Mr. Paine's opinions on that event are right;—whether according to the one, the National Assembly is a synod of political saints; or, according to the other, a bloody and ferocious democracy, are questions the importance of which to the gentlemen who stile themselves Whigs of the Capital, I shall not presume to determine: but it appears to me that the persons for whose edification they have subscribed towards a dissemination of Mr. Paine's pamphlet, are very little interested in any of these disquisitions, and when these gentlemen obtrude upon the public their approbation of this book, and volunteer a subscription to distribute its contents, at a price within the purchase of the husbandman and the mechanic, I cannot attribute their conduct to the

good wishes alone which they may feel for the success of France, in the subversion of its government. I think I can trace it to a higher cause, and shew that the magnitude of the end is proportioned to the industry of the means.

There is in this country, a description of men, whose principles in politics are republican, and in religion presbyterian,[2] enemies to monarchy in the government, and establishment in the church.—To this body a plausible dilation of their favourite tenets must have been particularly acceptable, and to their ears the bolder tone in which Mr. Paine has founded the trumpet of innovation, could not but be grateful. In a conviction of this, I find my mind amply satisfied as to the motives of dispersing over the country six-penny pacquets of sedition, for the study of a common people, but lately and scarcely emerging from the darkness of ignorance.—A panegyric upon innovation, a ridicule of establishments, a justification of rebellion, a libel upon the government and religion of their country, are good materials for a grammar for their infant information, and disinterested instructors have thrown it almost gratuitously into their hands.

These sentiments, my dear Sir, have tempted me to trouble you and the public with this book; the times are critical and the feeblest exertion cannot be unwelcome, when a factory of sedition is set up in the metropolis, and an upstart Club sends an inflammatory pamphlet through the kingdom.— When these state quacks infecting their country at the heart, circulate, by fomenting applications, the poison to the extremities, and reduce the price of the pestilence, least the poverty of any creature should protect him from its contagion.—The times are critical when such a book as Mr. Paine's ap-

---

[1] One of a great number of conservative replies to Paine which appeared in the years after Paine published *Rights of Man* Part One in 1791. Journals such as the *Analytical Review*, the *Monthly Review*, and the *Critical Review* devoted a great portion of their monthly publications to the pamphlet war in an attempt to keep readers abreast of the debate. Like many of these pamphlets, this was published anonymously.

[2] A reference to religious Dissenters, or non-Anglicans. The reformist nature of many Dissenters, who had failed in their recent struggle to have laws restricting their civic rights repealed, encouraged many conservatives to portray them as supporters of the French Revolution.

pears, and the consequences would be fatal, if its success was proportioned to the zeal of its author, or the industry of its propagators.—It is a system of false metaphysics, and bad politics—any attempt to carry it into effect, must be destructive of peace; and there is nothing practical in it, but its mischief.—It holds out inducements to disturbance, on the promise of improvement, and softens the prospect of immediate disorder in the cant of the empiric, *you must be worse before you can be better.*—It excites men to what they *ought not to do*, by informing them of what they *can do*, and preaches *rights*[†] to promote *wrongs*. It is a collection of unamiable speculations, equally subversive of good government and good thinking;—It establishes a kind of republic in the mind; dethrones the majesty of sentiment; degrades the dignity of noble and elevated feelings, and substitutes a democracy of mean and vulgar calculation.

(1791)

THOMAS PAINE
Letter Addressed to the Addressers on the Late Proclamation [1]

COULD I have commanded circumstances with a wish, I know not of any that would have more generally promoted the progress of knowledge, than the late Proclamation, and the numerous

rotten borough and corporation addresses thereon. They have not only served as advertisements, but they have excited a spirit of inquiry into the principles of government, and a desire to read the *Rights of Man*, in places where that spirit and that work were before unknown.

Much as the first part of *Rights of Man* impressed at its first appearance, the progressive mind soon discovered that it did not go far enough. It detected errors; it exposed absurdities; it shook the fabric of political superstition; it generated new ideas; but it did not produce a regular system of principles in the room of those which it displaced. And, if I may guess at the mind of the Government-party, they beheld it as an unexpected gale that would soon blow over, and they forbore, like sailors in threatening weather, to whistle, lest they should increase the wind. Everything, on their part, was profound silence.

When the second part of *Rights of Man, combining Principle and Practice*, was preparing to appear, they affected, for a while, to act with the same policy as before; but finding their silence had no more influence in stifling the progress of the work, than it would have in stopping the progress of time, they changed their plan, and affected to treat it with clamorous contempt. The speech-making Placemen and Pensioners, and Place-expectants, in both Houses of Parliament, the *Outs* as well as the *Ins*, represented it as a silly, insignificant performance; as a work incapable of producing any effect; as something which they were sure the good sense of the people would either despise or indignantly spurn; but such was the overstrained awkwardness with which they harangued and encouraged each other, that in the very act of declaring their confidence they betrayed their fears.

Ye silly swains, thought I to myself, why do you torment yourselves thus? The *Rights of Man* is a book calmly and rationally written; why then are

[†] There was a popular weapon sold throughout France, at the time of the revolution, for less than three livres.—This instrument too was called the Rights of Man, (*droits d'homme*) was sold at a reduced price, and contained within itself every principle of human annoyance.—It was something like a loaded whip, of about five feet in length, and concealed a cut-and-thrust sword.

By this contrivance every man was enabled to purchase for *a few livres*, a thing which armed him with power to knock down, cut, and stab his fellow creatures, as he pleased.—*It was long, heavy, pointed, sharp, and cheap.*

[1] Written in the summer of 1792, after Paine had fled to France. It responds to both the Royal Proclamation and his trial for seditious libel for *Rights of Man* Part Two.

you so disturbed? Did you see how little or how suspicious such conduct makes you appear, even cunning alone, had you no other faculty, would hush you into prudence. The plans, principles, and arguments, contained in that work, are placed before the eyes of the nation, and of the world, in a fair, open, and manly manner, and nothing more is necessary than to refute them. Do this, and the whole is done; but if ye cannot, so neither can ye suppress the reading, nor convict the author; for the law, in the opinion of all good men, would convict itself, that should condemn what cannot be refuted.

It is a dangerous attempt in any government to say to a nation, "*thou shalt not read.*" This is now done in Spain, and was formerly done under the old government of France; but it served to procure the downfall of the latter, and is subverting that of the former; and it will have the same tendency in all countries; because *thought* by some means or other, is got abroad in the world, and cannot be restrained, though reading may.

If *Rights of Man* were a book that deserved the vile description which promoters of the addresses have given of it, why did not these men prove their charge, and satisfy the people, by producing it, and reading it publicly? This most certainly ought to have been done, and would also have been done, had they believed it would have answered their purpose. But the fact is, that the book contains truths which those time-servers dreaded to hear, and dreaded that the people should know; and it is now following up the addresses in every part of the nation, and convicting them of falsehoods.

Among the unwarrantable proceedings to which the Proclamation has given rise, the meetings of the justices in several of the towns and counties ought to be noticed. Those men have assumed to re-act the farce of general warrants, and to suppress, by their own authority, whatever publications they please. This is an attempt at power, equalled only by the conduct of the minor despots of the most despotic governments in Europe, and yet those justices affect to call England a free country. But even this, perhaps, like the scheme for garrisoning the country by building military barracks, is necessary to awaken the country to a sense of its Rights, and, as such, it will have a good effect.

Another part of the conduct of such Justices has been, that of threatening to take away the licences from taverns and public-houses, where the inhabitants of the neighbourhood associated to read and discuss the principles of Government, and to inform each other thereon. This, again, is similar to what is doing in Spain and Russia; and the reflection which it cannot fail to suggest is, that the principles and conduct of any Government must be bad, when that Government dreads and startles at discussion, and seeks security by a prevention of knowledge.

I will here drop of the subject, and state a few particulars respecting the prosecution now pending, by which the Addressers will see that they have been used as tools to the prosecuting party and their dependents. The case is as follows:

The original edition of the First and Second Part of *Rights of Man*, having been expensively printed (in the modern stile of printing pamphlets, that they might be bound up with Mr Burke's *Reflections on the French Revolution*), the high price precluded the generality of people from purchasing; and many applications were made to me from various parts of the country to print the work in a cheaper manner. The people of Sheffield requested leave to print two thousand copies for themselves, with which request I immediately complied. The same request came to me from Rotherham, from Leicester, from Chester, from several towns in Scotland; and Mr James Mackintosh, author of *Vindiciae Gallicae*,[1] brought

---

[1] James Mackintosh (1765–1832), was educated at the University of Aberdeen, where he developed his liberal political views. Mackintosh joined the reformist Society for Constitutional Information in 1790

me a request from Warwickshire, for leave to print ten thousand copies in that country. I had already sent a cheap edition to Scotland; and finding the applications increase, I concluded that the best method of complying therewith, would be to print a very numerous edition in London, under my own direction, by which means the work would be more perfect, and the price be reduced lower than it could be by *printing* small editions in the country, of only a few thousands each.

And conscious as I now am, that the work entitled *Rights of Man*, so far from being, as has been maliciously or erroneously represented, a false, wicked, and seditious libel, is a work abounding with unanswerable truths, with principles of the purest morality and benevolence, and with arguments not to be controverted—Conscious, I say, of these things, and having no object in view but the happiness of mankind, I have now put the matter to the best proof in my power, by giving to the public a cheap edition of the first and second parts of that work. Let every man read and judge for himself, not only of the merits and demerits of the work, but of the matters therein contained, which relate to his own interest and happiness.

If, to expose the fraud and imposition of monarchy, and every species of hereditary government—to lessen the oppression of taxes—to propose plans for the education of helpless infancy, and the comfortable support of the aged and distressed—to endeavour to conciliate nations to each other—to extirpate the horrid practice of war—to promote universal peace, civilization, and commerce—and to break the chains of political superstition, and raise degraded man to his proper rank;—if these things be libellous, let me live the life of a libeller, and let the name of LIBELLER be engraved on my tomb.

(1792)

HANNAH MORE
Village Politics, Addressed to All the Mechanics, Journeymen and Day Labourers, in Great Britain.[1]

By WILL CHIP, A COUNTRY CARPENTER.

A DIALOGUE between JACK ANVIL the Blacksmith, and TOM HOD the Mason.

Jack. What's the matter, Tom? Why dost look so dismal?

Tom. Dismal indeed! Well enough I may.

Jack. What's the old mare dead? or work scarce?

Tom. No, no, work's plenty enough, if a man had but the heart to go to it.

Jack. What book art reading? Why dost look so like a hang dog?

Tom. (*looking on his book.*) Cause enough. Why I find here that I'm very unhappy, and very miserable; which I should never have known if I had not had the good luck to meet with this book. O 'tis a precious book!

Jack. A good sign tho'; that you can't find out you're unhappy without looking into a book for it. What is the matter?

---

when he moved to London to train as a lawyer. His *Vindiciae Gallicae* (1791) was one of the most respected of the many replies to Burke, in part because its learned style and literary allusions addressed itself to the same audience as Burke's *Reflections*.

[1] Hannah More (1745–1833), had been an active literary figure as a poet and dramatist, as well as a campaigner for causes such as Christian evangelicalism, education, and the anti-slavery movement for nearly two decades before she aided the anti-revolutionary cause with her 1792 pamphlet, *Village Politics*. Its success led to *Cheap Repository Tracts*, a series of pamphlets that was eagerly promoted by the Church of England, the Pitt government, and other conservative associations and individuals, as an antidote to radical pamphlets such as *Rights of Man*. The pamphlets were popular, partly because of this active support (which included subsidies designed to keep their price at a penny or less), but also because More had immersed herself in the milieu of popular broadsides in order to satisfy the literary taste of her plebeian audience.

Tom. Matter? Why I want liberty.

Jack. Liberty! What has anyone fetched a warrant for thee? Come man, cheer up, I'll be bound for thee.—Thou art an honest fellow in the main, tho' thou dost tipple and prate a little too much at the Rose and Crown.

Tom. No, no, I want a new Constitution.

Jack. Indeed! Why I thought thou hadst been a desperate healthy fellow. Send for the doctor then.

Tom. I'm not sick: I want Liberty and Equality, and the Rights of Man.

Jack. O now I understand thee. What thou art a leveller and a republican I warrant.

Tom. I'm a friend to the people. I want a reform.

Jack. Then the shortest way is to mend thyself.

Tom. But I want a *general reform*.

Jack. Then let every one mend one.

Tom. Pooh! I want freedom and happiness, the same as they have got in France.

Jack. What, Tom, we imitate them? We follow the French! Why they only begun all this mischief at first, in order to be just what *we* are already. Why I'd sooner go to the Negers to get learning, or to the Turks to get religion, than to the French for freedom and happiness.

Tom. What do you mean by that? ar'n't the French free?

Jack. Free, Tom! aye, free with a witness. They are all so free, that there's nobody safe. They make free to rob whom they will, and kill whom they will. If they don't like a man's looks, they make free to hang him with-out judge or jury, and the next lamp-post does for the gallows; so then they call themselves free, because you see they have no king to take them up and hang them for it.

Tom. Ah, but Jack, didn't their King formerly hang people for nothing too? and besides, wer'n't they all papists before the Revolution?

Jack. Why, true enough, they had but a poor sort of religion, but bad is better than none, Tom.

And so was the government bad enough too, for they could clap an innocent man into prison, and keep him there too as long as they would, and never say with your leave or by your leave, Gentlemen of the Jury. But what's all that to us?

Tom. To us! Why don't our governors put many of our poor folks in prison against their will? What are all the jails for? Down with the jails, I say; all men should be free.

Jack. Harkee, Tom, a few rogues in prison keep the rest in order, and then honest men go about their business, afraid of nobody; that's the way to be free. And let me tell thee, Tom, thou and I are tried by our peers as much as a lord is. Why the *king* can't send me to prison if I do no harm, and if I do, there's reason good why I should go there. I may go to law with Sir John, at the great castle yonder, and he no more dares lift his little finger against me than if I were his equal. A lord is hanged for hanging matter, as thou or I should be; and if it will be any comfort to thee, I myself remember a Peer of the Realm being hanged for killing his man, just the same as the man wou'd have been for killing him.[†]

Tom. Well, that is some comfort.—But have you read the Rights of Man?

Jack. No, not I. I had rather by half read the *Whole Duty of Man*.[1] I have but little time for reading, and such as I should therefore only read a bit of the best.

Tom. Don't tell me of those old fashioned notions. Why should not we have the same fine things they have got in France? I'm for a *Constitution*, and *Organization*, and *Equalization*.

Jack. I'll tell thee a story. When Sir John married, my Lady, who is a little fantastical, and likes to do everything like the French, begged him to pull down yonder fine old castle, and build it up in her

---

[†] Lord Ferrers was hanged in 1790, for killing his steward.

[1] William Beck (1684–1738), *The Whole Duty of Man, in all his stages, in a plain and familiar heroick verse* (1700).

frippery way. No, says Sir John; what shall I pull down this noble building, raised by the wisdom of my brave ancestors; which outstood the civil wars, and only underwent a little needful repair at the Revolution; and which all my neighbours come to take a pattern by—shall I pull it all down, I say, only because there may be a dark closet or an inconvenient room or two in it? My lady mumpt and grumbled; but the castle was let stand, and a glorious building it is, though there may be a trifling fault or two, and tho' a few decays may want stopping; so now and then they mend a little thing, and they'll go on mending, I dare say, as they have leisure, to the end of the chapter, if they are let alone. But no pull-me-down works.

Tom. I don't see why we are to work like slaves, while others roll about in their coaches, feed on the fat of the land, and do nothing.

Jack. My little maid brought home a story-book from the Charity-School t'other day, in which was a bit of a fable about the Belly and the Limbs. The hands said, I won't work any longer to feed this lazy belly, who sits in state like a lord, and does nothing. Said the feet, I won't walk and tire myself to carry him about; let him shift for himself, so said all the members; just as your levellers and republicans do now. And what was the consequence? Why the belly was pinched to be sure; but the hands and the feet, and the rest of the members suffered so much for want of their old nourishment, that they fell sick, pined away, and wou'd have died, if they had not come to their senses just in time to save their lives, as I hope all you will do.

Tom. But I say all men are equal. Why should one be above another?

Jack. If that's thy talk, Tom, thou dost quarrel with Providence and not with government. For the woman is below her husband, and the children are below their mother, and the servant is below his master.

Tom. I say we shall never be happy, till we do as the French have done.

Jack. The French and we contending for liberty, Tom, is just as if thou and I were to pretend to run a race; thou to set out from the starting post, when I am in already: why we've got it man; we've no race to run. We're there already. Our constitution is no more like what the French one was, than a mug of our Taunton beer is like a platter of their soup-maigre.

Tom. What then dost thou take French *liberty* to be?

Jack. To murder more men in one night, than ever their poor king did in his whole life.

Tom. And what dost thou take a *Democrat* to be?

Jack. One who likes to be governed by a thousand tyrants, and yet can't bear a king.

Tom. What is *Equality*?

Jack. For every man to pull down every one that is above him, till they're all as low as the lowest.

Tom. What is *the new Rights of Man*?

Jack. Battle, murder, and sudden death.

Tom. What is to be an *enlightened people*?

Jack. To put out the light of the gospel, confound right and wrong, and grope about in pitch darkness.

Tom. What is *Philosophy*, that Tim Standish talks so much about?[1]

Jack. To believe that there's neither God, nor devil, nor heaven, nor hell.—To dig up a wicked old fellow's†† rotten bones, whose books, Sir John

---

[1] This comment is typical of conservatives' denunciation of what they described as the arrogance of reformers' association of their cause with philosophy. In his *Reflections*, Burke made a great rhetorical show of being "a plain man" unimpressed by the "shallow speculations of the petulant, assuming, short-sighted coxcombs of philosophy." In *The Unsex'd Females* (1798), Richard Polwhele mocked "philosophism, the false image of philosophy…a phantom which heretofore appeared not in open day, though it now attempts the loftiest flights in the face of the sun."

†† Voltaire.

says, have been the ruin of thousands; and to set his figure up in a church and worship him.

Tom. And what mean the other hard words that Tim talks about—*organization* and *function*, and *civism*, and *incivism*, and *equalization*, and *inviolability*, and *imperscriptible?*

Jack. Nonsense, gibberish, downright hocus-pocus. I know 'tis not English; Sir John says 'tis not Latin; and his valet de sham says 'tis not French neither.

Tom. And yet Tim says he shall never be happy till all these fine things are brought over to England.

Jack. What into this Christian country, Tom? Why dost know they have no *sabbath?* Their mob parliament meets of a Sunday to do their wicked work, as naturally as we do to go to church. They have renounced God's word and God's day, and they don't even date in the year of our Lord.[1] Why dost turn pale, man? And the rogues are always making such a noise, Tom, in the midst of their parliament-house, that their speaker rings a bell, like our penny-postman, because he can't keep them in order.

Tom. And dost thou think our Rights of Man will lead to all this wickedness?

Jack. As sure as eggs are eggs.

Tom. I begin to think we're better off as we are.

Jack. I'm sure on't. This is only a scheme to make us go back in every thing. 'Tis making ourselves poor when we are getting rich.

Tom. I begin to think I'm not so very unhappy as I had got to fancy.

Jack. Tom, I don't care for drink myself, but thou dost, and I'll argue with thee in thy own way; when there's all equality there will be no superfluity; when there's no wages there'll be no drink; and levelling will rob thee of thy ale more than the malt-tax does.

Tom. And thou art very sure we are not ruined.

Jack. I'll tell thee how we are ruined. We have a king so loving, that he wou'd not hurt the people if he cou'd; and so kept in, that he cou'd not hurt the people if he wou'd. We have as much liberty as can make us happy, and more trade and riches than allows us to be good. We have the best laws in the world, if they were more strictly enforced; and the best religion in the world, if it was but better followed. While Old England is safe, I'll glory in her and pray for her, and when she is in danger, I'll fight for her and die for her.

Tom. And so will I too, Jack, that's what I will. (*sings.*)

"*O the roast beef of old England!*"

Jack. Thou art an honest fellow, Tom.

Tom. This is Rose and Crown night, and Tim Standish is now at his mischief; but we'll go and put an end to that fellow's work.

Jack. Come along.

Tom. No; first I'll stay to burn my book, and then I'll go and make a bonfire and——

Jack. Hold, Tom. There is but one thing worse than a bitter enemy, and that is an imprudent friend. If thou would'st shew thy love to thy King and country, let's have no drinking, no riot, no bonfires; but put into practice this text, which our parson preached on last Sunday, "Study to be quiet, work with your own hands, and mind your own business."

Tom. And so I will, Jack—Come on.

THE END

(1793)

---

[1] The French government's decision to begin time again with a new calendar was celebrated by reformers as a repudiation of an exploitative history of aristocratic tyranny, but mocked by conservatives as a very un-English act of arrogance that failed to appreciate the importance of inherited wisdom.

DANIEL ISAAC EATON
The Pernicious Effects of the Art of Printing Upon Society, Exposed [1]

BEFORE this diabolical Art was introduced among men, there was social order; and as the great Locke expresses it, some subordination-man placed an implicit confidence in his temporal and spiritual directors—Princes and Priests—entertained no doubts of their infallibility; or ever questioned their unerring wisdom. Indeed, the lower orders, though in other respects immersed in the most profound ignorance, knew full well (their superiors having taken care to inform them) that the existence of society depended upon distinctions of rank, fortune, &c. They therefore chearfully submitted without murmuring, to the basis upon which the pillar of society was erected, and patiently bore the wight of the shaft, cornice, frieze, and capital; nor ever complained of the expenses of supporting this structure, notwithstanding the taxes and contributions necessary for keeping it in repair, reduced them to the most abject poverty and dependence—to toil and labour for their superiors they never thought a hardship, sensible that submission was their duty, they never uttered a wish for a change in the order of things.

If their Prince engaged in war, without the least enquiry on their part, as to its justice or necessity, they not only furnished the means of carrying it on, but also at his command quitted the peaceful employment of cultivating the fields, to act a part in the field of battle, and take the chance of war, that they might crown with laurels the hero who led them on—the risk, the danger, and difficulties always theirs—the honour and profit his alone, or those in command under him, whose conduct he graciously condescended to approve and reward. If they returned in safety to their homes, they had recourse to their former means of subsistence, no provision ever being made for them.

In the times we are speaking of (the Golden Age), the feudal system prevailed—a system replete with blessings—by it the different orders of society were kept perfectly distinct and separate—there were kings, barons, priests, yeomanry, villains or slaves; and they were, I believe, with regard to rank and power, in the order in which I have named them. The villains, or lowest class, were what MR. BURKE so elegantly terms the *Swinish Multitude*, [2] but of rights or privileges as men they had not an idea; we may with propriety stile them the Jackalls of the times; they tilled the earth, and performed all manual labour; but in return, their superiors allowed them sufficient of the produce for subsistence—permitted them to take some rest, in order that they might be strong. To bear hardship and fatigue—took from them the trouble of thinking—indeed, from the very prudent manner in which they were brought up, I will not say educated, they were little capable of thought, of course

---

[1] Daniel Isaac Eaton (1753–1814), a radical publisher, bookseller, and author, and member of the London Corresponding Society. Eaton was tried and acquitted eight times for publishing, selling, or writing radical texts, frequently publishing the proceedings of the trial as a radical pamphlet in its own right. When in 1812 Eaton was tried and finally convicted for publishing *Age of Reason* Part Three, he was sentenced to eighteen months in jail and to stand in the pillory where he was cheered by the crowd. His weekly magazine, *Politics for the People* (1793–95), was an important element of the radical journalism of the 1790s. The hyperbolic rhetoric depicted in Eaton's satirical pamphlet, *The Pernicious Effects of the Art of Printing Upon Society, Exposed*, reflects his personal experience of the anti-revolutionaries' paranoia about the power of the radical press.

[2] Reformers made a great deal of Burke's reference to the "swinish multitude" as an unguarded admission of conservatives' arrogance in relation to their plebeian inferiors. Radical journals such as Thomas Spence's *Pig's Meat* and Eaton's *Politics for the People: A Salmagundy for Swine* embraced the phrase as an ironic definition of the lower orders. Burke's actual comment was that if "learning" was uprooted from the hierarchical social order that had nurtured it, it would be "cast into the mire, and trodden down under the hoofs of a swinish multitude." Arguably, however, Burke was referring to a particular faction of extremists rather than to the lower orders as social class.

exempt from the mental fatigues of study and reflections. The Scriptures having declared gold to be the root of every evil, they were very humanely prevented from possessing any. As to religion, the clergy taught them as much as they thought necessary, and they were without doubt the best judges, being in general good scholars.

In this beautiful scheme—this happy system of social order—what tender care, and generous concern—what almost parental anxiety and solicitude appear to have actuated the governors in every part of their conduct, in which the lower orders, or vassals, were concerned or interested. In my mind, their situation was equal, if not preferable, to that of the slaves in our West India islands—notwithstanding the friends of the slave-trade have lately represented the condition of the negroes to be so very enviable.

To enumerate all the advantages arising from hereditary distinctions in society would far exceed the bounds I have prescribed to myself; but what will my reader think, when I inform him, that the late government of France was feudal in the extreme; how will he pity and deplore the madness and folly of that deluded nation—no longer blessed with a king, nobles, or priests, but left, like a ship in a storm, without a pilot, to their own guidance—with hands uplifted he will exclaim, What will become of them!—Having briefly shewn a few of the advantages enjoyed before the art of Printing was discovered, or at least generally known, I come now to point out, as is expressed in my title, its Pernicious Effects upon Society.

Since Printing has been employed as the medium of diffusing sentiments &c. government has become more difficult—the governors are frequently, and insolently called upon, to give an account of the national treasure, its expenditure, &c.—and if they are in any respect tardy, or should circumstances render evasion necessary, it is astonishing, with what boldness some men will dare to revile and insult them.

The lower orders begin to have ideas of rights, as men—to think that one man is as good as another—that society is at present founded upon false principles—that hereditary honours and distinctions are absurd, unjust, and oppressive—that abilities and morals only should recommend to the first officers in a state—that no regard should be paid to rank and titles—that instruction, sufficient to qualify a man for being a member of society, is a debt due to every individual, and that it is the duty of every state to take care that he receive it—that every man has a right to a share in the government, either in his own person, or that of his representative, and that no portion of his property or labour ought to be taxed without his consent, given either by himself, or representative—that every one should contribute to the support of the state in proportion to his ability, and that all partial exactions are oppressive—that laws should be the same to all; and that no one, whatever may be his rank or station, should be allowed to offend them with impunity—that freedom of speech is the equal right of all; and that the rich have no right to dictate to the poor what sentiments they shall adopt on any subject—or in any wise prevent investigation and inquiry. This, with a great deal more such stuff, is called the rights of man—blessed fruits of the art of Printing—the scum of the earth, the swinish multitude, talking of their rights! and insolently claiming, nay, almost demanding, that political liberty shall be the same to all—to the high and the low—the rich and the poor—what audacity!—what unparalleled effrontery!—it ought to meet correction—With similar mistaken notions of liberty, even many women are infatuated; and the press, that grand prolific source of evil—that fruitful mother of mischief, has already favoured the public with several female productions on this very popular subject—one in particular, called Rights of Women, and in which, as one of their rights, a share in legislation is claimed and asserted— gracious heaven! to what will this fatal delusion lead, and in what will it terminate!

In politics, as I before observed, they say they are as much interested as the rich.—What will scarce be credited, those lenient sentences[1] passed by the Justiciary Court of Edinburgh upon seditious persons, have been most severely censured by them, and considered as an unwarrantable and despotic stretch of power:—the conviction of Mr. Winterbotham, in an English court has also met with severe animadversion; and the case of Mr. Holt, the Newark Printer, they universally reprobate, and for why?—because he only, as they say, reprinted what the Duke of Richmond and Mr. Pitt originally published.[2] What stuff and nonsense, as if there was no difference between a Duke, or the son of Chatham, and a pitiful low-bred fellow of a Printer, sprung, as I am informed, from the vulgar, plebeian loins of a gardener;—or that a duke, or the son and brother of a peer might not write and publish with impunity that, for which a printer or bookseller would meet the severest punishment.

But for Printing, those two disturbers of the repose of society, and rascally innovators, Calvin and Luther,[3] would never have been able to propagate their doctrines of Reform, as they audaciously called them—rebellion against the spiritual jurisdiction of his Holiness, the Pope, would have been a more proper expression, and to have punished as rebels those enemies to his sacred authority and the Catholic faith, upon the first promulging of their damnable heresies, would have been the only mode of preventing the further progress of opinions subversive of ecclesiastical power, and consequently of social order. Sure religion since that period has been gradually losing ground; and the reluctance with which tithes and church-dues are now paid, shew evidently its declining state, and how little the people respect their spiritual guides.

Had mankind remained ignorant of the use of types, those outcasts of society, Paine and Barlow,[4] would not have been able to publish their wicked inflammatory books—miscreants that treat with ridicule the most ancient establishment—Customs of such remote antiquity as to puzzel the deepest antiquaries to have their origin, they have even dared to speak of with levity—privileged orders and every species of hereditary destination (the Corinthian capital of polished society) they consider as encroachments upon the rights of others—nay, even kings and princes, to whom they know we are attached both from duty and interest, they have endeavoured to place in a contemptible and ludicrous point of view.

---

[1] An ironic reference to several notoriously harsh sentences given to reformers in 1793.

[2] William Winterbotham was convicted in July 1793 for uttering seditious words during a sermon; Daniel Holt, was tried twice (and convicted in both cases) in the same month for publishing Paine's *Address to the Addressers* and for publishing the *Address to the Tradesmen, Mechanics etc.* Charles Lennox, the third Duke of Richmond, had been an active proponent of parliamentary reform; William Pitt, first elected Prime Minister in 1784, had been an advocate for the same cause. These sorts of comparisons between the fates of different social classes of reformers were frequently cited as evidence of the class hypocrisy of British ideas about free speech. In his unsuccessful defense of Thomas Paine for seditious libel, Erskine had invoked the reformist legacies of Pitt and the Duke of Richmond as a way of legitimizing Paine's efforts: "The abuses pointed out by [Paine] led that Right Hon. Gentleman [Pitt] to associate with many others of high rank, under the banners of the Duke of Richmond, whose name stands at the head of the list, and to pass various public resolutions, concerning the absolute necessity of purifying the House of Commons."

[3] Jean Calvin (1509–64) and Martin Luther (1483–1546), leading members of the Reformation. Eaton is reminding his readers that Britain's fiercely Protestant character owed itself to the Reformation, and, therefore, to the work of these reformist activists. The reference also suggests the extent to which the Reformation was associated with the liberating effects of the mechanical art of printing, invented by Johann Gutenberg in the mid-fifteenth century.

[4] Joel Barlow (1754–1812), an American reformer, best known for his radical political tract *Advice to the Privileged Orders* (1792).

Prejudices, one of the strongest cements of a well ordered state, and which from the very circumstance of their being prejudices, Mr. Burke would recommend us to venerate and cherish—they would persuade us to get rid of—the knowing scoundrels, could they once accomplish this, our minds would be in a state to receive their seditious doctrines, and what, pray, would be the consequences?—we should become insolent, offend our superiors, and be punished with fine, imprisonment—the pillory, or transportation to Botany Bay.[1] Not a pillar or bullwark of well regulated society, in other words social order, but they have attacked as originally founded in injustice, and supported by fraud and imposition. Our glorious constitution, formed by the progressive wisdom of ages—the wonder and envy of surrounding nations—the *ne plus ultra*[2] in the science of government—the only human institution that ever perhaps was perfect, these sagacious gentlemen tell us, is full of defects and blemishes—that it is a system of deception, calculated to benefit the few at the expense of the many—they would, alas! be wicked enough to add, if it had occured to them, that it was in a great measure framed by men who had interests separate from the bulk of the people.

For all these, and numberless other evils, the natural consequence of a diffusion of knowledge and science, some remedy must be found; the present administration have made some trifling feeble attempts to check their progress—such as additional duties upon advertisements and newspapers, which almost preclude cheap publications—of the same nature I suppose the late tax upon paper to be—but these remedies are totally inadequate, at least they will be so exceedingly slow in their opera-

tion, that the present race have but little prospect of living to see any of their good effects.

To rid ourselves of such a monster, some strong efficient measure must be had recourse to—something that will strike at the root, and have an almost instantaneous effect—such a one, I think, I can point out.

Let all Printing-presses be committed to the flames—all letter foundries be destroyed—schools and seminaries of learning abolished—dissenters of every denominations double and treble taxed—all discourse upon government and religion prohibited—political clubs and associations of every kind suppressed, excepting those formed for the express purpose of supporting government; and lastly, issue a proclamation against reading, and burn all private libraries. To carry some part of this plan into execution, it will be necessary to employ spies and informers, which by many (Jacobins and Republicans) are thought to be signs either of a weak or wicked and corrupt government; they say, that governors, conscious of acting for the public good, of having it only in view in all their measure, would scorn using such unworthy and dishonourable means. I cannot be of this opinion, but am confident, that if the measures I have proposed be but speedily adopted, and rigorously pursued, the happiest consequences would soon be experienced; all the wild, idle theories, with which men are at present disturbed, would soon vanish—the lower orders would mind their work, become tractable and docile, and perhaps in less than half a century, that desirable state of ignorance and darkness, which formerly prevailed, might again restore to this Island that happy state of society with which it once was blessed.

(1793)

---

[1] Pillory: a wooden structure in which offenders were fastened by the neck and wrists and exposed to public ridicule; Botany Bay: a British penal colony in Australia.

[2] No higher good.

JOHN BOWLES
Letters of the Ghost of Alfred, Addressed to the Hon. Thomas Erskine, and the Hon. Charles James Fox, On the Occasion of the State Trials at the Close of the Year 1794, and the Beginning of the Year 1795.[1]

To the Right Hon. CHARLES JAMES FOX.

SIR,

IT required no great degree of discernment to foresee that the acquittal of the State Criminals at the Old Bailey,[2] would induce the necessity of providing new laws against Sedition and Treason: Laws, which should not only be too explicit to admit the perversion which had been so successfully employed in defeating the old ones, but which should have the effect of nipping Treason in the bud, instead of suffering it to arrive at a state of maturity. Some persons, indeed, were disposed to believe that the *all but convicted* Traitors could be won by lenity; that they could be wrought upon by a sense of their *wonderful* escape, and induced thereby to abandon their criminal projects, notwithstanding their frequent and peremptory declarations to the contrary; and that the Constitution might even derive fresh security from the impunity of those who plotted its destruction. These extravagant and absurd expectations, which displayed a total ignorance of the determined perseverance of the disciples of the new Philosophy, have been compleatly disappointed. The men, of whom such charitable hopes were formed, soon returned to their Seditious "vomitings," and to "their wallowing in the mire" of Treason. Insensible of the indulgence by which they had escaped the fate they most richly deserved, they have been rendered thereby but the more daring and indefatigable, in the pursuit of their mischievous designs. The Press has become more licentious and inflammatory, the Schools of Sedition have been more numerous, the Lecturers more animated, and their Pupils have been more frequently convened, not merely in their institutional Assemblies, where they learn the first principles of the science, but also in the field, in order to train them to habits of discipline; to inspire them with a consciousness of their strength by a sight of their numbers; to enlist all who are disposed for mischief, under the banners of Disloyalty; and, by enuring the public to such assemblages, to lessen that salutary dread, which all very numerous meetings, and particularly when so composed, are calculated to inspire.

The horrid attack on the person of HIS MAJESTY on the first day of the present Session, in his passage to and from Parliament, was the natural

---

[1] John Bowles (1751–1819), barrister, co-founder of the conservative Crown and Anchor Association, and political pamphleteer, began to publish his letters from "the Ghost of Alfred," in the *True Briton* in response to the Not Guilty verdicts in the 1794 treason trials (see note following). The letters continued to appear sporadically after that, and were addressed to the leader of the Opposition, Charles James Fox, rather than to Thomas Erskine, the Defense lawyer in the trials, as the first letters had been. They were published together in a 1798 edition, *Letters of the Ghost of Alfred.* Alfred, King of the Saxons (849–901), has a legendary place in English literary history because of his active role in the revival of letters in western England. Alfred translated various Latin works, in one case with a preface announcing his intention of reversing the decline of learning in England. This excerpt, which appeared as Letter IX, was first published in the *True Briton* in June 1796.

[2] Beginning on 25 October 1794, Thomas Hardy, the Leader of the London Corresponding Society, John Horne Tooke, a prominent member of the Society for Constitutional Information, and John Thelwall, a notorious radical with strong ties to both men, were tried for treason. When all three were acquitted, the nine other prisoners who had been arrested on the same charge were released. The trials marked the Pitt government's most significant attempt yet to repress the reform movement, but when they failed to convict its leaders, popular radicalism enjoyed new vitality until the government passed two highly restrictive pieces of legislation, known amongst reformers as "the Gagging Acts," late the next year.

fruit of such proceedings.[1] If that attack had been permitted by Providence to produce its intended effect, the unutterable calamity which it would have brought on the Nation, could only have been ascribed to the operation of those licentious doctrines and inflammatory discourses, which had seduced the multitude from their duty and allegiance; which had inspired them with contempt for whatever they had been accustomed to hold in reverence; and prepared them for acts of outrage and atrocity, at the very idea of which, without such incitements, they would have shuddered. The connection between such a cause and such an effect is too obvious to be denied by any but the most profligate. It is not necessary, indeed, in proof of such a connection, to suppose that the specific Treason which blackened that dreadful day, was actually hatched in the Committees of the Corresponding Society, or that the wretches who sought the life of His Majesty, were immediately employed for that purpose by the Lecturer of Beaufort Buildings, or the Orators of Chalk Farm, or of Copenhagen-House.[2] It is not on such modes of Treason that these men chiefly rely to accomplish their designs. That they would rejoice at the success of any attempt against the life of the Majesty, it is impossible to doubt, but they would not expose their plans to the failure of such an attempt, nor themselves to the proof of having instigated it.—They would be fools if they did. Theirs, though a more slow, is, in respect of themselves, a safer system, and much more sure in respect of its object. They know better than to place their dependence on the hand of a lurking Assassin, or on the savage fury of an enraged Mob. The horror, confusion and dismay attending the success of such means might be surmounted.—A successor might avenge the horrid deed—and the glorious scheme of Liberty and Equality might, in the result, lose ground. Their hatred is not against the person of the King, but his Throne: not against the Monarch, but the Monarchy. The crime of Regicide, in order to answer *their* purpose, must be preceded by indignity, insult, and dethronement—by the sentence of a pretended High Court of Justice, or of a Revolutionary Tribunal.—The Scaffold is their Altar of Liberty, where alone Royal Blood should flow, in solemn expiation of the unpardonable offence of wearing a Crown, and whence they might, at the same time, proclaim to the World, the subversion of the Throne, and the extinction of the Monarchy. Such are the scenes in which they aspire to act a distinguished part; they review with rapture and exultation, the atrocities of that nature which already stain the page of History; and they pant for an opportunity of adding to the list of Royal Martyrs. Impatient for the renewal of such atrocities, they are clamorous for Peace with the Murderers of the Gallic Monarch, who, by commemorating, have recently repeated their crime; and who by resolving that the insulting commemoration shall be annually repeated, have fairly and candidly announced to all Crowned Heads, their determination never to abandon their regicidal principles.

---

[1] On 29 October 1795, on his way to speak at the opening of Parliament, the window of the King's carriage was broken by an unidentified object. The small hole that it left in the window convinced the King that he had been shot at, a theory which the government used to sway public opinion on behalf of the royalist cause. More carriages windows were broken on the King's departure from Parliament.

[2] The Lecturer of Beaufort Buildings: John Thelwall lectured, first at 3 new Compton Street, Soho, and then as enthusiasm grew following his acquittal, at No. 2 Beaufort Buildings, Strand, in 1794–96; Chalk Farm: a meeting of about two thousand people held by the London Corresponding Society on 14 April, 1794; Copenhagen-House: two mass meetings (150,000 people reportedly attended the first) organized by the London Corresponding Society on 26 October and 12 November 1795, weeks before two bills designed to ban mass meetings and curb the radical press received royal assent. Thelwall spoke at both. An excerpt from Thelwall's speech at the 26 October meeting is included below.

But in order to bring about, in this Country, a state of things which would lead to such a crisis, these Conspirators are fully aware that they must cautiously abstain from intermediate violence, which, by exciting general disgust and alarm, would tend only to frustrate their projects. They have too much sagacity, and too intimate a knowledge of the nature of man and of society, not to discover that their best chance for success is by corrupting the public opinion and principle. To effect this, they want nothing but an uninterrupted access to the public mind. If they could, by an unlimited license in speech and writing, obtain permission to utter whatever sentiments, to promulgate whatever opinions, and to inculcate whatever principles they please, upon all subjects relating in any respect to Government, they are morally certain of being able, by degrees, to poison the minds, to excite the discontent, and to inflame the passions, of the mass of the People, to such a degree, that it would become impossible to restrain the exercise of the "*sacred right of insurrection.*" They, therefore, with great wisdom and consistency, avoid every thing that savours of commotion; they cautiously refrain from present violence, because it might interfere with their schemes of future and more complete violence.—They are perpetually boasting of the open and peaceable manner in which their followers assemble and disperse. They are constantly repeating that the only weapons which they employ are reason and argument; and, with great earnestness, and equal sincerity, they exhort their pupils to avoid every appearance of tumult and disorder.†

In short, they artfully profess to confine all their pretensions to the sacred right of free discussion; and they disclaim, in the most solemn manner, all recourse to other means. This is all they appear to require, and, indeed, all they actually want, in order to enable them to effectuate their designs. They well know, that this fair and specious privilege, harmless in appearance as it seems to be, nay, valuable and beneficial as it really is, when subjected to wholesome regulations and restraints, is capable of producing the utmost extremes of violence, confusion, and anarchy: consequences so different from the mild and gentle character it assumes, that it requires more penetration, and a greater faculty of reasoning from cause to effect, than mankind in general possess, to be able to foresee them. But the active and expert Professors of the New Philosophy are better instructed;—they are fully aware, that discussion, in the unlimited sense in which they claim the right, and in the excess to which they mean to carry it, is a powerful engine for the subversion of Government—a mighty Lever, sufficient, if judiciously applied, to overturn the Social Order of the whole World.

But although the Seditious Clubs, and Affiliated Societies, with their active and indefatigable Leaders, may, for the reasons above stated, be fairly acquitted of any direct interference, and indeed of any privity, in the flagitious[1] attempt recently made against the most valuable Life in the Kingdom, they must, in the judgment of every thinking person, be convicted of having produced the danger to which that life has been exposed. They were the primary

---

† The Lecturer, who makes a livelihood by the sale of his Seditious Poison, shortly before his labours were interrupted by the calls of justice, suffered himself (rather unguardedly, it is true), to avow his confidence in the means employed by him and his coadjutors. Wishing to discourage some symptoms of impatience, which his audience had manifested rather boisterously, on the delay of his appearance beyond the appointed hour, he took the opportunity to caution them against every appearance of tumult or commotion; observing, that "the means

they professed to employ, were not only more safe and easy, but also infinitely more efficacious than open force; that, by continuing, in a quiet and peaceable manner, to exercise the inestimable privilege of *free discussion*, they would do more to promote the attainment of the important objects they had in view, than by the aid of myriads of men in arms, or by the most powerful artillery, *were they disposed to resort to such means.*"

[1] Wicked or criminal.

and predisposing, though not the operative, cause, of the shocking outrage. They had excited the spirit of disloyalty, which broke forth on the occasion, and which, though it be necessary for their future purpose, it would have been their interest to restrain, until the time had come when it might be let loose with more certainty of effect. The Mine they had been long preparing, exploded before it was complete: but although it failed, for that reason, to produce its intended effect, and although they were unprepared to take advantage of the sudden explosion, it is not the less true that the combustibles were collected and arranged by themselves.—Thus the designs of the wicked are sometimes defeated by the very means employed for their accomplishment.

(1795)

JOHN THELWALL
Peaceful Discussion, and Not Tumultuary Violence the Means of Redressing National Grievance [1]

PREFACE

THERE needs, I believe, no further apology for sending this Speech into the world than will be found in the first pages of the Speech itself. For if the motives that stimulated me to deliver it are good, they apply with still greater force to the propriety of its publication; and if they are inadequate in the former case, they must, of course, be impotent in the latter. I shall only add, therefore, that frequent and numerous meetings of the people for purposes of political discussion, however alarming to the *pretended* supporters, but real *destroyers*, of British Liberty, have long appeared to me necessary to keep alive the spirit, and, consequently, to preserve the privileges of a free Nation: especially when such meetings are not confined to a particular sect or party, but lie open to the public at large, or to all such, at least, as have any common bond of union or object of pursuit. Accordingly, I no sooner perceived, by the advertisement in the Morning Chronicle, that not only the Corresponding Society, but the Friends of Parliamentary Reform in general, were invited, than the motives explained in the ensuing pages produced a strong anxiety in me to attend—an anxiety from the uneasiness of which nothing could relieve me till I had yielded to its impulse.

My experience, however, of the base and unfounded perjuries of the agents of "*Gentlemen high in office;*" [2] and my consciousness of the eagerness with which certain powerful individuals thirst for my blood, having long since determined me, never, while the present inquisitorial system lasts, to subject myself again to their misrepresentations, I took the precaution to carry my short-hand writer with me, that I might be able at all times to prove what were the real sentiments I delivered: and, as it appears to me that nothing is so important to the cause of Liberty as to enforce the preservation of peace and order, I seize the opportunity which this precaution furnishes, of sending the following pages into the world.

Extensive circulation is undoubtedly my object; and I should, therefore, have been glad to have sent this pamphlet abroad at a still cheaper rate: for he

---

[1] John Thelwall (1764–1834), a radical activist and lecturer and poet. Thelwall was one of the leading members of the 1790s reform movement, both in his work with the London Corresponding Society and as one of the most fearless and charismatic public lecturers of his time. He was one of three radicals tried for treason in 1794, but he returned to radical politics, offering a well-attended series of lectures throughout the next two years. Thelwall was a friend of S.T. Coleridge and William Wordsworth for a brief time in the late 1790s but struggled with ignomy as public reaction turned against the radical movement. This excerpt is from Thelwall's speech at a mass meeting of the Friends of Parliamentary Reform, called by the London Corresponding Society, on October 26, 1795. See John Bowles' reference, above.

[2] Source unidentified.

who disseminates right principles and right sentiments (and such I believe these to be) most widely among the common people, is the best friend to the peace and happiness of Society.

SPEECH, &C.

Citizens,

IF I had the lungs of *Stentor* and the breath of *Æolus* himself,[1] I should not be able to make myself heard to the extent I wish on the present occasion. When men assemble together to exalt the *energies of reason* against the *force of oppression*, one cannot but lament that they have not a voice that might resound from the Equator to the Poles, and make the far Antipodes[2] reverberate the accents of Truth, and the maxims of Liberty and Justice.

It was therefore impossible that a meeting of the Friends of Liberty could be called while I was in London, without my feeling a longing anxiety to be present at their deliberations and assistant in promoting the great cause to which I trust we are devoted. The truth, then, Citizens, is, that I came to this meeting because I could not help it: for till I had made up my mind to come, (and I did not so make up my mind till yesterday) I was the most wretched being on the face of the earth. It seemed like a crime against nature, that the friends of liberty should meet, and I not be present to share in their deliberations.

Citizens, there is another reason why I am present at this meeting. I am not ignorant of the machinations of the tools and advocates of corruption. I know that it is impossible for such a meeting as this to be summoned, but that there must be some conspiracy in existence. Yes, Citizens, conspir-

acies there are; but they are not the friends of liberty who are the conspirators, but the friends of the tottering cause of despotism and corruption. Those are the wretches who will conspire together, in the vain hope of making the friends of liberty, by plunging them into tumult and disorder, the instruments of their detestable machinations. They are the wretches who hope from our meetings and assemblies to pick out pretences for establishing that system of military despotism which they wish to establish over us. I had, therefore, the vanity to hope that I might be, in some degree, assistant in the preservation of that peace, order, and legal moderation of conduct, which will set at open defiance the vain machinations of those who wish for tumult; because, without the pretences which tumult might afford them, it is impossible for them to introduce that military coercion necessary for the support of their rotten borough system of corruption, peculation, and monopoly, under the weight of which we groan.

Let it not, however, be supposed, that while I wish to recommend to you a scrupulous respect for peace and order, that I wish to repress the generous ardour and enthusiasm in behalf of liberty, with which I know your bosoms are at this time burning. No, Citizens, I would increase that enthusiasm, I would disseminate that ardour, and I would steel with tenfold fortitude that determination which I know you feel—that resolution with which I know you have all solemnly sworn, upon the altar of your own generous hearts, to live free or die! I would fan, not extinguish, that sacred fire of freedom, which should glow in every bosom—"flame in the breath, and lighten in the eyes"[3] of all who call themselves Britons!—nay, of all who wear the form of man! But I am convinced, Citizens, that the most ardent enthusiasm in the cause of liberty is perfectly consistent with the utmost zeal for humanity and benevo-

[1] Stentor: a Greek warrior celebrated for the strength of his lungs; Æolus: the god of wind.

[2] Places diametrically opposite.

[3] Source unidentified.

lence. Nay, humanity and benevolence are indeed the soul of that virtuous system of which liberty is but the organ: for what is the object of our enquiries, our anxieties, and our labours? Is it not to promote the happiness of mankind? Which of us would neglect his ordinary occupations, fly from the embraces of a wife, and the endearments of his family, forego the peaceful calm of obscurity and domestic enjoyment, and with a bastille before his eyes, and an axe over his head, bathe his soul in the troubles of political controversy, for an object less important than the rights and happiness of man? And can this happiness be enjoyed; can these rights be secure in the midst of carnage and devastation? No: The liberty you seek is the emancipation and happiness of the human race. This alone can satisfy you.

It is the substance, then, not the word that you are to pursue; and that substance is the happiness, welfare, and prosperity of mankind. The universal diffusion of equal rights and equal laws, which smooth the rugged asperities of unequal conditions, and make man, wherever he beholds the form of man, perceive a brother, a friend;—a being, in short, entitled to the same rights with himself, and to the same protection in the enjoyment and maintenance of his opinions.

These, Citizens are the principles I wish to enforce. I would teach you how to obtain, upon these principles, the redress of all your grievances; for I am as well aware as any man present, how great your miseries and disasters are: nay, I will venture to say, that few of you know the extent and desperation of your calamity.

The pressure of your present misery you feel—for who can be insensible to the sharp and biting anguish with which War and Corruption have assailed the vitals of the Country? But you know not (unless you have seriously studied the history of past and present ages) the rapid strides with which Oppression is advancing to your final dissolution.

Thus convinced, and thus feeling for the miseries of my fellow beings; perceiving, as I think I do, the political forces of these calamities, and convinced of the necessity of speedy and effectual redress, believe me I do not mean to damp the ardor with which you pursue that object; but I will tell you, according to my judgement, what is the line of conduct by which we may obtain it. It is not by tumult. It is not by violence. It is by reason; by turning our serious attention to facts and principles; by bold and determinate investigation, not to be checked by idle threats, nor turned aside by actual danger. It is by the resolution to proceed like enlightened, bold, and peaceable Citizens, determined to respect in our own conduct the sacred laws of humanity and good order, but rather to die than suffer the turbulence, injustice, and persecuting fury of others to drive us from those principles of Liberty and Justice which the force of conviction has incorporated with our existence:—principles upon which the happiness—nay, the bread, of our children, and our children's children, through all successive generations, may depend.

Adhere then to reason and to the principles of truth and justice; for these are the principles of Liberty: and be well assured, that when the principles of Liberty shall be well understood throughout the country, when facts shall be known, and causes properly investigated, it will be no longer in the power of tyrannical ministers to oppress you under the semblance of Liberty; or in words of the Poet to "Make us slaves and tell us 'tis our charter."[1]—When those principles shall be properly understood, mankind will see and abhor the wickedness and deformity of the present system, and the instruments will be no longer to be found by whom the oppressions we groan under can be carried on.

---

[1] Thomas Otway (1652–85), *Venice Preserv'd* (1682): I: i: 164.

And be assured, it is by the discussion of principle alone, by laying the axe of reason to the root of the tree of corruption, that the blasting foliage of luxury, and the poisonous fruit of oppression can be destroyed. And this is not to be done by tumultuary rashness, by personal animosity, malevolence, or faction. It is to be effected only by a steady adherence to reason, truth and justice: and whosoever, by the violation of these principles, gives a handle to the tools of despotism for exercising their beloved system of oppressive coercion, whatever may be his motives, his sincerity, or his zeal, is, in effect, an enemy to the cause of freedom, and not a friend.

Mark then, I pray you, what misfortunes have fallen upon a neighboring country, from the neglect of these precautions—from being, in fact, less influenced by principle than by faction. Glorious principles, it is true, have been broached by the struggles of that country; and whatever danger may in this age of persecution attach to so honest a declaration, I proclaim in the face of heaven and earth, in the broad blaze of day, and what more than all I reverence, in the presence of this concourse of my fellow beings, that I venerate, I esteem, I adore the principles upon which the French Revolution has been established. But those principles, though talked of by a few, have unhappily never been considered by the many; and the people of *France*, though they were sensible of their wrongs, and easily found out the way to rid themselves of one tyranny, have not yet found out the effectual means of preventing the usurpations of another. Neither can it be disguised, that from the disastrous circumstance of being led by personal faction, and stimulated by suspicion, animosity and ambition, it has hitherto happened, that the men with the best principles have adopted the worst conduct.

What has been the consequence? Faction after faction has triumphed in the blood of its predecessors—the mountain had prevailed over the valley and the valley over the mountain; and during the space of six successive years they have been cutting each others throats, upon personal disputes, and questions of ambitious ascendancy, till the public mind appears to have grown sick and weary of the contest, and the real object of their first and wise pursuit has vanished almost out of sight. This is, I confess, a melancholy, but it is too evident a truth: for look at their newly accepted Constitution, and tell me—what have they done at last? Have they not abandoned the glorious principle of equality? Have they not quietly resigned the principle of universal suffrage? a principle which, I hope, from the long and peaceful discussion we have enjoyed, is becoming so deeply engrafted in our hearts, that we shall never part with it but with our existence; nor ever cease by every manly exertion to seek the full enjoyment of a right so important and indispensable.

Citizens, for this and many other errors which have blemished the bright course of the French Revolution, they have an excuse in *France* which can never be pleaded in *England*, if we should suffer ourselves to be plunged into similar calamities. From the particular circumstances and situation of that country, political discussion, was, in reality, what it has been attempted to make it here, a crime; and the people were obliged to begin to act before they began to reason. This must always be the case where despotism silences the voice and the press. When men are forbidden to seek redress from reason and enquiry, they have no other resource but to break their chains on the heads of their oppressors: they are obliged to plunge into tumult and violence before they can begin to speak; and, when tumult and violence begin, the level course of reason and enquiry cannot properly flow. That candour, that moderation, that disposition to tolerate opposing sentiments, so necessary for the discovery of truth, and the understanding of expansive principles, can never be expected in the heat and fury of insurrection. Faction, the child of Turbulence and misguided Zeal, usurps the dominion of the public mind, and intellectual improvement, with an exception alone to the talent of popular eloquence, is almost at a stand. But we, in England, in this respect are happier. Political discussion has long been common among Englishmen; and, for the last five or six years, we have been rapidly weaning ourselves from those personal disputes which too long engrossed our attention, and have been turning our minds to general principles. For us, therefore, to lose sight of these principles, in the factious contentions of personal attachment or personal anonymity, would be an offence without pardon, and into which nothing but precipitate violence can possibly plunge us. Keep clear then, citizens, of all tumultuary proceedings and violent resolutions; keep clear also of personal factions, groundless suspicions, rancour, animosity, and furious denunciation. Fix your attention on principles, not on men. Remember that no man ought to be of so much consequence as to draw your attention from the general object: and remember also, that you fall into this error as completely when you precipitately denounce, as when you implicitly confide. Keep these principles, citizens, in view, and you must triumph; for the cause of liberty is the cause of Truth—and Truth, when she exerts her perfect energies, is omnipotent.

(Here some interruption took place, in consequence of an enraged bull being driven into the field, which threw the people into some confusion, to which, after restoring order, the speaker thus alluded—)[1]

Behold an apt similitude, Citizens—

Would you know why *John Bull*[2] has been disposed to foam and run so fiercely of late? He is saddled with taxes and goaded by oppression. His provender[3] runs short, and his blows encrease. And, not being properly informed as to the means of redress, he is desirous of getting rid of his oppressions by rage and impetuous fury. This is natural to the brute, but let it not be so with the man.—Let yonder *John Bull* therefore, run that way: you *John Bull* keep your ground while I proceed to shew you that the way to attain liberty is neither by running away from your drivers, nor your reason. Let me shew you that the way to attain liberty, is not by being mad and desperate; but by calmly exerting your intellect in acquiring a just knowledge of the nature and cases of your oppressions. I have told you that this was one of the most glorious days I ever beheld, and I will tell you why it is so. It is from this circumstance, that it demonstrates, to the confusion of calumniators, that so many people of all ages, sexes, classes, and orders of society can meet together, without tumult or disorder, with but one heart, one voice, one sentiment:—that every pulse can beat, at once for the liberty, the peace, and the happiness of the human race; for the abolition of corruption, violence and persecution; and for the triumph of equal rights, equal laws, and consequently of virtue and happiness, exalted by reason, and united by peace.

(*1795*)

---

[1]   This parenthetical note is included in Thelwall's text.

[2]   "John Bull" was often used as a synonym for the prototypical Englishman.

[3]   Food for cattle.

WILLIAM GODWIN

Considerations on Lord Grenville's And Mr. Pitt's Bills, Concerning Treasonable And Seditious Practices, And Unlawful Assemblies. By a Lover of Order.[1]

HUMAN society is a wonderful machine. How great are the inequalities that prevail in every country in Europe! How powerful is the incitement held out to the poor man, to commit hostility on the property of the rich; to commit it in detail, each man for himself, or by one great and irresistible effort to reduce every thing to universal chaos! Political wisdom, when it is found such as it ought to be, is the great and venerable power, that presides in the midst of turbulent and conflicting passions, that gives to all this confusion the principles of order, and that extracts universal advantage from a nearly universal selfishness.

He that deliberately views the machine of human society, will, even in his speculations, approach it with awe. He will recollect with alarm, that in this scene,

—Fools rush in, where angels fear to tread.[2]

The fabric that we contemplate is a sort of fairy edifice, and, though it consists of innumerable parts, and hide its head among the clouds, the hand of a child almost, if suffered with neglect, may shake it into ruins.

There is no good reason to conclude, that speculative enquiries ought not to be tolerated, or even that they may not, if consulted with soberness, afford materials for general utility. But it is with soberness and caution that the practical politician will alone venture to consult them. Do you tell me, "that there are great abuses in society?" No wise man will dispute it. But these abuses are woven into the very web and substance of society; and he that touches them with a sacrilegious hand, will run the risk of producing the widest and most tremendous ruin. Do you tell me, "that these abuses ought to be corrected?" Every impartial friend to mankind will confirm your decision with his suffrage, and lend his hand to the salutary work.

Yes, my countrymen, abuses ought to be corrected. The effort to correct them ought to be incessant. But they must be corrected with judgment and deliberation. We must not, for the sake of a problematical future, part with the advantages we already possess; we must not destroy, faster than we rear.

There are persons indeed, to whom the edifice of society appears as nothing but one mass of deformity. With such persons it is not necessary here to enter into any regular argument. Is all that distinguishes the most enlightened genius of modern Europe from the American savage, nothing? Is the admirable progress of light and knowledge, that has been going on almost uniformly for centuries, and that promises to go on to an unlimited extent,— is this nothing? Where is the man hardy and

---

[1] William Godwin (1756–1836), the most prominent of the middle-class reformers, was famous for his philosophical vision of social change, *An Enquiry concerning Political Justice, and its Influence on General Virtue and Happiness* (1793), for his political thriller novel *Caleb Williams* (1794) and for other more journalistic efforts in the cause of reform. But Godwin's pamphlet, *Considerations on Lord Grenville's And Mr. Pitt's Bills, Concerning Treasonable And Seditious Practices, And Unlawful Assemblies,* also epitomized the complex position of radicals intellectuals, eager for change but ambivalent about a mass reform movement. *Considerations* was a response to the two acts named in its title, passed by the government in an attempt to curtail the reform movement. In it Godwin positioned himself as a champion of reform, but he identified as equal enemies the tyranny of the Pitt government and the violent tendencies of popular radicalism. For Godwin, reform could only be achieved through robust intellectual debate, but this required a degree of reflection that was irreconcilable with the mob mentality of a mass movement.

[2] Alexander Pope (1688–1744), *Essay on Criticism* (1711): 625.

brutish enough to put all this to peril, to set this immense and long earned treasure upon a single throw, for the chance, if universal anarchy and barbarism be introduced, of the more generous and auspicious scenes that will grow out of this barbarism?

If the most important duty of those who hold the reins of government, be, at all times, to take care of the public security, it is peculiarly so in the present crisis. We are never so well insured against anarchy and tumult, but that it is incumbent upon government to be vigilant. But the dangers of anarchy and tumult are greater now, than at any ordinary period. The foundations of society have been broken up in the most considerable kingdom of Europe. Dreadful calamities have followed. A great experiment has been made, and the happiness of mankind is eminently involved in the issue of the experiment. But there is something so beautiful and fascinating, to a superficial observation, in the principles that produced the French revolution, that great numbers of men are eager to adopt and to act upon them. The calamities that have attended their operation in France, do not deter them.

In the mean time, the success of the experiment of the French revolution has not been so unmixed and brilliant, but that a man of reflection will deliberate long, before he desires to see the experiment repeated in any other country. It is the duty of the governors of the earth, particularly at this time, to set their faces against rash and premature experiments. They will not seek to preclude men from the exercise of private judgment. They will not involve in an undistinguishing censure all projects of better economy and moderate reform. But, if they remark with a certain degree of applause the high blood and impetuous mettle of the racer, they will, at least, look to the boundary posts, and endeavour to prevent his running out of the course.

Let us apply these common and unanswerable topics of reasoning to the objects embraced in Lord Grenville's and Mr. Pitt's bills. These objects are, the influx of French principles, and the dangers accruing from these principles to public security. There are two points, in which this influx of principles and their concomitant dangers have been more particularly conspicuous.

The first of the two points to which we alluded above, is the institution of the London Corresponding Society. Respecting the nature of extensive political societies we have received a memorable instruction, which no lover of the happiness of mankind will easily persuade himself to forget, in the institution of the Jacobin Society in Paris. It is too notorious to admit of being reasonably questioned, that the London Corresponding Society has in several respects formed itself upon the model of the societies which have produced such memorable effects in France. They have adopted the language of these societies. They have copied their actions. They may, without the imputation of uncharitable construction, be suspected of a leaning to republican principles. But, what is most material, they have endeavoured, like the society of Jacobins, to form lesser affiliated societies in all parts of the island; and they have professed to send missionaries to instruct them. The very name indeed of London Corresponding Society presents to us this idea.

Let us consider what idea we ought to form of this extraordinary institution. It is extremely numerous in the metropolis, split and divided into a variety of sections. It boasts, that it weekly gains an accession of numbers. Its recruits are chiefly levied from the poorer classes of the community. It has abundance of impetuous and ardent activity and very little of the ballast, the unwieldy dulness, of property.

Political enquirers might have been induced to pay less attention to this extraordinary machine, than its magnitude deserves. But it has forced itself upon public notice, by the immense multitudes it has collected together in the neighbourhood of the metropolis, at what have been stiled its general meetings. The speeches delivered at these meetings, and the resolutions adopted, have not always been of the most temperate kind. The collecting of immense multitudes of men into one assembly, particularly when there have been no persons of eminence, distinction, and importance in the country, that have mixed with them, and been ready to temper their efforts, is always sufficiently alarming. We had a specimen of what might be the sequel of such collecting, in the riots introduced by Lord George Gordon and the Protestant Association in the year 1780.[1]

If ever a delicate and skilful hand were necessary in managing the public concerns, it was peculiarly necessary upon the present occasion. Lord Grenville's bill relates to the most important of all human affairs, the liberty of the press.

The title of Lord Grenville's bill is, *An Act for the safety and preservation of his majesty's person and government, against treasonable and seditious practices and attempts.* Its professed object is to provide additional securities, for the safety of the royal person, and against such proceedings and language, as may lead to popular tumult and insurrection. It consists of two parts, one enacting new treasons, or definitions of treason, and the other providing against seditious practices under the denomination of misdemeanours.

The liberty of the press! If any thing human is to be approached with awe, it is this. If other men deserve censure for trifling with public security, what censure do not ministers deserve, if they have so trifled? If lesser offences, if a train of personal scurrilities, ought not in some cases to be passed over without notice, what denomination shall we give to his offence, who offends against the liberty of the press, and who, while he offends, possesses the functions of government, can strike as soon as threaten?

If in reality any provisions be necessary against seditious writings, Heavens! with what caution, with what almost morbid sensibility ought such provisions to be constructed? I would say to the author of such a bill, "Consider well what it is that you are doing. You enter upon the most sacred of all human functions. Do not, while you pretend to be a friend to the public welfare, stab the frame of the public welfare to the very heart!"

The manner in which the provisions of Lord Grenville's bill are worded, may be satisfactorily illustrated. For that purpose, I will suppose these very pages, to be construed by the king's minister to have a tendency "to incite or stir up the people to hatred or dislike" (What a word is this dislike! What malignant genius introduced it into the bill? What a sweeping term, that may mean anything or everything that the prosecutor shall be pleased to understand by it!)—"to incite or stir up the people to hatred or dislike of the person of his majesty, his heirs or successors, or the established government and constitution (where is the philologist that will give me a secure definition of these two words?) of this realm." Well, in that case, I am to be "liable to such punishment as may by law be inflicted in cases of high misdemeanours," and "for the second offence, I am to be transported for seven years." The only security I have against the infliction of these penalties, the moment a prosecution is commenced against me, consists in the hope, that the judge may be unbiased and impartial; that the arguments of my counsel may be found in the experiment to be irresistible; or that my jury in whole or in part may be persons of a firm, independent, and intrepid temper. In the meantime the

---

[1] The Gordon Riots were a reaction to legislation designed to enfranchise Catholics.

prosecution commenced against me is a crown prosecution; it is attended in the course of it with the popular clamour against republicans and levellers; and people are to be reminded every day in the treasury prints, that, upon the conviction of such persons as I am, depends the security of property, and all that is valuable in social existence.

Who does not see, that, if I write a pamphlet or book in which any political question is treated or incidentally mentioned, I may suffer the penalties of this act? Who does not see, that, if the king's minister do not like my pamphlet, or do not like my face, if he have an old grudge against me for any past proceeding, if I have not proved a fortunate candidate for his general good-will, or if, by any distortion of understandings, or excessiveness of alarm, he be led to see in my pamphlet things it does not contain, I may suffer the penalties of this act? My after hopes are in the judge, that he shall have no inclination to gratify his majesty's minister; in my counsel, that he shall be able to convince men who may be predetermined against conviction; or in the jury, that they shall be undecided by hopes or fears, from government, or any of the intemperate and indiscriminate friends of government; or that the honest part of them shall be more enlightened, more determined, and better able to endure hunger and fatigue, than those who are disposed to consult only the voice of interest? This is the lottery, from which I am to draw my ticket. This is the game, at which I am to play for the liberties of an Englishman. The words of the bill are expressly calculated to afford the widest field for sophistry, and the most convenient recipe for quieting the awakened conscience of a delinquent jury or judge.

Was it design? Did they intend to have all the literature of England, original or translated, and all its votaries at their mercy?

But the matter lies deeper than we have yet seen. It is worth our while to enquire what would be the penalty awarded to the author of Hume's Idea of a Perfect Commonwealth, or Rousseau's Treatise of the Social Compact,[1] if they were living, and if these works were published during the operation of Lord Grenville's bill.

Hume and Rousseau appear in these treatises to have been republicans. Republicanism is a doctrine mischievous and false. Be it so. But there can be no enquiry, and no science, if I am to be told at the commencement of my studies, in what inference they must all terminate. Labouring under this restraint, I cannot examine; labouring under this restraint I cannot, strictly speaking, even attempt to examine. No matter how decisive are the arguments in favour of monarchical government; if men enter freely upon the discussion, there will be some, from singularity of temper, or peculiarity of prejudices which they are unable to correct, who will determine in favour of republicanism. The idea of combining uniformity of opinion in the sequel, with liberty of enquiry in the commencement, is the most impossible and frantic notion that ever entered into the mind of man.

What men imagine they see in the way of argument, they can scarcely refrain from speaking, and they ought to be permitted to publish. All republican writers (Hume is an eminent example) do not appeal to our passions; all appeals to our passions do not menace us with the introduction of universal anarchy. Considering how triumphant the arguments in favour of monarchy are affirmed to be, we surely ought not to be terrified with every philosophical debate. It is a well known maxim of literature, that no principle upon any controversial subject, can be so securely established, as when its adversaries are permitted to attack it, and it is found

---

[1] David Hume (1711–76), "Idea of a Perfect Commonwealth," in *Essays, Moral, Political, and Literary* (1777); Jean-Jacques Rousseau (1712–78), *A Treatise on the Social Compact; or the Principles of Political Law* (1761).

superior to every objection. A sober and considerate observer will have strange thoughts that suggest themselves to him, respecting the most venerable and generally received maxims, if he find that every person who ventures to enter upon an impartial examination of them, is threatened with the pillory.

A few words are due to those persons who, imbued with the scepticism incident to inquisitive habits, may be in doubt whether the monarchical or republican opinion will ultimately appear to be the most sound, or which of them will ultimately prove victorious. A doctrine opposite to the maxims of the existing government may be dangerous in the hands of agitators, but it cannot produce very fatal consequences in the hands of philosophers. If it undermine the received system, it will undermine it gradually and insensibly; it will merely fall in with that gradual principle of decay and renovation, which is perpetually at work in every part of the universe.

Philosophy and science, in all their most eminent branches, though venerable as the pillars of the world, are by this act sent to school to lord Grenville. He is to teach them good manners; he is to brandish over them the rod of correction; he is to subject them to the rigours of such discipline as to his judgment shall seem meet.

The most important object of lord Grenville's bill, is to impose certain restraints upon the liberty of the press. To what period does he recur for instruction upon that subject? What authorities does he consult? The reign of queen Elizabeth; the year 1571. Is this the consummation of ignorance, or are we to regard it in the light of unblushing sophistry? I will suppose that the reign of queen Elizabeth, had been as much distinguished by maxims of liberty, as it was by the maxims of arbitrary power. Lord Grenville's argument will gain nothing by that supposition.

In the year 1571, literature was not yet emancipated from its cradle: the liberty of the press had not yet been heard of. This important doctrine, so invaluable to times of knowledge and illumination, had not yet been invented. Men might have loved all other kinds of liberty, but this they could not love for they could not understand. The press, that great engine for raising men to the dignity of gods, for expanding and impregnating the human understanding, for annihilating, by the most gentle and salubrious methods, all the arts of oppression, was a machine thrust into an obscure corner, and which, for its unpolished plainness and want of exterior attraction, was almost regarded with contempt. Men knew scarcely more of the real powers of the press, and its genuine uses, than the savage would suspect of the uses of the alphabet, if you threw the four and twenty letters into his lap.[1]

And now, in the close of the eighteenth century, lord Grenville would bring us back to the standard of 1571. Does he think we are to be thus led? Does he believe that he will be permitted to treat men arrived at years of maturity, in the manner they were treated while children? Is the *imprimatur* of government to be a necessary preliminary to every publication? Are we to have an *Index Expurgatorius*, teaching us what books we may read, and what books must on no account be opened? Is government to appoint certain persons to draw up for us catechisms and primers, Whole Duties of Man, and elementary treatises of every science? And are we, by these publications from authority, to model our creed and fashion our understandings?

Little indeed do these ministers apprehend of the nature of human intellect! Little indeed have they followed its growth, to the vigorous sublimity of its present future! They are strangers come from afar, and cannot understand the language of the country. They are like the seven sleepers, that we

---

[1] Samuel Johnson's *Dictionary* (1755) conflates two sets of letters: "I" with "J" and "U" with "V."

read of in the Roman history, who, after having slumbered for three hundred years, knew not that a month had elapsed, and expected to see their old contemporaries, their wives still beautiful, and their children still in arms.[1] But they will be taught the magnitude of their error. This giant, the understanding, will rouse himself in his might, and will break their fetters, "as a thread of tow is broken, when it toucheth the fire."[2]

(1795)

---

[1] The tale concerns seven young Romans who, persecuted for their Christian beliefs, went into a cave to pray and prepare for death, at which point they fell asleep. The emperor had the cave closed and sealed. Years later, after the empire had become Christian, a rich landowner had the Sleepers' cave opened to use as a cattle-stall. The sleepers awoke and, thinking they had slept only one night, were shocked by the triumph of Christianity.

[2] Judges 16:9. From the story of Samson and Delilah. The reference is to Samson's strength.

SECTION TEN

A Revolution in Female Manners

The efforts of the French revolutionaries to reimagine the existing class hierarchy were integrally related to debates in the period about the social role of women. These had been evolving throughout the eighteenth century, but the intensity of the revolutionary debates in Britain infused them with a new urgency. This connection was accentuated by the tendency of many of these writers (some of whom had written polemics about the French Revolution itself) to link women's struggles to broader political controversies in overt ways, though their various interpretations of the nature of this connection reflected their political differences. For Mary Wollstonecraft, women's preference for the "illegitimate power" of youth and beauty over the more sober attractions of rational intelligence were merely a reflection of the mistaken priorities of a society where "kings and nobles" preferred "their gaudy hereditary trappings" to the "real dignity" of "enlightened reason." The democratic impulse which informed the class-based struggle for the rights of man would, therefore, encourage women to reject the false elevation of mindless femininity. For Hannah More, women's opportunity to become more active and more responsible social agents was also linked to the revolutionary struggles, but in a diametrically opposed way. Given women's unquestioned social influence, More argued, it was vital that they rise to the Jacobin challenge by opposing "the most tremendous confederacies against religion and order, and governments, which the world ever saw" with an unprecedented display of virtue and propriety.

If these opposed responses to the revolutionary debate reinforced what were in many ways very similar calls for women's improved social roles, this was partly because there was actually a considerable amount of common ground in the arguments of these writers. This was especially true in their shared emphasis on the importance of education and healthy reading habits as forces that could help women to pursue more meaningful lives. Catharine Macaulay's and Hannah More's works explicitly addressed the issue of education in their titles. It was the central focus of Wollstonecraft's notorious *Vindication of the Rights of Woman* and a favourite topic of Mary Hays. Each of these writers contrasted the power of rational women, whose intelligence rendered them endearing companions and useful citizens, with the corrosive influence of women whose minds were, as Hays put it, "occupied by trifles." This emphasis on the transformative power of education was influenced, however, by underlying assumptions about the extent to which the differences between the sexes was inherent or simply the product of cultural influence. Radical thinkers such as Macaulay, Wollstonecraft and Hays tended to insist that because these differences were largely cultural, they could be eradicated by giving women a proper education. For Hannah More, on the other hand, the point of a good education was to promote a more rational and virtuous femininity, rather than to encourage women to mimic those qualities which belonged uniquely to men. It was better "to be good originals, rather than bad imitators."

For each of these writers, the importance of education was crucially connected to the possibility of women becoming more productive members of the community. Priscilla Wakefield transformed this into a responsibility by citing Adam Smith's warning that "every individual is a burden upon the society to which he belongs, who does not contribute his share of productive labour for the good of the whole." She and Mary Ann Radcliffe addressed in very specific ways the sorts of occupations that women needed increased access to if they were to live up to Smith's challenge. Despite her radical reputation, Mary Wollstonecraft was largely silent on the issue of women's access to professions normally reserved for men, but like many of these writers, she challenged the hierarchical logic of public and private identities that structured assumptions about men's and women's work by insisting that "public virtue is only an aggregate of private"—a stance which undermined the distinction between male and female spheres and implied that women could expect to gain access to men's opportunities as they became more educated. Hannah More may have declared that she was not "sounding an alarm to female warriors, or exciting female politicians," but she nonetheless insisted that women embrace their "high and holy calling" in a way that emphasized their vital role in the political struggles of the day. Like Wollstonecraft, More implicitly challenged established demarcations between the public and private spheres by calling on women "to take the lead in society" by acting "as the guardians of public taste as well as public virtue."

This emphasis on education reflected a cluster of eighteenth-century assumptions about the power of knowledge: If it was true, as Enlightenment reformers suggested, that knowledge developed through reading was a form of power, then shouldn't women be allowed to have an Enlightenment too? If so, a number of more important questions arose, such as: What should the nature of their Enlightenment be? Would it be the same Enlightenment as men from the "polite classes" were entitled to? Would it be different for different classes? What practical social roles would it qualify women for? And who should get to decide the answers to these questions? These issues were sometimes debated in explicitly literary terms when they focussed on women's access to "masculine" fields such as history, politics, and philosophy. But even when the debates were not explicitly about literature, they turned on the essentially literary issue of the connections between knowledge and social usefulness. Despite her conservative emphasis on the inherent differences between the sexes, More encouraged women "to read the best books," not in order to become authors themselves, or to enter into any learned profession, but to enable women "to regulate" their own minds, "and to be useful to others."

If they were not always in complete agreement about the exact nature of the opportunities that an improved education would prepare women for, these writers did tend to be united in their sense that educational reform, and the social changes that would follow, was especially important as an antidote to what Hays called "the trifling and corruptive mode of education" that was "generally allowed" to women. Catharine Macaulay acknowledged that women had always suffered from "some degree of inferiority in point of corporeal strength," but, like Hays, she insisted that these differences had been exaggerated by "the defects of female education," which tended "to corrupt and debilitate both the powers of mind and body." Mary Wollstonecraft famously denounced "a false system of education gathered from the books written on this subject by men who, considering females rather as women than human creatures, have been more anxious to make them alluring mistresses than affectionate wives and rational mothers." Hannah More agreed that "it is a singular injustice which is often exercised towards women, first to give them a most defective Education, and then to expect from them a most undeviating purity of conduct."

These writers' rejection of "a false system of education" was reinforced by a widely shared opposition to the more informal but equally destructive literary influences to which women were exposed. The worst of these, they tended to agree, was what Priscilla Wakefield called "the baneful poison" of romantic novels "dressed up in the imagery of glowing language, filled with false sentiments of delicacy and sensibility, and presenting models of female perfection unfit for their imitation." Like Wakefield, Wollstonecraft castigated "the reveries of the stupid novelists, who, knowing little of human nature, work up stale tales, and describe meretricious scenes, all retailed in a sentimental jargon, which equally tend to corrupt the taste, and draw the heart aside from its daily duties." More agreed that "novels, which used chiefly to be dangerous in one respect, are now become mischievous in a thousand," but she extended this note of alarm to "that sober and unsuspected mass of mischief" which *seemed* to offer respectable instruction, but which was really being used to disseminate Jacobin principles. Whether it was the power of novels to encourage notions of false refinement, or of seditious literature to undermine proper religious and political beliefs, the problem was the same: the wrong sorts of literature tended to corrupt women's ability to become useful members of their society.

It is important to situate these debates about women within the wider backlash that developed in the 1790s. The image of an unstable and inherently transgressive femininity offered commentators a compelling means of understanding the unprecedented historical events of a revolutionary age. In *Proofs of a Conspiracy against all the Religions and Governments of Europe* (1798), John Robison argued that the clearest proof of the unnatural excesses of the French Revolution was that "the women have…taken the complexion of the men, and have even gone beyond them." Radical women reformers such as Macaulay, Wollstonecraft and Hays responded to this charge by distinguishing between masculine virtue, or the rational pursuit of moral independence, and masculine behaviour, which amounted to nothing more than an indulgence in the sorts of irrational behaviour (drinking, hunting, gambling) that were incompatible with virtue. For their critics, however, these positions were two sides of the same transgressive coin. These women's envious focus on male virtues was merely another symptom of their moral waywardness generally.

This backlash was reinforced by the popular trend of women dressing in men's clothing. An Edinburgh correspondent to the *Gentleman's Magazine* wrote to express his "disgust" to hear that "the military furore has actually so far seized on several young and beautiful females as to make them submit to be drilled and exercised (privately of course) by a common serjeant. Can any thing be more unworthy, or, I may add, more indelicate," he asked, "than for ladies with their petticoats kitted, to submit to be taught the movements of a soldier by a Highland-man without breeches?" For critics who considered the rights of women a contradiction in terms, this trend was ample proof of the contagious nature of women's desire to disregard the boundaries which made social order possible. Such a position had little to do with the question of what women ought to be reading and writing, but inevitably, the confusion between these two crises made it easier for alarmed conservatives to channel anxieties about social and political upheaval into the more manageable issue of threatened literary proprieties. If the spectre of radical women authors insisting on their rights was unsettling, then it could be most easily contained by confusing them with those other masculine women who, far from demonstrating any interest in the promotion of virtue, were really more interested in "being drilled and exercised…by a common serjeant."

⁏⁖⁏

CATHARINE MACAULAY
Letters on Education, with Observations on Religious and Metaphysical Subjects [1]

LETTER XXII

No characteristic Difference in Sex

THE great difference that is observable in the characters of the sexes, Hortensia,[2] as they display themselves in the scenes of social life, has given rise to much false speculation on the natural qualities of the female mind.—For though the doctrine of innate ideas, and innate affections, are in great measure exploded by the learned, yet few persons reason so closely and so accurately on abstract subjects as, through a long chain of deductions, to bring forth a conclusion which in no respect militates with their premises.

It is a long time before the crowd give up opinions they have been taught to look upon with respect; and I know many persons who will follow you willingly through the course of your argument,

---

[1] Catharine Macaulay (1731–91), historian and political and educational writer known for her republican or radical Whig values. Her *History of England from the Accession of James I* (8 vols., 1763–83) was regarded as an important reply to David Hume's Tory *History of Great Britain* (1754–62). Her *Letters on Education* (1790) helped to shape the terms of the debate about women and education in the 1790s.

[2] *Letters on Education* (1790) adopted the literary convention of an epistolary form, in this case to a fictitious correspondent named Hortensia.

till they perceive it tends to the overthrow of some fond prejudice; and then they will either sound a retreat, or begin a contest in which the contender for truth, though he cannot be overcome, is effectually silenced, from the mere weariness of answering positive assertions, reiterated without end. It is from such causes that the notion of a sexual difference in the human character has, with a very few exceptions, universally prevailed from the earliest times, and the pride of one sex, and the ignorance and vanity of the other, have helped to support an opinion which a close observation of Nature, and a more accurate way of reasoning, would disprove.

It must be confessed, that the virtues of the males among the species, though mixed and blended with a variety of vices and errors, have displayed a bolder and more consistent picture of excellence than female nature has hitherto done. It is on these reasons that, when we compliment the appearance of a more than ordinary energy in the female mind, we call it masculine; and hence it is, that Pope has elegantly said *a perfect woman's but a softer man.*[1] And if we take in the consideration, that there can be but one rule of moral excellence for beings made of the same materials, organized after the same manner, and subjected to similar laws of Nature, we must either agree with Mr. Pope, or we must reverse the proposition, and say, that *a perfect man is a woman formed after a coarser mould.* The difference that actually does subsist between the sexes, is too flattering for men to be willingly imputed to accident; for what accident occasions, wisdom might correct; and it is better, says Pride, to give up the advantages we might derive from the perfection of our fellow associates, than to own that Nature has been just in the equal distribution of her favours. These are the sentiments of the men; but mark how readily they are yielded to by the women; not from

humility I assure you, but merely to preserve with character those fond vanities on which they set their hearts. No; suffer them to idolize their persons, to throw away their life in the pursuit of trifles, and to indulge in the gratification of the meaner passions, and they will heartily join in the sentence of their degradation.

Among the most strenuous asserters of a sexual difference in character, Rousseau[2] is the most conspicuous, both on account of that warmth of sentiment which distinguishes all his writings, and the eloquence of his compositions: but never did enthusiasm and the love of paradox, those enemies to philosophical disquisition, appear in more strong opposition to plain sense than in Rousseau's definition of this difference. He sets out with a supposition, that Nature intended the subjection of one sex to the other; that consequently there must be an inferiority of intellect in the subjected party; but as man is a very imperfect being, and apt to play the capricious tyrant, Nature, to bring things nearer to an equality, bestowed on woman such attractive graces, and such an insinuating address, as to turn the balance on the other scale. Thus Nature, in a giddy mood, recedes from her purposes, and subjects prerogative[3] to an influence which must produce confusion and disorder in the system of human affairs. Rousseau saw this objection; and in order to obviate it, he has made up a moral person of the union of the two sexes, which, for contradiction and absurdity, outdoes every metaphysical riddle that was ever formed in the schools. In short, it is not reason, it is not wit; it is pride and sensuality that speak in Rousseau, and, in this instance, has lowered the man of genius to the licentious pedant.

---

[1] Alexander Pope (1688–1744), "Of the Characters of Women," *Moral Essays* (1732–34): 272.

[2] Jean-Jacques Rousseau (1712–78), originally from Geneva. Rousseau was a complicated figure for many radical women writers. They identified with his republican idealism but rejected the rigidly demarcated sex roles that informed his celebration of natural man over a corrupt modern society.

[3] Authority.

But whatever might be the wise purpose intended by Providence in such a disposition of things, certain it is, that some degree of inferiority, in point of corporal strength, seems always to have existed between the two sexes; and this advantage, in the barbarous ages of mankind, was abused to such a degree, as to destroy all the natural rights of the female species, and reduce them to a state of abject slavery. What accidents have contributed in Europe to better their condition, would not be to my purpose to relate; for I do not intend to give you a history of women; I mean only to trace the sources of their peculiar foibles and vices; and these I firmly believe to originate in situation and education only: for so little did a wise and just Providence intend to make the condition of slavery an unalterable law of female nature, that in the same proportion as the male sex have consulted the interest of their own happiness, they have relaxed in their tyranny over women; and such is their use in the system of mundane creation, and such their natural influence over the male mind, that were these advantages properly exerted, they might carry every point of any importance to their honour and happiness. However, till that period arrives in which women will act wisely, we will amuse ourselves in talking of their follies.

The situation and education of women, Hortensia, is precisely that which must necessarily tend to corrupt and debilitate both the powers of mind and body. From a false notion of beauty and delicacy, their system of nerves is depraved before they come out of their nursery; and this kind of depravity has more influence over the mind, and consequently over morals, than is commonly apprehended. But it would be well if such causes only acted towards the debasement of the sex; their moral education is, if possible, more absurd than their physical. The principles and nature of virtue, which is never properly explained to boys, is kept quite a mystery to girls. They are told indeed, that they must abstain from those vices which are contrary to their personal happiness, or they will be regarded as criminals, both by God and man; but all the higher parts of rectitude, every thing that ennobles our being, and that renders us both innoxious and useful, is either not taught, or is taught in such a manner as to leave no proper impression on the mind. This is so obvious a truth, that the defects of female education have ever been a fruitful topic of declamation for the moralist; but not one of this class of writers have laid down any judicious rules for amendment. Whilst we still retain the absurd notion of a sexual excellence, it will militate against the perfecting a plan of education for either sex. The judicious Addison[1] animadverts[2] on the absurdity of bringing a young lady up with no higher idea of the end of education than to make her agreeable to a husband, and confining the necessary excellence for this happy acquisition to the mere graces of person.

Every parent and tutor may not express himself in the same manner as is marked out by Addison; yet certain it is, that the admiration of the other sex is held out to women as the highest honour they can attain; and whilst this is considered as their *summum bonum*,[3] and the beauty of their persons the chief *desideratum*[4] of men, Vanity, and its companion Envy, must taint, in their characters, every native and acquired excellence. Nor can you, Hortensia, deny, that these qualities, when united to ignorance, are fully equal to the engendering and rivetting all those vices and foibles which are peculiar to the female sex; vices and foibles which have caused them to be considered, in ancient times, as

---

[1] Joseph Addison (1672–1719), best known for his co-authorship of the *Tatler* and the *Spectator*.

[2] Comments critically.

[3] Highest good.

[4] Desire.

beneath cultivation, and in modern days have subjected them to the censure and ridicule of writers of all descriptions, from the deep thinking philosophers to the man of ton[1] and gallantry, who, by the bye, sometimes distinguishes himself by qualities which are not greatly superior to those he despises in women. Nor can I better illustrate the truth of this observation than by the following picture, to be found in the polite and gallant Chesterfield. "Women," says his Lordship, "are only children of a larger growth. They have an entertaining tattle, sometimes wit; but for solid reasoning, and good sense, I never in my life knew one that had it, or who acted or reasoned in consequence of it for four and twenty hours together. A man of sense only trifles with them, as he does an engaging child; but he neither consults them, nor trusts them in serious matters."[2]

(1790)

Mary Wollstonecraft
Vindication of the Rights of Woman [3]

INTRODUCTION

AFTER considering the historic page, and viewing the living world with anxious solicitude, the

---

[1] Fashion.

[2] From the Earl of Chesterfield's notorious letters to his illegitimate son, Philip Stanhope, offering advice on manners and how to succeed in the world. First published by Stanhope's widow in 1774.

[3] Mary Wollstonecraft (1759–97), a well-known participant in the radical debates of the 1790s. Her response to Edmund Burke's conservative attack on the French Revolution, *Vindication of the Rights of Men* was followed two years later by the notorious *Vindication of the Rights of Woman*. Wollstonecraft was also a novelist, educational theorist and teacher (before becoming an author she had opened a school with her two sisters and a friend, Fanny Blood), travel writer, and literary critic for Joseph Johnson's *Analytical Review*. After her death she became a symbol for conservative critics of all of the worst excesses of the age, but in the early 1790s she was a prominent figure within the radical movement.

most melancholy emotions of sorrowful indignation have depressed my spirits, and I have sighed when obliged to confess, that either nature has made a great difference between man and man, or that the civilization which has hitherto taken place in the world has been very partial. I have turned over various books written on the subject of education, and patiently observed the conduct of parents and the management of schools; but what has been the result?—a profound conviction that the neglected education of my fellow creatures is the grand source of the misery I deplore; and that women, in particular, are rendered weak and wretched by a variety of concurring causes, originating from one hasty conclusion. The conduct and manners of women, in fact, evidently prove that their minds are not in a healthy state; for, like the flowers which are planted in too rich a soil, strength and usefulness are sacrificed to beauty; and the flaunting leaves, after having pleased a fastidious eye, fade, disregarded on the stalk, long before the season when they ought to have arrived at maturity.—One cause of this barren blooming I attribute to a false system of education gathered from the books written on this subject by men who, considering females rather as women than human creatures, have been more anxious to make them alluring mistresses than affectionate wives and rational mothers; and the understanding of the sex has been so bubbled by this specious homage, that the civilized women of the present century, with a few exceptions, are only anxious to inspire love, when they ought to cherish a nobler ambition, and by their abilities and virtues exact respect.

In a treatise, therefore, on female rights and manners, the works which have been particularly written for their improvement must not be overlooked; especially when it is asserted, in direct terms, that the minds of women are enfeebled by false refinement; that the books of instruction, written by men of genius, have had the same tendency as more frivolous productions; and that, in the true style of Mahometanism,[1] they are treated as a kind of subordinate beings, and not as a part of the human species, when improveable reason is allowed to be the dignified distinction which raises men above the brute creation, and puts a natural sceptre in a feeble hand.

I am aware of an obvious inference:—from every quarter have I heard exclamations against masculine women; but where are they to be found? If by this appellation men mean to inveigh against their ardour in hunting, shooting, and gaming, I shall most cordially join in the cry; but if it be against the imitation of manly virtues, or, more properly speaking, the attainment of those talents and virtues, the exercise of which ennobles the human character, and which raise females in the scale of animal being, when they are comprehensively termed mankind; —all those who view them with a philosophic eye must, I should think, wish with me, that they may every day grow more and more masculine.

This discussion naturally divides the subject. I shall first consider women in the grand light of human creatures, who, in common with men, are placed on this earth to unfold their faculties; and afterwards I shall more particularly point out their peculiar designation. I wish also to steer clear of an error which many respectable writers have fallen into; for the instruction which has hitherto been addressed to women, has rather been applicable to *ladies*, if the little indirect advice, that is scattered through Sandford and Merton,[2] be excepted; but, addressing my sex in a firmer tone, I pay particular attention to those in the middle class, because they

appear to be in the most natural state. Perhaps the seeds of false-refinement, immorality, and vanity, have ever been shed by the great. Weak, artificial beings, raised above the common wants and affections of their race, in a premature unnatural manner, undermine the very foundation of virtue, and spread corruption through the whole mass of society!

My own sex, I hope, will excuse me, if I treat them like rational creatures, instead of flattering their *fascinating* graces, and viewing them as if they were in a state of perpetual childhood, unable to stand alone. I earnestly wish to point out in what true dignity and human happiness consists—I wish to persuade women to endeavour to acquire strength, both of mind and body, and to convince them that the soft phrases, susceptibility of heart, delicacy of sentiment, and refinement of taste, are almost synonymous with epithets of weakness, and that those beings who are only the objects of pity and that kind of love, which has been termed its sister, will soon become objects of contempt.

Chapter Two
THE PREVAILING OPINION OF A SEXUAL CHARACTER DISCUSSED

To account for, and excuse the tyranny of man, many ingenious arguments have been brought forward to prove, that the two sexes, in the acquirement of virtue, ought to aim at attaining a very different character: or, to speak explicitly, women are not allowed to have sufficient strength of mind to acquire what really deserves the name of virtue. Yet it should seem, allowing them to have souls, that there is but one way appointed by Providence to lead *mankind* to either virtue or happiness.

If then women are not a swarm of ephemeron triflers, why should they be kept in ignorance under the specious name of innocence? Men complain,

---

[1] Islamic cultures were frequently cited by British writers as examples of societies which systematically mistreated women.

[2] A three volume novel by Thomas Day (1748–89; published 1783–9) which contrasted the fate of the rich but unlikeable Tommy Merton and the poorer but more compelling Harry Sandford. It was designed to suggest the moral potential of sound education.

and with reason, of the follies and caprices of our sex, when they do not keenly satirize our headstrong passions and groveling vices.—Behold, I should answer, the natural effect of ignorance! The mind will ever be unstable that has only prejudices to rest on, and the current will run with destructive fury when there are no barriers to break its force. Women are told from their infancy, and taught by the example of their mothers, that a little knowledge of human weakness, justly termed cunning, softness or temper, *outward* obedience, and a scrupulous attention to a puerile kind of propriety, will obtain for them the protection of man; and should they be beautiful, every thing else is needless, for, at least, twenty years of their lives.

Thus Milton describes our first frail mother; though when he tells us that women are formed for softness and sweet attractive grace,[1] I cannot comprehend his meaning, unless, in the true Mahometan strain, he meant to deprive us of souls, and insinuate that we were beings only designed by sweet attractive grace, and docile blind obedience, to gratify the senses of man when he can no longer soar on the wing of contemplation.

How grossly do they insult us who thus advise us only to render ourselves, gentle, domestic brutes! For instance, the winning softness so warmly, and frequently, recommended, that governs by obeying. What childish expressions, and how insignificant is the being—can it be an immortal one? who will condescend to govern by such sinister methods!

Consequently, the most perfect education, in my opinion, is such an exercise of the understanding as is best calculated to strengthen the body and form the heart. Or, in other words, to enable the individual to attain such habits of virtue as will render it independent. In fact, it is a farce to call any being virtuous whose virtues do not result from the exercise of its own reason. This was Rousseau's

opinion respecting men. I extend it to women, and confidently assert that they have been drawn out of their sphere by false refinement, and not by an endeavour to acquire masculine qualities. Still the regal homage which they receive is so intoxicating, that till the manners of the times are changed, and formed on more reasonable principles, it may be impossible to convince them that the illegitimate power, which they obtain, by degrading themselves, is a curse, and that they must return to nature and equality, if they wish to secure the placid satisfaction that unsophisticated affections impart. But for this epoch we must wait—wait, perhaps, till kings and nobles, enlightened by reason, and, preferring the real dignity of man to childish state, throw off their gaudy hereditary trappings: and if then women do not resign the arbitrary power of beauty—they will prove that they have *less* mind than man.

CHAPTER FIVE
ANIMADVERSION[2] ON SOME OF THE WRITERS WHO HAVE RENDERED WOMEN OBJECTS OF PITY, BORDERING ON CONTEMPT

DR FORDYCE'S sermons have long made a part of a young woman's library; nay, girls at school are allowed to read them; but I should instantly dismiss them from my pupil's, if I wished to strengthen her understanding, by leading her to form sound principles on a broad basis; or, were I only anxious to cultivate her taste; though they must be allowed to contain many sensible observations.[3]

Dr Fordyce may have had a very laudable end in view; but these discourses are written in such an affected style, that were it only on that account, and had I nothing to object against his *mellifluous* precepts, I should not allow girls to peruse them,

---

[1] John Milton (1608–74), *Paradise Lost* (1667) IV: 296–98.

[2] Critical reflections.

[3] James Fordyce (1720–96), *Sermons to Young Women* (1765).

unless I designed to hunt every spark of nature out of their composition, melting every human quality into female meekness and artificial grace. I say artificial, for true grace arises from some kind of independence of mind.

In declamatory periods Dr Fordyce spins out Rousseau's eloquence; and in most sentimental rant, details his opinions respecting the female character, and the behaviour which woman ought to assume to render her lovely.

Throughout there is a display of cold artificial feelings, and that parade of sensibility which boys and girls should be taught to despise as the sure mark of a vain little mind. Florid appeals are made to heaven, and to the *beauteous innocents*, the fairest images of heaven here below, whilst sober sense is left far behind.—This is not the language of the heart, nor will it ever reach it, though the ear may be tickled.

As these volumes are so frequently put into the hands of young people, I have taken more notice of them than, strictly speaking, they deserve; but as they have contributed to vitiate the taste, and enervate the understanding of many of my fellow-creatures, I could not pass them silently over.

Indignantly have I heard women argue in the same track as men, and adopt the sentiments that brutalize them, with all the pertinacity of ignorance.

When women are once sufficiently enlightened to discover their real interest, on a grand scale, they will, I am persuaded, be very ready to resign all the prerogatives of love, that are not mutual, speaking of them as lasting prerogatives, for the calm satisfaction of friendship, and the tender confidence of habitual esteem. Before marriage they will not assume any insolent airs, or afterwards abjectly submit; but endeavouring to act like reasonable creatures, in both situations, they will not be tumbled from a throne to a stool.

Mrs Chapone's Letters[1] are written with such good sense, and unaffected humility, and contain so many useful observations, that I only mention them to pay the worthy writer this tribute of respect. I cannot, it is true, always coincide in opinion with her; but I always respect her.

The very word respect brings Mrs Macaulay[2] to my remembrance. The woman of the greatest abilities, undoubtedly, that this country has ever produced.—And yet this woman has been suffered to die without sufficient respect being paid to her memory.

Posterity, however, will be more just; and remember that Catharine Macaulay was an example of intellectual acquirements supposed to be incompatible with the weakness of her sex. In her style of writing, indeed, no sex appears, for it is like the sense it conveys, strong and clear.

I will not call hers a masculine understanding, because I admit not of such an arrogant assumption of reason; but I contend that it was a sound one, and that her judgment, the matured fruit of profound thinking, was a proof that a woman can acquire judgment, in the full extent of the word. Possessing more penetration than sagacity, more understanding than fancy, she writes with sober energy and argumentative closeness; yet sympathy and benevolence give an interest to her sentiments, and that vital heat to arguments, which forces the reader to weigh them.[†]

---

[1] Hestor Chapone (1727–1801), *Letters on the Improvement of the Mind* (1773).

[2] See page 234, note 1.

[†] Coinciding in opinion with Mrs Macaulay relative to many branches of education, I refer to her valuable work, instead of quoting her sentiments to support my own.

Chapter XIII

SOME INSTANCES OF THE FOLLY WHICH THE IG-
NORANCE OF WOMEN GENERATES; WITH
CONCLUDING REFLECTIONS ON THE MORAL IM-
PROVEMENT THAT A REVOLUTION IN
FEMALE MANNERS MIGHT NATURALLY
BE EXPECTED TO PRODUCE

ANOTHER instance of that feminine weakness of character, often produced by a confined education, is a romantic twist of the mind, which has been very properly termed *sentimental*.

Women subjected by ignorance to their sensations, and only taught to look for happiness in love, refine on sensual feelings, and adopt metaphysical notions respecting that passion, which lead them shamefully to neglect the duties of life, and frequently in the midst of these sublime refinements they plump into actual vice.

These are the women who are amused by the reveries of the stupid novelists,[1] who, knowing little of human nature, work up stale tales, and describe meretricious scenes, all retailed in a sentimental jargon, which equally tend to corrupt the taste, and draw the heart aside from its daily duties. I do not mention the understanding, because never having been exercised, like the lurking particles of fire which are supposed universally to pervade matter.

Females, in fact, denied all political privileges, and not allowed, as married women, excepting in criminal cases, a civil existence, have their attention naturally drawn from the interest of the whole community to that of the minute parts, though the private duty of any member of society must be very imperfectly performed when not connected with the general good. The mighty business of female life is to please, and restrained from entering into more important concerns by political and civil oppression,

sentiments become events, and reflection deepens what it should, and would have effaced, if the understanding had been allowed to take a wider range.

But, confined to trifling employments, they naturally imbibe opinions which the only kind of reading calculated to interest an innocent frivolous mind, inspires. Unable to grasp any thing great, is it surprising that they find the reading of history a very dry task, and disquisitions addressed to the understanding intolerably tedious, and almost unintelligible? Thus are they necessarily dependent on the novelist for amusement. Yet, when I exclaim against novels, I mean when contrasted with those works which exercise the understanding and regulate the imagination.—For any kind of reading I think better than leaving a blank still a blank, because the mind must receive a degree of enlargement and obtain a little strength by a slight exertion of its thinking powers; besides, even the productions that are only addressed to the imagination, raise the reader a little above the gross gratification of appetites, to which the mind has not given a shade of delicacy.

Moralists have unanimously agreed, that unless virtue be nursed by liberty, it will never attain due strength—and what they say of man I extend to mankind, insisting that in all cases morals must be fixed on immutable principles; and, that the being cannot be termed rational or virtuous, who obeys any authority, but that of reason.

To render women truly useful members of society, I argue that they should be led, by having their undertakings cultivated on a large scale, to acquire a rational affection for their country, founded on knowledge, because it is obvious that we are little interested about what we do not understand. And to render this general knowledge of due importance, I have endeavoured to shew that private duties are never properly fulfilled unless the under-

---

[1] This was a favourite theme of Wollstonecraft's in her reviews for the *Analytical Review.*

standing enlarges the heart; and that public virtue is only an aggregate of private. But, the distinctions established in society undermine both, by beating out the solid gold of virtue, till it becomes only the tinsel-covering of vice.

That women at present are by ignorance rendered foolish or vicious, is, I think, not to be disputed; and, that the most salutary effects tending to improve mankind might be expected from a REVOLUTION in female manners, appears, at least, with a face of probability, to rise out of the observation. For as marriage has been termed the parent of those endearing charities which draw man from the brutal herd, the corrupting intercourse that wealth, idleness, and folly, produce between the sexes, is more universally injurious to morality than all the other vices of mankind collectively considered.

Contending, therefore, that the sexual distinction which men have so warmly insisted upon, is arbitrary, I have dwelt on an observation, that several sensible men, with whom I have conversed on the subject, allowed to be well founded; and it is simply this, that the little chastity to be found amongst men, and consequent disregard of modesty, tend to degrade both sexes; and further, that the modesty of women, characterized as such, will often be only the artful veil of wantonness instead of being the natural reflection of purity, till modesty be universally respected.

From the tyranny of man, I firmly believe, the greater number of female follies proceed; and the cunning, which I allow makes at present a part of their character, I likewise have repeatedly endeavoured to prove, is produced by oppression.

Asserting the rights which women in common with men ought to contend for, I have not attempted to extenuate their faults; but to prove them to be the natural consequence of their education and station in society. If so, it is reasonable to suppose that they will change their character, and correct their vices

and follies, when they are allowed to be free in a physical, moral, and civil sense.

(1792)

MARY HAYS
*Appeal to the Men of Great Britain
on Behalf of Women.*[1]

ADVERTISEMENT TO THE READER.

IT is necessary to inform the reader, that the greater part of the following pages, was written and arranged nearly in the present form, some years ago. The subject though at all times of general concern, had then likewise some degree of novelty to recommend it; in so far at least as that no work had appeared, I believe, for the professed purpose of advancing and defending the pretensions of women, to a superior degree of consideration in society, to that which they at present enjoy.

THE public too at that time was at leisure, and seemed disposed, to encourage the endeavours of individuals to instruct or amuse; and in such circumstances the following little work, without any claim to extraordinary attention, except in the interesting nature of its subject, might have come in for its share of notice, with other things of the same degree of merit. But times and circumstances are now so different, that some apology is necessary for obtruding it on the public; after having kept it back at a moment, when it might have been better received.

---

[1] Mary Hays (1760–1843), a novelist and critic, Hays combined a radical Enlightenment faith in rational inquiry with a compelling emphasis on sympathy. In 1793 she published *Letters and Essays, Moral and Miscellaneous*, whose radical tenor reflected the advice of her mentor, Mary Wollstonecraft. *Appeal to the Men of Great Britain on Behalf of Women* returned to the feminist aspects of this earlier, wide-ranging work, in what had by 1798 become a backlash against women radicals. She was a regular contributor to the *Monthly Magazine* on a range of topics.

While I was pursuing my work with all the enthusiasm common to a first attempt, and to my natural disposition; a gentleman of distinguished abilities and learning, but not one of those who wish to confine all knowledge to their own sex, sent me—Letters from *Barbary, France, Spain, Portugal,* &c. by an English officer.[1] Perhaps the most singular part of that very sensible and spirited performance, is the author's opinions with regard to women; and I was at first highly flattered to find that the sentiments I had pre-conceived on that subject, were *nearly* similar to those of one, whose abilities, in every point of view, appeared so respectable. And who was certainly less liable to prejudices, which—however much I endeavoured to guard against them,—I always feared might influence my own opinions.

These were my first reflections on reading Major Jardine's Letters; but those which succeeded were not so agreeable, and retarded for a considerable time the finishing of this sketch. For, it could not but occur to me, that, as he had—though, but incidentally—treated the subject of it so well; those who should come immediately after him, could have little claim to notice.

As it is not however an easy matter to give up a favourite pursuit, upon which the mind has accustomed itself to dwell with complacency and partiality, after a pretty long recess I found it not difficult, to reason myself into my own good opinion again; and in fact, resumed the business, with more ardor than ever.

Just at this period, and when I had the goal almost in view; and, as if the very *demon* of *intelligence* were let loose, to persecute me with information, though in an obscure corner of the kingdom——the Rights of Woman by Miss Wollstonecraft was sent by a friend, for my perusal.

[1] Lieutenant-Colonel Alexander Jardin (d. 1799), *Letters from Barbary, France, Spain, Portugal,* &c. By an English officer. 1788.

Mortified still more I must candidly acknowledge, by this second anticipation; because by its pointed title, and declared purpose, it was more likely than even the first, to impede the success of an attempt, which now had less claim to that novelty which ensures at least temporary notice; I flung aside my little sketch in favour of women, with a degree of disdain, which, I begin to hope, it did not deserve. I likewise hope, nay I most sincerely believe, that one spark of envy, did not lurk at the bottom of this conduct; though we have it from too good authority, that, the heart is desperately wicked. Be this as it may, sufficiently discouraged, and despairing of being able at the time, to give it the finishing touches with that degree of spirit, which, only, can render a work of any kind acceptable to the public; I laid aside all thoughts of it for a considerable time.

But though a still greater interval than the last elapsed, before I could prevail on myself to finish the sketch as it now appears; yet I had gone too far, and bestowed too much pains upon it, easily to relinquish my purpose. Indeed, when we consider how many books are written, and read upon every subject—I may rather say how many myriads of books of every different degree of merit, are absolutely necessary, to suit the different tastes, capacities, and judgments of mankind—before the public opinion is influenced to any great degree, far more before any new doctrine can be firmly established; there is perhaps no great presumption in supposing, that each may in some degree, more or less, have its effect.

I would have it understood, however, that I found my pretensions, whatever they may be, rather upon the merits, than,—as is too often the case among writers,—upon the alleged defects of those who have treated the same subjects. So far indeed, are works of very superior merit, from superseding the necessity of others; that on the contrary, it is too evident, that such are not *always* the most popular; or, at least that some time generally elapses before they become so. That which raises them in the eyes of the few, either sets them beyond the reach of the multitude; or, what is infinitely worse, renders them obnoxious to its hatred and persecution. If any thing indeed can be objected to, in the works to which I have alluded, it is an error but too commonly attendant on genius; who seldom designs, by managing, and sympathizing with, the prejudices of mankind, to make new and unexpected truths palatable to common minds.

YET to manage with some degree of tenderness the prejudices of the generality of mankind; to respect even *these* till the multitude can be persuaded that ALL PREJUDICES are inimical to its happiness and interests; can neither justly be esteemed immoral, or deceitful. It is only doing that by gentle means and by degrees, which can never be done *well* by any other.

THE task be mine then, of presenting a sketch, which presumes to recommend this gradual reformation, this gentle emancipation from error; and from error too as *deeply rooted*, and as *fondly cherished*, as any in the whole circle of humanity.

INTRODUCTION

IT may at first sight appear absurd to address the following pages in behalf of women, to the men of Great Britain; whose apparent interest it perhaps is, in common with that of all other men, that things should remain on the footing they are. But as the men of Great Britain, to whom in particular I chuse to appeal, have to their everlasting honor, always been remarkable for an ardent love of liberty, and high in their pretensions to justice with regard to themselves; it is not to be believed, if the subject of the present work were taken into their serious consideration, but that the same sentiments would be

freely and generously extended to that class of beings, in whose cause I though unworthy appear. A class, upon whom the Almighty has stamped so sublime, so unequivocal marks of dignity and importance, that it is difficult to conceive why men should wish to counteract the benevolent designs of Providence in their favour; by leading them in chains, too often galling to their sensible and tender natures, those, whom heaven having in its wisdom formed their equals, could never surely, save in its wrath, doom to be the slaves of man.

KNOW, however, that I come not in the garb of an Amazon,[1] to dispute the field right or wrong; but rather in the humble attire of a petitioner, willing to submit the cause, to him who is both judge and party. Not as a fury flinging the torch of discord and revenge amongst the daughters of Eve; but as a friend and companion bearing a little taper to lead them to the paths of truth, of virtue, and of liberty. Or if it lead not to these, may it be utterly extinguished. "If the arguments here advanced appear chimerical, unfounded, or irrational; let it perish, let it be obliterated, let no memorial of it remain."[2]

WHAT WOMEN OUGHT TO BE

I APPREHEND, that independent of their maternal character;—I mean as mothers of the human race, which cannot be taken from them, though it is reduced to as low a pitch in point of consequence as possible;—that independent of this, women are considered in two ways only.—In the lower classes as necessary drudges—In the higher as the ornaments of society, the pleasing triflers, who flutter through life for the amusement of men, rather than for any settled purpose with regard to themselves; and are accordingly as it suits the caprice of their masters, the objects of adoration, or of torment, or

---

[1] A female warrior.

[2] Source unidentified.

of a passion unworthy of a name, or a place, in civilized society. In plain language, women are in all situations rendered merely the humble companions of men,—the tools of their necessities,—or the sport of their authority, of their prejudices, and of their passions. Women viewed in this degrading light, are perhaps as well off with the trifling and corruptive mode of education generally allowed them; as with one which would rouse those talents, and increase that desire after knowledge, with which God and nature has from the beginning, so liberally endowed them.

WHEN men however deign to argue more to the point, they allege, that when women are educated too much upon an equality with them, it renders them—presuming and conceited;—unless[1] in their families;—masculine, and consequently disgusting in their manners.

THESE are very heavy charges indeed; but women do not allow them to be well founded, nor unanswerable.

THE first objection advanced, is,—that knowledge and learning render women presuming and conceited. I beg leave to say that both reason and experience contradict this assertion; for it has never been proven, that knowledge in a general view, favoured or produced presumption, though in particular instances it may no doubt be found to have done so. Much it must be confessed depends on the subject acted upon, and knowledge may be compared with respect to its effects on the mind, to wholesome food upon the body; for a diseased habit will turn the purest aliments to corruption, instead of nourishment. But this only confirms what has been so often and so well said, that there is no rule without exception.

INDEED knowledge, learning, and all solid acquirements, are as yet so very rare among the female sex, that it is by no means surprising if some who really possess these advantages, know it, and feel it. Nor is it surprising, nor perhaps altogether out of nature, though by no means commendable or pleasing, if they at times endeavour to let others know it, and feel it too. Yet to the honor of both sexes be it said,—to the honor of human nature and learning be it spoken,—instances of proud and presumptuous persons of real abilities and solid acquirements, are but rare, in comparison of the numbers; who are the delight of their friends, the ornaments of society, and the benefactors of mankind. It were possible to enumerate names well known to the world, and dear to their own circle, who are equally admired in an amiable, as in a literary point of view. Suffice it to say, that the experience of the present times as well as of past ages fully justify us in maintaining, that a few exceptions granted, which prove nothing, knowledge does improve every one, man or woman, who is blessed with common sense for a foundation—that presumption and conceit are rather the offspring of ignorance than knowledge—and that knowledge of almost every description is better than ignorance. Always without a doubt however preferring, that kind most suited to situation and circumstances; and which as far as human foresight can judge, is most likely to be useful and ornamental through life.

THE charge which we shall next endeavour to prove erroneous, is, that the pursuit and possession of knowledge, occasion in women, a neglect of their families and domestic duties. Perhaps this is the charge of all others the worst founded; the consequence the least likely to happen were we to trust to theory, and the most decidedly contradicted when we appeal to facts and experience. Surely knowledge, learning, and science, give a solidity to the mind, a turn for reflection, which must be highly favorable to the best feelings of humanity, and consequently to the most amiable of all the affec-

---

[1] Probably intended to be "useless."

tions, the parental. Not that I mean to say that women are wanting in this virtue, who have no pretensions to those; though to say the truth, the parental fondness of many mothers, often more resembles animal instinct, blind partiality, and personal vanity, than that rational affection which leads to the improvement, as well as to the preservation of the human species. And when added to that ignorance of the powers of the mind, to which most part of the female sex are condemned, we take into consideration, the flimsy, inconsequent education generally bestowed upon them; we cannot be surprised if instead of training, it unfits them for the important task,—the serious attention— requisite to form the minds, as well as to care for the bodies of their children.

THAT eternal round of giddy intercourse with the world, in which it is the fashionable mode for fashionable females to pass their time,—and indeed the *rabbia*[1] has reached almost all ranks but the industrious poor;—those frivolous, yet expensive amusements, in which they place their chief delight, and in which to say the truth they are but too well kept in countenance by the men; are totally inconsistent with attention to domestic concerns. They must therefore of course in a great degree neglect their offspring and families, and commit to others these, which they are disposed to sacrifice to those wretched substitutes for duty, commonly called pleasures; and those indeed totally engage their time, and their thoughts. For, it is too true that minds occupied by trifles, are as completely engrossed by them; as minds of a superior cast, by the most momentous concerns.

HAVING said as much on the two first charges, as the limited nature of this sketch will admit; I shall now consider the last—That knowledge renders women masculine, and consequently disgusting in their manners.—In doing this I think my argument will prove a two-edged sword. I think it must prove,

that neither has learning a direct, and inevitable tendency to render women masculine; nor if it did so, would it render them consequently, and infallibly disagreeable to the men.

PERHAPS to define the terms used, is one of the first duties of writers; and if they always understood themselves, and made their readers clearly comprehend the precise meaning of them, much labored reasoning, and many false and presumptuous conclusions might be spared. For example when we speak of a masculine woman, it is considered as a term of reproach; yet we do not consider whether it deserves to be so or not. We allow ourselves to be run away with by a vague idea,—an undefined term—of which we do not take the trouble to know the precise meaning, or the exact bounds.

IF therefore we are to understand by a masculine woman, one who emulates those virtues and accomplishments, which as common to human nature, are common to both sexes; the attempt is natural, amiable, and highly honorable to that woman, under whatever name her conduct may be disguised or censured. For even virtue and truth, may be misnamed, disguised, and censured; but they cannot change their natures, in compliance with the tyranny of fashion and prejudice. These may indeed for a time throw a shade over them; but this once removed we find them still the same,—IMMUTABLE, and ETERNAL. It is in vain perhaps therefore, honestly speaking and impartially, to attempt to make any very serious distinctions, between the virtues and accomplishments of the sexes. We may indeed dress out these somewhat differently, to suit a reigning taste, or through love of variety, and we may call this manners; by which if women can please the other sex; without materially injuring themselves, they ought most certainly to do so. But such vain distinctions vanish before the superior light of reason and religion; and women in all the different stations in life, find scope for the exercise

---

[1] Rage.

of every virtue, of which human nature is capable. And under the passive characters of humility, resignation, and absolute submission to their authority—under these do men expect to see exercised and exerted—every thing which they in their proud moments arrogate to themselves, and fondly claim as sole proprietors.

If then my reasoning is well founded it appears, that if we use the term masculine woman, for characters such as I have been describing, it is undeniably true, that knowledge does naturally produce such. But I will not so far insult the common sense of men,—to whose common sense indeed and humanity, the whole of this Appeal is addressed,—I will not I say so far insult it, as to suppose, even for a moment; that because a woman is rational, though perhaps in a superior degree than is absolutely necessary, that she must of course be disagreeable to them.

But if on the other hand we mean by a masculine woman, one who apes the exercises, the attributes, the unrestrained passions, and the numberless improprieties, which men fondly *chuse* to think suitable enough for their own sex—and which excesses to say the truth after all, chiefly distinguish their moral characters from those of women—I must say that knowledge has no tendency whatever to produce such aukward imitations; and I must confess, that such are masculine in the worst sense of the word, and as we should imagine consequently disagreeable. This however as we hinted before would be a hasty and ill-grounded conclusion, though apparently founded in reason, for the fact is otherwise; and the present age furnishes examples enough, that women may be truly masculine in their conduct and demeanor, without wounding the delicacy of the men. Nay that thus adorned, such women meet their full approbation, if at the moment the fluctuating tide of fashion be in their favor.

If then I have been able to prove, that those acquirements, the propriety, or at least the admission of which, I have been so ardently contending for, can have no unavoidable tendency to render women masculine in any disagreeable sense of the term, but much otherwise; and if I have been likewise able to prove that even if they had so, that this does not always, nay does not generally speaking, render them hateful in the eyes of the men; I think if I have proved all this, that the last objection that I have undertaken to examine, against women being educated with a view to the enlargement of their understandings, and the acquisition of knowledge in a superior degree—viz. that it renders them masculine, and consequently disgusting in their manner—falls with double force to the ground.

Without presumption then I hope I may be permitted to repeat; that neither knowledge, nor learning, nor science—with exceptions dictated by nature, by common sense, by delicacy and by peculiar circumstances, or by all united;—can reasonably, or generally speaking, be said to render women less amiable, than comparative ignorance, or superficial accomplishments.

(1798)

Priscilla Wakefield
Reflections on the Present Condition of the Female Sex; With Suggestions for its Improvement [1]

Chapter I.
Introductory observations, shewing the claim which Society has on Women to employ their time usefully; pointing out the characteristic perfection of the mental qualifications of both Sexes, and the necessity which there is for the talents of Women being directed to-

[1] Priscilla Wakefield (1751–1832), an author of instructive children's books and philanthropist active in causes for the working classes.

wards procuring an independent support; with an attempt to mark the line which bounds their exertions.

Introduction

I T is asserted by Doctor Adam Smith, that every individual is a burden upon the society to which he belongs, who does not contribute his share of productive labour for the good of the whole.[1] The Doctor, when he lays down this principle, speaks in general terms of man, as a being capable of forming a social compact for mutual defence, and the advantage of the community at large. He does not absolutely specify, that both sexes, in order to render themselves beneficial members of society, are equally required to comply with these terms; but since the female sex is included in the idea of the species, and as women possess the same qualities as men, though perhaps in a different degree, their sex cannot free them from the claim of the public for their proportion of usefulness. That the major part of the sex, especially of those among the higher orders, neglect to fulfil this important obligation, is a fact that must be admitted, and points out the propriety of an enquiry into the causes of their deficiency.

In civilized nations it has ever been the misfortune of the sex to be too highly elevated, or too deeply depressed; now raised above the condition of mortals, upon the score of their personal attractions; and now debased below that of reasonable creatures, with respect to their intellectual endowments. The result of this improper treatment has been a neglect of the mental powers, which women really possess, but know not how to exercise; and they have been contented to barter the dignity of reason, for the imaginary privilege of an empire, of the existence of which they can entertain no reasonable hope beyond the duration of youth and beauty.

Of the few who have raised themselves to pre-eminence by daring to stray beyond the accustomed path, the envy of their own sex, and the jealousy or contempt of the other, have too often been the attendants; a fate which doubtless has deterred others from attempting to follow them, or emulate, even in an inferior degree, the distinction they have attained.

But not withstanding these disadvantages, and others of less perceptible influence, the diffusion of christianity, and the progress of civilization, have raised the importance of the female character; and it has become a branch of philosophy, not a little interesting, to ascertain the offices which the different ranks of women are required to fulfil. Their rights and their duties have lately occupied the pens of writers of eminence; the employments which may properly exercise their faculties, and fill up their time in a useful manner, without encroaching upon those professions, which are appropriate to men, remain to be defined. There are many branches of science, as well as useful occupations, in which women may employ their time and their talents, beneficially to themselves and to the community, without destroying the peculiar characteristic of their sex, or exceeding the most exact limits of modesty and decorum. Whatever obliges them to mix in the public haunts of men, or places the young in too familiar a situation with the other sex; whatever is obnoxious to the delicacy and reserve of the female character, or destructive, in the smallest degree, to the strictest moral purity, is inadmissable.

But, under these restrictions, there may be found a multitude of objects adapted to the useful exertions of female talent, which it will be the principal design of these Reflections to point out, after making some remarks upon the present state of female education, and suggesting some improvements towards its reformation.

---

[1] This is a general summary of Smith's argument in *The Wealth of Nations*, rather than a particular quote.

Chapter VI.

Lucrative Employments for the first and second classes suggested, recommending as agreeable means of procuring a respectable support,—Literature.—Paintings; Historic, Portrait, and Miniature.—Engraving.— Statuary.—Modelling.—Music.—Landscape.— Gardening.—With Strictures on a Theatrical Life.

Transitions in private life from affluence to poverty, like the fable pageantry of death, from their frequency, produce no lasting impressions upon the beholders. Unexpected misfortunes befall an acquaintance, who has been caressed in the days of prosperity: the change is lamented, and she is consoled by the visits of her friends, in the first moments of affliction: she sinks gradually into wretchedness; she becomes obscure, and is forgotten. The case would be different, could avocations be suggested, which would enable these, who suffer such a reverse of fortune, to maintain a decent appearance, and procure them a degree of respect.

Numerous difficulties arise in the choice of occupations for the purpose. They must be such as are neither laborious nor servile, and they must of course be productive, without requiring a capital.

For these reasons, pursuits which require the exercise of intellectual, rather than bodily powers, are generally the most eligible.

Literature affords a respectable and pleasing employment, for those who possess talents, and an adequate degree of mental cultivation. For although the emolument is precarious, and seldom equal to a maintenance, yet if the attempt be tolerably successful, it may yield a comfortable assistance in narrow circumstances, and beguile many hours, which might otherwise be passed in solitude or unavailing regret. The fine arts offer a mode of subsistence, congenial to the delicacy of the most refined minds, and they are peculiarly adapted by their elegance, to the gratification of taste. The perfection of every species

of painting is attainable by women, from the representation of historic facts, to the minute execution of the miniature portrait, if they will bestow sufficient time and application for the acquisition of the principles of the art, in the study of those models, which have been the means of transmitting the names and character of so many men, to the admiration of posterity. The successful exercise of this imitative art requires invention, taste, and judgment: in the two first, the sex are allowed to excel, and the last may be obtained by a perseverance in examining, comparing, and reflecting upon the works of those masters, who have copied nature in her most graceful forms.

The stage is a profession, to which many women of refined manners, and a literary turn of mind have had recourse. Since it has been customary for females to assume dramatic characters, there appears to have been full as great a proportion of women, who have attained celebrity, among those who have devoted themselves to theatrical life, as of the other sex; a fact which argues that there is no inequality of genius, in the sexes, for the imitative arts; the observation may operate as a stimulant to women to those pursuits which are less objectionable than the stage; which is not mentioned for the purpose of recommending it, but of proving that the abilities of the female sex are equal to nobler labours than are usually undertaken by women. The profession of an actress is indeed most unsuitable to the sex in every point of view, whether it be considered with respect to the courage requisite to face an audience, or the variety of situations incident to it, which expose moral virtue to the most severe trials.

The presiding over seminaries for female education, is likewise a suitable employment for those, whose minds have been enlarged by liberal cultivation, whilst the under parts of that profession may be more suitably filled by persons whose early views have been contracted within narrower limits. After all that can be suggested by general remarks, the different circumstances of individuals must decide the profession most convenient to them. But it is a consolatory reflection, that amidst the daily vicissitudes of human life, from which no rank is exempt, there are resources, from which aid may be drawn, without derogating from the true dignity of a rational being.

Chapter VII.

On the duties, attainments, and employments of Women of the third Class.—Censuring the giving of greater rewards to Men than Women, for similar exertions of time, labour, and ingenuity; and the necessity there is for ladies of rank encouraging their own sex.—Recommending the teaching girls, the serving of retail shops; the undertaking for the female sex; turnery, and farming, as eligible means of support; with an extract from Sir F. M. Eden, of an account of a Female Farmer.[1]

THE next class of women which comes under animadversion,[2] includes several gradations, involving the daughters of every species of tradesmen below the merchant, and above the meaner mechanic: consequently, very different degrees of refinement befit the individuals who form the extreme links, which are separated, insensibly as it were, from the other divisions towards which they approximate.

Reading fluently, and spelling correctly will form a sufficient knowledge of the English language; and as their avocations will not admit of an extensive course of reading, the books selected for them should be such as are addressed to the understanding, rather than to the imagination. A complete acquaintance with the practical parts of scripture is essentially

necessary, and should be taught them daily, as lessons for the conduct of life.[†] Plays and novels, with every work tending to inflame the passions, and implant sentiments of the omnipotence of love and beauty, should be most carefully excluded from their sight, AS CONTAINING A BANEFUL POISON, DESTRUCTIVE OF EVERY PRINCIPLE THAT IS ADAPTED TO DEFEND THEM FROM THE ALLUREMENTS OF VICE. The relative situation of the four continents, and the kingdoms which they contain; the principal cities, rivers, and mountains of Europe, with the manners of the different nations, and the produce of each, both natural and artificial, and a more accurate knowledge of the divisions and chief towns of our own island, would form a study, at once useful, entertaining, and unobjectionable. A general acquaintance with the leading events of English history, collected from some well written compendium, might also be admitted as an occasional recreation from business.

Civilization would be much advanced, by bestowing such a rational mode of education upon this order of the sex, as shall teach them just notions of their duties and offices, and of the proper place they hold in society. Ignorance, and a vague manner of thinking, are the springs of many errors in conduct among them, which are increased by pernicious publications, containing improbable

---

[†] *The following books are suitable to form part of the library of young women, who have but little leisure to devote to reading:*
Trimmer's Bible, with Annotations and Reflections.
Œconomy of Human Life.
Penn's Reflections and Maxims.
Hanway's Virtue in Humble Life.
Sturm's Reflection for every Day in the Year.
Barbauld's Hymns.
Watts's Poems.
A Collection of Poems for young Persons, by Rachel Barclay.
Aikin's England delineated.
Robinson Crusoe.
Trimmer's Family Magazine.
Trimmer's Servant's Friend, and two Farmers.
Hannah More's Repository.

---

[1] Sir Frederick Morton Eden (1766–1809), author of *The State of the Poor* (1797).

[2] Consideration.

fictions, dressed up in the imagery of glowing lan-guage, filled with false sentiments of delicacy and sensibility, and presenting models of female perfec-tion unfit for their imitation; for nothing can be more distant from the plain, sober, useful qualities of a housewife, than the excellencies of the heroine of a novel. Errors of opinion are of all kinds the most dangerous, as they lead to improper conduct, even when the intentions are upright; whilst the modest virtues of industry, frugality, and simplicity of behaviour, are regarded with contempt, in vain will the practice of them be enforced. The refinement of manners and extravagant appearance of young women of small expectations is a discouragement to marriage; for what prudent tradesman would venture to burthen himself with a wife, who, by her mistaken ambition of gentility, would consume all the pro-duce of his industry, without contributing her endeavours to increase the common stock.

(1798)

MARY ANN RADCLIFFE
The Female Advocate; or, an Attempt to Recover the Rights of Women From Male Usurpation.[1]

TO THE READER

So various and complicated are the scenes of this life, that seven years have elapsed since the fol-lowing pages were written; a period, perhaps, more favourable for publishing than the present; but timidity, or other hinderances, have repeatedly prevented their appearing before the public, during which time, the author hoped some more able advocate would have taken up the cause, to do justice to a subject of such importance to society at large, and particularly a much injured part thereof. For, alas! it is too well known, that female educa-tion in general is confined within very narrow limits, and seldom permitted to extend to classical accomplishments.

The writer of this volume being a female, with only a female's education, is sufficiently aware of her inadequacy to the undertaking; but trusts the importance of the subject will claim some attention; at the same time, reposing a full confidence in the candour and unbounded goodness of some part of her readers at least, she is once more encouraged to resume the pen, to add or amend such remarks as the nature of the times and circumstances require, and at length has so far surmounted her timidity, as to submit the following sheets, with all their imper-fections, to the inspection of a generous public, who are more ready to appreciate the works of individu-als from the rectitude of intention, than the beauty of composition. The attempt, she must acknowl-edge, has cost her many a painful emotion; for, surrounded by all the disadvantages peculiar to the sex, seems to her to require no small share of cour-age, and which, indeed nothing but the importance of the subject should have induced her to encoun-ter.

All women possess not the Amazonian spirit of a Wolstonecraft; but, indeed, unremitted oppres-sion is sometimes a sufficient apology for their throwing off the gentle garb of a female, and assum-ing some more masculine appearance; yet, when the curtain of misrepresentation is once withdrawn, it is to be hoped (not doubted) that the cause of complaint will quickly be removed.

---

[1] Mary Anne Radcliffe (*c.* 1746–1810). *The Female Advocate* emerged out of Radcliffe's struggle to provide for her family through a series of frustrating ventures including running a school, selling patent medi-cines, and working as a governess, where she was the victim of sexual harassment.

Part First.
The Fatal Consequences of Men Traders Engrossing Womens' Occupation.

When we look around us, nothing is more conspicuous in the eyes of the world, than the distresses of women; I do not say those whom a kind Providence hath placed under the immediate care of a tender father, or an affectionate and kind husband; or, *by chance*, a friend, or brother. But these, alas! comprise only one part of the community. Notwithstanding all are of the same nature, and were formed by the same Divine Power, yet their comforts differ very widely indeed. Still, as women seem formed by nature to seek protection from man, why, in the name of justice, refuse the boon? Does it not become highly worthy the attention of men in general, to consider in what manner to redress the grievances *already within their notice*?

But before I proceed with my Hunt for erecting any established plan, for the restoration of peace and happiness to the, perhaps, once happy, but now most miserable of beings, I cannot help making a remark, that, in order to lay a good foundation, every builder must find it necessary, first, to remove the rubbish out of the way—Therefore let us proceed to the ground-work of the design; and, before any further steps are taken, ask, What can be said of men-milliners, men-mantuamakers, and men stay-makers? besides all the numerous train of other professions, such as hairdressers, &c. &c.; all of which occupations are much more calculated for women than men. But, thanks to the fashions of the times, (which have nearly exploded that disgraceful custom of men dressing ladies' heads), by the introduction of all the brutuses and chignons,[1] of so many denominations, which have found their way to the toilets of all descriptions of females.—Where is there a Stevens now?[2] was there ever a wider field for the display of his talents? Yet, if perukes[3] are the fashion of the day, what is to prevent a woman from displaying her taste upon a lady's head as well as a man, who is much better calculated for a more masculine employment.

"Look," says an observer, "to the shops of perfumers, toymen, and others of a similar situation; and, above all, look to the haberdashery magazines, where from ten to twenty fellows, six feet high, may be counted in each, to the utter exclusion of poor females, who could sell a toothpick, or a few ribbons, just as well."

Then, pass no longer, so unconcernedly and without notice, the distressed and wretched situation of the most helpless part of the creation, who are not impowered by any means whatever to defend themselves; having, by the strong power of custom, so long been deemed unworthy of notice.

O! may that auspicious day arrive, when the curtain may be withdrawn, and the tragic scene be exposed to open view; when every true Briton, who reveres his maker, or his king, may cheerfully exert himself in the general cause.

What says the Vagrant Act?[4]—"Persons who beg in the streets are idle and disorderly; and any person who apprehends and carries such a beggar before a justice, shall receive five shillings, when the said justice may commit them to a house of correction."

---

[1] Brutus: a rough-cropped type of wig, after the Roman politician and general; Chignon: a knot or roll of hair worn at the back of the head by women.

[2] In 1764 a relatively minor actor named George Alexander Stevens (1710–84) had an enormous popular success with his *Lecture on Heads*, a monologue which satirized, amongst other things, the popularity of wigs. The fashion for wigs declined in subsequent years but returned in the 1790s, thus threatening women's employment as hairdressers.

[3] Wigs.

[4] The Rogues, Vagabonds, and other Idle and Disorderly Persons Act (1744) offered a reward of five shillings for apprehending anyone who had abandoned their wives and children, lived idly and refused work or begged alms.

However shocking the sentence, what numbers of these poor objects have been dragged away by the ruthless hand of the unfeeling savage, to some loathsome prison without regard to the more refined or delicate sensations of one or another? Good heavens? there surely needs no Siddonian powers[1] to heighten such a tragic scene. She who, perhaps was reared with all the gentle softness and maternal care of a fond parent; she, who so lately was looked upon as an ornament to her sex, until the pressure of misfortunes compelled her to seek for bread, to be at once confined in a dark prison, there to be obliged to hear all the opprobrious language of the very lowest set of beings, and that under a storm of oaths and imprecations, which, of itself, must pierce her very soul. There to have her ears grated with the rattling of bolts and bars, and all the adamantine fetters of misery. Good God! is it possible we can see our fellow creatures debased so low! Can we see the tender and delicate frame, which was formerly accustomed to ease and tranquillity, and which was formed by nature to participate in others misfortunes! can we let these innocent and helpless beings pass unnoticed, and not commiserate their distress, and ask, from whence the cause?—No! it is impossible the eyes can any longer be shut to their sufferings, or the ears to their piercing cries of "Have pity on me! Oh! ye, my friends, have pity on me!"

That political and private happiness are invariably connected, is beyond a doubt; and that the morals of this nation are very corrupt, is but too visible, from the vast numbers of disgraceful women who infest the face of the country. As for the number of these miserable beings, it cannot be an easy matter to ascertain: but suppose, from the prodigious numbers, that are seen scattered about, like sheep having no shepherd, that in London, for example, there are five or six thousand: Nay; I have either read, or heard it said, ten thousand! but how that

calculation can be made, I shall not take upon me to say; yet, suppose we call it half that number; are not five thousand destitute females too many to suffer through so poor a cause, and will not a much less number suffice to contaminate the morals of more than half the youths in town, and prove a source of destructive oppression to a vast number of inhabitants? for, without morals, how can we expect happiness, or what is to support the public good?

(1799)

HANNAH MORE
Strictures on the Modern System of Female Education.[2]

INTRODUCTION

IT is a singular injustice which is often exercised towards women, first to give them a most defective Education, and then to expect from them the most undeviating purity of conduct;—to train them in such a manner as shall lay them open to the most dangerous faults, and then to censure them for not proving faultless. Is it not unreasonable and unjust, to express disappointment if our daughters should, in their subsequent lives, turn out precisely that very kind of character for which it should be evident to an unprejudiced by-stander that the whole scope

---

[1] Sarah Siddons, heralded as the greatest actress of the age.

[2] Hannah More (1745–1833) has frequently been remembered as Mary Wollstonecraft's conservative antagonist, but this appraisal has been complicated by a recognition of the reformist vision implicit in her critique of fashionable society, a stance which had a surprising amount in common with Wollstonecraft's own middle-class antagonism to contemporary excesses. A growing estimation of More's importance also reflects an awareness of her central literary status in the period as a dramatist, poet, educational pioneer, and political writer in the Rights of Man and Rights of Woman controversies, but also in the struggle to abolish the slave trade. She was an eminent member of the Blue Stocking Circle, a group of learned women committed to the eighteenth-century ideal of polite conversation.

and tenor of their instruction had been systematically preparing them?

Some reflections on the present erroneous system are here with great deference submitted to public consideration. The Author is apprehensive that she shall be accused of betraying the interests of her sex by laying open their defects: but surely, an earnest wish to turn their attention to objects calculated to promote their true dignity, is not the office of an enemy: so to expose the weakness of the land as to suggest the necessity of internal improvement, and to point out the means of effectual defence, is not treachery, but patriotism.

Let it not be suspected that the Author arrogantly conceives herself to be exempt from that natural corruption of the heart which it is one chief object of this slight work to exhibit; that she superciliously erects herself into the impeccable censor of her sex and of the world; as if from the critic's chair she were coldly pointing out the faults and errors of another order of beings, in whose welfare she had not that lively interest which can only flow from the tender and intimate participation of fellow-feeling.

With a deep self-abasement arising from a strong conviction of being indeed a partaker in the same corrupt nature; together with a full persuasion of the many and great defects of these Volumes, and a sincere consciousness of her inability to do justice to a subject which, however, a sense of duty impelled her to undertake, she commits herself to the candour of that Public which has so frequently, in her instance, accepted a right intention as a substitute for a powerful performance.

BATH
March 14, 1799.

Chap. I.

Address to women of rank and fortune, on the effects of their influence on society.—Suggestions for the exertion of it in various instances.

THE general state of civilized society depends more than those are aware, who are not accustomed to scrutinize into the springs of human action, on the prevailing sentiments and habits of women, and on the nature and degree of the estimation in which they are held.

In this moment of alarm and peril,[1] I would call on them with a "warning voice,"[2] which should stir up every latent principle in their minds, and kindle every slumbering energy in their hearts; I would call on them to come forward and contribute their full and fair proportion towards the saving of their country. But I would call on them to come forward, without departing from the refinement of their character, without derogating from the dignity of their rank, without blemishing the delicacy of their sex: I would call them to the best and most appropriate exertion of their power, to raise the depressed tone of public morals; to awaken the drowsy spirit of religious principle; and to re-animate the dormant powers of active piety. They know too well how imperiously they give the law to manners, and with how despotic a sway they fix the standard of fashion. But this is not enough; this is a low mark, a prize not worthy of their high and holy calling. For, on the use which women of the superior class may be disposed to make of that power delegated to them by the courtesy of custom, by the honest gallantry of the heart, by the imperious controul of virtuous affections, by the habits of civilized states, by the usages of polished society; on the use, I say,

---

[1] Although the threat of revolution had diminished in England by 1799, they remained in what had become a protracted war with France.

[2] The Christian concept of a divine warning. A call for repentance.

which they shall hereafter make of this influence, will depend, in no low degree, the well-being of those states, and the virtue and happiness, nay perhaps the very existence of that society.

At this period, when our country can only hope to stand by opposing a bold and noble *unanimity* to the most tremendous confederacies against religion and order, and governments, which the world ever saw; what an accession would it bring to the public strength, could we prevail on beauty, and rank, and talents, and virtue, confederating their several powers, to come forward with a patriotism at once firm and feminine for the general good! I am not sounding an alarm to female warriors, or exciting female politicians: I hardly know which of the two is the most disgusting and unnatural character. Propriety is to a woman what the great Roman critic says action is to an orator;[1] it is the first, the second, the third requisite. A woman may be knowing, active, witty, and amusing; but without propriety she cannot be amiable.

I do not wish to bring back the frantic reign of chivalry, nor to reinstate women in that fantastic empire in which they then sat enthroned in the hearts, or rather in the imaginations of men. Common sense is an excellent material of universal application, which the sagacity of latter ages has seized upon, and rationally applied to the business of common life. But let us not forget, in the insolence of acknowledged superiority, that it was religion and chastity, operating on the romantic spirit of those times, which established the despotic sway of woman; and though she now no longer looks down on her adoring votaries, from the pedestal to which an absurd idolatry had lifted her, yet let her remember that it is the same religion and chastity which

once raised her to such an elevation, that must still furnish the noblest energies of her character.

While we lawfully ridicule the absurdities which we have abandoned, let us not plume ourselves on that spirit of novelty which glories in the opposite extreme. If the manners of the period in question were affected, and if the gallantry was unnatural, yet the tone of virtue was high.

But in an age when inversion is the order of the day, the modern idea of improvement does not consist in altering, but extirpating. We do not reform, but subvert. We do not correct old systems, but demolish them, fancying that when every thing shall be new it will be perfect. Not to have been wrong, but to have been at all is the crime. Excellence is no longer considered as an experimental thing which is to grow gradually out of observation and practice, and to be improved by the accumulating additions brought by the wisdom of successive ages. *Our* wisdom is not a child perfected by gradual growth, but a goddess which starts at once, full grown, mature, armed cap-a-pee,[2] from the heads of our modern thunderers.

In animadverting[3] farther on the reigning evils which the times more particularly demand that women of rank and influence should repress, Christianity calls upon them to bear their decided testimony against every thing which is notoriously contributing to the public corruption. It calls upon them to banish from their dressing rooms, (and oh, that their influence could banish from the libraries of their sons and husbands!) that sober and unsuspected mass of mischief, which, by assuming the plausible names of Science, of Philosophy, of Arts, of Belles Lettres, is gradually administering death to the principles of those who would be on their guard, had the poison been labelled with its own pernicious title. Avowed attacks upon revelation are

[1] Asked what the chief part of an orator was, the Greek orator Demosthenes (*c.* 384–322 B.C.) answered, "action; what next? action; what next again? action. He said it that knew it best, and had by nature himself no advantage in that he commended." Found in Francis Bacon (1561–1626), "Of Boldness," *Essays or Counsels, Civil and Moral* (1625).

[2] From head to foot.

[3] Commenting critically.

more easily resisted, because the malignity is advertised. But who suspects the destruction which lurks under the harmless or instructive names of *General History*, *Natural History*, *Travels*, *Voyages*, *Lives*, *Encyclopedias*, *Criticism*, and *Romance?* Who will deny that many of these works contain much admirable matter; brilliant passages, important facts, just descriptions, faithful pictures of nature, and valuable illustrations of science? But while "the dead fly lies at the bottom,"[1] the whole will exhale a corrupt and pestilential stench.

Novels, which used chiefly to be dangerous in one respect, are now become mischievous in a thousand. They are continually shifting their ground, and enlarging their sphere, and are daily becoming vehicles of wider mischief. Sometimes they concentrate their force, and are at once employed to diffuse destructive politics, deplorable profligacy, and impudent infidelity. Rousseau was the first popular dispenser of this complicated drug, in which the deleterious infusion was strong, and the effect proportionably fatal. For he does not attempt to seduce the affections but through the medium of the principles.

The rare mischief of this author consists in his power of seducing by falsehood those who love truth, but whose minds are still wavering, and whose principles are not yet formed. He allures the warm-hearted to embrace vice, not because they prefer vice, but because he gives to vice so natural an air of virtue: and ardent and enthusiastic youth, too confidently trusting in their integrity and in their teacher, will be undone, while they fancy they are indulging in the noblest feelings of their nature. Many authors will more infallibly complete the ruin of the loose and ill-disposed; but perhaps (if I may change the figure) there never was a net of such exquisite art and inextricable workmanship, spread to entangle innocence and ensnare inexperience, as

the writings of Rousseau: and, unhappily, the victim does not even struggle in the toils, because part of the delusion consists in imagining that he is set at liberty.

Some of our recent popular publications have adopted all the mischiefs of this school, and the principal evil arising from them is, that the virtues they exhibit are almost more dangerous than the vices. The chief materials out of which these delusive systems are framed, are characters who practise superfluous acts of generosity, while they are trampling on obvious and commanded duties; who combine sentiments of honour with actions the most flagitious:[2] a high-tone of self-confidence, with a perpetual breach of self-denial: pathetic apostrophes to the passions, but no attempt to resist them. They teach that no duty exists which is not prompted by feeling: that impulse is the main spring of virtuous actions, while laws and principles are only unjust restraints; the former imposed by arbitrary men, the latter by the absurd prejudices of timorous and unenlightened conscience.

But there is a new and strong demand for the exertion of that power I am humbly endeavouring to direct to its true end. Those ladies who take the lead in society are loudly called upon to act as the guardians of public taste as well as public virtue, in an important instance. They are called upon to oppose with the whole weight of their influence, the irruption of those swarms of publications that are daily issuing from the banks of the Danube; which, like their ravaging predecessors of the darker ages, though with far other arms, are overrunning civilized society.

The writings of the French infidels were some years ago circulated in England with uncommon industry, and with some effect: but the good sense and good principles of the greater part of our countrymen resisted the attack, and rose superior to

---

[1] Ecclesiastes 10:1.

[2] Wicked or criminal.

the trial. Of the doctrines and principles here alluded to, the dreadful consequences, not only in the unhappy country where they originated and were almost universally adopted, but in every part of Europe where they have been received, have been such as to serve as a beacon to surrounding nations, if any warning can preserve them from destruction. In this country the subject is now so well understood, that every thing which issues from the *French* press is received with jealousy;[1] and a work, on the first appearance of its exhibiting the doctrines of Voltaire[2] and his associates, is rejected with indignation.

But let us not on account of this victory repose in confident security. The modern apostles of infidelity and immorality, little less indefatigable in dispersing their pernicious doctrines than the first apostles were in propagating gospel truths, have only changed their weapons, but they have by no means desisted from the attack. To destroy the principles of Christianity in this island, appears at the present moment to be their grand aim. Deprived of the assistance of the French press, they are now attempting to attain their object under the close and more artificial veil of German literature. Conscious that religion and morals will stand or fall together, their attacks are sometimes levelled against the one and sometimes against the other. With occasional strong professions of attachment to both of them, the feelings and the passions of the reader are engaged on the side of some one particular vice, or some one objection to revealed religion. Poetry as well as prose, romance as well as history; writings on philosophical as well as political subjects, have thus been employed to instil

the principles of *illuminatism*,[3] while incredible pains have been taken to obtain able translations of every book which it was supposed could be of use in corrupting the heart, or misleading the understanding. In many of these translations, the strongest passages, which, though well received in Germany, would have excited disgust in England, are wholly omitted, in order that the mind may be more certainly, though more slowly prepared for the full effect of the poison at another period.

Let not those to whom these pages are addressed deceive themselves, by supposing this to be a fable; but let them inquire most seriously whether I speak the truth, when I assert that the attacks of infidelity in Great Britain are at this moment principally directed against the female breast. Conscious of the influence of women in civil society, conscious of the effect which female infidelity produced in France, they attribute the ill success of their attempts in this country to their having been hitherto chiefly addressed to the male sex. They are now sedulously labouring to destroy the religious principles of women, and in too many instances they have fatally succeeded. For this purpose not only novels and romances have been made the vehicles of vice and infidelity, but the same allurement has been held out to the women of our country, which was employed by the original tempter to our first parent —Knowledge. Listen to the precepts of the new German enlightenment, and you need no longer remain in that situation in which Providence has placed you! Follow their examples, and you shall be permitted to indulge in all those gratifications

---

[1] Suspicion.

[2] The name assumed by François Marie Arouet (1694–1778) and by which he was generally known. French satirical writer known for his atheism and associated, in the 1790s, with radical Enlightenment skepticism that prepared the way for the French Revolution.

[3] A sarcastic reference to what conservatives derided as the philosophical pretensions of Enlightenment radicals. In *Proofs of a Conspiracy against all the Religions and Governments of Europe, Carried On in the Secret Meetings of Free Masons, Illuminati, and Reading Societies* (1798), John Robison denounced the Order of Illuminati, based in the Masonic Lodges in Germany, as a group of infidels intent on toppling all existing forms of government and religion.

which custom, not religion, has too far overlooked in the male sex!

We have hitherto spoken only of the German *writings;* but as there are multitudes who never read, equal pains have been taken to promote the same object through the medium of the stage: and this weapon is, of all others, that against which it is at the present moment the most important to warn my countrywomen. As a specimen of the German drama, it may not be unreasonable to offer a few remarks on the admired play of the *Stranger.*[1] In this piece the character of an *adultress*, which, in all periods of the world, ancient as well modern, in all countries heathen as well as christian, has hitherto been held in detestation, and has never been introduced but to be reprobated, is for the first time presented to our view in the most pleasing and fascinating colours.

About the same time that this first attempt at representing an adultress in an exemplary light was made by a German dramatist, which forms an era in manners; a direct vindication of adultery was for the first time attempted by a *woman*, a professed admirer and imitator of the German suicide Werter.[2] The Female Werter, as she is styled by her biographer,[3] asserts in a work, intitled "The Wrongs of Woman," that adultery is justifiable, and that the restrictions

placed on it by the laws of England constitute part of the *wrongs of woman.*[4]

But let us take comfort. These fervid pictures are not yet generally realised. These atrocious principles are not yet adopted into common practice. Though corruptions seem to be pouring in upon us from every quarter, yet there is still left among us a discriminating judgment. Clear and strongly marked distinctions between right and wrong still subsist.

CHAP. II.

On the education of women.—The prevailing system tends to establish the errors which it ought to correct.—Dangers arising from an excessive cultivation of the arts.

NOT a few of the evils of the present day arise from a new and perverted application of terms; among these perhaps, there is not one more abused, misunderstood, or misapplied, than the term *accomplishments*. This word in its original meaning, signifies *completeness, perfection*. But I may safely appeal to the observation of mankind, whether they do not meet with swarms of youthful females, issuing from our boarding schools, as well as emerging from the more private scenes of domestic education, who are introduced into the world, under the broad and universal title of *accomplished young ladies*, of *all* of

---

[1] *Menschenhass und Reue*, a 1789 hit by the German playwright, August von Kotzebue (1761–1819), it was adapted into English in 1798 as *The Stranger* by Richard Brinsley Sheridan. It set off a brief craze for German drama in the London theaters.

[2] The protagonist of Johann Goethe's novel, *The Sorrows of Young Werther* (1774), an extremely popular novel about a sensitive young artist who commits suicide because of unrequited love.

[3] In *Memoirs of the Author of a 'Vindication of the Rights of Woman'* (1798), which appeared the year after her death, Wollstonecraft's widowed husband William Godwin described her misery and two suicide attempts after the collapse of her prior relationship with Gilbert Imlay: "we not unfrequently meet with persons, whose minds seem almost of too fine a texture to encounter the vicissitudes of human affairs, to whom pleasure is transport, and disappointment is agony indescribable. This character is finely portrayed by the author of *The Sorrows of Werter*. Mary was in this respect a female Werter."

[4] In Wollstonecraft's unfinished novel, *Maria: Or, The Wrongs of Woman*, the protagonist, incarcerated after she attempts to separate from her libertine husband, George Venables, becomes romantically involved with a fellow prisoner, Henry Darnford. In the novel, Wollstonecraft had actually been careful to establish a more careful moral position than More's reference would suggest. Maria, having tolerated the infidelities and domestic tyranny of her husband, rejects the advances of one of her husband's friends. It is when she realizes that her husband has encouraged these advances in return for a £500 loan, that Maria determines to end the relationship, setting off the chain of events which culminates in her imprisonment. Godwin published the unfinished novel as part of *Posthumous Works of the Author of A Vindication of the Rights of Woman* (1798).

whom it cannot very truly and correctly be pronounced, that they illustrate the definition by a completeness which leaves nothing to be added, and a perfection which leaves nothing to be desired.

This phrenzy of accomplishments, unhappily, is no longer restricted within the usual limits of rank and fortune; the middle orders have caught the contagion, and it rages with increasing violence, from the elegantly dressed but slenderly portioned curate's daughter, to the equally fashionable daughter of the little tradesman, and of the more opulent, but not more judicious farmer. And is it not obvious, that as far as this epidemical mania has spread, this very valuable part of society declines in usefulness, as it rises in its unlucky pretensions to elegance? And this revolution of the manners of the middle class has so far altered the character of the age, as to be in danger of rendering obsolete the heretofore common saying, "that most worth and virtue are to be found in the middle station." For I do not scruple to assert, that in general, as far as my little observation has extended, this class of females, in what relates both to religious knowledge and to practical industry, falls far short both of the very high and the very low. Their new course of education, and the habits of life, and elegance of dress connected with it, peculiarly unfits them for the active duties of their own important condition; while, with frivolous eagerness and secondhand opportunities, they run to snatch a few of those showy accomplishments which decorate the great. This is done apparently with one or other of these views; either to make their fortune by marriage, or if that fail, to qualify them to become teachers of others: hence the abundant multiplication of superficial wives, and of incompetent governesses.

Fashion then, by one of her sudden and rapid turns, instantaneously struck out sensibility and affectation from the standing list of female perfections; and, by a quick touch of her magic wand, shifted the scene, and at once produced the bold and independent beauty, the intrepid female, the hoyden,[1] the huntress, and the archer; the swinging arms, the confident address, the regimental, and the four-in-hand.[2] These self-complacent heroines made us ready to regret their softer predecessors, who had aimed only at pleasing the other sex, while these aspiring fair ones struggled for the bolder renown of rivalling them. The project failed; for, whereas the former had sued for admiration, the latter challenged, seized, compelled it; but the men, as was natural, continued to prefer the more modest claimant to the sturdy competitor.

It were well if we, who have the advantage of contemplating the errors of the two extremes, were to look for truth where she is commonly to be found, in the plain and obvious middle path, equally remote from each excess; and, while we bear in mind that helplessness is not delicacy, let us also remember that masculine manners do not necessarily include strength of character nor vigour of intellect. Should we not reflect also, that we are neither to train up Amazons[3] nor Circassians,[4] but to form Christians? that we have to educate not only rational but accountable beings?

Would not a stranger be led to imagine by a view of the reigning mode of female education, that human life consisted of one universal holiday, and that the grand contest between the several competitors was, who should be most eminently qualified to excel, and carry off the prize, in the various shows and games which were intended to be exhibited in it? And to the exhibitors themselves, would he not be ready to apply Sir Francis Bacon's observation on the Olympian victors, that they were so excellent in these unnecessary things, that their perfection

---

[1] A boisterous or ill-mannered girl.

[2] A two-horse carriage requiring the driver to manage four reins.

[3] Female warrior.

[4] Tribes in the north Caucasus, whose women were noted for their beauty.

must needs have been acquired by the neglect of whatever was necessary?[1]

CHAP. XIII.
The practical uses of female education.—A comparative view of both sexes.

THE chief end to be proposed in cultivating the understandings of women, is to qualify them for the practical purposes of life. Their knowledge is not often like the learning of men, to be reproduced in some literary composition, nor ever in any learned profession; but it is to come out in conduct. A lady studies, not that she may qualify herself to become an orator or a pleader; not that she may learn to debate, but to act. She is to read the best books, not so much to enable her to talk of them, as to bring the improvement she derives from them to the rectification of her principles, and the formation of her habits. The great uses of study are to enable her to regulate her own mind, and to be useful to others.

It is because the superficial mode of their education furnishes them with a false and low standard of intellectual excellence, that women have sometimes become ridiculous by the unfounded pretensions of literary vanity: for it is not the really learned but the smatterers, who have generally brought their sex into discredit, by an absurd affectation, which has set them on despising the duties of ordinary life. There have not indeed been wanting (but the character is not common) *precieuses ridicules*[2] who, assuming a superiority to the sober cares which ought to occupy their sex, claim a lofty and supercilious exemption from the dull and plodding drudgeries

Of this dim speck called earth![3]

who have affected to establish an unnatural separation between talents and usefulness, instead of bearing in mind that talents are the great appointed instruments of usefulness; who act as if knowledge were to confer on woman a kind of fantastic sovereignty, which should exonerate her from female duties.

But *they* little understand the true interests of woman who would lift her from the duties of her allotted station, to fill with fantastic dignity a loftier but less appropriate niche. Nor do they understand her true happiness, who seek to annihilate distinctions from which she derives advantages, and to attempt innovations which would depreciate her real value. Each sex has its proper excellencies, which would be lost were they melted down into the common character by the fusion of the new philosophy.[4] Why should we do away distinctions which increase the mutual benefits and satisfactions of life? Whence, but by carefully preserving the original marks of difference stamped by the hand of the Creator, would be derived the superior advantage of mixed society? Have men no need to have their rough angles filed off, and their harshnesses and asperities smoothed and polished by assimilating with beings of more softness and refinement? Are the ideas of women naturally so very judicious, are their principles so invincibly firm, are their views so perfectly correct, are their judgments so completely exact, that there is occasion for no additional weight, no superadded strength, no increased clearness, none of that enlargement of mind, none of that additional invigoration which may be derived from the aids of the stronger sex? What identity could advantageously supersede an enlivening and interesting variety of character? Is it not then more wise as well as more honourable to move contentedly in the plain path which Prov-

---

[1] Unidentified.

[2] Precious fools.

[3] John Milton (1608–74), *Comus* (1634): 5–6.

[4] A sardonic term for a range of opinions that were associated with the Revolution.

idence has obviously marked out to the sex, and in which custom has for the most part rationally confirmed them, rather than to stray awkwardly, unbecomingly, and unsuccessfully, in a forbidden road? to be the lawful possessors of a lesser domestic territory, rather than the turbulent usurpers of a wider foreign empire? to be good originals, rather than bad imitators? to be the best thing of one's own kind, rather than an inferior thing even if it were of an higher kind? to be excellent women rather than indifferent men?

Is the author then undervaluing her own sex?—No. It is her zeal for their true *interests* which leads her to oppose their imaginary *rights*. It is her regard for their happiness which makes her endeavour to cure them of a feverish thirst for fame. A little Christian humility is worth all the wild metaphysical discussion which has unsettled the peace of vain women, and forfeited the respect of reasonable men. And the most elaborate definition of her ideal rights, and the most hardy measures for attaining them, are of less value in the eyes of an amiable woman, than "that meek and quiet spirit, which is in the sight of God of great price."[1]

Though it be one main object of this little work, rather to lower than to raise any desire of celebrity in the female heart; yet I would awaken it to a just sensibility to honest fame: I would call on women to reflect that our religion has not only made them heirs to a blessed immortality hereafter, but has greatly raised them in the scale of being here, by lifting them to an importance in society unknown to the most polished ages of antiquity.

(1799)

Thomas Gould
A Vindication of the Right Honourable Edmund Burke's Reflections on the Revolution in France, in Answer to All His Opponents [2]

I REJOICE in the French Revolution, only as it has given birth to the most eloquent production I have read in any language. From the nature of its subject, and the quality of the persons to whom it alludes, men naturally foretold a multiplicity of answers to its sublime author. Of each of these, I mean to take distinct separate notice; and shall begin with a pamphlet entitled "Vindication of the Rights of Men, in a Letter to the Right Honourable Edmund Burke, occasioned by his Reflections on the Revolution in France.[3]

The following paragraph is no contemptible instance of this lady's pathetic powers: "I cannot avoid expressing my surprize, that when you recommended our form of government, you did not caution the French against the arbitrary custom of pressing men into the sea service; you should have hinted to them that property in England is more secure than liberty; and not have concealed that the liberty of an honest mechanic, his all, is often sacrificed to secure the property of the rich, and how cruel it is to be obliged to pull a strange rope at the surly command of a tyrannic boy?" This entire paragraph is written in a strain of such exquisite feeling, that without pretending to any superior degree of inspiration, I will venture to say, I could nearly divine the peculiar case of this lady's bitter invective: the press was certainly very hot last summer: this lady, no doubt, has friends.

---

[1] Peter 1:3.4.

[2] Thomas Gould (*c.* 1766–1846), an Irish MP who had squandered his inheritance.

[3] By Mary Wollstonecraft.

After regaling her readers with no small portion of female inconstancy, such as asserting on one page, that Mr. Blackstone[1] was of her opinion, and in the next, saying he was of Mr. Burke's, she kindly allows, that Blackstone thought the *law* leaned to Mr. Burke's side of the question: this, however, she qualifies in the true Amazonian spirit. "But a blind respect for the law is no part of my creed." The ladies have no doubt the exclusive privilege of saying and doing what they please; but were any of those *gentlemen,* whose cruel situation this lady so feelingly describes in the foregoing paragraph, tempted to adopt her principle, and give life to it; I would not hesitate to assure him, that he would have but little occasion to dread the arbitrary custom of impressing men for the sea service; and instead of "being obliged to pull a strange rope, at the surly command of a tyrranic boy," he would be likely to partake of the sympathetic intercourse of virtue in distress at Botany Bay.[2]

For my own part, were I a legislator, I should undoubtably place more confidence in the long and approved experience of mankind, than in, at best, the hazardous resource of untried experiment. There are philosophers that, in their airy speculations, fritter away the substance of good government, and of course the happiness of mankind. From the little that is formed of the French constitution, it appears entirely novel, and evidently unrecommended by the experience of ancient or modern times.[††]

I am now to make a few remarks on a pamphlet, entitled, "Observations on the Reflections of the Right Honourable Edmund Burke, on the Revolution of France, in a Letter to the Right Honourable the Earl of Stanhope." This pamphlet is, it seems, the production of a lady, well known in the literary world.[3] She sets out with telling his Lordship, that "her observations are not directed to *captivate*; but to *convince.*" For my own part, I have ever been taught to believe, that to *captivate* was the peculiar province of the sex, and that its appeals to the *heart* were *always* successful; whatever might have been the fate of its efforts to *convince* the understanding. This lady, however, seems to pique herself less in those delicate touches of female sensibility, that are so well calculated to persuade, even a stubborn mind, than in the *masterly strokes of vigorous conception,* which, if unable to convey *lasting* conviction,

some embrace of one of the female legislators. It is well known that no trifling sums have been given to these ladies of the Halle, to purchase an exemption from their amorous follies. The ladies of our fish-market here, are, I believe, without any disparagement to this sober, gentle, decent, orderly part of the community, the last objects that could provoke the embrace of a man of taste or fashion: they are, however, much superior to their amiable sisters at Paris. I cannot help mentioning here an anecdote of these ladies, of which I was an eye-witness. In the month of July last, being at dinner with some gentlemen, our ears were assailed with some of the most horrid execrations I had ever heard (this it seems was owing to the very ungallant resistance on the part of the servants); immediately after, in rushed these polished Amazons, who amply redeem their total inability of appealing to the feelings, by the irresistible effects their presence produces on the senses; one of the most glaring of which was, in our part, sudden and total loss of appetite. Nothing was left undone by these accomplished damsels, that could display their talents. To please the sight, they danced; to please the ear, they sung; and last, though not the least of their powers, was given with such exquisite feeling, that I am really at a loss to give it a determinate name. I know at the time we called it strangling: I remember the ladies called it embracing. This friendly intrusion had not been safely rewarded with a smaller sum than twelve livres—half a guinea.—I know not what a nobleman of this country would say, if a band of fishwomen should force themselves, in spite of the servants, into his dining-room, where he had company at dinner—he might call it liberty—I think it a very unpardonable one.

---

[1] William Blackstone (1723–80), preeminent legal historian.

[2] Penal colony in what is now Australia.

[††] I believe the Revolution in France is the only one that has happened in the world, in which the fishwomen have taken a very leading part. They also have much influence on the Jacobins, who certainly are the governors of the country, and of course, in a great measure, the authors of the constitution. It may not be unworthy of remark, that in the very country that furnishes such a copious subject of panegyric to the Revolution Society, on the acquisition of an enlightened liberty, there are the most violent outrages committed on the taste, the feelings, and the ordinary habits of life. I have myself seen, on the Boulevards of Paris, a woman of fashion, youth, and beauty, forced to the unwhole-

[3] Catharine Macaulay (1731–91).

give at least temporary satisfaction.

I cannot think of taking my leave of this lady, without saying how much I admire her talents. Her ingenuity is obvious. Her style is easy and elegant. I could wish she had employed her numerous qualifications to a better purpose. When she says, she *will* convince, and is determined not to captivate, she has mistaken her forte. She has *captivated* me long since. I cannot, will not say, she has *convinced* me. There is in the female character a certain *je ne sais quoi,* that few men of any soul are able to resist. It is the peculiar and enchanting privilege of the sex, that their *weakness* is their *strength.* 'Tis it, that makes our *stubborn* natures bend. If it be not the shield that defends, it is the arrow that mortally wounds. It is the source of peaceful victory: we yield to what we know we are unable to resist. When this *natural* and *delightful* peculiarity, is superseded by an *affection* of manliness, the female character loses all its charm, it loses all its lustre: our former *vanquishers* become our equals.

(1791)

RICHARD CUMBERLAND
The Observer:
Being a Collection of Moral, Literary,
and Familiar Essays [1]

I HAVE not been inattentive to the interests of the fair sex, and have done my best to laugh them out of their fictitious characters: On the plain ground of truth and nature they are the ornaments of creation, but in the maze of affectation all their charms are lost. Where vice corrupts one, vanity betrays an hundred.

They have associated with our sex to the profit of

their understandings and the prejudice of their morals: We are beholden to them for having softened our ferocity and dispelled our gloom; but it is to be regretted that any part of that pedantic character, which they remedied in us, should have infected their manners. A lady, who has quick talents, ready memory, an ambition to shine in conversation, a passion for reading and who is withal of a certain age or person to despair of conquering with her eyes, will be apt to send her understanding into the field, and it is well if she does not make a ridiculous figure before her literary campaign is over. If the old stock of our female pedants were not so busy in recruiting their ranks with young novitiates, whose understandings they distort by their training, we would let them rust out and spend their short annuity of nonsense without annoying them, but whilst they will be seducing credulous and inconsiderate girls into their circle, and transforming youth and beauty into unnatural and monstrous shapes, it becomes the duty of every knight-errant in morality to sally forth to the rescue of these hag-ridden and distressed damsels.

It cannot be supposed I mean to say that genius ought not to be cultivated in one sex as well as in the other; the object of my anxiety is the preservation of the female character, by which I understand those gentle unassuming manners and qualities peculiar to the sex, which recommend them to our protection and endear them to our hearts; let their talents and acquirements be what they may, they should never be put forward in such a manner as to overshadow and keep out of light those feminine and proper requisites, which are fitted to the domestic sphere and are indispensable qualifications for the tender and engaging duties of wife and mother; they are not born to awe and terrify us into subjection by the flashes of their wit or the triumphs of their understanding; their conquests are to be effaced by softer approaches, by genuine

---

[1] Richard Cumberland (1732–1811), dramatist, novelist, and periodical writer. The *Observer* was comprised of a series of essays on a range of literary and general subjects. It first appeared as a one-volume edition in 1785. Subsequent multi-volume editions appeared in the following years.

delicacy of thought, by a simplicity and modesty of soul, which stamp a grace upon every thing they act or utter. All this is compatible with every degree of excellence in science or art; in fact it is characteristic of superior merit, and amongst the many instances of ladies now living, who have figured as authors or artists, there are very few, who are not as conspicuous for the natural grace of character as for talents; prattlers and pretenders there may be in abundance, who fortunately for the world do not annoy us any otherwise than by their loquacity and impertinence.

Our age and nation have just reason to be proud of the genius of our women; the advances they have made within a short period are scarcely credible, and I reflect upon them with surprize and pleasure: It becomes every young man of fashion now to look well to himself and provide some fund of information and knowledge, before he commits himself to societies, where the sexes mix: Every thing that can awaken his ambition, or alarm his sense of shame call upon him for the exertions of study and the improvement of his understanding; and thus it comes to pass that the age grows more and more enlightened every day.

Away then with that ungenerous praise, which is lavished upon past times for no other purpose than to degrade and sink the time present upon the comparison!

(1791)

GENTLEMAN'S MAGAZINE
Letter: Strictures on National Vices, Follies, and Inadvertencies

MR. URBAN,   *Edinburgh, Jan. 20.*

THERE are many men of a speculative turn of mind, and of melancholy dispositions, who consider the present times as the worst that have ever been; and men of the like temper have existed in every age. A little attention to history, however, and to the absurd consequences that might be drawn from such a representation of things, will induce us to think somewhat differently, and perhaps to conclude that, in every age, mankind (though their pursuits have been somewhat different) have, on the whole, been very much alike; and that the sum of virtue and vice in the world has, at every period, been nearly equal. If, indeed, we bring into the account the alarming depravity of a neighbouring nation, which almost exceeds every thing which history records, or which sober men can conceive; the present age will probably appear to posterity in blacker colours than most of those that have preceded it. But even then much extraordinary virtue in the many illustrious sufferers, and much extraordinary benevolence in the bystanders, may be found; if not sufficient to wipe out the stain (for this is impossible), yet sufficient to make a very considerable balance to it.

In our nation (not withstanding the late incessant endeavours to pervert the public mind, and to hide or deny the plainest facts) there is yet much political excellence, and much private virtue. Without private virtue and individual religion, indeed, the best schemes of politicks must eventually be ineffectual, and the wisest civil constitution must quickly decay. Had our modern reformers paid due attention to this, and had they, instead of attempting to raise dissatisfactions and convulsions in the State, directed their abilities and their influence to moral reformation (where much unquestionably remains to be done), they would have done a real service to their country, and essential good to their Constitution. But, from men who possess little virtue themselves, who can neither govern their passions, nor reform their vicious habits, and who can defend the atheism and immoralities of modern Frenchmen, such attention and endeavours were not to be expected. From such violent changes, and reformations of such dubious effect as some men certainly intended, I trust the general good sense of the nation will at present preserve us; and it is to be hoped, when the turbulence of party has subsided, and we are left at liberty to judge with coolness, that we shall all, from the highest to the lowest, learn, by the horrid scenes which have for some years past deluged Europe with blood, to render our public Constitution truly permanent by the reformation of our private vices. The influence of the virtue or vice of individuals on the communities of which they are members is too obvious to be denied; and I trust Mr. Urban will, therefore, excuse the following strictures on vices, follies, or inadvertencies, which really exist in the nation, and the reformation of which would be a public benefit.

It has often been remarked, and it is certainly true, that women, though they take no active share in the government of nations, have yet a mighty influence in every civilized State. Their influence, though it is not always of such a public nature as to attract general attention, certainly leads to important consequences, as it affects the private scenes of life, and determines the virtue or vice or numerous individuals. To the ladies of Great Britain much praise is unquestionably due; for, though our streets are crowded with unfortunates, and our courts of law disgraced by numerous trials for adultery, yet much of the guilt certainly lies at the door of our own sex, who, by the vilest means, are often the infamous seducers of those whom by the laws of true honour they are bound to protect. Truth, however, requires it to be added, that the fair sex are themselves often liable to considerable blame, and that they are often the real abettors and encouragers of vice when they are not practically vicious, and even, perhaps, when they do not mean it.

Softness, delicacy, benevolence, piety, and, I may add, timidity (the guardian of virtue), are the natural characteristics of women. Such endearing qualities touch the heart of the hero, awe the profligate, and extort respect from the most abandoned; whilst she in whom they are wanting creates only disgust; she appears to be an unnatural and monstrous being, and, instead of love and the softer passions, she excites only contempt, and meets but with neglect. No man, who sincerely respects the female character, would wish to see their amiable qualities and natural sensibility annihilated; and it is with sincere regret that their best friends observe, among the ladies of the present day, a tendency to masculine manners which is highly disgusting, and an insensibility to masculine vice which is of the worst consequence. A more unpleasant sight can scarcely be seen than that of a woman imitating the dress of our sex; and it is infinitely worse when they so far forget themselves as to imitate that of a soldier. Yet in this part of the country (and similar sights are sometimes to be seen in England) I have often seen them with short petticoats, short coats with epaulets, a Highland bonnet and feathers, and even with a sword by their side. Such infringements on the other sex, so uncongenial to their natural frame both of body and mind, deserve the severest reprehension, and the most marked contempt. But even this infringement, indecent and disgusting as it unquestionably is, is not quite so bad as that of learning the military exercise. Yet, Mr. Urban, it is a fact that, in this town,[1] since the corps of volunteers (who are men of the highest respectability, and most of them of independent fortunes) were embodied, the military furor has actually so far seized on several young and beautiful females as to make them submit to be drilled and exercised (privately of course) by a common serjeant. Can any thing be more unworthy, or, I may add, more indelicate, than for ladies with their petticoats kitted, to submit to be taught the movements of a soldier by a Highland-man without breeches? Their intentions

---

[1] Edinburgh.

may possibly be innocent, and I doubt not are so, but the consequences may be guilt. At all events, in such a course they must lose much of their natural timidity and amiable softness, and acquire many masculine, and perhaps some indelicate, notions; and, were the custom to become general, the consequences would neither be pleasant nor friendly to virtue. Let them then leave military duties, and the defence of our national dignity, to their fathers, their brothers, and their countrymen. War is always a great evil; but its consequences would be worse than we have yet found them, if the gentle bosoms of the fair sex were reduced from the quiet scenes of domestic life to riot in scenes of blood; and if, instead of the amiable qualities and bashful air for which they are admired, they were to learn to appear in all the fierceness of a hero.

The acquiescence of the ladies in masculine vices, as it is more general than the follies I have now attempted to expose, is also of worse consequence to the State. I have asserted indeed, and it is true, that the miserable condition of the unfortunate women who crowd our streets is the immediate effect of the savage and unprincipled cruelty of our own sex; but it is equally true that, if the great body of our women would shew their indignation and contempt for the perpetrators of those horrid crimes, they would be less frequent. On the contrary, however, it is found in fact that men of this stamp are received into their company without the least hesitation, and even with equal (I fear I might have said greater) pleasure as those who abhor the thought of such crimes.

Your fair readers, Mr. Urban, will, I trust, excuse the freedom of these strictures, which refer to follies and vices which have a real existence, and which is certainly in their power, in some measure, at least to check. Such a reformation is neither chimerical, impracticable, nor dangerous. On the whole, though I may have expressed myself strongly, I have intended no offence, Mr. Urban, to any of your readers, and least of all to the fair part of them; the influence of women in the State I well know, and their natural goodness of heart I admire and respect; and I have only attempted to persuade them to direct their influence into a proper channel. Though I am not yet so far advanced in life as to have acquired gloomy notions of things, or to be insensible to the charms of my fair countrywomen, I think the danger of the times requires our utmost exertions; and, as the present war is in defence of our religion and natural liberty, and as another Fast is proclaimed to implore success on our arms, it cannot be improper to request attention to our morals, and to the regaining our freedom from the slavish bands of vice.

ΦΙΟΣ ΤΗΣ ΣΟΦΙΑΣ.[1]

(1795)

RICHARD POLWHELE
The Unsex'd Females: a Poem, Addressed to the Author of The Pursuits of Literature[2]

SURVEY with me, what ne'er our fathers saw,
A female band despising Nature's law,[†]
As "proud defiance"[††] flashes from their arms,

---

[1] Friend of wisdom.

[2] Richard Polwhele (1760–1838), Anglican cleric, antiquarian, and pamphleteer, was best known for this poem which drew on a misogynist reference in T.J. Mathias's The Pursuits of Literature (see Section One). *The Unsex'd Females* was part of a vehement reaction that had developed against Wollstonecraft after her death the year before, and against radical politics generally. In the poem, Polwhele distinguished between a group of women such as Wollstonecraft, whose transgressive opinions he condemned, and an alternative group of conservative women such as Hannah More, whom he approved of for their moral integrity.

[†] Nature is the grand basis of all laws human and divine: and the woman, who has no regard to nature, either in the decoration of her person, or the culture of her mind, will soon "walk after the flesh, in the lust of uncleanness, and despise government." [Peter 2:10]

[††] "A troop came next, who crowns and armour wore,
    And proud defiance in their looks they bore." Pope ["The Temple of Fame" (1711) lines 342–43]

And vengeance smothers all their softer charms.
15   *I* shudder at the new unpictur'd scene,
Where unsex'd woman vaunts the imperious mien;
Where girls, affecting to dismiss the heart,
Invoke the Proteus of petrific art;
With equal ease, in body or in mind,
20 To Gallic freaks or Gallic faith resign'd,
The crane-like neck, as Fashion bids, lay bare,
Or frizzle, bold in front, their borrow'd hair;
Scarce by a gossamery film carest,
Sport,[†] in full view, the meretricious breast;[††]
25 Loose the chaste cincture, where the graces shone,
And languish'd all the Loves, the ambrosial zone;
As lordly domes inspire dramatic rage,
Court purient Fancy to the private stage;
With bliss botanic[†††] as their bosoms heave,

30 Still pluck forbidden fruit, with mother Eve,
For puberty in sighing florets pant,
Or point the prostitution of a plant;
Dissect[††††] its organ of unhallow'd lust,
And fondly gaze the titillating[†††††] dust;[††††††]
35 With liberty's sublimer views expand,[†††††††]
And o'er the wreck of kingdoms[††††††††] sternly stand;

The Amazonian band—the female Quixotes of the new philosophy, are, here, too justly characterised. Nor could they read, I suspect, some passages in the sixth satire of Juvenal without an uneasy sensation:

Quem praestare potest mulier galeata pudorem?
[What modesty can a woman show who wears a helmet?
Juvenal, Satire 6, line 252]

I have seen in MS. Mr. Gifford's masterly translation of this satire. Our expectations, I hope, will soon be gratified by his entire version of Juvenal.

[†] To "sport a face," is a cant phrase in one of our Universities, by which is meant an impudent obtrusion of a man's person in company. It is not inapplicable, perhaps, to the open bosom—a fashion which we have never invited or sanctioned.

[††] The fashions of France, which have been always imitated by the English, were, heretofore, unexceptionable in a moral point of view; since, however ridiculous or absurd, they were innocent. But they have now their source among prostitutes—among women of the most abandoned character. "See Madam Tallien come into the theatre, and other beautiful women, laying aside all modesty, and presenting themselves to the public view, with bared limbs, a la sauvage, as the alluring objects of desire." Robinson's Proofs of a Conspiracy, &c. &c. Edit. 2. P. 252. [John Robison, *Proofs of a Conspiracy against all the Religions and Governments of Europe* (1798)]

[†††] Botany has lately become a fashionable amusement with the ladies. But how the study of the sexual system of plants can accord with female modesty, I am not able to comprehend.

I had, at first, written:
More eager for illicit knowledge pant,
With lustful boys anatomise a plant;

The virtues of its dust prolific speak,
Or point its pistill with unblushing cheek,

I have, several times, seen boys and girls botanizing together.

[††††] Miss Wollstonecraft does not blush to say, in an introduction to a book designed for the use of young ladies, that, "in order to lay the axe at the root of corruption, it would be proper to familiarize the sexes to an unreserved discussion of those topics, which are generally avoided in conversation from a principle of false delicacy; and and that it would be right to speak of the organs of generation as freely as we mention our eyes or our hands." To such language our botanizing girls are doubtless familiarized: and, they are in a fair way of becoming worthy disciples of Miss W. If they do not take heed to their ways, they will soon exchange the blush of modesty for the bronze of impudence. [Mary Wollstonecraft, "Introductory Address to Parents," *Elements of Morality, For the use of Children* (1792). Polwhele misrepresents Wollstonecraft's position.]

[†††††] "Each pungent grain of titillating dust." Pope. [*Rape of the Lock* (1712) 5:84.]

[††††††] "The prolific dust"—of the botanist. [From Erasmus Darwin *The Botanic Garden* (1791), Canto XI:466.]

[†††††††] Non vultus, non color unus,
Non comptae mamsere comae: sed pectus anhelum
Et rabie fera corda tument; majorque videri, &c.
[Her expression and colour changed
Nor her kempt hair remained, but her breast was panting
And her wild heart swelled with madness and she seemed taller
Virgil, *Aeneid* 6:47–49.]

Except the non color unus, Virgil's Sibyll seems to be an exact portrait of a female fashionist, both in dress and philosophism.

[††††††††] The female advocates of Democracy in this country, though they have had no opportunity of imitating the French ladies, in their atrocious acts of cruelty; have yet assumed a stern serenity in the contemplation of those savage excesses. "To express their abhorrence of royalty, they (the French ladies) threw away the character of their sex, and bit the amputated limbs of their murdered countrymen.—I say this on the authority of a young gentleman who saw it.—I am sorry to add, that the relation, accompanied with looks of horror and disgust, only provoked a contemptuous smile from an illuminated British fair-one." See Robinson—p. 251.

And, frantic, midst the democratic storm,
Pursue, Philosophy! thy phantom-form[†]
   Far other is the female shape and mind,
40 By modest luxury heighten'd and refin'd;
Those limbs, that figure, tho' by Fashion[††] grac'd,
By Beauty polish'd, and adorn'd by Taste;
That soul, whose harmony perennial flows,
In Music trembles, and in Color glows;
45 Which bids sweet Poesy reclaim the praise
With faery light to gild fastidious days,
From sullen clouds relieve domestic care,
And melt in smiles the withering frown of war.
Ah! once the female Muse, to NATURE true,

50 The unvalued store from FANCY, FEELING drew;
Won, from the grasp of woe, the roseate hours,
Cheer'd life's dim vale, and strew'd the grave with flowers.
But lo! where, pale amidst the wild,[†††] she draws
Each precept cold from sceptic Reason's[††††] vase;
55 Pours with rash arm the turbid stream along,
And in the foaming torrent whelms the throng.[†††††]

   .   .   .   .

See Wollstonecraft, whom no decorum checks,
Arise, the intrepid champion of her sex;
65 O'er humbled man assert the sovereign claim,
And slight the timid blush[††††††] of virgin fame.

(1798)

[†] Philosophism, the false image of philosophy. See the pseudo Eneas of the Eneid, 10. b. imitated from the Iliad, 15. b.

   . . . .Nube cava tenuem sine viribus umbram. . . .
   . . . . .Dat inania verba,
   Dat sine mente sonum. . . .
   […from hollow mist a thin phantom without strength…
   . . . . .she gives it empty words,
   She gives it sound without thought…

                Aeneid, 10: 636–40]

A true description of Philosophism; a phantom which heretofore appeared not in open day, though it now attempts the loftiest flights in the face of the sun. I trust, however, to English eyes, it is almost lost in the "black cloud" to which it owed its birth.

   — Levis haud ultra latebras jam querit imago,
   Sed, sublime volans, nubi se immiscuit atrae.
   [But now the airy phantom no longer sought hiding-places,
   But flying aloft it melted into the dark clouds.

                Aeneid, 19: 663–64]

[††] I admit that we are quickly reconciled to the fashion of the day, and often consider it as graceful, if it offend not against delicacy.

[†††] "A wild, where flowers and weeds promiscuous shoot;
   A garden tempting with forbidden fruit." Pope. [*Essay on Man, Book* I:7–8 (1733).]

[††††] A troubled stream only, can proceed from the vase of scepticism; if it be not "the broken cistern that will hold no water." [Jeremiah 2:13]

[†††††] "Raging waves, foaming out their own shame"—St. Jude [1:13]. Such were those infamous publications of Paine and others, which, like the torrents of December, threatened to sweep all before them—to overwhelm the multitude.

[††††††] That Miss Wollstonecraft was a sworn enemy to the blushes, I need not remark. But many of my readers, perhaps, will be astonished to hear, that at several of our boarding-schools for young ladies, a blush incurs a penalty.

SECTION ELEVEN

The Second Wave of Reform

The debates that accompanied the French Revolution in the 1790s returned with a vengeance after the conclusion of the Napoleonic War in 1815. The mass disenfranchisement of soldiers, economic hardship, and growing doubts about what exactly so many people had died for, all contributed to a renewed atmosphere of political upheaval. As before, the spectre of insurrection was met with a wave of arrests and an array of legislative interventions. The controversy was exacerbated by the fact that old royal powers had been returned to the throne in France and elsewhere. The war had been fought, it turned out, not for liberty in any socially progressive sense, but so that the historical clock could be turned back to a pre-Revolution social order characterized by the preeminence of royalty and the aristocracy. Radicals referred to this renewed status quo satirically as "Legitimacy" or simply as "Corruption." As before, this controversy was in many ways a literary one. Samuel Taylor Coleridge, once a radical activist but now a prominent conservative, insisted that "the evils of a rank and unweeded Press" were all the more distressing because of "the greater love we bore to literature." Coleridge was not the only familiar name from the earlier political crisis to play an active role in the renewed struggle. Robert Southey, Coleridge's good friend and fellow radical in the 1790s, was the author of an anonymous article in the *Quarterly Review* decrying political radicals who, "by imposing upon the ignorance of the multitude, flattering their errors and inflaming their passions, are exciting them to sedition and rebellion."

Many of these debates addressed general theoretical and political issues such as the desirability of universal suffrage and annual parliaments, and complaints about undue taxation, in ways that were grounded in specific incidents. Southey's review essay in the *Quarterly* appeared just days after the Spa Fields riot and addressed various radical responses to the event which had already appeared. Reformers held two meetings at Spa Fields on 15 November and 2 December, 1816. The first was conducted peacefully, but the 2 December meeting, called to address the Prince Regent's refusal to consider a petition for reform passed on the previous occasion, was more controversial. Surrounded by the red, white, and green flags of the future British republic, James Watson, the erratic and apparently drunken son of one of the leaders of the reform movement, seized the largest tri-colour flag and led some of the protestors to capture the Bank and Tower, though their efforts largely amounted to looting and rioting.

The riot may have confirmed Southey's doubt about these radicals' intellectual capacities, but like Coleridge, he understood how high the stakes were: "Of all engines of mischief which were ever yet employed for the destruction of mankind, the press is the most formidable, when perverted in its uses, as it was by the Revolutionists in France, and is at this time by the Revolutionists in England." Coleridge's and Southey's old ally, William Hazlitt, remained unswerving in his radical allegiances, but whatever their political differences two decades later, the three men shared a common sense of the importance of the literary dimension in these struggles. They simply interpreted the nature of that importance in diametrically opposed ways. In an anonymous article in *The Examiner*, Hazlitt lambasted William Gifford, the editor of the conservative *Quarterly Review*, for being a "*Government Critic*, a character nicely differing from that of a government spy—the invisible link, that connects literature with the police."

Not all political converts were defectors from the radical cause. William Cobbett had been a violent opponent of the American and French revolutions, but by the nineteenth century, he had become a leading reformer. Cobbett may have disagreed with Southey's characterization of reformers as "apostles of anarchy," but he could not have agreed more that "a cry of discontent has gone forth." Cobbett's weekly magazine, the *Political Register*, was notorious with conservatives, but regardless of their political persuasion, few people doubted its influence. Dissatisfied with his already sizeable audience, and alarmed by reports that government officials were threatening to revoke the licenses of publicans who stocked the *Register*, Cobbett began to issue a cheaper broadside version of it for two pence. The intricacies of the mass reading public are epitomized by Cobbett's recognition that he was appealing to people who could not afford to buy the *Register* at its full price, and so would not have access to it if they could not read it at their local pub. Nor were financial constraints the only limitation faced by this plebeian readership. Cobbett's reference to "my readers, or *hearers*" suggests the complicated overlap between literate and aurol audiences that made up this audience for political information on the margins of the public sphere. His determination to cut the *Register*'s price in order "to make it move *swifter*" reflected a shrewd understanding of the social importance of the ways texts circulated.

For Cobbett, as for so many others on both sides of the political divide, the controversy was primarily about the power of the printed word. "The *success of the cause of Reform*, and of course, the happiness and peace of the country, must now," he insisted, "in a great degree, depend upon the efforts of the press." Another radical weekly, *The Gorgon*, insisted in similar terms that "CORRUPTION has not yet encountered a more formidable and dangerous enemy, than in the circulation of cheap, weekly publications." If many aspects of the political and literary controversies of this period were familiar from a generation earlier, the most important new element, as the *Gorgon*'s reference to "cheap, weekly publications" implied, was the powerful presence of the weekly radical press. Radical journals such as *Pig's Meat; or, Lessons for the Swinish Multitude* and *Politics for the People, or a Salmagundy for Swine* (both titles referred to Edmund Burke's reference to "the swinish multitude") had played an important role in the 1790s. But by the early nineteenth century, weekly radical journals had become a formidable presence. Cobbett's *Political Register* began in 1802, and Leigh Hunt's *Examiner* in 1808, but many of these journals, such as *The Briton*, *The Cap of Liberty*, the *Democratic Recorder*, and the *London Alfred*, sprung into life within a few months or even weeks of each other as political pressures intensified in 1819.

These radical journals were often inspired by particular atrocities that galvanized the radical movement, such as the Peterloo Massacre on August 16, 1819, in which soldiers on horseback killed unarmed protesters at a reform meeting in St. Peter's Field in Manchester, but they also focused on the broader issue of the power of extended debate in print and in conversation to renovate Britain's social order. Whatever their more particular concerns, they were animated by a shared sense that change was as unstoppable as it was imminent. The January 3, 1819 edition of *The Examiner* announced that "this is the commencement, if we are not much mistaken, of one of the most important years that have been seen for a long while." Its insistence that "a spirit is abroad, stronger than kings, or armies, or all the most predominant shapes of prejudice and force.... This spirit is knowledge," looked back to the Enlightenment faith in the transformative power of knowledge, and forward to the rhetorical urgency of Marx and Engel's *Communist Manifesto* (1848). *The Examiner* hardly needed to remind its largely Protestant readership that this "spirit" was fortified by the ominous presence of "an universal press, with a hundredth part of which LUTHER undid the despotism of Authority." Reform did not come as swiftly or as radically as these sorts of predictions suggested. The changes initiated by the 1832 Reform Bill fell far short of establishing the sort of universal male democracy envisioned by radicals. But whatever the political outcome, these debates marked a crucial historical moment of widespread deliberation on the power and propriety of the printed word—a discussion that extended well past the question of the inherent character of particular texts or of literary authority to considerations of readership and modes of textual dissemination that have returned as critical priorities in our own age.

࡞ࡁࡂ

EDINBURGH REVIEW
Liberty of the Press and its Abuses

A Review of *The Law of Libel, in which is contained a General History of this Law in the Ancient codes, and of its Introduction and successive Alterations in the Law of England: Comprehending a Digest of all the leading Cases upon Libels, from the earliest to the present Time.*
By THOMAS LUDLOW HOLT, Esq. Of the Middle Temple, Barrister-at-Law.

THE great subject which we are now about to discuss, presents so many difficulties to the view, that we frankly acknowledge the boldness of the task we have undertaken. The works of former writers afford but slender assistance, consisting generally of vague declamation or sweeping theory, in which the grand object of practical utility has been lost sight of. The labours of legislators have been still more defective, varying only between the opposite and almost equally pernicious extremes of strict prohibition and unrestrained license; nor has any attempt been made, as far as we know, even in the codes fashioned by speculative men for new communities, to reconcile the two great objects of protecting free discussion, and checking attacks upon character.

We shall, however, be told, that the press is in no danger, at least in England; that the discussion is unnecessary; that whatever defects may appear to exist in the system of our laws with regard to it, there are none in practice sufficient to require any material change; and that, at all events, there is nothing urgent in the question, so as to require its being pressed upon our attention peculiarly at the present moment. We purpose to begin by showing how extremely ill founded the two former observations are; and with regard to the others, our whole inquiries will have a strict reference to practical evils; and we only desire the attention of the public to them, and its favour to their results, in so far as they proceed upon plain matters of fact, of daily and familiar occurrence. With respect to the time, we certainly choose it purposely; for, not only will the attention of Parliament be turned towards this subject in its next session, in consequence of the bill lately introduced,[1] but it is at this moment the topic to which the regards of legislators and politicians in every part of Europe are most eagerly and anxiously directed. The slavery which is almost every where sought to be reestablished, by the admirers of the dark ages, rests its sole hope upon the destruction of the press; while the only chance of placing the general tranquility upon a sure basis, is sought by enlightened men all over the world, in a judicious extension of its freedom. The problem, then, which they are seeking to solve, is the one which we are about to investigate, namely, to find the quantity of liberty, and the species of restraint, which will secure to the press the greatest amount of free discussion, consistent with the tranquility of the community, and the safety of private character. Besides, the very circumstance of there being so few state trials connected with the subject for the last two or three years, even if it proved that no attacks were now likely to be made upon the press, would form an additional inducement to undertake the inquiry at the present time; for all great questions of jurisprudence, and especially of constitutional law, are most advantageously examined at a distance from the actual commission of the offences, or the exercise or the abuse of the powers to which they relate. We shall begin by stating precisely the most material provisions of the law of England, as now carried into practice, upon the subject of *Discussion*—under which term may be comprehended every thing that can give rise in its abuse to any of the offences known by the name of Libel—that is, written defamation, whether against the State or against individuals; or of seditious words, and slander—that is, spoken defamation against the State and against individuals.

It is manifest, that a statement, either against the Government, or an individual, may be libellous; or, to use a phrase which no one can object to, may be criminal, although founded in truth. Undoubted facts may be involved in furious or inflammatory invective. Some cases may be conceived (though they are exceedingly rare) in which a simple statement of facts respecting the government would be an offence against the public tranquility; but innumerable cases may be put, in which the publication of the truth, without any comment, would be an offence against private individuals. Things disclosed in confidence, or discovered by corruption, and things concealed from motives of prudence or humanity, may be maliciously promulgated, to the infinite injury or utter ruin of innocent persons. It is not therefore to be maintained, that the law would be erroneous, if it merely enacted that truth

---

[1] The bill, which was passed in 1817, laid increasingly severe penalties on those found guilty of uttering treasonable or seditious words.

might be a libel; and only refused to all men the unbounded license of publishing whatever is true. But it goes a great deal farther; it says, not that the truth of the statement shall be no justification in itself, but that the truth or falsehood is in all cases wholly immaterial to the question of malicious or innocent intention; that it shall be entirely excluded from the consideration of the Jury, who must proceed to pronounce upon the motives of the publisher, and, generally, upon the guilt or purity of the act of publication, without once inquiring whether the thing published be strictly true or utterly false. Now, instead of the truth of the statement being in every instance foreign to the question of guilt, which the law presumes it to be, the cases are extremely few, if indeed there be any at all, in which the question of guilty or not guilty is not materially connected with the question of true or false, always supposing the composition to bear reference to a matter of fact. Thus it is impossible to put a case in which the falsehood of a statement, injurious in its nature, whether to Government or individuals, would not at once be decisive of a malicious intent. If so, the Jury, when called upon to pronounce upon a publication, without any evidence either of its truth or falsehood, are placed in a very extraordinary predicament. One means of investigation, which *might* be decisive, is withdrawn from them; that which might be a criterion, and preclude all further inquiry, they must not resort to; they must not use an instrument which at least *might* show them the way.

The rule which now prevails, operates most injuriously to the great interests of liberty, and of good government in general. It tends to the prevention of publick discussion, beyond all the fetters that ever were invented for the press. It may be questioned, whether a previous censureship would

cramp its freedom much more effectually.[1] In that case, the writer is at least secure that what he is allowed to publish cannot afterwards, with the varying caprices of the day, or changes in the ruling powers, rise in judgment against him. He labours under no anxiety; he is either at once prevented from publishing, or he knows that he is safe. The uncertainty of our Libel law,—the *jus vugum atque incognitum*[2] which regulates this vital part of our constitution, is a most serious evil. No man can tell whether he shall be punished for daring to discuss the measures of Government freely and fairly, or not: and a great part of the uncertainty is owing to the maxim, that the truth may not be proved. If it could, the author would be pretty secure against any prosecution for a writing upon publick affairs; or if prosecuted, he would have little to fear from the result. As far as the facts bear him out, he might safely go; and his only care would be to avoid misstatements, and to keep some proportion between the vehemence of the invective and the conduct against which it was pointed. As the law now stands, there is something quite revolting in the powers given to rulers. A minister of state who has committed, in the face of day, the grossest injustice or oppression, or whose incapacity has been testified by the most notorious blunders, may unblushingly avow his wrongs, or his incapacity, and punish whoever conscientiously and calmly states it to the contrary; or he may obtain the same end, by denying with still greater effrontery what is indubitably true, but what he knows must not be proved. The utmost readiness to prosecute, accordingly, has at different times been found, in persons conscious that the truth only had been proclaimed against them. Thus, informations,[3] to the amount

[1] Libel laws did not prohibit publications beforehand. Once published, texts became susceptible to the charge of libel.

[2] Rights unnoticed and unknown.

[3] Criminal charges.

of above twenty, were once filed against persons who had accused a publick officer of malversation;[1] and these would no doubt have been tried without the possibility of the facts being proved, had not events in the mean time occurred which made that officer resign. These events showed, that had the trials gone on, the defendants would have been convicted for publishing statements not destitute of foundation, though incapable, by law, of being proved.

Some persons affect to see great danger to the peace of the community, and the stability of the government, in an unlimited discussion of public measures. But the rule for which we are contending, would not remove all bounds from the discussion; because the defendant might still be convicted, although he had proved his facts. We are willing, however, to admit that its adoption would greatly extend those bounds, inasmuch as rulers would be far less prone to order State prosecutions. The only check which at present represses such proceedings, and to which the liberty of printing actually enjoyed is wholly owing, is the fear of bad ministers, lest their conduct should be canvassed, irregularly and indirectly, on the trial. This fear, indeed, may frequently operate to prevent prosecutions in themselves just, because at present the defendant, though he can prove nothing, may insinuate any thing; but were proof allowed, no unjust prosecution would be undertaken; the inducement to silence would be imperative, and the limits of discussion greatly enlarged. In truth, we might go further, and ask what danger can ever result from the most unlimited discussion of publick measures? In what circumstances must a government be which ought to fear it? "My government," said Cromwell,[2]

"is not worth preserving if it cannot stand against paper shot." The sagacious usurper, accordingly, trusted to the strong arm of power, and never prosecuted for libels; but a good government, founded upon free principles, and planted in the hearts of the people by the blessings it conferred upon them, would have far less to fear from paper shot than the military despotism of Cromwell, who, after all, lived to feel that the press is the appointed scourge of evil rulers, when it dared to tell him, in the face of the country, that the people could only enter upon the inheritance of their birth-right by his death.[†] To hamper the press may serve the purposes of the usurper, or a wretched and incapable ruler; a just and lawful government may safely, and even advantageously, encourage the freest discussion. The influence of those at the head of affairs secures them at least an attentive hearing in their own defence; it ensures them also the support of a portion of the press. Even if they are in the wrong, they have so many circumstances in their favour, that it requires all the native vigour of truth, aided by time, to prevail against them. If they are in the right, how much more safely may they trust their support to reason, and rest satisfied with repelling or retorting the attack, by weapons of the same kind? What is there so very captivating in error—what so bewitching in excessive violence—what so attractive in gross and palpable injustice—as to make those tremble, who stand firm in the consciousness of being right? Surely truth and sense have, at the least, an equal chance in this contest; and if the refutation of sophistry may be entrusted to argument, the exposure and condemnation of literary excesses may be left to good taste, without much fear of their proving hurtful to any cause, but that which they are intended to befriend. The only risk that just and wise rulers can incur

---

[1] Misconduct in public office.

[2] Oliver Cromwell (1599–1658), leader of the Parliamentary side during the English civil war in the seventeenth century. In 1653 he became Lord Protector of England, a virtually absolute ruler of what

---

was essentially a military government.

[†] This was the definition of *paternal* government given in those days.

from discussion, is to be found in the consequences of its restriction. Hamper it, and even the best measures, the purest systems of government, have some reason to fear. No rules of law can prevent something of the truth from getting out; and, if a blunder is accidentally committed, the less free the press is, the more likely are distorted and exaggerated statements to prevail. A people kept in the dark, are sure to be easily disquieted; every breath makes them start; all objects appear in false shapes; anxiety and alarm spread rapidly without a cause; and a government, whose conduct might bear the broadest glare of day, may be shaken by the delusions which have sprung from unnecessary concealment. There are a few supposeable cases, in which such a government may have an interest in preventing the truth from being published; but they are rare in the extreme, and nearly exceptions to the rule. There can be no case in which, when the truth has been published, it can be its interest to prevent it from being proved upon the published trial.

(SEPTEMBER 1816)

QUARTERLY REVIEW
Parliamentary Reform

A Review of:

1. *An Inquiry into the Causes of the General Poverty and Dependance of Mankind; including a full Investigation of the Corn Laws.* By William Dawson. Edinburgh. 1814.
2. *A Plan for the Reform of Parliament, on Constitutional Principles.* Pamphleteer. No. 14.
3. *Observations on the Scarcity of Money, and its effects upon the Public.* By Edward Tatham, D.D. Rector of Lincoln College, Oxford. 1816.
4. *On the State of the Country, in December, 1816.* By the Right Hon. Sir John Sinclair, Bart.

5. *Christian Policy, the Salvation of the Empire. Being a clear and concise Examination into the Causes that have produced the impending, unavoidable National Bankruptcy; and the Effects that must ensue, unless averted by the Adoption of this only real and desirable Remedy, which would elevate these Realms to a pitch of Greatness hitherto unattained by any Nation that ever existed.* By Thomas Evans, Librarian to the Society of Spencean Philanthropists. Second Edition. London. 1816.
6. *The Monthly Magazine.*
7. Cobbett's *Political Register.*[1]

IF the opinions of profligate and of mistaken men may be thought to reflect disgrace upon the nation, of which they constitute a part, it might verily be said that England was never so much disgraced as at this time. Never before had the country been engaged in so long or so arduous a struggle; never had any country, in ancient or in modern times, made such great and persevering exertions; never had any country displayed more perfect magnanimity, and scarcely ever had any contest been terminated with such consummate and transcendent glory:—this at least is universally acknowledged:—it is confessed as much by the rage and astonishment of the ferocious revolutionist, and the ill-disguised regret of a party whom the events of the war have stultified as well as soured, as by the gratitude and admiration of all true Britons, and of the wise and the good throughout the civilized world. Yet at this time, when the plans of government have been successful beyond all former

---

[1] Launched in 1809, the *Quarterly Review* espoused a strong Tory perspective. This article, though published anonymously, was widely and correctly attributed to Robert Southey (1774–1843), a poet, historian, and essayist, and a former radical who, like Wordsworth and Coleridge (with whom he was associated), was reviled by radicals for his political apostasy. It is famous for Southey's hard line on the radical press, which went far beyond the positions adopted by his fellow apostates, Coleridge and Wordsworth.

example—when the object of a twenty years war—the legitimate object of a just and necessary war—has been attained, and England, enjoying the peace which she has thus bravely won, should be left at leisure to pursue with undistracted attention those measures, which, by mitigating present evils and preventing crimes in future, may as far as human means can be effectual, provide for an increasing and stable prosperity;—at this time a cry of discontent is gone forth, the apostles of anarchy take advantage of a temporary and partial distress, and by imposing upon the ignorance of the multitude, flattering their errors and inflaming their passions, are exciting them to sedition and rebellion.

During the great struggle between Charles I. and his parliament, the people required an appearance of least of devotion and morality in their leaders; no man could obtain their confidence unless he observed the decencies of life, and conformed in his outward deportment to the laws of God and man. There was much hypocrisy among them, as well as much fanaticism, but the great body of the nation were sincerely religious, and strict in the performance of their ordinary duties; and to this cause, more than to any other, is it owing that no civil war was ever carried on with so few excesses and so little cruelty, so that the conduct of the struggle was as honourable to the nation as the ultimate consequences have been beneficial. It is a melancholy, and in some respects an alarming thing, to observe the contrast at the present crisis, when the population looks for no other qualification in their heroes than effrontery and a voluble tongue. Easily deluded they have always been; but evil-minded and insidious men, who in former times endeavoured to deceive the moral feelings of the multitude, have now laboured more wickedly and more successfully in corrupting them. Their favourite shall have a plenary dispensation[1] for as many vices as he can

afford to entertain, and as many crimes as he may venture to commit. Among them sedition stands in the place of charity and covereth a multitude of sins.

Were it not that the present state of popular knowledge is a necessary part of the process of society, a stage through which it must pass in its progress toward something better, it might reasonably be questioned whether the misinformation of these times be not worse than the ignorance of former ages. For a people who are ignorant and know themselves to be so, will often judge rightly when they are called upon to think at all, acting from common sense, and the unperverted instinct of equity. But there is a kind of half knowledge which seems to disable men even from forming a just opinion of the facts before them—a sort of squint in the understanding which prevents it from seeing straightforward, and by which all objects are distorted. Men in this state soon begin to confound the distinctions between right and wrong—farewell then to simplicity of heart, and with it farewell to rectitude of judgment! The demonstrations of geometry indeed retain their force with them, for they are gross and tangible—but to all moral propositions, to all finer truths they are insensible—the part of their nature which should correspond with these is stricken with dead palsy. Give men a smattering of law, and they become litigious; give them a smattering of physic, and they become hypochondriacs or quacks, disordering themselves by the strength of imagination, or poisoning others in the presumptuousness of conceited ignorance. But of all men, the smatterer in philosophy is the most intolerable and the most dangerous; he begins by unlearning his Creed and his Commandments, and in the process of eradicating what it is the business of all sound education to implant, his duty to God is discarded first, and his duty to his neighbour presently afterwards. As long as he confines himself to private practice the mischief does not extend

---

[1] Official pardon.

beyond his private circle,—his neighbour's wife may be in some danger, and his neighbour's property also, if the distinctions between *meum* and *tuum*[1] should be practically inconvenient to the man of free opinions. But when he commences professor of moral and political philosophy for the benefit of the public,—the fables of old credulity, are then verified—his very breath becomes venomous, and every page which he sends abroad carries with it poison to the unsuspicious reader.

We have shewn, on a former occasion,[†] how men of this description are acting upon the public, and have explained in what manner a large part of the people have been prepared for the *virus* with which they inoculate them. The dangers arising from such a state of things are now fully apparent, and the designs of the incendiaries, which have for some years been proclaimed so plainly, that they ought, long ere this, to have been prevented, are now manifested by overt acts. On this point, therefore, it cannot be necessary to enlarge.

We have shewn also that as the constitution of Parliament has not been the cause of the existing distress, so no change in that constitution could in the slightest possible degree alleviate that distress, or otherwise benefit the people. If every office, sinecure, and pension, which the boldest reformer has yet ventured to proscribe, were abolished, the whole saving would scarcely be felt as a feather in the scale: and, as directly tending to exclude talents from the Government, and confine places of great trust to the aristocracy, such an abolition would be most injurious to the commonwealth. They who seek to lessen the influence of the crown, keep out of sight the increased power which has been given to public opinion by the publication of the parliamentary debates, and the prodigious activity of the press.— The first of these circumstances alone has intro-

duced a greater change into our government than has ever been brought about by statute; and on the whole, that change is so beneficial as to be worth more than the additional expense which it entails upon us during war. This momentous alteration gives, even in ordinary times, a preponderance to the popular branch of our constitution: but in these times, when the main force of the press is brought to bear like a battery against the Temple of our Laws; when the head of the government is systematically insulted for the purpose of bringing him into contempt and hatred; when the established religion is assailed with all the rancour of theological hatred by its old, hereditary enemies, with the fierceness of triumphant zeal by the new army of fanatics, and with all the arts of insidious infidelity by the Minute Philosophers of the age; when all our existing institutions are openly and fiercely assaulted, and mechanics are breaking stocking-frames in some places,[2] and assembling in others to deliberate upon mending the frame of the government,—what wise man, and what good one but must perceive that it is the power of the Democracy which has increased, is increasing, and ought to be diminished?

Of all engines of mischief which were ever yet employed for the destruction of mankind, the press is the most formidable, when perverted in its uses, as it was by the Revolutionists in France, and is at this time by the Revolutionists in England. Look at the language which is held by these men concerning the late transactions and see if falsehood and sedition were ever more audacious. "Perhaps," says the Examiner, "there may be a plot somewhere,—in some tap-room or other; like the plot of Despard, who was driven to frenzy by ill-treatment, and then conspired with a few brick-layers in a public-house, for which he was sent to the gallows, instead of the

---

[1] Mine and yours.

[†] No. XVI. Inquiry into the Poor Laws.

[2] Rebellious workers broke new textile machinery in the belief that mechanization was creating unemployment.

care of his friends!"[1] "We feel," says this flagitious[2] incendiary, "for the bodily pains undergoing by Mr. Platt,[3] and think his assassin, (unless he was mad with starvation) a scoundrel, and some of the corruptionists, who in luxury and cold blood can *provoke* such excesses, *greater scoundrels*!" As if of all "scoundrels" the man who can in this manner attempt to palliate insurrection, treason and murder, were not himself the greatest. Mr. Cobbett goes farther than this: with an effrontery peculiar to himself, notorious as it is that the rioters were led from Spafields by the man who harangued them there, and that the tricolour flag which they followed, was carried to Spafields to be hoisted there for their banner—he says, "it is well known to everyone in London, that the rioters had no connexion whatever with the meeting in Spafields."[4]

Another of this firebrand's twopenny papers is before us, in which he says that ministers, the noblesse, and the clergy of France wilfully made the revolution, in order to prevent the people from being fairly represented in a national council. "It was *they* who produced the confusion; it was *they* who caused the massacres and guillotinings; it was *they* who destroyed the kingly government; it was *they* who brought the king to the block!" And in the same spirit which dictated this foul and infamous falsehood, he asks, "was there any thing too violent, any thing too severe, to be inflicted on these men?"[5]

Why is it that this convicted incendiary, and others of the same stamp are permitted week after week to sow the seeds of rebellion, insulting the government, and defying the laws of the country? The press may combat the press in ordinary times and upon ordinary topics, a measure of finance, for instance, or the common course of politics, or a point in theology. But in seasons of great agitation, or on those momentous subjects in which, the peace and security of society, nay the very existence of social order itself is involved, it is absurd to suppose that the healing will come from the same weapon as the wound. They who read political journals, read for the most part to have their opinions flattered and strengthened, not to correct or enlighten them; and the class of men for whom these pot-house epistles are written, read nothing else. The Monthly Magazine asserts that from 40 to 50,000 of the two-penny Registers are sold every week, and the editor thinks it his duty to assist the sale by recom-

---

[1] *The Examiner* 467 (December 8, 1816): 772. This part of the *Quarterly*'s argument, and the articles in the *Examiner* and the *Political Register* that it cites, deal with the Spa Fields riot. *The Examiner* was responding to suggestions in the loyalist newspaper, the *Courier,* that the riot was evidence of an underlying plot to seize control through violent insurrection. Colonel Despard, was a descendant from an Irish landowning family and a British military veteran with a distinguished record, but by the 1790s, Despard had become actively involved in radical politics. He was involved with the London Corresponding Society, and in the more radical groups, the United Irishmen and United Englishmen in London. Despard was arrested in November 1802 and executed the next year. In his trial, the Crown argued that Despard was involved in a plan to stage an armed rebellion, seizing the Tower and the Bank, assassinating or imprisoning the King, and throwing open the prisons. The Crown made much of the fact that he had visited a series of working-class taverns in London during months before his arrest, possibly in order to promote this plan of armed insurrection.

[2] Wicked or criminal.

[3] *The Examiner* 467 (December 8, 1816): 769. The comments about Platt appeared in the lead article, which explored the political implications of the Spa Fields riot. Platt, who ultimately recovered, was shot while trying to discourage rioters who were robbing a gun shop.

[4] William Cobbett's *Political Register* 31.23 (Dec. 7, 1816): 733. Like many reformers, Cobbett was being careful to distinguish between the legitimate protests of the majority of the crowd, who remained at Spa Fields to hear Henry "Orator" Hunt's speech, and the disreputable but small minority who followed Watson and engaged in rioting.

[5] *Political Register* 31.18 (Nov. 2, 1816): 557. Cobbett's point was a common one in reformist accounts of the beginnings of the French Revolution: the privileged orders had precipitated the crisis by ignoring an important opportunity for more gradual change when the King had summoned the Estates-General in May 1789 to deal with France's growing financial crisis. The commoners who comprised the Third Estate had been forced to proclaim themselves a National Assembly on 17 June 1789, less than a month before the storming of the Bastille, because they had not been adequately incorporated into the decision-making process at the Estates-General.

mending it to his "liberal and enlightened readers." The statement may probably be greatly exaggerated,—this being an old artifice;—but if only a tenth of that number be circulated, among the populace, for it is to the populace that this ferocious journal is addressed, the extent of the mischief is not to be calculated. Its ignorant readers receive it with entire faith: it serves them for law and for gospel—for their Creed and their Ten Commandments. They talk by it, and swear by it;—they are ready to live by it; and it will be well if some of these credulous and unhappy men are not deluded to die by it; they would not be the first victims of the incendiary press. We have laws to prevent the exposure of unwholesome meat in our markets, and the mixture of deleterious drugs in beer.—We have laws also against poisoning the minds of the people, by exciting discontent and disaffection;—why are not these laws rendered effectual and enforced as well as the former? Had the insolence of the French journalists been checked at the commencement of the Revolution, those journalists would not have brought their king to the guillotine, and have perished themselves among the innumerable victims of their folly, their falsehood, their extravagance, and their guilt. Men of this description, like other criminals, derive no lessons from experience. But it behoves the Government to do so, and curb sedition in time; lest it should be called upon to crush rebellion and to punish treason. The prayer in the Litany will not deliver them from these things, unless they use the means which God and man have entrusted to them for delivering us and themselves.

How often have we heard that the voice of the people is the voice of God, from demagogues who were labouring to deceive the people, and who despised the wretched instruments of whom they made use! But it is the Devil whose name is Legion. *Vox Populi, vox Dei!* When or where has it been so? Was it in England during the riots in 1780?[1] Has it been in France during the last six and twenty years? Or was it in Spain when the people restored the Inquisition?[2]—for it *was* the people who restored that accursed tribunal, spontaneously and tumultuously—*not* the government, which only ratified what the people had done; still less were they assisted by that "base engine of our corrupt statesmen, the standing army,"[3] by which is meant the soldiers who fought and conquered with Wellington, as some of the city resolutioners have asserted with equal regard to truth, and to the honour of their country—What will not these men traduce! *Vox Populi, Vox Dei!*[4]—Was it so in the wilderness when the people gathered themselves together unto Aaron and said unto him, Up, make us Gods which shall go before us? Was it so at Athens when Socrates and Phocion were sacrificed to the factious multitude?[5] Or was it so at Jerusalem when they cried, Crucify Him! Crucify Him![6] The position is not more tenable than the Right Divine,[7] not less mischievous, and not less absurd. God is in the populace as he is in the hurricane, and the volcano, and the earthquake!

(OCTOBER 1816)

---

[1] The Gordon Riots (2–10 June, 1780), led by Lord George Gordon but characterized most memorably by the extensive mob violence in the days that followed, were a response to the government's refusal to repeal pro-Catholic legislation.

[2] The Inquisition was abolished in 1808 and restored in 1814.

[3] Source unidentified.

[4] The voice of the people is the voice of God.

[5] Socrates (469–399 B.C.) died from drinking hemlock after being sentenced to death, in part because his unswerving determination to discuss ethical question in public places threatened Athens' political and intellectual elites; Phocion (402–318 B.C.) fell victim to hostile political developments in Athens, though soon after his death, a statue was erected in his honour.

[6] Pontius Pilate offered the people a chance to save Jesus by invoking their right to release one prisoner, but the tide of popular opinion had changed and they rejected the offer.

[7] The doctrine of the divine right of kings argued for absolute power based on the contention that kings were God's deputies on earth.

POLITICAL REGISTER

To the Readers of The Register.

On the means of overcoming the difficulties experienced by those who are opposed to Corruption, and especially on the means adopted by me for obtaining fair play as to the use of the Press.[1]

Botley, 12th Nov. 1816

THE Register, No. 18, which was reprinted on an open sheet, to be sold for *two-pence* by retail,[2] having been found to be very useful, it is my intention to continue that mode of proceeding until *the Meeting of Parliament*, or, perhaps, until *the Reform shall have actually taken place.* I will detail the manner of doing this by and bye, after I have made some observations as to the causes of my having adopted this new method.

The Register in its *usual form* and at its *usual price* I shall continue; at least, I shall make no alteration in the price of it at present. The form is valuable, because, being capable of being collected into *volumes*, and easily referred to, the contents have effect long after their dates; and, while the country was in a state of comparative insensibility, I was less anxious about being read. I put my statements, my arguments, and my opinions upon record, and there I left them, quite satisfied that a time would come which would do justice to them all. But *now* the scene is changed. Now events are pressing upon us so fast, that my Register, loaded with more than half its amount in *stamp*[3] and other expences incidental to the stamp, does not move about *sufficiently swift* to do all the good that it might do. I have, therefore, resolved to make it move *swifter*.

Of the *shilling and a half-penny*, which is the present retail price of the Register, a very small portion is left to the *Author*. Not more, perhaps, than *two-pence half-penny*, if every expence be reckoned. I have no *advertisements*, no *paid for paragraphs*, and I publish little but what I myself write. It is impossible to publish *with the stamp* cheaper than I do, unless I go quite without compensation for my labour and time. Yet this *high price* must necessarily narrow the circulation; and, indeed, this is the obvious effect of such *heavy taxes* on the *paper* first, and, next, on the *stamp*. Still, as the Register was read in *meetings* of people in many towns, and one copy was thus made to convey information to scores of persons, I was somewhat satisfied; or, at least, I thought I was doing all that it was possible for me to do. But I have recently been informed, that, at *three* public-houses in one country town, the landlords have objected to *Meetings for Reading the Register being held at their houses*, for fear they should LOSE THEIR LICENCES. This was what had never struck me. I had heard of the Register having been banished from *Officer's Mess-Rooms*, from the *Mess Rooms on board of Ship*, from numerous *Reading-Rooms*, which must necessarily be under the control chiefly of the busy Clergy, the Pensioners, the Taxing People, and the like; but satisfied that all these are but as dust in the balance when we are talking of *the public, the energetic people*, I disregarded all these marks of hostility, and all the obstacles thus thrown in the way of circulation, seeing that thousands upon thousands of *real men* were *hearing* in the *Reading Meetings* at Public-houses. But I had not yet heard of the alarm about the LICENCES! The moment I heard of that, which was not more than nine days

---

[1] The *Political Register*, founded in 1802, was written and published by William Cobbett (1763–1835), the best known of the radical journalists in this period.

[2] By selling a cheaper version of his *Political Register* on a single open sheet, Cobbett was able to evade taxes that applied to periodical publications.

[3] The Stamp Act of 1712 imposed a tax on periodicals depending on the number of pages used. The tax was increased in 1797 and again in 1815 in an attempt to curb the circulation of the radical press.

back, I saw, at once, that my readers, or *hearers*, (or, at least, a great part of them) must either be driven out into the high-roads and waste-lands, or that they must be supplied with reading at a *cheap rate*. Two or three journeymen or labourers cannot spare a shilling and a half-penny a week; but they can spare a half-penny or three farthings each, which is not much more than the tax which they pay upon a good large quid of tobacco. And besides, the expence of the thing itself thus becomes less than the expence of going to a public-house to hear it read. Then there is the time for reflection, and opportunity of reading over again, and of referring to interesting facts. The *children* will also have an opportunity of reading. The expence of other books will be saved by those who have this resource. The wife can sometimes read, if the husband cannot. The women will understand the causes of their starvation and raggedness as well as the men, and will lend their aid in endeavouring to effect the proper remedy. Many a father will thus, I hope, be induced to spend his evenings at home in instructing his children in the history of their misery, and in warming them into acts of patriotism.

But there was still another motive to this measure. I saw the COURIER[1] and other hireling prints strenuously recommending the *circulating of little, cheap publications* in populous towns. This was, in one respect, a good sign. It showed how hard Corruption[2] felt herself to be pushed. What! Had she not advantages enough before? Did she stand in need of this extraordinary effort? However, if she was preparing for this sort of warfare, it was advisable to meet her at once. This is what I have now resolved to do. I hereby challenge her forth, and let the public be umpire of the battle.

---

[1] The Courier was conspicuous in its unswerving support of the government. It was a frequent satirical target in radical journals such as Cobbett's *Political Register* and Leigh Hunt's *Examiner*.

[2] Sarcastic term for the political establishment.

Those gentlemen who are of opinion, that the Register in this reprinted form and at the low price is likely to do good, will most effectually advance its circulation by pointing out to shop-keepers to *sell* it in towns and villages. The distributing of a thing *gratis* is not nearly so good as the selling of it at a price which everyone can reach who is not absolutely a beggar. The publisher in London will always be ready to supply retailers in the country, and the order from any particular retailer might be given for such a number to be sent *every week*, so that a new order need not be sent *weekly*, and postage would thus be saved. For instance, a retailer at York might send the Publisher an order to supply him with 1000 of each number. The thousand would cost only *6 pounds 5s.* and the profit to the retailer would be about *2 pounds*, or about 100 pounds a year without *capital* or *risk*; and so on for a smaller number in proportion. Whoever applies for a regular supply should write particularly to the Publisher, give him *very plain* directions as to the *coach* which he ought to send by, and as the *inn* whence the coach starts in London.

Nothing further occurs to me at present upon this part of the subject. The *success of the cause of Reform*, and of course, the happiness and peace of the country, must now, in a great degree, depend upon the efforts of the press. The COURIER has just again *called upon the government* to spread *cheap tracts* about the country. The government is very welcome to do this. Mr. JABET at Birmingham *has* done it. This I do not complain of. Let us only have *fair play*, and I am in no fear for the success of the *truth*. The COURIER complains of our *cheap publications*. The spies have, I dare say, found out that *twenty thousand* copies of the Register, No. 18, have already been sold. I dare say the spies have discovered this fact: and this it is, principally, I dare say, which has led to the complaint. However there is a better way of silencing these cheap publications;

and that is, by *removing all ground of public complaint* by granting a reform of the Parliament. This would knock us all up in the twinking of an eye. All our statements, all our eloquence, all our exhibitions of sinecures,[1] &c. would lose their interest at once. But, until this take place, the COURIER will find it very difficult to suggest to the government any measure for counteracting the cheap publications.

The days are past, never to return, when big wigs and long robes and gilded chariots could make the mass of mankind believe themselves an inferior species of animals. When I hear an able speech, or read an able book; when my mind receives conviction, or my heart is penetrated by the powers of the one or the other, am I to be so sorry a beast as to ask whether the speaker or the writer be a *weaver or a lord*? Or, at least, am I to be so base a being as to have my conviction or my feeling diminished by the circumstance of the want of rank on the part of the person who has produced such effects upon me? Can the tears and sobs, which the scenes of OTWAY[2] would wring even from the heart of a Castlereagh,[3] be stopped by telling the audience that the author died a beggar?

But, though we despise these sorrowful notes of Corruption, we ought to be very active in guarding against her various tricks. If she moves in any part of the country, I shall be glad to receive an account of her operations. She will not produce much effect; but her motions ought to be watched. Therefore, I shall be obliged to any one, who will send me up a copy of any publications that may appear, directed to the publisher in London. The time will now become very *busy*. Every thing will be put in motion, that promises the least help in the defeating of *Reform*. We, on the other hand, must neglect nothing that we are able lawfully to do in its favour. There is *no man* who may not be able to assist; and no man ought to be neglected. The *puffs*[4] which the emissaries are putting forth are contemptible.—These emissaries are idiots, or they are cheats. It is now become manifest, that a *change of some sort* must take place; and, I am certain, that it wants nothing but steady perseverance on the part of the friends of reform to make that change prove the salvation of the country. No town or county should desist from meeting again because it has *met once*. Meeting after meeting, petition after petition, remonstrance on remonstrance, until the country be saved!

W.M. COBBET.

P.S.—I wish again to press it upon the *Friends of Reform*, that, if they think that these publications tend to advance the interest of the country, the most *effectual* way, in which *they* can promote the circulation, is, by their carrying a few of the Numbers to Booksellers or any *other persons*, in the *towns* and *villages*, and *pointing out to them the way to go to work to obtain a regular supply*. With every parcel which goes to the country in the future, there will be sent a *placard* to be put up at the window of the retailer, in order to let the public know that Registers are to be had at that house.—In future, every Register, in succession, will be ready to send, in open sheets, to the country, on the *Saturday* on which it will be first published; so that it may be even in *Scotland* by the following *Tuesday*.—Orders will be supplied to *Ireland* with great pleasure; but very particular directions will be necessary as to the

---

[1] Well-paid but undemanding government positions.

[2] Thomas Otway (1652–85), a playwright known for tragedies such as *Don Carlos* (1676), *The Orphan* (1680) and *Venice Preserv'd* (1682), and comedies such as *Friendship in Fashion* (1678), *The Soldier's Fortune* (1678) and *The Atheist* (1684).

[3] Viscount Castlereagh (1739–1822), a leading figure in the Napoleonic War and senior government minister, appointed Secretary of War in 1805, and Foreign Secretary in 1812, a post which he held until committing suicide ten years later.

[4] Unduly positive reviews calculated to serve vested interests.

channel of conveyance.—If the quantity received by any person should fall short of the demand, a fresh supply may be had by sending a further order, because the press will be kept standing for the space of *three weeks*; and, indeed, in order that no means may be neglected which are within my reach, it is resolved to *re-print* after three weeks, rather than suffer any considerable portion of demand to go unanswered.—If a man in any little town, or in a village, sell 50 copies a week, why that sale gives him about *five pounds a year clear money;* and, where is he to get five pounds a year for doing really nothing but receiving and paying the money? Which may be done by his wife or his child. If, in this way, many of the Provincial Papers are lowered in their sale, do not their publishers deserve it? They, for the far greater part, convey no instruction to the people. They are either "*blind guides,*" or no guides at all. They are some of them tools of Corruption; and some of them "*dumb dogs,*" that have not the courage to take the part either of right or wrong. They are neither one thing nor the other; they are quite vapid; and, therefore, will the public "spew them out of their mouths."[1] Not, indeed, such papers as the *Nottingham Review,* the *Stamford News,* the *Liverpool Mercury,* and some others, the proprietors of which do honour to the press, and the pages of which will always be read with pleasure and advantage. There are also some good papers in London. The STATESMAN, a daily evening paper; the GLOBE too, and another or two of the daily papers; and, amongst the weekly papers, the *News,* and also the INDEPENDENT WHIG, contain a good deal of excellent matter. The proprietor of the latter frequently speaks very harshly of *me,* for what *reason* I am sure I cannot imagine; but even his illtreatment of me I regard as a good, if it at all tend to promote the circulation of the useful matter contained in his work. Some gentlemen have spoken with great anger against the proprietor for his conduct in this respect. I do not participate in that angry feeling. I hope that the gentleman in question has the cause of *his country* at heart, and, that being the case, his attacking of me, whether right or wrong, I shall always be ready to excuse.

(NOVEMBER 16, 1816)

S.T. COLERIDGE
A Lay Sermon[2]

ORTHLESS persons of little or no estimation for rank, learning, or integrity, not seldom profligates, with whom debauchery has outwrestled rapacity, easy because unprincipled and generous because dishonest, are suddenly cried up as men of enlarged views and liberal sentiments, our only genuine patriots and philanthropists: and churls, that is, men of sullen tempers and surly demeanor; men tyrannical in their families, oppressive and troublesome to their dependents and neighbours, and hard in their private dealings between man and man; men who clench with one hand what they have grasped with the other; these are extolled as public benefactors, the friends, guardians, and advocates of the poor! Here and there indeed we may notice an individual of birth and fortune

(For great estates enlarge not narrow minds)[3]

---

[1] Revelation 3:16.

[2] A well-known poet, literary critic and social commentator, Coleridge was hired in 1816 by the publisher Rest Fenner to write three Lay Sermons addressing the social and political unrest that had begun to grow after the end of the Napoleonic war. These sermons were to be directed to "the higher classes of society" in the first, "the higher and middle classes" in the second, and the labouring classes in the third, which remained unwritten. This extract is from the second Lay Sermon, which addressed "the existing distresses and discontents."

[3] Sir Fulke Greville (1554–1628), *Alaham* in *Workes* (1633): I: i: 72.

who has been duped into the ranks of incendiaries and mob-sycophants by an insane restlessness, and the wretched ambition of figuring as the triton of the minnows.[1] Or we may find perhaps a professional man of shewy accomplishments but of a vulgar taste, and shallow acquirements, who in part from vanity, and in part as a means of introduction to practice, will seek notoriety by an eloquence well calculated to set the multitude agape, and excite *gratis* to overt-acts of sedition or treason which he may afterwards be fee'd[2] to defend! These however are but exceptions to the general rule. Such as the Prophet has described, such is the *sort* of men; and in point of historic fact it has been from men of this sort, *that profaneness is gone forth into all the land.* (Jeremiah, xxiii. 15.)

In harmony with the general character of these false prophets, are the particular qualities assigned to them. First, a passion for vague and violent invective, an habitual and inveterate predilection for the language of hate, and rage and contumely, an ungoverned appetite for abuse and defamation! THE VILE WILL TALK VILLAINY.[3]

But the fetid flower will ripen into the poisonous berry, and the fruits of the hand follow the blossoms of the slanderous lips. His HEART WILL WORK INIQUITY.[4] That is, he will plan evil, and do his utmost to carry his plans into execution. The guilt exists already; and there wants nothing but power and opportunity to condense it into crime and overt-act. *He that hateth his brother is a murderer!* says St. John:[5] and of many and various sorts are the brother-haters, in whom this truth may be exemplified.

Whether in spoken or in printed Addresses, whether in periodical Journals or in yet cheaper implements of irritation, the ends are the same, the process is the same, and the same is their general line of conduct. On all occasions, but most of all and with a more bustling malignity, whenever any public distress inclines the lower classes to turbulence, and renders them more apt to be alienated from the government of their country—in all places and at every opportunity pleading *to* the Poor and Ignorant, no where and at no time are they found actually pleading *for* them. Nor is this the worst. They even plead against them. Yes! Sycophants to the *crowd*, enemies of the *individuals*, and well-wishers only to the continuance of their miseries, they plead *against* the poor and afflicted, under the weak and wicked pretense, that we are to do nothing of what we can, because we cannot do all, that we would wish. Or if this sophistry of sloth (*sophisma pigri*) should fail to check the bounty of the rich, there is still the sophistry of slander in reserve to chill the gratitude of the poor. If they cannot dissuade *the Liberal from devising liberal things,*[6] they will at least blacken the motives of his beneficence. If they cannot close the hand of the giver, they will at least embitter the gift in the mouth of the receivers. Is it not as if they had said within their hearts: the sacrifice of charity has been offered indeed in despite of us; *but with bitter herbs shall it be eaten!* (Exod. xii. 8.) Imagined Wrongs shall make it distasteful. We will infuse vindictive and discontented fancies into minds, already irritable and suspicious from distress: till the fever of the heart shall coat the tongue with gall and spread wormwood on the palate?

Such, I assert, has been the general line of conduct pursued by the political Empirics of the day: and your own recent experience will attest the truth of the assertion. It was affirmed likewise at the same time, that as the conduct, such was the *process*:

---

[1] William Shakespeare (1564–1616), *Coriolanus* (1607–09): III: i: 88.

[2] Hired.

[3] Isaiah 32:6.

[4] Isaiah 32:6.

[5] John 3:15.

[6] Isaiah 32:8.

and I will seek no other support of this charge, I need no better test both of the men and their works, than the plain question: is there one good feeling, to which they do—is there a single bad passion, to which they do not appeal? If they are the enemies of liberty in general, inasmuch as they tend to make it appear incompatible with public quiet and personal safety, still more emphatically are they the enemies of the liberty of the PRESS in particular; and therein of all the truths human and divine which a free press is the most efficient and only commensurate means of protecting, extending and perpetuating. The strongest, indeed the only plausible, arguments against the education of the lower classes, are derived from the writings of these incendiaries; and if for our neglect of the light that hath been vouchsafed to us beyond measure, the land should be visited with a spiritual dearth, it will have been in no small degree occasioned by the erroneous and wicked principles which it is the trade of these men to propagate. Alas! it is a hard and a mournful thing, that the Press should be constrained to call out for the harsh curb of the law against the Press! for how shall the Law predistinguish the ominous screech owl from the sacred notes of Augury,[1] from the auspicious and friendly birds of Warning? And yet will we avoid this seeming injustice, we throw down all fence and bulwark of public decency and public opinion. Already has political calumny joined hands with private slander, and every principle, every feeling, that binds the citizen to his country, the spirit to its Creator, is in danger of being undermined.—Not by reasoning, for from that there is no danger; but—by the mere habit of hearing them reviled and scoffed at with impunity. Were we to contemplate the evils of a rank and unweeded Press only in its effects on the manners of a people, and on the general tone of thought and conversation, the greater love we bore

[1] The art of foretelling by omens.

to literature, and to all the means and instruments of human improvement, the more anxiously should we wish for some Ithuriel spear[2] I that might remove from the ear of the ignorant and half-learned, and expose in their own fiendish shape those reptiles, which *inspiring venom and forging illusions as they list,*

——— thence raise,
At least distemper'd discontented thoughts,
Vain hopes, vain aims, inordinate desires.
PARADISE LOST.[3]
(MARCH, 1817)

THE GORGON[4]

Let not, whatever ills assail,
A damned aristocracy prevail.[5]

CORRUPTION has not yet encountered a more formidable and dangerous enemy, than in the circulation of cheap, weekly publications; and the malignant, but abortive attempts, that have been made to suppress these lights and guides to the poor, prove with what detestation and alarm their progress has been viewed by the tools of power. It is the lively apprehension of mountebanks and priests, who dread nothing so much as the exposure of their juggling tricks to the *vulgar gaze*. Possessing as the English system of Government does, in its form, all the features of vice, it is———

[2] In *Paradise Lost* (IV:799–819), Ithuriel is an angel sent by Gabriel to search for Satan, who is lurking in the Garden of Eden disguised as a toad. A touch of the spear returns him to his own likeness.

[3] *Paradise Lost* IV:802–808.

[4] The *Gorgon* (1818–19) espoused a radical utilitarian insistence on the links between economic and political exploitation. It was one of many cheap weakly magazines that emerged in the years after Cobbett reduced the price of his *Political Register* in 1816.

[5] Charles Churchill (1731–64), *The Farewell* (1764): 365–66.

——————— of such a frightful mien,
That to be hated, needs but to be seen.[1]

Before the commencement of these weekly papers, the labouring classes were, in a great measure, precluded from political information. They felt, indeed, the iron hand that was crushing them to the earth, and they beheld misery, poverty, and embarrassment spreading in every direction, but they had no means of judging of the precise causes that produced these extensive calamities. The public papers were generally in the pay of the two Sections, who were united to plunder and deceive, and conveyed little useful knowledge to the people. But how wonderfully is the scene changed during the last eighteen months! What a glare of light has been cast into every cottage and workshop of the kingdom! What a feeling of contempt and indignation has been excited in the breasts of Englishmen! The whole herd of peculators,[2] impostors, and hireling scribes have been successively held up to the scorn and execration of an insulted and deluded people. The praises that have been lavished on the reformers of convents and monks, are no less due to those meritorious individuals, whose unwearied efforts have exposed the injustice and corruptions of the English Government.

Every one must have read over the list of public paupers, placemen, pensioners,[3] and seen the amount of these enormous sums, which make the head giddy to think of, lavished in the support of gamblers and debauchees. The mysteries, too, of public credit, or rather public delusion, with the whole bubble of our paper system, have been made as clear as noon-day. Just notions have been inculcated on the nature of a war, undertaken from a dread of liberty at home, and to perpetuate slavery and tyranny abroad. Above all, the people have learnt the extent of their constitutional rights, as purchased by the blood of their ancestors, and of which they have been deprived by a proud and insolent aristocracy.

In the prudent, steady, and persevering conduct of the people, we observe the value of that information, which has been so carefully disseminated; and although the hydra[4] of corruption still rears its accursed head amongst us, we are persuaded, that it must ultimately fall beneath general indignation and contempt. Strong in all the arts of long-practised villainy, the honest and undisguised attempts of the people, have proved unequal to the attack of a system of such complicated fraud and guilt—defended, by all the artifices of swindlers, the craft of priests, and the ferocity of a Nero.[5] But nature is at war with such a system; and though it may continue for a time to "vex the mind and grieve the heart,"[6] it cannot long exist, opposed as it is to the sacred claims of justice, and the happiness of the community. One advantage we derive from "hope deferred," is, that it will teach us the value of our inheritance. Premature possession might have led to abuse; but we shall now enter upon it after repeated trials, contests, and privations, and shall know both how to defend and how to enjoy it.

It is in order to promote the great work of enlightening the minds of the people, and preparing them for those changes which must infallibly come, that we have commenced the present publication. In giving it to the public, we feel very little concern about its fate; if our intentions are good we know time will discover them, and they will be duly appreciated; if we have merit it will meet its reward.

---

[1] Alexander Pope (1688–1744), *Essay on Man* (1733–34): 2: 217–18.

[2] Embezzlers.

[3] Placemen and pensioners: recipients of government patronage.

[4] In Greek mythology, a nine-headed serpent that grew two-heads for each one that was cut off.

[5] Nero (A.D. 54–68), a Roman emperor remembered for his tyranny and brutality.

[6] Source unidentified.

Whatever may be the success of our undertaking, we engage, that our promises shall not exceed the extent of our abilities to perform,—nor will we begin with lofty professions of unchangeable virtue and patriotism which the end might belie. We do not pledge ourselves either to live or die by our present opinion, which time may prove to be false or erroneous. Nothing is so irksome as a first introduction. Even knaves are at a loss under what new shape to invade public credulity. Should we at once disclaim all intention to promote the public good, our conduct would certainly be novel, but imply such a degree of self-crimination, as our judges would hardly approve; and on the other hand, to begin with more flattering professions, we should justly incur suspicion and mistrust. Patriotism has long been the beaten path to popular favour; the glory of God to ecclesiastical ambition and emolument; and outward professions of honour and morality to the most afflicting inroads on domestic peace. We shall pride ourselves on none of these.

However, as the reader may reasonably expect a more strict account of our principles and opinions, we declare, without reserve, that we detest and abhor the vile oligarchy which has trampled on the rights and privileges of the people, and whose shameless system of corruption and injustice, are alike incompatible with the interests and welfare of society; nor less do we hate and despise, as the worst enemies of reform, those incorrigible fools whom experience has not taught wisdom, and who still pester mankind with their crazy and delusive theories. Though we intend to steer clear of the two extremes of injustice and corruption on one hand, and political fanaticism, think not, reader, we shall follow some middle, compromising course, that we have no definite opinions, but shape them to the "varying taste and fashion of the times."[1] No: our aim is to lash with unsparing and equal severity error and injustice, the designs of presumptuous ignorance, and hireling knavery. Even good intentions accompanied with mischievous doings, shall, with us, find no mercy. Measures shall be judged by their effects, and men by their actions. We make no professions ourselves, nor shall we value them in others. We care not to be called patriots, philanthropists, or citizens of the world, no more than we do Spenceans, republicans, or antiquity worshippers.[2] We may write from ambition, interest, or revenge, but let our arguments be the test of truth, and our actions our virtues.

(MAY 23, 1818)

THE EXAMINER
The Editor of the Quarterly Review [3]

THIS little person is a considerable cat's-paw; and so far worthy of some slight notice. He is the *Government Critic*, a character nicely differing from that of a government spy—the invisible link, that connects literature with the police. It is his business to keep a strict eye over all writers who differ in opinion with His Majesty's Ministers, and to measure their talents and attainments by the standard of their servility and meanness. For this office he is well qualified.—The Editor of the *Quarterly*

---

[1] Source unidentified.

[2] Followers of the agrarian reformer and political activist Thomas Spence grouped together in the year after his death in 1814 to form the Society of Spencean Philanthropists. The Spenceans were an important element of the radical movement in the years of political unrest that followed. The *Gorgon* rejected the nostalgic tendency of some radicals to celebrate an earlier era of social harmony in Britain.

[3] This article, about William Gifford, editor of the *Quarterly Magazine*, was by William Hazlitt (1778–1830), a leading essayist known for his radical political sympathies. *The Examiner*, a weekly radical periodical founded by Leigh and John Hunt, distinguished itself by its combination of political journalism and original poetry and criticism by authors such as Hazlitt, Percy Shelley, John Keats, and Charles Lamb. *The Examiner* ran from 1808–81, with Leigh Hunt as editor until 1821.

Review is also Paymaster of the Band of Gentle-man-Pensioners; and whenever an author comes before him in the one capacity, with whom he is not acquainted in the other, he knows how to deal with him. He has his cue beforehand. The distinction between truth and falsehood is lost upon him; he knows only the distinction between Whig and Tory. The same set of thread-bare common-places, the same second-hand assortment of abusive nick-names, are always repeated; and the ready convenient lie comes in aid of the lack of other resources, and passes off, with impunity, in the garb of religion and loyalty. He is under the protection of *the Court*; and his zeal for his King and country gives him a right to say what he pleases of every public writer who does not do all in his power to pamper the one into a tyrant, and to trample the other into a herd of slaves. Without wit or understanding in himself, he derives his weight with the great and powerful from the very circumstance that takes away all real weight from his opinion, viz. that it has no one object but to flatter their folly and vices in the grossest manner, by holding up to hatred and contempt whatever opposes in the slightest degree, or in the most flagrant instances of abuse, their pride and passions. Accustomed to the indulgence of his mercenary virulence and party-spite, he seems to have lost all relish as well as capacity for the ordinary exercises of the understanding, and makes up for the obvious want of ability by the barefaced want of principle. There is something in the nature of the man that suits with his office. He is in no danger of exciting the jealousy of his patrons by a splendid display of extraordinary talents, while his sordid devotion to their will, and to his own interest, at once ensures their gratitude and contempt. Of an humble origin himself, he recommends his performances to persons of fashion by always abusing *low people*, with the smartness of a lady's waiting-woman, and the independent spirit of a travelling tutor. Raised from the lowest rank to his present despicable eminence in the world of letters, he is indignant that any one should attempt to rise into notice, except by the same regular trammels and servile gradations, or go about to separate the stamp of merit from the badge of sycophancy. The silent listener in select circles, and menial tool of noble families, has become the oracle of Church and State. The purveyor to the prejudices of a private patron succeeds, by no other title, to regulate the public taste. Having felt the inconvenience of poverty, this man looks up with low and groveling admiration to the advantages of wealth and power: having had to contend with the mechanical difficulties of ignorance, he sees nothing in learning but its mechanical uses. A self-taught man naturally becomes a pedant, and mistakes the means of knowledge for the end, unless he is a man of genius; and Mr. Gifford is not a man of genius. From having known nothing originally, he thinks it a great matter to know anything now, no matter what or how small it is—nay, the smaller and more insignificant it is, the more curious he thinks it, as it is farther removed from common sense and human nature. The collating of points and commas is the highest game his literary ambition can reach to, and the squabbles of editors are to him infinitely more important than the meaning of an author. —He thinks more of the letter than the spirit of a passage; and in his eagerness to show his minute superiority over others, misses both. There cannot be a greater nuisance than a dull, envious, lowbred man, who is placed in the situation of the Editor of the *Quarterly Review*. Conscious that his reputation stands on very slender and narrow foundations, he is naturally jealous of the pretensions of others. He insults over unsuccessful authors; he hates successful ones. He is angry at the faults of a work, more angry at its excellences. If an opinion is old, he treats it with supercilious indifference; if it is new, it provokes his rage. Having but a limited range of understanding, every thing beyond that range appears to him a paradox and an absurdity: and he resents every suggestion of the kind as an imposition on the public, and an insult on his own sagacity. He cavils at what he does not comprehend, and misrepresents what he knows to be true. Bound to go through the periodical task of abusing all those who are not, like himself, the abject tools of power, his irritation increases with the number of obstacles he meets with, and the number of sacrifices he is obliged to make of common sense and veracity to his interest and self-conceit. Every instance of prevarication he wilfully commits makes him more in love with hypocrisy, and every indulgence of his hired malignity makes him more disposed to repeat the insult and the injury. His understanding becomes more and more distorted, and his feelings more and more callous. Grown old in the service of corruption, he drivels on to the last with prostituted impotence, and shameless effrontery; salves a meagre reputation for wit, by venting the driblets of his spleen and impertinence on others; answers their arguments by confuting himself; mistakes habitual obtuseness of intellect for a particular acuteness, not to be imposed upon by shallow pretensions; unprincipled rancour for zealous loyalty; and the irritable, discontented, vindictive and peevish effusions of bodily pain and mental infirmity, for proofs of refinement of taste and strength of understanding.

(JUNE 14, 1818)

THE EXAMINER
State of The World [1]

Party is the madness of many for the gain
of a few.—*POPE*

THIS is the commencement, if we are not much mistaken, of one of the most important years that have been seen for a long while. It is quiet; it seems peaceable to us here in Europe; it may even continue so, as far as any great warfare is concerned; but a spirit is abroad, stronger than kings, or armies, or all the most predominant shapes of prejudice and force. It is like the interval described by the poet:—

> Nor war, nor battle's sound,
> Was heard the world around;
>   The idle spear and shield were high up hung;
> The hooked chariot stood
> Unstained with hostile blood;
>   The trumpet spake not to the armed throng;
> And kings sat still with awful eye,
> As if they surely knew their sovran Lord was by. [2]

This spirit is knowledge. The "sovran Lord" is that gigantic sense of the general good which has awaked for the first time in the known history of the world, and is stretching his earth-thrilling limbs from Caucasus to the Andes. So completely do all classes feel that something, as the phrase is, must be done; or rather, that this knowledge, and this sense of the general good, must go on increasing, in consequence of the diffusion of the press and the enormous growth of scientific power, that the kings and their ministers would willingly persuade us of the commencement of a sort of millenium under *their* auspices. Some of them and their advocates, who have not yet recovered the fright of their own success, are even inclined to believe, if they do not actually do so, in the approach of the millenium itself, that is to say, the reign of the saints upon earth for a thousand years, a religious golden age. The Emperor ALEXANDER [3] is a known mystic.

---

[1] This excerpt is from the lead article in the first edition in 1819.

[2] John Milton (1608–74), "On the Morning of Christ's Nativity" (1629): 53–60.

[3] Alexander Pavlovich (1777–1825), Emperor of Russia.

Madame KRUDENER,[1] a polite Joanna South-cotte,[2] whose person he is said to have admired formerly till converted by the more seasonable beauties of her mysticism, openly preaches a new order of things, of which "kings are the nursing fathers."[3] And even the *Courier*, sly but at the same time bare-faced rogue, announces an era which is to "realize the utmost dreams of philanthropic enthusiasm." We quote from memory, but his words are quite as strong. The meaning of all this is,—first, that the "great men of the earth" have really been put into a state of superstitious wonder by their success and apparent re-establishment;—secondly, that they dare not go to war for sometime to come, because their broken promises have lost them their momentary popularity; and thirdly, that if they do not lead the world, something else will. They make Holy Alliances;[4] are willing nevertheless to be thought knowing in all liberal matters; and meanwhile, on the very threshold of their Eden, betray the worldly effects of their religious system and the poor opinion it generates of the Divine Power; for observe,—they keep possession of foreign countries to which they have no more right than BONAPARTE had to his: they pray, they withhold, they grasp, they deceive, they trample, they preach, they regret, they laugh and they lie. It is the old joke come to court. Have you tied up the Poles? Have you deceived the Italians? Have you battered and trucked up the Norwegians? Have you cribbed the Saxons? Have you cheated the universe? Then come up to prayers.

Now the world at large are far beyond their leaders in the knowledge of their own interests,—a natural consequence of the progress of knowledge itself, which the privileged orders are of necessity slow to follow. And we repeat our firm conviction, that if the leaders can continue to remain at their head, so much the better for themselves; if not, the world will do without them. Divine Right, Loyalty, and other perverted terms, are found to have no meaning separate from the general good; and having no such meaning, they have no longer any meaning to serve the purposes of the few. Legitimacy[5] stands them in more stead. It is merely substituting one name for another, because the thing named by it has been found wanting;—and *because* it has been found wanting, the name will not do. When the people ask for more equal rights and enjoyments, and are answered with such words as Legitimacy, they might as well be told of the Sign of the Leg.[6] The thing has nothing to do with the question. It had; but it is done with; and if kings chuse to discuss it with each other, the world will quit them, and go on, as it is prepared to do already. If all the queens of all the kings that ever lived were as chaste as icicles (which it appears, was not the case),—if they had been dumb, deaf, blind, and insensible to all the enticements of courts, times, manners and opinions; and in continued meditations on the united virtues of Legitimacy and Chastity, had even

Made themselves marble with too much conceiving,[7]

---

[1] Baroness Juliana von Krüdener (1764–1824), a Russian novelist and mystic. An aristocrat by birth, in 1801 she left her husband, a diplomat, and immersed herself in the literary and social life in Paris and Switzerland. She claimed to have inspired the formation of the Holy Alliance of Russia, Austria, and Prussia.

[2] Joanna Southcott (1750–1814), a religious visionary whose prophecies earned her a large following. She distanced herself from popular radicalism, but the considerable overlap between other religious visionaries or enthusiasts and the radical movement made Southcott an object of government attention.

[3] Isaiah 49:23.

[4] An alliance formed in 1815 by Russia, Austria, and Prussia, aimed at preserving the peace settlement at the end of the Napoleonic War, it reinvigorated monarchical rule in Europe.

[5] Sarcastic term for the attempt of government leaders to restore the old, pre-Revolutionary status-quo of monarchical governments after the end of the Napoleonic War.

[6] William Shakespeare (1564–1616), *2 Henry IV* (1600): II: iv: 249.

[7] John Milton (1608–74), "On Shakespeare" (1630).

the result would have been of no consequence to the spirit and demands of the present age. The last representatives and *residuums*[1] of dynasties might have been twice the *mortuum caputs*[2] they are (we beg pardon of Latin plurals), and they would not have kept their ground. The purest, ten-thousandth "transmitter of a foolish face"[3] would really not have been worshipped.

The Methodists have a phrase of "sweet experiences."[4] The world has had it's "sweet experiences," till it is sick; and it is these which together with it's more happily acquired knowledge will produce whatever millenium it is about to enjoy. In Spain, for instance, there is the sweet experience of King FERDINAND,[5] alias the Grateful, alias the Embroiderer, alias the Creature. In Poland, there is the very sweet experience of Russia, Austria, and Prussia.[6] In France there is the experience of the Revolution and the BOURBONS.[7] In South America, there is the experience of the Mother Country, who burned the very produce of the soil lest it should make its colonies independent for common comfort.[8]

In short, the world has now

1st. The experience of despots.

2d. The experience of *French* revolutions.

3d. A sense of it's wants.

4th. A knowledge of it's means.

5th. The examples of North and South America.

6th. An universal press, with a hundredth part of which LUTHER undid the despotism of Authority.[9]

And 7th. The astonishing growth of that experimental philosophy, which has such an effect both on the production of means and the diffusion of knowledge; and which it's illustrious father, Lord BACON, prophecied, would alter the world.

(JANUARY 3, 1819)

---

[1] Dregs.

[2] Worthless residue. Alchemist's term for the residue after distillation.

[3] Richard Savage (1697?–1743), "The Bastard: A Poem" (1728).

[4] A moment of immediate communication with God, often resulting in religious conversion or the intensification of one's existing beliefs.

[5] Ferdinand I (1751–1825), King of the Two Sicilies (1816–25). Ferdinand's government, which was reinforced by royalist powers after Napoleon's defeat, was infamous for its reactionary spirit. His policies provoked an insurrection in 1820, though with Austria's aid, he was able to reinforce his authority in 1821, when he intensified his persecution of all liberal reformers.

[6] A liberal constitution established in Poland in 1791, was terminated in 1793 by a displaced elite acting with the help of the Russian military. Two years later, Poland was divided up between Russia, Austria, and Prussia, a situation which lasted until 1830.

[7] The Royalist powers that defeated Napoleon used their victory to reinstate the Bourbons, who had been on the throne before the Revolution, as France's monarchy.

[8] Spain's conduct in its war with its South American colonies was a recurring topic in the radical press.

[9] The Reformation was widely associated with the advent of the press.

SECTION TWELVE

British India

The struggles over the nature of English literature did not happen in a national context alone. Nor were the imperial dimensions any less complicated. The connections between literature and empire in the Romantic period were necessarily developed within the complex and often turbulent debate about the moral character of empire. Tensions over the American war, the trial of Warren Hastings, the debates over the 1793 and 1813 renewal of the East India Company's monopoly license, and the rebellion in Ireland all helped to ensure that there would be no easy consensus on the issue of England's presence beyond its own borders. But if this proved to be problematic, most commentators were able to find common ground in their celebration of the disinterested work of authors toiling to develop a greater understanding of subaltern cultures.

Commentators stressed that the more information that Orientalists such as Sir William Jones, Charles Hamilton, Thomas Maurice, and Nathaniel Halhed gathered, the more humanely imperial administrators would be able to adapt themselves to local customs. Jones and his colleagues took this role seriously. They insisted that the main point of their efforts was to make it possible to rule in more tolerant ways by developing an awareness of Oriental literature and culture. In this way, they were as reformist in their mind-set as many authors were in Britain. The difference, however, was that the sovereignty of the imperial administration was never called into question. For Asian populations to be liberated, these writers insisted, they needed to be ruled by governors (the British) who understood the importance of liberty.

These efforts offered a convenient justification for apologists who remained worried by the recurring news of imperial violence as the East India Company consolidated its hold in the Asian subcontinent. The problem with this justification was that it remained haunted by the uglier realities of military conquest which, as Charles Hamilton acknowledged in his *Preface to the Hedaya*, the exploratory work of the Orientalists implicitly relied upon. Public reaction to the outlandish profits made by commercial adventurers in India, many of whom returned to Britain to purchase landed estates and gain seats in parliament, made it all the more attractive to dwell on the important blessings gained for civilization as a whole as a result of the work of these authors. But critics complained that too often, the British reading public, by either ignoring Oriental texts or, at best, taking an interest in them as exotic novelties, replicated the conditions of those supposedly degenerate cultures which the Orientalists claimed to be saving this literature from. All of these dynamics helped to simultaneously promote and undermine the ideal of literature as a disinterested and universal sphere of knowledge

The image of the selfless author toiling at the outer edges of the empire for the good of both the subject people and civilization in general was attractive for several reasons, but there were other opinions about the connections between literature and empire. In his defence of John Stockdale for publishing the Rev. Logan's critique of the charges against Warren Hastings, the former governor of India, Thomas Erskine argued that it was hypocritical of the British to rule on Hastings's supposed excesses since the very nature of empire was itself a form of excess that contravened any respect for the sovereignty of foreign nations. Others were less critical than Erskine, but they had a range of different ideas about how to redeem the administration of the British empire from the scandals which continued to plague it. Thomas Macaulay's *Minute on India Education* marked a radical change in British policy because it argued that literature had an important role to play in the imperial administration, not as a source of information about native cultures, but as a basis of a cultural rather than religious evangelicalism. Insisting that "a single shelf of a good European library was worth the whole native literature of India and Arabia," Macaulay argued that true liberality did not mean pretending to respect the worth of cultures which were obviously inferior, but in saving those cultures from their own degeneracy by introducing them to the blessings of English culture. This altered the direction in which literary knowledge was supposed to flow, but for administrators, its cultural rather than religious focus had the advantage of forestalling demands for a Christian missionary presence. As the *Quarterly Magazine* suggested, those who accepted this plan often did so in the hope that a taste for English culture—including reports of "Shakspeare performed by Gentoos and Mahometans on the shore of the Ganges!"—would lead inevitably to a respect for the Christian faith.

❧❧❧

Sir William Jones
The Second Anniversary Discourse Delivered 24 February, 1785 by The President [1]

WHOEVER travels in *Asia*, especially if he be conversant with the literature of the countries

through which he passes, must naturally remark the superiority of *European* talents: the observation, indeed, is at least as old as ALEXANDER; and though we cannot agree with the sage preceptor of that ambitious Prince, that "the *Asiaticks* are born to be slaves,"[2] yet the *Athenian* poet[3] seems perfectly in the right, when he represents *Europe* as a *sovereign*

[1] Sir William Jones (1746–94), the leading British Orientalist of the period, was respected as a linguist for his knowledge of Sanskrit, but also as an authority on Hindu and Muslim law. He was a judge of the High Court at Calcutta from 1783 until his death eleven years later, and founder and first President of the Asiatic Society of Bengal. This excerpt is from the second of Jones's annual Anniversary Discourses, which he used as opportunities to map out the contours of Orientalist research.

[2] Aristotle (384–322 B.C.), a tutor of Alexander the Great (356–323 B.C.), argued in *Politics* (350 B.C.) that "the natives of Asia are intelligent and inventive, but they are wanting in spirit, and therefore they are always in a state of subjection and slavery" (Book 7, Part VII).

[3] *Euripides* (c. 480–406 B.C.), referred to Asia as "Europe's handmaid" in *Hecuba* (424 B.C.): chorus, 1st antistrophe 2.

Princess, and *Asia* as *her Handmaid*: but if the mistress be transcendently majestick, it cannot be denied that the attendant has many beauties, and some advantages peculiar to herself. The ancients were accustomed to pronounce *panegyricks* on their own countrymen at the expence of all other nations, with a political view, perhaps, of stimulating them by praise, and exciting them to still greater exertions; but such arts are here unnecessary; nor would they, indeed, become a Society[1] who seek nothing but truth unadorned by rhetorick; and although we must be conscious of our superior advancement in all kinds of useful knowledge, yet we ought not therefore to contemn the people of *Asia*, from whose researches into nature, works of art, and inventions of fancy, many valuable hints may be derived for our own improvement and advantage. If that, indeed, were not the principal object of your institution, little else could arise from it but the mere gratification of curiosity; and I should not receive so much delight from the humble share which you have allowed me to take in promoting it.

To form an exact parallel between the works and actions of the Western and Eastern worlds, would require a tract of no inconsiderable length; but we may decide on the whole, that reason and taste are the grand prerogatives of *European* minds, while the *Asiaticks* have soared to loftier heights in the sphere of imagination. The civil history of their vast empires, and of *India* in particular, must be highly interesting to our common country; but we have a still nearer interest in knowing all former modes of ruling *these inestimable provinces*, on the prosperity of which so much of our national welfare, and individual benefit, seems to depend. A minute *geographical* knowledge, not only of *Bengal* and

Bahar,[2] but, for evident reasons, of *all the kingdoms bordering on them,* is closely connected with an account of their many revolutions: but the *natural* productions of these territories, especially in the *vegetable* and *mineral* systems, are momentous objects of research not only to an *imperial*, but, which is a character of equal dignity, a *commercial* people.

All these objects of inquiry must appear to you, Gentlemen, in so strong a light, that bare intimations of them will be sufficient; nor is it necessary to make use of *emulation* as an incentive to an ardent pursuit of them: yet I cannot forbear expressing a wish, that the activity of the *French* in the same pursuits may not be superior to ours, and that the researches of M. SONNERAT,[3] whom the court of *Versailles* employed for seven years in these climates, merely to collect such materials as we are seeking, may kindle, instead of abating, our own curiosity and zeal. If you assent, as I flatter myself you do, to these opinions, you will also concur in promoting the object of them; and a few ideas having presented themselves to my mind, I presume to lay them before you, with an entire submission to your judgment.

No contributions, except those of the literary kind, will be requisite for the support of the Society; but if each of us were occasionally to contribute a succinct description of such manuscripts as he had perused or inspected, with their dates and the names of their owners, and to propose for solution such *questions* as had occurred to him concerning *Asiatick* Art, Science, and History, natural or civil, we should possess without labour, and almost by imperceptible degrees, a fuller catalogue of Oriental books than has hitherto been exhibited, and our

---

[1] The Asiatic Society of Bengal, founded by Jones in 1784 to promote Orientalist research.

[2] Indian territories controlled by Britain through the East India Company.

[3] Pierre Sonnerat (1748–1814), travelled in India and China from 1774–81 on behalf of the French king.

correspondents would be apprised of those points, to which we chiefly direct our investigations. Much may, I am confident, be expected from the communications of *learned natives*, whether lawyers, physicians, or private scholars, who would eagerly, on the first invitation, send us their *Mekámát* and *Risalahs*[1] on a variety of subjects; some for the sake of advancing general knowledge, but most of them from a desire, neither uncommon nor unreasonable, of attracting notice, and recommending themselves to favour. With a view to avail ourselves of this disposition, and to bring their latent science under our inspection, it might be adviseable to print and circulate a short memorial, in *Persian* and *Hindi*, setting forth, in a style accommodated to their own habits and prejudices, the design of our institution; nor would it be impossible hereafter to give a medal annually, with inscriptions, in *Persian* on one side, and on the reverse in *Sanscrit*, as the prize of merit, to the writer of the best essay or dissertation. To instruct others is the prescribed duty of learned *Bráhmans*,[2] and, if they be men of substance, without reward; but they would all be flattered with an honorary mark of distinction; and the *Mahomedans* have not only the permission, but the positive command, of their law-giver, *to search for learning even in the remotest parts of the globe*. It were superfluous to suggest, with how much correctness and facility their compositions might be translated for our use, since their languages are now more generally and perfectly understood than they have ever been by any nation of *Europe*.

(1785)

THOMAS ERSKINE
Speech for the Defense in the Case of the King against John Stockdale, for a Libel on the House of Commons.[3]

GENTLEMEN, the author having discussed all the Charges, article by article, sums them all up with this striking appeal to his readers:

"The authentic statement, of facts which has been given, and the arguments which have been employed, are, I think, sufficient to vindicate the character and conduct of Mr. Hastings,[4] even on the maxims of European policy. When he was appointed Governor General of Bengal, he was invested with a discretionary power to promote the interests of the India Company, and of the British empire in that quarter of the globe. The general instructions sent to him from his constituents were, *"That in all your deliberations and resolutions, you make the safety and prosperity of Bengal your principal object, and fix your attention on the security of the possessions and revenues of the Company."* His superior genius sometimes acted in the spirit, rather than complied with the letter, of the law; but he discharged the trust, and preserved the empire committed to his care, in the same way, and with greater splendor and success than any of his predecessors in office; his departure from India was marked with the lamentations of the natives, and

---

[1] Treatises or journals.

[2] Members of the first of the four Hindu castes in India, traditionally associated with religious authority and respected for their learned achievements.

[3] Thomas Erskine (1750–1823), was defending Stockdale for publishing a pamphlet responding to the Articles of Impeachment against Warren Hastings (1732–1818), the Governor General of Bengal from 1772. In doing so, he was placed in the implicit position of defending Hastings because Stockdale's publication was essentially a critique of Hastings's prosecutors. Erskine did so, however, not by denying Hastings's guilt, but by extending that guilt to the whole of Britain's imperial enterprise.

[4] Warren Hastings (1732–1818), Governor-General of Bengal from 1772, faced trial and impeachment by the House of Commons in England (the trial lasted from 1788–95) for the East India Company's often ruthless conduct as a conquering power. He was widely respected by Orientalist researchers, however, for his generous support of their work.

the gratitude of his countrymen; and on his return to England, he received the cordial congratulations of that numerous and respectable society, whose interests he had promoted, and whose dominions be had protected and extended."

Gentlemen of the Jury—If this be a wilfully false account, of the instructions given to Mr. Hastings for his governments and of his conduct under them, the author and publisher of this defense deserve the severest punishment, for a mercenary imposition on the public.—But if it be true that he was directed to make the safety and prosperity of Bengal the first object of his attention, and that, under his administration, it has been safe and prosperous;—if it be true that the security and preservation of our possessions and revenues in Asia were marked out to him as the great leading principle of his government, and that those possessions and revenues, amidst unexampled dangers, have been secured and preserved; then a question may be unaccountably mixed with your consideration, much beyond the consequence of the present prosecution, involving, perhaps, the merit of the Impeachment itself which gave it birth;—a question which the Commons, as prosecutors of Mr. Hastings, should in common prudence have avoided; unless, regretting the unwieldy length of their proceedings against him, they wished to afford him the opportunity of this strange anomalous defence.—For although I am neither his counsel, nor desire to have any thing to do with his guilt or innocence; yet, in the collateral defense of my Client, I am driven to state matter which may be considered by many as hostile to the Impeachment. For if our dependencies have been secured, and their interests promoted, I am driven in the defense of my Client to remark, that it is mad and preposterous to bring to the standard of justice and humanity, the exercise of a dominion founded upon violence and terror. It may, and must be true, that Mr. Hastings has repeatedly offended against

the rights and privileges of Asiatic government, if he was the faithful deputy of a power which could not maintain itself for an hour without trampling upon both:—he may and must have offended against the laws of God and nature, if he was the faithful viceroy of an empire wrested in blood from the people to whom God and nature had given-it:—he may and must have preserved that unjust dominion over timorous and abject nations by a terrifying, overbearing, insulting superiority, if he was the faithful administrator of your government, which having no root in consent or affection,—no foundation in similarity of interests,—nor support from any one principle which cements men together in society, could only be upheld by alternate stratagem and force. The unhappy people of India, feeble and effeminate as they are from the softness of their climate, and subdued and broken as they have been by the knavery and strength of civilization, still occasionally start up in all the vigour and intelligence of insulted nature:—to be governed at all, they must be governed with a rod of iron; and our empire in the East would, long since, have been lost to Great Britain, if civil skill and military prowess had not united their efforts to support an authority which Heaven never gave,—by means which it never can sanction.

These reflections are the only antidotes to those anathemas of super-human eloquence which have lately shaken these walls that surround us;[1]—but which it unaccountably falls to my province, whether I will or no, a little to stem the torrent of,—by reminding you that you have a mighty sway in Asia, which cannot be maintained by the finer sympathies of life, or the practice of its charities and affections what will they do for you when surrounded by two hundred thousand men with artillery, cavalry, and elephants, calling upon you

---

[1] A reference to the impassioned rhetorical styles of Edmund Burke and Thomas Sheridan in their speeches for the prosecution.

for their dominions which you have robbed them of! Justice may, no doubt, in such a case forbid the levying of a fine to pay a revolting soldiery:—a treaty may stand in the way of increasing a tribute to keep up the very existence of the government;—and delicacy for women may forbid all entrance into a Zenana[1] for money, whatever may be the necessity for taking it.—All these things must ever be occurring.—But under the pressure of such constant difficulties, so dangerous to national honour, it might be better perhaps to think of effectually securing it altogether, by recalling our troops and our merchants, and abandoning our Oriental empire. Until this be done, neither religion nor philosophy can be pressed very far into the aid of reformation and punishment.—If England, from a lust of ambition and dominion, will insist on maintaining despotic rule over distant and hostile nations, beyond all comparison more numerous and extended than herself, and gives commission to her viceroys to govern them with no other instructions than to preserve them, and to secure permanently their revenues; with what colour of consistency or reason can she place herself in the moral chair, and affect to be shocked at the execution of her own orders; adverting to the exact measure of wickedness and injustice necessary to their execution, and complaining only of *the excess* as the immorality, considering her authority as a dispensation for breaking the commands of God, and the breach of them as only punishable when contrary to the ordinances of man.

Such a proceeding, Gentlemen, begets serious reflections.—It would be better perhaps for the masters and the servants of all such governments, to join in supplication, that the great Author of violated humanity may not confound them together in one common judgment.

(1789)

---

[1] Women's apartments.

CHARLES HAMILTON
Preface to *The Hedaya, or Guide; a Commentary on the Mussulman Laws* [2]

THE diffusion of useful knowledge, and the eradication of prejudice, though not among the most brilliant consequences of extended empire and commerce, are certainly not the least important.—To open and to clear the road to science; to provide for its reception in whatever form it may appear, in whatever language it may be conveyed:—these are advantages which in part atone for the guilt of conquest, and in many cases compensate for the evils which the acquisition of dominion too often inflicts.

Perhaps the history of the world does not furnish an example of any nation to whom the opportunity of acquiring this knowledge, or communicating those advantages, has been afforded in so eminent a degree as GREAT-BRITAIN.—To the people of this Island, the accession of a vast empire in the bosom of ASIA, inhabited, not by hordes of Barbarians, but by men far advanced in all the arts of civilized life, has opened a field of observation equally curious and instructive.—Such researches must ever be pleasing to the speculative philosopher, who, unbiassed by the selfish motives of interest or ambition, delights in perusing the great variegated volume of society:—but to *us* they come recommended by no *ordinary* inducements; know-

---

[2] Charles Hamilton (*c.* 1753–92), traveled to India in 1776 as a cadet in East India Company's establishment in Bengal. Having applied himself to the study of oriental languages, Hamilton became one of the first members of the Asiatic Society. Hamilton's extensive legal commentary, *The Hedaya, or Guide; a Commentary on the Mussulman Laws*, which was commissioned by the Governor-General of Bengal and written during a five-year leave in Britain, reflected his belief (one which was shared by the Orientalists generally) that imperial governors, charged with administering populations whose legal and cultural traditions were foreign to their own, required a "means of consulting" local customs including "the principals on which the decisions of the Mussulman courts are founded."

ing, and feeling, as we ought, how much the preservation of what we have obtained depends upon the proper use of our power; and upon the right application of those means which PROVIDENCE has placed in our hands for continuing, and perhaps increasing, the happiness of a large portion of the human race.

The permanency of any foreign dominion (and indeed, the justification of holding such a dominion) requires that a strict attention be paid to the ease and advantage, not only of the *governors,* but of the *governed;* and to this great end nothing can so effectually contribute as preserving to the latter their ancient established practices, civil and religious, and protecting them in the exercise of their own institutes; for however defective or absurd these may in many cases appear, still they must be infinitely more acceptable than any *we* could offer; since they are supported by the accumulated prejudices of the ages, and, in the opinion of their followers, derive their origin from the Divinity himself.

This salutary maxim was wisely adopted by the servants of the EAST INDIA COMPANY on the first acquisition of out *BENGAL* territories; and to a steady adherence to it much of the present flourishing state of those provinces must be attributed.

(1791)

THOMAS MAURICE
Indian Antiquities, or Dissertations on Hindostan [1]

IN the year 1785, a singular phenomenon made its appearance, in the world of literature, under the title of BHAGVAT-GEETA or Dialogues of Creeshna and Arjoon. [2] This production was asserted to be a translation by Mr. Wilkins [3] from a Sanscreet [4] poem, denominated the MAHABBA-RAT, or Great War, of which poem it forms an episode, and the public were informed that it is believed in India to be of the venerable antiquity of four thousand years, and that it contained all the grand mysteries of the Hindoo Religion.

The GEETA was ushered into the world with all the importance which so invaluable a monument of Indian science seemed to merit: it was prefaced by a recommendatory letter from the Governor-General of Bengal to the Directors, and published at the expense of the Company. [5] The profound theological and metaphysical doctrines which were inculcated in it, with the date to which it laid claim, roused the attention and excited the curiosity of the public, whose eyes about that period began, in a more particular manner, to be directed towards the history and literature of India. It fell into my hands at a period when, from being engaged in writing upon a subject connected with an interesting period of Persian history, I had recently perused with attention the very learned work of Dr. Hyde, "De

---

[1] Thomas Maurice (1754–1824), a British cleric, was one of the first of the British Orientalists to popularize a knowledge of the history and religion of India.

[2] One of the principal sacred writings of the Hindus, probably from the 1st or 2nd century A.D. A section of the epic poem, *The Mahā-bhārata,* in which Krishna instructs and exhorts Arjuna before battle.

[3] Sir Charles Wilkins (1750–1836), traveled to Bengal in the service of the East India Company as a writer and became superintendent of the company's factories at Maldah. Inspired by Nathaniel Halhed's efforts, Wilkins played a central role in constructing a printing press of the oriental languages in 1778, and in helping Sir William Jones establish the Asiatic Society of Bengal in 1784.

[4] Sanskrit: the ancient and classical language of the Hindus in India.

[5] The East India Company was launched as a commercial venture in 1600 by a group of London merchants. It had a monopoly in Britain over the Asiatic trade. In the mid-eighteenth century, partly as a result of competition with French interests in India, the Company had developed a military presence that was reinforced by its own standing army. As it gained possession of an increasing share of India, the Company developed into a political infrastructure as well.

Historia Religionis Veterum Persarum,"[1] and, as I thought I traced a surprising similitude in the theological systems of ZOROASTER[2] and BRAHMA,[3] particularly in the mutual veneration of the SUN and FIRE, I was gradually led on to that more accurate investigation and comparison of their principles, of which the Dissertation on the Religion of Hindostan is the result.

From considering the Religion, I passed, by an easy and natural transition, to an attentive consideration of the History, the Philosophy, and Literature, of this wonderful and remote race of men. The light, which so strongly radiates from the page of classical antiquity upon most other abstruse points of literary research, cast but a glimmering ray on this obscure subject; and indeed its assertions were, in many instances, diametrically opposite to what, from the information of modern travellers of high repute, is known to be the fact. Whatever genuine information could possibly be obtained relative to India, its early history and literature seemed only to be acquired through the medium of faithful versions from the Sanscreet, the ancient original language of the country, and the grand repository of all its history and sciences; but, unfortunately, at that period, there were only three gentlemen who were supposed to be thoroughly acquainted with it, viz. Sir William Jones, Mr. Halhed[4] and Mr. Wilkins.

The scientific labours of these gentlemen are displayed in that grand repository of Sanscreet information, the two volumes of ASIATIC RESEARCHES, which have successively arrived in this country, the ministry of which never did a more wise or prudent thing than when they sent out the great Orientalist, their president, to superintend the jurisprudence of those Asiatic provinces, the prevailing languages and manners of which were so familiarly known to him. The early efforts of that Society were crowned with signal success. The buried tablet has been dug from the bowels of the earth; the fallen and mouldering pillar has been reared; coins and medals, struck in commemoration of grand and important events, have been recovered from the sepulchral darkness of two thousand years; and the obsolete characters, engraved on their superficies, have, with immense toil, been deciphered and explained. It is by the increasing and concentrated light, which those precious remains throw up on the classic page, that the footsteps of the historian must be guided and his path through the obscure maze of antiquity illumined.

Had there been any work at that time published, or had I known of any work intended to be published, that promised to include the ancient and modern history of India, according both to Sanscreet and classical writers, and present to the reader a comprehensive view of the wonderful transactions performed, during the period of near four thousand years, on that grand theatre, I should never have ventured upon an undertaking at once so arduous and so hazardous.

As soon as I had formed the resolution, in the best manner I might be able, to supply that defect, I communicated my intention to Sir William Jones, in India, with whose friendship I was honoured at an early period of life, and who returned me such an answer as encouraged me both to proceed with

[1] Thomas Hyde (1636–1703), orientalist. The *Historia Religionis* (1700) was his most important work.

[2] Zoroaster (c. 628–551 B.C.), a religious teacher and prophet of ancient Persia.

[3] Brahma, a god often identified, along with Vishnu and Shiva, as one of the three supreme gods in Hinduism. He is regarded as the creator and is periodically reborn in a lotus that grows from the navel of the sleeping Vishnu.

[4] Nathaniel Brassey Halhed (1751–1830), a renowned Orientalist, was encouraged to study Arabic by Sir William Jones, whom he met while studying at Oxford. Disappointed in love, he left England having obtained a writership with the East India Company. In 1776 he translated *A Code of Gentoo Laws*, and in 1788, he published *A Grammar of the Bengal Language*. Returning to England in 1785, he

served as an M.P. from 1790–95.

vigour and to aspire with ardour. He was at the same time so obliging as to impart a few hints for the conduct of the work, which I have anxiously endeavoured to follow. I likewise submitted the Proposals for my intended History to the Court of Directors of the East India Company, accompanied with a Letter, in which I took an extensive survey of the great outlines of that history. Nothing could be more flattering to an infant-undertaking than the applause which that Letter procured me from the most respectable quarters: and, indeed, as a proof that the distinguished body of men, to whom it was addressed, thought that the author had exerted laborious assiduity in the investigation of the obscure subject which he professed to elucidate, an immediate answer was returned, and *forty sets* of the History subscribed for.

I frankly own to the candid reader that I knew not, at the time, the full extent and magnitude of the undertaking in which I had embarked. At my very entrance into the grand historic field, through the whole ample circuit of which it became necessary for me to range, a field over-run with exotic and luxuriant vegetation, such a prospect unfolded itself, as, I confess, at once disheartened and terrified me. Such a variety of complicated and profound subjects pressed for discussion, before the way could be sufficiently cleared for an entrance upon the immediate path of History; so deeply were the wild fables of Indian Mythology blended with the authentic annals of regular History; that the *proper* execution of the arduous work seemed to demand the exertion of abilities, as well as the command of fortune, to which I could by no means lay claim.

To an undertaking thus comprehensive in its design and important in regard to its objects, an undertaking generally allowed to be, at this moment, a *desideratum in literature,* it might naturally have been expected, that not only the Court of

Directors themselves, who, in fact, manifested by their resolution so early and so flattering an attention to the address of the author, but that all those gentlemen in their service, or otherwise, who from situation or connection could not be indifferent to Indian concerns, would have extended their powerful support and patronage.

It was not unreasonable to suppose that the man of business would be interested by the faithful detail professed to be given of commercial transactions during so many revolving centuries, and that the man of letters would be induced decidedly to support a production recommended by a circumstance equally novel and gratifying; *that in one work, of small expense,* was to be combined the substance of all the most esteemed Persian and Arabian historians upon the subject, of whose productions correct and elegant versions have been yet presented to the public; productions mouldering upon the shelves of public libraries, or deposited in the inaccessible museums of learned individuals; productions equally high in value and difficult to be procured.

For myself, conscious that I had, by continued inquiry, by extensive reading, and intense application, endeavoured to prepare myself for the important task in which I had engaged, I too eagerly indulged those sanguine expectations of success which were entertained by the private circle of my friends. Enjoying from nature a very ample portion of those high and volatile spirits, which as they are often in early youth the occasion of many errors, afterwards regretted, so in riper years they too frequently buoy up with false hopes the deluded imagination, I suffered those spirits to betray me into the most fatal delusions. I exulted in the fair prospect that a life early marked by the vicissitudes of fortune, or rather continually passed in the extremes of gay hope and gloomy disappointment, as it approached its meridian,[1] was likely to be

---

[1] Middle age.

cheered with the dawn of success and a share of probable independence; that some moiety of the public applause would be the consequence of incessant efforts to merit it, and that an adequate portion of emolument would be the reward of severe literary toil. I therefore embarked in the purchase of the various books, charts, and engravings necessary for the composition or elucidation of my work, a considerable part of a small fortune, which fell to me by the untimely death of a near and beloved relative, and, as I was settled in the country, remote from the convenience of a public library, and was constantly in want of many expensive publications in regard to India, which, indeed, from their recent date no public library could furnish, I continued to accumulate expenses of this kind, till a sense of prudence compelled me to resort to the bookseller to know the result of the distribution of my proposals and the publication of my advertisements. Let it for ever repress the ardour of romantic ambition and the enthusiastic dreams of authors unknown to fame, and unprotected by patrons invested with the ensigns of power and stationed at the helm of political eminence, that, in the course of twelve months, THE HISTORY OF HINDOSTAN, a work sanctioned by the approbation of THE EAST-INDIA COMPANY in England and SIR WILLIAM JONES in India, was able to obtain only *a dozen* subscribers!—It was not, however, a little flattering to the author, that amongst that number of unsolicited subscribers was the Marquis of Landsdown,[1] who sent an agent to inquire concerning the author, and to express his Lordship's hope that "so meritorious a work might not sink for want of proper support." His Lordship could only form a judgement of its possible merit from my Letter to the Directors; of which I printed a thousand, at the expense of Forty Pounds, and

have since been obliged to distribute them *gratis*.

(1793)

Dissertations and Miscellaneous Pieces Relating to The History and Antiquities, the Arts, Sciences, and Literature of Asia [2]

PREFACE

IT is a consideration which cannot but afford the utmost pleasure to a reflecting mind, that the Arts and Sciences, which are rapidly advancing towards a state of perfection in EUROPE, are not confined to that quarter of the globe. In the East, where Learning seemed to be extinguished, and Civilization nearly lost, amidst the contention of avarice and despotism, a spirit of enquiry hath gone forth, which, aided by the ardour of Philosophy, promises to dissipate the gloom of ignorance, and to spread the advantages of knowledge through a region where its effects may be expected to be most favourable to the general interests of society.

To the exertions of one Gentleman,[3] whose various excellencies panegyric might display in the warmest terms, without being charged with extravagance, the ENGLISH settlements in the EAST INDIES are indebted for an institution which has already exhibited specimens of profound research, of bold investigation, and of happy illustration, in various subjects of literature;—subjects which, until the present times, had not exercised the faculties of EUROPEANS; but which, being produced to publick notice, will enlarge the bounds of knowledge, increase the stock of information, and furnish materials for future Philosophers, Biographers, and Historians.

---

[1] Henry Fitzmaurice, 3rd Marquess of Landsdowne (1780–1863).

[2] A compilation of works by members of the Asiatic Society formed by Sir William Jones.

[3] Sir William Jones.

That so much has been already achieved by an infant Society, will be a subject of surprize, to those who have not considered the powers of genius and industry to overcome obstacles. From what has already appeared at CALCUTTA, a judgment may formed of what may hereafter be expected. The stores of Oriental Literature being now accessible to those who have ability to make a proper use of them, intelligence hitherto locked up, it may be hoped, will delight and inform the enquirers after the History, Antiquities, Arts, Sciences and Literature of Asia.

Two Volumes of the Society's Transactions have been already published; but these have been so sparingly distributed in GREAT BRITAIN that few have had the opportunity of being informed of their contents, or of judging of their value. This circumstance had induced the Editor to select the contents of the present volumes from them and the Asiatic Miscellany, for the amusement and instruction of the publick. They are such as will confer honour on their authors, and afford entertainment to their readers. They contain a noble specimen of the talents of our countrymen inhabiting a distant quarter of the globe, employing themselves sedulously and honourably in extending the credit and establishing the reputation of BRITONS in new and unexplored regions of Science and Literature.

(1793)

BRITISH CRITIC
Review of *Travels in India, 1780, 81, 82, and 83.* By William Hodges, R.A.

IT is no less remarkable than true, that, till within these few years, very little authentic information has been communicated to Europe concerning the literature, antiquities, and customs of India. The veil of obscurity, however, which has so long been spread over that immense and interesting portion of the globe, seems now in a fair way of being effectually removed. Mr. Hastings[1] led the way, by his patronage of Mr. Wilkins and Mr. Halhed. Sir William Jones, with that unremitting zeal which characterizes genius, has since brought to light what has for ages been concealed. The successful labours of Mr. Maurice, already noticed by us, have produced a systematic arrangement of much curious and important matter. And lastly, the publication before us must not be suffered to pass without its due share of well-deserved praise, for that branch of information to which it is confined, the local illustration of those parts through which the author travelled. The work of Dr. Robertson, on India,[2] is of a different kind from all the rest. The learned had long been in doubt how far into ancient India the victorious and indefatigable Alexander had made his way: it was certain, that the knowledge which the ancients had of this portion of the globe was vague and inconclusive; and the helps on this subject, which the moderns might expect to receive from Ptolemy, Strabo,[3] and the ancient geographers, rather provoked than satisfied curiosity. The historical disquisition concerning India by Dr. Robertson, has removed many of these difficulties; has systematized the knowledge of the ancients, has often illuminated what was obscure, and made clear what was doubtful. We wanted however, and we still

---

[1] Warren Hastings (1732–1818), Governor-General of Bengal from 1772, faced trial and impeachment by the House of Commons in England (the trial lasted from 1788–95) for the East India Company's often ruthless conduct as a conquering power. He was widely respected by Orientalist researchers, however, for his generous support of their work.

[2] William Robertson (1721–93), author of *Historical Disquisition concerning the Knowledge which the Ancients had of India; and the progress of Trade with that country prior to the discovery of the Passage to it by the Cape of Good Hope* (1791).

[3] Ptolemy: Claudius Ptolemaeu, mathematician, astronomer and geographer in 2nd century A.D.; Strabo: historian and geographer in first century B.C.

require, the efforts of individuals, who, penetrating into the interior parts of a beautiful and picturesque region, will give us a faithful representation of ancient monuments and modern manners. Thus the progress of art, the change of manners, and the variation of national character, may be, more perspicuously understood, and the stock of universal knowledge extended and improved.

(1794)

Sir William Jones
The Preface to *Institutes of Hindu Law: or, the Ordinances of Menu, According to the Gloss of Callúca. Comprising the Indian System of Duties, Religious and Civil.*

IT is a maxim of the science of legislation and government, that *Laws are of no avail without manners,* or, to explain the sentence more fully, that the best intended legislative provisions would have no beneficial legislative effect even at first, and none at all in a short course of time, unless they were congenial to the disposition and habits, to the religious prejudices, and approved immemorial usages of the people for whom they were enacted; especially if that people universally and sincerely believed, that all their ancient usages and established rules of conduct had the sanction of an actual revelation from heaven: the legislature of *Britain* having shown, in compliance with this maxim, an intention to leave the natives of these *Indian* provinces in possession of their own Laws, at least on the titles of *contracts* and *inheritances*, we may humbly presume, that all future provisions, for the administration of justice and government in *India*, will be conformable, as far as the natives are affected by them, to the manners and opinions of the natives themselves; an object which cannot possibly be attained, until those manners and opinions can be fully and accurately known. These considerations, and a few others more immediately within my province, were my principal motives for wishing to know, and have induced me at length to publish, that system of duties, religious and civil, and of law in all it's branches, which the *Hindus* firmly believe to have been promulgated in the beginning of time by Menu, son of Brahmá, or, in plain language, the first of created beings, and not the oldest only, but the holiest of legislators.

The work, now presented to the *European* world, contains abundance of curious matter extremely interesting both to speculative lawyers and antiquaries, with many beauties which need not be pointed out, and with many blemishes which cannot be justified or palliated. It is a system of despotism and priestcraft, both indeed limited by law, but artfully conspiring to give mutual support, though with mutual checks; it is filled with strange conceits in metaphysicks and natural philosophy, with idle superstitions, and with a scheme of theology most obscurely figurative, and consequently liable to dangerous misinterpretation; it abounds with minute and childish formalities, with ceremonies generally absurd and often ridiculous; the punishments are partial and fanciful; for some crimes, dreadfully cruel, for others, reprehensibly slight; and the very morals, though rigid enough on the whole, are in one or two instances (as in the case of light oaths and of pious perjury) unaccountably relaxed: nevertheless, a spirit of sublime devolution, or benevolence to mankind, and of amiable tenderness to all sentient creatures, pervades the whole work; the style of it has a certain austere majesty, that sounds like the language of legislation, and extorts a respectful awe; the sentiments of independence on all beings but God, and the harsh admonitions, even to kings, are truly noble.

Whatever opinion in short may be formed of Menu and his laws, in a country happily enlightened by sound philosophy and the only true revelation, it must be remembered, that those laws are actually revered, as the word of the Most High, by nations of great importance to the political and commercial interests of *Europe*, and particularly by many millions of *Hindu* subjects, whose well directed industry would add largely to the wealth of *Britain*, and who ask no more in return than protection for their persons and places of abode, justice in their temporal concerns, indulgence to the prejudices of their old religion, and the benefit of those laws, which they have been taught to believe sacred, and which they alone can possibly comprehend.

(1796)

ELIZABETH HAMILTON
Translation of the Letters of a Hindoo Rajah[1]

PRELIMINARY DISSERTATION

IN the extensive plan which is carried on under the direction of the great Governor of the Universe, an attentive observer will frequently perceive the most unexpected ends, accomplished by means the most improbable, and events branch out into effects which were neither foreseen, nor intended by the agents which produced them. A slight view of the consequences which have hitherto resulted from our intercourse with the East-Indies, will sufficiently evince the truth of this assertion.

The thirst of conquest and the desire of gain, which first drew the attention of the most powerful, and enlightened nations of Europe toward the fruitful regions of Hindoostan, have been the means of opening sources of knowledge and information to the learned, and the curious, and have added to the stock of the literary world, treasures, which if not so substantial, are of a nature more permanent than those which have enriched the commercial.

The many elegant translations from the different Oriental languages with which the world has been favoured within these last few years, have not failed to attract merited attention; and the curiosity awakened by these productions, concerning the people with whom they originated, has been gratified by the labours of men, who have enjoyed the first rank in literary fame.

In the struggle of contending interests, though peace is sometimes lost, intellectual energy is roused, and while the strife of emulation, and restlessness of ambition disturb the quiet of society, they produce, in their collision, the genius that adorns it: it is accordingly pronounced, by one who must be allowed competent to the decision, that "Reason and Taste are the grand prerogatives of European minds, while the Asiatics have soared to loftier heights in the sphere of Imagination."[2]

But notwithstanding all the disadvantages under which they laboured, the many monuments that yet remain of their former splendour, the specimens of their literature, and the productions of their manufactures, sufficiently evince their advancement in

---

[1] Elizabeth Hamilton (1758–1816), wrote in a range of genres from educational tracts to political satires to a fictionalized biography designed to make Roman history appealing to young women readers. Dedicated to Warren Hastings, the impeached Governor-General of Bengal, and published four years after the unexpected death of her brother, the preeminent Orientalist Charles Hamilton, *Translation of the Letters of a Hindoo Rajah* (1796), used the familiar eighteenth-century narrative device of immersing a foreigner into Britain as a way of offering an often highly satirical account of British culture. But it was also a vindication of British conduct in India, particularly its controversial war against the Rohillas. Its "Preliminary Dissertation" offered a learned and polemical account of what she described as the redemptive role played by Orientalists such as her brother, whose research would help British administrators adapt themselves to local customs in a more humane way.

[2] See the excerpt from Sir William Jones's *Second Anniversary Discourse* in this section.

the sciences which dignify life, as well as in the arts that ornament it.

The Bramins,[1] to whom the cultivation of science was exclusively committed, seem to have made no contemptible use of their high privilege. In astronomy they are allowed to have excelled; many works of their ancient writers on metaphysics, and ethics, have already come to our knowledge; and, surely, no lover of poetry can peruse the specimens of that divine art, which have been presented to the public in an English dress; without feeling a desire to be more intimately acquainted with the productions of the Hindoo bards.

The degree of knowledge we already possess, concerning the antiquities of Hindoostan, has not been attained without efforts of the most indefatigable assiduity. But what obstacles are sufficient to deter the spirit of literary curiosity? When supported by philosophy, and guided by taste, it seldom fails to subdue every difficulty, and to see its persevering labours crowned with success!

How much of this observation has been verified in respect to the Asiatic Society, is well known to all who have perused the volumes of their Researches. It is thus briefly described by Mr. Maurice, in the Introduction to his Indian antiquities. "The buried tablet has been dug from the bowels of the earth; the fallen, and mouldering pillar has been reared; coins, and medals, struck in commemoration of grand, and important events, have been recovered from the sepulchral darkness of two thousand years; and the obsolete characters, engraved on their superficies, have, with immense toil, been decyphered and explained."[2]

In the contemplation of these scientific labours, the Governor General,[3] under whose auspices they were commenced, will have the deserved meed of grateful acknowledgment from every candid and philosophic mind; for although he declined complying with the wishes of the members, who were all solicitous to see him at the head of their society, he was eminently instrumental in promoting its success; and in this, as in every other instance, he stood forth the steady friend, the liberal patron, and zealous promoter of useful knowledge.

How much the world has been indebted to the learned Gentleman who was nominated to the Presidentship of the Society,[4] is too well known to require animadversion.[5] Long and deeply will his loss be deplored by every lover of literature, and friend to virtue.

A few of the original members of the Asiatick Society, still continue to pursue the great object of their undertaking with unremitted ardour, and undiminished success. Of the rest, some have returned to the bosom of their families, and native country, not enriched by the plunder, and splendid by the beggary and massacre of their fellow-creatures, as has been represented in the malevolent and illiberal harangues of indiscriminating obloquy;[6] but possessed of those virtues which ennoble human nature, and that cultivation of mind and talents, which dignify the enjoyment of retirement. Others of that society, equally honoured, and equally estimable, are, alas, no more! The generous esteem, the cordial fellowship, the warm admiration which

[1] Members of the first of the four Hindu castes in India, traditionally associated with religious authority and respected for their learned achievements.

[2] Thomas Maurice (1754–1824), author of *Indian Antiquities, or Dissertations on Hindostan* (1793).

[3] Warren Hastings. Hamilton's praise for Hastings is in part an implicit defense of Hastings in the context of the "rancorous misrepresentations" against him, which she refers to later in Preface.

[4] Sir William Jones.

[5] Extensive commentary.

[6] Returning commercial adventurers or "nabobs," who used fortunes accumulated in India to purchase landed estates in Britain and set themselves up as aristocrats, were a favorite topic of derision in the British press.

accompanied them thro' life, has not been extinguished in the silent grave; it lives, and will long live, in the hearts of many, calling for the tear of tender recollection, and of unextinguished, though, alas! unavailing sorrow.

In those provinces which, by a train of circumstances, totally foreign to our purpose to relate, have fallen under the dominion of Great Britain, it is to be hoped that the long-suffering Hindoos have experienced a happy change.[1] Nor can we doubt of this, when we consider, that in those provinces, the horrid modes of punishment, inflicted by the Mahommedans, have been abolished; the fetters, which restrained their commerce, have been taken off; the taxes are no longer collected by the arbitrary authority of a military chieftain, but are put upon a footing that at once secures the revenue, and protects the subject from oppression. The Banditti of the Hills, which used to molest the inoffensive inhabitants by their predatory incursions, have been brought into peaceable subjection. That unrelenting persecution, which was deemed a duty by the ignorant bigotry of their Mussulman rulers, has, by the milder spirit of Christianity, been converted into the tenderest indulgence. Their ancient laws have been restored to them; a translation of them, into the Persian and English languages, has been made, and is now the guide of the Courts of justice, which have been established among them. Agriculture has been encouraged by the most certain of all methods—the security of property; and all these advantages have been rendered doubly valuable, by the enjoyment of a blessing equal, if not superior, to every other—the Blessing of Peace, a blessing to which they had for ages been strangers.

These salutary regulations, originating with Mr. Hastings, steadily pursued by Sir John M'Pherson

and Lord Cornwallis, and persevered in by the present Governor General, will diffuse the smiles of prosperity and happiness over the best provinces of Hindoostan, long after the discordant voice of Party shall have been humbled in the silence of eternal rest; and the rancorous misrepresentations of envy and malevolence, as much forgotten, as the florid harangues, and turgid declamations, which conveyed them to the short-lived notice of the world.[2]

(1796)

MONTHLY REVIEW
Review of *Dissertations and Miscellaneous Pieces relating to the History and Antiquities, the Arts, Sciences, and Literature of Asia.*
By Sir William Jones and others. Vol. III.

WE always contemplate with renewed satisfaction the ingenious labours of our countrymen in the East. We consider them in the aggregate, as constituting the monument more durable than brass, which will survive the existence and illustrate the memory of our Eastern dominion. After the contingent circumstances to which we owe our present preponderance in that country shall have ceased to operate, and the channels of Indian knowledge and Indian wealth shall have again become impervious to the western world, the Asiatic Researches will furnish a proof to our posterity, that the acquisition of the latter did not absorb the attention of their countrymen to the

---

[1] British commentators typically described Hindu Indians as having been tyrannized by Islamic conquerors. The British portrayed themselves as liberating Hindus from this state of enslavement.

[2] Warren Hastings (1732–1818), Sir John Macpherson (1745–1821), and Lord Cornwallis (1735–1843), the first three Governor Generals of India. "The rancorous misrepresentations of envy and malevolence" is a reference to Edmund Burke's impassioned rhetoric in his arguments against Warren Hastings in Hastings' impeachment trial in England. See Thomas Erskine's defense of Stockdale for a similar reference.

exclusion of the former; and that the English laws and English government, in those distant regions, have sometimes been administered by men of extensive capacity, erudition, and application.

When we call to our recollection how far the boundaries of knowledge have been extended, in Europe, by the establishment of the various academies which instruct and adorn this enlightened quarter of the globe; we know not whether any thing could have happened, more favourable to the general interests of literature, than the establishment of a similar institution in the centre of Asia:—a learned society placed in the midst of a people preserving, at the close of the eighteenth century, the pristine dogmata of the primeval ages: from whom Pythagorus derived the tenets which he transmitted to the philosophers of the Italic school;[1] and by whom the same tenets are still taught, that were taught to Pythagorus. The votary of history, who has remarked that our knowledge of antiquity extends little beyond the shores of the Mediterranean, must be curious to pierce the veil which has hitherto enveloped the antiquities of the East, and the origins of nations. The natural historian must feel his attention arrested, by these researches prosecuted in a country "where many animals are found, and many hundreds of medicinal plants, which have either not been described at all, or what is worse, ill described by the naturalists of Europe."[2] The philosopher will direct his view to the singular moral phænomena exhibited by the Asiatic world; and while he remarks the shades of distinction which discriminate individual nations, he will contemplate the universal traits of character, opinion, and manners, which still more distinguish

them from ourselves; and he will observe, not without surprise, some tribes still sunken in the grossest barbarism, dwelling on the confines and even in the midst of nations, whose exquisite refinement has been transmitted from the earliest antiquity.

Those who have perused the first and second of this compilation will deem the third not inferior in variety of literary excellence. The essays of which it is composed claim very different degrees of commendation: but, in all, something will be found to instruct, or something to amuse.

(1797)

WILLIAM OUSELEY
Prospectus for *The Oriental Collections:
Consisting of Original Essays and
Dissertations, Translations and
Miscellaneous Tracts of Asia* [3]

AMONG the many considerations which give importance to the study of Asiatick Literature, and especially induce to the cultivation of the ARABICK and PERSIAN Languages, it is almost unnecessary to point out that of *National Interest*, since it not only occurs of itself, but has already been treated of by able writers: we shall not, therefore, dwell on the advantages resulting from a knowledge of those tongues, to whom all the affairs of Commerce, the administration of Government, or other publick or private business, may lead to visit our Indian Territories;—their utility is obvious, and sufficiently evinced by the munificence with which the cultivation of them has been en-

---

[1] Pythagoras, a philosopher who lived in the second half of the sixth century B.C., is generally credited for conveying Indian ideas to Greek culture. Sir William Jones suggested that "Pythagorus and Plato derived their sublime theories from the same fountain as the sages of India."

[2] Source unidentified.

[3] Sir William Ouseley (1767–1842), was educated privately until the age of twenty, when he was sent to Paris to pursue his studies, where he became fascinated with Oriental, and especially Persian cultures. In 1795 he published *Persian Miscellanies: an Essay to Facilitate the Reading of Persian Manuscripts. The Oriental Collections* was a three volume work published between 1797–99.

couraged, by the most enlightened and respectable commercial society in the world.

It will be found, that on almost every subject, the writers of ARABIA afford much interesting matter;—and whatever rapid advances towards perfection in Arts and Sciences our northern nations may have made in later ages, there was a time when the dark clouds of ignorance and superstition hung so thick on the intellectual horizon of Europe, as to exclude every ray of learning that darted from the East, and all that was polite or elegant in Literature was classed among the "*Studia Arabum.*"[1]

That those engaged in the study of GRECIAN Antiquities and Literature, may derive considerable aid from an acquaintance with the History and Language of Persia, we shall endeavour to demonstrate in successive Numbers of the ORIENTAL COLLECTIONS.

(1797)

MONTHLY REVIEW
Review of *Essays by the Students of the College of Fort William in Bengal.* Printed by the Honourable Company's Press. Imported by Debrett, London.[2]

To behold the victor bowing to the institutions, laws, and manners of the conquered people; and labouring to render their dialects familiar to him, in order to avoid offending their prejudices, that he may be better able to learn their complaints, and to redress their grievances; this is a novel sight, and highly gratifying to every lover of humanity:—it is a policy above all praise, a policy of which Britain sets the example, and on which she may

justly pride herself. May she pursue it, and ever persevere in it! It is also gratifying to contemplate this institution, as it engages youth in an early, regular, and systematic study of the several dialects of the East. May we not expect that, among them, there will arise those who will clear up whatever can be known of the antiquities, history, polity, science, letters, arts, customs, and manners of this most interesting portion of the globe, the cradle of mankind, the fountain of knowledge and civilization? Of this glory, Great Britain ought to be ambitious. The world has a right to require this service from her; it is a province most properly her own; and if she duly fills it, she may lay the literati of every country under obligations, while, at the same time, she advances her own political interests.

Though we highly applaud this condescension on the part of the conqueror, we cannot help observing that a pardonable national vanity would be indulged, and we do not perceive that any maxim of policy would suffer, if we were to encourage the natives, by gentle and inoffensive methods, to acquire our language, to study our literature, and to cultivate our sciences and arts. That this practice would prove injurious to the Indians no one will contend; and that it cannot prejudice us, we conceive is clearly shewn in the pages of this volume: where it is demonstrated that it is our interest to promote their mental cultivation, as well as any other measure which may advance their happiness. Acting on this plan, we may look to glory far more durable than that can possibly be, which is founded on our civil power; for in that case it may happen that monuments of our genius, or our wisdom, and of our justice, may live and flourish in these distant regions, when every trace of our political authority may have long disappeared.

The perusal of this collection awakens the recollection of, and as it were carries us back to, that enviable period of human life, when we behold

---

[1] Arabic Studies.
[2] Fort William College was founded in 1800 by Governor-General Wellesley, to promote Orientalist research.

nature arrayed in her best dress; when hope is sanguine, when our prospects are gay, when the bosom beats high to the calls of honour and the dictates of virtue, when temptation has not yet led astray, nor disappointment soured the temper, nor the conflicts of the world sombered our views and chastened our expectations.

The information with respect to the Natives, contained in the following extract from Mr. Newnham's Essay,[1] induces us to insert it:

"The Indians at present under the British dominion, particularly those near to the seats of Government, appear inclined to dismiss many of their prejudices. The richer Hindoos in particular, affect to despise many of their former customs, to which the destructive precautions of the Mahomedans only served to rivet their affections. They however rather copy the follies, than the virtues of Europeans, and endeavour to excel them in luxury and expense, rather than in knowledge. They have acquired the same freedom of behaviour, without the generosity and independence of spirit; and they are more eager in the acquirement of riches, without the same enterprize and honesty of principle. To over-reach the stranger by the lowest artifices of despicable chicane[2] and intrigue, is considered by the trading Hindoo as his *calling*. If the passions have not the same influence over him as over the more vigorous and impetuous European, the influence of the virtues is still less. If he is less quick in resenting injuries, he is utterly insensible to every feeling of gratitude. To vegetate in sloth is the delight of the Hindoo: and he is never roused to exertion but by the calls of necessity, or to gratify his ruling passion, avarice. He is dastardly in spirit, and will seldom stand a contest with an open foe; but is rather inclined to injure his enemy secretly.

When transported with anger, he vents his rage with feminine impotence in the vilest and foulest reproaches; but this fury is damped, if likely to be resented by force."

(1804)

QUARTERLY MAGAZINE
Review of :

1. *The Life of Bishop Reginald Heber, D.D., Bishop of Calcutta.* 1830.
2. *The Last Days of Bishop Heber.* By Thomas Robinson, A.M., Archdeacon of Madras, and late Domestic Chaplain to his Lordship. Madras, printed. London, reprinted, 1830.[3]

THE name of Reginald Heber now belongs to the history of the Christian church; it takes its place among those whose canonization have been demanded by the general sentiment; and, though in Protestant Europe no earthly power is recognized as having a right to pronounce on the final state of any human being, or to demand the veneration of posterity—yet the unanimous sentence of an enlightened age may well supersede, and would certainly derive no weight from, an authoritative ratification. He whose Christian virtues have thus enshrined his memory in the hearts of the wise and good in all ranks and classes, would gain nothing to his pure fame by the solemn judgement of a public tribunal.

We trust that this high view of his "heavenly calling" can excite in no bosom deeper admiration and sympathy than in our own. This entire devotion of his whole soul to its one great purpose is worthy of all praise; still we may be permitted to embody a "day-dream" of our own, which, under other circumstances, and had divine Providence been pleased to spare his valuable life, might, to a

---

[1] "Essay on the Character and Capacity of the Asiaticks, and particularly of the Natives of Hindoostan."

[2] Deception.

[3] Reginald Heber (1783–1826), Bishop of Calcutta.

certain degree at least, have been realized. Had it been possible, in two or three years, to have brought the affairs of the diocese into order, established a spirit of harmony and zealous co-operation among the various functionaries, so that the precious time of the bishop should not be wasted in reconciling paltry quarrels and jealousies—in short, had the Bishop of Calcutta been allowed those periods of relaxation which ought to be assigned to every public man, and which, instead of interrupting, would but restore him refreshed and reanimated to the discharge of his peculiar duties, so ardent and universal a scholar as Heber might have found time at least to encourage, if not to extend, the study of that ancient literature, in which we do not despair of finding a key to some of the most interesting questions connected with the history of man. It would have been no ungratifying sight to see an Indian bishop take the place of Sir William Jones, of Sir James Mackintosh, or Mr. Colebrook,[1] and direct, if not assist, the inquiries of less occupied scholars in the study of primitive language and antiquities of Hindostan; a study which, now that European scholars are grown out of the leading-strings of mercenary pundits, and are secure from their deceptions, may bring forth, if not more attractive, at least more genuine fruits.

As to the native population, it now seems almost universally admitted that little progress is likely to be made by direct conversion; while it is impossible to calculate the slower results of European inter-course, and the general advancement of education. There is an interesting passage in the Memoir of Bishop James, which shows the manner in which these innovating principles are working—we trust, for good.

"Meanwhile, though he had not personally visited them, he was no inattentive observer of what was going on in the Hindoo and Mahometan Colleges in Calcutta, both of which are largely assisted by the government from the annual supply for public instruction. The object of these two colleges is to instruct the Hindoo and Mahometan youth in English literature—but, alas! without the Scriptures. The exhibition of the students of the former institution, at the public distribution of their prizes, in January, had recently attracted much notice: they had acted scenes from Shakespeare with great success; and the astonishing progress they had made had been the subject of frequent discussion among the wealthier Hindoos. The Bishop, lamenting deeply the fear which caused the exclusion of the Scriptures, saw, from all that was passing around, that both these institutions, in their parent state, obviously led to deism;[2] still, as he observed that it was deism not directly opposed to Christianity, but to Hindoo polytheism, he could not but regard it as tending to remove the main bulwark of their idolatrous superstitions, and gradually opening a way for the admission of the *truth and the life.*"

How singular a spectacle—Shakspeare performed by Gentoos and Mahometans on the shore of the Ganges! It is altogether a very curious indication of the deep root which English manners and opinions are taking in the minds of the Asiatics; and it may be fairly expected that they will smooth the way for the reception of the religion of England. The silent undermining of the ancient edifice will give room for the new one to arise upon its ruins.

(1830)

---

[1] Sir James Mackintosh (1765–1832), well known for his reformist pamphlet *Vindiciæ Gallicæ*, moved to Bombay in 1804, where he received a commission as judge two years later. During his seven years in India he initiated the Literary Society of Bombay (1805), of which he became president, and worked to promote the study of Indian languages and culture. Henry Colebrook (1765–1837) received a writership from the East India Company in 1782. During his thirty-two years service in the Company, Colebrook was an active student of Hindu science and law, contributing to prestigious publications such as the *Asiatic Researches* and *Transactions of the Royal Asiatic Society*, which he had helped to found in 1823.

[2] Religious views not wholly reconcilable with Christianity.

Thomas Macaulay
Minute on Indian Education [1]

I HAVE no knowledge of either Sanscrit or Arabic.— But I have done what I could to form a correct estimate of their value. I have read translations of the most celebrated Arabic and Sanscrit works. I have conversed both here and at home with men distinguished by their proficiency in the Eastern tongues. I am quite ready to take the Oriental learning at the valuation of the Orientalists themselves. I have never found one among them who could deny that, a single shelf of a good European library was worth the whole native literature of India and Arabia. The intrinsic superiority of the Western literature is, indeed, fully admitted by those members of the Committee who support the Oriental plan of education.

Sanscrit poetry could be compared to that of the great European nations. But, when we pass from works of imagination to works in which facts are recorded and general principles investigated, the superiority of the Europeans becomes absolutely immeasurable. It is, I believe, no exaggeration to say, that all the historical information which has been collected from all the books written in the Sanscrit language is less valuable that what may be found in the most paltry abridgments used at preschools in England. In every branch of physical or moral philosophy the relative position of the two nations is nearly the same.

How, then, stands the case? We have to educate a people who cannot at present be educated by means of their mother-tongue. We must teach them some foreign language. The claims of our own language it is hardly necessarily to recapitulate. It stands pre-eminent even among the languages of the West. It abounds with works of imagination not inferior to the noblest which Greece has bequeathed to us; with models of every species of eloquence; with historical compositions, which, considered merely as narratives, have seldom been surpassed, and which, considered as vehicles of ethical and political instruction, have never been equaled; with just and lively representations of human life and human nature; with the most profound speculations on metaphysics, morals, government, jurisprudence, and trade; with full and correct information respecting every experimental science which tends to preserve the health to increase the comfort, or to expand the intellect of man. Whoever knows that language, has ready access to all the vast intellectual wealth, which all the wisest nations of the earth have created and hoarded in the course of ninety generations. It may safely be said that the literature now extant in that language is of far greater value than all the literature which three hundred years age was extant in all the languages of the world together. Nor is this all. In India, English is the language spoken by the ruling class. It is spoken by the higher class of natives at the seats of Government. It is likely to become the language of commerce throughout the seas of the East. It is the language of two great European communities which are rising, the one in the south of Africa, the other in Australasia; communities which are every year becoming more important, and more closely connected with our Indian empire. Whether we look at the intrinsic value of our literature, or at the particular situation of this country, we shall see the strongest reason to think that, of all foreign tongues, the English tongue is that which would be the most useful to our native subjects.

The question now before us is simply whether, when it is in our power to teach this language, we shall teach languages in which, by universal confession, there are no books on any subject which deserve to be compared to our own; whether, when we can teach European science, we shall teach systems which, by universal confession, whenever they differ from those of Europe, differ for the worse; and whether, when we can patronize sound Philosophy and true History, we shall countenance, at the public expense, medical doctrines which would disgrace an English Farmer—Astronomy, which would move laughter in girls at an English boarding school—History, abounding with kings thirty feet high, and reigns thirty thousand years long—and Geography, made up of seas of treacle and seas of butter.

I can by no means admit that, when a nation of high intellectual attainments undertakes to superintend the education of a nation comparatively ignorant, the learners are absolutely to prescribe the course which is to be taken by the teachers. It is not necessary, however, to say anything on this subject. For it is proved by unanswerable evidence that we are not at present securing the co-operation of the natives. It would be bad enough to consult their intellectual taste at the expense of their intellectual health. But we are consulting neither—we are withholding from them the learning for which they are craving; we are forcing on them the mock-learning which they nauseate.

This is proved by the fact that we are forced to pay our Arabic and Sanscrit students, while those who learn English are willing to pay us. All the declamations in the world about the love and reverence of the natives for their sacred dialects will never, in the mind of any impartial person, outweigh the undisputed fact, that we cannot find, in all our vast empire, a single student who will let us teach him those dialects unless we will pay him.

What we spend on the Arabic and Sanscrit colleges is not merely a dead loss to the cause of truth: it is the bounty-money paid to raise up champions of truth. It goes to form a nest, not merely of helpless place-hunters, but of bigots prompted alike by passion and by interest to raise a cry against every useful scheme of education. If there should be any opposition among the natives to the change which I recommend, that opposition will be the effect of our own system. It will be headed by persons supported by our stipends and trained in our colleges. The longer we persevere in our present course, the more formidable will that opposition be. It will be every year reinforced by recruits whom we are paying.

In one point I fully agree with the gentlemen to whose general views I am opposed. I feel, with them, that it is impossible for us, with our limited means, to attempt to educate the body of the people. We must at present do our best to form a class who may be interpreters between us and the millions whom we govern; a class of persons, Indian in blood and colour, but English in taste, in opinions, in morals, and in intellect. To that class we may leave it to refine the vernacular dialects of the country, to enrich those dialects with terms of science borrowed from the Western nomenclature,[1] and to render them by degrees fit vehicles for conveying knowledge to the great mass of the population.

I would strictly respect all existing interests. I would deal even generously with all individuals who have had fair reason to expect a pecuniary provision. But I would strike at the root of the bad system which has hitherto been fostered by us. I would at once stop the printing of Arabic and Sanscrit books; I would abolish the Madrassa and the Sanscrit college at Calcutta. Benares is the great seat of Brahmanical learning; Delhi, of Arabic learning.[2] If we retain the Sanscrit college at Benares

[1] Terminology.

[2] The Madrassa: a school for Islamic instruction. Macaulay was objecting to funding schools to educate natives in their own cultures, which, he argued, would die out without this artificial encouragement.

and the Mahomedan college at Delhi; we do enough, and much more than enough in my opinion, for the Eastern languages.

I believe that the present system tends, not to accelerate the progress of truth, but to delay the natural death of expiring error. I conceive that we have at present no right to the respectable name of a Board of Public Instruction. We are a Board for wasting public money, for printing books which are of less value than the paper on which they are printed was while it was blank; for giving artificial encouragement to absurd history, absurd metaphysics, absurd physics, absurd theology; for raising up a breed of scholars who find their scholarship an encumbrance and a blemish, who live on the public while they are receiving their education, and whose education is so utterly useless to them that, when they have received it, they must either starve or live on the public all the rest of their lives. Entertaining these opinions, I am naturally desirous to decline all share in the responsibility of a body which, unless it alters its whole mode of proceeding, I must consider not merely as useless, but as positively noxious.

(1835)

SECTION THIRTEEN

The Slave Trade

In its review of Captain Thomas Morris's *Quashy, or the Coal Black-Maid. A Tale* (1796), a poem in "easy and harmonious verse," relating "the affecting story of the loves of a Negro youth and damsel, interrupted by the cruelty of their task-masters, and fatally terminated by the death of the lover," the *Analytical Review* insisted that "the muses cannot be more worthily employed, than in pleading the cause of humanity; and humanity never demanded an advocate more importunately, than in the person of the Afric slave. Several excellent writers have employed the powers of poesy in this good cause" (24:482). Both of these points—the importance of the cause and the number of talented authors who had responded to it—were so widely acknowledged that they were, in many ways, two of the literary clichés of the age. Few issues better typified the reformist ideal of literature as a public forum capable of promoting what William Godwin described as "the collision of mind with mind." Even those authors who published arguments in support of the slave trade (and there were many of them) frequently began their defences by acknowledging the barrage of (as they put it) misguided propaganda with which they were forced to contend. The Jamaican clergyman Robert Nicholls characterized his pro-slavery pamphlet, *Observations, Occasioned by the Attempts Made in England to Effect the Abolition of the Slave Trade*, as a response to "the many calumnies, industriously propagated, against the proprietors of negro slaves in the West Indies" that were contained in the endless "magazines, newspapers, and reviews" that had been "sent from England to this island." The anonymous author of another pro-slavery pamphlet, *Thoughts on the Slavery of the Negroes*, allowed that "the champions of liberty and humanity, availing themselves of the popularity of the subject, have been remarkably successful in engaging the passions, in extolling their own feelings, and in representing, in the most odious light, every attempt to shake the infallibility of their belief."

Abolitionists invoked a range of authorities, including nature, religion, and Britain's celebrated affinity for liberty. For Hannah More, slavery was an occasion of "nature confounded," an "unnatural deed" which "broke…the fond links of feeling Nature" by separating mothers from their children and reducing human beings into commodities. To support the slave trade, she suggested, was to ignore "Nature's plain appeal." Helen Maria Williams warned that the dehumanizing nature of the trade had erased nature's "impressions" from slave traders' "hardened hearts." Thomas Clarkson agreed that those who profited from slavery had "violated the rights of nature." Appeals to nature were doubled by invocations of a religious imperative. S.T. Coleridge could take a kind of ironic consolation in the belief that "all evils in the moral and natural world" were part of a larger divine plan—these controversies would "awaken intellectual activity," forcing men and women to "develop the powers of the Creator, and by new combinations of those powers to imitate his creativeness." Nor, for Coleridge, was religion merely a broader context which converted even the worst of human sins into some kind of good—it was also a political injunction: "As you hope to live with Christ hereafter," he warned his readers, "you are commanded to do unto others as ye would that others should do unto you." Most abolitionists shared Coleridge's sense of heaven as an active moral presence that provided an ultimate judicial forum in which victory was inevitable. For More, heaven was an active force that ought to "forbid" the perpetuation of such unnatural circumstances; for Anna Barbauld, "Heaven's impartial plan" was both a compelling vision of social justice and a source of retribution—"vengeance yet to come"—for those who betrayed this ideal. Abolitionists exploited their association with the cause of liberty by drawing on the rhetorical appeal of Britain's mythical association with the cause of human freedom. "Shall Britain, where the soul of Freedom reigns,/Forge chains for others she herself disdains?" demanded More. Williams encouraged "Loved Britain, whose protecting hand,/Stretched o'er the globe," to extend its imperial benevolence to "Afric's strand." Even the anonymous author of the pro-slavery *Thoughts on the Slavery of the Negroes* acknowledged the inevitability that "a free and a generous people" such as the British would be drawn to a cause that seemed to have so much to do with others' aspirations for liberty.

Anti-abolitionists were frequently amongst the first to acknowledge the force of these various appeals, but this should not allow us to overlook their own considerable rhetoric achievements. The anti-slavery movement is today better remembered than its opposite, in part because it *was* so strong a movement, and in part, perhaps, because its values seem to us to be more palatable. But it is important to remember how many eloquent champions the anti-abolition movement had. The continuation of the slave trade was a difficult case to make without seeming to be so cynically self-interested that one alienated one's readers. Anti-abolitionists' most obvious response to this problem was to insist on the straightforward claim that slaves were treated well because, as a form of property, it was in their owners' financial self-interest to do so. That so many well-intended abolitionists could fail to recognize this, they suggested, was merely a sign of how uneducated these crusaders really were. Rewriting their own complicity as an informed perspective, they argued that people who preferred slogans to the sort of "personal knowledge and actual experience" that could only be gained by living in a slave colony were not to be trusted.

It was, anti-abolitionists acknowledged, a difficult cause for a people with a natural love of liberty and compassion for others to resist. But, they warned, this made the British all the more vulnerable to deception. The cause of "the sufferings of the Negroes" was merely a "story," allowed the author of *Thoughts on the Slavery of the Negroes*, which, "like any other fiction of the brain, often repeated, begins at last to be firmly believed." Even Charlotte Smith, a self-declared opponent of slavery, accepted that "dreadful as the condition of slavery is, the picture of its horrors is often overcharged." Exploiting the anti-

Jacobin fervour of the early 1790s, Alexander Geddes linked two different types of misguided extremism driven by the allure of novelty: "In this curious and inquisitive generation, when the most venerable and hoary prejudices seem to flee, with precipitancy, before that blazing meteor, called *The Rights of Man*; some rash and inconsiderate assertors of those rights have gone so far as to maintain, that the vile and barbarous *Blacks* of Africa have an equal claim to freedom with the rest of the human race." These extremists, he warned, imposed themselves upon the public with such "earnestness, energy and eloquence; that the world, I find, begins to listen to it with wonderful attention; and many weak souls seem, at length, disposed to believe it to be well grounded." Inverting the normal power relations of slavery, he positioned the advocates of slavery as underdogs, flinging "a few hard pebbles" at the "giant Goliath" of the abolitionist movement. Nor, pro-slavery writers argued, were the abolitionists guilty of a mere disregard for the truth, where intentional or otherwise. Worse, the author of *Thoughts on the Slavery of the Negroes* warned, activists inspired by "a mistaken benevolence" were in danger of giving "encouragement to evils of more serious consequence than any we are going to remedy."

In many ways, pro-slavery writers' most effective strategy was to counter the particular grounds of the abolitionists' arguments. Recognizing the futility of arguing with abolitionists' appeals to a British love of liberty, apologists instead warned of the dangers of assuming that African slaves felt the same way: "Men who enjoy the benefits of civilization, and who are protected in life, liberty, and property, by the wisdom of humane and equal laws, feel that spirit of liberty, and enthusiastic love of their country, which freedom only can inspire. Talk to them of banishment, and it is more terrible than death. Not so the poor African," suggested the author of *Thoughts on the Slavery of the Negroes*. Robert Nicholls insisted that imposing this agenda on people who did not share their inherent love of freedom amounted to an "attempt to cram liberty down the throats of people who are incapable of digesting it." This point could be made all the more convincingly by countering pitiable depictions of Negro suffering with what the author of *Thoughts on the Slavery of the Negroes* described as "melancholy picture" of Africa as a tyrannized world from which Negroes were fortunate to be delivered. He juxtaposed the "despotic" nature of Africa with the utopian condition of the Negro, "from the moment he is put on shore in an English colony, to the time he becomes the master of a family, and acquires property of his own....The African now, finding himself a family man, and in possession of house and land, he begins to rear hogs, poultry, and other small stock, and either sells them to his master at a fair price, or carries them to market, for which one day in the week is allowed him."

Addressing himself to another element of the abolitionists' arguments, Geddes acknowledged the rhetorical power of characterizations of slavery as "a manifest and cruel insult to *Nature*." But, anticipating Charles Darwin, he insisted that nature was a destructive as much as it was a nurturing power: "In truth, she seems to be a very whimsical capricious Madam, whose blandishments and bastings follow one another so speedily and unexpectedly, that we are totally at a loss to know, when she is in jest, or earnest. This, however, we know full well: when she happens to be in her sulky humours, which is very often, she kicks without mercy, and without the smallest appearance of feeling." Rejecting the tendency to anthropomorphize nature as "a Matron of exquisite tender feelings," he insisted that "we may fairly say of Nature, what an apostle says of God: *No one hath ever seen Her.* We can form no idea of her, but from her visible operations; and surely these give us little room to think, that she is either tear-eyed, or tender-hearted." Confronting the rhetorical power of invoking religion on the side of the abolition movement, Robert Nicholls cited a pamphlet by another clergyman, "the Rev. Mr. Harris, of Liverpool, who has…clearly proved, from the scriptures, that slavery is neither contrary to the law nor gospel."

Abolitionists had at least two very different reasons for rooting their appeals in the eighteenth-century vogue for sensibility. Emphasizing Negroes' emotional depth undermined arguments about their alleged intellectual inferiority. Rejecting "this cruel and stupid argument, that they do not *feel* the miseries inflicted on them as Europeans would do," More insisted that whatever one thought of Negroes' capacity for reason, it remained the case that "all mankind can feel," and ought, therefore, to be treated with equal decency. And appealing to their readers' sensibility, abolitionists sought to inspire what Williams called the "throb of sympathy" by confronting readers with graphic descriptions of human suffering that would provoke an emotional response through the sheer power of its vivid immediacy. In doing so, Barbauld insisted, they "forc'd" the country's "averted eyes" to confront the "bloody scourge" of the slaves' suffering. This strategy of unsettling their readers was intensified by the literary technique of performing their own shock at being exposed to the same offenses. "Whe'er to Afric's shores I turn my eyes," More exclaimed, "horrors of deepest, deadliest guilt arise." But in emphasizing their own anguished responses, abolitionists sometimes made themselves vulnerable to charges of a kind of moral ostentation. "Will these benevolent men forgive me," suggested the author of *Thoughts on the Slavery of the Negroes*, "if I insinuate, that, in their zeal for the cause of humanity, they have not been entirely indifferent to a display of their own feelings, and to the ambition of being distinguished from the mass of the people?" Nor was it merely the abolitionists who distrusted this emphasis on sharing a traumatic personal response. Coleridge declaimed against "a false and bastard sensibility that prompts [individuals] to remove those evils and those evils alone, which by hideous spectacle or clamorous outcry are present to their senses," but which permits "other miseries, though equally certain and far more horrible," to persist unchallenged.

It was a debate which spanned a range of genres, from poetry to novels to travelogues to prose pamphlets, uniting individuals of otherwise very different political perspectives such as Hannah More, on the one hand, and Helen Maria Williams and Anna Barbauld, on the other, who would soon be on opposite sides of the French Revolution debate. Nor was it merely a literary debate, in even the most extended sense of the word. The struggle against the slave trade spilled over into movements such as the anti-saccharites, who advocated the purchase of slave-free sugar, and spawned a variety of commercial memorabilia such as Wedgwood pottery adorned with a Negro profile. The literary debate itself was a far more complex one than the polarized nature of the struggle might suggest. The abolitionists' rhetorical strategies ranged from Hannah More's emotional appeal to Britons to "redeem our age," to Helen Maria Williams' note of qualified support in which she heralded a new law regulating the conditions of slave ships as a step in the right direction, to Anna Barbauld's angry injunction to the anti-slavery crusader, William Wilberforce, to "seek no more to break a Nation's fall." The approaches of the anti-abolitionists were equally varied, from Bryan Edwards' careful distinction between the cruelty of the slave-traders and the more paternal consideration of the plantation owners, to Alexander Geddes' characterization of himself as an underdog warding off the impositions of an uncaring multitude, to the uglier and more overt racism of Geddes' references to "the vile and barbarous *Blacks* of Africa" and the descriptions of Negroes' "unconquerable indolence" and "deplorable degeneracy" in *Thoughts on the Slavery of the Negroes*. Few issues better embodied the age's perception of literature as an engine of public debate facilitating "the collision of mind with mind."

ᏬᏮᎧ

HANNAH MORE
Slavery: A Poem [1]

O great design!
Ye Sons of Mercy! O complete your work;
Wrench from Oppression's hand the iron rod,
And bid the cruel feel the pains they give.
                    Thompson's *Liberty* [2]

---

[1] Hannah More (1745–1833), an active poet and dramatist, as well as a campaigner for causes such as Christian evangelicalism, education, the anti-slavery campaign, and in the 1790s, the anti-revolutionary movement. She was closely connected with William Wilberforce and his fellow Evangelicals in the Clapham sect. *Slavery* was published to coincide with the first Parliamentary debate on the slave trade. Abolitionists' expectations were raised when a Committee of the Privy Council started to take evidence on the "present state of the African trade" in February 1788.

[2] James Thomson (1700–48), a Scottish poet, wrote *Liberty* (1735–6), as a tribute to Britain.

IF Heaven has into being deign'd to call
Thy light, O LIBERTY! to shine on all;
Bright intellectual Sun! why does thy ray
To earth distribute only partial day?
5 Since no resisting cause from spirit flows
Thy penetrating essence to oppose;
No obstacles by Nature's hand imprest,
Thy subtle and ethereal beams arrest;
Nor motion's laws can speed thy active course,
10 Nor strong repulsion's pow'rs obstruct thy force;
Since there is no convexity in MIND,
Why are thy genial beams to parts confin'd?
While the chill North with thy bright ray is blest,
Why should fell darkness half the South invest?
15 Was it decreed, fair Freedom! at thy birth,
That thou shou'd'st ne'er irradiate *all* the earth?
While Britain basks in thy full blaze of light,
Why lies sad Afric quenched in total night?
          *   *   *

Perish th' illiberal thought which would debase
The native genius of the sable race!
Perish the proud philosophy, which sought
To rob them of the pow'rs of equal thought!
Does then th' immortal principle within
Change with the casual colour of a skin?
Does matter govern spirit? or is mind
Degraded by the form to which 'tis join'd?

   No: they have heads to think, and hearts to feel,
And souls to act, with firm, tho' erring zeal;
For they have keen affections, kind desires,
Love strong as death, and active patriot fires;
All the rude energy, the fervid flame,
Of high-soul'd passion, and ingenuous shame:
Strong, but luxuriant virtues boldly shoot
From the wild vigour of a savage root.

   Nor weak their sense of honour's proud control,
For pride is virtue in a Pagan soul;
A sense of worth, a conscience of desert,
A high, unbroken haughtiness of heart;
That self-same stuff which erst proud empires
   sway'd,
Of which the conquerors of the world were made.
Capricious fate of man! that very pride
In Afric scourg'd, in Rome was deify'd.
   No Muse, O† Qua-shi![1] shall thy deeds relate,
No statue snatch thee from oblivious fate!

For thou wast born where never gentle Muse
On Valour's grave the flow'rs of Genius strews;
And thou wast born where no recording page
Plucks the fair deed from Time's devouring rage.
Had Fortune plac'd thee on some happier coast,
Where polish'd souls heroic virtue boast,
To thee, who sought'st a voluntary grave,
Th' uninjur'd honours of thy name to save,
Whose generous arm thy barbarous Master spar'd,
Altars had smok'd, and temples had been rear'd.

   Whene'er to Afric's shores I turn my eyes,
Horrors of deepest, deadliest guilt arise;
I see, by more than Fancy's mirror shewn,
The burning village, and the blazing town:
See the dire victim torn from social life,
The shrieking babe, the agonizing wife!
She, wretch forlorn! is dragg'd by hostile hands,
To distant tyrants sold, in distant lands!
Transmitted miseries, and successive chains,
The sole sad heritage her child obtains!
Ev'n this last wretched boon their foes deny,
To weep together, or together die.
By felon hands, by one relentless stroke,
See the fond links of feeling Nature broke!
The fibres twisting round a parent's heart,
Torn from their grasp, and bleeding as they part.

   Hold, murderers, hold! nor aggravate distress;
Respect the passions you yourselves possess;
Ev'n you, of ruffian heart, and ruthless hand,
Love your own offspring, love your native land.
Ah! leave them holy Freedom's cheering smile,
The heav'n-taught fondness for the parent soil;
Revere affections mingled with our frame,
In every nature, every clime the same;
In all, these feelings equal sway maintain;

---

† It is a point of honour among negroes of a high spirit to die rather than to suffer their glossy skin to bear the mark of the whip. Qua-shi had somehow offended his master, a young planter with whom he had been bred up in the endearing intimacy of a play-fellow. His services had been faithful; his attachment affectionate. The master resolved to punish him, and pursued him for that purpose. In trying to escape Qua-shi stumbled and fell; the master fell upon him: they wrestled long with doubtful victory; at length Qua-shi got uppermost, and, being firmly seated on his master's breast, he secured his legs with one hand, and with the other drew a sharp knife; then said, "Master, I have been bred up with you from a child; I have loved you as myself: in return, you have condemned me to a punishment of which I must ever have borne the marks: thus only I can avoid them;" so saying, he drew the knife with all his strength across his own throat, and fell down dead, without a groan, on his master's body.
   Ramsay's *Essay on the Treatment of African Slaves*.

[1] Qua-shi: A story of a slave named Quashi who kills himself instead of killing his master in self-defence. Several other writers also depict this story, shaping Quashi into various tropes, including martyr, rebel, and the subaltern Other. In Bermuda, in 1784, a slave named Quashi was convicted of murdering his master John McNeill and was hanged on Gibbet Island.

120 In all the love of HOME and FREEDOM reign:
And Tempe's[1] vale, and parch'd Angola's[2] sand,
One equal fondness of their sons command.
Th' unconquer'd Savage laughs at pain and toil,
Basking in Freedom's beams which gild his native
        soil.
125   Does thirst of empire, does desire of fame,
(For these are specious crimes) our rage inflame?
No: sordid lust of gold their fate controls,
The basest appetite of basest souls;
Gold, better gain'd, by what their ripening sky,
130 Their fertile fields, their arts[†] and mines supply.
        What wrongs, what injuries does Oppression
                plead
To smooth the horror of th' unnatural deed?
What strange offence, what aggravated sin?
They stand convicted—of a darker skin!
135 Barbarians, hold! th' opprobrious commerce spare,
Respect *his* sacred image which they bear:
Tho' dark and savage, ignorant and blind,
They claim the common privilege of kind;
Let Malice strip them of each other plea,
140 They still are men, and men shou'd still be free.
Insulted Reason loaths th' inverted trade—
Dire change! the agent is the purchase made!
Perplex'd, the baffled Muse involves the tale;
Nature confounded, well may language fail!
145 The outrag'd Goddess with abhorrent eyes
Sees MAN the traffic, SOULS the merchandize!
        Plead not, in reason's palpable abuse,

Their sense of [††] feeling callous and obtuse:
From heads to hearts lies Nature's plain appeal,
150 Tho' few can reason, all mankind can feel.
Tho' wit may boast a livelier dread of shame,
A loftier sense of wrong refinement claim;
Tho' polish'd manners may fresh wants invent,
And nice distinctions nicer souls torment;
155 Tho' these on finer spirits heavier fall,
Yet natural evils are the same to all.
Tho' wounds there are which reason's force may
        heal,
There needs no logic sure to make us feel.
The nerve, howe'er untutor'd, can sustain
160 A sharp, unutterable sense of pain;
As exquisitely fashion'd in a slave,
As where unequal fate a sceptre gave.
Sense is as keen where Congo's sons preside,[3]
As where proud Tiber rolls his classic tide.[4]
165 Rhetoric or verse may point the feeling line,
They do not whet sensation, but define.
Did ever slave less feel the galling chain,
When Zeno prov'd there was no ill in pain?[5]
Their miseries philosophic quirks deride,
170 Slaves groan in pangs disown'd by Stoic pride.
        When the fierce Sun darts vertical his beams,
And thirst and hunger mix their wild extremes;
When the sharp iron[†††] wounds his inmost soul,
And his strain'd eyes in burning anguish roll;
175 Will the parch'd negro find, ere he expire,
No pain in hunger, and no heat in fire?

---

[1] A valley in North Thessaly, between Mt. Olympus and Mt. Óssa, celebrated by poets, including Virgil in the *Georgics*, for its sublime beauty. The Vale of Tempe was also sacred to Apollo, to whom a temple was erected on the right bank; laurel for the wreaths of victors of the Pythian games was gathered there.

[2] From the late sixteenth century until 1836, when Portugal abolished the trade, slave trading dominated the economy in Angola, the source of as many as two million slaves for the New World.

[†] Besides many valuable productions of the soil, cloths and carpets of exquisite manufacture are brought from the coast of Guinea.

[††] Nothing is more frequent than this cruel and stupid argument, that they do not *feel* the miseries inflicted on them as Europeans would do.

[3] The Congo is the second largest river in Africa.

[4] The Tiber flows through Rome and across much of Italy.

[5] Zeno of Citium (c. 334–c. 262 B.C.), Greek philosopher, founder of Stoicism.

[†††] This is not said figuratively. The writer of these lines has seen a complete set of chains, fitted to every separate limb of these unhappy, innocent men; together with instruments for wrenching open the jaws, contrived with such ingenious cruelty as would shock the humanity of an inquisitor.

*　　*　　*

Shall Britain, where the soul of Freedom reigns,
Forge chains for others she herself disdains?
Forbid it, Heaven! O let the nations know
The liberty she loves she will bestow;
5 Not to herself the glorious gift confin'd,
She spreads the blessing wide as humankind;
And, scorning narrow views of time and place,
Bids all be free in earth's extended space.
  What page of human annals can record
10 A deed so bright as human rights restor'd?
O may that god-like deed, that shining page,
Redeem OUR fame, and consecrate OUR age!

*　　*　　*

(1788)

HELEN MARIA WILLIAMS
A Poem on the Bill Lately Passed for Regulating the Slave-Trade [1]

The quality of mercy is not strained;
It droppeth, as the gentle rain from heav'n
Upon the place beneath. It is twice blessed;
It blesseth him that gives, and him that takes.
                 Shakespeare [2]

THE hollow winds of night no more
In wild unequal cadence pour
On musing fancy's wakeful ear
The groan of agony severe
5 From yon dark vessel which contains
The wretch new-bound in hopeless chains,
Whose soul with keener anguish bleeds

As Afric's less'ning shore recedes;
No more where ocean's unseen bound
10 Leaves a drear world of waters round,
Between the howling gust shall rise
The stifled captive's latest sighs;
No more shall suffocating death
Seize the pent victim's sinking breath
15 (The pang of that convulsive hour
Reproaching man's insatiate power—
Man, who to Afric's shore has passed
Relentless as the annual blast
That sweeps the Western Isles and flings
20 Destruction from its furious wings).
And woman—she, too weak to bear
The galling chain, the tainted air,
Of mind too feeble to sustain
The vast accumulated pain,
25 No more in desperation wild
Shall madly strain her gasping child
With all the mother at her soul;
With eyes where tears have ceased to roll,
Shall catch the livid infant's breath,
30 Then sink in agonizing death.
  Britain, the noble blessed decree
That soothes despair, is framed by thee! [3]
Thy powerful arm has interposed,
And *one* dire scene for ever closed;
35 Its horror shall no more belong
To that foul drama, deep with wrong.
Oh, first of Europe's polished lands
To ease the captive's iron bands;
Long as thy glorious annals shine,
40 This proud distinction shall be thine!
Not first alone when Valour leads
To rush on Danger's noblest deeds;
When Mercy calls thee to explore
A gloomy path untrod before,

---

[1] Helen Maria Williams (1761–1827), a well-known author and supporter of campaigns for political reform such as the abolition movement and, in the 1790s, the French Revolution and the related political struggles in Britain. *A Poem on the Bill Lately Passed for Regulating the Slave Trade* (1788) refers to the passing of Sir William Dolben's 1788 Slave Carrying Bill, which regulated the size of slavery ships on the Middle Passage.

[2] William Shakespeare, *The Merchant of Venice* (1596), IV:ii: 184–86.

[3] A reference to Britain's parliament passing Sir William Dolben's Slave Carrying Bill (1788), which decreed that the number of slaves carried in a vessel should be proportional to its tonnage.

45 Thy ardent spirit springs to heal
And, greatly gen'rous, dares to feel!
Valour is like the meteor's light
Whose partial flash leaves deeper night,
While Mercy, like the lunar ray,
50 Gilds the thick shade with softer day.

       *   *   *

    Who from his far-divided shore
210 The half-expiring captive bore?
Those whom the traffic of their race
Has robbed of every human grace,
Whose hardened souls no more retain
Impressions nature stamped in vain,
215 All that distinguishes their *kind*,
For ever blotted from their mind;
As streams that once the landscape gave
Reflected on the trembling wave,
Their substance change when locked in frost
220 And rest in dead contraction lost;
Who view unmoved the look that tells
The pang that in the bosom dwells;
Heed not the nerves that terror shakes,
The heart convulsive anguish breaks;
225 The shriek that would their crimes upbraid,
But deem despair a part of trade.
Such only for detested gain
The barb'rous commerce would maintain.
    The gen'rous sailor, he who dares
230 All forms of danger, while he bears
The British flag o'er untracked seas
And spreads it on the polar breeze;
He who, in glory's high career,
Finds agony and death are dear,
235 To whose protecting arm we owe
Each blessing that the happy know—
Whatever charms the softened heart,
Each cultured grace, each finer art,
E'en thine, most lovely of the train,
240 Sweet poetry, thy heav'n-taught strain—
His breast, where nobler passions burn

In honest poverty, would spurn
The wealth oppression can bestow,
And scorn to wound a fettered foe.
245 True courage in the unconquered soul
Yields to compassion's mild control,
As the resisting frame of steel
The magnet's secret force can feel.

       *   *   *

    Oh eloquence, prevailing art,
Whose force can chain the list'ning heart,
The throb of sympathy inspire
And kindle every great desire,
325 With magic energy control
And reign the sov'reign of the soul,
That dreams, while all its passions swell,
It shares the power it feels so well,
As visual objects seem possessed
330 Of those clear hues by light impressed—
Oh skilled in every grace to charm,
To soften, to appal, to warm,
Fill with thy noblest rage the breast,
Bid on those lips thy spirit rest,
335 That shall, in Britain's senate, trace
The wrongs of Afric's captive race!
But fancy o'er the tale of woe
In vain one heightened tint would throw;
For ah, the truth is all we guess
340 Of anguish in its last excess!
Fancy may dress in deeper shade
The storm that hangs along the glade,
Spreads o'er the ruffled stream its wing
And chills awhile the flowers of spring,
345 But where the wintry tempests sweep
In madness o'er the darkened deep,
Where the wild surge, the raging wave,
Point to the hopeless wretch a grave,
And death surrounds the threat'ning shore—
350 Can fancy add one horror more?
    Loved Britain, whose protecting hand,
Stretched o'er the globe, on Afric's strand

The honoured base of freedom lays,
Soon, soon the finished fabric raise!
And when surrounding realms would frame,
Touched with a spark of gen'rous flame,
Some pure, ennobling, great design,
Some lofty act, almost divine,
Which earth may hail with rapture high,
And Heav'n may view with fav'ring eye,
Teach them to make all nature free,
And shine by emulating thee!

(1788)

ANONYMOUS
Thoughts on the Slavery of the Negroes, as it Affects the British Colonies in the West Indies; Humbly Submitted to the Consideration of Both Houses of Parliament.

WHEN a subject becomes of sufficient importance to engage the public attention; when the Legislature itself is called upon to determine a question, which hath for its object the happiness or misery of thousands of our fellow creatures; it is only fair to suppose, that the promoters of the present enquiry into the slavery of the Negroes in the West Indies, are influenced by the best intentions, by an honest zeal for the cause of humanity, and an utter abhorrence of all tyranny and oppression. An enquiry, dictated by such principles, ought to have many advocates, and I trust will have the support of every good man, as long as it is conducted with temper and moderation, with a becoming regard to truth, and a sincere desire to investigate a subject, in itself sufficiently problematical to prevent any hasty opinion, lest, in pursuing a mistaken benevolence, we may give encouragement to evils of more serious consequence than any we are going to remedy.

It is exceedingly difficult to attempt to combat any popular prejudice or opinion. Like a new light in religion, it is eagerly followed by the credulous multitude, and for a while will tyrannize over the human mind. When the charms of novelty and infatuation are no more, we are shocked at the delusion, and ashamed of our own weakness. A free and a generous people, feeling the blessings of liberty and humanity themselves, are easily moved to compassionate the distresses of others—They patiently listen to the tale of woe, in whatever form it appears. If they behold a spectacle of uncommon distress, their honest indignation bursts into a flame. The very stories in romance, and the extravagancies of the stage, produce the most violent conflicts; and the fiction is lost in the struggle with contending passions: when the calm voice of reason succeeds, we can hardly believe the frailty and imbecility of our natures. This reasoning applies to the present enquiry into the slavery of the Negroes in the West Indies, on which so much has been said, and so little understood. The champions of liberty and humanity, availing themselves of the popularity of the subject, have been remarkably successful in engaging the passions, in extolling their own feelings, and in representing, in the most odious light, every attempt to shake the infallibility of their belief.—Men, who profess themselves the declared enemies of tyranny and oppression, begin with many advantages. To all their actions we are ready to attribute the purest intentions; and hardly reserving the right of private judgment, we are firmly persuaded they are invariably directed to the public good.

I congratulate my countrymen on the present union between the Dissenters and the Clergy of the established Church—It is a happy presage of universal peace—We shall banish from our remembrance every controversial point which hath at any time distracted this happy isle—The only contention will be, who shall most distinguish himself for his love of humanity, benevolence, charity, and every other Christian virtue! The first effusions of this philanthropic spirit will soon extend to the most distant regions, and the yet unborn will remember with gratitude the pious efforts of their unknown friends!

I am loth to disturb the reveries of these well-intentioned, but mistaken men. I am loth to deprive them of any happiness they can possibly derive from their own conceits. While their well-meant zeal was harmless to others, nothing could have induced me to interrupt their repose. Will these benevolent men forgive me if I insinuate, that, in their zeal for the cause of humanity, they have not been entirely indifferent to a display of their own feelings, and to the ambition of being distinguished from the mass of the people? To prepare the mind for the reception of this new phantom, its advocates are at infinite pains to represent the West Indians as cruel, avaricious, and tyrannical. If these were facts, there could be only one opinion upon the present question. Those who best know the West Indians, will do ample justice to their humanity, munificence, and hospitality.

The story of the sufferings of the Negroes, like any other fiction of the brain, often repeated, begins at last to be firmly believed. So would any other tale much more improbable, if the same trouble was taken to propagate it. If a surmise went forth, that every man who quitted his native country was infatuated and bewitched, and any one would be at the pains to enter into the detail, with peculiar circumstances of commiseration for all such unhappy objects, there is no doubt but it would readily obtain belief among individuals, and they would soon be tracing evident signs of witchcraft in the looks and actions of every man who returned again to his own country.

Let us endeavour to trace the source of this unhappy perversion of human reason. In northern Europe, whether it is from the density of the atmosphere, the scorbutic[1] tendency of the blood, or from any other physical and unknown cause, these countries always produce a number of gloomy, discontented people, who, brooding over their own infirmities, and viewing all nature through a melancholy medium, are continually hunting after imaginary evils of the most terrible kind. Restless and dissatisfied themselves, they believe all mankind in the same state. In a mood like this, if they hear of a house in flames, they immediately see the whole world on fire. If the sound of chains strike upon the ear, nothing short of universal bondage is thought of.

In looking for instances of cruelty in the West Indies, many have been found, and always will be found, under the best government upon earth. Is it fair, is it charitable, to form general conclusions from particular events which all mankind hold in abhorrence? Have we not had a Kirke,[2] a Jefferies,[3] and a Cole?[4] And are not monsters the growth of every soil? They appear in defiance of all human laws.

If I am able to shew that the blacks are really happy; that their condition (if the odious name of slave could be forgotten) is preferable to the lower orders of the people in Great Britain and Ireland; and that they enjoy the necessaries, and often the luxuries of life, I trust every honest man will feel a just indignation at any attempt to mislead his judgment, and to impose upon him an opinion of cruelty, which has no existence in any of the British West India islands.

Nothing can be more distant from my mind, than any attempt to outrage the feelings of human-

---

[1] Suffering from scurvy.

[2] Percy Kirke (1646–91), infamous for the severity of the punishments when, after the Battle of Sedgemoor in 1685, his troops hanged nineteen prisoners in the Taunton marketplace.

[3] George Jeffreys, (1648–89), an infamously brutal judge, appointed Lord Chief Justice in 1683.

[4] Probably a misspelt reference to Sir Edward Coke (1552–1634), an eminent English jurist with a reputation for severity.

ity. An idea so shocking to every civilized mind, can hardly be supposed. No motive could have engaged me, in the present investigation, but a desire to distinguish truth from falshood, happiness from misery, and declamation from argument, and to endeavour to undeceive my countrymen on a subject wherein so much pains has been taken to mislead them.

Let us take a view of the situation of the Africans, the nature of their country, their climate and government, and the genius and disposition of its inhabitants. The appearance of the slave-coast of Africa, when it was first visited by the Europeans, strongly marked the barbarous state of the people; a rude, inhospitable country, susceptible indeed of cultivation, but almost every way covered with thick, impenetrable forests. The wild luxuriance of nature was here pourtrayed in rich attire. The pruning hand of man was hardly seen. The peaceful labours of agriculture were little known.

It has been observed, that those countries most favoured by nature, often make the slowest progress to civilization; and that the people always groan under the weight of a cruel despotism. "This is an effect which springs from a natural cause. Great heat enervates the strength and courage of men, while in cold climates they have a certain vigour of body and mind, which renders them capable of long, painful, great, and intrepid actions. We ought not, then, to be astonished, that the effeminacy of the people in hot climates has almost always rendered them slaves; and that the bravery of those in colder regions has enabled them to maintain their liberties."[1]

In those countries between the tropics, and especially under the equator, "the excess of heat renders men so slothful and dispirited, that nothing but the most pressing necessity can induce them to perform any laborious duty."[2] An unconquerable indolence is universally felt and acknowledged. Sunk into the most deplorable degeneracy, they feel no incitements beyond the present moment. In vain may we represent to them the happiness of others. In vain may we attempt to rouse them to a sense of their own weakness. The soul, unwilling to enlarge itself, becomes the prey of every ignoble passion. Strangers to every virtuous and magnanimous sentiment, they are without fame—they are without glory.

The Africans have been always represented as a cruel and perfidious people, lazy, lascivious, faithless in their engagements, innate thieves, without morals, and without any just notion of any one religious duty. Their laws are founded on such principles as naturally flow from so impure a source. The government of the slave-coast of Africa is despotic. The will of the Prince must be obeyed. There is no appeal upon earth from his awful decree. The lives and fortunes of every one are absolutely at his disposal. These tyrants have thought fit to distinguish a number of crimes, but have taken no care to proportionate their degrees of punishment. Every offence is there punished with loss of life or liberty. Captives in war are deliberately murdered, or sold as slaves, as may most indulge the sanguinary caprice of the conqueror. Those convicted of adultery or theft, lose their liberty. He who is in debt, and unable to pay must either sell himself or his children to satisfy the creditor. It may be said, that the loss of life, or liberty, only commences with the injury done to society. I answer, "that in Africa, the civil liberty is

---

[1]   Charles de Montesquieu (1686–1755), French lawyer and political philosopher. From *The Spirit of Laws*, Book XVII, "How the Laws of Political Servitude Bear a Relation to the Nature of the Climate," Chapter 2, "The Difference between Nations in point of Courage."

---

[2]   Montesquieu, *The Spirit of Laws*, Book XV, "In What Manner the Laws of Civil Slavery Relate to the Nature of the Climate," Chapter 7, "Another Origin of the Right of Slavery."

already destroyed by the political slavery."[†] A country like this, doomed to bear the weight of human misery, will always present a history of the most shocking cruelties, and of the severest slavery upon earth.

After viewing this melancholy picture, we ought not to be surprized at the extent of the present intercourse between the Africans and Europeans. For want of proper consideration, and from the influence of certain prejudices, the slave-trade has long been considered the scandal and reproach of every nation who have been anywise engaged in it, but without sufficient reason.

Men who enjoy the benefits of civilization, and who are protected in life, liberty, and property, by the wisdom of humane and equal laws, feel that spirit of liberty, and enthusiastic love of their country, which freedom only can inspire. Talk to them of banishment, and it is more terrible than death. Not so the poor African—he has few motives for wishing any longer to behold the distresses of his country; he is, alas! perhaps, the last witness of the sad misfortunes of his house—Already deprived of family, friends, and every other tender endearment, he has no relief but in banishment or death.

It is pleasant to mark the progress of the barbarian, from the moment he is put on shore in an English colony, to the time he becomes the master of a family, and acquires property of his own. He is first of all clothed (a thing unknown to him in his own country) and then instructed in the necessity of cleanliness. When carried to the plantation, he is shewn how to work in common with others. In a little time he chuses himself a wife, and has a house given to him, much better, allowing for the difference of climate, than what the peasants have in this country. When he is sufficiently instructed in the management of ground, a certain portion is alotted to the exclusive use of himself and family, which, with a moderate share of industry, is not only sufficient to supply every personal want, but leave a considerable part to be sent to market, to be sold, or exchanged for either necessaries or luxuries. The African now, finding himself a family man, and in possession of house and land, he begins to rear hogs, poultry, and other small stock, and either sells them to his master at a fair price, or carries them to market, for which one day in the week is allowed him. There have been instances of slaves upon plantations leaving no less than five hundred pounds in money, among their children, besides other personal property, and exclusive of what they gave away in their own life time. So sacred is the separate property acquired by slaves, there are few instances of the master interposing his authority in its distribution. The African, no longer remembering a country to which he owes nothing but birth, becomes attached to the soil which is so propitious to his wants, and having few cares, and few desires, that are not compleatly satisfied, there is nothing so terrible to him as a change of situation. The master is the steward, the faithful guardian of all his wants and necessities. In sickness and in health—in youth and in old age, his assiduities are undiminished. The reader will anticipate the happiness of these people—and happy they must be, while their labours are directed by equity and humanity, and not by avarice.

God forbid that I should be an advocate for slavery, or servitude of any description, that can anywise limit the extent of human happiness: at the same time let me caution my countrymen against the weakness and folly of believing that happiness can only be sought in a constitution as free as their own. The history of all nations shew how extremely improper the laws of one country would be for

---

[†] Montesquieu. [A reference to *The Spirit of Laws*, Book XV, Chapter 6, which warns that "In all despotic governments...the political slavery annihilates the civil liberty." Montesquieu doesn't actually mention Africa by name.]

those of another. Let us see what Baron Montesquieu says upon this subject.—"Laws should be adapted to the climate of each country, to the quality of the soil, to its situation and extent, to the manner of living of the natives, whether husbandmen, huntsmen, or shepherds—they should have a relation to the degree of liberty which the constitution will bear, to the religion of the inhabitants, to their inclinations, riches, number, commerce, manners, and customs."[1]

VERITAS.

London, March 12, 1788.

(1788)

The Rev. Mr. Robert Boucher Nicholls, Dean of Middleham
Observations, Occasioned by the Attempts Made in England to Effect the Abolition of the Slave Trade; Shewing the Manner in Which Negroes Are Treated in the British Colonies, in the West-Indies [2]

"And why beholdest thou the mote that is in thy brother's eye, but considerest not the beam that is in thine own eye?"

"Or how wilt thou say to thy brother, let me pull out the mote out of thine eye; and behold, a beam is in thine own eye?"[3]

PREFACE.

THE author of the following pages having learned, from magazines, newspapers, and

[1] Montesquieu, *The Spirit of Laws*, Book I, "Of Laws in General," Chapter 3, "Of Positive Laws."

[2] Born in Barbados, Nicholls was also the author of *A Letter to the Treasurer of the Society Instituted for the Purpose of Effecting the Abolition of the Slave Trade* (1787).

[3] Matthew 7:3–4.

reviews, sent from England to this island, some of the many calumnies, industriously propagated, against the proprietors of negro slaves in the West Indies; and the attempts made to persuade men of humanity and religion, to exert their endeavours to procure a law to abolish slavery and the slave trade, as offensive to both: thought it might be useful to lay before the public, the real situation and treatment of slaves in the sugar colonies, an undertaking which a long and intimate knowledge of, and residence, at different times in most of the islands, from Barbadoes to Jamaica, particularly qualifies him for.

The account he has given, he is satisfied, will be acknowledged by every person, acquainted with the West Indies, to be a less favourable representation of the negroes' situation than the fact would justify; but, as he speaks only of general treatment, he has avoided mentioning the attention which particular people shew their slaves. It is now not uncommon, on sugar estates, in several of the islands, to have a kind of marquees, or tents pitched, or in their stead, thatched sheds erected in different places on the land for the negroes, in case of hasty and violent showers to retire to, and also to employ two or three boys with mules to bring grass, to prevent the gang having any thing to do after they leave the field; which is considered injurious to their healths, as they are often detained, in wet weather, till the whole gang are collected together, to be called over.

It was the author's original intention to have done no more than point out the extreme improbability, not to say absurdity, of the accounts given of the planters' cruelty to their slaves; but observing that not only individuals had united themselves upon this occasion; but that the two Universities, and other respectable public societies, had addressed the House of Commons to abolish the slave trade, as inconsistent with the Christian Religion; he could not help respecting such authorities, and having doubts how far he might venture to say any thing in favour of a commerce so generally condemned. He thought it incumbent on him first to search the scriptures, to learn whether slavery was inconsistent with the revealed will of the Deity. The result of his enquiry was perfectly satisfactory to himself, and he thought it but right to point out some few of the many passages, to be found in the sacred volumes, which justify that commerce. Since the following observations went to the press the author has the great satisfaction to find, that he might have pursued his original plan without any injury to the cause he has endeavoured to support, as he has seen a pamphlet by the Rev. Mr. Harris, of Liverpool,[1] who has so clearly proved, from the scriptures, that slavery is neither contrary to the law nor gospel, that it is scarcely possible for the most conscientious believer, who reads that tract, to doubt in future; whether the man servant or the maid servant is not as much a man's property as "*his ox or his ass, or any thing that is his.*"[2]

To a British subject the word *slavery* conveys an idea, in some measure different from what it raises in the minds of most other people in Europe. But it is to be doubted, if the idea entertained by my countrymen can be easily explained by many of them. Every submission to the will of another; every degree of servitude; every restraint upon a man's personal liberty; is in some sort a species of slavery—If this observation is just; which is the nation in Europe, where, in some instances, personal liberty is restrained by severer laws, than in England?

If by liberty is understood to be, *people being governed by laws to which they have given their assent by themselves, or their representatives*: Without entering into an enquiry, whether the bulk of the people in England have, or have not, that priviledge; it may, surely, be truly said, the inhabitants of these colonies, do not possess it, to any great extent; and if their property is to be taken from them or much lessened in value, which it certainly will be, if the present attempt should succeed, either in the whole, or in part; they will themselves become slaves, in the stead of those who are now *called* so.

About the time of Lord Mansfield's determination in the case of Mr. Stuart's negro,[3] the imaginations of the populace of London were as much heated by the cry of *liberty*, as they were a few years ago, by the name of the *Protestant Religion*,[4] and as those of the people in Great Britain seem, in general, to be now, with the idea of *humanity*; the exercise of which virtue they seem more earnest to recommend to the inhabitants of the East and West Indies, than to practice it themselves.

They have already, about the time of the decision above-mentioned, tried the effects of emancipating the negroes at home, and *found it would not do.* From that to the present time, the number of slaves, who have attended their masters and their families from North America and the islands to

---

[1] Rev. Raymond Harris (1753–1831), *Scriptural Researches on the Licitness of the Slave Trade, Shewing its Conformity with the Principles of Natural and Revealed Religion, Delineated in the Sacred Writings of the Word of God* (1788). The pamphlet, which used biblical references to prove that the slave trade conformed with scripture, was commissioned by Liverpool Council.

[2] From the Ten Commandments, in Exodus 20:17; also Deuteronomy 5:21—"Thou shalt not covet thy neighbour's house, thou shalt not covet thy neighbour's wife, nor his manservant, nor his maidservant, nor his ox, nor his ass, nor any thing that is thy neighbour's."

[3] In 1769, Charles Stuart, a customs official from Boston, came to London with one of his slaves, James Somerset. Somerset escaped in 1771. In November of that year, Stuart recaptured his "property" and brought him on board the Ann and Mary, to be shipped to Jamaica. With the swift actions of Somerset's friends, Lord Mansfield granted a writ of Habeas Corpus two days later, which meant that Somerset could not legally be taken from England. In June 1772, Lord Mansfield ruled in favour of Somerset, conceding that slavery was legal under colonial laws, but insisting that this had no application to the laws of England.

[4] The Gordon Riots, in 1780, were aimed at forcing Parliament to repeal a law passed in 1778 for the relief of Roman Catholics.

Great Britain and Ireland, cannot have been much less than 40,000; particularly, taking into the account, the many families who have been forced from the southern colonies of the American continent by the late unhappy contest. Notwithstanding the planters had every right to suppose they were authorised, by the laws of Great Britain, as well as those of the colonies to consider those people as their property; and that they had a right to their services in Europe, or to send, or accompany them back to the colonies, as they judged proper: They found themselves mistaken, and that it was permitted to debauch their slaves, to encourage or entice them to run away, with impunity. The ideas of liberty, the charms of novelty, and an ignorance of the country they had got to; where they found themselves upon a perfect equality, at least, with the inferior white people, could not fail of having pernicious effects upon their minds, and great numbers ran away from their masters. They in general plunged into vice and debauchery, and many of them, who were desirous of returning to their masters and mistresses, were refused to be received. The whole of those thus lost to their owners, and as to every useful purpose, to the community, cannot have been less in number than from 15,000 to 20,000.—As most of them were prime, young seasoned, or Creole slaves, the loss to their owners, the planters, have not been less than from 1,000,000 to 1,200,000 sterling. A large sum to be sacrificed, to the mere names of *liberty and humanity!* What has been the result of thus extending *the blessings of liberty* to so many *wretched slaves.* Let any body shew scarce a single instance of any one of these people being in so happy a situation as they were before. The greater part, it is known, died miserably, in a very short time. No parish was willing to receive them, so that the survivers, after begging about the streets of London, and suffering all those evils, and inconveniencies, consequent on idleness and poverty, famine, disease, and the inclemency of the weather; attracted the attention of the public, and government was prevailed upon to undertake the transportation of them to the country from whence they or their ancestors had been ravished *by the wicked traders* of London, Liverpool, and Bristol.

Equal unhappiness would be the lot of the slaves in the islands, if they were set free; what could they do to obtain a livelihood? To suppose they would hire themselves out to work, can only enter into the imagination of those who do not know the people, or the country: What has so lately passed in England is surely sufficient to shew that there can be no idea, they will, any of them, wish to return to their own country. Thousands of negroes have been made free by their masters in the colonies, and it may, with truth, be asserted, that, notwithstanding many of them were very capable of paying for a passage to any part of Africa they thought proper; scarce a single instance can be produced of any one of them desiring to return to the place of his nativity.[†]

[†] A negro woman was imported amongst a cargo of slaves from Anamaboa, about the year 1772. In the latter end of the year 1773, her brother, named Quashy, who is well known to all the masters of ships in the Gold Coast trade, as a kind of Broker or Interpreter, and who has more than once sailed in a ship from the Coast to the Islands, and home by the way of London; hearing his sister was in Jamaica, took his passage in a ship bound from the Coast to this Island for the sole purpose of endeavouring to discover her, obtain her freedom, and carry her back to her own country; he brought money with him for that purpose, and was lucky enough to find her out, she having been sold to a Miss Tindal, a lady in Kingston. He purchased her from Miss Tindal, and she was prevailed upon, though with great reluctance, to embark with him for England in the Nancy, Captain Brown, the latter end of 1773. Early in 1774, they took their passage from London to Anamaboa, in a scow belonging to John Shoolbred, Esq; called the Peggy, Robert Martin, Master, who landed them safe at that port. During Captain Martin's stay there, he had frequent opportunities of seeing this woman, who, after having been at home a short time, grew perfectly tired and disgusted with the place, and repeatedly requested Captain Martin to carry her back to Jamaica, and would even have returned as a slave, rather than stay where she was; but Captain Martin dared not comply with her desire, as the laws of the country do not permit the carrying away a free woman, or another's slave, without the

The present attempt to cram liberty down the throats of people who are incapable of digesting it, can with propriety, be resembled to nothing, so well as to the account of poor Gulliver, when he was carried out of his little cabinet to the top of the house, by the Brobdignag Monkey.[1]

(1788)

ANNA LETITIA BARBAULD
Epistle to William Wilberforce, Esq. on the Rejection of the Bill for Abolishing the Slave Trade.[2]

Master's permission.

This anecdote was communicated to the author by Robert Hibbert, Esq; of this town, who was personally acquainted with the former part of this history, from a servant of his being husband to the woman while he was in Jamaica; and the other part of it he had from Captain Martin, on his return from Anamaboa to Jamaica, who told it, at his table, in the presence of the negro, the husband, without having any previous knowledge of the connection between the parties.

The attestation of a man of Mr. Hibbert's reputation to such a fact, is surely, of more authority than the journals of twenty such surgeons of Guinea ships, as are said to have sailed from New York sixty or seventy years ago.

What can be a stronger proof of the truth of what is said above, of the reluctance of negroes to return from the West Indies to their own country, than that a young woman, who had been from it so short a time, and had so favourable an opportunity of returning to it under the protection of a brother, who shewed such an affection for her, should not only shew a reluctance to return home and enjoy her LIBERTY, but should express so strong a desire to leave Africa again, and return to Jamaica, and to SLAVERY.

(1788)

[1] Jonathan Swift (1667–1745), *Gulliver's Travels* (1726), "A Voyage to Bobdingnag." After Gulliver is bought by the queen of Brobdingnag, he is carried off by a monkey from his apartment at court to the roof of the palace, and rescued with great difficulty.

[2] Anna Letitia Barbauld (1743–1825), a Dissenting author well-known for her advocacy of many social and political issues such as religious toleration and democratic reform. *Epistle to William Wilberforce, Esq. on the Rejection of the Bill for Abolishing the Slave Trade* (1791) reflects abolitionists' disillusionment when, in April 1791, William Wilberforce's motion to abolish the slave trade, though strongly seconded by both Charles Fox, the leader of the Opposition, and William Pitt, the Prime Minister, was defeated in the House of

CEASE, Wilberforce,[3] to urge thy generous aim!
Thy Country knows the sin, and stands the shame!
The Preacher, Poet, Senator in vain
Has rattled in her sight the Negro's chain;
5   With his deep groans assail'd her startled ear,
And rent the veil that hid his constant tear;
Forc'd her averted eyes his stripes to scan,
Beneath the bloody scourge laid bare the man,
Claim'd Pity's tear, urg'd Conscience's strong controul,
10 And Flash'd conviction on her shrinking soul.
The Muse, too soon awak'd, with ready tongue
At Mercy's shrine applausive peans rung;
And Freedom's eager sons, in vain foretold
A new Astrean reign,[4] an age of gold:
15 She knows and she persists—Still Afric bleeds,
Uncheck'd, the human traffic still proceeds;
She stamps her infamy to future time,
And on her harden'd forehead seals the crime.
    In vain, to thy white standard gathering round,
20 Wit, Worth, and Parts and Eloquence are found:
In vain, to push to birth thy great design,
Contending chiefs, and hostile virtues join;
All, from conflicting ranks, of power possest
To rouse, to melt, or to inform the breast.
25 Where seasoned tools of Avarice prevail,
A Nation's eloquence, combined, must fail:

Commons by 163 votes to 88: a victory for arguments based on the economic benefits of slavery to Britain.

[3] William Wilberforce (1759–1833), a British MP, one of the leaders of the anti-slave trade movement. The Committee for the Abolition of the Slave Trade was formed in 1787, and Wilberforce was invited to fight for abolition in Parliament. He raised the issue annually, each time unsuccessfully. The Abolition of the Slave Trade bill was finally passed, with Wilberforce's active support, in March, 1807. The Anti-Slavery Society continued until 1833 when Parliament passed the Slavery Abolition Act that gave all British empire slaves their freedom.

[4] Also spelled Astraean. Daughter of Jupiter and Themis, Astraea is the Goddess of Justice. Astraea became offended by the corruption of mankind, and ascended from the earth to become the constellation Virgo, to begin a new Golden Age.

Each flimsy sophistry by turns they try;
The plausive argument, the daring lye,
The artful gloss, that moral sense confounds,
Th' acknowledged thirst of gain that honour
    wounds:
Bane of ingenuous minds, th' unfeeling sneer,
Which, sudden, turns to stone the falling tear:
They search assiduous, with inverted skill,
For forms of wrong, and precedents of ill;
With impious mockery wrest the sacred page,
And glean up crimes from each remoter age:
Wrung Nature's tortures, shuddering, while you tell,
From scoffing fiends bursts forth the laugh of hell;
In Britain's senate, Misery's pangs give birth
To jests unseemly, and to horrid mirth[1]——
Forbear!—thy virtues but provoke our doom,
And swell th' account of vengeance yet to come;
For, not unmark'd in Heaven's impartial plan,
Shall man, proud worm, contemn his fellow-man?
And injur'd Afric, by herself redrest,
Darts her own serpents at her Tyrant's breast.
Each vice, to minds deprav'd by bondage known,
With sure contagion fastens on his own;
In sickly languors melts his nerveless frame,
And blows to rage impetuous Passion's flame:
Fermenting swift, the fiery venom gains
The milky innocence of infant veins;
There swells the stubborn will, damps learning's fire,
The whirlwind wakes of uncontroul'd desire,
Sears the young heart to images of woe,
And blasts the buds of Virtue as they blow.

Lo! where reclin'd, pale Beauty courts the breeze,
Diffus'd on sofas of voluptuous ease;
With anxious awe, her menial train around,
Catch her faint whispers of half-utter'd sound;
See her, in monstrous fellowship, unite

At once the Scythian,[2] and the Sybarite;[3]
Blending repugnant vices, misally'd,
Which *frugal* nature purpos'd to divide;
See her, with indolence to fierceness join'd,
Of body delicate, infirm of mind,
With languid tones imperious mandates urge;
With arm recumbent wield the household scourge;
And with unruffled mien, and placid sounds,
Contriving torture, and inflicting wounds.

For you, whose temper'd ardour long has borne
Untir'd the labour, and unmov'd the scorn;
In Virtue's fasti[4] be inscrib's your fame,
And utter'd your's with Howard's honour'd name,[5]
Friends of the friendless—Hail, ye generous band!
Whose efforts yet arrest Heav'n's lifted hand,
Around whose steady brows, in union bright,
The civic wreath, and Christian's palm unite:
Your merit stands, no greater and no less,
Without, or with the varnish of success;
But seek no more to break a Nation's fall,
For ye have sav'd yourselves—and that is all.
Succeeding times your struggles, and their fate,
With mingled shame and triumph shall relate,
While faithful History, in her various page,
Marking the features of this motley age,

---

[1] A reference to an alleged incident in Parliament, in which some members of the House laughed at the story of an African woman who was forced to throw her baby overboard after it had been murdered.

[2] The people of ancient Scythia were notorious for their barbarity.

[3] The people of the ancient Greek city of Sybaris were noted for their luxury and self-indulgence.

[4] Festival days of the Roman calendar; Virtue's fasti was reserved for the abstract gods called Honos (Honour) and Virtus (Virtue).

[5] John Howard (1726–90), a well-known prison reformer. As a result of the evidence he collected, which he gave to the House of Commons, Parliament passed the 1774 Gaol Act, which suggested ways to improve the sanitation of prisons and the health of the prisoners. Over the next few years, Howard completed an exhaustive tour of foreign prisons. When he returned to England he toured its prisons to see if any of the 1774 reforms had been implemented. In 1777, he published the result of his investigations, *The State of Prisons in England and Wales, with an Account of some Foreign Prisons*, which was found to be so shocking that some countries, including France, refused to allow it to be published.

To shed a glory, and to fix a stain,
Tells how you strove, and that you strove in vain.

(1791)

ALEXANDER GEDDES
An Apology for Slavery; or, Six Cogent Arguments Against the Immediate Abolition of the Slave-Trade [1]

IN this curious and inquisitive generation, when the most venerable and hoary prejudices seem to flee, with precipitancy, before that blazing meteor, called *The Rights of Man;* some rash and inconsiderate assertors of those rights have gone so far as to maintain, that the vile and barbarous *Blacks* of Africa have an equal claim to freedom with the rest of the human race; and that we cannot, even indirectly, be accessory to the depriving them of that freedom, without disregarding the piteous cries of *Nature, Humanity,* and *Religion;* which are all vitally wounded (say they) by our enslaving our fellow creatures, or by conniving at that nefarious practice.

I have often, before now, observed, that vague and general imputations are generally overcharged; and have, therefore, less effect on the minds of those who think, than specific positive accusations: but the imputation in question has been so often urged and repeated with so much earnestness, energy and eloquence; that the world, I find, begins to listen to it with wonderful attention; and many weak souls seem, at length, disposed to believe it to be well grounded. The professed defenders of *Slavery* have been, comparatively, so few and so feeble, that their numerous and potent adversaries have often ob-

tained over them an easy triumph: so that, for some time past, I have not heard of a single pen, of any force, having been brandished on that side of the question.

Yet the cause, I apprehend, is far from being desperate. It only wants a proper and persevering champion: and to shew how easily, and, I trust, how successfully it may be defended; I, who am but a puny man, and no Quixotist,[2] will venture to undertake its defence.

The enemies of *Slavery* are, indeed, a formidable phalanx, and most expert in the use of every weapon that can be used in this sort of warfare. Greek and Latin, French and English, Philosophy and Oratory, Prose and Verse, have all been alternately and successfully employed to prepossess the unwary *Vulgar* against the Orthodox doctrine for which I combat. But I am not, in the least, dismayed: with *truth* and *stubborn* facts on my side, I fear not a legion of foes. Some gigantic Goliath may, haply, step forth to defy me; and may even curse me in the name of his Gods: but I flatter myself, that I have in my scrip a few hard pebbles, which, to use a common phrase, will do his business, if my trusty sling but serve me sufficiently on this occasion.

As, above all things, I love method, I will go to work as methodically as possible; and, as honest *Poliniere* was wont to say, "begin by the beginning, and end by the end:"[3] a rule which too many modern writers seem greatly to neglect; for they often begin where they should end, and end where they

---

1 Alexander Geddes (1737–1802), minister, Biblical scholar and author. In addition to the *Apology*, Geddes also wrote much biblical criticism, including a translation of the Bible for English Catholics (1792), which was received with great controversy by Protestants and Catholics.

2 An individual who is impractical in the pursuit of ideals; undertakes extravagant and absurd actions because of an extreme romantic ideal of duty or honour, as illustrated in *Don Quixote de la Mancha* (1605), a satirical romance by Cervantes.

3 Pierre Poliniere (1671–1734), scientist, French schoolmaster, lecturer at the College d'Harcourt and other colleges of the University of Paris. He began to demonstrate experiments in courses of philosophy in Paris in 1696. As one of the first in France to present public lectures on experimental natural philosophy, Poliniere argued that conclusions about causes must be based on experimentation.

should begin.

First of all then, as my opponents are continually affirming, that Slavery and the slave-trade are a manifest and cruel insult to *Nature,* whom they represent as a Matron of exquisite tender feelings, weeping and wailing over the misery of our *Negroes* as Rachel is said to have done over the murdered Innocents of Bethlehem;[1] it becomes necessary to enquire, what sort of a being this same *Nature* is, and through what channel her voice of lamentation has reached the ears of those good gentlemen.

Indeed, from the manner in which some of them talk and write, one would think they had discovered the recess of the old Lady, and found her tearing her hair, and beating her breast, and rending her garments, on account of the fabled sons and daughters of Africa. One writer, in particular, a member of the Jacobine Club, has pourtrayed her in the form of a naked Eve, weeping, not over a captured slave, but over a dead fawn; and crying out her poor eyes at the flagitiousness[2] of men for—eating animal food!—I will take upon me to say, that they never detected her in this, or any such like attitude; nor ever saw her at all, but in their own wild imaginations.

We may fairly say of Nature, what an apostle says of God: *No one hath ever seen Her.*[3] We can form no idea of her, but from her visible operations; and surely these give us little *room* to think, that she is either tear-eyed, or tender-hearted. She sometimes indeed shews symptoms of benevolence; but it is the stern benevolence of an indifferent step-dame, rather than the fond caresses of a partial mother. In truth, she seems to be a very whimsical capricious Madam, whose blandishments and bastings follow one another so speedily and unexpectedly, that we are totally at a loss to know, when she is in jest, or

earnest. This, however, we know full well: when she happens to be in her sulky humours, which is very often, she kicks without mercy, and without the smallest appearance of feeling.

When, heaving the surges of the sea, she plunges whole navies into the Deep—When, shaking the solid earth, she buries whole cities in their own ruins—When, opening her dreadful Volcanos, she overwhelms the adjacent towns and villages with liquid fire—When her lightning issues from the cloud, and blasts whatever it touches—When her rivers inundate the plains, and sweep away, in the course of a minute, the fruits of a whole year's labour; or her mildews, in a single morning, destroy all the husbandman's hopes—Are these marks of maternal affection? Are these proofs of a sympathetic disposition?

Nor is it only in her unanimate reign that she shews her cruel power. Is it not She that inspires the lion and the tyger to tear in pieces and devour their prey? Is it not She that excites the eagle to truss[4] the innocent lamb, and the kite to dart upon the harmless dove? Is it not She that makes the bloodthirsty beagle pursue the timid hare, and the wily spider entrap the unwary fly? Is it not She who bids the wolf ravage our fields, the fox steal our poultry, the locusts eat up our herbs, the rats and mice our grain; and the shark swallow—even ourselves? Is it not She who is daily tormenting us with head-achs, tooth-achs, heart-achs, gouts, gravels, rheumatisms, palsies, dropsies, epilepsies; and the whole catalogue of bodily evils that consume our brittle frame?—Yet this is the Being who is said to cry, forsooth, for the savage Negroes, because we force then to work for their own and our bread!—Let us hear no more of slave-making being a disregard to the cries of *Nature.*

That man is born in Slavery, lives in Slavery, and dies in Slavery, is a truth too obvious to be

---

[1] The children murdered in the search for the baby Jesus.

[2] Degrading acts or habits, with wicked or criminal connotations.

[3] John 1:18.

[4] To secure tightly, bind.

seriously called in question.

At the very first period of his vital existence, he finds himself shut up in a lightless dungeon, whence the midwife, even with her *Habeas Corpus*[1] (as my friend Malcolm M'Gregor wittily observes), cannot always rescue him, without danger to his little person.—No sooner is he relieved from this dismal situation, than he is violently ensheathed in swathings sufficient to bind Hercules, or a Samson; and put under the command of a mercenary Female *Slave-driver*, who turns, tosses, and torments him, according to her pleasure or caprice.—From under this petticoat-government he is removed to school, where a new tyrant awaits him with rods and ferulas[2]—From school he goes to a seven-years apprenticeship, or into a seven-years College-ship; in neither of which, he will not affirm, that he is not more or less a Slave.—Has he ever yet tasted of the *Rights of Man?*

He now arrives at manhood; and gets quit of his master, or his tutors; but is he free? No; if he be poor he must work, in subordination, for a longer term than that of his apprenticeship; perhaps, for all his life; if he be rich and independent, he will soon become the slave of idleness, dissipation, vice, and all their concomitants. Both will most probably be the slaves of Love, the most unmerciful of all tyrants. Ten to one, however, but they escape from his domination—to become the slaves of ambition; and, when ambition has lost its sway, they become the slaves of sordid avarice. There is, now, no hope of delivery; in their present fetters they will remain until tyrannic Death lay hold on them, and throw them breathless into a still more dismal prison than that from which they issued into life?

Such is the natural life of man: a continued series of successive slavery! nor let it be imagined that birth, rank, or riches, make any essential difference. There may be an accidental *plus* or *minus* in the *quotum* of servitude: but that depends not on any external advantage. The king may be a greater slave than the cobler; the first peer of the realm than the meanest peasant; and Lord Lonsdale, with all his mines, than the poor author of this essay. A facetious Latin poet introduces a Stoic philosopher proving, that all men are, more or less, mad—

—————————————— Huc prop ius me,
Dum doceo infanire omnes, vos ordine adite.[3]

With much greater reason I may affirm, that all men are, more or less, slaves.

But, if a certain degree of Slavery be the necessary portion of mankind, why should the *Negroes,* who are scarcely *men,* be exempted from any degree of Slavery that they can bear?—If the European race, who reflect so strongly their Maker's image in the whiteness of their skin, the nobleness of their features, and the symmetry of their limbs; in short, who are *little less* than angels, be, notwithstanding, doomed by Nature to live in a state of perpetual Slavery, with what decency can it be asserted, that the Africans, whose black complexion, beast-like lineaments, and mis-shapen members demonstrate them to be *little more* than incarnate devils, are naturally entitled to the same degree of freedom with ourselves?—Strange, unaccountable assertion!

(1792)

---

[1] Habeaus Corpus Act was passed by Parliament in 1679, guaranteeing that individuals detained by the authorities would have to appear in court to ensure the legality of the detention.

[2] Ferule: Flat ruler used for punishing boys. The word is misspelled in the original edition.

[3] Horace (65–8 B.C.), *Satires* 2.3: "Hither, come near to me, while I prove/that you are mad, all of you from first to last."

BRYAN EDWARDS
*The History, Civil and Commercial,
of the British Colonies in the West Indies* [1]

CHAP. II.

*Of Negroes in a state of Slavery.—Preliminary
Observations.—Origin of the Slave Trade.—Portuguese
Settlements on the African Coast.—Negroes introduced into
Hispaniola in 1502, and the Slave Trade revived at the
instance of Barth. de las Casas in 1517.—Hawkins's
Voyages to the coast, in 1562 and 1563.—African Com-
pany established by James I.—Second charter in 1631 by
Charles I.—Third charter in 1662.—Fourth charter in
1672.—Effect of the Petition and Declaration of Right in
1688.—Acts of the 9th and 10th of William and Mary, c.
26.—New regulations in 1750.—Description of the African
Coast.—Forts and Factories.—Exports from Great
Britain.—Number of Negroes transported annually to the
British Colonies.—State of the Trade from 1771 to
1787.—Number of Negroes at this time exported annually
by the different Nations of Europe.*

I AM not unapprized of the danger I incur at this
juncture in treating the subject of African Slavery,
and the Slave Trade. By endeavouring to remove
those wild and ill-founded notions which have been
long encouraged by misinformed writers in Great
Britain, to the prejudice of the inhabitants of the
British Sugar islands, I am conscious that I shall be
exposed to all that "bitterness and wrath, and anger
and clamour, and evil-speaking and malice," [2] with
which it has long been popular to load the unfortu-

nate slave-holder: yet nothing is more certain than
that the Slave Trade may be very wicked, and the
planters in general very innocent. Much the greatest
part of the present inhabitants of the British West
Indies came into possession of their plantations by
inheritance or accident. Many persons there are, in
Great Britain itself, who, amidst the continual
fluctuation of human affairs, and the changes
incident to property, find themselves possessed of
estates in the West Indies which they have never
seen, and invested with powers over their fellow
creatures there, which, however extremely odious,
they have never abused: some of these gentlemen,
unacquainted with local circumstances, and misled
by the popular outcry, have humanely given orders
to emancipate all their slaves, at whatever expence;
but are convinced that their benevolent purposes
cannot be carried into effect consistently even with
the happiness of the Negroes themselves. The
Reverend Society established in Great Britain for
propagating the Gospel in foreign parts, [3] are themselves under this very predicament. That venerable
society hold a plantation in Barbadoes under a
devise [4] of Colonel Codrington; [5] and they have
found themselves not only under the disagreeable
necessity of supporting the system of slavery which
was bequeathed to them with the land; but are

---

[1] Bryan Edwards (1743–1800), a supporter of the slave trade,
considered strong opposition by Wilberforce. Edwards lived in Jamaica
for several years before settling in England as a West India merchant.
In 1784 Edwards wrote *Thoughts on the late Proceedings of Government
respecting the Trade of the West India Islands with the United States of
America*, in which he attacked the restrictions placed by the government upon trade with the United States. In 1794 he published his
most esteemed work, *History, Civil and Commercial, of the British
Colonies in the West Indies*, and in 1797 published his *Historical Survey
of the French Colony in the Island of St. Domingo*.

[2] Ephesians 4:31.

[3] The Society for the Propagation of the Gospel in Foreign Parts,
begun by Rev. Dr. Thomas Bray, who travelled to Maryland at the end
of the seventeenth century on behalf of the Bishop of London and
found that the Church of England in the American Colonies lacked
spiritual rigour and institutional organization. In 1701, William III
issued a royal charter establishing the Society as an organisation able to
send priests and schoolteachers to America to help the Church's
ministry to the colonists and to take the message of the gospel to the
slaves and native Americans. After 1701, the Society expanded to the
West Indies, Canada, Australia, New Zealand and West Africa, and
then further afield to China (1863) and Japan (1873).

[4] A gift of real property by will.

[5] Colonel Christopher Codrington (1668–1710), founded Codrington College in Barbados, and bequeathed two estates to the Society for
the Propagation of the Gospel in 1710.

induced also, from the purest and best motives, to purchase a certain number of Negroes annually, in order to divide the work, and keep up the stock. They well know that moderate labour, unaccompanied with that wretched anxiety to which the poor of England are subject, in making provision for the day that is passing over them, is a state of comparative felicity: and they know also, that men in savage life have no incentive to emulation: persuasion is lost on such men, and compulsion, to a certain degree, is humanity and charity.

The question then, and the only question wherein the character of the planters is concerned, is this:—Making due allowance for human frailty under the influence of a degree of power ever dangerous to virtue, is their general conduct towards their slaves such only as necessarily results from their situation? If to this enquiry, an affirmative be returned, surely Christian charity, though it may lament and condemn the first establishment of a system of slavery among them, and the means by which it is still kept up and supported, will not hastily arraign those who neither introduced, nor, as I shall hereafter shew, have been wanting in their best endeavours to correct and remedy many of the evils of it.

CHAP. IV.

Means of obtaining Slaves in Africa—Observations thereon.—Objections to a direct and immediate abolition of the trade by the British Nation only.—The probable consequences of such a measure, both in Africa and the West Indies, considered.—Disproportions of sexes in the number of Slaves annually exported from Africa.—Causes thereof.—Mode of transporting Negroes to the West Indies, and regulations recently established by act of parliament.—Effect of those regulations.

THE chief objection to the slave trade arises from the great encouragement which I fear it un-avoidably holds forth to acts of violence, oppression, and fraud among the natives towards each other. Without doubt, this is the strong part of the petitioners case; and I admit it to be so, with that frankness which I trust no honest West Indian will condemn. At the same time it deserves very serious consideration, whether a direct and immediate discontinuance of the trade by the British nation only (the other nations of Europe continuing to purchase as usual) would afford a remedy to those miseries, the existence of which every enlightened mind cannot but admit, and every good mind must deplore; or rather, whether a partial and sudden abolition (so inveterate is the evil) would not aggravate them in a high degree.

In considering this question, we must have in view not only the circumstances attending the Slave Trade on the Coast, but also the situation of the enslaved Negroes already in the Sugar Colonies. On the first head, it is to be enquired whether, supposing Great Britain should abandon her share in this commerce, a less number of slaves would in consequence thereof be brought down for sale in Africa? Admiral Edwards, who served on the station, and was on shore seven months at a time, is decidedly of opinion that, so long as other nations continue to purchase, the number would not be diminished in the least; and a little reflection may perhaps convince us that his opinion is founded in reason, and the nature of the case. Among the commercial nations of Europe, it is true that, in most cases of purchase and barter, the demand and the supply grow up together, and continue to regulate and support each other: but these are the arrangements of well-informed and civilised men. In Africa, it is apprehended the slave merchants possess no ideas of this kind, neither does the nature of their traffic allow of such regulations. When two African states are at war with each other, the aim of each undoubtedly is to destroy as many enemies, or seize on as great a number of captives, as possible. Of these last unfortunate victims, all such as are able to travel, are commonly sent down to the coast for sale, the rest are massacred on the spot, and the same fate attends those unhappy wretches who, being sent down, are found unsaleable. The prices indeed on the coast have been known to vary as the market is more or less plentifully supplied; but, so long as ships from Europe create a market, whether the prices be high or low, it can hardly be doubted that wars will be as frequent as ever, and that the same acts of oppression, violence and fraud, which are said to be committed by princes on their subjects, and by individuals on each other, for the purpose of procuring slaves for sale, will exist as usual, without regulation or restraint.

Behold then an excess of 38,000 of these miserable people (the present annual export in British shipping) thrown upon the market, and it is surely more than probable that one or the other of these consequences will follow: Either the French, the Dutch, and the other maritime nations of Europe, by seizing on what we surrender, will encrease their trade in proportion to the encreased supply, or, having the choice and refusal of 38,000 more than they have at present, will become more difficult to please; confining their purchases to such only as are called prime slaves. Thus the old, and the very young, the sickly and the feeble, will be scornfully rejected; and perhaps *twenty* poor wretches be considered as unsaleable then, and sacrificed accordingly, to *one* that is so considered and sacrificed now.

That this latter supposition is not a mere speculative contingency, is abundantly proved by many respectable witnesses, whose examinations were taken by the committee of the privy council:—Being asked concerning the disposal of such slaves as are rejected by the European traders, either because their cargoes are already assorted, or be-

cause the miserable victims are considered as too old or too feeble for labour, it was given in evidence, as a fact too notorious to be controverted, that they are very frequently, if not generally, put to death. The slave merchant, not having the means of maintaining his captives for any length of time, makes no scruple to avow that it is his intention to destroy them, provided they are not sold by a certain day; and the *work of death*, on such occasions, is sometimes performed in sight of our shipping. Shocking as this account may seem, it is verified by undisputed testimony; and to suppose that a discontinuance of the trade by one nation only, will put an end to this enormity, is to suppose that the African slaveholder will become more merciful, as his slaves are rendered of less value; a conclusion which I am afraid experience will not warrant.

What I have thus deliberately written, is not, if I know my own heart, the language of selfishness, or party. I confess that, reflecting on the means by which slaves are very frequently obtained in Africa, and the destruction that formerly attended the mode of transporting them to the West Indies, I was at one time of opinion it became this great and renowned nation, instead of regulating her conduct by that of other states, to set a laudable example to *them*, by an immediate and unqualified suppression of this reprobated commerce; and I should still maintain and avow the same sentiments, were I not, on fuller enquiry and better information, led to suspect *that the means proposed are not adequate to the end*. I fear that a direct and sudden abolition, by one nation alone, will *not* serve the purposes of humanity in Africa; and I am fully convinced that such a measure will tend to aggravate, in a very high degree, the miseries of a great majority of the Negroes already in the West Indies; whose decreasing population is at present unavoidable; and who therefore, unless recruited by supplies from Africa, must find their labours augment, as their numbers diminish.

(1793)

CHARLOTTE SMITH
The Wanderings of Warwick.[1]

MUCH has been written by moralists against cruelty to animals, and much has been said of the horrors of slavery: but, alas! the people who exercise these cruelties read not the lucubrations of the essayist—The slave merchant studies nothing but his profit and loss; and if at any time something like a qualm of conscience should disturb the felicity he finds in acquiring wealth, he reconciles himself to his pursuit with reflecting, that if he did not drive this trade somebody else would—an argument which I have often heard used to justify every folly and every vice.

In Barbadoes, where I resided at the time I am now accounting for, it appears to be, and certainly is, so much the interest of the planters to be careful of the lives of their slaves, on whose labour their incomes depend, that in general they are not ill-treated;—and if there are some masters whose malignant disposition even avarice cannot controul, there are others whose humanity is not lessened even by the perverse and savage tempers of some of those unhappy beings who are their property.—But so much cannot be said of persons who hire the slaves of others:—these men seem to believe that lives which are not certainly to be spent in their

service are of no value; and a gang of hired negroes are often so overworked as to occasion them to perish in a very few years.—But it seems as if the general lot of this unfortunate race was more tolerable than we are led to suppose from a transient view of their situation: those who are born upon the estates they cultivate, having never any other idea than that of being destined to that labour which they behold going forward around them, are no more discontented with their lot than the peasants of England; and, unless provoked by any tyrannical exertion of their masters power, have no more malice against them than our day-labourers against the lord whose ground they cultivate. On the contrary, the idea of their being the property of their master makes them take a peculiar interest in whatever relates to *him*.—They are pleased if his house is better—his equipage finer—and his property greater than that of his neighbours; and seem to derive consequence themselves from the consequence of him to whom they belong.—This is particularly the case with house negroes, who never think that honour enough is done to those whose property they are; and indeed an infinite deal of pride and vanity is a principal ingredient in the temper of negroes; and a woman dressed for a negro ball, in her jacket of flowered linen, her bead necklace, and white cap, is more vain than the most beautiful Englishwoman on a birth-night ball. The strange attachment of some Europeans to these ebon beauties, but more particularly the preference given to mulatto women, feeds this excessive vanity at the expence indeed of every thing that resembles morals or decency; and perhaps in no part of the Christian world are appearances of morality so little attended to as in the West India islands.

The condition however of the negroes is certainly in some respects even preferable to that of the English poor.—An Englishman, born to no other inheritance than the labour of his hands, can with

---

[1] Charlotte Smith (1749–1806), author of several novels, including *The Wanderings of Warwick* (1794). Smith also wrote many educational books for children, and volumes of poetry that were influential in early Romanticism, including *Elegiac Sonnets* (1784), *The Emigrants* (1793), and *Beachy Head* (1807). Smith married the son of a Caribbean merchant in 1764, and had ten children by 1777; after her husband was imprisoned for debt and fled to France, Smith worked to support her family with her literary efforts.

difficulty earn enough to support even himself.—As soon as he is strong enough, he goes to a master as a ploughman or a carter, where he seldom serves longer than twelve months; by which indeed he gains a settlement in the parish where he so serves: but he usually seeks another service, with no other fortune than his round frock, and a change of coarse clothes.—He has now, however, higher wages in proportion to the increase of his strength; and falls in love with a fellow-servant, whom, before the end of his year's service, he is frequently compelled to marry.—The parish officers reluctantly find him a hovel, or a room;—and with less furniture than is seen even in a negro hut, he commences house-keeper. If his wife is notable, and he is himself industrious, he may exist for a year or two in tolerable comfort (living, however, upon little else than bread): but any remission in the labour of either, and an increasing family, expose him to the extremes of poverty:—he loses his health for want of proper nourishment;—and, becoming careless of his family, who are a burthen to him, mutual reproaches aggravate the bitterness of that poverty which gave rise to them.—He turns poacher or smuggler, yet is not the richer, for the ale-house consumes his illicit profits; and his family become chargeable to the parish. The impatience of those who now bear this load urges them to complaints against him; and he, all freeman as he is, is driven to labour—not indeed with stripes, but by the terrors of a gaol—From this species of tyranny he seeks his remedy in flight, leaving a wife and six or seven children to be maintained solely at the public expence—He enlists for a soldier, and, having sold himself for six-pence a day, becomes in reality as great a slave as the African—at least for the term of years for which he has engaged himself—at the end of which, if he does not return mutilated from the service (in which case indeed he is provided for), he may possibly go back to his parish, and finish his

life, which his mode of living has shortened, in a work-house.— Let any one who has ever inspected a work house compare his *then* situation with that of the negro, who it is true is a slave; but for whom all the necessaries of life are provided in his old age, and who is then established in a little hut of his own—possibly with a woman of nearly his own age, whom long habit has attached to him—where he is employed only in such work as his strength will admit—in teaching some kind of trade to younger negroes, or in taking care of children. If sick, he has medical assistance; and, if he has been a good servant, and has a master only of common humanity, he has many little indulgences to sweeten this last period of existence—to say nothing of the respect and affection with which people of his colour treat the aged among them.

I do not, however, mean to say, that the sole consciousness that, he is free—or rather the notion that he is so, is not to the Englishman more than adequate to every advantage which the slave under the kindest master can enjoy. I intend from this comparison only to infer, that, dreadful as the condition of slavery is, the picture of its horrors is often overcharged.—In one instance is strikes me as having been particularly so.—I recollect, among the representations that have often been made of the heavy tasks imposed on the negroes, great stress has been laid on the barbarous custom of sending out women and children, after a hard day's work, to collect meat for the cattle. That this is never done I do not assert: but I do not believe it is the general practice. In Jamaica, the plenty of forage which the extent and variety of the island afford renders it unnecessary. In Barbadoes, where such advantages do not exist, there are always, as far as I have observed, negroes, who are perhaps incapable of other work, whose business it is to gather forage—and who are called meat-pickers. But let me, after having enumerated all these circumstances of palliation, declare against every species of slavery: let me protect my belief that it brutalises, while it degrades, the human character, and produces at once servility and ferocity.[†]

It has been remarked in the army, that the most tyrannical officers have been almost invariably those most meanly obsequious to their superiors, and who have been raised from inferior life by patronage; and by a man of strong understanding, who had had an opportunity of observing for many years the manners of a great public school, I have been assured, that the boys who had themselves been the worst treated in their juniorships, by those whose age gave them the improper privilege of subjecting them to a state of temporary servitude, were almost always the greatest tyrants in their turn;—whereas it should seem that the very reverse would happen; and that those who had been thus injuriously treated when children, would feel for the defenceless condition of their juniors, when they themselves became young men.—It has been received as a maxim, that human nature is every where the same;—and if these observations are just, it is exemplified in remarking, that such of the negroes as are entrusted with any degree of authority over their unhappy countrymen, exercise that authority with infinitely more rigour than the white superintendents.

(1794)

[†] Notwithstanding my apprehensions that Novel-readers, in their eagerness for more narrative, will murmur at being detained by a sort of dissertation on negro slavery, I should have tempted their patience for a few pages more, if I had not, since I wrote this part, seen Mr. Edward's History of the West Indies, where clearness of style and accuracy of description are united with knowledge of the subject, integrity of heart, and general humanity—and where the English gentleman is not for a moment lost in the Jamaica planter.

C.B. WADSTROM
An Essay on Colonization, Particularly Applied to the Western Coast of Africa, with Some Free Thoughts on Cultivation and Commerce; Also Brief Descriptions of the Colonies Already Formed, or Attempted, in Africa, Including Those of Sierra Leona and Bulama.[1]

CHAP. II.
CHARACTER AND DISPOSITION OF THE AFRICANS.

CIVIL and religious government is allowed to be the principal cause which affects (and even forms) the characters of nations. Climate, diet, occupation, and a variety of other less considerable causes contribute their share to the general effect. It is not, however, by abstract reasonings alone, on the separate or combined influence of those causes that the character of a nation can be ascertained; but actual observations on their genius and conduct must also be attended to. Such observations cannot be too numerous; nor can general conclusions be too cautiously drawn from them.

That this important moral balance may be struck with perfect impartiality, the observer ought to dismiss every prejudice, and to leave his mind open to a full and fair impression of all the circumstances. Every well disposed man will allow the necessity of such procedure, who knows how grossly the very people of whom we are treating, have been misrepresented by those who first made merchandize of their persons, and then endeavoured, by

---

[1] Carl Bernhard Wadstrom (1746–99), a Swedish engineer who went to West Africa in 1788 to investigate slavery, leading to his *Observations on the Slave Trade and a Description of Some Part of the Coast of Guinea during a Voyage Made in 1787 and 1788...with Dr. A. Sparman and Capt. Arrhenius* in 1789, along with his *Essay on Colonization, Particularly Applied to the Western Coast of Africa* in 1794.

calumny, to justify their own conduct towards them. The accounts of African governors and other slave merchants, have been but too implicitly followed by authors of no small note, who never were in Africa, and who did not suspect that the writers they quoted were interested in misleading them. Hence it is to be feared, that many well meaning persons have been led to believe that the Africans are so insensible as not to feel their ill treatment, or so wicked as not to deserve better; and have therefore, without farther examination, left them to what they think a merited fate.

The author, aware of the difficulty of this part of his subject, has all along laboured to observe as minutely and extensively, and to judge as impartially, as he could. But, after all his diligence, he is only able to offer some short and imperfect sketches. Imperfect, however, as they are, he is conscious they are faithfully copied from the original.

He believes every man, who has made it his business to compare the conduct of civilized and uncivilized nations, will admit that the former are governed by reason, and the latter by their will and affections, or what are commonly called their passions—or at least that, upon the whole, reason influences mankind in proportion as they are civilized.

This observation may be applied very appositely to the Africans. Their understandings have not been nearly so much cultivated as those of the Europeans; but their passions, both defensive and social, are much stronger. No people are more sensible of disrespect, contempt, or injury, or more prompt and violent in resenting them. They are also apt to retain a sense of injury, till they obtain satisfaction, or gratify revenge. In this they resemble other imperfectly civilized tribes, and even the more refined Europeans, in whom that benevolent religion, which teaches forgiveness of enemies, has not yet produced it's full effect. For was not satisfaction to offended honour; that is, was not a certain mode

of revenge a distinguishing part of the system of chivalry? And do not our modern duelists, the polite successors of the ancient knights, still cherish a principle which they will not allow to be called revenge; but for which sober people cannot find a better name? Revenge causes wars in Africa: and are there no symptoms of its producing wars in Europe? But African wars are never protracted, with cold-blooded perseverance, to the length of the siege of Troy; nor is peace ever negociated with a view to future wars. The Africans have no particular tortures in reserve for their prisoners, like the North American Indians; nor do they ever devour them, like the natives of New Zealand.

But if they be charged with hatred to their enemies, kindness to their friends ought, in candour, to be stated to their credit; and their hospitality to unprotected strangers is liberal, disinterested, and free from ostentation; as I myself and many others have experienced. Their kindness, and respectful attention to white persons, with whose characters they are satisfied, arises to a degree of partiality which, all things considered, is perfectly surprising. Persons of this description may, and often do, reside among them in perfect security, receiving the best possible proofs of their good will, namely the most pressing solicitations to settle among them. This partiality to well disposed Europeans extends also to their dress, manners, and commodities; in short, to every thing that is European—a disposition which might long ago have been improved to the best purposes.

On those parts of the coast and country, where the slave trade prevails, the inhabitants are shy and reserved, as well they may! and on all occasions go armed, lest they should be way-laid and carried off.

In maternal, filial, and fraternal affection, I scruple not to pronounce them superior to any Europeans I ever was among: but, as they practice polygamy, their paternal and conjugal affections may be supposed less ardent.

As many of them have not sufficient employment either for their heads or their hands, they are apt to relieve listlessness by intoxication, when they can procure the means. So very successful, indeed, have the European slave-dealers been, in exciting in them a thirst for spirits, that it is now become one of the principal pillars of their trade; for the chiefs, intoxicated by the liquor with which they are purposely bribed by the whites, often make bargains and give orders fatal to their subjects, and which, when sober, they would gladly retract. A desire for spirituous liquors, however, is the failing of all uncivilized people. In particular, it has greatly thinned some American tribes, and almost annihilated others.

Their notions and practices respecting property are not more inaccurate or irregular than those of other men in the same stage of society; as is evident from the general conduct of such of them as are unconnected with this destructive commerce. But those who are, may be expected to be tainted with it's concomitant vices. As the whites practice every fraud upon them, in the quantity and quality of the goods delivered, and in trepanning[1] their persons, the blacks cannot carry on *this* trade, on equal terms, without resorting to similar practices. As to the injustice, cruelty and rapine which, at the instigation of the whites, they practice on one another, they are not more disgraceful than the well known trades of crimps, and kidnappers, and press-gangs, carried on, without foreign instigation, in several European countries, and even protected, or connived at, by their governments. At the worst, these practices are not so disgraceful to uncivilized men as to their *civilized*, European instigators.

Refined nations form systems, and rise to generals: unpolished tribes dwell on detail, and trifle in particulars. The Africans are unacquainted with the

dexterity and dispatch arising from the division of labour, and with the numerous advantages of combined exertions systematically conducted. Except in works which, without united efforts, cannot be performed at all, they do every thing in a solitary, desultory manner. Each individual or family, like the peasants in some parts of Europe, spins, weaves, sews, hunts, fishes, and makes baskets, fishing-tackle and implements of agriculture; so that, considering the number of trades they exercise, their imperfect tools, and their still more imperfect knowledge of machinery, the neatness of some of their works is really surprising.

Of their labour in concert, I shall give one example, of which I have been a spectator. The trees on the coast I visited, being generally bent in their growth by the sea-breeze, and wanting solidity, are unfit for canoes. A tree of the proper dimensions is therefore chosen, perhaps fourteen or fifteen miles up the country, which being cut into the requisite length, but not hollowed, lest it should be rent by accident, or by the heat of the sun, the people of the nearest village draw it to the next, and thus successively from village to village, till it reach the coast, where it is formed into a canoe. For this severe labour the villagers look for no other reward than a feast and merry-making, which they enjoy in the true style of rural simplicity.

The same happy mixture of united labour and festivity takes place at building their houses; also in cultivating, planting or sowing their fields, belonging to the same village, and in reaping the crop, which is considered as the common property of the inhabitants. Such a practice in Europe would generate endless disputes; but among this simple people, is the best bond of good neighbourhood. Such indeed is the amiable simplicity of manners which reigns in the villages remote from the slave-trade, that European visitors are ready to imagine themselves carried into a new world, governed by

---

[1] Trapping.

the purest maxims of patriarchal innocence. But though few of them unite their strength, except on these, and a few similar, occasions, and most of them turn their hands to different occupations, we are not thence to conclude unfavourably of their intellects, any more than of the intellects of those European peasants, (in Sweden, Norway, Scotland, &c.) whose practices are similar. On the contrary, Lord Kaimes has observed, I think with much truth, that such peasants are generally more intelligent than artificers, to whom the division of labour, in manufacturing countries, has assigned one, simple operation. A peasant, who makes and repairs ploughs, harrows, and harness, his household furniture, and even his cloaths, has an ampler scope for his understanding, and really becomes a more intelligent being than he who spends his whole life in forging horseshoes, making nails, or burnishing buttons. Such a being, confined for life to a few simple motions, may be said, in some degree, to lose the use of all his powers, but that of the muscles which perform those motions. His intellect lies dormant, for it's use is superseded by a mere animal habit. He becomes, in short, a kind of live machine, in the hands of some monied man, to contribute to the pride and luxury of drones, who posses no other talent than that of turning to their own account the activity of their poor brethren of mankind.[†]

I am unwilling to refine too much; but as the situation of the Africans approaches much nearer to that of intelligent peasants than that of stupid mechanics, I am inclined to think that their intellects may have been improved by being so variously exercised; for the natural way of improving the human intellect, is to afford it an ample field of action; and the sure way to cramp and contract it, is to keep it incessantly plodding in *one* dull pursuit. Certain it is, that though, on the whole, passion is more predominant in the African character than

reason; yet their intellects are so far from being of an inferior order, that one finds it difficult to account for their acuteness, which so far transcends their apparent means of improvement.

(1794)

S.T. COLERIDGE
On the Slave Trade[1]

I HAVE the firmest Faith, that the final cause of all evils in the moral and natural world is to awaken intellectual activity. Man, a vicious and discontented *Animal*, by his vices and his discontent is urged to develop the powers of the Creator, and by new combinations of those powers to imitate his creativeness. And from such enlargement of mind Benevolence will necessarily follow; Benevolence which may be defined "Natural Sympathy made permanent by an acquired Conviction, that the Interests of each and of all are one and the same," or in fewer words, "Natural Sympathy made permanent by enlightened Selfishness." In my calmer moments I have the firmest Faith that all things work together for Good. But alas! it seems a long and a dark Process.

> The early Year's fast-flying Vapours stray
> In shadowing Trains across the orb of Day:
> And we, poor Insects of a few short Hours,
>   Deem it a world of Gloom.
> Were it not better hope a nobler doom
> Proud to believe, that with more active powers
> On rapid many-coloured Wing
> We thro' one bright perpetual Spring
> Shall hover round the Fruits and Flowers

[†] See Lord Kaimes's Sketches of the History of Man.

[1] Samuel Taylor Coleridge (1772–1834), a well-known poet, literary critic, and social commentator. Coleridge's article on the slave-trade, which was based on a lecture given in Bristol on 16 June 1795, appeared in his political and literary magazine, *The Watchman*, No. IV, 25 March, 1796.

Screen'd by those Clouds & cherish'd by those
Showers!
From an unpublished Poem.[1]

I have dwelt anxiously on this subject, with a particular view, to the Slave-trade, which, I knew, has insinuated in the minds of many, uneasy doubts respecting the existence of a beneficent Deity. And indeed the evils arising from the formation of *imaginary* Wants, have in no instance been so dreadfully exemplified, as in this inhuman Traffic. We receive from the West-India Islands Sugars, Rum, Cotton, Logwood,[2] Cocoa, Coffee, Pimento, Ginger, Indigo, Mahogany, and Conserves. Not one of these articles are necessary; indeed with the exception of Cotton and Mahogany we cannot truly call them even useful: and not one of them is at present attainable by the poor and labouring part of Society. In return we export vast quantities of necessary Tools, Raiment, and defensive Weapons, with great stores of Provision. So that in this Trade as in most others the Poor are employed with unceasing toil first to raise, and then to send away the Comforts, which they themselves absolutely want, in order to procure idle superfluities for their Masters. If this Trade had never existed, no one human being would have been less comfortably cloathed, housed, or nourished. Such is its value— they who would estimate the price which we pay for it, may consult the evidence delivered before the House of Commons. I will not mangle the feelings of my readers by detailing enormities, which the gloomy Imagination of Dante would scarcely have dared attribute to the Inhabitants of Hell. For the honour of our common nature, I would fain hope that these accounts have been exaggerated. But, by the confession of all, these enormities might have been perpetrated and with impunity: and when was power possessed and not exercised? By the confession of all parties great cruelties have been inflicted: and therefore before I can suspect exaggeration, I must disbelieve the oaths of the humane and disinterested in compliment to the assertions of men from whose shoulders though I should take mountains of guilt, enough would remain to sink them to perdition.—These Facts have been pressed on the Public even to satiety.

The Abbe Raynal computes that at the time of his writing,[3] nine millions of slaves had been consumed by the Europeans—add one million since, (for it is near thirty years since his book was first published) and recollect, that for one procured ten at least are slaughtered, that a fifth die in the passage, and a third in the seasoning; and the calculation will amount to ONE HUNDRED and EIGHTY MILLION! Ye who have joined in this confederacy, ask of yourselves this fearful question—"if the God of Justice inflict on us that mass only of anguish which we have wantonly heaped on our brethren, what must a state of retribution be?" But who are they who have joined in this tartarean confederacy? Who are these kidnappers, and assassins? In all reasonings neglecting the intermediate links we attribute the final effect to the first cause. And what is the first and constantly acting cause of the Slave-trade? That cause, by which it exists and deprived of which it would immediately cease? Is it not self-evidently the consumption of it's products? And does not then the guilt rest on the consumers? And is it not an allowed axiom in morality, that wickedness may be multiplied, but cannot be divided; and that the guilt of all, attaches to each one who is knowingly an accomplice? Think not of

---

[1] This citation was the poem's only appearance in print during Coleridge's lifetime.

[2] Used for making dyes for fabrics, and therefore associated with luxury rather than necessity.

[3] Guillaume-Thomas-François Raynal, *A Philosophical and Political History of the Settlement and Trade of the Europeans in the East and West Indies.* 1770.

the slave-captains and slaveholders! these very men, their darkened minds, and brutalized hearts, will prove one part of the dreadful charge against you! They are more to be pitied than the slaves; because more depraved. I address myself to you who independently of all political distinctions, profess yourself Christians! As you hope to live with Christ hereafter, you are commanded to do unto others as ye would that others should do unto you. Would *you* choose, that a slave merchant should incite an intoxicated Chieftain to make war on your Country, and murder your Wife and Children before your face, or drag them with yourself to the Market? Would you choose to be sold? to have the hot iron hiss upon your breasts, after having been crammed into the hold of a Ship with so many fellow-victims, that the heat and stench, arising from your diseased bodies, should rot the very planks? Would *you*, that others should do this unto *you*? and if you shudder with selfish horror at the bare idea, do you yet dare be the occasion of it to others?

There is observable among the Many a false and bastard sensibility that prompts them to remove those evils and those evils alone, which by hideous spectacle or clamorous outcry are present to their senses, and disturb their selfish enjoyments. Other miseries, though equally certain and far more horrible, they not only do not endeavour to remedy—they support, they fatten on them. Provided the dunghill be not before their parlour window, they are well content to know that it exists, and that it is the hot-bed of their pestilent luxuries.—To this grievous failing we must attribute the frequency of wars, and the continuance of the Slave-trade. The merchant finds no argument against it in his ledger: the citizen at the crouded feast is not nauseated by the stench and filth of the slave-vessel—the fine lady's nerves are not shattered by the shrieks! She sips a beverage sweetened with human blood, even while she is weeping over the refined sorrows of Werter[1] or of Clementina.[2] Sensibility is not Benevolence. Nay, by making us tremblingly alive to trifling misfortunes, it frequently prevents it, and induces effeminate and cowardly selfishness. Our own sorrows, like the Princes of Hell in Milton's Pandemonium, sit enthroned "bulky and vast:"[3] while the miseries of our fellow-creatures dwindle into pigmy forms, and are crouded, an innumerable multitude, into some dark corner of the heart. There is one criterion by which we may always distinguish benevolence from mere sensibility—Benevolence impels to action, and is accompanied by self-denial.

(1796)

THOMAS CLARKSON
The History of the Rise, Progress, and Accomplishment of the Abolition of the African Slave-Trade By the British Parliament.[4]

AMONG the evils, corrected or subdued, either by the general influence of Christianity on the minds of men, or by particular associations of

---

[1] The protagonist of Johann Goethe's popular novel, *The Sorrows of Young Werther* (1774), a sensitive young artist who commits suicide because of unrequited love.

[2] A lady who goes temporarily mad in Samuel Richardson's novel, *The History of Sir Charles Grandison* (1754).

[3] John Milton (1608–74), *Paradise Lost* (1667), I: 196–97.

[4] Thomas Clarkson (1760–1846), abolitionist. In 1787, Clarkson formed the Society for the Abolition of the Slave Trade with Granville Sharp. Over the next two years, Clarkson gathered evidence against the slave trade, interviewing thousands of sailors and collecting equipment used on the slave-ships such as iron handcuffs, leg-shackles, thumb screws, instruments for forcing open slaves' jaws, and branding irons. He passed his evidence on to the Abolition Committee, which brought the campaign to Parliament, where William Wilberforce was leading the effort to outlaw the trade.

Christians, the African Slave-trade appears to me to have occupied the foremost place. The abolition of it, therefore, of which it has devolved upon me to write the history, should be accounted as one of the greatest blessings, and, as such, should be one of the most copious sources of our joy. Indeed I know of no evil, the removal of which should excite in us a higher degree of pleasure. For in considerations of this kind, are we not usually influenced by circumstances? Are not our feelings usually affected according to the situation, or the magnitude, or the importance of these? Are they not more or less elevated as the evil under our contemplation has been more or less productive of misery, or more or less productive of guilt? Are they not more or less elevated, again, as we have found it more or less considerable in extent? Our sensations will undoubtedly be in proportion to such circumstances, or our joy to the appreciation or mensuration of the evil which has been removed.

To value the blessing of the abolition as we ought, or to appreciate the joy and gratitude which we ought to feel concerning it, we must enter a little into the circumstances of the trade. Our statement, however, of these needs not be long. A few pages will do all that is necessary! A glance only into such a subject as this will be sufficient to affect the heart—to arouse our indignation and our pity,—and to teach us the importance of the victory obtained.

The first subject for consideration, towards enabling us to make the estimate in question, will be that of the nature of the evil belonging to the Slave-trade. This may be seen by examining it in three points of view:—First, As it has been proved to arise on the continent of Africa in the course of reducing the inhabitants of it to slavery;—Secondly, In the course of conveying them from thence to the lands or colonies of other nations;—And Thirdly, In continuing them there as slaves.

To see it as it has been shown to arise in the first case, let us suppose ourselves on the Continent just mentioned. Well then—We are landed—We are already upon our travels—We have just passed through one forest—We are now come to a more open place, which indicated an approach to habitation. And what object is that, which first obtrudes itself upon our sight? Who is that wretched woman, whom we discover under that noble tree, wringing her hands, and beating her breast, as if in the agonies of despair? Three days has she been there at intervals to look and to watch, and this is the fourth morning, and no tidings of her children yet. Beneath its spreading boughs they were accustomed to play—But alas! the savage man-stealer interrupted their playful mirth, and has taken them for ever from her sight.

But let us leave the cries of this unfortunate woman, and hasten into another district:—And what do we first see here? Who is he, that just now started across the narrow pathway, as if afraid of a human face? What is that sudden rustling among the leaves? Why are those persons flying from our approach, and hiding themselves in yon darkest thicket? Behold, as we get into the plain, a deserted village! The rice-field has been just trodden down around it. An aged man, venerable by his silver beard, lies wounded and dying near the threshold of his hut. War, suddenly instigated by avarice, has just visited the dwellings which we see. The old have been butchered, because unfit for slavery, and the young have been carried off, except such as have fallen in the conflict, or have escaped among the woods behind us.

But let us hasten from this cruel scene, which gives rise to so many melancholy reflections. Let us cross yon distant river, and enter into some new domain. But are we relieved even here from afflicting spectacles? Look at that immense crowd, which appears to be gathered in a ring. See the accused innocent in the middle. The ordeal of poisonous water has been administered to him, as a test of his innocence or his guilt. He begins to be sick, and pale. Alas! yon mournful shriek of his relatives confirms that the loss of his freedom is now sealed.

And whither shall we go now? The night is approaching fast. Let us find some friendly hut, where sleep may make us forget for a while the sorrows of the day. Behold a hospitable native ready to receive us at his door! Let us avail ourselves of his kindness. And now let us give ourselves to repose. But why, when our eyelids are but just closed, do we find ourselves thus suddenly awakened? What is the meaning of the noise around us, of the trampling of people's feet, of the rustling of the bow, the quiver, and the lance? Let us rise up and inquire. Behold! the inhabitants are all alarmed! A wakeful woman has shown them yon distant column of smoke and blaze. The neighbouring village is on fire. The prince, unfaithful to the sacred duty of the protection of his subjects, has surrounded them. He is now burning their habitations, and seizing, as saleable booty, the fugitives from the flames.

Such then are some of the scenes that have been passing in Africa in consequence of the existence of the Slave-trade; or such is the nature of the evil, as it has shown itself in the first of the cases we have noticed. Let us now estimate it as it has been proved to exist in the second; or let us examine the state of the unhappy Africans, reduced to slavery in this manner, while on board the vessels, which are to convey them across the ocean to other lands. And here I must observe at once, that, as far as this part of the evil is concerned, I am at a loss to describe it. Where shall I find words to express properly their sorrow, as arising from the reflection of being parted for ever from their friends, their relatives, and their country? Where shall I find language to paint in appropriate colours the horror of mind brought on by thoughts of their future unknown

destination, of which they can augur nothing but misery from all that they have yet seen? How shall I make known their situation, while labouring under painful disease, or while struggling in the suffocating holds of their prisons, like animals inclosed in an exhausted receiver? How shall I describe their feelings as exposed to all the personal indignities, which lawless appetite or brutal passion may suggest? How shall I exhibit their sufferings as determining to refuse sustenance and die, or as resolving to break their chains, and, disdaining to live as slaves, to punish their oppressors? How shall I give an idea of their agony, when under various punishments and tortures for their reputed crimes? Indeed every part of this subject defies my powers, and I must therefore satisfy myself and the reader with a general representation, or in the words of a celebrated member of Parliament, that "Never was so much human suffering condensed in so small a space."[1]

I now come to the evil, as it has been proved to arise in the third case; or to consider the situation of the unhappy victims of the trade, when their painful voyages are over, or after they have been landed upon their destined shores. And here we are to view them first under the degrading light of cattle. We are to see them examined, handled, selected, separated, and sold. Alas! relatives are separated from relatives, as if, like cattle, they had no rational intellect, no power of feeling the nearness of relationship, nor sense of the duties belonging to the ties of life! We are next to see them labouring, and this for the benefit of those, to whom they are under no obligation, by any law either natural or divine, to obey. We are to see them, if refusing the commands of their purchasers, however weary, or feeble, or indisposed, subject to corporal punishments, and, if forcibly resisting them, to death. We are to see them in a state of general degradation and

---

[1] Generally attributed to William Wilberforce.

misery. The knowledge, which their oppressors have of their own crime in having violated the rights of nature, and of the disposition of the injured to seek all opportunities of revenge, produces a fear, which dictates to them the necessity of a system of treatment by which they shall keep up a wide distinction between the two, and by which the noble feelings of the latter shall be kept down, and their spirits broken. We are to see them again subject to individual persecution, as anger, or malice, or any bad passion may suggest. Hence the whip—the chain— the iron-collar. Hence the various modes of private torture, of which so many accounts have been truly given. Nor can such horrible cruelties be discovered so as to be made punishable, while the testimony of any number of the oppressed is invalid against the oppressors, however they may be offences against the laws. And, lastly, we are to see their innocent offspring, against whose person liberty the shadow of an argument cannot be advanced, inheriting all the miseries of their parents' lot.

(1808)

INDEX OF AUTHORS AND TITLES